Economic Forecasting

The first edition of this book became a valuable reference tool in the field of economic forecasting. This new edition takes into account what the profession has learnt during this century's first Great Recession, which so few foresaw. It also restructures the material to make it more user-friendly. Policy-relevant analyses have been expanded, providing key insights for macroeconomic management and supervisory authorities.

The book offers a comprehensive overview of macroeconomic forecasting. It presents a wide range of approaches, including business cycle analysis, time series methods, macroeconomic models, medium- and long-run projections, and fiscal and financial forecasts. The book then explores the main issues surrounding the use of forecasts, including accuracy and communication challenges. All along, the economic policy implications are highlighted, together with a focus on their financial stability dimension. A tour of the economic data and forecasting institutions is also provided.

This book will be essential reading for economists and professional forecasters as well as students.

Economic Forecasting and Policy

Second Edition

Nicolas Carnot

Vincent Koen

and

Bruno Tissot

First edition 2005
Second edition 2011

Published by
PALGRAVE MACMILLAN

Palgrave Macmillan in the UK is an imprint of Macmillan Publishers Limited,
registered in England, company number 785998, of Houndmills, Basingstoke,
Hampshire RG21 6XS.

Palgrave Macmillan in the US is a division of St Martin's Press LLC,
175 Fifth Avenue, New York, NY 10010.

Palgrave Macmillan is the global academic imprint of the above companies and has
companies and representatives throughout the world.

Palgrave® and Macmillan® are registered trademarks in the United States, the United
Kingdom, Europe and other countries

ISBN 978–0–230–24321–7   hardback
ISBN 978–0–230–24322–4   paperback

This book is printed on paper suitable for recycling and made from fully managed
and sustained forest sources. Logging, pulping and manufacturing processes are
expected to conform to the environmental regulations of the country of origin.

A catalogue record for this book is available from the British Library.

Library of Congress Cataloging-in-Publication Data
Carnot, Nicolas.
Economic forecasting and policy / Nicolas Carnot, Vincent Koen,
Bruno Tissot.
   p. cm.
Published in 2005 under title: Economic forecasting.
Includes bibliographical references and index.
ISBN-13: 978–0–230–24321–7 (hbk)
ISBN-13: 978–0–230–24322–4 (pbk)
   1. Economic forecasting.   I. Koen, Vincent.   II. Tissot, Bruno.
III. Carnot, Nicolas. Economic forecasting.   IV. Title.
HB3730.C35 2011
330.9001'12—dc22   2011011750

10 9 8 7 6 5 4 3 2 1
20 19 18 17 16 15 14 13 12 11

Contents

List of Figures

List of Tables

List of Boxes

Foreword

While macroeconomic and economic policy handbooks abound, they rarely dwell on the important question of economic forecasting. Many even bypass it altogether. Yet scores of economists, in both the private and public sectors, spend their working days constructing forecasts, and worry at night whether they got them right. The techniques they use blend traditional macroeconomic analysis, statistical and econometric tools, microeconomic insights and a fair dose of eclectic judgement. Granted, some of them are described in journal articles, but few if any books pull these various strands of knowledge and expertise together in a comprehensive survey. Bruno, Nicolas and Vincent aptly fill the void with this book, drawing on their experience built up at first-hand, in particular at the BIS, the IMF and the OECD.

Economic Forecasting and Policy is accessible to anyone with a general background in economics, yet it is nuanced and state-of-the-art. It provides the complete toolkit for forecasters, with clear presentations of the technicalities and numerous up-to-date, real-life exhibits, and relates these to the challenges faced by economic policy makers. It covers a broad range of areas, including national accounting, monitoring of financial markets, business cycle analysis, macroeconomic model building and usage, long-term projections and fiscal forecasting.

But this book also steps back from the basics of day-to-day forecasting to put things in perspective. It sets out the theoretical underpinnings of forecasting models. It shows how forecasts feed into policy making or private agents' decisions. It discusses forecasting (in)accuracy, arguing convincingly that forecasts are essential even if forecasters are almost inevitably bound to be off the mark. It points out candidly the shortcomings of existing analytical frameworks and gives readers a glimpse of forthcoming developments on the frontier of national accounting, economic analysis and forecasting. It looks at some of the key lessons from the financial crisis that began in 2007, regarding in particular the feedback loop between the real economy and financial markets as well as the associated financial stability dimension. Last but not least, it offers a unique round-the-world tour of the institutions producing forecasts – a precious guide through what has become a crowded jungle.

An early version of this book was published by Economica in French in 2002 and received a prize from the French Academy of Moral and Political Sciences for the best book on economic policy. The first global edition, in English, was published in 2005 and rapidly became popular with students, academics and practitioners alike. I trust that this second global edition, which draws lessons from the profession's chastening failure to predict the Great Recession, will be even more successful.

JEAN-PHILIPPE COTIS
Head of the French National Statistical Institute
Former OECD Chief Economist

Acknowledgements

This book – both the first and the second, revamped, edition – owes a lot to what we learnt from colleagues as we built up forecasting experience since the 1990s as economists at the Bank for International Settlements (BIS), the International Monetary Fund (IMF) and the Organisation for Economic Co-operation and Development (OECD), but also in national policy making bodies, as government and central bank staff in Paris.

A number of current and former colleagues are quoted in the book, but attempting an exhaustive list of thanks would be as fastidious as it would be vain. We would none the less like to single out those who supported our efforts most directly – the former or current chief economists of the BIS, IMF and OECD, namely Bill White, Olivier Blanchard and Jean-Philippe Cotis. Our gratitude also extends to Jean Pavlevski and Frédéric Bobay as well as to our families, who bore with us during a long march.

While grateful for all the wisdom and backing, we take full responsibility for the views expressed in this book, as well as for any residual shortcomings, which should not be ascribed to the aforementioned institutions or individuals.

NICOLAS CARNOT
VINCENT KOEN
BRUNO TISSOT

List of Abbreviations

ABS	asset-backed security
ADB	Asian Development Bank; African Development Bank
AGE	applied general equilibrium (model)
AIG	American International Group
AR	autoregressive (model)
ARCH	autoregressive conditional heteroskedasticity (model)
ARIMA	autoregressive integrated moving average (model)
ARMA	autoregressive moving average (model)
AS/AD	aggregate supply/aggregate demand (model)
BEA	Bureau of Economic Analysis (USA)
BEER	behavioural equilibrium exchange rate
BEKK	Baba, Engle, Kraft, Kroner (volatility model)
BIS	Bank for International Settlements
BLS	Bureau of Labor Statistics (USA)
BNP	Banque Nationale de Paris (France)
BRIC	group of countries: Brazil, Russia, India and China
BRICS	group of countries: Brazil, Russia, India, China and South Africa
BVAR	Bayesian VAR (model)
CAE	Conseil d'Analyse Economique (France)
CANSIM	Canadian socioeconomic database
CASE	Center for Social and Economic Research (Poland)
CBI	Confederation of British Industry
CBO	Congressional Budget Office (USA)
CBOLT	CBO Long-Term (model)
CCC	constant conditional correlation (model)
CDO	collateralized debt obligation
CDS	credit-default swap
CEA	Council of Economic Advisors (USA)
CEO	chief executive officer
CEPII	Centre d'Etudes Prospectives et d'Informations Internationales (France)
CEPR	Centre for Economic Policy Research
CES	constant elasticity of substitution
CGE	computable general equilibrium (model)
c.i.f.	cost of insurance and freight
CLI	composite leading indicator

CPB	Central Planning Bureau (now Dutch Bureau for Economic Policy Analysis) (Netherlands)
CPI	consumer price index (see HICP)
DCC	dynamic conditional correlation (model)
DEER	desired equilibrium exchange rate
DGT	Direction Générale du Trésor (France)
DIR	Daiwa Institute of Research (Japan)
DIW	Deutsches Institut für Wirtschaftsforschung (German Institute for Economic Research) (Berlin)
DSGE	dynamic stochastic general equilibrium (model)
EBRD	European Bank for Reconstruction and Development
EC	European Commission
ECB	European Central Bank
ECM	error correction model
ECOFIN	Economic and Financial Affairs Council (EU)
ECRI	Economic Cycle Research Institute
EGARCH	exponential GARCH (model)
EMS	European Monetary System
ESA	European System of Accounts (EU)
ESRI	Economic and Social Research Institute (Ireland)
ETLA	Research Institute of the Finnish Economy (Finland)
EU	European Union
EVT	extreme value theory
FCI	financial conditions index
FDI	foreign direct investment
FEER	fundamental equilibrium exchange rate
f.o.b.	free on board
FOMC	Federal Open Market Committee (USA)
FSA	Financial Services Authority (UK)
FY	fiscal year
GARCH	generalized ARCH (model)
GDP	gross domestic product
GIMF	Global Integrated Monetary and Fiscal (model)
GLI	Global Leading Indicator (Goldman Sachs)
GNI	gross national income
GNP	gross national product
GPM	global projection model
GSE	government-sponsored enterprise (USA)
HBOS	Halifax Bank of Scotland
HDI	Human Development Index (UNDP)
HICP(CPI)	Harmonised Index of Consumer Prices (EU)
HP	Hodrick-Prescott (filter)

HSBC	Hongkong and Shanghai Banking Corporation
HWWI	Hamburgische Welt-Wirtschafts-Institut (Germany)
IADB	Inter-American Development Bank
IEA	International Energy Agency
IFL	Instituto Flores de Lemus (Spain)
IFO	ifo Institute for Economic Research (Munich, Germany)
IFS	Institute for Fiscal Studies (UK)
IfW	Institut für Weltwirtschaft (Kiel, Germany)
IGIER	Innocenzo Gasparini Institute for Economic Research (Italy)
IIF	International Institute of Forecasters
IKB	Industriekreditbank (Germany)
ILO	International Labour Organization (UN)
IMA	integrated moving average
IMF	International Monetary Fund
INSEE	Institut National de la Statistique et des Études Économiques (France)
IOSCO	International Organization of Securities Commissions
IRR	internal rate of return
ISAE	Istituto di Studi e Analisi Economica (Italy)
ISIC	International Standard Industrial Classification
ISM	Institute for Supply Management
ISTAT	National Institute of Statistics (Italy)
IT	information technology
IVCCA	inventory valuation and capital consumption adjustments
IWH	Institut für Wirtschaftsforschung Halle (Germany)
JCER	Japan Center for Economic Research
LFS	Labour Force Survey
LIBOR/Libor	London interbank offered rate
MA	moving average (model)
MAE	mean absolute error
MBS	mortgage-backed securities
MCI	monetary conditions index
ME	mean error
METI	Ministry of Economy, Trade and Industry (Japan)
MFCI	monetary and financial conditions index
MPC	marginal propensity to consume; Monetary Policy Committee (Bank of England)
MSE	mean squared error
NACE	Classification of Economic Activities in the European Community
NAICS	North American Industry Classification System

NAIRU	non-accelerating inflation rate of unemployment
NAPM	National Association of Purchasing Management (later ISM)
NATREX	natural real exchange rate
NBER	National Bureau of Economic Research (USA)
NCAER	National Council of Applied Economic Research (India)
NDRC	National Development and Reform Commission (China)
NIESR	National Institute of Economic and Social Research (UK)
NiGEM	NIESR Global Econometric Model
NIPA	National Income and Product Accounts (USA)
NPI	non-profit institution
NPISH	non-profit institutions serving households
NPV	net present value
OBR	Office for Budget Responsibility (UK)
OECD	Organisation for Economic Co-operation and Development
OEEC	Organisation for European Economic Co-operation (forerunner of OECD)
OEF	Oxford Economics (formerly Oxford Economic Forecasting) (UK)
OFCE	Observatoire Français des Conjonctures Économiques (France)
OFHEO	Office of Federal Housing Enterprise Oversight (USA)
OIS	overnight index swap
OLS	ordinary least squares (model)
OMB	Office of Management and Budget (USA)
ONS	Office for National Statistics (UK)
OPEC	Organization of the Petroleum Exporting Countries
PEER	permanent equilibrium exchange rate
PER	price-to-earnings ratio
PMI	Purchasing Managers' Index
PPP	purchasing power parity
PS	price-setting (equation)
QE	quantitative easing
R&D	research and development
RBC	real business cycle
RE	rational expectations
RIW	Rheinisch-Westfälisches Institut für Wirtschaftsforschung (Essen, Germany)
RMSE	root mean squared error
RPI	Retail Prices Index (UK)
RPIX	Retail Prices Index excluding Mortgage Interest Payments (UK)
S&P	Standard & Poor's
SEEA	system of integrated environmental and economic accounts
SETAR	self-exciting threshold auto-regressive (model)
SIFI	systemically important financial institution

SNA	system of national accounts
STAR	smooth transition autoregressive (model)
STING	short-term indicators of growth (model)
TAR	threshold auto-regressive (model)
TARCH	threshold GARCH (model)
TARP	Troubled Asset Relief Program (USA)
TFP	total factor productivity
UIP	uncovered interest parity
UN	United Nations
UNCTAD	United Nations Conference on Trade and Development
UNDP	United Nations Development Programme
VAR	vector autoregressive (model)
VaR	value at risk
VAT	Value Added Tax
VECM	vector error correction model
WEO	World Economic Outlook (IMF)
WIFO	Austrian Institute for Economic Research
WS	wage setting (equation)
WTO	World Trade Organization
ZEW	Center for European Economic Research

Introduction

All human errors are impatience, a premature breaking off of methodical procedure, an apparent fencing-in of what is apparently at issue.

Franz Kafka

Man approaches the unattainable truth through a succession of errors.

Aldous Huxley

In the past few years, professional forecasters and those who relay their predictions to the broader public have made the largest forecasting error in their lifetimes. Very few economists foresaw the 2007 financial crisis and the twenty-first century's first Great Recession. Some of the most prominent policy makers have since confessed that they just could not imagine a scenario as dire as the one that occurred. The former chairman of the US Federal Reserve, Alan Greenspan, testifying in Congress in October 2008, explained that the Fed failed to forecast a significant nationwide drop in house prices because such a decline had never been observed. With the benefit of hindsight, this shows that disaster myopia may blind even the most sophisticated forecasters. It is all too easy to forget the painful episodes of the past when times look good.

While the Great Recession has humbled the profession, the role of economic forecasts, which had become increasingly important in recent decades, is undiminished. Expected future economic developments continue to be discussed daily, both in specialized forums and more broadly. News about the economic outlook still can send financial markets into jitters at any time. Hence an assessment of economic prospects remains an indispensable ingredient in economic policy making, as well as for private-sector decisions. To cope with

1

uncertainty and anticipate the implications of their behaviour, nearly every agent or collective entity has to rely on some description of how the economy is likely to evolve; that is, on an economic forecast.

What is economic forecasting?

This book focuses mainly on the forecasting of macroeconomic phenomena. From a formal standpoint, economic forecasting can be defined as a set of hypothetical statements about future aggregate developments, such as the evolution of overall activity or prices. As a rule, economic forecasting involves:

- A view of the economic future, reflected in quantitative estimates for the main macroeconomic variables at different horizons.
- An underlying analytical 'story', including the assumptions underpinning the forecast, and an investigation of the risks that might materialize if some of them turned out to be wrong.
- A discussion of possible courses of action and their likely consequences, intended for policy makers and other forecast users.

Economic forecasting is basically a structured way of peering into the future using all available information, including recent outcomes, survey data on agents' mood and plans, prior knowledge of economic relationships, and so on. Obviously, forecasting requires economic and econometric expertise. But it also draws on history as well as on political and social science, while the forecaster's own judgement plays a crucial role.

The book's aims

This book covers all aspects of economic forecasting. It is aimed both at non-specialists wishing to better understand this field and at forecasters looking for a comprehensive and up-to-date compendium on the subject. It thus fills a void between specialized econometric or statistics textbooks and more general economic textbooks. The perspective here is that of practitioners presenting their profession's contribution to analysis and decision-making, in particular economic policy making.

The book describes and discusses most current forecasting techniques. It tries to be comprehensive, but with an emphasis on those approaches that are most commonly used in practice. In general, the mathematical material is kept to a minimum and appears in boxes, technical appendices or annexes. The forecasting tools are not presented in isolation but motivated by empirical observations and related to theoretical intuitions, in the vein of applied economic policy textbooks. In addition, important advice is given on the practical implementation of forecasting methods.

The book explains and discusses the role of economic forecasts in policy making, which is often misunderstood. Granted, any economic forecast is inherently shrouded in uncertainty – as the unexpected Great Recession has shown. But when properly prepared and used, it helps to improve the quality of decision-making. Indeed, the value of any particular forecast has less to do with specific numbers than with its ability to structure public debate in a simple, yet rigorous fashion.

Roadmap

The book reviews both the methods and the uses of economic forecasting. It is structured as follows:

Chapter 1 provides an overview of the book, explains what, why and how to forecast, and answers a set of frequently asked questions about forecasting. Chapter 2 focuses on macroeconomic monitoring and business cycle analysis for the purpose of near-term forecasting.

The book then turns to the forecaster's usual tools. Chapter 3 is devoted to the modelling of real sector economic behaviour. Chapter 4 focuses on the financial sector, whose importance is even more obvious today than before the Great Recession. Chapter 5 is devoted to fiscal forecasts, against the backdrop of the additional challenges stemming from the 2007 financial crisis. Chapter 6 presents the techniques used in medium- and long-run projections.

Chapters 7 and 8 offer perspectives on the contribution of economic forecasts to decision-making. Chapter 7 discusses forecasting accuracy, in the light of the profession's largest-ever error. Chapter 8 explains how forecasts are used in practice by economic policy makers and other agents, and discusses the communication of economic forecasts. It is supplemented by a tour of the institutions producing forecasts.

Annex I goes over the economic data, and in particular national accounts, which constitute the general framework for economic forecasting. Annex II presents the main time series methods used in forecasting. Annex III offers a primer on the various types of macroeconomic models that underpin story-based forecasts.

Each chapter and annex is relatively self-contained, allowing readers to go explore them in the order that best suits their needs – with a range of figures, tables, boxes and appendices providing the opportunity for a more in-depth focus on issues of particular interest. Each of the chapters also ends with some pointers for further reading.

Chapter 1

Overview

Contents

Macroeconomics in this original sense has succeeded: its central problem of depression prevention has been solved, for all practical purposes, and has in fact been solved for many decades.

Robert Lucas (2003)

We are in the midst of a once-in-a-century credit tsunami ... We were wrong quite a good deal of the time.

Alan Greenspan, Testimony to US House of Representatives Committee on Oversight and Government Reform, October 2008

Economic variables tend to bounce around, especially over shorter horizons. The forecaster's challenge is to make sense of these movements in order to predict where economies are heading, be it in the course of the cycle or over the longer run. His or her toolbox to do so includes models of various degrees of sophistication and comprehensiveness, ranging from simple equations with a single variable to heavy macroeconomic models with hundreds of them. Forecasts serve national and international economic policy makers, but also private firms and households. Ex post, forecasts usually turn out to be off the mark, sometimes by large margins. Even so, they are indispensable ex ante, *to provide a quantified framework for decision-making in the face of an uncertain world.*

This chapter provides an overview of the main themes covered in the book. It revolves around three basic questions:

- First, what is being forecast? In this book, the focus is on forecasting macroeconomic variables. Aggregate changes are thus primarily of concern, with sectoral developments being considered only in so far as they have a significant impact at a more global level. These forecasts are underpinned by traditional macroeconomic analysis, especially as it relates to cyclical fluctuations and long-run growth theory (section 1.1).
- Second, why forecast these variables? Forecasting as a specific professional activity has emerged for both intellectual and practical reasons. The latter have become increasingly important with the growing sophistication of modern economies. Indeed, forecasts constitute a convenient framework to bring together assessments regarding the future and to evaluate the consequences of possible decisions (section 1.2).
- Third, how are forecasts produced? As a rule, a forecast combines informed judgement and model-based predictions. Well-digested information is key: the best forecaster is often the one with the most documented and sharpest

reading of the facts. But the role of the model(s) is also essential: models impart a healthy dose of discipline and help to draw lessons for the future from observations of the past. Finally, it is important to note that forecasting involves much more than merely coming up with a set of numbers. The forecaster must be able to explain how the numbers hang together, to weave a compelling story around them, to identify the risks surrounding the central scenario and to map out alternative courses of action (section 1.3).

1.1 What to forecast?

The main variables forecasters try to pin down include output growth, inflation, unemployment, interest rates, exchange rates, international trade flows, fiscal balances and public debt. This section defines the scope of economic forecasting, starting with a few basic facts.

1.1.1 Growth trends and business cycles

When looking at growth in advanced economies, two features stand out. First, over a period of several decades, and putting aside the recent major recession, economic activity as measured by real gross domestic product (GDP) expands fairly steadily (see Figure 1.1). Using this measure, the US economy was four-and-a-half times as large in 2008 as it was in the early 1960s, the euro area economy over four times as large and the Japanese economy seven-and-a-half times as large. In general, economic expansion has far exceeded demographic growth, implying a substantial improvement in GDP per capita and thus in individual living standards.[1]

Second, over shorter periods, growth rates fluctuate, as economies are hit by shocks and experience slowdowns or even outright recessions (see Figure 1.2). Growth in the advanced economies was generally rapid from the late 1940s to the mid-1970s, when the first oil shock occurred and many countries entered a recession. A few years later, the second oil shock heralded another sharp slowdown. For a variety of reasons, including a brief, geopolitically-induced spike in oil prices as well as idiosyncratic shocks in some major countries, the early 1990s saw a number of economies slowing down again, though this time the recessions were far from synchronized. Following a spell of rapid growth in the latter part of the 1990s, the bursting of the 'new economy' bubble translated into a shallow but none the less significant slowdown. Most recently,

---

[1] Over the very long run, the increase in output has been even more enormous. Estimates suggest that real GDP per capita has been multiplied by 15 or so since 1820 in Western countries (Maddison, 2001). Some regions tend to grow faster than others, however, even over long periods (with Africa, for example, standing out as a low-growth area).

Figure 1.1   Real GDP levels since the 1960s

Over the long run, economies expand substantially, though not all at the same pace

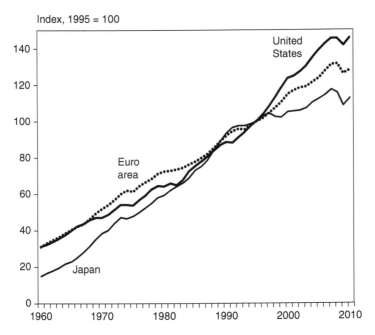

Index, 1995 = 100

Source: OECD.

Figure 1.2   Real GDP growth rates since the 1960s

Over the shorter run, economies experience booms and busts, synchronised or not

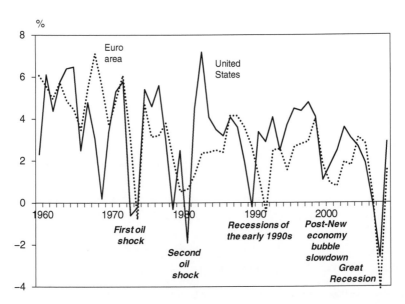

Source: OECD.

the triple whammy of soaring commodity prices, bursting housing market bubbles and the 2007 financial crisis together triggered the Great Recession, the worst global downturn since the 1930s, with almost simultaneous, deep and protracted contractions in most of the world's economies.

These phases of acceleration and deceleration in activity point to the existence of economic cycles. Four different types of cycles are usually distinguished, depending on the horizon under consideration:

- Kondratieff cycles (or waves), which last about half a century, correspond to the transition from one set of dominant technologies to the next (for example, steam power and railways, electricity, information technology);
- Kuznets cycles, spanning about two decades, were mainly associated with the US construction industry before the First World War; they are derived looking at population changes, capital formation and incomes;
- Kitchin cycles, which are much shorter (two to four years), are primarily related to fluctuations in inventories and wholesale prices; and
- Juglar cycles, lasting five to ten years, are what is usually understood under the generic term 'cycle', when it is not further specified. This is also referred to as the 'business cycle' or the 'conjunctural cycle'.

1.1.2 Horizons

The concepts of trend growth and cycles play a key role in macroeconomic analysis as well as in forecasting. Trend growth refers to long-run tendencies. Cyclical fluctuations are temporary departures from the longer-run trend. Against this backdrop, four different forecasting horizons are traditionally distinguished:

- The very short run, from the latest observations to two quarters ahead;
- The short run, from six months to two years down the road;
- The medium run, generally understood as two to five years ahead (sometimes ten); and
- The long run, beyond the five- or ten-year horizon.

As regards the very short run, the objective of what is widely called 'business cycle analysis' is first to pin down recent or ongoing developments. Indeed, since indicators of economic activity are published with a lag, there is a need to 'forecast', or estimate, the present and recent past (unlike in weather forecasting). This is sometimes referred to as 'nowcasting'. On the basis of this tentative assessment, a forecast is built up for the next few months, which itself then serves as the starting point for longer-run forecasts.

Routine forecasting exercises usually look at the short run, which implicitly encompasses the very short run. Typically, published macroeconomic forecasts cover the current year and the following one.

Medium- and long-run projections are produced less frequently, albeit still quite regularly, in particular by public bodies. Occasionally, large firms also prepare such projections; for example, when they need to evaluate a big investment project.

1.1.3 Basic mechanisms

Forecasting relies on the analysis of economic facts in the light of economic theory, with the exact combination depending on the time horizon.

Over the short run, stock variables such as the productive capital that is in place are more-or-less fixed. Therefore the analysis focuses on flow variables, with most forecasters sharing relatively similar assumptions. Specifically:

- The conventional wisdom is that the business cycle is shaped, first and foremost, by changes in aggregate demand. Of particular importance in this respect are changes in fixed investment and inventories, as well as changes in foreign demand. Some components of household consumption, particularly purchases of durables, are also rather volatile.
- But aggregate demand may meet a supply constraint, notably when factors of production are already fully used or when enterprise profitability is deemed too weak to warrant new investment. Then, prices increase and/or domestic buyers turn to foreign suppliers.
- Macroeconomic policies act on aggregate demand. Fiscal policy operates directly via public spending and indirectly via taxation. An unsustainable fiscal stance can push up financial market spreads, with dire consequences for the real economy. Monetary policy influences financial variables, including interest rates, exchange rates, credit and stock prices (see Chapter 4). Overly loose monetary policy can fuel asset price bubbles and lead to a boom-and-bust cycle, especially if regulation and supervision are deficient. Conversely, overly tight monetary policy can delay or derail a recovery or abort an expansion. Such effects have become increasingly important with the growing role played by financial markets in today's economies, leading to complex and powerful feedback between the real economy and financial variables.
- Employment usually follows the ups and downs in output with a bit of a lag and in a more subdued fashion. As a result, labour productivity is normally pro-cyclical. The same holds for the productivity of capital and for the usual indicators of economic slack (capacity utilization rate, duration of equipment's use, overtime).
- In the short run, prices and wages do not react directly to real disequilibria. But over time, and with a lag, they do. In contrast, exchange rate shifts and changes in the price of imported goods (in particular, oil) have an impact on domestic inflation fairly rapidly. Changes in domestic prices in turn affect the real side: via competitiveness, which influences foreign trade flows; via

real balances, which influence household consumption (the so-called 'Pigou effect'); and via the impact of changes in costs on factor demand. Overall, however, these various feedback effects play a minor role in explaining cyclical turnarounds.

- Finally, the shares of wages and profits in total income fluctuate over the business cycle. The profit share tends to increase when exiting recession and in the early stages of an expansion, and vice versa for the wage share. This affects investment and consumption patterns.

These stylized features of the business cycle are not always observed in practice, and forecasters differ on the relative importance of the various mechanisms (see Chapter 3). Moreover, each cycle has its idiosyncrasies, and may come with its own set of effects. Furthermore, the growing interactions between the real economy and the financial sphere are rather hard to depict.

Looking several years ahead, the degree of uncertainty is such that the term 'projection' is generally preferred to that of 'forecast'. Strictly speaking, a projection is an extrapolation of past trends, while a forecast can include *ad hoc* modifications that are thought to improve accuracy. In practice, this distinction is less clear-cut. Instead, the horizon typically determines the choice of the term.

Over the medium run, economic structures are not deemed to change much. Therefore a natural approach to medium-run projections is to examine what happens when the trends that are forecast at an 18-month or two-year horizon are prolonged. If the economy is seen to be close to its steady state path at the end of the short-run projection period, the usual approach is to forecast a continuation of its trend. But if this is not the case, it suggests that some of the short-run trends are unlikely to be sustained because they translate into ever-larger disequilibria; for example, an inflationary spiral or a protracted recession. Such disequilibria may be related to unsustainable macroeconomic policies (say, excessive fiscal deficits) or to exuberant private agent behaviour (say, in the case of a stock or housing market bubble). The projections would then suggest that a correction has to take place. But it is difficult to predict when. There are then two ways to proceed:

- One is to present a projection that simply extrapolates current trends. This may not be realistic, but it can serve to raise awareness of their unsustainability and thereby prompt some reactions, especially on the part of policy makers.
- The other is to introduce an assumption as to when and how adjustment will come about that will steer the economy back to equilibrium by the end of the projection period. This is what is often done, implicitly, when the projection is constructed around a gradual closing of the output gap and the unwinding of other imbalances (see Chapter 6).

In this context, however, there is no point in fine-tuning by trying to foresee cyclical fluctuations three or four years in advance, as they are inherently unpredictable at that horizon.

Over the long run – that is, beyond the five- to ten-year horizon – economies can undergo substantial structural transformations. These are difficult to forecast. But one way to look at the long run is to use growth models, which focus on the supply side and disregard cyclical fluctuations. In this context, labour force resources and technical progress are the two key determinants of future trend growth. The latter can thus be estimated by combining demographic assumptions and their implications for labour force growth with assumptions on total factor productivity growth, based on what has been observed in the past.

Going into more detail is tricky. Indeed, when looking at long-run phenomena, causes and effects are difficult to disentangle. For example, progress in education unquestionably boosts growth prospects, but higher growth in turn allows more resources to be devoted to education. More generally, over the long run, each variable depends on all the others, and there are no truly 'exogenous' ones left on which to anchor a forecast.[2]

In a nutshell, and whatever the time horizon, any forecast thus revolves around two questions: where is the economy in the cycle, and what is the underlying growth trend? Forming a view on both is at the heart of any forecasting endeavour. It is also a prerequisite in order to proceed with more specific forecasts, such as forecasts of tax revenues (see Chapter 5) or of a particular sector (see Chapter 3).

1.2   Why forecast?

Forecasting started around the time of the Second World War, as a way to test economic theories, but it also has very concrete uses and has played an increasing role as an input in decision-making.

1.2.1   Intellectual and practical reasons

Economic forecasting emerged in the late 1930s and 1940s, when researchers built the first forecasting models (Tinbergen, 1939; Klein, 1950), for intellectual as well as practical reasons.

The scientific objective was to test the empirical relevance of economic theories, in particular the Keynesian synthesis that was taking off at the time, using statistical

---

[2] There is also a literature that goes beyond economics *in the narrow sense* and tries to foresee changes in technology, social structures or the environment. This type of so-called 'prospective' analysis goes well beyond the aim of this book.

data generated by the fledgling national accounts systems. The forecasts were intended to play the role that experiments play in the hard sciences: invalidate the underlying model if unreliable, or corroborate it when on the mark.

The practical objective was to provide new economic tools for policy-makers, in the form of instruments to assess the cyclical situation and to gauge the impact on the aggregate activity of their potential decisions. This concern was obviously sharpened by the painful experience of the Great Depression of the 1930s.

Both the intellectual and practical reasons remain important today. However, many things have changed since the early days of economic forecasting. One is that it has become clear that forecasting the economy cannot be as safe as predicting the trajectory of inanimate objects using the laws of physics. Uncertainties abound, some quantifiable and others not.

Recognizing this uncertainty has to some extent diminished the enthusiasm of academics for forecasting.[3] As for policy, it has changed the perception of how forecasting may be useful but certainly not diminished the appetite for forecasts. Routine forecasts are now (rightly) understood as a basic input into policy decisions, but risk analysis and attention to medium-run imbalances are perhaps even more essential for policy advice.

What is more, it appears that economic forecasts could also fulfil many other needs than macroeconomic stabilization, as well as helping agents in the private sector – for example, a firm deciding to invest or a household wishing to anticipate its future earnings. As a result, forecasts started to be used more widely and in a growing number of specialized areas. Financial markets have become important consumers of economic and financial forecasts. Hence, forecasting is these days more a practitioner's than a researcher's activity, with thousands of forecasters in the public and private sectors delivering their diagnoses to decision-makers and stakeholders.

1.2.2 The need for forecasts

The demand for forecasts stems from a need to form an educated view of the future before making decisions. More precisely, in the economic sphere, it arises from two basic constraints (see Chapter 8):

- Lags: economic relationships are complex and the impact of actions initiated today may not materialize for some time. It is therefore necessary to anticipate these effects in some way.

---

[3] Academics have generally become less inclined to engage in macroeconomic forecasting since the disappointing experiences of the 1970s, when efforts to build large-scale econometric models failed to provide the expected results. In recent decades, most of the research efforts have been focusing on time series techniques, especially those related to volatility forecasts (see Annex II).

- Uncertainty: the future is inherently uncertain. Forecasts cannot eliminate the uncertainty but they can help to assess risks, thus enabling agents to deal with them better.

Prior to making choices for the future, agents simply need to better understand the environment in which their actions will unfold. That said, the required degree of sophistication and detail of the forecast depends on the circumstances. In some cases, informal or even implicit assessments may suffice, but in others, specific and well-reasoned assumptions are called for, and quantitative methods must be brought to bear. The forecasts then constitute a useful framework, drawing together all the relevant information and spelling out the costs, benefits and risks associated with economic agents' behaviour.

1.2.3   Impact of the forecasts

Forecasts affect agents' behaviour in two, non-mutually-exclusive, ways:

- Adaptation: agents will seize an opportunity, or try to protect themselves against the consequences of an adverse event. For example, faced with a forecast decline in demand for its products, a firm will adjust its production schedule and its budget accordingly, not unlike an individual who is informed that rain is on the way and chooses to take along an umbrella or to stay at home.
- Retroaction: when agents can influence what is forecast, they might act on it. For example, governments and central banks can take initiatives to alter the course of macroeconomic events. Of course, some adaptation remains in order even then, since the authorities' powers are limited.

This leads to the distinction between 'conditional' and 'unconditional' forecasts. Conditional forecasts are based on specific and possibly somewhat unrealistic assumptions regarding economic agents' behaviour. The idea is to explore their implications for the shape of the forecast, often by trying out alternative sets of hypotheses. The results can help agents to decide which course of action is preferable. Unconditional forecasts are closer to what is commonly understood by 'forecasts': they attempt to describe the most likely scenario. Implicitly, they rest on assumptions concerning the most plausible behaviour of all agents, including policy makers.

1.2.4   Forecasting and decision-making

While forecasting plays an important and sometimes decisive role in decision-making,[4] decisions may depart from what the forecast would suggest. One reason is that individuals' objectives go far beyond the variables usually included in the forecast. For example, a government may care at least as much about its

---

[4] Elections have been triggered or lost on the basis of erroneous forecasts.

own popularity as about the country's economic performance, and may therefore prefer not to take the painful measures that a forecast might call for.

Moreover, even if decision-makers acted only on strictly 'economic' grounds, disagreements could arise on the forecast itself. And agents may weigh policy objectives differently; for example, when considering the trade-off between more inflation and more growth, or their degree of risk aversion.

Hence it is best for forecasters to stick to a clear division of labour. They should outline the various plausible scenarios and quantify the associated costs and benefits. Decision-makers then have to take responsibility for their actions, based on this information and on their objectives (see Chapter 8).

1.2.5   Why is the short run important?

In practice, institutions producing forecasts devote many more resources to short-run and very short-run forecasts than to medium- and long-run projections, which are done less frequently and receive less publicity. This is a paradox, given that growth is somewhat erratic in the short run, and that in the end structural trends matter the most. Indeed, classical economists cared mainly about the expansion of the supply side, viewing cycles as no more than temporary disturbances. Until the 1930s and the advent of J. M. Keynes' ideas, this meant that cyclical analysis was confined to some very specific phenomena, such as the hog cycle in agriculture, for example, or to a narrowly descriptive approach, limited to recording the ups and downs of the stock market and of inflation to characterize the cycle.

In fact, there are three sets of reasons why short-run prospects matter. First, business cycle fluctuations are important in and of themselves, and may have consequences going beyond mere disturbances. Slowdowns and recessions aggravate social problems, not least through the rise in unemployment. And macroeconomic statistics may understate the pain because they mask disparities between sectors or groups of individuals. Moreover, some slowdowns are far worse than average, notably the Great Depression in the 1930s and the Great Recession that began around 2007, but also, albeit to a lesser extent, the sluggish growth rates in Japan, Germany and Italy during the 1990s. The fact that economies eventually recover is cold comfort: 'In the long run we are all dead', as Keynes famously put it.

Second, the ground lost during downturns may not be offset by higher growth later. On the contrary, short-run macroeconomic instability may undermine investment, and thereby lead to lower growth over the long run. Therefore, improving short-run stability is important from a long-run perspective.

Finally, assessing short-run prospects is crucial for economic policy purposes, especially with regard to fiscal and monetary policy. The forecasts provide an indispensable framework for the preparation of budgets, and their quality affects that of macroeconomic stabilization policy (see Chapters 5 and 8).

1.3   How to forecast?

Economic forecasting draws on a variety of methods, each of them hingeing on some specific theoretical or statistical assumptions, with their pros and cons. There is no single optimal way to proceed, if only because reality is so complex and ever in a state of flux. In practice, a variety of methods are therefore brought to bear. To the extent that they can be combined, they provide for a more robust forecast.

The preparation of a forecast involves three steps: observing the facts, selecting a model (or models) to interpret them, and using this model (or these models) to forecast the future. In practice, these steps tend to overlap somewhat.

1.3.1   Deciphering the facts

Any forecast rests on an understanding of past developments. Hence it is conditioned by a phase of active observation, devoted to measuring and interpreting the facts.

The usefulness of proper measurement has become obvious. Economic indicators these days receive intense media coverage, but this was not always the case. For example, the economic information and understanding among European citizens in the 1930s was extremely poor, and this led to serious policy mistakes. The production and dissemination of economic data has made considerable progress since then, and national statistical systems now offer a wealth of information. At their core lie the national accounts, which offer a rich and coherent summary picture (see Annex I towards the back of this book). In addition, there are numerous administrative and survey data, some of which are published well ahead of the national accounts. Yet the 2007 financial crisis showed that there are still substantial data gaps to properly asses the situation in financial markets, the role of specific institutions, the strength of balance sheets of various economic agents, and the feedback channels between the real economy and the financial sphere.

While the profusion of measures allows for more rigorous and sophisticated interpretations, far greater efforts than in the past are needed to sift through the maze of indicators and make sense of the data (see Chapter 2). A good understanding of economic history is also necessary to read the facts correctly. Quantitative tools, such as the macroeconomic models discussed below, can help to store this knowledge and facilitate the interpretation of new observations by offering benchmarks. For example, when abnormal fluctuations seem to occur (such as surges in investment or sharp drops in consumption), it is useful to compare them to average past movements. This helps to characterize and explain these fluctuations, and says something about their likely future developments.

This task of interpreting incoming information is the challenge faced daily by business cycle analysts. A certain degree of urgency as well as the volatility of short-term indicators, coupled with sometimes considerable publication lags, tend to obscure underlying trends. Getting the recent past right is thus in itself quite difficult.

1.3.2 The various approaches

Broadly speaking, four types of quantitative approaches are used in economic forecasting: subjective methods, indicator-based methods, time series models and structural models.

Subjective methods call exclusively on the forecasters' common sense, intuition or experience, without bringing in any explicit model. Such forecasts are not necessarily inaccurate, but they can only take into account a limited information set while resting on implicit assumptions. Hence they are difficult to interpret and discuss.

Indicator-based methods exploit the information provided by 'advance' indicators that are published before the forecast variables, in order to anticipate the latter. Such methods are used mainly in business cycle analysis, in particular for the early detection of turning points. One example of such advance indicators is export orders in small, open economies, which often foreshadow activity trends.

Most indicators used in this context come from business cycle surveys, such as surveys of investment plans, or from administrative records; for example, customs data on foreign trade flows. Composite indicators can also be constructed, combining several indicators to better gauge trends. A well-known example is the German Ifo Institute for Economic Research's business climate index.

The predictive power of any single indicator is limited, and in practice business cycle analysts tend to look at a whole range of indicators. However, these often diverge: what if, say, business sentiment and household confidence move in opposite directions? Both intuition and past experience may be of help when gauging the respective merits of each indicator, but it is sometimes hard to reconcile such divergences.

Time series models are based solely on the statistical properties of the series under consideration, irrespective of any interpretation or causal relationships informed by economic theory (see Annex II of this book). Generally, the only assumption needed in this approach is that the probabilistic model describing the past behaviour of the series remains valid when going forward. There are two types of time series methods:

- Univariate methods: in this case, the forecast of a variable depends solely on its past realizations. These methods encompass so-called 'naïve' forecasts (say, forecast growth equals average past growth), simple techniques such as moving averages or smoothing algorithms, but also more general approaches such as ARIMA models, which combine autoregressive and moving average models. These methods can be well suited to dealing with variables subject to random disturbances.
- Multivariate methods: these jointly forecast several variables based on their past behaviour. This allows the taking into account of the correlations between series. Vector autoregressive (VAR) models are the most popular among such methods, being very simple to use.

Time series methods offer clear advantages: they are simple, require few data, allow the capture of statistical relationships among variables, and can be relatively successful even if the analyst knows little about the phenomenon under consideration. Therefore, they can be used to quickly obtain a quantitative forecast for a small number of variables.

A drawback, however, is that these methods fail to explain how they reach their conclusions: the forecast is generated by simply prolonging past correlations. The results cannot be interpreted in the sense that the forecast cannot be decomposed to show the contributions of various explanatory factors. Hence these methods are ill-suited for the construction of scenarios based on alternative assumptions or for the analysis of the sensitivity of the forecast to changes in structural parameters.

Structural models try to explain as much as to forecast.[5] They feature causal relationships among variables and distinguish between 'endogenous' ones, which are determined by the model, and 'exogenous' ones, which are treated as given (see Annex III in this book). The model delivers a forecast of the endogenous variables based on assumptions made, outside the model, on the evolution of the exogenous variables.[6]

---

[5] These methods are sometimes referred to as 'econometric'. This is confusing, however, in so far as econometric techniques are also used for time series analysis and in indicator-based approaches.

[6] These assumptions can themselves be established using one of the forecast approaches described here, or they may be set more judgementally.

Building a structural model involves three stages: design, estimation and testing. First, the model is written up in the form of a set of equations spelling out the relationships between variables, based on some theoretical priors and a clear distinction between endogenous and exogenous variables. Second, values of the parameters appearing in these equations are estimated using econometric regressions, calibration techniques and the like. Then, the validity of the model is tested to see whether it describes observed past behaviour accurately, whether the simulations it generates are plausible, and so on. In practice, these three stages are interdependent and require the analyst to go back and forth among them.

The size of structural models ranges from very small to enormous. At one extreme, single-equation models are often estimated to assess a particular behavioural pattern, while at the other, so-called macroeconomic (or 'macroeconometric') models contain up to hundreds of equations. Their purpose is to provide an overall picture of the economy, showing its main interdependencies. The endogenous variables typically include such key economic indicators as GDP, inflation, employment, the fiscal deficit, export and imports, financial market indicators and so on. The exogenous variables tend to relate to demography, technical progress, the international environment (including the price of raw materials) and economic policy decisions.

The main advantage of macroeconomic models is that they bring together in a common framework a vast quantity of information. They allow for a coherent forecast of all the variables that are traditionally taken into account to appraise economic developments, including growth and its main components, prices, jobs and incomes, public finance aggregates and the increasingly important role played by the flows of funds among economic agents. They are useful to compare alternative scenarios and to evaluate the impact of policy measures. But such models do require a high degree of expertise, are costly to set up and to maintain, and sometimes produce relatively poor value for money in terms of forecast accuracy (on the latter, see Chapter 7).

1.3.3 Building a forecast

In practice, forecasts are rarely based on the mechanical implementation of any one of the above methods. Rather, different approaches are usually combined and raw model outputs are adjusted to take outside judgements into consideration. Moreover, the numbers normally have to come with a story spelling out the underlying assumptions, the main driving forces of the forecast, the risks surrounding the central scenario and the room for manoeuvre.

Fundamentally, economic forecasting is an attempt to anticipate the future by using a large variety of information sources. In so doing, it would not be sensible to rely on only one model, whatever its merits. As far as possible, it is advisable to test different methods so as to obtain a more robust forecast.

One way to proceed is to carry out separate experimental forecasts using various tools, such as advance indicators, simple or more sophisticated extrapolations and structural models. Divergences typically surface when the results are compared, highlighting the problems associated with this or that forecasting approach. Such problems do not necessarily disqualify the tool used, since it is often possible to adjust the results; for example, methodological shortcomings associated with a given approach may be spotted at this stage, leading to technical refinements and more robust evaluations.

Eventually, though, one central method has to be selected for the practical purpose of structuring the forecast. But it is of great importance that the forecast takes into account the weaknesses of the chosen method that have been brought to light by other approaches. At the same time, judgement will typically have to be incorporated, to reflect information or knowledge that is not embodied precisely in the model. In that sense, the science of forecasting may require some degree of craftsmanship.

Exercising judgement is done using an array of techniques designed to amend 'spontaneous' model results that are only partly satisfactory. For example, one technique is the use, at the margin, of add-on factors or of multiplicative corrections (see Annex III of this book).

It may be surmised that such judgemental adjustments denote a lack of rigour. In fact, they are a rational response to the known limitations of models, as the latter can only be simplified representations of reality. Corrections may thus be appropriate and legitimate when there are compelling reasons to believe that in some ways the model lacks realism. However, these corrections are best done transparently – if possible, on the basis of quantifications undertaken outside the model.

As judgement often has the last word, the forecast should be viewed as the economist's more than the model's. What, then, is the role of the model? The following chapters will shed light on this, but three aspects can be underlined here:

- The model imposes discipline. It obliges the forecaster to think about the underlying assumptions and greatly facilitates the discussion on the forecast with other economists and with users.
- The model memorizes the past. Its structure and parameters reflect the behavioural patterns that have been observed so far. Thus, the forecast has a historical anchor. The model also allows for the keeping of a track-record of past forecasting errors and their associated lessons.

- As noted earlier, the model, especially if it is a macroeconomic one, constitutes a tool to assemble a great deal of information into a coherent and common framework.

In sum, the model needs to be complemented by the economist's judgement, but conversely, judgement is exercised better when underpinned by a model. The model instils discipline and transparency into the forecasting process even if, ultimately, the forecast is served by the model rather than the reverse.

When a forecast is presented, it is usually described in terms of raw economic figures. However, users also need an explanation of the economic mechanisms at work, a review of the underlying assumptions, and a description of the associated risks. For this purpose, the traditional macrodynamic interactions listed above (in section 1.1) have to be presented, showing in particular how they unfold in the specific context of the period under consideration. The forecast thus comes across as a story articulated around some key behavioural relationships (investment accelerator, consumption and saving, impact of the international environment and of economic policies, wage-price setting, and so on). The coherence and plausibility of that story contribute to the credibility of the forecast.

The story has to start with a rationale for the assumptions that have been chosen. Their nature differs according to the type of model used. Indicator-based and time series approaches rest on the premise that historical statistical regularities will endure. Structural methods rely on a greater variety of hypotheses, both related to exogenous variables and to the validity of the model used, so that it can be difficult to define them concisely. A good forecaster understands his or her own assumptions well.

In practice, experts are often asked about the main risks associated with their forecast. This is closely linked to the identification of the assumptions. One answer is to elaborate model-based 'variants' around the central scenario, using a different set of assumptions and quantifying the resulting impact on the forecast. Another way to characterize the risks is to provide confidence intervals for the key variables, which can convey a sense of the overall uncertainty surrounding the forecast.

1.4 Frequently asked questions

Even before the Great Recession, forecasters often faced questions about the usefulness and relevance of their work. As Robert Solow remarked, 'Forecasting is hard and dangerous, and I don't do it', though he went on in the very next sentence of the same interview to make a assessment of the economy's position in the economic cycle, followed by a prediction about its future course.[7] To round up this overview, below are a few of the most frequently asked questions on this topic, with answers.

1.4.1 Aren't forecasters bound to always get it wrong?

Sometimes, they are lucky and forecast just right. Most of the time, they are off somewhat, or even by a large margin, especially at longer horizons. However, an approximately correct forecast is more valuable than a random guess. And coming close to the outcome is good enough, keeping in mind the substantial revisions that many (though not all) macroeconomic series undergo after their initial release. In addition, the forecast is often much more than a specific value for a specific variable, in so far as it is part of a scenario, with a rationale.

1.4.2 Are forecasters held hostage by their modelling tools?

They shouldn't be, if they are good. Good forecasts are informed by models of one sort or another, but they should also involve a degree of judgement, not least in light of the recent performance of the models used, but also taking into account the known limitations of those models. For example, a forecasting model that lacks any financial variables may not perform well in times of financial stress and should be used with more caution than usual under such circumstances.

1.4.3 Aren't official forecasts always too rosy?

Government growth forecasts are often somewhat optimistic, in part because the authorities believe they should guard against unpleasant self-fulfilling prophecies and not undermine private agents' sentiment by painting an overly bleak outlook. However, this bias may become counterproductive, if firms and households internalize it. Therefore, and to promote fiscal rectitude, some prudent governments prefer systematically to build in a 'margin' and tend to produce forecasts that deliberately err on the low side.

Central bank inflation forecasts are usually less affected by such considerations, in contrast to government inflation forecasts (some of which have tended to display a downward bias). In such cases, the motivation may be to contain public spending growth, or to try to keep workers' wage claims in check.

---

[7] The interview ran as follows:
'Q. What is your assessment of the economy now, and where is it going?
A. Forecasting is hard and dangerous, and I don't do it. But it appears that the worst of the recession is over. However, the economy will be getting better slowly'. *MIT News*, 7 October 2009 (http://web.mit.edu/newsoffice/2009/3q-solow.html).

1.4.4　Is it possible to forecast severe crises?

The vast majority of forecasters failed to anticipate the financial crisis that erupted in 2007. Rather, they kept revising their forecasts frantically downwards as the scope and magnitude of the downturn became evident. This was not the first large-scale crisis that took forecasters by surprise, nor is it likely to be the last. Indeed, *ex post*, it is fairly easy to point out some of the causes of the Great Recession. However, *ex ante*, most experts did not see the financial meltdown coming. As former Federal Reserve Chairman, Alan Greenspan, in his testimony before the US House of Representatives Committee on Oversight and Government Reform, said on 23 October 2008: 'Those of us who have looked to the self-interest of lending institutions to protect shareholders' equity, myself especially, are in a state of shocked disbelief.' Granted, a handful of observers did display greater foresight and warned of an impending disaster. Shiller (2005) warned early on against the bursting of the housing bubble, and Roubini (2006) highlighted several of the risks that in the event did materialize – and was derided as 'Dr Doom' when he did. Similarly, the BIS had warned in its *Annual Reports* for many years before the 2007 crisis against the build-up of financial imbalances and excessive risk-taking. But no observer is on record as having identified all of the determinants of the crisis in advance, nor were any of the more perceptive individuals in a position to forecast its timing with any accuracy.

Further reading

A far more technical and detailed handbook on economic forecasting, based on contributions from leading academics in the field, is Elliott *et al.* (2006). Two specialized journals track the evolution of forecasting techniques: the *Journal of Forecasting* and the *International Journal of Forecasting*. Two relevant websites are forecasters.org and forecastingprinciples.com.

Chapter 2

Business Cycle Analysis

Contents

One of the first challenges faced by forecasters is to find out the actual position of the economy in a cycle, given that many of the hard data appear with considerable lags and are later revised, often substantially. Indeed, a good grip on the starting point is key, as the recent past carries over into quarterly and annual averages. For this purpose, forecasters need to sift through a wealth of data, both 'soft' (opinions) and 'hard' (facts). Filtering this information is an art as much as a science, as some of the incoming data are potentially misleading, or just irrelevant. One of the main difficulties is to adjust the raw data properly for seasonal variations of various sorts. There are different ways of using the filtered information. Synthetic indicators aggregating a number of series provide summary statistics that can help to assess the economy's position in the cycle ahead of national accounts releases. More sophisticated tools can also be used, including advanced methods allowing for non linearities. Alternatively, bridge models based on the links between various indicators and the headline variable to be forecast can be used to estimate where the economy is, and will be in the very short run.

The first step in economic forecasting is to establish the actual position of the economy. This is a prerequisite for a proper forecast of where it is heading (section 2.1). The starting point is therefore the collection of a great variety of economic information with a view to assessing the state of the economy before national accounts data become available, weeks or months later (section 2.2). Survey data can provide precious insights, almost in 'real time', and usefully complement the 'hard data' due to be released later (section 2.3). Once a range of reasonably comprehensive information has been gathered, the challenge is to make sense of it, by adjusting the raw data in various ways and combining some of them to build summary indicators (section 2.4). In this context, bridge models are especially useful for near-term forecasting purposes (section 2.5). Even so, macroeconomic monitoring involves difficult trade-offs between abundant but often seemingly inconsistent bits of information (section 2.6).

2.1 Monitoring the ups and downs

Understanding recent economic developments is the first building block for longer-run forecasts.

2.1.1 Capturing ongoing trends

Gauging where the economy is at present is difficult, since many of the key data appear with considerable lags. In fact, even the recent past has to be estimated, or 'forecast' (this exercise is usually referred to as 'nowcasting'). This is important in many settings. Policy makers need to assess the state of the economy in order to make decisions long before the statistical office renders its *ex post* verdict. Thus central banks dedicate considerable resources to monitoring incoming data. Governments also scrutinize them; for example, to check whether budget execution is on track and to take measures if it isn't. Financial market participants, whose trades are quintessentially forward-looking, are equally eager to find out where things stand and where the next economic inflection point lies. Bond market 'vigilantes', in particular, follow closely all the ups and downs, trying to anticipate what will come next. And, in turn, reactions in financial markets are closely monitored by decision-makers, be they public authorities or business leaders, and at times these influence their behaviour.

2.1.2 Laying down the basis for longer-run forecasts

Understanding the recent past offers clues about the immediate future. For example, an acceleration of output is likely to translate into a pick-up in hires a few months or quarters ahead, which itself will boost household income and therefore consumption. Conversely, some phenomena may foreshadow a subsequent correction. For example, involuntary stock building signals future destocking.

More mechanically, recent developments have direct near-term implications, since the way the data have evolved in the past will to some extent shape future statistical releases. Consider a strong increase in activity at the beginning of year t. This will have a major impact on average annual growth in year t, but not much of an impact on growth in year $t + 1$. But if activity rises sharply towards the end of year t, average annual growth in year t will not be affected much, while average annual growth in year $t + 1$ will be significantly higher, reflecting the so-called carry-over effect (see Appendix 2.1). In that sense, and barring exceptionally steep recessions or booms, average annual growth in a given year is almost a done deal once the GDP data for the third quarter of that year are available, and already much is known about average annual growth in the following year once the GDP data for the last quarter of the current year are published.

In sum, short-term monitoring lays the foundation for forecasting in two ways: by drawing lessons from recent developments, not least to understand why past forecasts were off the mark; and by using fresh information to anticipate near-term evolutions.

2.2 Collecting economic information

Recent economic information typically consists of bits and pieces of variable quality, many of which are subject later to substantial revisions, and some of which are related only loosely to the national accounts framework described in

Annex I. Sifting incoming data is a heavy job, with no end in sight. In addition, it requires making tricky judgement calls, given the trade-off between timeliness and reliability. Yet it is an indispensable and crucial step.

Broadly speaking, the data that need to be collected can be grouped into five categories: domestic production; the international environment; economic policy variables; prices; and private demand. These are analysed using a number of standard statistical descriptors (see Appendix 2.1).

Monitoring supply-side developments in 'real time' is difficult, since the quarterly national accounts data appear with a lag and sometimes do not even provide a detailed decomposition by sector. Hence one needs to work from gross output data, making assumptions about intermediate consumption to derive estimates of value added. Supply-side indicators are readily available for industry (output, orders), agriculture, construction (housing starts and completions) and trade (turnover), but less so for services, which account for the lion's share of GDP. In Japan, however, an indicator of service sector output has been developed analogous to the industrial output index, and efforts are under way in a number of OECD countries to monitor service sector output more efficiently.

The incompleteness of the supply-side statistics can be remedied in two ways. One is by using sectoral labour market data and, in particular, statistics on hours worked (for example, the very detailed monthly reports released by the US Bureau of Labor Statistics). The other is by exploiting survey information (see section 2.3). In addition, comparing the supply-side information with that obtained on the demand side is key, though the latter is often incomplete at the monthly frequency. In principle, data on the income side too can serve as useful checks, but these tend to be even less complete, even at the annual frequency.

On the external side, forecasters need to take into account:

- World demand for the output produced by the country under consideration; that is, the imports of that country's trading partners. This information is available at current prices for almost all countries (and easily accessible in the IMF's Direction of Trade Statistics), and in volume terms – though only for a number of them and with significant lags and uncertainty.
- The evolution of the country's competitiveness, which depends on exchange rate, price and cost developments in that country and in its trading partners. Relatively sophisticated indicators such as cost-competitiveness in manufacturing are available for almost all OECD countries, and consumer price index (CPI)-based real effective exchange rates are available for virtually all economies.
- Financial variables, such as interest rates and equity prices in the major countries (see Chapter 4).

- Commodity price developments, in particular with regard to oil (see Appendix 3.2).

One problem is that these data are not strictly comparable across countries and appear at different times. To some extent, using OECD, IMF or BIS statistics allows this difficulty to be overcome, but at the expense of delays. In practice, therefore, there is a trade-off between data timeliness and consistency.

Turning to fiscal data, a wealth of information is generally released by governments on budgetary developments at monthly, quarterly and annual frequency. Some of it is useful to gauge the evolution of private sector demand; for example, value-added tax (VAT) receipts. But its heterogeneity and pitfalls make it difficult to exploit effectively. Among the complications associated with this type of data are that:

- Some of the most important fiscal variables are available only at an annual frequency, and with delay.
- There are important differences between the budget and the national accounts. For example, privatization receipts are treated as revenue in the budget accounts but not in national accounts (where they are the counterpart of an asset transfer). More generally, budgets are often drawn up in cash terms, whereas national accounts are based on accrual accounting.
- There is usually a whole range of public sector entities: as well as the central government, there are subnational governments and social security bodies, which publish less information and less frequently. This is particularly problematic in federal countries, such as the USA or Germany, where central government typically represents less than half of the general government sector.

In contrast, monetary and financial variables are more readily available. However, this information is not that easy to factor into a short-run forecast, since these variables tend to influence activity and spending with lags and through complex channels. For example, monetary aggregates are available on a monthly basis but they are at best correlated with inflation two or three years later. That said, some financial variables are more relevant for short-run monitoring; for example, credit aggregates and interest rate spreads.

Price data are usually very abundant, as most countries publish numerous monthly and quarterly indices. However, the relevance and quality of this type of data varies, as underlined in Annex I. Moreover, information on asset prices (especially for housing) is often not readily available from a single source. Besides prices, a number of other variables are indicative of the tensions between supply and demand: capacity utilization rates, margins, the unemployment rate, or job offers.

As far as household demand is concerned, data on purchases of goods and some services are readily available (such as car registrations, retail sales), as are data on housing investment. But they are very volatile, and highly sensitive to special factors such as the weather, sales and so on. Household purchases are also difficult to relate to incomes, as the saving rate often displays considerable short-run variation. In addition, incomes themselves are not captured that precisely: while headline wage series are often available, information on benefits is scarcer; in addition, labour compensation is an imperfect proxy for households' total income, since the share of non-wage incomes may fluctuate significantly (partly but not exclusively as a function of the cycle). Furthermore, many of the data are at current prices and on a cash basis, rather than in volume terms and on an accruals basis.

Enterprise investment and stockbuilding is even harder to monitor. Investment indicators appear with long lags and some of them are not aligned with national account concepts or refer to longer-run horizons (multiyear projects). Two specific problems are that a substantial chunk of capital spending is undertaken by new firms, whose activities are not captured well, and that investment outlays tend to be concentrated over time, as they take place at discrete intervals rather than on a continuous basis. While investment in transportation capital goods is relatively well measured, spending on other types of equipment is often estimated indirectly (as a residual based on output and international trade data). In some cases (notably in the USA and Germany), it can be monitored through statistics on orders of durable goods. With regard to investment in buildings, data on the delivery of permits can be used, based on some assumptions as to average construction times (as for households' residential investment). Data on stockbuilding are usually very poor, even taking into account the quantitative information available on the inventories of certain goods (raw materials and agricultural products, for example) or enterprise-level data, as well as the more qualitative information provided by business surveys. Given that investment, and in particular stockbuilding, is very volatile and contributes far more than proportionately to fluctuations in GDP (see section 3.1), these data problems are very serious.

2.3   Business and consumer surveys

Against the backdrop of the shortcomings of the 'hard' high-frequency data, survey evidence, which describes many facets of economic activity, can be extremely helpful – provided it is used properly.

2.3.1   How surveys are carried out

Business and consumer surveys have become very important tools for short-run forecasting purposes. They are conducted regularly by public or private bodies, who ask economic agents how they perceive the current situation and near-term outlook, be it in general or as far as their own prospects are concerned. Though a few are quantitative, the questions are mainly of a qualitative nature. Indeed, qualitative questions (for example, is production up, stable or down?) allow for faster answers and, in the case of firms, they make it possible for managers rather than subordinates to reply. The information is then presented in the form of balances of opinions – also called diffusion indices – which, broadly speaking, can be thought of as the difference between percentages of respondents giving favourable and unfavourable answers; these balances measure to what extent the indicated change is prevalent throughout the sample population.

The samples are usually quite small and stable, so as to increase speed and enhance consistency over time: having the same person answer the questionnaire facilitates prompt replies and means that the questions, especially the qualitative ones, will be understood in the same way from one month or quarter to the next. Small samples, however, imply that the results will be particularly sensitive to the methods used to aggregate individual replies – an issue for firms more than for households, however, since there are a variety of ways to weight the former (usually by taking into account both the relative size of the firm and the economic importance of its sector) while the latter all receive the same weight. Another tricky issue is how to deal with missing replies: one technique is to retain only those respondents who answered in both months when computing month-on-month changes.

In the European Union (EU), the European Commission has long published EU-wide business and consumer survey results, putting much effort into ensuring that the underlying data are as comparable as possible across countries (see Box 2.1). The institutions providing inputs for this purpose are typically leading public or private bodies, such as national statistical institutes (in the case of France) or prominent think tanks which conduct surveys that are well-known in their own right (such as IFO in Germany).

Other prominent European indices include the Purchasing Managers' Index (PMI) indices, published on the first working day of each month for manufacturing and on the third day for services, both for many individual countries and for the euro area as a whole (see Table 2.1). These series are based on surveys conducted by Markit Economics in conjunction with national members of the purchasing associations. The PMIs are diffusion indices, with a reading above 50 suggesting growth and a reading below contraction (just like the PMI of the Institute for Supply Management (ISM) in the USA, described below). They reflect 'hard' evidence only ('is your output up, stable or down?'), and no 'softer' opinions about the future, and are therefore less forward-looking

Box 2.1 European Commission surveys

Since the early 1960s, the European Commission has co-ordinated and published the results of harmonized business surveys across member countries, and since the early 1970s also for consumer surveys. At the time of writing, 125,000 firms are surveyed during the first fortnight of every month in the industry, construction, retail trade and service sectors, alongside 40,000 consumers. In addition, 44,000 industrial firms are polled twice a year in an investment survey. The responses are used as they are, but are also summarized in synthetic confidence indicators, typically defined as arithmetic means of seasonally adjusted balances of the responses to questions closely related to the reference variable they track. EU-wide and euro-area-wide indicators are calculated as weighted averages of the country-aggregate replies, and the weights are updated annually. More specifically, the balances are computed as the difference (in percentage points of total answers) between positive and negative options. If a question has three alternative options, 'positive' (the exact wording varies and may also be 'up', 'more', 'more than sufficient', 'good', 'too large', 'increase', 'improve' and so on), 'neutral' ('unchanged', 'as much', 'sufficient', 'satisfactory', 'adequate' and so on) and 'negative' ('down', 'less', 'not sufficient', 'too small', 'decline' and so on), and if P, E and M stand for the shares of respondents having chosen, respectively, the positive, neutral or negative option, the balance is $B = P - M$. A similar type of calculation applies to questions with a richer menu of options. Hence, balance values range from -100 (all respondents choose the (most) negative option) to $+100$ (all respondents choose the (most) positive option). Though in theory the questions refer explicitly to a 'normal' situation for a given period of time, the opinions recorded may still be influenced by events taking place at the same time every year – for example, Christmas or certain public holidays. This is filtered through seasonal adjustment procedures.

The broadest survey indicator published by the European Commission is the EU economic sentiment indicator, which combines judgements and perceptions of firms and consumers by aggregating the opinion balances of the confidence indicators for industry (with a weight of 40 per cent), services (30 per cent), consumers (20 per cent), construction (5 per cent) and retail trade (5 per cent).

The industrial confidence indicator, for example (shown in Figure 2.1), is the arithmetic average of the balances of the answers to the following questions (the last one with an inverted sign):

- Do you consider your current overall order books to be more than sufficient (above normal), sufficient (normal for the season) or not sufficient (below normal)?
- Do you expect your production over the next three months to increase, to remain unchanged or to decrease?
- Do you consider your current stock of finished products to be too large (above normal), adequate (normal for the season) or too small (below normal)?

than business sentiment measures. They are highly regarded but still have a relatively short history, starting in 1998.

The USA has an even longer-standing tradition of surveying businesses and households. The most prominent surveys include those conducted by the ISM, the University of Michigan and the New York-based Conference Board (see Box 2.2). The ISM's PMI for manufacturing has been available on a monthly basis since 1948, but the index for non-manufacturing sectors is more recent, starting in 1998. The monthly series for the consumer confidence indices published by the University of Michigan and the Conference Board go back to the late 1970s (and much earlier for lower-frequency data).

In Japan, the most prominent business survey is the Bank of Japan's Tankan survey of business sentiment (see Box 2.3). One of its limitations is that it is quarterly. Monthly surveys include NTC Research's manufacturing PMI, based on a sample of 300 companies, which is internationally comparable and is also released on the first working day of each month. However, it began later, in 2001, so its performance is more difficult to assess. Consumer and business confidence surveys are also conducted by the government, in collaboration with the Economic and Social Research Institute (ESRI).

PMIs are also available for the BRIC countries (Brazil, Russia, India and China) and at the global level (see Table 2.1). Global PMIs are produced by Markit Economics, in association with the ISM. They appear in a monthly *Global*

Box 2.2   Some leading US surveys

The ISM was formerly known as the National Association of Purchasing Management (NAPM). Issued on the first business day of each month, its manufacturing PMI is one of the most closely watched near-term economic barometers. On the third business day of the month, the ISM releases its non-manufacturing index, which covers agriculture, mining, construction, trade, finance and many other service sectors. Respondents to ISM surveys (around 350 purchasing agents in both sectors) indicate each month whether particular activities for their organization have increased, decreased or remained unchanged from the previous month. This allows the diffusion indices for each activity to be computed, calculated as the percentage of respondents reporting 'positive' (for example, that activity has increased) plus half of the percentage reporting 'no change'. The composite PMI index is compiled on the basis of the seasonally adjusted diffusion indices for the following five indicators, which since a methodological change in 2008 are equally weighted: new orders, production, employment, supplier deliveries, and inventories. The composite non-manufacturing index is constructed in a similar way, but does not include inventories. An index above 50 denotes expansion compared with the prior month, while a reading under 50 suggests contraction. Other indicators are computed (in particular, for price developments and export orders) but they do not enter the composite indices.

The University of Michigan publishes a widely monitored monthly index of consumer sentiment based on a sample of about 500 telephone interviews. It appears relatively early in the month but is revised later in the same month. The overall index is based on five questions:

1. Are you (and your family living there) better or worse off financially than a year ago?
2. A year from now, will you (and your family living there) be better or worse off financially than now, or just about the same?
3. Turning to business conditions in the country as a whole, will the next 12 months be good or bad financially?
4. Will the next five years more likely see continuous good times, periods of widespread unemployment or depression, or something else?
5. Is now a good or a bad time for people to buy major household items?

In addition, an index of current economic conditions is compiled, averaging the scores for the first and last question, as well as an index of consumer expectations, averaging those for the other questions.

The Conference Board also publishes a monthly consumer confidence index, based on a survey of some 5,000 households. It is usually released on the last Tuesday of the month. The five underlying questions relate to respondents' appraisal of:

1. Current business conditions.
2. Expected business conditions six months hence.
3. Current employment conditions.
4. Expected employment conditions six months hence.
5. Expected total family income six months hence.

For each question, the reply can be positive, negative or neutral (the response proportions are seasonally adjusted) and the positive figure is divided by the sum of the positive and negative to yield a proportion, the 'relative value'. The average relative for 1985 is then used as a benchmark to yield the index value for that question. The consumer confidence index is the average of all five indices. A present situation index is also compiled, as the average of the indices for the first and third questions, as well as an expectations index, which averages the indices for the other questions.

Box 2.3   The Tankan survey

The Tankan is a short-term economic survey of Japanese enterprises carried out in March, June, September and December each year. Firm coverage has varied somewhat over time, with about 10,300 enterprises in the sample in mid-2009. Companies are divided into three groups (large, medium-sized and small), based since 2004 on capitalization rather than employment. The survey also provides a sectoral decomposition: manufacturing is divided into 16 categories and non-manufacturing into 14, following the Japan Standard Industrial Classification introduced in 2002. Hence the results are decomposed into 90 strata (30 industries times three sizes). In addition, a sample of financial institutions is also surveyed (covering about 200 institutions, divided into 18 strata).

The survey contains some 40 questions, grouped into four types: judgemental questions, quarterly data, annual projections and number of new graduates hired (the latter question asked only in June and December). The questions generally cover both the assessment of the current situation and the outlook. Financial institutions are subject only to a subset of these questions. The qualitative judgements (favourable, not so favourable or unfavourable for business conditions; excessive, balanced/adequate or insufficient for demand conditions, inventory levels, production capacity and employment; easy, not so tight or tight for corporate finance; accommodative, not so severe or severe for the lending attitude of financial institutions) are used to calculate diffusion indexes, obtained as the balance of responses with a positive tone minus those with a negative tone (thus ignoring the intermediate answers).

Report on Manufacturing, based on surveys covering more than 7,500 purchasing executives in 29 countries (which together account for some 90 per cent of global manufacturing output). There is also a monthly *Global Report on Services*, based on surveys covering around 3,500 executives in a smaller number of countries (which together account for some 80 per cent of global service sector output). And, last but not least, a global PMI for manufacturing and services combines the two.

2.3.2   Interpreting survey results

Paradoxically, qualitative questions tend to be more informative than quantitative ones, despite it being difficult to summarize their answers using simple averages. This is because firm managers have an overall sense of how the enterprise is doing, but a less a precise knowledge of detailed numbers. It also

Table 2.1 Global manufacturing PMI coverage*

Broad-based PMIs provide a timely gauge of the global cycle

Country	Percentage share in global GDP**	Producer	In association with	Website
United States	28.8	ISM	–	ism.ws
Japan	12.8	Markit	Nomura/JMMA	nomura.co.jp, jmma.gr.jp
China	6.5	Markit	HSBC	hsbc.com
Germany	5.2	Markit	BME	bme.de
United Kingdom	4.3	Markit	CIPS	cips.org
France	3.8	Markit	–	markit.com
Italy	2.9	Markit	ADACI	adaci.it
Brazil	2.1	Markit	HSBC	hsbc.com
India	2.0	Markit	HSBC	hsbc.com
South Korea	1.9	Markit	HSBC	hsbc.com
Spain	1.8	Markit	AERCE	aerce.org
Mexico	1.7	HSBC	–	hsbc.com
Australia	1.3	AIG	PriceWaterhouse Coopers	aigroup.asn.au, pwcglobal.com/au
Netherlands	1.1	Markit	NEVI	nevi.nl
Russia	1.1	Markit	VTB Capital	vtb.com
Turkey	1.0	Markit	HSBC	hsbc.com
Taiwan	0.8	Markit	HSBC	hsbc.com
Switzerland	0.7	SVME	Credit Suisse	svme.ch, credit-suisse.ch
Poland	0.6	Markit	HSBC	hsbc.com
Austria	0.6	Markit	BA Creditanstalt/ OPWZ	ba-ca.com, einkauf. opwz.com
South Africa	0.5	BER	IPSA/Kagiso	ber.sun.ac.za, ipsa. co.za, kagiso.com
Denmark	0.4	DILF	Kairoscommodities	dilf.dk, kairos commodities.com
Greece	0.4	Markit	HPI	hpi.org
Israel	0.4	IPLMA	Bank Hapoalim Ltd	iplma.org.il, bankhapoalim.co.il
Ireland	0.3	Markit	NCB Stockbrokers	ncbdirect.com
Singapore	0.3	SIPMM	–	sipmm.org.sg
Czech Republic	0.2	Markit	HSBC	hsbc.com
New Zealand	0.2	Business NZ	Bank of New Zealand	businessnz.org.nz, bnz.co.nz
Hungary	0.2	HALPIM	Hungarian National Bank	logisztika.hu

* As at mid-2010.
** As estimated by the World Bank (2008 data, in US dollars, at market exchange rates).
Sources: Markit, JPMorgan Chase Bank.

reflects problems of comparability across firms and sectors, which render aggregation more hazardous. The quantitative surveys on investment conducted under the aegis of the European Commission are a good illustration: expectations and outcomes often differ radically. Similarly, the quantitative information provided by managers on prices and wages does not add much to what is already known from the detailed price and wage statistics. One exception relates to capacity utilization rates, for which respondents are asked for a point estimate: this sort of information is usually not available elsewhere and is very useful.[1]

As indicated above, some of the qualitative surveys are conducted somewhat differently across countries and sectors. For purposes of comparability, it is useful to normalize them; that is, to translate the results into departures from a long-run average, divided by the standard deviation of the series (this is done in Figure 2.1). This also allows the analyst to control for any structural bias in the responses (for example, if for some reason there is a propensity to err on the pessimistic side). But even then, a number of caveats need to be borne in mind:

- Depending on the period within the month when the survey is actually conducted, it may reflect the previous calendar month more than the current month, or vice versa.
- The horizon over which respondents actually reason may not be the one stated in the question: French businesses asked about their own production prospects are supposed to indicate what they expect over the next three months, compared to six months in Germany, but in practice they tend to look implicitly at a similar horizon.
- Answers to questions about firms' own situation are generally more informative than those about the respondents' perception of the economy-wide outlook.
- The vaguer questions posed to households about their view of overall economic conditions may be coloured by political or other non-economic news. In fact, consumer confidence is less closely correlated with actual economic trends than business confidence and, based on the information available at the time of the forecast, consumer confidence often fails to improve forecasts

---

[1]There is more than one way to define capacity utilization. For example, the US Federal Reserve's measure of capacity utilization assumes the availability of additional labour, if needed, as is standard practice in most other countries. In contrast, the Institute of Supply Management measures the capacity of plants to produce with their current labour force. Following a significant cyclical contraction in manufacturing employment, a definition of capacity relying on workers in place will indicate much less slack than one that does not consider current employees as a limiting factor.

Figure 2.1   Business confidence*

Business sentiment is one of the better indicators of the cycle

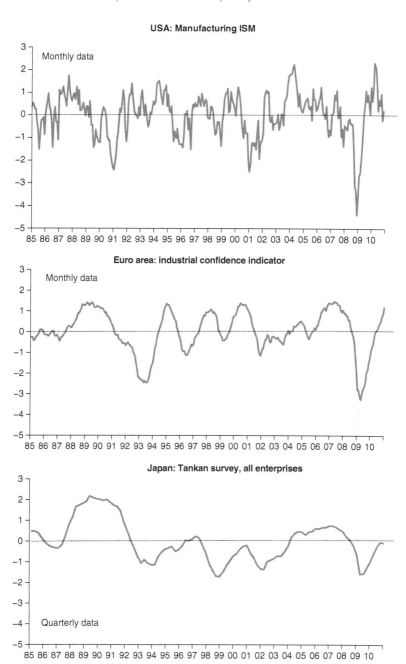

USA: Manufacturing ISM

Euro area: industrial confidence indicator

Japan: Tankan survey, all enterprises

*Deviation from long-run average, in units of standard deviation.
Sources: Institute for Supply Management, European Commission, Bank of Japan.

of consumer spending (Croushore, 2005; Cotsomitis and Kwan, 2006).[2] Similarly, business surveys of the trade sector are less reliable than surveys of industry.

- A given balance of responses may have a different meaning depending on the cyclical context; for some questions, there may be a tendency to over-react when the cycle turns sour but to underreact when prospects take a turn for the better. And a given balance value might have different implications depending on the relative importance of the 'neutral' responses. Questions on inventories are also difficult to interpret: the rule is that inventories are deemed to be on the low side the more that orders increase, but by how much depends on the level of activity.

- With the expansion of multinational firms and the globalization of activity, the replies to questions on their own situation by a respondent in establishment X of firm Y increasingly tend to reflect the overall situation rather than just their own. This should serve to nuance the results region by region or sector by sector. Similarly, surveys conducted in small, open economies may be less informative about the economies themselves than about the situation more broadly: for example, industrial confidence in Belgium is seen as more useful as a bellwether of the situation in the euro area at large than as an early indicator of developments in that country (also because Belgian industry is relatively specialized in cyclically-upstream intermediate goods).

- Since any balance value is limited on both the downside and the upside, both its level and its change have to be considered when assessing the state of the business cycle.

For all these reasons, normalizing the responses may not be enough, and more sophisticated techniques may be needed to exploit survey information fully (see section 2.5).

2.4   Making sense of the data

Once the raw data have been collected, they need to be processed. First, they need to be adjusted for seasonality and working days if this has not already been done. While the data practitioners download are often already adjusted in this sense, this is not always the case and how exactly such adjustment is carried out matters. Next, they can be combined to form synthetic indicators

---

[2] This finding, however, may at least partly reflect the shortcomings of the models used to forecast consumer spending. In addition, using the answers to the individual component questions of consumer surveys may work better, especially around cyclical turning points (Wilcox, 2007).

characterizing overall cyclical conditions, or turning-point indicators which signal possible inflections in the cycle.

2.4.1 Adjusting the raw data

Smoothing

The raw data, especially at high frequencies, may be very volatile, reflecting short-run shocks of various kinds (strikes or extreme weather, for example) and/or measurement problems. One way to smooth the series – if indeed the view is that it is unduly bumpy – is then simply to remove the outliers. For this solution to be warranted, however, truly exceptional factors have to be identifiable, and, even then, outright removal may be unsatisfactory.

A more common technique is to use moving averages. Let X_t be the variable under consideration. The centred and uniformly weighted moving average is then:

$$(X_{t-k} + X_{t-k+1} + \cdots + X_{t-1} + X_t + X_{t+1} + X_{t+2} + \cdots + X_{t+k}) / p$$

where $p = 2k + 1$ and k is chosen as a function of the desired degree of smoothness. Depending on how forward- or backward-looking the moving average is to be, it can be computed asymmetrically. For example, if it is intended to capture recent trends, it can be computed as:

$$(X_{t-k} + X_{t-k+1} + \cdots + X_{t-1} + X_t) / (k+1)$$

The drawback of this formulation is that it overstates past developments and tends to lag actual data. Alternatively, it is possible to assign smaller weights to periods further away from time t. For example, one could define the moving average as:

$$(X_{t-2} + 2 X_{t-1} + 3 X_t + 2 X_{t+1} + X_{t+2}) / 9$$

All in all, many different types of specifications can be used. The choice of the averaging method can matter greatly, especially around turning points, as illustrated by the case of US industrial output: the centred moving average distinctly precedes the lagged one both during the downturn in 2007–8 and once activity started to turn around in 2009 (see Figure 2.2). *A priori*, symmetric averaging seems preferable, but of course, in real time, the analyst does not know the forthcoming observations that enter the moving average. In practice, therefore, asymmetric averaging is often used. Alternatively, one can forecast the required $X_{t+1}, \ldots, X_{t+k}$ (for example, by using the time series methods presented in Annex II).

Seasonal adjustment

One reason for the bumpiness of the raw data may be seasonal variations, when these are not already controlled for. A simple way to remove their impact – or at least most of it – is to look at cumulative data or changes over the previous 12 months rather than at month-on-month or quarter-on-quarter data.[3] One drawback, however, is that this amounts to focusing on a lagging variable. Consider a variable that is steadily increasing, then suddenly drops, and then starts growing again but at a slower rate (see Figure 2.3). If the focus is on year-on-year changes, the analyst will initially perceive less of a slowdown than is in fact occurring. Subsequently, he or she will measure a further slowdown even though growth has already resumed, and will be almost one year late in identifying the upturn.

Alternatively, the series itself can be deseasonalized (only when appropriate, however – some series, such as certain financial data, are not obviously subject

Figure 2.2   Alternative ways to average*
Lagging moving averages fail to capture turning points early enough

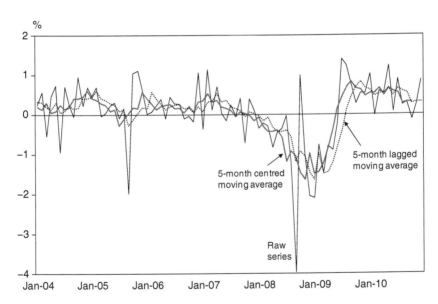

*Month-on-month rate of change in US industrial output, seasonally adjusted.
Source: Federal Reserve.

---

[3] Seasonality may not be removed entirely, however, for example when Easter matters for the series under consideration and falls in a different month from one year to the next (see below). And even if seasonality is removed, the analyst needs to be fully aware of the nature of the corrections that have been implemented.

Figure 2.3   Year-on-year versus quarter-on-quarter changes*
Changes over the previous year may be misleading

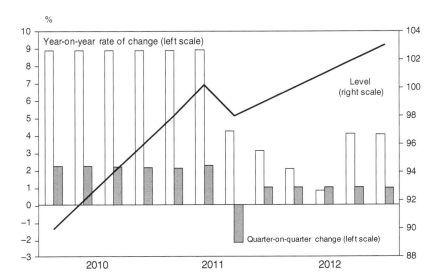

*Hypothetical economy.

to significant seasonal oscillations). This can be done in multiplicative or additive fashion. The former amounts to decomposing the series as the product of a trend T_t, a seasonal coefficient S_t (which in the absence of seasonality equals 1) and a random or irregular component I_t:

$$X_t = T_t\, S_t\, I_t$$

Alternatively, the decomposition can be carried out additively, with:

$$X_t = T_t + S_t + I_t$$

The seasonally adjusted series, respectively X_t / S_t or $X_t - S_t$, will not be smooth if I_t moves around significantly. Moreover, what is called trend here is in fact the combination of cyclical movement and a long-run trend (on the latter, see Annex II). The choice between the multiplicative and additive approach depends on whether T, S and I are roughly proportional or not. If they are, as is often the case, the multiplicative formula is advisable. If not, the additive one is to be preferred. Also, when X takes on negative values, only the additive formula can be used.

In both cases, the aim of deseasonalization is essentially to derive S_t by comparing developments in a given month (quarter) with those in the same month (quarter) of other years. In this respect, it is first necessary to have sufficient data – say five years' worth. In addition, one has to extend the available series by at least a few months to be able to smooth the latest observations using centred moving averages or similar procedures implemented by seasonal adjustment software. Another reason is the need to derive seasonal adjustment coefficients that can be applied to future raw data. These coefficients are usually not stable over time, as the impact of seasonal factors evolves; in France, for example, August used to be a 'dead month' when a large proportion of the population was on holiday, implying a large seasonal adjustment; but, as the French have tended to spread out their holidays more over the year, the size of the adjustment has declined.

In practice, there are several deseasonalization software packages. A widely-used programme is X-12 (see Appendix 2.1), developed by the US Bureau of Census. It can be downloaded from census.gov/srd/www/x12a.

There are other packages, notably those based on the spectral decomposition of time series, such as the so-called BV4 method, or the Baxter and King filter (see Annex II). Different methods can yield very different results, as is evident when comparing the GDP growth estimates available for Germany using one or the other method, which at times diverge quite considerably (see Figure 2.4).

Deseasonalization is important to properly assess the shape of the cycle, including possible turning points. It also facilitates international comparisons, given that seasonal oscillations differ from one country to another. Three complications deserve to be underlined, however:

- The usual procedures rely on smoothing techniques that typically suffer from end-point problems. More generally, deseasonalization is a statistical procedure which by its very nature is subject to uncertainty.
- Standard push-button procedures ignore idiosyncratic irregularities, such as a drop in output resulting from a strike. Proper deseasonalization requires an intimate knowledge of the series.
- Some seasonal oscillations vary over time. For example, this is the case in Germany, where school holiday dates change from one year (and one *Land*) to the next, causing seasonally adjusted industrial production to move rather erratically over the summer months.

Working-day adjustment

Another important factor that needs to be taken into account when 'cleaning up' the raw data is that the number of working (or 'trading') days varies from one month, one quarter or one year to the next (in the case of annual data, leap

Figure 2.4   Two incarnations of German real GDP*

The choice of the deseasonalization method matters

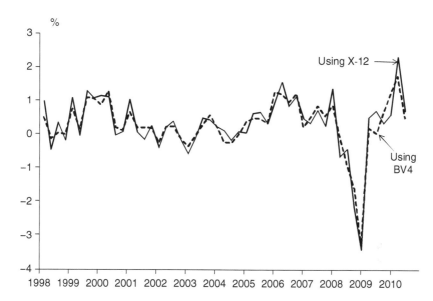

*Quarter-on-quarter rate of change, seasonally and working-day adjusted.
Sources: Bundesbank, DIW.

years are a well-known problem in this respect).[4] How many of these there are in a given period may not matter for the consumption of food or for rents, but it does for retail sales, for example. In the case of industrial output, one extra working day can push up monthly production mechanically by as much as 5 per cent or so (given that there are around 20 working days per month).

Correcting for the number of working days is particularly tricky, however. To some extent, working-day effects are seasonal, and deseasonalization therefore already takes them into account. Christmas, for example, always falls in December. However, it does not always fall on a Sunday. In fact, only once in every 28 years is the calendar identical in terms of dates and days of the week. Moreover, some holidays are set according to the lunar cycle, which is not synchronized with the (solar) calendar of economic activity. This is the case for a few celebrations in Europe and North America (Easter in particular). It is more of a problem in Asia,

---

[4] For example, 2004 was a leap year and in addition several public holidays fell at weekends, leading to 2.8 more working days than average in the euro area. The ECB estimated the implied calendar effect on GDP growth to around ¼ per cent, albeit with considerable differences across countries, ranging from ½ per cent in Germany to ¼ per cent in France and even less in some other euro area members (ECB, 2004a).

as well as in Muslim countries because of the length of Ramadan. Furthermore, the elasticity of economic variables with respect to the number of working days is not necessarily fixed. It may depend in particular on the economy's position in the cycle.[5] Hence, fully correcting for working-day effects can be an impossible task and might only be feasible on a qualitative basis.

In practice, working-day correction starts with the identification of the series that are likely to be affected by this problem, such as industrial output, exports and imports (except for dealing with tourists, customs offices are not open seven days a week), retail sales and so on. Four different types of methods can then be applied to these series:

- The first is to adjust the individual components of the relevant series directly; for example, production industry by industry, drawing on specialized knowledge of the practices in each. The raw data are then adjusted proportionately based on a standardized number of working days.
- Alternatively, one can test econometrically to check whether the number of Mondays, Tuesdays and so on in a month has a statistically significant influence on the raw monthly series. If so, the latter can be adjusted accordingly. To some extent, this type of test is in fact embedded in most deseasonalization packages.
- The third approach is to calculate for each month the number of working days in excess of or below the long-run average, and to adjust the raw data proportionately. De facto, however, this tends to lead to overcorrections.
- Yet another approach is to first identify and adjust for the working-day effects that are controlled for by the deseasonalization procedure, and then to deal with the residual irregular component to see if it still contains some working-day effects. This type of treatment of the data can be applied iteratively.

Caveats

Users should, of course, be careful to establish whether the series they work with are seasonally and/or working-day adjusted or not, and what sorts of corrections were indeed implemented, and try to avoid mixing genres. Several presentational problems may also arise. For example, annual growth rates may differ when using adjusted quarterly figures and raw data, not least for leap years. Or the balance between two adjusted series may not match the adjusted raw balance.

---

[5] See Lin and Liu (2002), who note that the date of the three most important Chinese holidays (Chinese New Year, Dragon-Boat Festival and Mid-Autumn Holiday) are determined by a lunar calendar and move between two solar months, strongly affecting consumption and production in countries with large Chinese populations. They also document that when unemployment rises, the magnitude of holiday and seasonal factors declines.

A last note of caution is in order: even when the raw data are not, or no longer, revised, the seasonally and/or working-day adjusted series can continue to change as new observations lead to the re-estimation of adjustment coefficients, which are then applied retroactively to the historical raw data. This is referred to as the 'wagging tail' problem.

2.4.2   Synthetic indicators

The data can be combined or used in a variety of ways to produce synthetic leading, coincident or lagging indicators of the business cycle. The confidence indices and the composite PMIs described above are in effect one example of such synthetic indicators and are intuitively appealing for broader audiences in that they seem to capture prevalent moods. However, they are rather *ad hoc*, and to the extent that they do move with the cycle, the leads or lags vary across countries and over time. Hence, while they do help to identify major swings and are a useful tool to characterize economic agents' psychological condition, other indicators may in some cases signal changes in activity more effectively.

One possible short-cut of sorts to try to anticipate cyclical developments is to focus on financial variables, and specifically on equity prices (which in principle embody future profits and therefore reflect growth prospects), interest-rate spreads between riskier and less risky bonds (with a presumption that a smaller spread denotes a lower probability of default, and hence a more favourable outlook for activity) and the difference between long- and short-term interest rates, the so-called 'yield curve', or 'term spread' (see Box 2.4).

A more comprehensive approach is to use a much broader range of variables to construct synthetic cyclical indicators. This approach was already quite popular at the start of the twentieth century, when some crude 'business barometers' were computed. At the time of the Great Depression, the NBER, having dated the US cycle, developed a more rational approach, by classifying economic statistics that distinguished leading, coincident and lagging series (Burns and Mitchell, 1946). The series were then combined into composite indicators correlated with the cycle, in order to depict the economic situation in real time. Aggregating a variety of series reduced the risk that noise in any one of them would send incorrect signals. To be considered, the series had to have sufficient coverage, timeliness, correlation with the cycle, and economic relevance. Other important selection criteria included their susceptibility to revisions and short-run variability.

Since the 1980s, the OECD publishes this type of synthetic indicators, in the form of monthly composite leading indicators (CLIs). These are constructed to predict turning points in the cycle of a reference series that is chosen as a proxy measure for aggregate economic activity. Industrial (or in a few cases, manufacturing) output is used as the reference series as it correlates fairly well with GDP,

Box 2.4 What does the yield curve say about future growth?

A number of analysts put considerable emphasis on the yield curve alone, based on the striking empirical correlation between the term spread and GDP growth several quarters down the road, both in the main advanced economies and more globally (Harvey, 1991). The canonical linear regression used in this context is $g = \alpha + \beta s$, where g stands for real GDP growth over some future period, s for the current yield spread and α for the expected growth rate when short- and long-term interest rates are identical. Alternatively, a probit equation is used where the spread determines the probability of recession several quarters hence (Estrella and Trubin, 2007).

In practice, every US recession (as defined by the NBER) since the late 1960s has been preceded by a negative (or 'inverted') term spread, albeit with a variable lag ranging from two to six quarters (see Figure 2.5). Moreover, every yield curve inversion has been followed by a recession (suggesting that this indicator rarely sends 'false signals'), and longer inversions have tended to be followed by longer recessions. Hence, the yield curve seems to provide useful early warnings of business cycle turning points and, in practice, many forecasters closely monitor this curve.

Figure 2.5 Yield spread and recessions*
The slope of the term spread seems to be a fairly good predictor of recessions

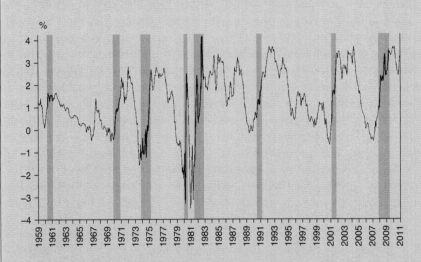

*10-year T-bond rate minus three-month T-bill rate, monthly averages.
**Shaded areas indicate the recessions as identified by the NBER.
Source: Federal Reserve Bank of New York.

Several types of economic rationale tend to be invoked to explain this pattern. The first pertains to agents' portfolio choices: if they expect a recession, they will adjust their portfolio away from short-term bonds towards longer-term ones with a view to earning interest later to cushion future income losses; this pushes short-term yields up and longer-term yields down, thus flattening or even inverting the yield curve. The second rationale is that, during recessions, short-term interest rates are low, as the central bank tries to counter the downturn, while long-term interest rates are higher, since agents expect future short-term interest rates to rise. Hence an upward-sloping yield curve is associated with bad times today but better times tomorrow, while the reverse holds during economic expansions. A third rationale is that a falling term spread discourages banks (inasmuch as they borrow short and lend long) from engaging in new lending, thus leading to lower credit creation and activity – and vice versa.

However, the situation is far from clear-cut. These explanations often rely on the assumption that private agents can anticipate future developments relatively well, which is far from obvious, notably least when compared to monetary authorities. Moreover, interest rates are quite volatile and the lags between changes in term spreads and activity vary and can be relatively long – at least for those forecasters who look mainly at the very short run. Therefore, the yield curve should not be seen as more than just one useful advance indicator among others.

constitutes the most cyclical subset of economy-wide activity and – unlike GDP – is available at a monthly frequency for most OECD countries.

The CLI for a given economy combines a set of series selected on the basis of their economic relationship with the reference series, their cyclical behaviour (their cycle should lead that of the reference series, with no missing or extra cycles, and the lead at turning points should not vary too much over time) and data quality (coverage, frequency, availability, absence of breaks, and limited revisions). If necessary, quarterly components are converted into a monthly series by linear interpolation. For most countries, variables such as share prices, interest rates, car registrations and business/consumer survey data will be included, as well as variables for a key foreign country in a few cases. The list of component series is revised regularly, if only because over time some components are suspended by the national source, but also because they may gradually lose relevance.

Each component of the CLI is equally weighted in the aggregation process. Before they are aggregated, however, they are deseasonalized, and outliers (caused, for example, by strikes or changes in regulations) are removed. In addition, each component has to be de-trended. Since 2008, this has been done using a Hodrick–Prescott filter (described in Chapter 6), which is run as a band-pass filter with parameters set so that cycles shorter than 12 months and longer than 120 months are filtered out (OECD, 2008). The components are then normalized, by subtracting from the filtered observations the mean of the series, and dividing this by the mean absolute deviation of the series.

As this approach rests on the concept of 'growth cycles', defined as recurrent fluctuations in the series of deviations from trend, it produces different results from the 'classical' approach (say, the NBER's) of cycles: growth cycle contractions include slowdowns as well as absolute declines in activity, in contrast with classical contractions, which include only absolute declines (recessions). The difference is illustrated in Figure 2.6, which shows that growth peaks tend to precede level peaks, whereas growth troughs tend to occur after level troughs.

In turn, once its components have been assembled, the CLI itself is adjusted to ensure that its cyclical amplitude matches on average that of the de-trended reference series. The OECD presents information on each CLI in three different forms:

- By comparing the amplitude-adjusted CLI to the de-trended reference series. The adjustment rescales the CLI so that its amplitude matches that of the reference series.

Figure 2.6 Activity versus growth cycle: turning points
Turning points in level and growth terms differ

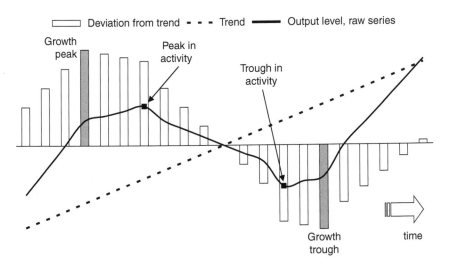

- The 'trend-restored' CLI – reincorporating the trend component – allows direct comparisons with the evolution of the reference series.
- The '12-month rate of change' of the trend-restored CLI is directly comparable with year-on-year GDP or industrial output rates of change.

This information needs to be handled with care. In particular, a turning point in the CLI needs to be sufficiently marked and durable – not least with respect to its past developments – and widely shared among its components before inferring that a turning point in the reference series is imminent. Moreover, the ability of the CLI to predict turning points may vary over time and across countries. A good example of the difficulties in analysing such indicators is provided by the US Great Recession, which, according to the NBER, started in December 2007 and ended in June 2009. The OECD CLI for the USA did in fact peak in June 2007; that is, almost six months before the recession. However, the indicator declined only slowly during the initial first year; it was only after spring 2008 that it dropped sharply, in line with the severity of the ongoing recession. Similarly, the indicator rebounded markedly after February 2009, again several months in advance compared to actual output. But the strength of this rebound was somewhat misleading: the indicator went back to close to its pre-crisis levels by early 2010, though the real US economy remained significantly weaker (with a persistently large output gap).

In addition, the OECD CLIs have some limitations. Publication of timely CLIs generally entails the use of an incomplete set of component series, with the minimum percentage of component series required being 60 per cent. This reduces the precision or stability of turning-point signals. Moreover, these indicators are revised substantially over time, which makes it difficult, when looking at the latest observations, to distinguish turning-point signals from erratic CLI fluctuations. Furthermore, industrial production accounts for a shrinking share of GDP and is one of its more volatile building blocks. Last but not least, the composition of the CLIs is often significantly modified *ex post* to improve the tracking of past cycles. Nevertheless, as a practical matter, other leading indicators for major economies based on somewhat different methodologies do not outperform the OECD CLIs. For example, the OECD's CLI for the USA evolves in tandem with the leading indicators developed by the Conference Board (see Box 2.5).

Similar CLIs are also produced elsewhere. For example, Goldman Sachs monitors a Global Leading Indicator which combines high-frequency information such as US weekly job claims, monthly South Korean exports (which are published very quickly), and business and consumer confidence surveys to predict changes in industrial production three to six months ahead.

Box 2.5 The US Conference Board's composite indicators

Every month, the US Conference Board releases a widely watched set of composite leading, coincident and lagging indicators for the USA and several other large economies. The standardization factor of each component is inversely related to the historic standard deviation of its month-to-month change over recent decades and the factors are normalized to sum to one (see Table 2.2). To address the problem of lags in data availability, those indicators that are not available at the time of publication are estimated by using an auto-regressive model. The resulting indices thus incorporate

Table 2.2 Leading, coincident and lagging indicators for the US economy
Some high-frequency indicators are far more forward-looking than others

	2010 standardization factor
Leading index	
Average weekly working hours in manufacturing	0.2725
Average weekly initial claims for unemployment insurance	0.0322
Manufacturers' new orders (consumer goods and materials)	0.0809
Vendor performance (slower deliveries diffusion index)	0.0715
Manufacturers' new orders (non-defence capital goods)	0.0192
Building permits for new private housing units	0.0263
Stock prices (500 common stocks)	0.0373
Money supply (M2)	0.3248
Interest rate spread (10-year Treasury bonds less federal funds)	0.1058
Index of consumer expectations	0.0295
Total	1
Coincident index	
Employees on non-agricultural payrolls	0.4949
Personal income less transfer payments	0.2615
Industrial production	0.1346
Manufacturing and trade sales	0.1090
Total	1
Lagging index	
Average duration of unemployment	0.0356
Inventories-to-sales ratio (manufacturing and trade)	0.1192
Labour cost per unit of output in manufacturing	0.0631
Average prime rate charged by banks	0.2731
Commercial and industrial loans	0.1071
Ratio of consumer instalment credit to personal income	0.2117
Consumer price index for services	0.1902
Total	1

Source: The Conference Board.

actual and estimated data, and are revised later on as the data unavailable at the time of publication are subsequently released.

One interpretation of the Conference Board's leading index, from Vaccara and Zarnowitz (1978), is that if it declines for three months in a row, it signals an impending downturn. While crude, this type of rule of thumb is not necessarily outperformed by more sophisticated methods (Filardo, 2004).

2.4.3 More advanced techniques

Techniques have been developed since the late 1980s – in particular, following an influential contribution by Stock and Watson (1989) – to overcome some of the problems highlighted above, in the form of more rigorous statistical procedures and the replacement of judgemental characterizations of the current situation by more formal and probabilistic ones (quantifying the likelihood of being in a recession or an expansion, or to face either of these). These new tools are quite sophisticated, however, and some of them are still somewhat experimental.

One avenue is dynamic factor analysis, which builds on the insight that when a set of macroeconomic time series clearly tend to move together, the evolution of each can be represented as a linear combination of the evolution of a small number of common latent variables which drive the co-movements (the so-called common factors), and of an uncorrelated residual term (the idiosyncratic component). More specifically, if X^i_t is the ith series being observed:

$$X^i_t = a^i\, C_t + \varepsilon^i_t$$

where C_t is the ($k \times 1$) vector of k common factors, a^i a ($1 \times k$) vector of parameters and ε^i is white noise. The model is then written in so-called state-space form, as the variables are unobservable, and the parameters are estimated through a maximum likelihood procedure, using a Kalman filter. This allows for the derivation of a relatively smooth synthetic indicator. It also sheds light on the contribution of each series to the overall outlook; for example, if in a recovery order books in industry are buoyant, they may at first glance seem to be one of the drivers of the upturn, but once the common factor is taken into account, it may well appear that they are in fact a drag.

This type of analysis is carried out in a number of central banks. For example, the Federal Reserve Bank of Philadelphia monitors and publishes a business conditions index to track the cycle (Aruoba *et al.*, 2009). It rests on six underlying indicators, blending different frequencies and stock and flow data: weekly initial jobless claims; monthly payroll employment; industrial production; personal income less transfer payments; manufacturing and trade sales; and quarterly real GDP.

In Europe, the Euro-STING model has been developed at the Spanish central bank, where STING stands for Short Term INdicators of Growth (Camacho and Perez-Quiros, 2008). This model allows for daily updates of the quarterly GDP forecast for the yet-to-be-released quarter and the two subsequent ones. In a somewhat similar vein, Frale *et al.* (2009) set out a monthly measure for euro area GDP based on a small-scale factor model for mixed frequency data, featuring two factors, one driven by hard data and the other capturing the contribution of survey variables as coincident indicators.

A related, though different, approach underpins the new EuroCOIN index for the euro area, introduced in 2007 by the Banca d'Italia (Altissimo *et al.*, 2007). It uses a very large dataset and is based on generalized principal components, to extract the common, longer-run information on GDP that it contains. Indeed, the purpose here is to provide a real-time estimate of GDP growth purged of short-run oscillations (defined as not exceeding one year).

Another class of studies has focused on the probability of facing a cyclical turning point. Artis *et al.* (1995) followed this route, setting up a framework that treats turning-point prediction as a problem of pattern recognition, based on a variant of the Bayesian forecasting method developed by Neftçi (1982). First, a business-cycle chronology is constructed to describe the past as an oscillation between two regimes – downturns and upturns.[6] A turning point is said to occur when the regime shifts. Then, a leading indicator is scrutinized to try to recognize early on that a turning point in the reference series lies ahead. In addition to the statistical delay for obtaining the leading data, two types of lags come into play: the time needed to realize that a turning point in the leading series has been reached (the 'recognition lag'), and the lead time between turning points of the leading and the reference series (the 'signal lead time'). They involve a trade-off: attempting to increase the signal lead time by reducing the recognition lag runs the risk of issuing false signals. This risk, however, can be reduced by exploiting the cumulative information provided as observations come in, taking into account the distributions observed in past regimes. This allows for the derivation of a probabilistic indicator of being in one regime or the other that varies in intensity, rather than simply flashing 'on' or 'off'. Yet the user still has to decide on a threshold value for the probabilistic indicator

---

[6] It is also possible to use existing chronologies, such as those produced by the Business Cycle Dating Committee of the NBER or the CEPR for classical cycles in the USA and the euro area, respectively, or the ones published by the Economic Cycle Research Institute (ECRI) for growth cycles in several countries.

at which to issue a turning-point call. Moreover, the choice of the indicator as well as the pre-determination of the cycles leave some room for discretion.

One of the key elements in predicting the turning point is the assumption made regarding the expected lifetime of the reference series' regime: is a regime more likely to end as it ages? More formally, is the conditional probability or 'hazard' of a regime ending at time *t*, given that it has survived up to that time, increasing, decreasing or constant? If it is increasing (decreasing) within a regime, there is said to be positive (negative) duration dependence in that regime; if it is constant, there is said to be duration independence. The empirical studies quoted in Artis *et al.* (1995) suggest, perhaps somewhat counter-intuitively, that in practice the latter can be assumed. Indeed, duration independence is not inconsistent with the notion that the longer a regime persists, the rarer it is.

More recent work in the probabilistic vein (albeit with a different functional set-up) has emphasized cross-country links. Sensier *et al.* (2004) looked at classical business cycles in Germany, France, Italy and the United Kingdom, with regimes defined as binary variables (recessions, expansions); and Osborn *et al.* (2004) have done the same for growth cycles. In both cases, foreign variables enter significantly into the national leading indicators. In this context, it is worth noting that growth cycles typically exhibit more frequent regime changes than do classical cycles. This is not surprising, since a spell of slow growth may be sufficient to define a growth recession even in the absence of the output decline that defines a classical recession. Growth cycles are also closer to being symmetric, in the sense of approximately the same number of observations falling in recessions and expansions.

A somewhat different approach to turning points is based on the so-called hidden Markov-switching models, a statistical tool originally developed in the 1960s for speech recognition purposes. The idea, again, is that the economy moves back and forth between two regimes, with a probability that varies over time, depending on the evolution of an unobserved 'state' variable. Observed statistical series (say, business confidence) are characterized by two different probability distributions, depending on the type of regime and thus on the unobserved state variable. Each new data point is treated as a 'surprise' compared to the assumed probability distribution of the observed series. It will therefore give some information regarding the probability of the unobserved variable being in one state or another. A sudden change in this probability will signal that a turning point is imminent. This methodology is applied to French business survey data by Gregoir and Lenglart (2000), to UK data by Simpson *et al.* (2001), and to German data by Bandholz and Funke (2003). Andersson *et al.* (2004) evaluate the merits of this and related approaches using the Swedish recession of the early 1990s as an example. While Markov-switching non-linear effects have some intuitive appeal, Harding and Pagan (2002) argue that this approach in fact fails to outperform simpler, linear models.

Finally, another non-linear approach has been explored, known as neural network models, developed initially in computer science and widely used in medical science and engineering, which have powerful pattern-recognition abilities (Kaashoek and van Dijk, 2003). This approach is also premised on the view that linear, constant-parameter models are not adequate for forecasting turning points. In principle, this class of models offers a very general framework which can approximate any type of non-linearity in the data. Qi (2001) applies this methodology with some success to US data, and Heravi *et al.* (2004) to European data. However, because of their very flexibility in approximating different functional forms, neural network models run the risk of 'overfitting'. This raises the likelihood that, despite a near-perfect in-sample fit, the representation of the data-generation process might be incorrect, leading to poor out-of-sample predictions.

In a nutshell, these advanced techniques present several advantages, not least the estimation of various 'signals' that nicely complement more traditional monitoring exercises. There are, however, two drawbacks. First, the emergence of any signal often appears to come from a 'black box', implying that it is difficult to present a convincing economic story. And a second, related, problem is that communicating this information to forecast users is often challenging.

2.5   Bridge models

Business and consumer surveys provide the earliest economic information but it is mainly of a qualitative nature, whereas forecasters aim for quantification. One way to bridge this gap is to use econometric techniques to pin down the relationship between 'soft' survey evidence and 'hard' economic indicators, so as to extrapolate it over the forecast period. Generally, such bridge models are estimated equation by equation, but joint estimation is also possible. The interpretation of this type of equations, however, is not straightforward. Survey data are imperfect measures of agents' expectations, because of sampling errors and the phrasing of the questions, and expectations themselves may be wrong (Nardo, 2003). Also, how does causality run? It is not clear, for example, whether business managers' views determine future production, or whether their answers to survey questions are shaped by the outlook but do not 'cause' it.

The first step is to select the most relevant survey indicators. Generally, balances of opinion are used, both in level terms and in first difference. The choice among survey questions is based on the forecaster's experience, but it can also be informed by elaborate statistical testing along the lines discussed in Section 2.4, or drawing on vector auto-regression (see Annex II). In practice, most of the useful information for forecasting is often embodied in a small subset of questions and answers.

Before linking up soft and hard variables, a few checks are in order, including:

- Sectoral coverage, which may not be similar. In some countries, statistical coverage differs in the monthly and in the quarterly data for what at first sight might look like one and the same indicator.
- The period under consideration. While it is fairly unambiguous for hard data, it is sometimes less so for soft data. For example, it is not always obvious whether firm managers' answers are more reflective of the ongoing month or quarter, the previous one or the next. This depends partly on when exactly during the period they are polled. In the case of the German IFO survey, for example, the answers for month m can be influenced by the outcome in the previous month rather than developments in month m itself.
- Possible working-day distortions: in principle, firms' answers should not be influenced by the number of working days, but in practice they sometimes are – for example, in the retail sector. Also, in some cases, the hard series is itself not adjusted for working days.
- The statistical properties of the series: opinion balances are typically stationary and bounded, whereas quantitative variables are often integrated of order one (see Box 3.1 and Annex II), implying that their rate of growth rather than their level is stationary and has to be related to the survey data.
- Frequencies, which may differ. Surveys are often, albeit not always, monthly, while the hard data used in bridge models are generally quarterly, to ensure consistency with the quarterly national accounts data.

The canonical equation used in linear bridge models is of the form:

$$\Delta \log Y_t = \Sigma_{i \geq 1} (a_i X_{t+1-i} + b_i \Delta \log Y_{t-i}) + c$$

where X is the qualitative exogenous variable (opinion balance), assumed to be leading other variables, Y the quantitative endogenous variable, $\Delta \log Y$ the growth rate of Y, and c a parameter reflecting the systematic bias in respondents' answers (which can be zero).

This general formulation can be amended in various ways, depending on circumstances:

- Some lags may be eliminated if the associated parameter values are unstable.
- The lagged values of the endogenous variable may be excluded. Then only the survey data appear on the right-hand side, which may be welcome,

for example, when there are doubts as to how accurately the latest values of the endogenous variables are measured (say, if the preliminary estimate of GDP looks awkward). Hence, Y will be determined only by current and past values of the exogenous qualitative variable. But recent developments (exceptional weather, say) might have caused Y to deviate from this underlying trajectory; ignoring the information provided by Y_{t-i} might therefore affect the equation's forecasting power.

- Conversely, it may be appropriate to add other exogenous variables.
- *A priori*, the change in the opinion balance is more important than its level to explain the growth in Y, especially around turning points. But taking its level into account may serve to amplify or dampen the estimated impact. One can switch easily from a formulation in level terms to a hybrid one, as $\Delta \log Y_t = a_1 X_t + a_2 X_{t-1} + c$ can be rewritten as $\Delta \log Y_t = a_1 \Delta X_t + (a_1 + a_2) X_{t-1} + c$.
- In principle, these growth rates can be expressed in year-on-year or in quarter-on-quarter terms. Practices differ across institutions and depend in part on how survey questions are put (for example, on whether the survey is explicitly comparing one time period to another).

The forecaster has an incentive to try to have the largest possible lag between the survey data and the hard indicators, so as to extend the forecasting horizon. But the best fit for the above equations is for short lags, so there is a trade-off.

In practice, the following steps can be distinguished, assuming output is the variable under consideration (Y_t):

- The coincident variables are first used to estimate output in the current quarter, T, say, by benchmarking output in quarter T on the latest balance of opinion on produced output observed in T.
- Then the forecast is extended directly, by benchmarking – more tentatively – production in quarter $T+1$ on the latest balance of opinion on firms' own output prospects (ideally, opinions expressed in T regarding output in $T+1$).
- Or the forecast is extended more indirectly, by extrapolating the latest balance of opinion on firms' own output prospects in $T+1$ and expressed in T to derive an estimate of the balance of opinion that will be expressed in $T+1$ on produced output in quarter $T+1$, and then benchmarking output in quarter $T+1$ on this estimate. When the balance of opinion on produced output for the first month or two of quarter $T+1$ is already known, or when extraneous information on the likely results of the coming surveys becomes available, it may be better to try to proceed along such lines (adjusting the extrapolation accordingly, to take this information on board).

Generally, bridge models appear to be better suited to forecast some components of aggregate supply (industrial output, construction) than to forecast components of aggregate demand or GDP directly (Baffigi *et al.*, 2004). This implies that it is necessary to build a framework for the forecast that can incorporate the benchmarked estimates for each separate component, to derive a forecast for GDP. While this may be more time-consuming, it can also help to build up the economic story associated with the forecast.

Turning to some practical examples, the OECD twice a year publishes nowcasts and near-term forecasts for real GDP in the G7 countries plus the euro area as a whole, based on a similar but more elaborate approach (Sédillot and Pain, 2005; Mourougane, 2006). Again, both soft indicators, such as business surveys, and hard ones, such as industrial production and retail sales, are fed into the equations (see Table 2.3). Consumer confidence is not included, as it is not found to add sufficient information. These high-frequency indicators are recast into quarterly GDP figures using bridge models. For each country, there are several indicator models. For the current quarter, models with only hard indicators, or combining these with survey data, tend to outperform models relying solely on survey data. For the one-quarter-ahead forecasts, in contrast, the inclusion of hard indicator data adds little to the information provided by surveys. To produce the published forecast, the OECD first makes residual adjustments to the raw forecasts of each of the hard, soft and mixed models (based on the average residual from the past eight quarters) and then takes a simple average of these three adjusted forecasts. Notwithstanding its sophistication, this approach cannot forecast the quarterly rate of GDP growth very precisely (see Annex I).

Similar models are used in other institutions, notably at the ECB, as noted by Hahn and Skudelny (2008), who emphasize that over the forecasting cycle for GDP in a given quarter the optimal set of bridge equations evolves with data availability.

An alternative approach is to select synthetic indicators that serve directly as forecasts of output in the coming quarter(s) and mix both benchmarked variables and leading indicators. The idea is to combine the information provided by benchmarking components of overall activity and that embodied in the leading indicators, which on their own are only indicative of trends or possible turning points.

Such synthetic indicators have been developed in Europe in the form of Euroframe's euro area growth indicator for the current quarter and the following one, compiled for the *Financial Times* by the Observatoire Français des Conjonctures Économiques (OFCE), in co-operation with nine research institutes across Europe.[7] The first step is to provide a quarterly coincident

---

[7] WIFO in Austria, ESRI in Ireland, ETLA in Finland, IfW and DIW Berlin in Germany, Prometeia in Italy, CPB in the Netherlands, CASE in Poland and NIESR in the United Kingdom. See Appendix 8.1 for more information on some of these institutes. The indicator is available on euroframe.org.

Table 2.3   Variables used by the OECD in nowcasting and near-term forecasting*

Depending on the country, different sets of variables are used to estimate the recent past and the near future

	Indicator(s) selected	Sources
Surveys		
United States	ISM for manufacturing, home builders' sentiment survey	ISM, National Association of Home Builders
Canada	US and domestic confidence indicators and new orders	CANSIM database
Euro area	Level of order books, level of stocks	European Commission
Germany	IFO business climate index	IFO
France	Production tendency, future production tendency	INSEE
Italy	Level of order books	ISAE, Eurostat
United Kingdom	Future production tendency, level of order books	CBI
Japan	Sales diffusion index, cash flow index	Japan Finance Corporation for Small Businesses
Hard indicators		
United States	Industrial production, consumption volume, retail sales, new construction put in place, monthly export volumes, non-farm employment, total monthly level of stocks, building permits	Federal Reserve, BEA, Census Bureau
Canada	Employment, retail sales, lagged industrial production, production of motor vehicles, terms of trade	CANSIM database
Euro area	Industrial output, construction output, retail sales volumes	Eurostat, OECD calculations
Germany	Industrial production, construction output, retail sales volumes, manufacturing orders	Bundesbank, Statistische Bundesamt
France	Industrial production, consumption of manufactured goods	INSEE
Italy	Italian and German industrial production, new car registrations	ISTAT, Bundesbank, Eurostat
United Kingdom	Industrial production, retail sales volumes, real house prices	National Statistics, Lloyds Banking Group
Japan	Real living expenditure, tertiary industry activity, industrial production of investment goods, job-offers-to-applicants ratio, inventory shipments ratio in industry	Japan Statistics Bureau, METI, Ministry of Labour

*As at 2009.
Source: OECD.

indicator for GDP growth in the current quarter. Then, one- and two-quarters ahead forecast equations are estimated, depending on the incoming monthly information that is available. The variables considered incorporate an industry survey factor (obtained as the first factor in a principal component analysis of the series of the monthly survey of industry in the euro area), information provided by surveys in other sectors, as well as rapidly available variables such as the relative term spread in the euro area compared with the USA, the euro's real exchange rate *vis-à-vis* the dollar, and the price of oil in euros.

2.6 Final health warning

In sum, business cycle analysts can use very different empirical approaches, which ultimately become a blend of rather heterogeneous hard and soft variables and are not underpinned by any single economic model. Moreover, the available statistical information might change rapidly over time, in sharp contrast with longer-run forecasting exercises, which are more squarely based on a 'fixed' set of economic data. Finally, short-term economic analysis is forced to deal with a lack of sufficient statistical information in several sectors and, when data are available, high volatility.

This has several implications. First, short-term macro monitoring requires the following of disparate but complementary approaches. Second, analysts have to make the most of all the incoming information, not least because of large carry-over effects. Third, some prudence is necessary when deciding whether a new piece of information is altering the outlook – by foreshadowing a new trend, say – or whether it has to be disregarded, at least for the time being. The best way to address these challenges is to build a structured framework, derived, for example, from the quarterly national accounts, in an attempt to integrate all this information in a consistent way and to try to make sense of seemingly contradictory signals.

Further reading

Wheelock and Wohar (2009) survey recent research on the ability of the term spread to forecast output growth and recessions. European Commission (2007) explains in greater depth how EU-wide surveys are conducted. Similar information is available on ism.ws for the ISM surveys, on sca.isr.umich.edu for the Reuters/University of Michigan consumer confidence index, and on conference-board.org for the Conference Board surveys. Details on the OECD's CLI methodology are provided in OECD (2008), and their performance in the context of globalization is assessed by Fichtner *et al.* (2009).

Adams *et al.* (2010) explain how the Conference Board's coincident and leading indicators set was recently extended to China. Erkel-Rousse and Minodier (2009) assess the extent to which business tendency surveys in industry and services help to forecast GDP growth. Gelper and Croux (2010) compare forecasts of activity based on the European Commission's economic sentiment index with forecasts based on dynamic factor analysis. Using a large factor model combining data of different frequencies, Schumacher and Breitung (2008) show how to estimate monthly German GDP in real time, with a discussion of nowcast/forecast accuracy and of the role of data revisions. The EuroCOIN index and associated information are available on eurocoin.cepr.org. Angelini *et al.* (2008) evaluate alternative nowcasting methods using timely monthly data. Up-to-date information and events related to business cycle analysis in Europe is available on eabcn.org.

Appendix 2.1 Some useful concepts and tools

Carry-over effects

Carry-over effects can be thought of as 'what's in the bag' going forward, assuming that the variable under consideration (usually GDP, but also the price level or other variables) stays flat. Take, for example, US real GDP from the start of 2008, once the advance estimate for the last quarter of 2007 was published (at the end of January 2008). The carry-over effect was then the average annual growth rate that would have applied in 2008 had real GDP remained flat throughout 2008 at its end-2007 level. Since real GDP grew substantially during the course of 2007, its average level in 2008 was set to be 1 per cent higher than its average level in 2007 even in the absence of any further growth during the course of 2008 (see Figure 2.7).

In the event, however, the US economy was entering the worst recession in decades at the end of 2007, and GDP contracted in 2008. If only for that reason, taking 'what's in the bag' for granted can turn out to be rather dangerous.

Arithmetically, let g^1_{-1}, g^2_{-1}, g^3_{-1} and g^4_{-1} be the quarter-on-previous-quarter (non-annualized) growth rates of real GDP in year $t - 1$ and g^1, g^2, g^3 and g^4 be those in year t. Let Y^i_{-1} be the level of real GDP in quarter i of year $t - 1$, Y^i its level in quarter i of year t, and g the average annual growth rate of real GDP in year t over year $t - 1$. Then:

$$g = (Y^1 + Y^2 + Y^3 + Y^4) / (Y^1_{-1} + Y^2_{-1} + Y^3_{-1} + Y^4_{-1}) - 1$$
$$= Y^1 [1 + (1 + g^2) + (1 + g^2)(1 + g^3) + (1 + g^2)(1 + g^3)(1 + g^4)]/$$
$$\{Y^1 [1/(1 + g^1) + 1/(1 + g^1)(1 + g^4_{-1}) + 1/(1 + g^1)(1 + g^4_{-1})(1 + g^3_{-1})$$
$$+ 1/(1 + g^1)(1 + g^4_{-1})(1 + g^3_{-1})(1 + g^2_{-1})]\} - 1$$

Figure 2.7 Inherited growth

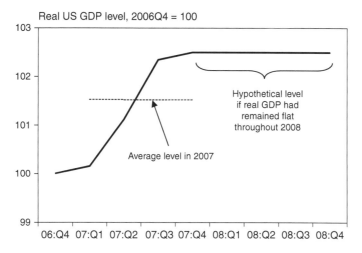

Real US GDP level, 2006Q4 = 100

Given that quarter-on-previous-quarter growth rates are typically small, one can use first-order approximations of the type $(1 + x)(1 + y) \approx 1 + x + y$, $1 / (1 + x) \approx 1 - x$ and $(1 + x) / (1 + z) \approx 1 + x - z$. Thus, simplifying by Y^1:

$$g \approx [1 + (1 + g^2) + (1 + g^2 + g^3) + (1 + g^2 + g^3 + g^4)] /$$
$$[(1 - g^1) + (1 - g^1 - g^4_{-1}) + (1 - g^1 - g^4_{-1} - g^3_{-1}) + (1 - g^1 - g^4_{-1} - g^3_{-1} - g^2_{-1})] - 1$$

$$\approx (4 + 3g^2 + 2g^3 + g^4) / (4 - 4g^1 - 3g^4_{-1} - 2g^3_{-1} - g^2_{-1}) - 1$$

$$\approx (1 + 0.75g^2 + 0.5g^3 + 0.25g^4) / (1 - g^1 - 0.75g^4_{-1} - 0.5g^3_{-1} - 0.25g^2_{-1}) - 1$$

$$\approx g^1 + 0.75(g^2 + g^4_{-1}) + 0.5(g^3 + g^3_{-1}) + 0.25(g^4 + g^2_{-1})$$

Hence the average annual growth rate of real GDP in year t over year $t - 1$ can be approximated as a weighted average of quarterly growth rates, with the weights being 1 for the first quarter of year t; 0.75 for the second quarter of year t and the fourth quarter of year $t - 1$; 0.5 for the third quarter of year t and the third quarter of year $t - 1$; and 0.25 for the fourth quarter of year t and the second quarter of year $t - 1$. It is influenced far more by developments towards the end of year $t - 1$ than by what happens towards the end of year t.

Going back to the first example, the US advance estimate for the fourth quarter of 2007 published in early 2008 showed that US GDP had been growing by 3.8 per cent, 4.9 per cent and 0.6 per cent, respectively, in the second, third and fourth quarters of 2007 at annual rates (and by 0.9 per cent, 1.2 per cent and 0.2 per cent at quarter-on-quarter rates). Hence, one can calculate the carry-over effect for the average annual growth rate in 2008 at the end of 2007 using the above formula, with $g^2_{-1} = 0.9$, $g^3_{-1} = 1.2$, $g^4_{-1} = 0.2$ and $g^1 = g^2 = g^3 = g^4 = 0$: $g \approx 0.75 \times 0.2 + 0.5 \times 1.2 + 0.25 \times 0.9 \approx 1$ per cent.

This carry-over effect was more than offset, however, by the sharp decline in real GDP over the course of 2008.

Statistical workhorses

Let A_a denote the value observed in year a for some economic variable, $Q_{a,q}$ its value observed in quarter q of year a, and $M_{a,m}$ its value in month m of year a (or $M_{q,m}$ its value in month m of quarter q). When frequency does not matter, the variable is simply called X_t. The following concepts are commonly used in forecasting.

Summary statistics

- The mean M of the series X_t between $t = 1$ and $t = T$ is its 'first moment': $M = (\Sigma_t X_t) / T$.
- The median of X_t is another measure of central tendency, namely the dividing point such that half of the observations of X_t are above and half below.
- The standard deviation σ is a measure of dispersion such that $\sigma^2 = [\Sigma_t (X_t - M)^2] / T$. Note that σ^2 is also known as the variance or 'second moment'. When M is not known but estimated based on the observations X_t, the sum of squares has to be divided by $(T - 1)$ instead of T to obtain an unbiased estimator of σ^2.

- The skewness S or 'third moment' characterizes the degree of asymmetry of a distribution around its mean: $S = \{\Sigma_t\ [(X_t - M) / \sigma]^3\} / T$. A curve is said to be skewed to the right, or positively skewed if it tails off towards the high end of the scale. While the mean and standard deviation are dimensional quantities – that is, they have the same units as X_t – the skewness is non–dimensional. It is a pure number that describes only the shape of the distribution.
- The kurtosis K or 'fourth moment', which is also a pure number, measures the heaviness of the tails of a distribution, compared with a normal distribution: $K = \{\Sigma_t\ [(X_t - M) / \sigma]^4\} / T$. For a normal distribution, $K = 3$. If $K > 3$, the distribution is said to be leptokurtic and if $K < 3$, it is said to be platykurtic.

Values and volumes

- Let N_t denote the nominal value of a variable; that is, its value at the prices prevailing in the period or at date t.
- Let V_t be the corresponding volume; that is, its value at the prices of some base period or date: V_t is obtained by deflating N_t by the change in the relevant price index since that time.
- Let I_t denote the index value of a series X_t, be it a nominal value, a volume or a price. Often I_t is set at 100 for the base period: $I_0 = 100$. Then $I_t = (X_t / X_0)\ 100$.
- If I_t is the relevant price index, the following relationship must hold: $N_t/N_{t-1} = V_t/V_{t-1} \times I_t/I_{t-1}$.

Growth rates

- Growth of X_t between $t = 1$ and $t = 2$, percent: $(X_2 - X_1) / X_1 \times 100$. 'Growth' is often implicitly referring to the change in real GDP (which can be negative, of course).
- Year-average growth refers to A_a / A_{a-1}, or $(Q_{a,1} + ... + Q_{a,4}) / (Q_{a-1,1} + ... + Q_{a-1,4})$ for quarterly observations, or $(M_{a,1} + ... + M_{a,12}) / (M_{a-1,1} + ... + M_{a-1,12})$ for monthly observations.
- Year-on-year growth generally refers to growth over the past four quarters or 12 months in quarter q or month m of year a; that is, to $Q_{a,q} / Q_{a-1,q}$ or $M_{a,m} / M_{a-1,m}$.
- Within-year growth, or growth over the four quarters of year a, is growth observed in the course of the elapsed year, when standing at the end of year a; that is, $Q_{a,4} /Q_{a-1,4}$, with quarterly data and $M_{a,12} / M_{a-1,12}$ with monthly data.
- Quarter-on-quarter growth typically refers to $Q_{a,q} / Q_{a,q-1}$, month-on-month growth to $M_{a,m} / M_{a,m-1}$ and within-quarter growth to $M_{q,3} / M_{q-1,3}$ (where 3 stands for the latest month of the quarter).
- Intra-annual rates of growth are often corrected for seasonal oscillations (see section 2.4). In this context, they can sometimes be annualized (as it is often the case in the USA), to get a sense of what the pace of change would be if growth continued for four quarters or 12 months at the same rate: $[(Q_q / Q_{q-1})^4 - 1] \times 100$ for quarterly data,[1]

---

[1] This will often be characterized as quarterly growth 'in annualized terms' or, in the USA, 'at annual rates' (not be confused with year-on-year growth).

$[(M_m / M_{m-1})^{12} - 1] \times 100$ for monthly data, or $[(M_m / M_{m-3})^4 - 1] \times 100$ for the annualized rate of change over the past three months.

- The contribution of a variable X_t to the growth of a variable Y_t is defined as $(X_t - X_{t-1}) / Y_{t-1} \times 100$, and is thus expressed in percentage points of Y_{t-1}.
- The base effect refers to an evolution of X_t that reflects what happened one year earlier. For example, suppose that month-on-month inflation is 0.1 per cent (or approximately 1.2 per cent annualized) at all times apart from in January 2009, when, because of a rise in value-added tax, the consumer price level in addition shifts upwards by 5 per cent (see Figure 2.8). Then year-on-year inflation jumps from 1.2 per cent to 6.3 per cent in January 2009 and stays there for one year, falling back to 1.2 per cent in January 2010. The fall in January 2010 is then attributed to a base effect (implicitly caused by what happened one year earlier).

Figure 2.8   The base effect*

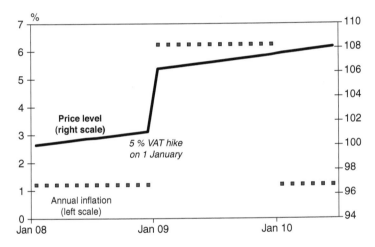

*Impact of a one-off price level shift on inflation.

Seasonal-adjustment software: X-12

The X-12 programme, like its X-11 predecessor, follows an iterative estimation procedure, based on a series of moving averages. The user has numerous choices as to the length of the averages.

Initially, the user is given the option to 'preadjust' the series for outliers, level shifts, known irregular events and calendar-related effects using adjustment factors supplied by the user or that can be estimated using built-in estimation procedures. The so-called RegARIMA part of the programme then allows the user to extend the series by backcasts and forecasts so that less asymmetric filters can be used at the beginning and the end of the series than in the original X-11 programme (this drawback was so significant that an intermediate X11-ARIMA version had to be implemented).

The preadjusted series subsequently goes through three rounds of filtering. This represents the core of the programme and has not changed very much compared with X-11, even if X-12 does provide some enhancements. In the case of a multiplicative decomposition of the time series, the three rounds unfold as follows (where T_t is the trend, S_t a seasonal coefficient (which in the absence of seasonality equals 1) and I_t a random or irregular component):

1. The trend T_t is calculated as a moving average, providing an estimate for $S_t \times I_t$; the latter is smoothed for the same months of several years to derive a set of seasonal coefficients S, which are normalized so that their product equals one; an initial seasonally adjusted series thus obtains.
2. A new trend is computed based on this initial seasonally adjusted series, which is treated in the same way as in the first round.
3. The same procedure is then repeated once more.

Finally, various diagnostics and quality control statistics are computed, tabulated and graphed. This is an important step in the procedure, not least to assess whether the user made the right choices from among the many options offered along the way.

In practice, the seasonal adjustment coefficients are refreshed once a year rather than after each new high-frequency observation. The programme provides the extrapolated coefficients needed for the coming year, which are applied to the incoming raw data.

X-12 can be combined with other procedures such as TRAMO/SEATS (signal extraction in ARIMA time series, developed by the Bank of Spain and promoted by Eurostat). The associated interface, called DEMETRA, can be downloaded from circa.europa.eu/irc/dsis/eurosam/info/data/demetra.

Chapter 3

Real Sector Building Blocks

Contents

> *To prepare growth forecasts, GDP may be decomposed into major components that can each be examined using standard economic and econometric analysis. Business investment responds to perceptions of global demand and the profitability of installing new equipment. Household spending depends on purchasing power and variables that affect the propensity to consume, such as wealth, inflation, interest rates or unemployment. The contribution of external trade reflects competitiveness and the relative strength of foreign and domestic demand. Beyond GDP components, real sector building blocks include employment and price developments, which are interrelated via Phillips curve effects.*

This chapter focuses on the forecasting of private real sector developments, including private consumption and investment, trade flows, employment, and wage and price inflation. These variables, which are close to ultimate policy goals such as a higher standard of living, full employment or low inflation, are of key interest to policy makers; they are thus central outcomes of forecasting exercises.

Understanding real developments requires the deciphering of agents' behaviour, block by block. This means, for example, analysing households' aggregate spending decisions, given income, wealth and other developments; or firms' aggregate investment and recruiting choices, given their perception of demand or profitability.

This chapter presents the specifications that are generally adopted to describe private agents' economic behaviour. Section 3.1 deals with business investment (fixed and stockbuilding), which plays a prominent role as a driver of economic fluctuations. Section 3.2 deals with household spending (consumption and residential investment). Section 3.3 discusses imports, exports, world demand and competitiveness. Section 3.4 covers employment and section 3.5 wage–price dynamics. In the process, this chapter surveys the commonly used specifications, including their theoretical underpinnings and typical results. The presentation draws heavily on error correction equations, as they are intuitive, enlightening and frequently used by practitioners (see Box 3.1). Estimation methods *per se* are beyond the scope of this book but are presented in standard econometrics textbooks.

Some of the theoretical mechanisms will be shown to hold up well empirically. Examples include the effect of expected demand on investment, the effect of growth abroad on exports, or the influence of wages on prices and vice versa. Other purported mechanisms are more difficult to document in practice. For example, the impact of a change in interest rates on investment, and more

Box 3.1 Error-correction models: a primer

Error-correction models (ECMs) allow analysts to account both for the links between economic variables over the long run and for the short- or medium-run dynamics around these equilibrium relationships. They are well suited to the statistical properties of macroeconomic time series, in particular with regard to their frequent nonstationarity.

First, recall the following definitions:

- A stochastic process is said to be (weakly) stationary if its first and second moment (mean and covariances) are constant over time.
- A process is said to be integrated of order 1, and is denoted $I(1)$, if it is non-stationary and if differenced once it becomes stationary, that is, $I(0)$; similarly, it is $I(d)$ if it needs to be differenced d times to become stationary.
- A set of $I(d)$ processes are said to be cointegrated if at least one linear combination of these processes is stationary.

The existence of such a cointegration relationship is the statistical counterpart of an economic equilibrium between the variables under consideration. For example, consumption and income are both generally considered to be $I(1)$, but the ratio of consumption to income – the average propensity to consume – may be $I(0)$: if this is the case, while consumption and income grow indefinitely, and partly randomly, their ratio would deviate only temporarily from its long-run average.

Economic theories suggest that *a priori* many such relationships may exist: between the capital stock and GDP, between prices, wages and productivity, between imports, world demand and the relative price of imports, and so on. The empirical relevance of these various equilibrium relationships has to be examined by using cointegration tests.

When several variables are cointegrated, this relationship does not hold exactly at all times. That would only be the case in a fictional economy devoid of any disturbances and where each variable would expand at a constant rate. In practice, unanticipated shocks and variable adjustment lags entail deviations from these long-run paths. The difference between the cointegrating linear combination and its long-run mean then measures the distance from equilibrium. The idea underlying ECMs is that, when there is such a gap, forces tend to pull the relevant variables back towards equilibrium.

Consider the example of consumption and suppose that the saving ratio (equal to one minus the average propensity to consume) is stationary. Then one can assume that consumption c and income y (both in logarithms) may be cointegrated. Let U denote the unemployment rate; an ECM of consumption could then be written as:

$$\Delta c_t = \alpha + \beta\,\Delta y_t + \gamma\,\Delta U_t - \eta\,(c_{t-1} - y_{t-1})$$

The term $\eta\,(c_{t-1} - y_{t-1})$ is the error correction term, where η stands for the adjustment in each period back towards equilibrium. If there were no other term in the equation, one would simply have a partial adjustment model. In addition, the short-run dynamics of Δc_t is captured by the term $\beta\,\Delta y_t$, which increases the speed of convergence towards the long-run equilibrium, and by the term $\gamma\Delta U_t$, which is added in to illustrate that variables that are not part of the long-run relationship may none the less have an impact over the short run.

The equation could also include other dynamic terms, such as lagged changes in consumption and income or other stationary variables. In fact, the selection of the appropriate specification is largely empirical. The practice is usually to include variables that seem sensible from an economic standpoint and prove to be statistically robust, while ensuring that the equation residuals eventually be approximately white noise.

More generally, when a group of $I(d)$ variables admits a single cointegration relationship, it can be shown that each of them has an error correction representation akin to the example above (this is the so-called Engle and Granger representation theorem). When there are several cointegration relationships, each error correction term may affect the evolution of all the other variables.

Note also that an equation in which only the level of variables would appear (here, regressing the level of consumption on the level of income) would allow analysts to identify the cointegration relationship between these two variables, but would not depict accurately the short-run fluctuations in consumption. Conversely, an equation featuring only first differences of these variables might properly account for their short-run dynamics but would overlook their tendency to move towards the long-run equilibrium when they are away from it. The usefulness of ECMs may be limited for very short-run forecasts, however, since gravitation towards the long-run equilibrium is often relatively slow. Hence, ECMs are in principle more relevant for longer forecast horizons.

generally on aggregate demand, is hard to pin down, as is the impact of a wage hike on labour demand.

The equations presented in this chapter seek to reflect the main determinants of economic behaviour as they have been observed in the past. They constitute the backbone of the structural forecasting methods which combine economic reasoning and econometrics (see section 1.3). When assembled, these equations lead to the macroeconometric models that can be used to produce overall forecasts (see Annex III).

This chapter is closely linked to other parts of the book. First, the approach followed here typically helps to inform short- to medium-run forecasts that are plugged into the high(er) frequency analysis covered in Chapter 2, while also feeding into the more long-term-oriented methods of Chapter 6. Second, and most important, developments in real variables are interlinked with financial evolutions (Chapter 4). Indeed, while splitting things up may be unavoidable for presentational purposes, it is crucial to acknowledge the interaction between real and financial dynamics, with the 2007 financial crisis providing a prominent example of such connections. Finally, three appendices go beyond the macroeconomic issues and focus on sectoral forecasting, commodity prices (which have been an important source of aggregate shocks in the recent past) and NAIRU estimates.

3.1   Business investment

This section deals with investment by private firms, as opposed to public sector investment, and to residential investment by households. Fixed investment involves replacing or increasing firms' productive capital stock (structures and equipment). Stockbuilding is the change in the volume of inventories held by firms and has its own laws of motion.

3.1.1   Fixed investment

The dynamics of investment are often considered to be at the core of the economic cycle. In the traditional view, investment accelerates during a recovery, when capacity is deemed to be insufficient to meet future demand, and declines when the slowdown begins and the need for capital is more than met. Investment thus both reflects and drives the economic cycle; it depends on the fluctuations in demand and, at the same time, is a major contributor to these ups and downs. It is this underlying dynamic of investment that the econometric analysis seeks to capture, discounting high-frequency movements which affect investment erratically (for example, in the case of bunched aircraft deliveries).

Box 3.2   Investment and the capital stock: theories

There are at least five different theoretical approaches to investment, under-stood as the outlays necessary to increase the stock of capital, over and above depreciation through ordinary use ('wear and tear') or obsolescence:

- *The accelerator model*: if the desired capital–output ratio is a constant k (usually, $k > 1$) and if GDP is expected to rise by x per cent, the required stock of capital will rise by kx per cent of GDP; with investment aver-aging, say, one fifth of GDP, the percentage point increase in investment ($5kx$) needed to raise the capital stock to its new desired level is much larger than the percentage point increase in GDP. This model captures the stylized fact that investment 'accelerates' in response to a variation in output and is therefore more volatile. It can be augmented to take into account the cost of capital and construction lags.
- *The effective demand model*: firms are assumed to minimize costs for a given level of production. The optimal capital stock then depends on the latter (proportionately in the case of constant returns to scale) and on the cost of capital relative to the cost of labour.
- *The neo-classical model*: under perfect competition, a firm maximizes its profits by equalizing the marginal product of capital and its cost. The corresponding equation could be seen as giving the optimal level of capital, the two determinants being the level of production and the real cost of capital. But the optimal level of output itself depends on the profit maximization programme. To solve it, two cases need to be distin-guished. Under decreasing returns to scale, the optimal level of capital ultimately depends on the (real) cost of labour and capital; empirically, however, such a specification without a demand term tends to perform poorly. Under constant returns to scale, the optimal level of capital remains undetermined, since profits are zero at any level of output; only the optimal capital–output ratio can be determined, which is of no use empirically to pin down the level of capital.
- *Imperfect competition models*: under imperfect competition and with a con-stant price-elasticity of the demand for goods, each firm maximizes profit by jointly deciding on its prices, the quantity of factors used in produc-tion and its level of output, while considering aggregate demand as an exogenous variable. In this framework, aggregate demand and the real cost of capital are the ultimate determinants of aggregate investment.
- *Models based on Tobin's q theory*: firms invest as a function of the differ-ence between the expected return on the new investment and the cost of its financing (or the return on a financial asset, if the firm does not need

to borrow to invest). This difference is defined as profitability. While in principle it is constant over the long run, it can vary in the short run, leading to investment cycles.

In addition, one generally considers that investment is sensitive to firms' financial situation, and specifically to their short-run liquidity position, as documented, for example, by Ashworth and Davis (2001) for the G7 countries. Indeed, firms may not have unrestricted access to external financing, because of various credit and capital market imperfections. The current level of profits may therefore influence investment, in so far as profits allow an increase in the share of the project that can be financed by internal cash flow, and facilitate access to outside finance. This, however, pertains more to the feasibility than to the desirability of investment.

A variety of theories may guide the econometric specification of investment demand (see Box 3.2 and Chirinko, 1993). Most of them derive an expression for firms' optimal capital stock, which is generally considered as a long-run target. The determinants of the optimal capital stock vary according to the approach, but the following are usually emphasized:

- expected demand (for the goods or services that the capital under consideration will help to produce), leading to the principle of the 'accelerator';
- the user cost of capital, defined as the cost of renting one unit of capital;
- firms' profitability, defined as the difference between expected return and capital cost; and
- their financial situation, as revealed *inter alia* by the level of profits or balance sheet indicators.

In practice, econometric tests almost always corroborate the notion that demand is one of investment's main determinants. In contrast, it is often more difficult to find a robust relationship with the other factors. One problem is that the time needed for capital to adjust to them is often considerable compared to the length of the available data set. Besides, investment may be driven by a variety of other considerations, depending in particular on the type of capital considered (new technologies versus old ones, for example). As a result, the specifications used in practice in forecasting are fairly parsimonious given the diversity of the theoretical explanations. They rest principally on the accelerator mechanism, though profits, the user cost or profitability are sometimes also taken into account.

A typical ECM equation for the stock of capital is:

$$\Delta k_t = \alpha + \Sigma_j \, \alpha_j \, \Delta k_{t-j} + \Sigma_j \, \beta_j \, \Delta y_{t-j} - \mu \, (k_{t-1} - \varepsilon_k \, y_{t-1}) + \gamma_k \, z_t^k \qquad (3.1)$$

Similarly, for investment, a typical ECM equation is:

$$\Delta i_t = \alpha + \Sigma_j \, \alpha_j \Delta i_{t-j} + \Sigma_j \, \beta_j \Delta y_{t-j} - \mu \, (i_{t-1} - \varepsilon_i \, y_{t-1}) + \gamma_i \, z_t^i \qquad (3.2)$$

where k, i and y are the logarithms of the capital stock, investment and a variable standing for aggregate demand, while z^k and z^i are vectors of other explanatory variables (which may play a role in the short-run dynamic term of the equation as well as in the long-run one, but are subsumed into a single vector here, for the sake of simplicity).

In practice, the dependent variable can be either the stock of capital K or the flow of investment I. The first option comes closest to the usual theories, based on the concept of an optimal capital stock. The second option has the advantage of not requiring a series for the stock of capital, which is important given how difficult it is to properly measure capital and the poor quality of many capital stock series. It is also possible to adopt a specification in terms of the rate of accumulation of capital, I/K, since:

$$I_t = K_t - (1 - \delta_t) \, K_{t-1}$$

where δ_t is the rate of depreciation. The latter is usually treated as exogenous and projected by extrapolating past depreciation rates. This formulation is very close to one in Δk, since $\Delta k = \Delta \log K \approx \Delta K/K = I/K - \delta$, where the depreciation rate is assumed to be constant.

While the long-run relationship in Equations (3.1) or (3.2) is generally associated with one of the above theories, their dynamic part can be interpreted in two ways. On the one hand, it reflects the existence of technical or organizational delays when installing new equipment, implying that it is not possible to jump immediately to the optimal level of capital: building a factory, for example, can take years. On the other hand, it is necessary to take into account the time it takes to reach the investment decision itself. The purchase of expensive machinery or the creation of a new plant are risky and largely irreversible decisions. To go ahead, entrepreneurs and those who finance them need to be confident enough that the investment will be profitable. In practice, these different types of lags cannot be distinguished lest the equations become excessively complicated. The dynamics are therefore estimated globally, letting the data determine the adjustment coefficients. One may expect, in particular, that some of the factors considered here, such as the cost of capital or profitability, have their full impact only if they are sustained for quite some time. Hence one should not expect the coefficient μ to be high, especially for specifications in terms of capital stock or rate of accumulation.

It is worth discussing the various explanatory variables in greater detail.

Demand

Different measures of demand are used in practice, including gross output, value-added and GDP. Since the left-hand-side variable is enterprise investment, it may be preferable, however, to focus on the demand of the private sector, rather than overall demand. Econometric estimates usually confirm the accelerator mechanism described in Box 3.2; that is, that in the short run investment increases more than proportionately in response to rising demand. This pattern explains why investment tends to be so volatile and procyclical. Typically (albeit far from universally), a sustained 1 per cent increase in demand would translate, after a lag of two to four quarters, into a 2–2.5 per cent increase in investment. The capital stock instead reacts much less rapidly, with an average adjustment lag of five to ten years. Finally, it is often considered that the capital–output ratio and the investment ratio should be stable over the long run, as predicted by constant returns to scale growth theories (see section 6.2). This is indeed more or less the case in practice. It can be tested by testing the restriction $\varepsilon_k = 1$ or $\varepsilon_i = 1$ in the long-run term of the above equations.

The user (or rental) cost of capital

Though it is sometimes proxied by an interest rate, the usual definition of the user cost of capital – consistent with a set-up where the value of the firm is maximized – is:

$$C_t = (1 + R_t) P_{t-1}^i - (1 - \delta) P_t^i \approx P_t^i (R_t + \delta - \pi_t)$$

where P_t^i is the investment deflator, R_t the nominal interest rate and π_t inflation. In words, the cost of one unit of capital in period t has three components: the unit of capital, which is bought in $t - 1$ at the price P_{t-1}^i; the interest rate R_t, which reflects the cost of borrowing funds (or by which the firm's own funds would otherwise have been remunerated); and the value of the capital stock that remains after depreciation $(1 - \delta)$ and that can be sold in t at price P_t^i.

This formula can be augmented to take taxes into account. This can make a big difference, as suggested by Cummins *et al.* (1996), who document that in many OECD countries taxes do matter at the firm level. Even so, the impact of taxation is often ignored in practice because estimating the relevant effective tax rates, which often vary frequently over time, is very complicated.

The way this is taken into consideration when conducting empirical estimations reflects to some extent the theoretical views of the forecaster. As noted in Box 3.2 for the neo-classical model, the optimal capital stock depends on the real cost of capital. The latter may be measured as the ratio of the nominal user cost divided by the price of the produced goods. In a Keynesian model, stressing the role of demand, the optimal capital stock rather depends on the cost of capital relative to that of labour.

Numerous empirical studies have attempted to find evidence supporting one or the other approach, and to quantify the elasticity of substitution between capital and labour (Chirinko, 2008, offers a survey and tentative consensual estimates). The results are mixed because of several practical complications over and above the difficulty of estimating the incidence of taxation. Which interest rate should one use? Should it include a risk premium, and if so, how large? Is the price of investment, notably that of computers, adequately measured? If the cost of labour enters the picture, what is a good assumption for the evolution of labour productivity? In addition, adjustment lags imply that changes in factor costs have only a very gradual effect on the production–input mix. It is easier to document substitution between capital and labour at the microeconomic level, but then the results cannot be readily extended to the macroeconomic level.

Profitability

Profitability may be defined as the difference between the expected return on new investment and its cost. The most frequently cited indicator of profitability is Tobin's q, which is the ratio of the stock market valuation of a firm (or group of firms) to the replacement value of their capital stock. Firms invest until, at the margin, $q = 1$.[1] An alternative indicator, proposed by Malinvaud (1983), is the difference between the after-tax profit rate net of depreciation and the long-term interest rate. These two indicators are in fact equivalent when stock prices correctly price in future profits (then the profit rate equals the interest rate times Tobin's q). Malinvaud's indicator is not sensitive to stock market over- or under-valuations, but whether this is an advantage in this context is a moot point, since investment cycles are precisely influenced by stock market bearishness or bullishness.

In principle, profitability should sum up all the determinants of investment: if a project is profitable, it should be undertaken. But empirically, investment equations containing solely profitability on the right-hand side perform poorly. One reason may be that the above indicators capture average rather than marginal profitability, whereas investment is driven by the latter. But marginal profitability cannot be observed directly at the macroeconomic level.

---

[1] The intuition underlying q theory was articulated by Keynes (1936): 'daily revaluations of the Stock Exchange... inevitably exert a decisive influence on the rate of current investment. For there is no sense in building up a new enterprise at a cost greater than that at which a similar existing enterprise can be purchased; whilst there is an inducement to spend on a new project what may seem an extravagant sum, if it can be floated off on the Stock Exchange at an immediate profit'.

A more pragmatic approach is then to test the significance of (average) profitability alongside the traditional accelerator effect.

Financial conditions

While economic decisions such as investment are traditionally seen as being driven by real factors, an alternative view that has gained ground since the 1990s gives a larger role to conditions in financial markets and firms' financial situation. A key idea of this 'financial accelerator' theory literature is that firms prefer to finance investments from internal funds rather than external resources (Bernanke *et al.*, 1996). Any development that either reduces internal funding options (such as lower cash flows) or raises the external funding premium (such as falling asset values that depress collateral, stretched capital markets or sheer uncertainty) may therefore act as a drag on investment spending.

From this perspective, a broad range of financial variables may be tested in investment equations. One such is firms' debt level (measured, for example, as a share of value added or, to reflect leverage, as a share of equity). However, structural trends and breaks may well blur the empirical significance of such balance-sheet indicators: until the 2007 financial crisis, financial liberalization made it possible to sustain higher indebtedness or leverage, whereas the perceived need to deleverage afterwards may have worked in the opposite direction.

A more traditional modelling strategy is to include profits in the investment equation. Profits may influence investment both because current profits foreshadow future profits, rendering investment more attractive, and because profits improve firms' cash flow and allow them to finance a significant share of investment by using retained earnings (which makes a difference when firms lack unfettered access to outside funding). One commonly used empirical measure of profits is the profit rate, defined as the gross operating surplus divided by the capital stock valued at replacement cost. Another option is to use real profits (the gross operating surplus divided by the value-added deflator). Profits can also be measured in net terms (meaning deducting the consumption of fixed capital) and after corporate income taxes. The significance of the chosen profit indicator can be tested in the short-run as well as in the long-run term of the investment equation.

Accelerator-profit models

Models where investment depends both on demand and profits are referred to as accelerator-profit investment models. Such equations can work well for forecasting purposes and are therefore popular. Yet they have some drawbacks. First, the cost of capital, or even simply the interest rate, is ignored. Given that investment is generally thought to be sensitive to changes in interest rates, this is a problem, notably when analysing the short-run effects of monetary policy. Second, it is difficult to disentangle the impact of demand from that of profits, given that the two are highly correlated. And last but not least, profits themselves are hard to predict with any accuracy, particularly if after-tax profits are considered, which fluctuate greatly and are affected by firms' efforts to minimize the tax burden and smooth it over time.

3.1.2 Stockbuilding

Inventories can comprise raw materials, energy, semi-finished products and finished products that have yet to be sold. While the level of inventories is small relative to GDP, arithmetically, they contribute significantly to the high-frequency cyclical ups and downs. Blinder (1990) even goes as far as to write that 'business cycles are, to a surprisingly large degree, inventory cycles'. Yet, stockbuilding is a very noisy series, hard to analyse and forecast.

Recall first that it is not the level of the stock S but stockbuilding ΔS that is added to the components of final demand FD (consumption, fixed investment and net exports) to form GDP, noted Y:

$$Y = \Delta S + FD$$

Information on inventories is relatively poor, which complicates their analysis. Indeed, in many countries, the national accounts, especially at the quarterly frequency, partly estimate stockbuilding as a residual, namely as the difference between GDP estimated from the supply side and GDP estimated as the sum of the components of final demand.

Indeed, inventories contribute significantly to cyclical fluctuations, as illustrated in Figure 3.1 in the case of the USA. The decline in stockbuilding during the downturn in 2001, for example, was larger than the contraction in GDP. This feature did not repeat itself during the subsequent downturn in 2008 but, in late 2009 and early 2010, inventories contributed very strongly to the recovery. In general, and over longer periods than shown here, stockbuilding tends to be procyclical (although at times it may exert a countercyclical influence, as analysed below). Formally, its contribution to output growth can be computed by differencing the above equation. Dividing by GDP, this yields:

$$\Delta Y/Y = \Delta^2 S/Y + \Delta FD/Y$$

While stockbuilding tends to be procyclical, this does not necessarily imply that it magnifies output fluctuations. That depends on whether it tends to amplify the movements in GDP in response to variations in final demand, or to dampen them. In the former case, output should be more volatile than

Figure 3.1   Stockbuilding: contribution to US GDP growth*
Stockbuilding often accounts for a large share of short-run GDP swings

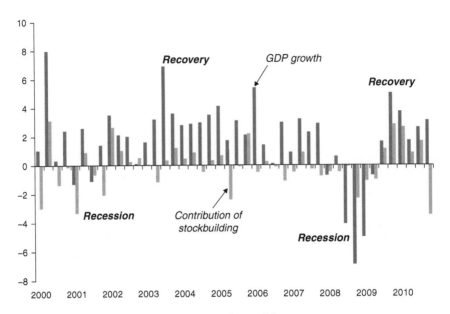

*Quarter-on-quarter, seasonally-adjusted annualized rates of change, percentages.
Source: US Bureau of Economic Analysis.

sales – Var(Y) > Var(FD) – and stockbuilding should be positively correlated with final demand – Cov(ΔS, FD) > 0. In the latter case, the opposite should hold.

Theory itself is ambivalent, with two competing views of stockbuilding:

- One is that the accumulation or decumulation of inventories is a voluntary response on the part of firms to expected fluctuations in demand. If a firm anticipates rising demand, it will increase its inventories *ex ante*, with a view to be able to meet the extra demand while keeping the inventories-to-demand ratio roughly constant *ex post*. In the case of adaptive expectations, an increase in demand causes an increase in expected demand, and therefore also in inventories. This notion of an 'inventory accelerator' is consistent with the first of the above empirical hypotheses.
- Alternatively, inventories are seen as a buffer. Faced with changes in demand, firms can draw down or build up inventories to smooth the level of production over time. This helps to maximize profits in so far as production is subject to a fixed schedule of increasing marginal costs (though the costs of holding stocks should also be considered, as discussed below). Inventories would then decline in response to an unanticipated demand surge, and vice versa. At first glance, this seems to be consistent with the second of the above hypotheses.

In reality, the two views can be reconciled to some extent, by distinguishing anticipated and unanticipated changes in demand. An unanticipated rise in demand may first lead to a decline in inventories, if it is too expensive for the firm to step up production rapidly. But if the higher level of demand has been anticipated to last, some restocking may be undertaken and the inventories-to-output ratio will rise (especially if *ex post* the upturn in demand proves to be more ephemeral than foreseen). Ultimately, it is thus mainly the gap between expected and actual demand that influences stockbuilding.

For the practitioner, one way to exhibit these effects is to run the following type of equation, where the *i* denotes the statistically significant lags:

$$\Delta S_t = \Sigma_i \, \alpha_i \, \Delta S_{t-i} + \Sigma_i \, \beta_i \, \Delta FD_{t-i}$$

Generally, the coefficients are then interpreted in light of the above considerations. In particular, β_0 measures the contemporaneous correlation between stockbuilding and the change in sales. *A priori*, a negative sign for β_0 is consistent with the production-smoothing/buffer-stock view, and a positive sign with the amplification view. In the latter case, however, it may be that short-run buffer effects are actually at work but that the frequency of the series used is insufficient to show it, especially if the series is an annual one. When the equation is run on quarterly data, one often obtains (Wen, 2005) a buffer effect over the very short run ($\beta_0 < 0$) and an accelerator effect over more distant horizons (for $i \geq 1$, $\beta_i > 0$ and $\Sigma_i \beta_i > -\beta_0$).

Other possible explanatory factors can be brought in, notably speculative behaviour: firms may wish to build up inventories if they expect that their value will rise more than enough to offset the cost of financing them, the latter being related directly to the level of interest rates. This warrants testing a real interest rate variable in the equation, calculated as the nominal interest rate minus the anticipated increase in the output price (often proxied by the recently observed increase). The sign of the associated coefficient is expected to be negative: the more costly it is to carry inventories, the lower they will be. If that fails, one can try to quantify the influence of the nominal interest rate and the inflation rate separately, the expectation being that the coefficient for the former will be negative and the coefficient for the latter positive.

On the whole, this type of equation does not perform that well, however, not least because of the crude and purely backward-looking way in which expectations of demand are introduced. One alternative is to relate the evolution of inventories to business survey results; for example, to businesses' sentiment regarding future demand. This helps in forecasting them over the very short run, but not beyond, as it would be hazardous to forecast business sentiment itself. Another solution would be to define a long-run target for the inventories-to-sales ratio, for example, by extrapolating its recent trend.

3.2 Household spending

Household spending is by far the largest component of aggregate demand, and therefore plays a central role in forecasting the cycle. It includes current consumption, purchases of durables (cars in particular) and spending on new housing. The latter is usually treated as a category on its own, labelled residential investment. Purchases of durables are sometimes also analysed separately, as they do not behave like the rest of household consumption (see, for example, Palumbo *et al.*, 2002).

3.2.1 Household consumption

There are two measures of household consumption (see Annex I): final consumption expenditure, which encompasses all purchases of goods and services; and a broader one that also includes final consumption expenditure of the non-profit institutions serving households plus that of the general government that can be attributed to households individually. The focus here is on the former, which is linked more closely to household income. Generally, it represents well over half of GDP. When durables are treated separately, consumption in the equation below is restricted to expenditure on non-durable goods and services.

The Keynesian approach has emphasized the link between consumption and current income and the associated multiplier: an increase in activity, driven for example by rising investment, boosts income and therefore consumption, which in turn amplifies the initial increase in activity. In this framework, current household income is a key determinant of consumption. Subsequent theories, however, have highlighted other factors. Specifically, according to the permanent income hypothesis (Friedman, 1957) and the life-cycle hypothesis (Ando and Modigliani, 1963), households' consumption decisions are governed by the present value of their wealth, which alongside current income takes into account expected future income streams as well as existing assets holdings. Households are thus described as smoothing consumption over time, saving when their income is relatively high (in mid-career, for example) and borrowing, or dissaving, when it is low (in youth and retirement).

This analysis can be enriched by bringing in liquidity constraints, unequal access to credit, bequest motives, risk aversion and uncertainty (notably about life expectancy), but the basic intuition can be tested by running an equation of the following type:

$$\Delta c_t = \alpha + \Sigma_i \alpha_i \Delta c_{t-i} + \Sigma_i \beta_i \Delta y_{t-i} - \mu (c_{t-1} - \eta y_{t-1}) + \gamma z_t \qquad (3.3)$$

where c is the volume of consumption and y real income, both in logarithms, and z is a vector of other explanatory variables which may be relevant over the short or longer run, including real wealth, inflation, real interest rates and unemployment. Consider each of these in turn.

Income

Income is usually defined as household disposable income; that is, the income left after taxes and social contributions have been deducted. Hence, the equation indicates how households divide their income between consumption and saving. Income itself is sometimes split up into wages, current income from assets (including dividends and interest, but not capital gains) and transfer income (social benefits), as the propensity to consume may vary across these different components. In particular, it is usually deemed to be lower in the short run for asset-related income.

If the equation does not contain any wealth term, it is natural to test whether the long-run elasticity of consumption to income (η) equals 1. If this is the case, the long-run component of the equation implicitly defines a target for the saving rate, which can be constant or depend on the long-run component of z. The short-run coefficients (α_i, β_i) indicate how quickly consumers react to changes in income, thus providing an empirical characterization of consumption smoothing behaviour. The mean lag for the adjustment of consumption to income is typically in the order of one year.

While income clearly influences consumption, using Equation (3.3) for forecasting purposes is not straightforward, since income itself then needs to be forecast with sufficient accuracy. But income depends on activity, which in turn depends on consumption. Proper forecasting thus requires the joint examination of consumption, activity and income. This can be done by using a full macroeconomic model (see Annex III), or iterations between the various elements of the forecast, until it converges.

Furthermore, some components of income are difficult to assess, notably stock options. Also, households' perception of their income may matter more than actual income. Consider realized capital gains. In the national accounts, these are not handled as income, but as a change in the composition of wealth. However, the taxes levied on these capital gains are deducted from income. This treatment, while it has its logic, probably does not reflect households' perception of their income.

Wealth

Alongside income, wealth plays a role in determining consumption, referred to as the 'wealth effect'. Wealth effects have attracted much attention since the beginning of the 1990s because of large upward and downward movements in stock and housing market valuations (translating into large changes in financial and housing wealth, respectively) and the likely effect of these on consumer spending. Theory suggests that rising wealth could, sooner or later, trigger higher consumption. However, gauging the size of such effects in reality is challenging.

The existence of wealth effects is rarely disputed. Unexpected windfalls (arising from higher stock or home prices) give more resources to households over their lifetime, part of which they can use to increase current purchases. That fraction is measured by the so-called marginal propensity to consume (MPC). For example, with an MPC of 5 per cent, an increase in wealth by US\$ 1 would translate into higher current consumption by 5 cents.[2]

The wealth variable used should in principle represent households' net wealth (assets minus liabilities) in real terms. A key distinction is between financial and housing wealth. Indeed, empirical studies carried out on large samples of OECD countries suggest that these two types of wealth may have different effects on consumption. As timely data are at best incomplete, proxies are often used: for example, financial wealth would be proxied by the capitalization of the stock market (which does not include bonds or unlisted securities), or simply by stock price indices (admittedly a rather crude proxy).

There is, however, considerable uncertainty as to the empirical size of wealth effects. Recent surveys point to widely different estimates and no clear conclusion regarding the relative sizes of financial versus housing wealth channels (CBO, 2007; Skudelny, 2009).

There are several reasons for such uncertainty, both conceptual and empirical. First, to change current consumption decisions through a wealth effect *per se*, wealth variations have to be both unanticipated and regarded as permanent. This occurrence is rather infrequent, though a good example would be

---

[2]The MPC is equal to $\Delta C/\Delta W$ (where C and W stand for consumption and wealth, respectively) and should not be confused with α, the elasticity of consumption to wealth as would be estimated in an equation in log terms such as in Equation (3.3) – leading to $\Delta C/C = \alpha \Delta W/W$. The MPC and elasticity are linked through the consumption/wealth ratio (that is, MPC = $\alpha C/W$), and the latter may move over time. Indeed, as the MPC is theoretically stable, it may be argued that Equation (3.3) is misspecified, since the wealth elasticity varies as the consumption/wealth ratio changes.

information technology in the 1990s and its implications for financial wealth. Second, however, housing wealth effects, in contrast, seem to work through indirect channels (Muellbauer, 2008). Indeed, appreciating home prices are accompanied by a matching increase in housing costs and therefore the cost of living. To the extent that their lifetime horizon is limited, home owners may benefit from these dual changes and increase their spending; but first-time buyers, who are affected negatively, may maintain their consumption levels only through rising indebtedness. However, the physical stock of houses changes only slowly, and housing rents tend to rise with house prices. Hence, in aggregate, it is not obvious that a rise in house prices implies that the household sector is better off, since it merely leads to a redistribution of wealth, from current and future users of housing in favour of current home owners.

While, in theory, it is therefore not clear that higher housing prices should affect consumption, balance sheet effects might still provide an important transmission channel. Higher house prices raise the value of households' fixed assets relative to their liabilities, allowing them to take on more debt (especially in English-speaking advanced economies, but less so in continental Europe) or to realize capital gains from selling homes (for example, through mortgage equity withdrawals), thereby easing their financial constraints. From this perspective, the housing wealth channel works via growing household debt, which, as evident in the recent crisis, may not be sustainable.

Such analysis suggests that wealth effects may vary considerably over time (and countries), especially with structural transformations such as financial liberalization and development. Moreover, one could also expect a non-linear impact of asset price changes because of asymmetric effects of increases and declines. Furthermore, asset price changes perceived as being permanent should have greater effects than those seen as merely temporary. To complicate things further, data issues often blur the analysis, and sensible data may not be available over long time periods, despite a better data situation in some countries (such as the USA) and ongoing progress overall.

Therefore, it may be advisable for empirical economists to focus on a limited time period, accepting as a lesser evil the implied lack of statistical precision. In some cases, the best that can be achieved is to estimate an order of magnitude rather than a point estimate. In calculations such as Equation (3.3) the inclusion of a wealth variable tends to weaken the sensitivity of consumption to current income, though often not by a great deal. What is obtained is a so-called 'hybrid' consumption function, reflecting both Keynesian and more 'classical' behaviour, whose relative weights are to be determined empirically. The weights are important when it comes to evaluating the incidence of fiscal policies, particularly the likely incidence of changing taxes on aggregate consumer spending.[3]

In sum, the presence of a wealth term is satisfying from an analytical standpoint but is fraught with empirical difficulties. Measurement errors may be substantial, and forecasting wealth (in particular, asset prices) is perilous, not to mention that there is much disagreement on the exact potency of wealth effects. And while it makes sense to believe that rising wealth should ultimately boost consumption, the timing of the impact is quite uncertain (Poterba, 2000).

Inflation

Inflation has an obvious impact on consumption, since households' purchasing power and wealth is eroded by increases in the general level of prices. But, even though consumption and wealth are therefore expressed in real terms in Equation (3.3), inflation may need to be included on the right-hand side, because of two possible additional effects. One is that expected inflation could encourage households to front-load purchases. The other goes in the opposite direction and is called the 'Pigou effect': inflation eats into households' real balances (since liquid assets are not indexed one-for-one to inflation), which will be restored by higher saving. Empirically, the second effect of inflation dominates. In fact, the early Keynesian consumption functions that simply related c to y failed to capture the increase in the saving rate in the main advanced countries in the 1970s, which was interpreted retrospectively as a consequence of the Pigou effect in a context of rising inflation.

Looked at in this way, rising inflation depresses consumption both through a reduction in real income (if nominal income is not fully indexed) and via the real balance effect. Since the mid-1980s, however, the macroeconomic environment in OECD countries has changed: central banks have gained more independence and inflation as well as inflation expectations have declined to low levels and remained there. In addition, the Pigou effect is somewhat analogous to a negative wealth effect (with real wealth losses stemming from higher inflation in this particular case) and may therefore already be captured by the inclusion of a wealth variable in the consumption equation. Therefore, econometric estimates sometimes fail to document any real balance effect.

---

[3] It is also possible to test whether the sum of the long-run elasticities of consumption to income and wealth equals 1, and to impose this as a constraint if the data corroborate this assumption. This would mean, quite logically, that a 1 per cent increase in income and in wealth would push consumption up by 1 per cent over the long run.

Real interest rates

Real interest rates appear in Equation (3.3) as they may affect household consumption through a substitution, an income and a wealth effect. First, a rise in the real interest rate means that the present price of future consumption declines compared to that of current consumption: this substitution effect causes saving to increase. But at the same time, an income effect is also at work: the interest rate rise boosts the return on households' savings, thus easing their budget constraint and allowing for higher consumption both in the present and in the future. The key reason is that households' financial assets on aggregate exceed their liabilities. As net creditors, their interest income increases following a rise in interest rates, exceeding the adverse impact of higher debt service. Finally, higher interest rates may affect consumption via a third channel, by reducing the value of the assets – stocks and bonds, but also housing – held by households. The ensuing negative wealth effect can be expected to depress consumption.

Which of the effects dominates is an empirical question. In practice, econometric estimation tends to be carried out using real long-term interest rates – though measuring real long-term rates is difficult since ideally one needs to consider long-term inflation expectations. In addition, a short-term rate is also occasionally introduced. Indeed, in some countries – notably the United Kingdom and Australia – short-term interest rates play a more prominent role, given that bank lending to households is largely at variable rates.

Other variables

Unemployment U, in addition to influencing current income (which is already captured in y), reduces expected future income, and therefore current consumption, according to the permanent income hypothesis. Unemployment also adds uncertainty, prompting risk-averse households to increase their precautionary savings. Hence it is sensible to test for the significance of ΔU in the short-run component of the equation, and of U in the long-run component.

Finally, dummy variables may improve the quality of the econometric estimates by explicitly taking into account policy measures or exceptional events ignored in traditional consumption equations. Examples are the time-bound incentives introduced by several OECD countries during the 1990s, and the 2007 financial crisis to stimulate purchases of new, less-polluting motor vehicles, which gave a temporary boost to the acquisition of durables. Another example is weather conditions: an unusually cold winter, for example, would drive up energy consumption (which represents a sizeable share of overall household consumption). Once again, this has to be tested empirically, since the impact of these sectoral effects on total consumption may also depend on cross-sector elasticities (higher car purchases could be compensated by lower consumption of other items).

3.2.2   Residential investment

Residential investment includes households' purchases of new housing as well as their spending on major improvements to existing dwellings. It represents a large chunk of household investment (which *inter alia* also includes unincorporated business capital formation if the self-employed are included in the household sector, as recommended by international national accounts guidelines).

As illustrated in Figure 3.2, residential investment is far more volatile than GDP or household consumption, as demonstrated in the recent Great Recession, which was characterized by a sharp correction in housing prices. Therefore, the importance of housing in business cycles can hardly be overemphasized, with strong implications for the conduct of macroeconomic policies, particularly monetary policy. Unfortunately, housing dynamics are hard to forecast and even harder to control.

From a theoretical standpoint, residential investment can be thought of in life-cycle terms, like consumption. The relevant determinants *a priori* include households' real gross disposable income y, real wealth, and the real interest rate r. Generally, an equation of the following sort is estimated:

$$\Delta k_t = \alpha + \Sigma_i \, \alpha_i \, \Delta k_{t-i} + \Sigma_i \, \beta_i \, \Delta y_{t-i} - \mu \, (k_{t-1} - \eta \, y_{t-1} + \theta \, r_{t-1}) + \gamma \, z_t \qquad (3.4)$$

Figure 3.2   US GDP, household consumption and residential investment*
Housing investment is far more volatile than GDP

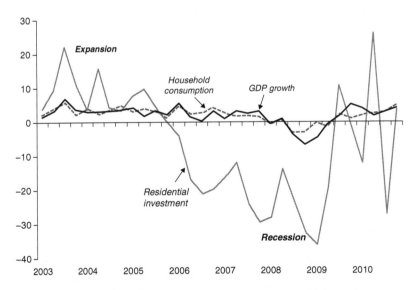

*Quarter-on-quarter, seasonally-adjusted annualized rates of change, percentages.
Source: Bureau of Economic Analysis.

where y and the (real) stock of housing k are in logarithms, and the vector z includes other explanatory variables, such as the relative price of housing (which influences households' arbitrage between housing and consumer goods or services).

Note that Equation (3.4) models the stock of housing rather than investment in housing. However, it is possible to model the accumulation rate instead, or the investment flow, since, as for business fixed investment, $I_t = K_t - (1 - \delta_t)K_{t-1}$. In addition, it is often not convenient to rely on balance-sheet information, which is published with long lags. A quick fix is to construct an *ad hoc* series for the stock of housing, using the permanent inventory method, which, starting from the stock in a base year (K_0, provided by the latest financial accounts available) adds up the subsequent net investment flows to obtain K_t.

The deflator used in this context is ideally the residential investment deflator, though it can also in practice be some index of house prices. A rise in the real interest rate is expected to have a negative impact: it increases the cost of purchasing housing for households who borrow to finance the acquisition, while for owners renting out property it reduces the relative return on housing. The real interest rate is included here in the long-run component of the equation but can also feature in the short-run component. It is typically a long-term interest rate, except in countries where mortgages are predominantly at variable rates, such as the UK.

A major problem with calculations such as Equation (3.4) is that residential investment is much more volatile than any of its putative determinants: some of the brutal swings in residential investment cannot be fully explained by the relatively smooth evolution of real incomes and even of interest rates. The only way to do so would be to have highly variable short-run elasticities. But this would be technically difficult and in any event is hard to justify theoretically: why would decisions to purchase a new house, which are eminently long-run decisions, be so sensitive to short-run ups and downs in income? Part of the explanation may be related to financial constraints and the occasional presence of real estate market bubbles. How banks lend to households, compared to firms, is also likely playing a part in this.

The basic model has been augmented in several ways. Demographics have been incorporated, to reflect the observation that younger working-age cohorts invest more than retirees. Attempts have been made to factor in the numerous tax and other incentives that in most countries influence the housing market (tax breaks, subsidies, low interest rate loans, for example). However, it is very difficult to quantify these properly in the context of a regression, and they may affect house and land prices more than the volume of housing consumption or home ownership rates (Hendershott and White, 2000). Another, partly related, avenue for improving Equation (3.4) has been to model the psychological factors impinging on investment decisions. Income or interest rate developments may affect households' mood and inclination to take the risk involved in the purchase of housing. One way to incorporate this dimension is to include unemployment (U or ΔU) on the right-hand side, as for consumption. Finally, the impact of mortgage financing arrangements (which are estimated to have contributed substantially to the rise in US property prices prior to the burst of the housing bubble in 2006–7) has been factored in explicitly.

To conclude, it should be noted that over short horizons (a year or less), the econometric approach is generally less helpful for forecasting purposes than extrapolation based on variables that are known to foreshadow residential construction (such as building permits), taking into account the usual gestation lags in this sector (see Chapter 2 and Appendix 3.1).

3.3   Imports and exports

Identifying what drives exports and imports is a long-standing research area that received renewed attention during the decade of the 2000s with the emergence of large trade imbalances, including large US deficits and Chinese surpluses. In particular, assessing the policy implications of such imbalances and their unwinding depends on a good understanding of trade flow determinants, such as output growth and exchange rates.

The theoretical background for foreign trade equations is relatively uncontroversial. On the import side, the standard underlying model features a representative consumer facing the choice between a foreign and a domestic good, which are imperfect substitutes, and deciding how much to spend on each. Utility maximization subject to budget constraints allows for the derivation of the demand for imports as a function of real income and the relative price of imports. Export behaviour is analysed symmetrically, as the imports from the rest of the world. Exports are therefore a function of world income and their relative price. Hence, two variables take centre stage in empirical foreign trade equations: a demand variable and a variable measuring the competitiveness of domestic production.

The specifications used sometimes split up goods and services (and within goods, they may concentrate on manufactures). Indeed, manufactures are often viewed as being more cyclically sensitive than other items, such as energy or some services. Nevertheless, this traditional distinction may have partly lost its relevance in recent years, while in some contexts working on aggregate series may be simpler with little loss in information. For example, the OECD has moved to focusing on relationships for total trade in goods and services in its global trade model (see Pain *et al.*, 2005, who also provide comprehensive empirical results that can serve as a benchmark).

The typical equations for real imports (*m*) and exports (*x*), both in logarithms, are:

$$\Delta m_t = \alpha^m + \Sigma_i\, \alpha_i^m\, \Delta m_{t-i} + \Sigma_i\, \beta_i^m\, \Delta y_{t-i} + \Sigma_i\, \xi_i^m\, \Delta c_{t-i}^m$$
$$- \mu^m\, (m_{t-1} - \eta^m\, y_{t-1} + \theta^m\, c_{t-1}^m) + \lambda^m\, t + \gamma^m\, z_t^m \qquad (3.5)$$

$$\Delta x_t = \alpha^x + \Sigma_i\, \alpha_i^x\, \Delta x_{t-i} + \Sigma_i\, \beta_i^x\, \Delta y_{t-i}^* + \Sigma_i\, \xi_i^x\, \Delta c_{t-i}^x$$
$$- \mu^x\, (x_{t-1} - \eta^x\, y_{t-1}^* + \theta^x\, c_{t-1}^x) + \lambda^x\, t + \gamma^x\, z_t^x \qquad (3.6)$$

where *y* is now domestic demand, y^* foreign demand, c^m import competitiveness, c^x export competitiveness (all in logarithms), *t* a time trend, and z^m and z^x vectors including other relevant variables, such as the domestic capacity utilization rate. We shall consider each of these in turn.

Demand

Starting with demand and the import equation, *y* is often defined empirically as total aggregate demand, including exports, rather than GDP or domestic demand. This allows analysts to take into account the import content of exports, which is large not only in small, open economies (and very large even in countries such as the Netherlands or Belgium) but also in those regions such as Asia where the production chain is highly integrated across countries. It is often useful to distinguish the different components of demand (consumption, investment and exports) since the associated propensities to import differ: in particular, the import content of investment is roughly twice that of consumption in a number of OECD countries, and the import content of exports is higher than that of consumption (Claus and Li, 2003).

The estimated coefficients α_i^m and β_i^m show how aggregate demand is distributed between imports and domestic production. This is important in practice: high β_i^m coefficients imply that demand shocks (say, a fiscal boost) will largely leak out to trading partners, and that the stimulative impact on domestic activity will be limited.

On the export side, there are no readily available indicators of demand, so these need to be constructed. A short-cut is to proxy world demand addressed to the country under consideration by world GDP. But it is better to take into account the country's foreign trade structure, and to estimate how rapidly exports would grow if market shares remained unchanged (see Box 3.3). This provides export market growth for the national economy under consideration. The evolution of market shares is then captured in Equation (3.6) by the competitiveness term.

Box 3.3 World demand

World demand in period t, WD_t, is defined as the weighted sum of the imports (M_t^i) of trading partners i, the weights being the country's market share (MS^i) in each of these trading partners:

$$WD_t = \Sigma_i MS^i M_t^i$$

where $MS^i = X_0^i / M_0^i$ is the ratio, in the base year, of the exports of the country to partner i over total imports of partner i. In the base year, this world demand equals the country's exports. Its subsequent growth is not that of total world trade, but rather that of world trade seen from the perspective of the country, so to speak.

Building this type of indicator is not straightforward. In practice, disentangling prices and volumes is not easy, as different concepts are used across countries. The data are not only surrounded by significant uncertainty but also appear with substantial lags and are subject to large revisions. By the time world demand was properly estimated, the cycle would have moved on.

From an analytical standpoint, it is tempting to restrict the analysis to manufactures, which allows analysts to leave aside the (often different) dynamics of services and special factors, such as those related to the energy markets. Yet, in practice, up-to-date data are often limited to customs flows of overall goods, in US dollars, for a selection of countries (OECD plus some emerging market countries). Conversion into volumes requires difficult assumptions to be made on the changes in deflators. In addition, a reliable decomposition between manufactures and other goods may not be at hand and data on traded services may be incomplete. It is certainly simpler to look only at national accounts data for goods and services but this may be too much of a shortcut, as it implies long lags and may be an overly aggregate approach.

How can world demand be forecast? One useful option in the very short run is to use the survey data collected from businesses (see Chapter 2). Their assessment of export prospects and order books are usually a good predictor of export market growth in the coming quarters. A second option is to build an overall growth scenario that allows analysts to estimate future imports from the various trading partners. This runs into two problems, however. One is that the accounting framework tends to give a significant weight to countries that are not key players in world trade, but rather 'followers'. France, for example, trades a great deal with Switzerland and relatively little with the USA. But the evolution of US imports is more informative on world demand, given the spillover effects to France's other trading partners. The other problem is circularity caused by trade interactions between countries. This can be particularly damaging in highly integrated trade zones such as the euro area. A third, lighter and possibly more robust option is to run a regression of world demand on domestic demand in a few key trading partners, and use the estimated equation to forecast world demand.

Trends

A time trend is often included in the import equation to take into account the growing openness of economies (that is, the tendency for the ratio of imports to GDP to rise). This reflects the gradual dismantling of tariffs, the mounting importance of multinational firms and increasing specialization. These factors are difficult to quantify but a time trend can serve as a proxy. The associated coefficient is, of course, expected to be positive. The time trend is usually introduced linearly, but can also be represented in logistic form, to reflect that the scope for and pace of further opening might decrease as openness rises. The inclusion of such a trend tends to reduce the apparent elasticities of imports to world demand, especially over the long run. In the absence of a trend, estimates often point to long-run elasticities as high as 2 or 3 while, with a trend, the assumption of unitary elasticity ($\eta^m = 1$) is often accepted (a result in line with theory). The estimated short-run elasticities, and therefore the leaks following positive demand shocks, also tend to be lower in the presence of a trend term.

A time trend is also sometimes added to the export equation, but for somewhat different reasons. Indeed, world demand being constructed based on the imports of the trading partners, it already incorporates the openness trend effect. The role of a time trend in the export equation is rather to capture any long-running changes in market shares linked to changes in non-price competitiveness. The time trend then proxies for product quality in the wider sense, which is difficult to measure. The expected sign of the associated coefficient can be positive or negative, depending on the circumstances. As in the case of imports, the inclusion of a time trend may help to validate the hypothesis of unitary long-run elasticity ($\eta^x = 1$), which may also seem natural. In a forecasting context, however, extrapolating this time trend may not be warranted, or at least involves substantial judgement.

Competitiveness

Price or cost competitiveness can be measured in various ways, by comparing domestic conditions with some averages of conditions abroad (see Box 3.4). Changes in competitiveness can amplify or offset changes in demand. Forecasters, however, often assume that nominal or real exchange rates will remain unchanged in the future (see section 4.7), which implies that forecast changes in competitiveness are limited. Then, competitiveness mainly affects forecast trade flows via the lagged impact of past changes, which themselves largely reflect past nominal exchange rate movements.

While competitiveness clearly influences foreign trade, there is no consensus on the empirical estimates of the respective elasticities and lags, nor on the stability of elasticities over time. Econometric estimation usually generates surprisingly low elasticities, given that the law of one price (premised on perfect

Box 3.4   Competitiveness indicators

From a short- to medium-run perspective, competitiveness is measured traditionally by the real exchange rate, which can be calculated in a variety of ways, involving prices or unit costs expressed in the same currency:

- Indices of relative consumer prices are easy to construct and to update, since the data are readily available for virtually any countries and are published rapidly (see, for example, bis.org/statistics/eer/index). A drawback, however, is that the associated basket of goods and services includes a large share of non-traded items (though it might also be argued that part of the competitiveness of a country's exporters is influenced by domestic costs in its non-tradable sectors).
- Relative export price indices overcome this problem, since by definition they only cover tradables. Export price competitiveness is usually computed by comparing the average of foreign countries' export prices with national export prices. Import price competitiveness is obtained by comparing the price of national imports with the price of domestic production. These measures, however, ignore the trade flows which are not observed, partly because of a lack of competitiveness.
- Relative cost indices are sometimes preferred because they avoid both of the problems mentioned above. The most frequently used indicator is the ratio of unit labour costs (possibly restricted to manufacturing). This indicator, however, may mismeasure short-run competitiveness developments because it ignores changes in profit margins. For example, exporters may prefer to absorb a rise in domestic costs by accepting lower margins, thereby keeping export price competitiveness constant. The same holds, *mutatis mutandis*, for importers. Over the longer run, however, margins cannot expand or shrink indefinitely, so that cost and price competitiveness tend to move in tandem.

These various indicators can be computed using weights reflecting bilateral competition, or preferably using a double-weighting scheme that also takes into account competition in third-country markets (Lafrance and St-Amant, 1999). Indeed, firms in country X may not export much to country Y but may compete fiercely with firms from country Y in country Z, which is ignored if bilateral competition alone is taken into account. The OECD, among others, uses this methodology: for a given country, the procedure calculates the relative importance of each of its competitors in its domestic and foreign markets (which is determined by the pattern of supply on these markets), and then weighs it according to the relative share of the different markets in the total demand directed at this country.

substitutability, however) would imply infinitely elastic flows. This is the case for long-run elasticities and even more so for short-run elasticities, as shown, for example, by Hooper *et al.* (2000). More generally, such findings may result from the fact that Equations (3.5) and (3.6) assume that imports and exports depend on demand but not on supply (which might be the case if, for example, imports arise because of domestic producers' inability to produce exactly the types of goods demanded by consumers).

Domestic capacity utilization is therefore sometimes included among the determinants of manufacturing imports and exports, as a measure of supply constraints. If it is high, one would expect more imports than otherwise, implying a positive coefficient in Equation (3.5). One might also expect lower exports, and therefore a negative coefficient in Equation (3.6), if indeed domestic producers tend to serve domestic clients first when they cannot fully satisfy demand. Whether this is in fact the case must be tested empirically.

3.4 Employment

Employment generally follows activity with a lag. On average, however, employment grows more slowly than value added, because of the trend productivity gains stemming from technical progress. Other factors, notably the cost of labour, may also affect employment.

From a theoretical standpoint, employment is usually thought of as firms' demand for labour, in a framework similar to the one discussed above for the optimal stock of capital. The determinants of employment are activity and the real cost of labour when targeted employment is derived from the profit maximization behaviour of firms; or activity and the cost of labour relative to that of capital when demand is limited and firms minimize costs for a given level of activity. Technical progress enhancing productivity per head is often simply represented as a time trend. Employment is assumed to adjust gradually to its targeted level, but the adjustment process is in principle faster than for the capital stock, labour being a more flexible input.

Alternatively, the production function can be inverted to yield an employment equation. In this case, no maximization behaviour needs to be assumed. The targeted level of employment is then a function of output, the other available factor inputs and technical progress. The cost of labour does not enter this 'technical' relationship.

Implicitly, these two approaches assume that labour demand determines employment (irrespective of labour supply developments) and can be modelled along the following lines:

$$\Delta l_t = \alpha + \Sigma_i \, \alpha_i \, \Delta l_{t-i} + \Sigma_i \, \beta_i \, \Delta y_{t-i} + \Sigma_i \, \xi_i \, \Delta w_{t-i}$$
$$- \mu \, (l_{t-1} - \eta \, y_{t-1} + \theta \, w_{t-1} + \lambda \, t) + \gamma \, z_t \qquad (3.7)$$

where l is employment, y output and w the real cost of labour (all in logarithms), while t is still a time trend and z a vector of other explanatory variables.

This type of equation usually has private sector employment on the left-hand side (or employment in a specific private industry), since public sector employment has different determinants. Employment is usually also restricted to wage earners; to the extent that the number of those who are self-employed evolves more smoothly, it can be forecast through simple extrapolation.

A more delicate choice has next to be made for l between number of employees and number of hours worked. Modelling the latter seems more sensible from the standpoint of firms' demand for labour; the problem in this case is that average working times need to be estimated and forecast in order to derive a forecast for employment. This is usually done using a more-or-less robust accelerator-type relationship between activity and average working hours. In practice, forecasting the number of employees directly is simpler, in so far as, ultimately, it is the variable that is focused on the most. However, this approach may run into difficulties in periods when hours per person change dramatically, either as a response to the business cycle or because of policy changes. Regarding the latter case, Dixon *et al.* (2004) suggest that changes in 'standard' hours of work should be incorporated in the long-run component of the employment equation.

Demand

Turning to demand (y), it is usually defined as gross output or value added (restricted to the business sector if private employment alone is modelled). The dynamic component of Equation (3.7) indicates the speed at which employment adjusts to changes in y. During a cyclical upturn, employment tends to increase with a lag, and when it does it rises less than y, so that productivity is procyclical: this is the so-called 'productivity cycle' as documented by Skoczylas and Tissot (2005). Note, however, that in many countries the take-off of more flexible forms of employment (such as fixed-term contracts and temporary work) are likely to render employment more sensitive to cyclical fluctuations and hence could reduce the length of the productivity cycle. Moreover, it may be of interest to test for asymmetries in the short-run response to activity between downturns and other periods. In the same way as for capital, the long-run restriction $\eta = 1$, which corresponds to constant returns to scale, is usually tested.

Labour cost

Equation (3.7) features the real cost of labour on the right-hand side, computed as the nominal cost (which should normally include the social contributions paid by employers and employees) deflated by producer prices. Alternatively, the relative cost of labour (compared to the cost of other production inputs) can be used. The choice between these two options depends on which of the above two analytical frameworks applies. Empirically, however, it is often difficult to decide which of the two is the most suitable.

The elasticity θ measures the sensitivity of the demand for labour to its cost over the long run, for a constant level of production. In the particular case of perfect competition with only two factors of production (labour and capital), θ could also be interpreted as the elasticity of substitution between capital and labour. This kind of identification with structural parameters is risky, though. In principle, one should go for a consistent model of the main decisions of the firm (capital and labour demand, price setting, for example), estimate them simultaneously and jointly identify the structural parameters, provided, of course, that this can be done and that the data support the selected theoretical set-up.

Technical progress

As noted, technical progress, which increases trend productivity, can be captured by a time trend. But even in this simple framework, caution is called for: the interpretation of the coefficient attached to the technical progress term depends on the exact specification of the equation, and in particular on the presence or absence of the cost of labour among the explanatory variables, as illustrated in Box 3.5.

3.5 Prices and wages

Forecasters focus on a variety of inflation measures, including those associated with consumer prices, producer prices (possibly disaggregated by sectors), prices of capital goods, housing prices, import and export prices, and wages (which is the price of labour services). There are also different theories of inflation. In a perfectly competitive world, prices adjust to instantly equilibrate all markets at all times. But in the real world, prices display inertia. Theoretical models offer several possible explanations for price stickiness, including the infrequency of contracting, menu costs and strategic pricing behaviour in imperfectly competitive markets. Hence, prices react only gradually to real sector imbalances, even if they do indeed help to redress them over the longer run. In the short run, there can thus be some disconnect between real and nominal variables. It should also be stressed that some prices are much more volatile than others, notably oil and raw material prices, as well as some food prices (see Appendix 3.2). This can have a significant effect on short-run movements in 'headline' inflation. Measures of core inflation, which one way or another control for the high-frequency volatility of some components of the overall price index, are more stable (though the definition of core inflation can vary across countries or analysts).

Box 3.5   Technical progress: three long-run employment relationships

Consider the following three alternative formulations for the long-run employment target, where $e = bt$ is trend technical progress and $b > 0$ measures the pace of growth in productivity per capita:

$$l = y - e$$
$$l = y - e - \theta (w - e)$$
$$l = y - w$$

The first does not feature the cost of labour. It assumes constant returns to scale. Employment simply depends on output, with a unitary elasticity, and on trend technical progress. This equation would be consistent with an assumption of full complementarity of the factor inputs or with the inverted production function approach coupled with the hypothesis that the stock of capital per head is constant.

The second equation is consistent with the maximization of profits in a perfectly or imperfectly competitive market, under the assumption of a constant elasticity of substitution θ between capital and labour. In this context, when the real wage rises in line with productivity ($w = e$), $l = y - e$ (which is the first formulation). The second equation can be rewritten as $l = y - (1 - \theta) bt - \theta w$. Hence, the coefficient associated with the time trend is not the pace of per capita productivity growth b, as in the first equation, but $(1 - \theta) b$. The inclusion of the cost of labour thus alters the interpretation of the technical progress coefficient.

The third equation is a special case of the second one, where it is assumed that $\theta = 1$, as when the production function is a Cobb–Douglas one. Then, the technical progress term vanishes completely and the equation amounts to stating that the share of wages in value added is a constant.

These equations assume 'disembodied' technical progress. One could think instead that technical progress can only bear fruit when embodied in new capital. Then productivity growth depends on the speed at which the stock of capital is renewed. A simple way to take this possibility into account is to test the significance in Equation (3.7) of a variable representing the average age of the capital stock.

Prices and wages are usually considered jointly, given their high degree of interdependence. Wages are negotiated with an eye on past and expected inflation. At the same time, prices are influenced by costs – particularly labour costs, which on average are the single largest component of total costs. More generally, various prices interact with wages (see Figure 3.3). The supply side features deflators associated with aggregates such as value added, gross output and imports, while on the demand side deflators appear that pertain to final consumption, intermediate consumption, investment and exports. The underlying intuition is that, on the supply side, prices are essentially set in the light of costs, with firms deciding on the mark-up to apply, depending on the conditions prevailing in their product markets. On the demand side, prices depend on what is charged by producers, on the relative weight of the various components of demand and on mark-up behaviour in the distribution sector. Figure 3.3 ignores international trade: in an open economy, one would have to add the influence of foreign prices on import prices (and therefore, indirectly, on the other demand prices) and on export prices (in so far as national producers are price-takers on their export markets).

Figure 3.3   Wage–price dynamics in a closed economy

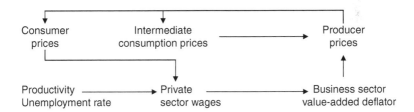

Wage–price dynamics can be explored in greater or lesser detail. A fairly elaborate representation can be obtained in a macroeconomic model such as those discussed in Annex III, with a distinction between the various sectors and several interrelated feedback loops. But in many cases a more parsimonious approach may suffice, of the kind illustrated in Figure 3.4. A popular extension of the basic loop presented in Figure 3.4 is the so-called 'triangle model' of inflation, in which inflation depends on three main determinants: past inflation, demand and cost shocks (notably commodity price shocks).

Figure 3.4   Reduced forms of the wage–price dynamics

The remainder of this section presents commonly used models of supply prices, demand prices and wages. None of them accounts fully for observed inflation, giving practitioners some latitude to pick and choose the framework that best fits their needs. The focus here is on traditional approaches of price dynamics where lags play a significant part in capturing inflation inertia. Indeed, while an extensive literature has recently explored the theoretical implications of the 'new-Keynesian Phillips curve', lessons from this research for daily empirical forecasting of inflation are somewhat inconclusive; in contrast, traditional inflation models have proved themselves to be rather robust tools (Rudd and Whelan, 2007).

3.5.1   Price equations

Supply prices

Starting with supply, a choice has to be made between the value-added deflator and the producer price index (since the price of intermediate consumption is set on the demand side, knowledge of one of the two ensures knowledge of the other). The main difference between these two approaches is related to the coefficient associated with intermediate consumption in the price equation. If producer prices are modelled, this coefficient can be expected to be positive. Alternatively, if the focus is on value added, the coefficient is likely to be zero, or even negative (if firms react to an increase in the cost of intermediates by reducing mark-ups). For illustrative purpose, producer prices are considered below.

The usual assumption is that the equilibrium price is obtained by applying a given mark-up ratio to the production cost per unit of output. This is consistent with profit maximization by producers in a perfectly competitive market (the mark-up is then nil) or in an environment of monopolistic competition à la Dixit–Stiglitz (1977) (the mark-up then depends negatively on the elasticity of demand). While the mark-up rate may be constant over the long run, it can fluctuate with the cycle over the shorter run, and more generally with macroeconomic conditions.

A typical equation is:

$$\Delta p_t^s = \alpha + \Sigma_{i \geq 1}\, \alpha_i\, \Delta p_{t-i}^s + \Sigma_{i \geq 0}\, \beta_i\, \Delta uc_{t-i} + \Sigma_{i \geq 0}\, \xi_i\, c_{t-i}$$
$$- \mu\, (p_{t-1}^s - uc_{t-1}) + \gamma\, z_t \tag{3.8}$$

where p^s is the price of output and uc the unit cost of production, both in logarithms, while c is an indicator of cyclical conditions and z a vector or other explanatory variable.

In practice, uc is taken to include at least labour costs, but also the cost of the intermediates (since in this example p^s is the price of gross output) and possibly the cost of the physical capital used (see above). The unit labour cost, for example, is a deflator defined as the wage bill (including employer-paid social contributions) divided by the volume of output. The various components of costs can be lumped together, as in Equation (3.8), or identified separately, if there are reasons to think that they are not all passed through into producer prices with the same mark-up. Econometric tests can help to settle this question empirically.

In the long-run term of Equation (3.8), prices are often indexed with a unitary elasticity on costs. This is the so-called static homogeneity property. In other words, a lasting increase in unit costs is ultimately passed on in full, in line with the theoretical assumption of constant mark-up rates in the long run.

The short-run coefficients α_i and β_i reflect the speed at which prices adjust to changes in costs. The lower and more spread out they are, the slower the reaction of prices. These coefficients are usually estimated freely, without trying to impose any *a priori* theoretical structure on them.

That said, the dynamic homogeneity constraint ($1 - \Sigma_{i\geq1}\alpha_i = \Sigma_{i\geq0}\beta_i$) is sometimes tested. This means that prices and costs are fully indexed over the periods covered by the lags featuring in the equation. Given that producers tend to determine their prices with respect to past but also to future costs developments, this constraint can be interpreted as a sign of economic agents' ability to form consistent inflation expectations. Moreover, if the number of lags is limited, the indexation is fairly rapid. Whether this is in fact the case has to be tested empirically.

The variable c features in Equation (3.8) because of the presumption that the state of demand (relative to potential supply) does influence the price mark-up. Accordingly, the coefficients ξ_i are generally expected to be positive, and the larger they are, the greater the responsiveness of prices to tensions in the product market. The upward pressures on mark-up ratios from strong demand may nevertheless be mitigated on the supply side. A higher intensity of competition may in particular act as a drag on mark-ups even when the economy is accelerating, as documented by Oliveira Martins and Scarpetta (2002).

The choice of the right indicator for the cycle is generally guided by the data, depending on what seems plausible and holds up well econometrically. Typical examples are the rate of capacity utilization, which is available rapidly, or the output gap, though the latter is not observable and can only be estimated. Similar indicators in first-difference (rather than level terms) are also used.

Demand prices

On the demand side, prices can be thought of as set by the distribution sector, as a function of domestic producer and import prices, according to an equation of the following sort:

$$\Delta p_t^d = \alpha + \Sigma_{i\geq1}\, \alpha_i\, \Delta p_{t-i}^d + \Sigma_{i\geq0}\, \beta_i\, \Delta p_{t-i}^s + \Sigma_{i\geq0}\, \xi_i\, \Delta p_{t-i}^m$$
$$- \mu\,(p_{t-1}^d - \eta\, p_{t-1}^s - \theta\, p_{t-1}^m) + \gamma\, z_t \tag{3.9}$$

where p^d is the retail price, p^s still the producer price and p^m the import price expressed in domestic currency, while z again stands for a vector of control variables. The static homogeneity condition is $\eta + \theta = 1$, which ensures that a lasting 1 per cent increase in producer and import prices translates into a 1 per cent increase in the retail price. In principle, η and θ should reflect the shares of demand met, respectively, by domestic and foreign suppliers, and it is useful to check whether the estimated coefficients indeed broadly match these market shares.

In many countries, recent movements in inflation have been related to import prices, and more specifically to commodity prices (including oil). Moreover, the pass-through of changes in commodity prices to domestic inflation is likely to be higher than for non-commodity imports, for which domestic goods can more easily be substituted and pricing-to-market behaviour is more widespread. To capture these differences, it is standard practice to split import prices in Equation (3.9), between, say, energy commodity, non-energy commodity and non-commodity import prices (see Vogel *et al.*, 2009). In such a framework, the inflation responses to commodity price shocks (or exchange-rate shocks) may be decomposed between so-called 'first-round' effects on consumer prices, and waves of 'second-round' effects that transit via the prices of intermediate inputs and possible wage indexation to higher consumer prices.

3.5.2   Wage equations

Turning to the modelling of wages, the first problem facing the forecaster is to choose between wage per hour and wage per capita. *A priori*, the former might seem preferable. Indeed, if hours worked change one would expect the wage per capita to move in the same direction. In practice, the choice between the two options depends largely on the trustworthiness of the data. As in the case of employment, discussed above, both options can be problematic. Modelling wages per capita without having working time in the equation may be misleading when hours worked change significantly, as was the case in France around the turn of the millennium. But focusing on hourly wages requires analysts to have a reliable measure of hours. However, data on working time are typically unreliable and are published with long lags. Hence, some analysts prefer to use wages per capita and to ignore developments in average worked hours. It should also be borne in mind that a given change in working time may have different effects on productivity and wages, depending on its cause (trend decline, legislated reduction in hours worked, expansion of part-time work and so on).

A second choice pertains to sectoral coverage and disaggregation. One option is to take the average wage in the business sector (public sector wages should be modelled separately, given that they usually behave somewhat differently). Alternatively, the wage can be modelled sector by sector, depending on how wage formation processes differ across sectors. An intermediate approach is to focus on one robust overall equation (for the business sector or for manufacturing, say) and to derive sectoral equations as variants; for example, by introducing sector-specific intercepts or trends. This makes sense when sectoral differences are significant but stable over time (because of, for example, long-run discrepancies in productivity levels or changes across sectors).

Finally, it is customary to model gross wages, including employee-paid social contributions but excluding those paid by employers, on the grounds that this corresponds to what wage-earners bargain for. But it is sometimes preferable to reason on total labour cost or, in contrast, on the wage net of any social contributions.

Phillips curves

In a famous article, Phillips (1958) described a negative relationship, over the long run, between unemployment and nominal wage growth in the United Kingdom. Various types of 'Phillips curves' have been used in the literature since. A typical one is:

$$\Delta w_t = c + \Sigma_{i \geq 1} \, \alpha_i \, \Delta w_{t-i} + \Sigma_{i \geq 0} \, \beta_i \, \Delta p_{t-i} - \lambda \, U_{t-1} + \gamma \, \Delta z_t \qquad (3.10)$$

where w is the gross nominal wage and p the consumer price index (both in logarithms), U the rate of unemployment, and z a vector of other explanatory variables, typically including import price inflation (somewhat artificially, the notation Δz instead of z is used here because the explanatory variables are expected to affect the changes in wages, not their levels – see below). This specification does not incorporate any long-run equilibrium wage level.

Normally, $\lambda > 0$: low unemployment translates into high wage inflation, and vice versa. The value of λ indicates how sensitive wage demands are to labour market tensions. The latter can be captured, alternatively, by a transformation of U (for example, log U) or by other indicators, such as the ratio of the number of unemployed to the number of job vacancies.

Wage earners aim for a certain level of purchasing power, hence their demands incorporate inflation expectations. In Equation (3.10), these expectations are assumed to depend on the inflation rates observed in the recent past (Δp_{t-i}). This term did not feature in the original Phillips curve and its inclusion is reflected in the 'augmented Phillips curve' label used for Equation (3.10) and others like it.

When agents do not suffer from any money illusion, a change in the pace of inflation does not alter their real wage demands. In this case, one would expect that $1 - \Sigma_{i\geq 1}\,\alpha_i = \Sigma_{i\geq 0}\,\beta_i$, in other words, that wages be fully indexed on prices, albeit with some lag. This condition means that there is no long-run trade-off between inflation and unemployment, an intuition dear to many economists. It has to be met if a NAIRU is to be computed (see Box 3.6 on page 104). In practice, however, empirical estimates do not always support this condition, and the forecaster faces a trade-off between obtaining a better statistical fit and imposing more consistency with economic theory.

Equation (3.10) can be enriched by adding a number of other determinants on the right-hand side. In some cases, inserting ΔU in lieu or in addition to U is warranted. This increases the estimated sensitivity of wages to ups and downs in activity and may significantly enhance the equation's fit, in particular when the labour market is of the insider–outsider type (in which case the wage claims of the insiders – whose jobs are relatively protected – are not influenced greatly by the level of unemployment affecting the outsiders but more by changes in the level of unemployment, which reflect the probability of job losses for insiders). A number of more specific effects can also be taken into account explicitly. One would typically test for the influence of changes in minimum wages, wages in the public sector, and tax and social contribution rates. It is also common practice to include dummies for particular episodes (such as important wage agreements), so as to avoid biasing the estimation of the structural coefficients with outlier data for which there is an idiosyncratic explanation. But even with such additions, wage equations are often not that robust, and should be used with caution when forecasting.

The wage curve

Phillips curves have been criticized on theoretical grounds. They are interpreted most readily as showing the adjustment of wages when the labour market is out of equilibrium: for example, when labour is in excess supply, competition for jobs among the unemployed will drive down, or at least slow down, nominal wages. But this Walrasian supply-versus-demand logic fails to acknowledge that unemployment tends to moderate wage claims in more indirect ways, notably by affecting the probability of job loss for the incumbent workers, which they take into account when formulating their wage claims. Most modern labour market theories (including those based on efficiency wages or on bargaining) rather point to a 'wage curve' relating the level – instead of the growth rate – of wages to its determinants (Blanchard and Katz, 1999). This leads to the following type of equation:

$$w_t = p_t + \alpha\, \pi_t + \eta\, \omega_t - \varphi\, U_t \tag{3.11}$$

where π stands for the productivity of labour. Equation (3.11) is usually described as a wage-setting (WS) equation. The average wage and the unemployment rate are related negatively provided $\varphi > 0$, which one would normally expect. Wage claims take workers' productivity into account, with $\alpha > 0$. If $\alpha = 1$, changes in productivity are fully reflected in wage claims, both on the way up and on the way down. The other relevant variables, featuring in vector ω, may be very diverse, potentially including the unionization rate (as a proxy for unions' bargaining strength), the level of unemployment benefits or more generally of replacement incomes, the mismatch between demand and supply of skills, the tax and social contribution wedge (computed as the difference between the total cost of labour for the employer and the income after social contributions and taxes received by the wage earner), and the terms of trade.

Assuming that Equation (3.11) properly describes the long-run determinants of wages, one can insert it into Equation (3.10) and obtain the following dynamic wage equation:

$$\Delta w_t = c + \Sigma_{i \geq 1}\, \alpha_i\, \Delta w_{t-i} + \Sigma_{i \geq 0}\, \beta_i\, \Delta p_{t-i} + \gamma\, \Delta z_t$$
$$- \mu\, (w_{t-1} - p_{t-1} - \alpha\, \pi_{t-1} - \eta\, \omega_{t-1} + \varphi\, U_{t-1}) \tag{3.12}$$

This form is more general than the augmented Phillips curves and more consistent with modern labour market theories.

Combined with a price-setting (PS) equation as in Equation (3.9), a wage-setting (WS) equation such as Equation (3.12) implies an equilibrium unemployment rate that differs from the NAIRU obtained from a Phillips curve (see Box 3.6). The merit of the WS/PS approach is that it allows for a richer model. However, the empirical robustness of Equation (3.12) is far from guaranteed: is μ significantly positive, as one would want, and is it stable over time? The great diversity of explanatory variables potentially included in ω and influencing the targeted wage may also complicate estimation considerably (L'Horty and Rault, 2003).

Yet another approach is the 'semi-structural method' which combines the information contained in the Phillips curve with changes of the NAIRU over time (see Appendix 3.3). In practice, it is often difficult to evaluate which of several specifications is best.

Box 3.6   The NAIRU and the equilibrium unemployment rate

The NAIRU (non-accelerating inflation rate of unemployment) is the rate of unemployment compatible with stable inflation. It can be derived from a wage–price loop combining a mark-up producer price PS equation and a Phillips curve as a WS equation. For example, keeping the same variable names as above:

$$p_t^s = w_t - \pi_t + z_t + \alpha \qquad \text{(producer price equation)}$$
$$\Delta w_t = \Delta p_{t-1} - \lambda\, U_{t-1} + \Delta z_t' + \beta \qquad \text{(Phillips curve)}$$

where z and z' are variables exerting inflationary pressures (there could be more than one in each equation), while α and β are constants. For the sake of simplicity, the producer price p^s is assumed to instantly reflect any change in unit wage cost, whereas the wage w follows consumer prices p with a one-period lag.

Differencing the producer price equation yields: $\Delta p_t^s = \Delta w_t - \Delta \pi_t + \Delta z_t$. Define the wedge between consumer and producer prices, which reflects the influence of imports prices and of indirect taxes, as ψ. Hence $\Delta p_t = \Delta p_t^s + \Delta \psi_t$. Then the producer price equation in first difference can be rewritten as $\Delta p_t = \Delta w_t - \Delta \pi_t + \Delta \psi_t + \Delta z_t$. Inserting the latter into the Phillips curve leads to:

$$\Delta p_t - \Delta p_{t-1} = -\lambda\, (U_{t-1} - U^*)$$

where

$$U^* \equiv (\beta - \Delta \pi_t + \Delta z_t + \Delta z'_t + \Delta \psi_t) / \lambda$$

is the NAIRU.

When $U_{t-1} = U^*$, consumer price inflation is stable. The NAIRU is inversely proportional to λ, the sensitivity of wages to unemployment. It increases with the difference between average wage award demands (β) and productivity gains. The NAIRU also depends on the other variables that exert inflationary pressures, such as changes in import prices or in taxation. Therefore, U^* may vary over the short run.

The concept of the NAIRU has significant implications for policy debates. In principle, when unemployment exceeds the NAIRU, there can be some scope for macroeconomic policy to stimulate demand without stoking inflationary pressures on the labour market. In contrast, if unemployment is at or below the NAIRU, expansionary demand policies would translate into higher inflation, and the ensuing losses in competitiveness and/or wealth would have a contractionary effect that offsets the stimulus.

U^* as defined above is rather volatile, since transient inflation shocks (changes in Δz_t, $\Delta z_t'$ or $\Delta \psi_t$) move it around. It is often preferable to abstract from such disturbances, and to assume that $\Delta z_t = \Delta z_t' = \Delta \psi_t = 0$. This yields a long-run NAIRU U^{**} which varies only with productivity:

$$U^{**} = (\beta - \Delta \pi_t) / \lambda$$

Moreover, if $\Delta \pi$ is added into the above Phillips curve, as in the case for a WS formulation, and if it has a unitary long-run elasticity, then it cancels out in the NAIRU, which then becomes a constant (β/λ).

Turning to the concept of equilibrium unemployment, which is derived by combining a producer price level equation with a WS curve, one can start, for example, from the following long-run relationships:

$$p_t^s = w_t - \pi_t + z_t$$
$$p_t = p_t^s + \psi_t$$
$$w_t = p_t + \pi_t + z'_t - \varphi\, U_t$$

Through substitution, this leads to:

$$U^{eq} = (z + z' + \psi) / \varphi$$

In contrast to the NAIRU, the explanatory variables enter the price and wage equations in level terms, rather than as changes. A permanent shock on oil prices, taxation or any other variable contained in z or z' will therefore have a lasting impact on unemployment, rather than a temporary one. The determinants of equilibrium unemployment are more diverse than in the Phillips curve framework.

An obvious question is whether the equilibrium rate of unemployment described above can also be considered as a (long-run) NAIRU, in the sense of being the rate compatible with stable inflation. In a number of studies, the two concepts are in fact implicitly treated as if they were equivalent. In the ECMs, such as those presented in this chapter, however, equivalence only obtains when dynamic homogeneity holds in all price and wage equations. The OECD (Gianella *et al.*, 2008) has promoted a two-stage empirical methodology that reconciles both approaches: first, a NAIRU is estimated on the basis of a Phillips-curve type equation, relating inflation to the gap between the NAIRU and actual unemployment; second, the obtained NAIRU is regressed on a set of likely explanatory variables such as the tax wedge, product market regulation and indicators of labour market rigidities.

Further reading

This chapter has concentrated on the major components of real sector behaviour. For a deeper understanding, the reader can plunge into the literature on macroeconomic models (see also Annex III and the references there) or turn to the specialized literature on each major component. On corporate investment, Chirinko (1993, 2008) describes empirical strategies and standard results. Household consumption behaviour has been studied at length over time, but recently the focus has been very much on wealth effects (see CBO, 2007 for the US evidence; and Skudelny, 2009 on Europe). On trade flows, Pain *et al.* (2005) is a good starting point. Alquist *et al.* (2011) provide a comprehensive review of the pitfalls of forecasting oil prices. As regards wage and price inflation, as well as Phillips curve estimation, a rich source is the empirical research carried out under the aegis of the ECB's inflation persistence and wage dynamics networks, see ecb.int/home/html/researcher_ipn_papers.en and ecb.int/home/html/researcher_wdn.en. In addition, Fair (2007) tests various empirical price equations on US data.

Appendix 3.1   Sectoral forecasting

This book deals mainly with macroeconomic forecasting. In contrast, sectoral forecasts follow a more microeconomic approach. Here, the focus is on sectors, or even on one particular sector. This is a relevant perspective for a firm concerned with the outlook its sector faces, or for a local government wondering how much needs to be spent on infrastructure to ensure that firms in the area can grow without encountering local bottlenecks (such as road congestion).

Sectoral forecasts are useful in at least three ways. First, they offer a more concrete reading of economic developments. Macroeconomic analysis is often somewhat abstract: a given growth rate of GDP, for example, can reflect a steady, broad-based expansion, with all sectors doing well; or it can mask considerable divergence across sectors, with some booming and others in recession. A sectoral approach thus sheds light on important differences across sectors, reflecting both exposure to dissimilar shocks and heterogeneous behavioural responses.

It also makes it possible to check on the internal consistency of economy-wide forecasts by explicitly factoring in the interdependence across sectors. Indeed, sectoral forecasting was used actively during eras when some form of central planning played a significant role. For example, in France, a concern in the 1950s and 1960s was that some sectors, such as steel, might not grow fast enough to meet the demands of other sectors. Input–output matrices were used to forecast steel demand by sector for a given pace of GDP growth, with a view to ensuring sufficient supplies of steel. This approach remains of interest today in some cases, albeit in a different spirit – for example, when looking at the emergence of new sectors.

Finally, short-run sectoral forecasts are crucial for economic agents involved in the given sector. Managers and investors have to think ahead and prepare budgets, or decide on inventory levels and working schedules. Similarly, investment and hiring decisions that lock in resources over a longer period require careful, longer-run sectoral forecasts.

This appendix reviews two approaches to sectoral forecasting: the microeconomic one, which zooms in on one particular sector, subsector or firm; and the cross-sectoral one, which looks jointly at the different sectors and their interrelationships, typically using input–output analysis. While the emphasis is on production, value added and intermediate consumption, similar techniques can be used to forecast consumption, investment, prices or employment by sector.

Microeconomic forecasts

The microeconomic approach focuses on production or value added in a given sector, in the sense of a set of activities as defined in the national accounts classification (see Annex I) or at a more disaggregated level. The sectoral forecast can then incorporate specialized microeconomic expertise and idiosyncratic information. This does not mean, however, that macroeconomic developments are necessarily ignored.

In fact, there are two ways to carry out this exercise. Let Q be the value added in the sector under consideration, S a vector of relevant sector-specific variables (including, for example, past values of Q, prices, inventories and so on), and Y a macroeconomic variable, say GDP. Then Q can be forecast, either in 'partial equilibrium' fashion, as $Q = f(S)$, or taking into account macroeconomic developments, as $Q = f(S,Y)$.

The second specification generally ensures a better fit to past observations, as fluctuations in a given sector are often fairly strongly correlated with overall movements in activity. Even when the correlation is negative (the sector behaves countercyclically), taking it into account improves the fit. But this does not, by that very fact, imply that, for forecasting purposes, the second specification will deliver superior results. For that to be the case, the forecast of Y itself should be sufficiently accurate. An illuminating parallel is the usefulness of taking into account world demand when forecasting national GDP, especially for small, open economies. This can improve the GDP forecast substantially but, of course, it can also worsen it if the international environment is assessed incorrectly. Similarly, here, a poor forecast of Y can increase the forecast error on Q.

'Partial equilibrium' approaches

One way to forecast Q for a given sector independently of the global outlook is to use one of the time series methods presented in Annex II, notably when no other detailed statistical information is available. This, however, does require the purging the series from its seasonal component (when the frequency is greater than annual) and controlling for any identified exceptional factors. The adjusted series can then be subjected to simple extrapolation techniques or to modelling *à la* Box and Jenkins (1976).

An alternative and more structural approach is to look for the factors that have accounted for the evolution of Q in the past, and at how they are set to evolve over the forecast period. A classic example is the use of data on housing starts to forecast activity in the construction sector, since there is a strong positive correlation between the former and output several months later.

More generally, this type of sectoral forecast tends to exploit available survey information, such as enterprises' answers to questions regarding their investment plans, the evolution of capacity and their own production forecasts. Household surveys on intended durable goods purchases might be useful, for example, when forecasting sectors such as that of motor vehicles. In this context, survey data foreshadow future behaviour and play the role that leading indicators take at the macroeconomic level (see Chapter 2). How successfully they can be used depends, however, on how robust is the correlation between the surveys and actual developments. And, in practice, the forecast of Q can be improved by adjusting for any extraneous news – for the likely impact of announced tax measures in a given economic sector, say.

Taking the macroeconomic environment into account

A simple way of bringing in the macroeconomic context is to write demand for the sector (or firm) under consideration as $Q = f(Y,P)$, where Y is economy-wide income and P the relative price of output in that sector. Suppose the sector produces a given set of consumer goods or services. Then:

- Q is usually taken to be output (in volume terms) rather than value added, as demand pertains to the product including the embodied intermediates; an ancillary assumption would thus be needed to go from output to value added (for example, one would assume fixed technical coefficients);

- *Y* would typically be real disposable household income (using the CPI as a deflator), or the volume of total household consumption (when the view is that households first split up income between saving and spending and then decide how to allocate their spending across goods and services); and
- *P* would normally be the price of *Q* relative to the CPI. As microeconomic demand functions are typically homogeneous of degree one, a similar increase in all prices would not change the composition of real demand, so what matters here is the relative rather than the absolute price.

It is standard practice to estimate the demand function in logarithmic form, to obtain the underlying elasticities directly:

$$\log Q = \eta \log Y + \beta \log P + \varepsilon \tag{1}$$

where ε is a residual, η is income elasticity and β price elasticity. For 'normal' goods or services, $\eta > 0$, while for 'inferior' ones $\eta < 0$. When $\eta > 1$, they are said to be 'luxury' goods or services. Besides, β is generally expected to be negative. Note also that, in this simplified framework, demand for a given good does not depend on that for other goods, so that no cross-elasticities come into play.

The above formulations are static in nature. As such, they represent long-run rather than short-run relationships. A standard way to add some short-run dynamics is to consider Equation (1) as the long-run component in an error-correction equation:

$$\Delta q_t = \alpha + \Sigma \alpha_j \Delta q_{t-j} + \Sigma \beta_j \Delta y_{t-j} - \mu \left[q_{t-1} - \eta \, y_{t-1} - \beta \, p_{t-1} \right] + \varepsilon_t \tag{2}$$

where small letters are used to denote logarithms ($q = \log Q$, and so on) and it is assumed for simplicity that the relative price does not affect the short-run dynamics.

Equation (2) is similar to the types of equations presented in Chapter 3. Such equations are frequently used, in isolation or within a model, to forecast output in a given sector as part of a more global scenario. Conversely, macroeconomic analysis can usefully be complemented by checking whether sectoral developments implied by the global outlook appear to be sensible and coherent.

Input–output analysis

In principle, the above techniques can be applied across all sectors. The results can then be summed up, provided the adding-up constraint is met (that is, that the aggregation does equal GDP). But there is an alternative approach, based on input–output matrices. In addition to sectoral value added, it provides, for each sector, the detail of what goes in as intermediate consumption and the decomposition of what goes out between final demand and the intermediate consumption of other sectors.

The method

The input–output matrix is identical to the input–output table described in Annex I. For the sake of simplicity, it is helpful to assume that sectors and products overlap, abstracting from the distribution sector, and to ignore indirect taxes and subsidies. Then, for each group of products (hereafter 'product'), the input–output matrix shows:

- How much is supplied overall, through domestic production and imports;
- How much is used per sector, including the one producing it, as intermediate consumption; and
- The final uses: consumption, fixed capital formation and exports.

For each product, the sum of the intermediate and final uses equals total supply.

The way to proceed with this analysis is as follows, bearing in mind that this is essentially an accounting method, and a static one, which can be applied to values as well as to volumes. The first step is to extract from the input–output table the matrix of technical coefficients, called A. If there are n sectors, A is a square, n-by-n, matrix. The coefficient a_{ij}, at the intersection of the ith line and jth column, is the ratio of the intermediate consumption of product i by sector j that produces output j.

Three n-dimensional column vectors are then introduced (where T is the transpose symbol, indicating that a line vector is turned into a column vector or vice versa): $Y = (Y_1, ..., Y_n)^T$, the outputs of products 1 to n, $M = (M_1, ..., M_n)^T$, the imports of products 1 to n, and $D = (D_1, ..., D_n)^T$, the final uses of products 1 to n.

Then $A \times Y$ is the n-dimensional column vector of intermediate consumption by product. Its first term, for example, is $a_{11}Y_1 + a_{12}Y_2 + ... + a_{1n}Y_n$, which is equal to the total consumption across sectors of product 1.

The equality between supply and uses of each product can then be summed up as follows:

$$M + Y = A \times Y + D \tag{3}$$

where each term is an n-dimensional column vector. Equation (3) says that imports plus domestic production of each product equals its intermediate plus final consumption. This can also be written as:

$$Y = (Id - A)^{-1} \times (D - M) \tag{4}$$

where Id is the n-by-n identity matrix (with ones along the diagonal and zeros everywhere else), and noting that the matrix $(Id - A)$ is assumed to be invertible (which is indeed the case in practice).

Equation (4) allows the derivation of the production by sector, given final demand and imports. Then, having derived Y, the intermediate consumption of each product can be computed as $A \times Y$. Value added by sector is then the difference $Y - A \times Y = Y \times Y (Id - A)$.

However, in practice, forecasts for M and D are rarely available. Rather, what are available are forecasts for total imports, m, and the components of final demand: final consumption, c; fixed investment, i; and exports, x. In order to forecast M and D, they need to be split up among products. This can be done by using another matrix related to the input–output table, the matrix of final demand coefficients. Here, this matrix, named B, would have n rows (one per product) and 4 columns (for imports, final consumption, fixed investment and exports). Coefficient b_{31}, for example, would be the share of the imports of product 3 in total imports. Hence:

$$M = B \times (m, 0, 0, 0)^T \text{ and } D = B \times (0, c, i, x)^T \tag{5}$$

It is thus possible to forecast M and D once imports and the main components of final demand have been forecast, on the assumption that the final demand coefficients are unchanged. From there, sectoral output can be forecast using Equation (4).

Pros and cons

Input–output analysis enables the translation of the forecast of the components of final demand into a forecast of the intermediate and final demand addressed to each sector. It also provides a forecast of the inputs that each sector will need from the others. The inbuilt consistency of this approach is appealing: by construction, the resulting sectoral forecasts add up to the macro picture.

This is particularly interesting for sectors that are important suppliers or heavy users of intermediates. For the former, the method allows for the estimation of the traction they get from changes in final demand. For the latter, it provides estimates of the volume and costs of the inputs they will need. In the context of economy-wide planning, this allows the forecasting of import requirements and the identification of potential future bottlenecks that could stifle overall economic expansion.

As presented above, however, input–output analysis rests on the stringent assumption that both the technical coefficients and the final demand coefficients are fixed over the forecast horizon. In other words, it is assumed that the structure of production and demand does not evolve. This is unrealistic in at least two cases:

- When the forecast extends for only a few quarters: in the short run, the technical and final demand coefficients are unstable, because of lags between the production of intermediates and their incorporation into final products, and into inventory fluctuations.
- When the forecast spans many years: over time, technological progress and new investments alter production patterns, while consumption habits change, not least in response to shifts in relative prices (for example, in the case of information technology goods). It may then be necessary to use time-varying technical and final demand coefficients.

Therefore, the most relevant horizon for input–output analysis is the medium run. Over periods of a few years, firms are generally not going to overhaul their *modus operandi*: once a piece of equipment is installed, it will be used for some time before being replaced. Similarly, clients' behaviour will probably not change that much. On the whole, however, this type of tool is not used routinely in macroeconomic forecasting, even if it does offer useful insights into the workings of the economy.

Appendix 3.2   Commodity prices

Commodity prices are an important variable in many macroeconomic forecasts, given that they affect core variables such as output and inflation significantly. Indeed, total trade in commodities accounts for a large share of overall world trade. Commodities encompass such diverse items as unprocessed agricultural products, energy, metals, textiles and, in broader definitions, computer chips. Forecasters often focus on the oil price, as oil alone accounts for about one tenth of world trade and because of the prominent role oil price shocks have played since the 1970s. Hamilton (2003) documents this, showing also that the effect of oil prices on activity is non-linear, with oil price increases depressing output more than similarly sized oil price declines boost it, and that increases have significantly less predictive content if they simply correct earlier decreases.

Oil prices

Historically, the price of oil was very low until 1973–4, when OPEC implemented production cuts, largely for political reasons. The price of a barrel of crude oil jumped from US$3 to US$12 (see Figure 3.5). In 1979–80, it soared to US$37 against the backdrop of the revolution in Iran and the Iran–Iraq war. The mid-1980s witnessed a reverse price shock, as OPEC eased the restrictions on output. In the early 1990s, with the first Gulf War, the price jumped again, but fell back rapidly and eventually skidded to a low of US$12 in 1998 in the wake of the Asian financial crisis.

Oil prices have trended up strongly since the late 1990s, albeit with considerable volatility. Prices hovered around US$30 in 2000–4, responding to hiccups in global demand as well as climatic and geopolitical factors, including the second Gulf War in early 2003.

Figure 3.5   Oil prices*
Oil prices tend to trend up over the long run but with considerable volatility

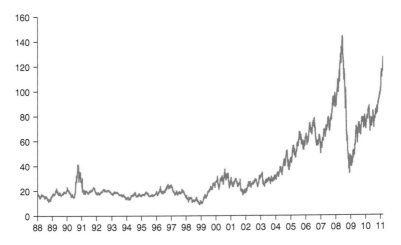

*Daily Brent spot price, f.o.b., in US$ per barrel.
Source: US Energy Information Administration.

Against the backdrop of surging demand in emerging market economies, prices rose from 2004 onwards. The first half of 2008 witnessed a breathtaking spike, with the oil price culminating at US$145 in July before receding even more abruptly in the next few months as global output and confidence slumped. Prices subsequently rebounded, reverting in early 2011 to the high levels comparable to those observed in the early stages of the 2008 spike. In real terms (for example, deflated by the US consumer price index), however, oil prices have increased far less than in US$ terms over the past few decades.

Against this turbulent background, how can oil prices be forecast? To approach this question it is helpful to distinguish projections of long-run trends from short-term influences on prices.

Long-run projections of the oil market and the oil price

A somewhat theoretical view of long-run oil price developments is based on the so-called Hotelling rule: in principle, the price[1] of a rare and non-renewable resource such as oil should rise at a rate equal to the interest rate. Indeed, if the price was seen as being set to rise faster, producers at the margin would want to keep the oil in the ground and let it appreciate, rather than extracting it immediately and investing the proceeds in financial assets. Lower production in turn would push up the spot price, reducing the expected pace of oil price increases. Conversely, if the price was expected to rise by less than the interest rate, it would be profitable to extract and sell more oil, and to earn a higher financial return on the proceeds. This would push the spot price down, making for more rapid expected price increases.

In practice, however, this theoretical principle is of limited help, given that the future levels of reserves and interest rates are uncertain, that rates of time preference may not accord with theory, and that producers may be liquidity constrained. Moreover, even leaving aside short-lived ups and downs, Hotelling's theory is at odds with some of the data, notably the fall in prices in 1982–6 and the subsequent period of depressed prices. As a result, many economists think of oil prices as having been influenced very little by resource exhaustibility. Nevertheless, with the change in demand from emerging countries and growing recognition of the finiteness of the resource, it has been argued that the scarcity rent emphasized by Hotelling may now be becoming more relevant (Hamilton, 2009).

A more pragmatic approach is to assess the fundamentals of the oil market, namely physical supply and demand over various horizons:

- Trend consumption growth may be seen as a function of potential GDP growth, of its energy intensity and of the share of oil in total energy use. For example, strong demand from emerging economies as a result of rapid income and GDP growth has been a major feature of recent developments that is likely to continue in the future. In contrast, demand has decelerated in OECD economies since the first oil shock, reflecting a steady decline in the intensity of oil production.

---

[1] Or, more precisely, the marginal revenue associated with its sale minus its marginal extraction cost. In a competitive market, the marginal revenue equals the price. However, in so far as the oil market is dominated by a few large players, the market price exceeds the marginal revenue from oil sales.

- Supply-side factors come into play, including technical changes and market structure. For example, because of its larger reserves, OPEC will control an increasing share of the market, which will give it more monopoly power.

Over the medium to long run, both demand and production capacity are endogenous, in the sense that they respond to prices. When production is falling behind demand, the price rises, encouraging higher-cost producers to expand capacity. With a lag (because of the time needed to build new wells) output rises and prices decline, which in turn reduces investment in the oil sector and thus supply, and so on. At the same time, demand reacts to oil prices over the medium run, given the prices' impact on growth and on the energy intensity of production. Moreover, because of policies to stem greenhouse gas emissions, energy tends to be taxed more heavily as time goes on. This also feeds back on supply and demand and is likely to play a growing role in coming decades.

Empirical models of supply and demand are used to incorporate these various elements. For example, the International Energy Agency's long-run model has demand as a function of GDP growth, prices (including an allowance for the taxation of carbon dioxide emissions), technological progress and other factors, and supply as a function of ultimately recoverable resources (which themselves depend on the price of oil and on improvements in drilling, exploration and production technologies). Long-run income and price elasticities of demand and supply are key parameters of these models (Wurzel *et al.*, 2009).

These models suggest that the rise in oil prices over the 2000s stemmed from vigorous demand growth from emerging markets and a sluggish price response in oil supply. Looking ahead, projections typically conclude that global dependence on oil will not diminish in the 2010s or 2020s, despite gains in efficiency and the growing use of alternative energy sources. However, sensitivity scenarios also suggest a wide range of possible outcomes. Of importance are assumptions on market responses (elasticities) as well as policies (including those endeavouring to mitigate climate change and the strategic choices of major oil producers). Given such uncertainties, it is not surprising that medium- to long-run oil price forecasts are often widely off the mark.

Short-run developments

The volatility of oil prices is high and increased during the 2000s, with 2008 seeing the largest swing observed to date. One major reason is that the underlying supply and demand curves appear to be price-inelastic in the short run. Demand responds to activity but is rather price-insensitive, as fuel-consuming equipment cannot easily be altered. Oil supply is price-inelastic, since it takes time to raise productive capacities or explore new fields. In addition, supply varies depending on OPEC cohesion, on the tactics of non-OPEC producers, and on Saudi Arabia's behaviour as a 'swing producer'; such factors can only be forecast by drawing on market expertise.

Given that quantities do not respond much to prices in the short run, large price effects may be obtained with seemingly small shocks, including geopolitical uncertainties, supply disruptions and demand pressures. Short-run models built on these features give clues to recent developments and forecasts, though they fail to explain all the observed volatility in prices. Part of the adjustment between supply and demand may also take the form of changes in stocks. However, inventories are costly to hold, and the development of financial derivatives based on oil contracts has reduced the role of stocks as a buffer. It has also led to lower stock levels, making for more precarious equilibria on the spot market.

While the supply and demand models provide some useful explanatory tools, they nevertheless struggle to capture the most radical swings, most notably the spike in 2008 (Smith, 2009). This has raised the suspicion that other factors, in particular 'speculation', contributed to such fluctuations. The fact that large volumes of transactions no longer pertain to physical flows on the spot market facilitates self-fulfilling speculative behaviour before the fundamentals have time to play their equilibrating role (for financial variables in general, see Chapter 4). Indeed, it has been observed that the net long positions held by non-commercial traders stood at record levels between mid-2007 and mid-2008, indicating expectations of ever-rising prices.

However, the idea that speculation on futures markets drives the spot price is generally regarded with scepticism. For speculation to be profitable in an environment of rising prices, the oil price future curve would have to slope upwards (a situation described as 'contango'). This was not the case in the run-up to the 2008 peak: futures prices were most often lower than spot prices (the market is then said to be in 'backwardation'). Moreover, the oil spot price equilibrates supply and demand in the physical market. This suggests that prices cannot stray from the fundamentals in a sustained manner. In this sense, it might in fact be the spot price that drives the futures price, with 'speculation' actually bringing forward movements of prices toward equilibrium. Under this interpretation, financial activity would fuel price volatility in the near term by accelerating the market response to changes in fundamental drivers.

Non-oil commodity prices

Similar price formation mechanisms are observed for other non-renewable resources. The fact that they are exhaustible would suggest that their price should increase over the long run. But as in the case of oil, a number of factors stand in the way of Hotelling's rule, including the existence of producing countries' cartels, fluctuations in the evaluation of available world reserves and changes in demand behaviour. Consider gold: in some developing countries with untrustworthy banks it has long served as the principal saving instrument; but if the financial systems of such countries become more reliable, demand for gold as a store of value could decline, everything else being equal.

As regards renewable resources and the commodities whose value has less to do with rarity, it is often claimed that their price is on a trend decline relative to the price of industrial goods, for several reasons and in particular because of the low income elasticity of demand for commodities. This is referred to as the Prebisch–Singer hypothesis. It is consistent with the fact that, from the 1860s to the 1990s, real non-energy commodity prices had been declining on average by about 1 per cent per year (Cashin and McDermott, 2002).

However, many non-oil commodity prices trended upwards during the 2000s. As with oil, their prices collapsed in the wake of the financial crisis but subsequently staged a recovery. Medium-run expectations are for these prices to remain high by historical standards, as a result of sustained demand from emerging economies and sluggish capacity growth.

Price volatility around these trends is enormous. It has even increased since the end of the Bretton Woods fixed exchange rate regime of the early 1970s, since most commodity prices are quoted in US dollars, implying that the prices in other national currencies began to fluctuate with their exchange rate *vis-à-vis* the US dollar. In addition, various price regulation mechanisms put in place after the Second World War (agreements between producer and consumer countries, stabilization funds and so on) gradually lost whatever effectiveness they might have had. The secular downward trend is therefore of little practical relevance for forecasters, the associated change in prices being dwarfed by large and long-lasting booms and slumps. Microeconomic expertise on specific markets – based on intimate knowledge of weather conditions (for agricultural products), stocks and demand – can be more useful in this context than blanket assumptions about a return to trend. A key element in this respect is estimating supply capacity in light of past investments in the sector under consideration. The mechanism at play is that strong prices initially stimulate investment, pushing supply up and, in turn and with a lag, prices down.

For forecasting purposes, three frequencies are distinguished in the modelling of commodity price fluctuations:

- In the (very) short run, stock movements, speculative behaviour and information constraints play a major role. Information from commodity futures markets might also be useful, as argued by Bowman and Husain (2004).
- Over the medium term, stocks matter less. Demand depends positively on the position in the cycle of consumer countries, on the price of the goods using the commodities as inputs and on the price of their substitutes; and negatively on commodities' dollar price and on the strength of the dollar *vis-à-vis* consumer countries' currencies. Supply depends positively on commodities' dollar price, on the strength of the dollar *vis-à-vis* producer countries' currencies and on expected demand; and negatively on production costs. These relationships are usually more stable for commodities such as metals than for agricultural products, given the strong impact of weather conditions on the latter.
- Long-run fluctuations are more clearly driven by structural trends, such as changes in consumption patterns, productivity trends and the evolution of producers' capacity (which is shaped, with a lag, by prices). Structural models are usually built to capture these forces, including computable general equilibrium (CGE) models, which take into account simultaneously the different commodities and regions and their interactions.

Appendix 3.3 Semi-structural estimation of the NAIRU

The NAIRU can be estimated using an unobservable component model including a Phillips curve. It is based on the assumption that the unemployment rate U can be decomposed into a trend component, identified as the NAIRU, U^*, and a cyclical one, C, which is not observed but is assumed to affect inflation, π:

$$U_t = U_t^* + C_t + e_t$$
$$\Delta \pi_t = \Sigma \alpha_i \, \Delta \pi_{t-i} + \gamma \, C_t + \delta \, z_t + u_t$$

where lagged inflation is introduced to take inflation inertia into account and z is a vector of variables further explaining inflation (supply shocks, for example), while e and u are error terms. The unobserved component C enters both equations and γ indicates how strongly it affects inflation.

Estimation of the model (parameters α_i, γ and δ as well as U^*, C and e) requires the analyst to make assumptions about the statistical properties of trend and cyclical unemployment, and about correlations. A simple but representative example would be as follows:

- The trend follows a random walk with drift: $U_t^* = U_{t-1}^* + \beta + \eta_t$ (this assumption would be consistent with the probable non-stationarity of the NAIRU – consider, for example, its tendency to rise in continental Europe through the mid-1990s: a case of positive drift).
- The cycle is an ARMA stationary process, that is an AR(2) process of the form $B(L) C_t = v_t$, with $B(L)$ a second-order polynomial distributed lag and v_t white noise.
- The error term is nil: $e_t = 0$.
- Trend and cycle are uncorrelated: $E(v_t, \eta_{t'}) = 0$ for any (t, t').

Based on such a set of assumptions, the model is written in state space form, which allows Kalman filter estimation (see Annex II). Unlike univariate trend-cycle decompositions, this allows for the use of information contained in the Phillips curve and thus comes closer to the theoretical NAIRU concept. At the same time, and in contrast with traditional Phillips curve analysis, allowance is made here for the fact that the NAIRU may change over time, even if nothing is said about why. This time-varying NAIRU approach is therefore often dubbed 'semi-structural'.

This approach can serve to shed light on the key drivers of structural unemployment across countries. Working on a panel of OECD countries, Gianella *et al.* (2008) use their estimates of time-varying NAIRUs to test for the influence of various policy and institutional variables, using in particular OECD structural indicators related to the level of rigidities of labour and product markets. The findings first confirm that unemployment has a significant impact on the change in inflation in almost all countries, highlighting the usefulness of semi-structural approaches based on Phillips-curve-type equations and time-varying NAIRUs. Second, they suggest that the main factors influencing structural unemployment are the level of the tax wedge (defined as the combined labour and consumption tax rate) and, to a lesser extent, union density as well as the cost of capital (proxied by long-term real interest rates).

In practice, however, the hypotheses underpinning this type of approach are somewhat arbitrary, notably with regard to the statistical properties of the cycle (which may be less symmetrical than is assumed). More generally, such methods are complicated to implement properly and difficult to communicate to outsiders, so that transparency is limited. Finally, there is uncertainty caused by the estimation techniques themselves – in particular surrounding the setting of the initial parameters of the estimation process, and because the results of these filtering techniques can be altered substantially by future revisions to the data, especially at the end of the sample. The estimates by Gianella *et al.* (2008) point in fact to an average standard error for the NAIRU of about 1 percentage point at a 90 per cent confidence interval level, with significant variation across countries.

Chapter 4

Financial Sector Dynamics

Contents

There are several ways to project financial variables and to take into account their high volatility compared with other economic variables. Short-term interest rates can be projected by anticipating central banks' actions, and then extending the forecast to longer horizons for 'risk-free' bonds and yield spreads. Stock prices are harder to deal with as they often display large and sudden movements, while real estate prices can experience impressive booms and busts, each lasting many years. Exchange rates are among the most volatile variables and are almost impossible to predict in the very short run.

Financial indicators play a key role in forecasting exercises: the evolution of major asset prices such as interest rates (which relate to the price of a short-term loan or a bond), equities, house prices and exchange rates has large implications for how the macroeconomic outlook evolves. As stressed in Chapter 3, asset prices can exert substantial wealth effects on consumption behaviour, since a large share of household wealth is held in the form of bonds, stocks and housing. Asset prices also play an important role in driving business investment. In turn, asset prices are driven by various forces including macroeconomic developments, and in particular by interest rates, taxation, demography and international factors (such as the portfolio strategies of global fund managers).

The importance of these interrelations has come to the fore in the context of the global financial crisis that erupted in 2007 – not only during the crisis itself, but also in the periods preceding and following it. Another major lesson from this crisis is that it will have long-lasting implications for the conduct of monetary policy, and thus also for the determination of short-term interest rates (and indirectly of other asset prices). However, the ways in which this will in practice change forecasting methods and tools is, at this stage, still unclear. On the one hand, monetary policy-makers are likely to take into consideration a wider set of objectives than previously when setting interest rates. On the other hand, it can be expected that these policy makers will employ a broader set of instruments to pursue their policy objectives.

This chapter focuses on the specific way that financial indicators are forecast, which differs significantly from the methods used for real economic indicators, such as national accounts aggregates. The main reason is that asset prices are far more volatile and very much driven by market participants' expectations. Fads or other forces can at times push asset prices far above or below what is warranted by the fundamentals. Hence, their forecasts are surrounded by considerable uncertainty. It is therefore advisable to draw on a great variety of tools to analyse and forecast financial variables, ranging from traditional economic models of interest rate determination to pure time series techniques and 'heterodox' methods such as chartism.

The chapter first discusses what distinguishes financial variables and the methods used to forecast them (section 4.1). It then goes on to explore the modelling and forecasting of short-term (section 4.2) followed by long-term interest rates (section 4.3). Bond, stock and house prices are covered next (respectively in sections 4.4, 4.5 and 4.6), followed by exchange rates (section 4.7). The chapter does not cover other economic variables to which the techniques used for financial indicators can be also applied, such as commodity prices, which are dealt with in Appendix 3.2. The reader interested in using time series methods with a specific focus on highly volatile financial markets data can refer to Annex II of this book.

This chapter is complemented by two appendices, expanding on the lessons learnt from the 2007 financial crisis that may be useful in understanding financial sector dynamics over a longer-term perspective (Appendix 4.1), and on a class of specific forecasting methods called 'technical analysis' (Appendix 4.2). A third appendix discusses country risk analysis and how rating agencies assess financial risks (Appendix 4.3).

4.1 Dealing with volatility

Financial indicators exert a strong and sometimes even decisive influence on the real sector variables that are at the heart of macroeconomic forecasting. But financial prices are volatile and at times seem only remotely connected to macroeconomic fundamentals (see Box 4.1). Hence, their evolution is difficult to predict.

Broadly speaking, six different approaches are followed to project financial variables:

- The first is to freeze them at some recently reached level, or at the average level observed over a given period of time. As noted in Annex II, this is good practice when the variable under consideration follows a random walk, and this method is frequently used for exchange rates in particular. It is also occasionally adopted for stock prices. Central banks long liked it for interest rates because it allowed them to avoid tying their hands as regards their future policy actions. However, in practice, forecasters can select the period that serves to set the assumption so that they retain some leeway to decide which value suits their forecast best.
- Expert judgement calls are the second way to go. This is particularly the case for those asset prices that are difficult to measure on an aggregate basis, given the heterogeneity of the market (for example, for house prices at a

Box 4.1   Bubbles, noise and herds

Financial markets are notoriously prone to excesses, manias and crashes. The 2007 financial crisis was a powerful reminder that bubbles arise recurrently, in the sense of a widening divergence between economic fundamentals and the quoted price, with the latter far exceeding what even an optimistic assessment of the fundamentals – which are themselves uncertain – would warrant. Paradoxically, bubbles are not synonymous with irrationality on the part of traders, who can make a fortune as long as they get out before the market turns around. Bullish expectations become a self-fulfilling prophecy once a sufficient number of agents share them. So a bubble can continue to inflate for a surprisingly long time after irrational exuberance has been diagnosed, with each trader knowing that the asset is overvalued but believing that he will be able to sell to one who has not yet realized it. At some point, however, a triggering event occurs, causing the bubble to burst. Awkwardly enough, this event may well be a 'sunspot', unrelated to any fundamentals but highly visible and serving as a co-ordination device to trigger the collapse (similarly, the event that sparked the onset of the bubble may also be unrelated to fundamentals).

The specificities of financial markets, surveyed by Brunnermeier (2001), include:

- Herd behaviour, which can be rationalized as resulting from traders attempting to make short-run profits by following others and thereby amplifying market swings. In fact, traders are disinclined to depart from the average view: if they sell too early in a rising market, they will be blamed for underperforming their competitors, while if they record losses in the context of a general market collapse, they will not be singled out. As Keynes (1936, p. 158) put it: 'Worldly wisdom teaches that it is better for reputation to fail conventionally than to succeed unconventionally'. This feature has been particularly important in the recent financial crisis, which highlighted the perverse incentives in compensation practices in the financial industry: short-term profits are rewarded on a non-risk-adjusted basis, while financial market participants' pay should be better aligned with the long-term profitability of their operations. Such long-term, risk-adjusted profits are often smaller than indicated by the apparent financial performance of financial firms in periods of booms and excessive risk-taking (Financial Stability Forum, 2009).
- The fact that access to information is key. Two types of market participants can be distinguished, with asymmetric information: on the one hand, informed or professional traders, who are in a position to exploit

arbitrage opportunities; and on the other, 'noise traders' or amateurs, who are less well-informed. If the latter are numerous, even efficient behaviour on the part of the informed traders will not be sufficient to prevent prices from deviating from what the fundamentals would warrant. Moreover, even sophisticated traders may engage in herd behaviour if they are risk-averse and have short horizons, thus contributing to the formation of bubbles.

- Expectations play a key role in driving asset prices. This can lead to long-lasting deviations from 'fundamentals' and seemingly irrational behaviour that, in fact, is quite rational from the perspective of market participants. A seminal example of self-fulfilling prophecy is the United Kingdom's exit from the European exchange rate mechanism in 1992. The British pound was not wildly overvalued, compared to the levels it subsequently reached in the late 1990s. However, speculative attacks on the currency led market operators to believe that defending the pound by raising interest rates would be untenable in a context where activity was already weak, which only reinforced speculators' pressure, so that ultimately the authorities abandoned the exchange rate peg. Another, more recent, example was the speculation in the US housing market in the 2000s that preceded the 2007 crisis. New home owners were granted credit facilities (especially risky 'subprime' mortgages) to buy houses even though their repayment capacity was obviously insufficient. This was caused by a variety of factors, including inadequate consumer protection, excessive liberalization in the US mortgage industry, and low interest rates that pushed down the cost of credit. Expectations also played a major role: in a general context of what looked like a secular upward trend in house prices, both debtors and creditors believed that future capital gains would be more than sufficient to service the loans. When prices started to fall, borrowers' repayment capacity proved much more limited than anticipated, foreclosures surged, and house prices fell, leading to a downward spiral.

Globalization and financial innovation have further complicated the relationships between financial variables, making them even harder to analyse and forecast:

- With regard to globalization, a number of domestic financial variables are increasingly determined by the behaviour of global investors. A well-known example observed on several occasions in the past few decades is that a rise in oil prices will affect the financial holdings of oil-exporting countries and therefore the demand for dollars; the recycling of such 'petrodollars' can then have large-scale consequence in the global economy and on financial variables.

- Turning to the consequence of financial innovation, a key element relates to portfolio management. Investors have tended to pursue risk diversification objectives, aiming at keeping the weights of the different asset classes in their portfolio at some desired level. When the risk of a component of their portfolio increases, investors may reduce their holdings of some other risky assets (thereby affecting their prices) even though the latter's risk/return profile has not changed.

- Analysing the interactions between globalization and financial innovation is becoming increasingly challenging. At times, a link has been observed between the price of certain domestic US assets (such as high tech shares or Treasury bonds), and capital flows to and from emerging markets. Increased savings in Asia in the 2000s (the 'global saving glut' reflected in the unprecedented accumulation of large forex reserves in this region) was combined with a global reduction in investors' home bias (because of increased opportunities for emerging market savers to diversify their holdings and hold an increasing share of foreign securities in their portfolios). This helped to push down interest rates and fuelled excessive risk appetite and a search for yield in industrial economies that arguably contributed to bringing about the 2007 financial crisis (Bernanke, 2005).

Since financial prices are so unpredictable in the short run, many forecasters prefer to work with a simple technical assumption; for example, freezing them at some level rather than trying to forecast them.

national level) or when these asset prices have displayed huge, seemingly unwarranted swings: sound judgement based on past experience (long-term trends, correction patterns and so on) can be useful to anchor the forecast. This approach is used in particular when building alternative scenarios: for example, the central scenario could be a freeze, and an alternative scenario could be a correction to a recent boom, or a return to some longer-term trend.

- Market expectations, as reflected in futures prices, can serve as an anchor and are indeed used explicitly by some central banks in their forecasts. The price of futures contracts, however, may not be a good predictor of the spot prices that will prevail down the road. Moreover, it incorporates a risk premium, implying that it does not coincide with the price actually expected by agents. The price of options (which give the buyer the right to sell or to buy a financial asset) also contains information about agents' expectations, especially with regard to perceived risks. In practice, however, derivatives markets may not be deep enough for price quotes to be very informative, especially at longer horizons. Furthermore, market expectations may be at odds with the baseline scenario contemplated by the forecaster.

- Financial price forecasts can be derived in the context of a full macroeconomic model. This is done at times for interest rates or, to a lesser extent, for other variables.
- Alternatively, they can be forecast outside the model, by trying to relate them to their key determinants. This provides equilibrium, or target values with which the variable under consideration will be assumed to converge over time.
- Finally, the time series techniques described in Annex II can be used, especially those techniques that have been developed to model volatility patterns.

In practice, the distinction between these different approaches is not that clear-cut, and some combination of them is commonly put to work.

Regarding more specifically public sector forecasters, they often refrain from publishing any forecasts for asset prices, so as not to interfere with the operation of the markets and unduly influence participants' expectations. Indeed, an official exchange rate forecast, for example, could be interpreted as a policy objective the authorities will defend rather than as a purely technical hypothesis. Similarly, central banks have often been reluctant to produce forecasts of short-term interest rates as this could be seen by market participants as a commitment – though this has changed somewhat in recent years. For all these reasons, conventional working assumptions of one type or another are generally used for forecasting financial indicators.

4.2 Short-term interest rates

The spectrum of interest rates is very broad, depending on the quality of the security or loan, and on the time horizon. The focus of this section will be on short-term rates, which are very much influenced by monetary policy.

Short-term interest rates are highly sensitive to central bank decisions or announcements, with the policy-controlled rates (often referred to as the central bank's repo rates) playing a key role. In practice, however, the measure used for short-term interest rates is typically a three-month interbank rate, such as the London interbank offered rate (Libor) (depicted in Figure 4.1). The key assumption for this choice used to be that interbank rates move in a less discontinuous fashion than the central banks' rate(s) and are less volatile than the overnight rates in the money market, which occasionally spike or plummet depending on liquidity conditions. However, a key and unexpected

Figure 4.1   Short-term interest rates*

Short-term interest rates came down to very low levels in major regions during the Great Recession

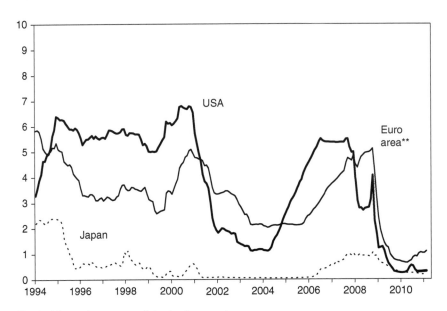

*Nominal 3-month money market rates, in percentages.
**Germany until end-1998, euro area since then.
Sources: ECB, Bundesbank.

characteristic of the 2007 crisis was that (uncollateralized) interbank markets dried up as banks became very risk adverse and were no longer willing to lend to each other without posting some collateral (Michaud and Upper, 2008). As a result, large gaps – so-called Libor/OIS spreads – appeared between the rates in the interbank market at, say, a three–month horizon and the rates derived from the overnight interest-rates swap markets (that is, the three-month ahead interest rates calculated as the result of the successive expected overnight rates over the period). After 2009, major interbank markets have roughly normalized (see Figure 4.2) though they remained volatile from time to time – for example, Libor/OIS spreads widened somewhat in 2010 when fiscal worries intensified in the euro area. Moreover, it is unclear whether these unsecured interbank markets will still represent a key benchmark in the future, or whether this role could instead be played by swap markets.

In forecasting, short-term interest rates are treated in a variety of ways. The first avenue is to monitor closely what monetary policy makers are themselves communicating. For example, the OECD as well as many private sector forecasters map out a trajectory for short-term interest rates over the forecast

Figure 4.2   Libor minus OIS spreads in major financial centres*

Interbank market spreads soared with the onset of the financial crisis in 2007, and spiked even more dramatically after of the collapse of the investment bank Lehman Brothers in September 2008

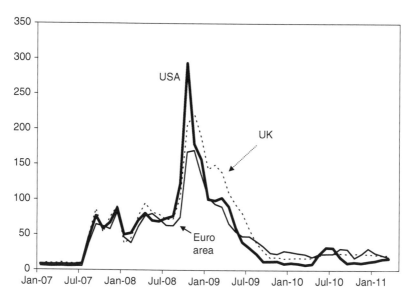

*Three-month Libor rate minus corresponding OIS rate, in basis points.
Source: Bloomberg.

period, based on what is perceived as the policy stance consistent with central banks' objectives.

4.2.1   Monetary policy transparency

Forecasting short-term interest rates basically means anticipating the decisions of one economic agent, the central bank (taken either by one person, its governor, or a governing body, which comprises a limited number of people). From this perspective, the aim is quite different from other forecasting exercises, where the task is usually to forecast a variable that is result of the aggregation of the decisions of numerous individual agents.

One difficulty is that central banks are discrete institutions. Accordingly, they often prefer to use an unchanged interest rate assumption, which does not reveal their thinking about possible future policy moves. However, a number of central banks, including the ECB and the Bank of England, have abandoned this conventional assumption and replaced it with the use of some measure of the interest rate path expected by markets. In fact, a few central banks have gone a step further and publish their own forecasts of interest rates: the central bank of New Zealand started to do so in 1997, and Norway, Sweden and Iceland have followed suit. But these are still exceptions in the global central banking community.

In addition to the issue of which interest rate path to use in making their forecasts, central banks communicate their analysis and intentions in various and more-or-less transparent ways (Minegishi and Cournède, 2009). The trend since the late 1990s has been for more openness about the future orientation of monetary policy, and with more verbal guidance, even if central banks do not commit themselves to a well-defined pattern of future policy actions. The idea is to attempt to anchor market expectations of future interest rates by committing to specific actions depending on objective conditions outside the control of the central bank. Enhanced policy predictability can help both to anchor private-sector long-term inflation expectations in the face of short-term blips, and to avoid policy surprises that could lead to unwelcome market volatility. The US Federal Reserve ('the Fed') is one of the major central banks that have followed this approach increasingly in recent years. The progressive and measured pace of tightening of US policy rates in the mid-2000s was clearly communicated in advance to avoid unsettling bond markets (in contrast to what happened in 1994, when the decision to tighten led to a sharp sell-off). Following the 2007 financial crisis, the Fed as well as many central banks also felt the need to communicate explicitly about how long their unconventional policy measures would remain in place. Again, such guidance was not an absolute commitment but rather conditional on evolving circumstances: central banks wanted to assure markets in advance that they would not withdraw unconventional operations before the turmoil in financial markets had receded.

As noted, another approach to the forecasting of short-term interest rates, instead of focusing on central bank actions, is to rely on market data. For example, the term structure and quotes for derivatives can be used to infer market expectations, even though the latter cannot be pinned down perfectly in this way, because of the existence of unobservable and time-varying risk premia. But at the end of the day this basically results in relying on others' expectations of future monetary policy moves.

4.2.2   Endogenizing the interest rate forecast

Given that there is significant room for judgement when forecasting policy rates, yet another approach is to endogenize the interest rate by estimating the central banks' reaction function (see Box 4.2). This basically means that the forecasts will be made using standard economic modelling techniques, such as for real-economy variables. Such monetary reaction functions are therefore usually embedded in macroeconomic models.

An alternative to estimating a reaction function is simply to posit that the central bank follows some kind of rule. When monetarism was in vogue, the normative rule was to keep the stock of narrow or broad money growing at

Box 4.2 Monetary policy reaction functions

A monetary reaction function relates short-term interest rates to the fundamentals that the central bank, according to empirical observations, is supposed to take into account. This can be done either explicitly or implicitly – for example, when it says it is targeting a specific variable but acts on a different basis in practice. A prominent example is the Deutsche Bundesbank before the advent of the euro: it had an explicit objective for the growth rate of broad money M3 but in fact set interest rates more as a function of inflation, unemployment and exchange rate considerations. In such a case, the explicit objective may be excluded from the estimated reaction function if data confirm that it is not statistically significant.

A typical ECM reaction function equation (see Box 3.1) would be as follows:

$$\Delta i_t = \alpha + \Sigma_j\, \beta_j\, \Delta i_{t-j} + \Sigma_j\, \gamma_j\, \Delta FC_{t-j} + \Sigma_j\, \delta_j\, F_{t-j} - \mu\,(i_{t-1} - \eta_i\, FC_{t-1}) \quad (4.1)$$

where i is the short-term interest rate, F the vector of relevant fundamentals, and FC the vector of the fundamentals that are cointegrated with the short-term interest rate, possibly with some lag structure (not shown here, for the sake of simplicity).

The fundamentals that are natural candidates to enter Equation (4.1) include real sector variables (such as output growth, the output gap, capacity utilization or unemployment), cost and price variables (such as consumer prices, import prices, producer prices or unit labour costs), the fiscal stance (although this is *a priori* more relevant for long-term interest rates), and variables depicting the international environment. The fundamentals may, of course, also include deviations from the central bank's policy objectives, when such objectives are known explicitly.

External environment variables are particularly important for open economies with capital mobility, where domestic interest rates depend heavily on interest rates abroad. As is apparent from Figure 4.1, short-term interest rates often tend to fluctuate at the same time across the main countries. This was particularly striking in the 1980s and 1990s among the countries that eventually adopted the euro in 1999. But it is also noticeable when looking at transatlantic interest rate relationships, with econometric tests often showing that US interest rates influence European ones. Therefore, key foreign interest rates are often included in Equation (4.1), possibly alongside other external sector variables such as the exchange rate, foreign exchange reserves or the current account balance.

The form of the long-run cointegrating relationship depends on the nature and statistical properties of the series under consideration, as well as on the time period. Nominal variables such as inflation or nominal interest rates are often not stationary but $I(1)$, so that it is sensible to estimate a long-run relationship between the domestic interest rate, inflation and possibly some foreign interest rate.

Furthermore, when searching for the best specification for Equation (4.1), it is important to bear in mind some of the defining features of monetary policy. Central bank interest rate moves impact macroeconomic aggregates with a lag, and gradually. In addition, central banks often tend to smooth their interest rate adjustments, opting for a progressive rather than a hyperactive approach, to give them time to gauge the effect of their decisions and not to surprise agents too much. From this perspective, interest rates are 'path-dependant', as they rely on their own past developments and not just on fundamentals. In terms of modelling techniques, this suggests the introduction of significant lags into forecasting equations.

Moreover, and as highlighted by the 2007 financial crisis, there can be important non-linearities in monetary policy reaction functions. For example, the central bank will not react similarly to a decline in inflation by one percentage point if inflation is at 5 per cent or 1 per cent: in the latter case it is likely to react more forcefully, to avoid deflation, given the constraint of the zero lower bound for nominal interest rates. Similarly, the impact on policy rates of exchange rate appreciation and depreciation might not be symmetric. One way to deal with this issue is to include in the specification of Equation (4.1) the possibility that the economy may switch from one regime to another depending on economic circumstances. This can be done, for example, by using a dummy variable. Another way is to insert non-linear specifications into the equation – for example, the squared inflation gap if one wants to allow for the possibility that the central bank reacts more to extreme developments in inflation than to modest ones.

a certain rate, leaving little room for discretionary action on the part of the central bank, at least in principle. But inferring the interest rate for forecasting purposes was not so simple, since in practice central banks continued to use discretion, *inter alia* because the relationship between money and output or inflation was insufficiently stable or even very weak.

Gradually, however, the focus shifted towards less normative and more descriptive types of rules, intended to capture rather than to prescribe central banks' behaviour.[1] Most prominent in this genre is the 'Taylor rule' (see Box 4.3).

---

[1] In this sense, the term 'rule' may be confusing, as the 'neutral' state refers to what is traditionally observed and not to optimality.

Box 4.3 The Taylor rule

Taylor (1993) described the Fed's behaviour between 1987 and 1992 in terms of a rule, as if the Fed was setting monetary policy directly, and solely, as a function of inflation and output deviations from target:

$$r = r^* + 0.5 \ (\pi - \pi^*) + 0.5 \ (y - y^*)/y^* = r^* + 0.5 \ (\pi - \pi^*) + 0.5 \ gap$$

where r is the real short-term interest rate, r^* its 'neutral' level (consistent with full employment), π annual inflation, π^* targeted inflation, y GDP and y^* potential GDP, noting that $(y - y^*)/y^*$ is the output gap ('*gap*').

The rule states that the real interest rate should be above its neutral level if inflation exceeds the target and/or output is above potential, and vice versa. At times, the inflation and output goals are in conflict; for example, when inflation is above target while the economy is below full employment. Then the rule shows how these competing considerations are balanced in setting the interest rate.

The Taylor rule can be recast in nominal terms:

$$i = r^* + \pi + 0.5 \ (\pi - \pi^*) + 0.5 \ gap$$

Furthermore, since the rule above is backward-looking, it can be set in a more forward-looking fashion and use the expectations of inflation and/or output. For example, and with π^e standing for expected inflation, one can have the choice between the two following specifications for inflation:

$$i = r^* + \pi + 0.5 \ (\pi - \pi^*) + 0.5 \ gap \ \ \text{(backward-looking)}$$

$$i = r^* + \pi^e + 0.5 \ (\pi^e - \pi^*) + 0.5 \ gap \ \text{(forward-looking)}$$

Moreover, the rule can be rewritten more simply in terms of changes:

$$\Delta i = 1.5 \ \Delta\pi + 0.5 \ \Delta gap$$

Suppose that inflation picks up from 1 per cent to 2 per cent (or is expected to), and that growth is running at 3 per cent while potential growth is only 2 per cent. Then the rule would predict that the central bank will raise rates by 2 percentage points. The advantage of this reasoning, everything else being equal, is that one can have a view about the future path of interest rates without having to qualify the current monetary stance.

While appealing, the Taylor rule is not devoid of problems with regard to its contribution to forecasting:

- The neutral rate is often computed as some historical average, or as trend output growth, but whether this is the best assumption is not obvious.

- The inflation target may not be spelt out by the central bank. The US Federal Reserve in particular does not have a well-defined numerical inflation target, even if it is widely assumed that it has an implicit objective of 2 per cent.
- Output gap estimates are surrounded by considerable uncertainty (see Chapter 6). Moreover, the central bank's estimates of these magnitudes may not be in the public domain.
- Inflation may not be that straightforward to measure, nor is expected inflation. In many cases, there is scope for interpretation as to what is the most pertinent index (headline versus core inflation in particular), and this can have important policy implications – see Kohn (2010) for the debate on this issue in the USA.
- Other variables influencing the central bank's decision are ignored, notably unemployment and exchange rates.
- The weights are not universal but often simply those Taylor set as a rough approximation in the US case. In addition, central banks do not all share the same monetary policy targets; for example, the Federal Reserve has an explicit mandate to focus on inflation and activity, whereas the ECB is first and foremost focusing on price stability.

One way around some of these problems is to generalize the Taylor rule so as to take into account explicitly a broader set of variables of concern to the central bank. For example:

$$i = c + \alpha \pi + \beta p + \gamma \, gap + \delta \, \Delta y$$

where c is a constant, p the log of the price level ($\Delta p = \pi$), and Δy is real GDP growth.

Depending on the value of the coefficients, the following rules obtain:

- $\beta = \delta = 0$: Taylor-type rule, with a target for inflation and for the level of activity (with the latter sometimes interpreted as an advance indicator of inflation);
- $\beta = \gamma = 0$: Taylor-type rule, but with a target for output growth rather than for the level of activity;
- $\alpha = \delta = 0$ and $\beta = \gamma$: nominal GDP or money stock targeting (depending on the assumptions made regarding the income velocity of money);
- $\delta = 0$ and $\beta = \gamma$: inflation and money stock target; and
- $\beta = \gamma = \delta = 0$: inflation target.

Going one step further, one could estimate econometrically, rather than impose, the coefficients. But then, in essence, one is estimating a monetary reaction function.

Such rules may appear to be a useful forecasting device, even if the central bank denies following any of them. However, in practice, policy-controlled interest rates move only rarely in accordance with formal rules. It is thus preferable for forecasting purposes to estimate reaction functions rather than to assume that a given rule – the specification and parameters of which are somewhat arbitrary – will apply universally.

That said, a rule can be useful for several reasons:

- In contrast to reaction functions, it is formulated in a simple and easily understandable way – a great advantage in terms of communication.
- It allows for the assessment of the stance of monetary policy compared with the rule; the difference between the observed interest rate and the one the rule would imply signals how tight or loose policy is, or how much discretion is being exercised by the central bank as compared to a 'neutral' stance that merely reflects fluctuations in the variables entering the rule. In the years preceding the 2007 crisis, for example, short-term interest rates in the USA were significantly below what most formulations of a Taylor rule would have predicted, as the Fed attempted to guard against the risk of deflation (see the debate between Bernanke, 2010 and Taylor, 2010).
- A rule also serves as a guidepost in an uncertain environment or a new regime, in which previously estimated reaction functions become obsolete. Since the 1970s, the environment surrounding central banks has changed enormously, and so have their individual independence and credibility. A good example was in Europe at the end of the 1990s: the advent of a new currency area completely altered the landscape, making it impossible initially to estimate the new central bank's reaction function over some past period (in so far as the ECB's actions depart from the simple aggregation of the decisions of the euro area national central banks). When such a regime change occurs, a rule can be quite helpful.

A third way to forecast monetary policy is to consider that the central bank takes its decisions depending on the wide range of financial conditions prevailing in the economy. This was highlighted when the financial crisis occurred in 2007, as policy rates in major jurisdictions moved well out of line with what could be anticipated using monetary reaction functions or simple monetary rules. To consider the wider range of financial conditions, one can use a monetary conditions index, which aims at summarizing the factors that can matter for the central bank when it sets its interest rate (see Box 4.4). For example, the central bank will be less likely to tighten interest rates if the exchange rate is appreciating (leading to a tightening in the MCI), everything else being equal.

Box 4.4   Monetary and financial conditions indices

In its simplest form, a monetary conditions index (MCI) encompasses only r, the real short-term interest rate, and q, the log of the real effective exchange rate (where a rise represents an appreciation):

$$MCI_t = \theta_r (r_t - r_0) + \theta_q (q_t - q_0)$$

where r_0 and q_0 are reference values, corresponding to a base period or some historical average. The weights θ_r and θ_q reflect the importance of the two variables from the point of view of monetary policy; for example, if the central bank wants to stabilize activity (and hence inflation), the coefficients could be proportional to the impact on aggregate demand of changes in r and in q, respectively.

A few small open economy central banks have actively used MCIs (Canada, Sweden and New Zealand), and many central banks monitor MCIs, even if they do not publish them. Private sector analysts also frequently compile them. A good example was the Bank of Canada's headline MCI which, in contrast with the formulation above, was expressed in nominal terms and comprised the interest rate (measured as the 90-day commercial paper rate) and the effective exchange rate (measured against Canada's six main trading partners). The weights applied (respectively, 1 and 1/3) reflected the view that a one percentage point change in the short-term interest rate was estimated to have about the same effect on the policy goal as a 3 per cent change in the effective exchange rate. However, the Bank of Canada dropped the MCI at the end of 2006 as an input into monetary policy decisions.

The MCI concept has been broadened to incorporate other key financial variables, such as long-term interest rates and stock price indices (Gauthier *et al.*, 2004). The MCI is then typically referred to as an MFCI (monetary and financial conditions index) or, more curtly, an FCI. The 2007 financial crisis has reinforced interest in incorporating an even broader set of variables to gauge the evolution of financial conditions that can have an impact on the behaviour of economic agents. Guichard *et al.* (2009), for example, include indicators such as credit availability (derived from survey-based measures of banks' credit standards), corporate bond spreads and household wealth in their index. They find evidence that a substantial loosening of financial conditions occurred across all countries in the years preceding the 2007 financial crisis, and that the subsequent tightening in financial conditions was unprecedented in its severity, subtracting 5 per cent to 8 per cent from the level of GDP in major industrial economies.

From a forecaster's standpoint, the MCI (or MFCI) sums up information in a convenient way and is quite informative. It can be computed almost instantaneously and is not subject to significant revisions later. Given the lags between changes in interest rates and exchange rates and their impact on activity, the current value of the index can help to predict developments over the coming few quarters. Also, one can assess what a reversion of the index to its long-run historical average would require in terms of the developments of the financial variables entering the index.

Notwithstanding these advantages, such indices have weaknesses, particularly the fact that the choice of the included variables and of the associated weights is model-dependent – or judgement-based – and therefore somewhat arbitrary (Batini and Turnbull, 2002). This choice also depends on the time horizon considered (it is generally assumed that the impact of financial conditions on 'real' indicators has its full effect after two years, though significant uncertainty surrounds this lag). Furthermore, international comparisons can be difficult as the weights of the various components may vary significantly from one country to another (for example, reflecting the different wealth effects stemming from the holding of financial assets); one solution is therefore to compare changes in the indices rather than their absolute levels.

Moreover, defining where 'neutrality' lies for the index is tricky. For policy purposes, a movement in an MCI or MFCI has very different implications depending on which component of the index has shifted, and why. Indeed, the index averages a rate of return and an asset price, which may affect inflation at different speeds. Hence the policy implications that can be inferred from the index's behaviour are limited. This is why many central banks such as the Bank of Canada, the Sveriges Riksbank and the Reserve Bank of New Zealand no longer base their decisions and communication on an MCI.

4.2.3 How to capture central bank objectives

In practice, forecasting central bank actions can be more complicated than is indicated by simple reaction functions or rules, and involves a degree of judgement. One solution is to try to incorporate a wider range of information – sometimes beyond the strict universe of macroeconomic aggregates – by monitoring closely the sentiment of those in charge of monetary policy decisions. This is what 'central bank watchers' do. For example, they will focus on the balance of power between 'doves' and 'hawks' in monetary policy committees, look at how central banks and central bank officials behave, at governance arrangements, and at the (implicit or explicit) distribution of responsibilities within these institutions.

Yet another complication is that, strictly speaking, policy interest rates are not determined solely by monetary policy considerations. The 2007 financial crisis highlighted the importance of other objectives – in particular financial stability objectives (see Box 4.5). In the future, it seems likely that, in order to forecast policy rates, greater attention will have to be paid to these considerations.

Box 4.5   Central banks' objectives

The starting point to assess central banks' objectives is to look at their mandates. Central banks typically pursue an objective of price stability. This objective can be defined strictly, as for inflation-targeting central banks (such as the Bank of England), or more vaguely, as for the ECB (below but close to 2 per cent in the medium-term) and the Bank of Japan (operational inflation target range of 0 per cent to 2 per cent, to be reviewed regularly).

But a number of central banks have additional objectives related to the real economy. In particular, the Federal Reserve's mandate, in addition to fostering stable prices, is to 'promote effectively the goal of maximum employment'. Moreover, other central banks are not completely indifferent to the situation in the real economy. In the euro area, the ECB's first pillar aims at short- to medium-term price stability, with the objective of avoiding prolonged inflation and deflation and, 'without prejudice to the maintenance of price stability', excessive fluctuations in output and employment. In Japan, the two-perspective approach to monetary policy adopted in 2006 comprises as the first perspective a focus on expected developments in inflation and activity (Bank of Japan, 2006a). In addition, central banks can have other objectives. The 2007 crisis showed that almost all of them have an explicit or implicit financial stability mandate.

- In the USA, as reported above, the central bank is primarily following 'real objectives'; that is, employment and stable prices. Nevertheless, the Federal Reserve Act also states that it 'shall maintain long run growth of the monetary and credit aggregates commensurate with the economy's long run potential'. In other words, attention should also be paid to financial aggregates to foster economic stability.
- At the ECB, the second policy pillar (the so-called monetary analysis) focuses on the long-run link between money and prices, considering factors that might affect inflation beyond the medium-term time horizon, such as the presence of financial imbalances and asset price misalignments. From this perspective, the ECB has acknowledged that it could take decisions that might have an impact on price stability at horizons extending well beyond conventional policy horizons (ECB, 2004b). To

this end it looks at a wide range of indicators (broad monetary aggregates, growth rates of credit and asset prices) that may provide early information on developing financial instability.

- In Japan, the second monetary perspective includes the various long-term risks deemed to have a significant impact should they materialize, though their probability is low. The Bank of Japan's monetary framework does not refer explicitly to financial stability but it has stated that medium- to long-term price stability should be understood as a way of avoiding falling in a vicious cycle of declining prices and deteriorating economic activity, and to preserve stability in the financial system.

In sum, major central banks do in fact have a variety of objectives and this makes it more difficult to forecast policy interest rates. Yet another complication arises from the fact that central banks do not care only about their objectives but also about how they can achieve them. Indeed, monetary policy influences the economy via various channels (Cournède *et al.*, 2008):

- The interest rate channel: this relates to the 'traditional' impact of interest rates on macroeconomic aggregates such as household consumption (for example, impact on loan demand and on saving/consumption decisions) and business investment decisions (for example, impact on the user cost of capital and cash flow constraints). As analysed in Chapter 3, higher interest rates generally dampen domestic demand and thus also output growth. However, this can be complicated by balance sheet effects. An interesting example is Japan, where gross government debt has exploded since the 1990s, and now approaches some 200 per cent of GDP. Since most of this debt is owned by Japanese residents, it has been argued that the negative impact of higher interest rates on demand can be significantly offset by the impact of higher interest income for Japanese households.
- The credit channel: here the focus is on commercial banks' supply of loans because of the impact of the monetary policy stance on banks' deposits and capital position as well as on borrowers' positions (balance sheets, cash flows and the ability to borrow against collateral). This channel has evolved in recent years as a result of financial innovation, with, in particular, the greater ability of borrowers to access disintermediated savings.
- The asset price channel: this relates to the specific impact of policy interest rates on various asset prices (as analysed in the rest of this chapter) and in particular on the exchange rate.
- The risk-taking channel (Borio and Zhu, 2008): this aspect was prominent during the 2007 crisis. The mechanism here is that interest rates

influence risk premia in the economy. For example, low interest rates induce economic agents – in particular those who target nominal rates of return – to find new, innovative ways to obtain higher returns by taking more risks, in turn pushing down risk premia for a wide range of assets. Dubecq *et al.* (2009) argue that one key feature of this risk-taking channel is through the interaction with financial regulation: financial intermediaries increase risk-taking through higher leverage and/or regulatory arbitrage. These intermediaries are able to do this without being penalized by the market when they benefit from lax monetary conditions and the associated misperception of risk by investors.

While the objectives of central banks are likely to become broader, with more weight assigned to financial stability, the set of instruments they resort to is also becoming more diversified, compounding the challenge faced by forecasters. The traditional instruments are used to steer money market interest rates up or down (see Box 4.6). However, when short-term interest rates approach the zero bound and inflation is low and/or activity is weak, these instruments reach their limits and other measures are needed.

Box 4.6   Central banks' traditional policy apparatus

The specific features of traditional instruments differ across countries, but in general the objective of central banks is to influence the overnight interest rates at which deposit institutions ('banks') can have access to funding. In the USA, for example, the federal funds rate is the rate under which depository institutions lend their balances at the Federal Reserve to other depository institutions overnight. When a bank needs more currency for its customer, it receives Federal Reserve notes and at the same time this reduces the quantity of reserve balances held in its Fed account, therefore pushing up the federal funds rate, everything else being equal. Developments in this specific interbank market segment are considered to influence indirectly conditions in the money market more broadly (defined by maturities of less than one year, in opposition to capital markets).

Central banks use several tools to influence the demand for, and supply of, reserve balances. One is open market operations, by which they buy and sell high-quality securities. This can take the form of outright purchases/ selling (when the central bank increases its holding of securities, the reserves of deposit institutions grow); repurchase agreements ('repos'), where the central bank buys a security under the agreement to sell it back later (which is equivalent to a collateralized loan); reverse repurchase agreements ('reverse repos'), where the central bank sells high-quality securities temporarily to the market; or pure credit operations, such as lending against collateral. The aim is to affect the level of reserve balances and indirectly to drive the federal funds rate. A side effect of these operations is also to modify the quantity of securities available to private agents that can be used as collateral for their own transactions; this can be of particular importance in times of financial stress, as was the case in 2007.

A second tool is to provide access to a given institution to financing facilities in case of need. Such lending is usually on a very short-term basis and secured by collateral, often with haircuts – a percentage is subtracted from the market value of the collateral when calculating the secured amount. In general, banks borrow at such windows in order to meet (unexpected) short-term liquidity needs, and pay a 'discount rate' exceeding the going short-term market interest rates. The central bank can decide to modify the spread between the related lending rates and the market rate, and there can be various discount window programmes depending on the specific type and quality of the institution involved.

In such dire circumstances, central banks have indeed used other measures, dubbed 'unconventional' or 'unorthodox'. This has been the case in Japan in the early years of the twenty-first century, under the (slightly odd) name of 'quantitative easing', and more spectacularly and more generally during the 2007 crisis, under the name of 'credit easing' (see Box 4.7). As acknowledged by US Fed Chairman Bernanke (2009b), 'we no longer live in a world in which central bank policies are confined to adjusting the short-term interest rate. Instead, by using their balance sheets, the Federal Reserve and other central banks are developing new tools to ease financial conditions and support economic growth'.

As a result, the balance sheets of major central banks swelled enormously during the 2007 financial crisis. The total assets on the US Federal Reserve's balance sheet almost tripled in size, while their composition changed dramatically (see Figure 4.3). These unorthodox monetary operations were accompanied by large government rescue packages and explicit public guarantees to the private financial system (see Chapter 5).

As noted earlier, central banks are also mindful of financial stability, whether or not it is enshrined in their mandate as an explicit objective. In the context of the 2007 crisis, the importance of financial regulation came to the fore, and greater attention is now being paid by central banks to prudential tools and their macroeconomic implications, whether these tools are under the control

Figure 4.3 Balance sheet of the US Federal Reserve*

Since the beginning of the financial crisis, the Federal Reserve's balance sheet has grown tremendously in size

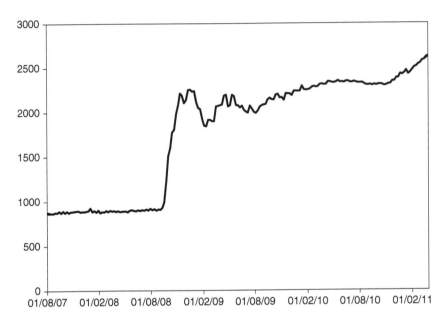

*Total assets of the Federal Reserve, in billions of dollars.
Source: Board of Governors of the US Federal Reserve System.

Box 4.7   Central banks' unconventional instruments

Depository institutions hold reserves at the central bank to satisfy compulsory reserve requirements (which are a function of the institutions' characteristics) as well as reserves in excess of this minimum. These reserves are generally remunerated (including in the USA since 2008). When the zero interest rate bound is in sight, the central bank can decide to target the quantity of banks' reserves, as did the Bank of Japan from 2001 to 2006, as part of its 'quantitative easing' policy. This consisted of shifting the main operating target from the uncollateralized overnight call rate to the banks' current account balances at the Bank of Japan and supplying ample liquidity far in excess of required reserves.

During the 2007 financial crisis, the major central banks also expanded lending considerably, even if they did not pursue a policy of directly targeting banks' reserves. By doing this, they triggered a sharp increase in reserve balances, consistent with their target of very low market interest rates. The aim was to support the liquidity of specific financial institutions and enhance financial market conditions: in other words, basically to support the price of certain financial assets, and in particular to influence the unsecured interbank markets (and alleviate the problems caused by the sharp widening in Libor/OIS spreads) as well as the long end of the yield curve. These measures were clearly marked as exceptional and began to be unwound progressively around the turn of 2009/10. However, renewed tensions in financial markets in 2010 led to delays in this exit strategy, and major central banks in industrial countries even decided to expand their toolkit of unconventional measures.

In the case of the US Federal Reserve, the main aspects of this policy of 'credit easing' were:

- The provision of short-term liquidity to banks and other financial institutions, involving the reduction of the cost of these credits; the opening of facilities to specific institutions (for example, the primary dealer credit facility); the expansion of the maturity of term lending facility operations – for example, the term auction facility allowed banks to receive funds with a maturity of up to 84 days; and the launch of a securities lending programme to provide high-quality securities to financial market participants in need of good collateral.
- The provision of direct liquidity to borrowers and investors in key markets (beyond the 'traditional' area of deposit institutions that normally have access to the Fed). For example, various lending facilities were set up to finance the purchase of high-quality asset-backed commercial paper, to provide short-term liquidity to issuers of commercial paper and asset-backed securities and for money market mutual funds, and to provide loans for a period of up to five years to specific holders of eligible asset-backed securities.
- Direct purchases of long-term securities to support the functioning of credit markets – in particular, a key element of this 'shock and awe' approach was the decision to purchase up to US$1.25 trillion of mortgage-backed securities, US$200 billion of government-sponsored enterprise debt and US$300 billion of longer-term Treasury securities. In November 2010, the Fed announced a second round of asset purchases (referred to as 'QE2'; that is, Quantitative Easing Part Two) and its intention to further buy US$600 billion of longer-term Treasury securities, at a rate of around US$75 billion per month.
- Bilateral currency swap agreements between the US Fed and 14 foreign central banks, in order to allow the latter to provide dollar liquidity to their domestic banks. These swap lines obliged foreign central banks to

buy back their domestic currencies at a specified date at the same exchange rate (the foreign central banks had to pay interest and to bear the credit risk of the loans provided to their commercial banks). Conversely, foreign currency liquidity swap lines were set up (but not drawn) to offer liquidity to US institutions in foreign currency. Though the US arrangements with 14 foreign central banks were terminated in February 2010, dollar liquidity swap lines were reactivated in May 2010 with five major central banks and were subsequently extended to August 2011.

- Various forms of support to specific US institutions: to JP Morgan to facilitate the acquisition of Bear Sterns; a credit line to AIG; and credit to commercial banks such as Citigroup and Bank of America.

The ECB also embarked on large-scale non-standard measures, unprecedented in nature, scope and magnitude. However, its policy of 'enhanced credit support' (Trichet, 2009) differed from the US credit easing policy – in particular with regard to the provision of direct lending facilities to market participants – and was initially aiming at enhancing the flow of credit through:

- The unlimited provision of liquidity at the policy rate (the 'fixed rate full allotment' tender procedure).
- The extension of both the list of securities accepted as collateral and of the list of counterparties eligible for liquidity operations.
- The lengthening of the maturity of refinancing operations (up to one year).
- The provision of liquidity in foreign currencies, most notably in US dollars (using the swap lines arranged with the US Federal Reserve) and agreements with other central banks to provide euro liquidity to their banking sectors.
- The outright purchase of covered bonds (debt securities backed by cash flows from mortgages or public-sector loans which are de facto asset-backed securities that remain on the issuer's consolidated balance sheet and are thus deemed to be safer).

As severe strains re-emerged in certain euro area market segments (especially sovereign debt) in May 2010, the ECB took further, bolder steps to safeguard the monetary policy transmission mechanism and thereby the effective conduct of its monetary policy. In particular, it reintroduced some of the non-standard measures that had been withdrawn earlier and began interventions in the euro area public and private debt securities markets, under a Securities Markets Programme. These new measures, especially the direct purchase of long-term government paper, proved quite controversial within European policy-making circles, though they were sterilized and designed to avoid affecting the monetary policy stance. Furthermore, the temporary liquidity swap lines with the Federal Reserve System were reactivated.

The policies followed after 2007 by the Fed and the ECB focused on the asset side of their balance sheet and in particular on the mix of loans and securities, in contrast to Japan's quantitative easing approach, which aimed initially at expanding the central bank balance sheet on the liability side (the commercial banks' reserves). However, the distinction between the two approaches is in fact not that clear cut. Indeed, the Bank of Japan in 2001–6 did not focus solely on banks' target reserves: various additional measures included the expansion of the monetary base through outright purchases of long-term government bonds, asset-backed securities, corporate bonds and equities. During the 2007 financial crisis, the Bank of Japan in effect moved closer to 'credit easing', extending its purchases of government bonds, widening the range of eligible collateral (to corporate debt in particular), offering complementary deposit facilities (including securities lending facilities and US dollar funds supplying operations), purchasing corporate commercial paper and bonds, resuming its purchases of stocks held by banks, and providing subordinated loans to banks. These measures were reinforced in 2010 as renewed uncertainties in financial markets were accompanied by strong appreciation pressures on the yen. In particular, in October 2010, the Bank of Japan adopted its 'Comprehensive Monetary Easing' policy, which included the establishment of an asset purchase programme on a temporary basis, and which was further expanded after the March 2011 earthquake and tsunami. The aim of this programme was to purchase financial assets, including government bonds, corporate bonds and other risk assets (with a total maximum amount outstanding envisaged at about 40 trillion yen by mid-2012) so as to ensure a decline in long-term market interest rates and in various risk premia.

of the central bank or of one or several separate supervisors (see Box 4.8). This raises a new set of issues, however. Financial and business cycles interact, and macroeconomic (monetary and fiscal) and macro-prudential policies influence each other and can, in some cases, have conflicting effects. Moreover, the transmission channels of these policies might change. Finally, the clarity of the mandates can be at stake, leading to credibility problems regarding the joint pursuit of price and financial stability objectives.

Box 4.8   Macro-prudential tools

Macro-prudential instruments can be defined as those prudential instruments that apply to individual financial institutions but have a broader macroeconomic impact. It is important to focus on two key aspects of macro-prudential surveillance (Crockett, 2000): the stability of the financial system as a whole, or systemic stability (as opposed to the stability of the individual institutions); and the macroeconomic risks associated with the behaviour of financial institutions (the micro-prudential approach instead focuses on the risk of failure of a single institution).

Systemic risk has a time dimension and a cross-sectional dimension. The time dimension relates to the progressive build-up of financial fragility and how aggregate risk evolves over time; one of the main associated policy problems is how to address the pro-cyclicality of the financial system. The cross-sectional dimension relates to how the structure of the financial system at a given point in time influences how it responds to, and possibly amplifies, shocks; such spillover effects can arise, for example, from common exposures across institutions or from network interconnections. The policy problem is how to address such common exposures and interlinkages among financial institutions (Caruana, 2010).

Many of the instruments at the disposal of central banks/financial supervisors have a macro-prudential dimension:

- Communication tools: assessment of macro-financial risks and provision of information on credit conditions, so as to influence the behaviour of market participants.
- Limitations to volatile capital flows (reserve requirements, forex interventions); some have argued that this could include capital controls, but their pros and cons remain controversial.
- Actions to address pro-cyclicality: request for banks' capital requirements and/or provisions to go up in line with the credit cycle, imposition of liquidity ratios (loans to deposits, limits to currency and duration mismatches).
- Actions to address interconnectedness (leverage ratios, specific requirements – for example, to have additional cushions and thereby greater loss-absorbing capacity – for institutions deemed to be of systemic importance, limits on inter-institution exposures).
- Actions to contain the credit cycle: limits to borrowers' access to credit (loan-to-value ratios) or sectoral caps to credit growth (for example in the real estate sector).

How central banks/financial supervisors will use such macro-prudential instruments in the future remains unclear.* But the essence of a macro-prudential framework would be to prevent financial instability in two ways (CGFS, 2010): (i) by enhancing the resilience of the financial system in case of shock; or (ii) by preventing this shock from happening in the first place so as to 'lean against the wind' (that is, to try pre-emptively to avoid the build-up of incipient financial bubbles).

The first goal can be achieved by using micro-prudential instruments (norms for the capital or liquidity of banks, or maintenance of the quality of loans, say) with a macro view to ensure that the prudential standards provide enough buffers for the system as a whole. The second goal means reducing the inherent volatility in the financial sector. However, this is difficult to put in place in an *ad hoc* way, not least because of political pressures and recognition lags. Moreover, it is unclear what kind of automatic stabilizers (such as the fiscal stabilizers) can be set up to damp the financial cycle automatically. Under the new Basel III package, banks will be required by national supervisors to hold countercyclical capital buffers in periods of rapid credit growth and this will help to reduce the amplitude of the financial cycle. Other tools could also be developed. For example, some countries, such as Spain, have implemented dynamic provisioning banking rules in recent years that link the provisioning of bank loans not to observed loan delinquencies but to some dynamic view of their likely evolution over the course of the cycle.

---

*It has been argued that one lesson of the 2007 financial crisis is that alongside its main policy instrument (that is, short-term interest rates) a central bank should target an aggregate equity ratio for the banking system (Gersbach and Hahn, 2009).

4.3   Long-term interest rates

A key financial variable in macroeconomic forecasting is the long-term interest rate. In practice, the benchmark used for that purpose is the 10-year government bond yield (often, though somewhat misleadingly, referred to as the 'risk-free' rate). When forecasting government bond yields, it should be borne in mind that they are increasingly subject to global influences, and are sensitive to current and foreseeable public indebtedness.

4.3.1 Three angles

Long-term interest rates can be approached from the angle of financial markets, as averages of current and expected future short-term rates, or from a macroeconomic angle, as the price that equilibrates saving and investment. In practice, forecasters tend to combine the two approaches; they also often take a short-cut by modelling the yield curve directly (see Box 4.9).

***

Box 4.9   Modelling long-term interest rates

Financial markets' angle

The link between expected short-term interest rates and current long-term interest rates stems from the fact that agents arbitrage between the expected return from rolling over short-term deposits (namely, the compounded expected short-term rates during the bond's life) or bills and the known yield on long-term fixed-rate bonds. The proliferation of financial innovations and rising substitutability between financial assets has probably strengthened this connection. Arithmetically:

$$1 + i_t^\ell = [\Pi_j (1 + E_t \, i_{t+j}^s)]^{1/(T-t)} + \varphi_t^T$$

where i_t^ℓ is the long-term nominal interest rate at time t and for time horizon T, $E_t \, i_{t+j}^s$ the expectation as of time t of the one-period interest rate that will prevail at time $t + j$, and φ_t^T the $(T - t)$ period ahead risk premium (all interest rates being expressed at annualized rates).

The risk premium is very difficult to pin down, not least because it can vary substantially over time. It reflects agents' preference for liquidity and their degree of risk aversion, since the premium should compensate for the risk of a commitment to extend credit far in the future. It can be influenced by two types of factors: idiosyncratic features connected with the bond's issuer and the characteristics of the market the bond is traded on; and more macroeconomic factors such as investors' portfolio preferences, general liquidity features, appetite for credit risk, inflation expectations, cyclical conditions, saving/investment balance and demographics (for example, as a result of the impact of retirement prospects on saving propensity).

Ahrend *et al.* (2006) find that the compression in the term premia is an important factor underlying the low bond yields in the early 2000s. This is consistent with Kim and Wright (2005), who find evidence of a clear downward trend in the US risk premia since the early 1990s. This could be explained by some combination of low and stable inflation, higher *ex ante* net saving at a global level (especially in Asia after the crisis in the region in

1997/8), and portfolio shifts (demand for US government bonds from Asia and oil exporters). A key factor often put forward is that monetary policy entered a new era after the 1960–80 period of high inflation and poor central bank credibility (Kroszner, 2007). From this perspective, low and less volatile inflation would have contributed to flattening the yield curve by reducing inflation expectations. Combined with greater central bank credibility and predictability, this could have durably reduced perceived inflation risk, resulting in a lower premium. There can be other factors, and indeed Hördahl and Tristani (2007) use information from both nominal and index-linked yields to decompose the influence on term premia of 'real' risks and inflation risk.

Institutional changes can also play an important role in driving investors' portfolio preferences. For example, recent accounting rules have had important implications for pension funds funded though defined-benefit schemes, and more generally insurers with long-term liabilities – a growing number of these institutions have reacted by changing the structure of their assets, by buying longer-term debt, and by reducing the duration mismatch between their assets and liabilities. This reportedly also contributed to the low levels of long-term government bonds rates in the 2000s.

Macroeconomic angle

From a macroeconomic perspective, expected short-term interest rates and the risk premium can be viewed as depending on:

- International interest rates: in so far as investors arbitrage between domestic and foreign financial assets, domestic interest rates will be influenced by those prevailing abroad, exchange rate expectations and various associated factors (for example, capital flows and saving/investment patterns, though these might be difficult to incorporate into forecasting equations). Econometrically, and as can be seen in Figure 4.4, long-term US interest rates are commonly found to be a significant determinant of the interest rates observed in other OECD countries (more so than for short-term interest rates).
- Fiscal policy: a fiscal expansion may foreshadow rising inflation and therefore push up expectations of future short-term rates; it also increases the supply of long-term bonds so that a rise in long-term rates is required to balance saving and investment. In cases where fiscal sustainability looks threatened, the risk of ultimate default adds to the risk premium.
- Monetary policy: if, for example, interest rates are below what a rule or an estimated reaction function suggests, they may be expected to rise. Interest rate expectations may also be influenced by the degree of credibility

148

of the central bank: the more credible it is, the less it needs to raise rates to reach its objectives. An important issue is the one of possible regime shifts.

Figure 4.4   Long-term interest rates*
Major 10-year government bond yields have come down significantly since the early 1990s

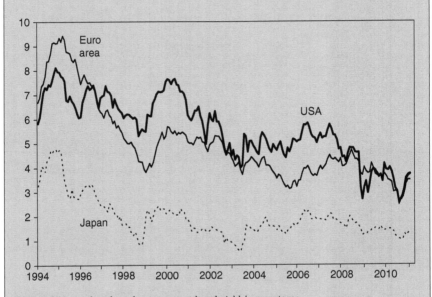

*Nominal 10-year benchmark government bond yields' percentages.
Source: ECB.

These influences can be quantified jointly through econometric estimation in a similar way to that described above for short-term interest rates.

Yet another channel highlighted after the 2007 financial crisis relates to the direct impact of central banks' purchases of government securities on long-term interest rates. This is particularly difficult to gauge, not least because these central bank actions were taken in uncharted territories. In theory, the direct purchase of securities can influence long-term rates by reinforcing the transmission mechanism of short-term policy rates (via a 'signalling effect' and a strengthened monetary policy commitment). The impact can be also more indirect, via portfolio effects (for example, if the government bonds purchased by central banks are imperfectly substitutable with other financial assets) and private agents' reactions. In the case of the USA, the Fed has estimated that the November 2010 decision to purchase another US$600 billion worth of Treasuries may have lowered the 10-year Treasury yield by 25 basis points, all else being equal. It should be noted, however, that while US long-term rates had been moving downwards before November 2010 as investors had increasingly been anticipating the Fed's new round of quantitative easing, they rose sharply in the subsequent period, underscoring the complexity of the factors influencing long-term rates.

Yield curve approach

A less ambitious approach is to start from a forecast for the short-term interest rate and to model the spread s between the long- and the short-term rate. In its crudest form:

$$s_t = \alpha\, i_t + \beta$$

where i_t is again the short-term nominal interest rate. *A priori*, $\alpha < 0$: all else being equal, a higher short-term interest rate means that the central bank is serious in the pursuit of its price stability objective, so that the component of the risk premium corresponding to inflation risk, and hence the spread, is lower. This can be extended to include other determinants of the spread on the right-hand side, such as the aforementioned variables (expected inflation, foreign interest rates or the fiscal position).

This type of equation can be improved upon, depending on the statistical properties of the series under consideration. Nominal interest rates and inflation are often cointegrated, so that the spread and the real short-term interest rate r are stationary, which suggests the use of the real rather than the nominal rate in the equation above. This allows the analyst to look for a long-term relationship between the two, of the form:

$$s_t = a\, r_t + b$$

This specification could be augmented to include a richer menu of explanatory variables. The full equation, including the short-run dynamic component, then becomes:

$$\Delta s_t = \Sigma_i\, \alpha_i\, \Delta s_{t-i} + \Sigma_i\, \beta_i\, \Delta r_{t-i} + \gamma\, Z - \mu\, (s_{t-1} - a\, r_{t-1} - b)$$

where Z is a vector, with the other variables entering the short-run dynamics.

4.3.2   Financial globalization

One issue of growing importance in recent years relates to the impact of financial globalization on long-term rates: the saving/investment equilibrium is progressively more realized at the global level, implying that asset prices in general – and US government bond yields as a key benchmark in particular – are increasingly determined internationally. Policy attention has focused on exceptionally high saving and forex reserve accumulation in Asia after the 1997–8 Asian financial crisis, partly as a means for Asian economies to build up 'self-insurance' against future shocks and avoid reliance on IMF assistance. This resulted in what has been dubbed a 'global saving glut'; that is, an excess of *ex ante* global saving relative to global investment (Bernanke, 2005).

In addition, it has become easier for investors around the world to diversify their portfolios, which so far has tended to support global demand for US assets. Indeed, traditionally, investors display a strong home bias, preferring to hold the bulk of their portfolio in domestic assets even though they could theoretically achieve a better trade-off by diversifying internationally. Despite the difficulties involved in measuring such home bias, empirical studies suggest that it has declined over time, in part because of falling information costs and the liberalization of international capital flows (Ahearne *et al.*, 2004). The associated higher demand for external assets in emerging countries could represent a structural factor supporting the demand for US assets in general and for US public bonds in particular, contributing to downward pressures on US long-term rates.

These two factors are estimated to have contributed significantly to the low levels of US long-term rates in the 2000s. Warnock and Warnock (2005), for example, estimate that official capital flows into the USA lowered US long-term rates by around 60 basis points in the mid-2000s.

4.3.3 The fiscal debate

The 2007 financial crisis revived the issue of the impact of fiscal positions on government bond yields. A huge amount of public debt was issued to mitigate the impact of the recession and to rescue failed financial institutions. Many observers feared this might unsettle bond markets, but in the event long-term interest rates remained fairly low in most major economies.

In theory, fiscal expansion affects long-term interest rates via its impact on saving/investment, inflation expectations and risk premia. In practice, however, the effect of fiscal policy is difficult to capture empirically. The available studies give different results, though several of them have found a positive and significant impact of fiscal expansion on long-term rates. A review conducted by the IMF (2009c) highlights the following results:

- For industrial countries, a one percentage point increase in the primary fiscal deficit as a share of GDP could lead to a 10 basis points increase in nominal long-term interest rates, though results differ across studies and countries.
- The impact of an increase in public debt is non-linear: it is econometrically insignificant for countries with relatively low public debt/GDP ratios; but

where public debt exceeds GDP, the impact could be of around 20 basis points for a 10 percentage point increase in the debt ratio.

For the USA, Laubach (2003) estimated that, other things being equal, a 10 percentage point increase in the projected ratio of US public debt to GDP will push long-term interest rates up by 40 basis points, a result broadly confirmed by Engen and Hubbard (2004). This is perhaps not that much, however, for the purpose of forecasting, given the volatility of long-term interest rates. Moreover, Stehn (2010) notes that the very sharp deterioration in US fiscal positions in 2007–10 was accompanied by extremely low long-term rates, apparently contradicting these results. Controlling for economic variables such as short-term policy rates and real GDP growth, but also for country fixed effects and the fact that there are global risk shocks common to all countries, he finds that a 10 percentage point increase in the US public debt-to-GDP ratio (respectively, deficit ratio) might raise yields by only 10 basis points (respectively, 90 basis points).

An intriguing case in point in this regard is that of Japan. The gross public debt ratio in Japan has soared to close to 200 per cent of GDP. Yet Japanese government bond yields have remained very low, fluctuating in a narrow range of 1 per cent to 2 per cent since the late 1990s (well below those in the USA and Europe). This suggests that other factors are involved that are difficult to model. In the case of Japan, these may include the country's large net external creditor position, the very low proportion of government debt held abroad (estimated at less than 10 per cent, compared to around 50 per cent in the case of the USA), the fact that in net terms the Japanese government debt is only about half of its gross value, the strong home bias of domestic investors and the importance of household savings channelled into government paper through the Post Office. Moreover, the Bank of Japan's long-standing policy of keeping the short-term interest rate at the zero bound in order to fight enduring deflation means that expected short-term rates are extremely low.

However, a more worrying explanation may be that bond markets can also experience bubbles, in the sense that yields can fall significantly below what the fundamentals would suggest is sustainable. Hence there is a risk that bond prices would collapse at some point, as yields back up in major countries. Given the size of the global outstanding bond portfolio, this would have serious adverse repercussions, not least on bank balance sheets.

4.4 Bond prices and yield spreads

Forecasting bond prices is essentially equivalent to forecasting long-term interest rates, given that they are directly related. While long-term interest rates can be highly volatile over the very short run, they tend to move relatively smoothly over longer periods. Hence, over longer horizons, foreseeable changes in bond wealth are usually not particularly abrupt, so that forecasters often pay little attention to bond holdings, extrapolating their value in accordance with some simple algorithm.

When long-term interest rates undergo large and lasting shifts, however, the associated wealth effect is sizeable. This was the case with the durable decline in bond yields recorded during the 1990s in Japan (against the background of prolonged economic anaemia) and in Italy (in the context of the run-up to monetary union, when Italian bond rates converged towards German ones). In both countries, households, who had large holdings of bonds, enjoyed a temporary positive wealth effect.

Given that, for the forecaster, the price of long-term risk-free bonds is key, the interest rate forecasting techniques presented in section 4.3 may often be sufficient. But, as was seen during the 2007 financial crisis, forecasting the price of riskier bonds can also be important. That price is a function of the spreads between their yields and the risk-free rate. Much of the focus here is typically on corporate (including financial institutions) spreads, for high-quality (high grade) or lower-quality (high yield) borrowers, and on spreads for lower-quality sovereigns: traditionally emerging markets spreads for dollar bonds, but also spreads for industrial countries – for example, within the euro area in the aftermath of the 2007 financial crisis.

These spreads are related to the risk premia of the institutions/countries, which can in turn reflect two different factors:

- An idiosyncratic factor, namely the risk presented by the individual borrower (or a specific asset class) because of its fundamentals. This component can be modelled as a function of cyclical developments, liquidity, short-term interest rates and expectations of credit risk (expected default rate).
- A general risk premium in the market segment under consideration, influenced by macroeconomic developments.

One possibility is to try to distinguish the role of fundamentals for each asset class versus the common factors; based on such an analysis, Sløk and Kennedy (2004) concluded that, in the early 2000s, bonds' low risk premia were driven down further by abundant liquidity.

One prominent issue in this context is how corporate credit spreads evolve during the business cycle. According to the 'financial accelerator' theory put forward by Bernanke *et al.* (1996), an economic shock characterized by a fall in asset prices leads to a deterioration in firms' balance sheets and thus also to an increase in their cost of external finance (debt) relative to internal finance (equity): this increase in the 'external finance premium' reinforces the credit crunch and the initial shock. As argued by Kannan (2010), stressed credit conditions are an important factor constraining the pace of economic recoveries, and the spread between the commercial paper rate and the short-term interest rate on government-issued bills can be employed as a useful proxy for measuring this effect. From this perspective, the determination of the factors driving credit spreads in general (and thereby influencing bond prices) is of interest in order to gauge the evolution of the financial conditions in the economy adequately. One key factor identified in the literature is policy interest rates, which influence both the cost of capital but also – through balance sheet effects – the credit loan cycle (through the external finance premium and the actual supply of loans by banks).

4.5 Stock prices

Stock prices are also subject to gyrations over and beyond what the associated fundamentals may warrant. This was the case in most OECD countries at the end of the 1990s, when the 'new economy' euphoria gave way to a sharp correction as the IT bubble burst, and more recently in the context of the 2007 financial crisis (see Figure 4.5 overleaf). Hence the forecaster faces a dilemma. In principle, it would be logical to anticipate a correction to values that look more in line with fundamentals (see Box 4.10). But such fundamentals are hard to assess, and a forecast based on a correction would probably be wrong, since experience suggests that stock prices can depart from these equilibrium levels for quite a long time. In addition, domestic prices are heavily influenced by developments in foreign markets.

Box 4.10   Modelling stock prices

One way to analyse stock prices is to start from the return expected by their owner. The rate of return r on a stock priced P is the sum of the dividend D plus the capital gain ΔP over the considered holding period, divided by P; hence:

$$r = (D + \Delta P) / P$$

The expected rate of return on stock prices should exceed government bond yields, which are normally considered as the risk-free benchmark asset; so:

$$r = (i^\ell + \varphi)$$

where i^ℓ is the nominal risk-free long-term interest rate and φ the risk premium.

Figure 4.5　Stock prices*
Stock prices display significant volatility

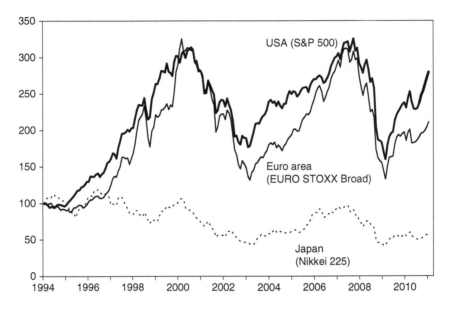

*Broad stock market indices, January 1994 = 100.
Source: ECB.

Assuming a constant dividend $\bar{D}$, the equilibrium value for P ($\Delta P = 0$) equals $\bar{D}/(i^\ell + \varphi)$. The equity premium is thus:

$$\varphi = \bar{D} / P - i^\ell$$

But this is of limited help in practice, since interest rates, risk premia and dividends all vary over time and are uncertain. An alternative approach uses the Gordon–Shapiro formula for the equilibrium stock price. Let dividends now be assumed to grow at a constant rate d. Then:

$$P = D / (i^\ell + \varphi - d)$$

where D is now today's dividend. If the ratio c of dividends to profits Π is a constant, then the price–earnings ratio (PER), P/Π, equals $c/(i^\ell + \varphi - d)$ and one can look for a cointegration relationship between $\log P$, $\log \Pi$ and $\log i^\ell$. In principle, this relationship can then be used to forecast stock prices as a function of forecast profits and interest rates. In practice, however, this may not work well, since c and φ are not constant.

One way to proceed from here is, as financial analysts do, to carefully examine the firms that issued the stock and to evaluate how well they and their stock price are likely to perform. From the standpoint of the macroeconomic forecaster, however, it is not clear how to aggregate the profit forecasts published by financial analysts, both because the information is often very idiosyncratic and because the concepts used differ from those embedded in the national accounts. In addition, analysts' forecasts are not always that reliable, as cruelly illustrated in the emblematic case of Enron in 2001: until just a few days before the firm's collapse, a number of analysts were still advising investors to buy or to continue to hold its stock, touting Enron's wonderful prospects. Financial analysts are in fact often viewed by macroeconomists as being too close to the traders and therefore likely to get carried away by market fads.

Therefore, a common assumption in forecasting is instead that stock prices are unchanged, either in nominal or in real terms, or that, going forward, they are indexed on nominal GDP or profits. Recourse to more sophisticated but more precarious assumptions tends to be confined to alternative scenarios as opposed to the baseline forecast.

4.6   Real estate prices

As with stock prices, real estate prices experience momentous swings. While some of their determinants are identical, they do not necessarily move in unison; consider, for example, the remarkable resilience or even buoyancy of house prices following the stock market collapse that began around 2000 (see Figure 4.6).[2] Moreover, real estate prices are less fickle, given that some of their determinants are very slow-moving, or even fixed (as is usually the case for the quantity of land available in a country, apart from some exceptions such as Dutch polders). But when property markets do collapse, as they did in Japan in the early 1990s, then, on average, the pain lasts twice as long and the impact on output is twice as great according to some estimates (Helbling and Terrones, 2003).

House prices are normally a function of the present value of expected rents. Over the short run, the supply of real estate is quite inelastic, because of construction lags and the limited availability of land, so that rents are largely demand-driven, reflecting developments in real income and real interest rates. Other fundamental factors affecting house prices include the efficiency of

---

[2] It should be borne in mind that, in many countries, house price indices make insufficient allowance for changes in quality, so that measured house price inflation is upward-biased compared to CPI inflation. This bias varies across countries, which distorts straight cross-country comparisons.

Figure 4.6   Real house prices*

Real house prices can experience large swings, over long periods of time

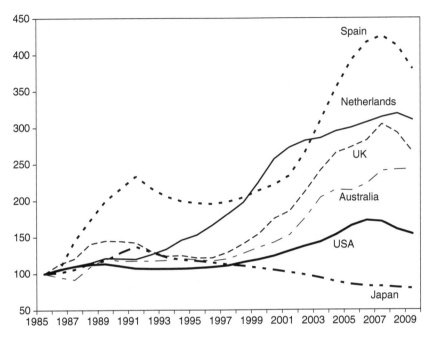

*House prices deflated by the overall consumer price index, 1985 = 100.
Sources: OECD; authors' calculations.

mortgage markets, taxation of real estate transactions and capital gains, mortgage interest rate deductibility, zoning and building code restrictions, tenancy and lease laws, demography and so on (see Box 4.11). But they are harder to quantify and therefore also to include in empirical specifications.[3]

Some of the features of property markets increase the risk of boom and bust (Herring and Wachter, 2003):

- Imperfect information, in a context of supply rigidities, allows prolonged spells of euphoria or depression before enough agents reach the conclusion that a market reversal is in order.

---

[3] One difficulty is that some evidence points to a secular upward trend in real house prices, at least in industrial countries in recent decades, coupled with a high degree of cyclicality leading to sudden price corrections. This may reflect several factors, including statistical difficulties regarding the measurement of house prices adjusted for quality improvement, land scarcity, marginally higher demand for housing as incomes rise, financial innovation, deregulation and so on.

Box 4.11   Modelling real estate prices

Borrowing from Girouard *et al.* (2006), one can distinguish three ways of modelling the determinants of house prices: macroeconomic relationships, affordability indicators and the asset-pricing approach.

Macroeconomic relationships

These modelling techniques will often be included in general macroeconomic models. The equilibrium (real) price of houses will be a function of macroeconomic indicators driving supply (housing stock) and demand (household disposable income; interest rates; and demographics – population size/age, migrations). Other factors can be considered, such as real household wealth, stock prices, unemployment, credit/money or construction costs. The problem is to find precisely the variables that affect those supply and demand conditions, and that can be incorporated into macroeconomic models. This task can become quite complex, depending on changes in public regulation, land supply, demographic developments, taxation and so on. Financial deregulation and innovation (new lending processes, innovative mortgage instruments, greater ability to borrow against collateral, competition among creditors and so on) can also play an important role, and in fact contributed to the 2007 crisis in the US subprime market.

Housing affordability

The idea here is to estimate an equilibrium based on past evidence on housing affordability. For this, one can compare the ratio of (per capita) household income to the average house price to its long-term trend. An alternative is to consider the ratio of mortgage interest payments to disposable income to assess the cost of mortgage debt financing for households.

Asset-pricing approach

The aim of this approach is to compare the price of the asset (the level of the housing price) to the income this asset generates that is, the rental price (for example, the rental component of the CPI). The assumption here is that there is some kind of arbitrage for a buyer between purchasing a house and renting one. Hence, the equilibrium price should equalize the cost of renting a house and the cost of buying and occupying one. But while the former is usually available in CPI statistics, the latter (the user cost of ownership) depends on a number of factors (such as taxation, depreciation of the house, and expected future real estate price developments).

The user cost of housing C for a house with a price P can be computed as the sum of the following:

- the net mortgage interest rate i: that is, the cost for the owner of forgone interest – after deduction of the benefit reflecting possible tax deductions;

- the property tax rate t on owner-occupied houses;
- the depreciation costs d of the house (though a well-known feature of housing prices is that they are imperfectly corrected for quality improvements); and
- the expected capital gains g.

In equilibrium, the user cost of owning should equal the cost of renting R:

$$R = C = P\,(i + t + d - g)$$

And so one can compare the actual price-to-rent ratio P/R observed in the market to the determinants of the user cost of housing:

$$P/R = 1/(i + t + d - g)$$

- Moral hazard arising from explicit or implicit deposit guarantees and weaknesses in financial regulation or oversight leads banks (especially when they are considered to be 'too big to fail') to lend too much, thus fuelling booms.
- Adverse selection works in the same direction, with the riskiest investors most actively seeking loans.
- The real estate cycle is amplified by banks' behaviour: rising house prices increase the value of banks' capital (in so far as they hold real estate) and of real estate lending collateral, leading banks to lend more, which in turn pushes house prices up further. These feedback effects go into reverse when the market turns, and may be aggravated when regulators or supervisors react by tightening real estate loan classification and provisioning rules, or when interest rates go up.

Against this backdrop, forecasters often try to play it safe by adopting a technical assumption similar to the one used for stock prices (constant nominal or real prices, or indexation to wages), and shy away from attempting to judge where prices are headed based on fundamentals. A simple way of checking for possible overheating is to compare the prices to their long-term trend. A more refined approach is to bring in the price-to-rent ratio indicator, analogous to the PER, and to assume, for example, that over a certain period it will converge to some long-run average. But again, this is usually left for alternative scenario purposes rather than being built into the baseline forecast.

Finally, increasing attention is being paid to commercial real estate prices, not least because of their importance for business activities and financial institutions' balance sheets. However, the information available is even less reliable than for housing prices, which makes it difficult for macroeconomic forecasters to factor in explicitly what happens in this sector.

4.7   Exchange rates

The exchange rate is one of the key variables in any open economy model and forecast. Since the end of the Bretton Woods system in the early 1970s, it has also been one of the most volatile variables, not least because of the huge scale of transactions observed in forex markets (dwarfing the magnitude of transactions in goods and services). Hence, exchange rates present modellers and forecasters with a major challenge. For example, the euro's rollercoaster ride since its launch in 1999 (see Figure 4.7) is difficult to capture in an econometric equation, and its very-short-run jitters may be even harder to explain in a rigorous fashion (though casual stories abound).

Moreover, several studies have shown that exchange rate forecasts based on fundamentals do not outperform a random walk – as argued long ago by Meese and Rogoff (1983). However, some more recent literature has suggested that the exchange rate may be more predictable based on fundamentals at longer horizons (Mark, 1995).

Figure 4.7   Real effective exchange rates*
Real effective exchange rates display significant short-term gyrations

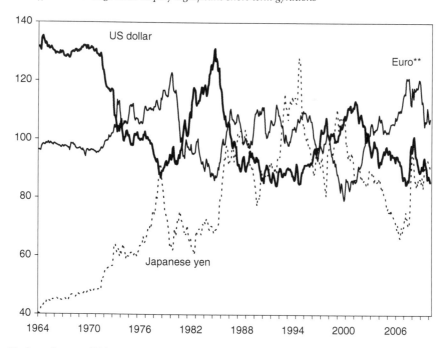

*Indexes, January 1999 = 100.
**Synthetic euro prior to January 1999.
Source: BIS.

This section reviews the main exchange rate determination theories, highlighting their practical limitations, and discusses the options facing the forecaster.

4.7.1   Exchange rate theories

The simplest relationship between the exchange rate and the fundamentals is that of purchasing power parity (PPP), which in its modern form dates back to the 1920s. In its absolute version, it states that, when converted in a common currency, a given good should have the same price everywhere, as any difference would be arbitraged away. If this holds for all goods, and with P standing for the domestic price level (for example, the price in US dollars of a basket of goods in the USA), P^* the foreign price level (for example, the price in euros of the same basket in the euro area), and E the value in the foreign currency of one unit of the domestic currency (for example 1 US dollar = E euros):

$$P^* = P\,E$$

or, in log form:

$$p^* = p + e$$

As a result of trade barriers, imperfect competition, transportation and distribution costs, and different consumer preferences across countries, absolute PPP does not hold in practice. An infamous test of PPP is the regular cross-country comparison of the price of a Big Mac sandwich by the publication *The Economist*: even for a such a homogeneous product, the price differs substantially from what PPP would imply, partly because a substantial portion of the cost of a Big Mac corresponds to non-tradable services, but also for a host of other reasons. Finally, indirect evidence against PPP is provided by the low price elasticities typically obtained in export and import equations (see section 3.3).

As a result, less demanding versions of PPP have emerged, though they are not fully convincing either. The first is relative PPP, which states that exchange rate movements reflect changes in relative prices:

$$\Delta p^* = \Delta p + \Delta e$$

This formulation implies that the change in the real exchange rate is equal to zero.

Another version is PPP restricted to the tradable sector. Most researchers, however, prefer an even looser version of PPP, which simply states that, over the long run, real exchange rates are mean-reverting. The problem is that even if indeed that is the case, it takes a long time for relative prices to move back to equilibrium, so that PPP offers little guidance to forecasters. In addition, for many countries and periods, the real exchange rate is not stationary, not least because of the so-called 'Balassa–Samuelson' effect, which posits that productivity catch-up in the less advanced countries' tradable sectors causes faster overall wage and price increases: as result, their currency should display a trend appreciation in real terms.

A derived approach is the monetary approach to the exchange rate (Frenkel, 1976) with an 'asset view' of exchange rate determination. It rests on the relationship between the exchange rate, the nominal money stock, inflation expectations and foreign prices. The reasoning is rather intuitive and derives from the PPP logic, namely that the exchange rate between two countries is determined by the relative price levels: if goods cost on average twice as much in US dollars than in euros, 1 euro should be equal to 2 dollars. Hence, if the money supply M increases in the USA, everything else being equal, the US price level will rise and the dollar will depreciate against the euro. Conversely, if US output Y rises, everything else being constant (money supply thus being unchanged), the price level will fall and the dollar will appreciate. Hence a general specification of the model will be:

$$E = \alpha \, (M^*/M)^\beta \, (Y^*/Y)^\gamma$$

or in log form:

$$e = \alpha + \beta \, (m^* - m) + \gamma \, (y^* - y)$$

Various specifications can be added – for example, in order to focus on expected exchange rates. While monetary models of exchange rate determination long ago lost their prominence, in particular after the 1983 Meese–Rogoff critique, recent work using more sophisticated techniques, such as panel cointegration analysis, has found that monetary models can beat the random walk (Cerra and Saxena, 2008b).

More recently, the literature has focused on incorporating Taylor rules into exchange rate models. Let the home country (say, the USA) follow a standard Taylor rule:

$$i_t = c_t + \alpha \, \pi_t + \beta \, gap_t$$

and the foreign country (*) follow a Taylor rule with the same specifications plus an exchange rate target e_{Tt}^*:

$$i_t^* = c_t^* + \alpha^* \, \pi_t^* + \beta^* \, gap_t^* + \gamma^* \, (e_t^* - e_{Tt}^*)$$

One can then assume, for example, that the monetary authorities target PPP (so that $e_{Tt}^* = p_t - p_t^*$). One can also test whether the inflation and gap coefficients are the same for the two countries. In addition, some interest rate smoothing can be incorporated: for example, $i_t = (1 - \lambda)\, i_T + \lambda\, i_{t-1}$, where i_T is the target interest rate as derived from the Taylor rule.

The Taylor-rule-based forecasting equation is then derived by looking at the difference between the two interest rate functions (that is, $i_t - i_t^*$) and by retaining one specific determination of the expected exchange rate. For example, one can retain the interest rate parity relation (see Box 4.13 below):

$$E_t(e_{t+1}) - e_t = i_t - i_t^* + \rho_t$$

where ρ_t here represents the deviation from rational expectations uncovered interest rate parity.

Molodtsova and Papell (2009) retain the following exchange rate forecasting equation with a more general specification of the exchange rate:

$$\Delta e_{t+1} = \omega - \alpha\, \pi_t + \alpha^*\, \pi_t^* - \beta\, gap_t + \beta^*\, gap_t^* + \gamma^*\, e_t - \delta\, i_{t-1} + \delta^*\, i_{t-1}^* + \eta_t$$

They compare this model with a set of other models of exchange rate determination (interest rate parity, monetary model, PPP) and find that models which incorporate Taylor rule fundamentals display significant and better evidence of short-term predictability (with the strongest result for Taylor models with heterogeneous coefficients between countries and interest rate smoothing).

Wang and Wu (2009) also find that the benchmark Taylor rule model performs better than other models and better than the random walk. They focus on interval forecasting (rather than point forecasts), arguing that there is a connection between economic fundamentals and the prediction of the ranges in which future exchange rates can be.

The important role played by exchange rate expectations in models has been emphasized by Engel and West (2005). Their starting point is the 'asset-market approach to exchange rates', by which the exchange rate is influenced by expectations of future fundamentals. They model the exchange rate e_t at time t as:

$$e_t = (1 - b)\, (o_{1t} + u_{1t}) + b\, (o_{2t} + u_{2t}) + b\, E_t(e_{t+1})$$

where o_1 and o_2 are observable economic fundamentals, u_1 and u_2 unobservable economic fundamentals or shocks, $E_t(e_{t+1})$ the expected future exchange rate and b the discount factor. Imposing a no-bubbles condition ($b^j\, E_t(e_{t+j})$ goes to 0 as $j \to \infty$) yields a present-value relationship for e_t modelled as the discounted infinite sum of the expected combination of fundamentals and unobservable shocks, as in conventional asset pricing models.

From this perspective, Engel *et al.* (2007) argue that fundamentals models are not that bad if one incorporates changes in expectations. The reasoning is that standard models do in fact imply near random walk behaviour in exchange rates, meaning that the question of whether these models beat the random walk is irrelevant. Once expectations of future fundamentals are integrated, the fit is better, and exchange rates are more predictable at longer horizons. To do so, one possibility is to use survey data. Another is to incorporate expectations of economic fundamentals indirectly through changes in expectations in monetary policy, confirming the interest of Taylor-based exchange rate models. Chen *et al.* (2008) also emphasize the importance of expectations for 'commodity currency' exchange rates: since the exchange rate depends on the present value of exogenous fundamentals, it is fundamentally forward-looking and therefore embodies useful information about future commodity prices movements (see also Appendix 3.2).

In addition, there is the issue of parameter instability and non-linearities. Rossi (2005) argues that finding exchange rate causality relationships fails because of the presence of underlying parameter instabilities. Sarno and Valente (2009) also emphasize the frequents shifts in the set of fundamentals driving exchange rates that reflect swings in market expectations over time: market participants look at fundamentals but frequently change the list of variables considered and attribute an excessive weight to a 'scapegoat' variable but only for a limited period of time. Indeed, Kilian and Taylor (2003) estimate that the apparent failure of forecasting models is caused by non-linearity in forex data, in particular because the economy adjusts in a non-linear fashion to the long-run equilibrium. Using a specific model allowing for non-linearity – modelling the deviation of the exchange rate from its PPP fundamental and incorporating transition functions depending on the level of the real exchange rate and its equilibrium level – they are quite successful at forecasting exchange rates at two- to three-year horizons for a significant number of countries. In this context, Clarida *et al.* (2002) recommend the use of Markow regime-switching modelling techniques to deal with non-linearities when producing exchange rate forecasts.

However, these recent approaches are complex and difficult for the forecaster to use in practice. Moreover, there are serious measurement problems and it can be difficult to disentangle fundamentals from measurement errors in the estimations, as Engel and West (2005) recognized. Indeed, some of the key fundamentals are not measured in the same way across countries, notably productivity or capital stock (Schnatz *et al.*, 2004). Others are measured with error, in particular current accounts, since they fail to add up to zero internationally. And others are simply unobservable – for example, risk premia. Moreover, several crucial indicators are subject to large revisions over time. Ironically, however, models based on real-time statistics (that is, on those available at the time the spot exchange rate was observed) tend to fit better than those estimated using final and more accurate data, possibly because market participants' behaviour is shaped by the information they have rather than by what will ultimately become the definitive series.[4] But real-time data sets are rare and most models are estimated on subsequent data vintages. Finally, another challenge relates to the importance of the evaluation criteria for judging the quality of competing models. Cheung *et al.* (2005) acknowledge that no single model/specific combination is very successful, and at best some models seem to do well at certain horizons on certain criteria.

Faced with these challenges, the forecaster may find it useful to focus on long-term fundamentals rather than on modelling more short-term patterns that are highly uncertain. Indeed, many promising avenues have been explored that focus primarily on modelling the real equilibrium exchange rate as a function of economic fundamentals (see Box 4.12).

Box 4.12 Long-run exchange rate equilibria

Williamson (1985) proposed a macroeconomic balance approach, estimating a fundamental equilibrium exchange rate (FEER) defined as the rate ensuring internal as well as external equilibrium over the medium term. The former obtains when the level of activity is consistent with full employment and low inflation, while the latter means that the underlying, or 'structural', current account balance should match desired, or 'sustainable', capital flows – derived from several factors, such as the state of development or demography. For this to apply, the exchange rate should bring about the requisite levels of imports and exports, which is where trade elasticities come into play – first to estimate the current account position that would occur should the output gap be closed, and second to estimate the exchange rate movements that would be needed to obtain the required external balance. The FEER thus allows the abstraction from Keynesian cyclical effects and other transient shocks.

Empirically, the FEER can be calculated in a number of ways, but the most widely used approach is based on a partial equilibrium analysis, which plugs exogenous estimates of trend output and structural capital flows into a trade model. Wren-Lewis (2003), for example, used this approach to calculate an equilibrium rate for the British pound *vis-à-vis* the euro, in the context of an assessment of the United Kingdom's readiness to join the euro area: assuming

---

[4] See Faust *et al.* (2003), who document this starting from the following, widely used, ECM: $\Delta e_t = \alpha + \beta \left[(m_t - m_t^*) - (y_t - y_t^*) - e_t \right] + \varepsilon_t$ (where all variables are in logs, m stands for the money stock, y for output and an asterisk denotes foreign), and then extending it to include the short-term interest rate, inflation and the accumulated current account balance (as a measure of the net external investment position).

that the sustainable current account level was zero in the United Kingdom, the conclusion was that the FEER was €1.37/£1 sterling, implying that the pound was significantly overvalued at the time. A variant of the FEER is the DEER, where D stands for desired and is in essence the FEER incorporating an optimal fiscal policy trajectory (Artis and Taylor, 1995).

The great advantage of the FEER is that it is operational in the context of model-based forecasting, given that estimates of output gaps and trade elasticities are usually available within macroeconomic models. However, treating trend output and the structural current account as exogenous may be an extreme assumption, since it ignores the possible feedback from the exchange rate on these variables. More importantly perhaps, estimating structural capital flows involves very substantial judgement.* A final complication is that the structural external balance of a given country interacts with those of other countries, since current account positions should sum to zero at the global level.

Attempting to extend the FEER analysis, Stein (1994) put forward a natural real exchange rate (NATREX) model, which endogenizes the interaction between the flows considered in the macroeconomic balance approach and the capital and foreign debt stocks. The NATREX models the exchange rate as moving from a medium-run FEER-type equilibrium (where flows are balanced) to a long-run equilibrium (where net foreign debt is constant at its steady-state level). In the process, it highlights the determinants of the medium-run capital flows, notably:

- The propensity to consume: higher consumption increases interest rates and hence capital inflows, causing exchange rate appreciation.
- Technical progress: accelerating productivity raises investment and therefore also pushes up capital inflows and the exchange rate.

However, the increase in external indebtedness caused by rising consumption cannot be sustained indefinitely, so that over the long run the exchange rate depreciates, allowing for an increase in net exports that serves to pay the extra interest due. The long-run impact of technical progress is more ambiguous: external debt service also increases, but higher potential growth generates higher national saving.

The NATREX is usually tested in reduced form, which again means that the feedback effects are not accounted for rigorously. One example is the structural estimation of the euro's equilibrium exchange rate by Detken *et al.* (2002), who found that at its end-2000 trough, and measured against the euro area's four largest trading partners, the euro was some 25 per cent weaker than its medium-run equilibrium level, and some 28 per cent weaker than its long-run equilibrium level. Such precise estimates, however, should be taken with a pinch of salt, since they are quite sensitive to small changes in the behavioural equations.

Both the FEER and the NATREX approach may impose too much theoretical structure, and focus on horizons extending far beyond standard forecasting periods. A popular alternative are behavioural equilibrium exchange rate (BEER) models, which can be applied with shorter time horizons. They amount to reduced-form modelling and test for the significance of a vast array of variables, such as productivity differentials, interest rate differentials, relative fiscal stance, the price of oil and the current account balance. Maeso-Fernandez *et al.* (2002) apply this to the euro. Since most of these variables are non-stationary, they estimate VECMs. Their study confirms that the euro was greatly undervalued in late 2000. In this context, it is possible to distinguish:

- The predicted value of the exchange rate based on the actual values of the explanatory variables, which can be thought of as the current and cyclical equilibrium exchange rate. This one is the most relevant for forecasting purposes.
- Its value based on the 'permanent' component of the explanatory variables, namely the so-called permanent equilibrium exchange rate (PEER), which is smoother, since it is purged of transitory effects.

To summarize, Bénassy-Quéré *et al.* (2008) recommend distinguishing three long-run horizons: the very long run, for which PPP holds (and the real exchange rate goes back to its constant level);** the long run, for which the net foreign asset position matters and is stabilized at some level (net external liabilities being associated with a weak currency in such a long run); and the medium long run, during which the net foreign asset position is changing through current account variations and valuation effects and is slowly moving to its long-run, stable value.

---

*It has long been held that older and more advanced economies should have a structural current account surplus and finance the investments that younger emerging market economies cannot fund out of their own saving and for which the return on capital should be higher. However, the 2007 financial crisis gave some weight to the argument that emerging countries should run current account surpluses and build forex reserves to absorb shocks in times of financial crises and sudden stops in international capital flows.

**This applies to economically integrated economies (the authors look at the euro/dollar exchange rate). However, for less developed economies that are catching up, the real exchange rate should normally appreciate over a rather long period of time (see Chapter 6, section 6.2.5 for an application to medium- to long-term world growth projections).

4.7.2   Practical approaches

All these difficulties lead the many forecasters who focus on relatively short time horizons (say, up to two years) to rely on an implausible but simple and transparent constant nominal (or real) exchange rate assumption, and others to base their forecast on the forward rates quoted on the foreign exchange market (see Box 4.13). As noted, these can be good practices when the variable under consideration is very volatile.

Box 4.13   Uncovered interest parity

One simple approach to exchange rate modelling is to take a pure financial market view and not to refer to any real sector equilibrium. This is what the Bank of England, for example, had long done in its core macroeconomic model (Bank of England, 1999), where the exchange rate was determined by a risk-adjusted uncovered interest parity (UIP) condition. Let e now denote the effective nominal exchange rate (in log), e^a its anticipated value, i the domestic one-period interest rate and φ a risk premium. Then:

$$e^a_{t+1} = e_t + i^*_t - i_t + \varphi_t$$

UIP posits that an investor has to be indifferent between holding the domestic currency, earning i_t and benefiting from its expected appreciation $(e^a_{t+1} - e_t)$, or holding the foreign currency and earning i^*_t. But the investor may believe that the domestic currency will appreciate by more than the interest rate differential, in which case s/he will only be ready to hold the foreign currency if s/he also receives a positive risk premium φ. The latter can be defined as a function of the current account balance, inflation and other variables, or for simplicity it can be assumed to equal zero, as the Bank of England did in its exchange rate equation (though its *Inflation Report* assumes that the nominal exchange rate will evolve along a path halfway between an unchanged rate and the path implied by the UIP condition).

The freezing assumption can be justified by the Meese and Rogoff (1983) critique. The use of forward rates may seem to disregard the literature's long-standing finding that the forward rate is a poor predictor of the future spot rate (see Hansen and Hodrick (1980), who rejected the 'efficient markets hypothesis' for exchange rates). However, the issue is still controversial. Since the 1980s several studies have pointed to the valuable information contained in forward rates for forecasting purposes, provided the structural wedge between forward and expected spot rates or any non-linearities are taken into account. For example, looking at the US dollar/Deutschmark and US dollar/£ sterling pairs, Clarida and Taylor (1993) note that the information in the forward exchange premia can be used to reduce the forecast error for the spot rate (relative to a random walk forecast). But other studies (see Aggarwal *et al.*, 2009 for a recent one) continue to find evidence of the poor ability of the forward exchange rate to forecast spot rates, even after accounting for various statistical properties and even for the most liquid foreign exchange markets.

In practice, however, the above simplified relationships may not be observed over the time horizon of the forecasts. Indeed, UIP failed to hold during much of the 2000s. As explained in Box 4.13, UIP would suggest that, if interest rates are higher in a country B than in A, investors should anticipate a depreciation of the exchange rate of country B so as to equalize the rate of returns. However, in practice, they have often had an inclination to prefer to take the risk of borrowing in A and to invest at higher rates in so-called 'carry trades' (McCauley and McGuire, 2009). A classic carry trade was to buy an Australian dollar bond yielding 5 per cent with Swiss francs borrowed at 1 per cent. The profit from such trades over extended periods stands in stark contradiction with interest rate parity. These are thus very risky strategies, which raise questions of financial stability. This is even more so as carry trades appear to rest on a false sense of comfort among investors in periods of cheap funding conditions and excessive liquidity and risk-taking.

The inadequacies of long-term structural models have generated much interest in using the purely statistical methods described in Annex II. There has also been a growing interest in recent years for neural network statistical techniques. But these methods also present significant drawbacks – not least their complexity and the absence of an economic story underlying the forecasts – and generally it seems reasonable for forecasters to stick to simpler and more transparent assumptions.

Further reading

The thinking about monetary policy in the aftermath of the 2007 crisis is evolving rapidly. It therefore pays to monitor the websites of the largest central banks, notably the US Federal Reserve, the ECB and the Bank of Japan. Bernanke (2009b) offers a brief guided tour of the Federal Reserve balance sheet, explaining the Fed's policy strategy and instruments in the aftermath of the crisis. BIS (2009a) provides a detailed description of various monetary policy arrangements, and IMF (2011) is similarly a useful review of issues related to macro-prudential policy. For an overview of the functioning of financial markets, and in particular of the behaviour of interest rates and related securities prices, Van Horne's (2001) textbook is a key reference. On derivatives, Hull (2008) is very helpful. A comprehensive overview of housing markets is provided by André (2010). A good textbook focusing on exchange rates is Sarno and Taylor (2002).

On the interaction with financial stability issues, Minsky (1982), Kindleberger and Aliber (2011) and White (2009) provide a useful background, while Reinhart and Rogoff (2009) put the 2007 financial crisis into historical perspective. The BIS (2009b) and the UK FSA (2009) review the lessons to be drawn from this crisis, especially with respect to financial regulation.

Appendix 4.1   Integrating the financial stability perspective – lessons from the 2007 financial crisis

Renewed interest for financial stability issues

The financial crisis that began in summer 2007 and led to a severe global recession was a wake-up call for the forecasters' community. The crisis erupted quite suddenly and went through various stages (see Table 4.1). It was largely unexpected and missed by almost all forecasters despite significant evidence of mounting problems in the US subprime market that ultimately triggered the turmoil.

Table 4.1   The 2007 financial crisis: key stages

Period	Main developments
Up to 2006 **Formation and peak of the US housing bubble**	• US house prices rose threefold from the mid-1990s to 2006.* • Sharp increase in subprime lending (to borrowers with weak credit histories and greater risk of default), to around 20 per cent of total US mortgage origination from around 7 per cent before 2004. • Relaxation of regulations for US investment banks leading to higher leverage and issuance of mortgage-backed securities (MBS). • Financial innovation: surge in the issuance of subprime MBS and collateralized debt obligations (CDOs). • Predatory lending associated with the engineering of new, sophisticated mortgage products.
2006–May 2007 **Bursting of the US bubble**	• US house prices peak in mid-2006 (subsequently falling by 34 per cent to spring 2009). • Sharp increase in delinquency rates for borrowers, even those with prime credit ratings; surge in foreclosures, particularly in the subprime segment. • Sharp widening of spreads on non-investment grade tranches of home equity CDOs from November 2006, associated with increased concerns about their valuation. • Increased number of subprime lender bankruptcies; US subprime lender Novastar announces large losses; funds put aside by HSBC to cover subprime portfolio losses (February 2007). • Volatility in global financial markets (sharp sell-off in February/March 2007).
June 2007– August 2008 **First stages and contagion**	• Moody's downgrades the ratings of 131 asset-backed securities (ABSs) backed by subprime home loans (June 2007). • Two hedge funds managed by US investment bank Bear Stearns are close to being shut down (June 2007); rising valuation losses marked in banks' balance sheets. • Dislocation in interbank money markets (Libor/OIS spreads widen); pressure on asset prices. • Germany's IKB warning of US-related losses (30 July 2007) followed by a publicly-supported rescue plan (1 August 2007); three investment funds frozen by French BNP Paribas (9 August 2007). • Interest rate cut by the US Federal Reserve (17 August 2007).

(continued)

Table 4.1 Continued

	• Northern Rock receives liquidity support from the Bank of England as depositors' panic triggers the first run on a UK bank in 150 years (14 September 2007).
	• Co-ordinated action by advanced economies' central banks (12 December 2007).
	• Onset of the longest post-Second World War US recession (December 2007).
	• Northern Rock taken into state ownership (22 February 2008); liquidity shortage at Bear Stearns leads to a government-facilitated takeover by JP Morgan (16 March 2008).
	• Spillover of the US recession to the other advanced economies.
	• Trouble surfaces at US monoline insurers (June 2008).
	• US government-sponsored enterprises (GSEs) require government help (13 July 2008); government takes formal control of the GSEs (7 September 2008).
	• False signs of stabilization in financial markets.
September–October 2008 Global loss of confidence	• US investment bank Lehman Brothers files for bankruptcy (15 September 2008).
	• US government support for AIG, a large insurer heavily involved in CDS markets; investor run on US money market funds as a large fund (the Reserve Primary Fund) 'breaks the buck' and reports a net asset value below $1 (16 September 2008).
	• Collapse in financial markets; severe disruptions in interbank money markets and foreign exchange swap markets.
	• Co-ordinated set-up of central bank forex swap lines.
	• Rescue of UK bank HBOS (18 September 2008).
	• US Treasury guarantee for money market funds and Troubled Asset Relief Program (TARP) to remove bad assets from banks' balance sheets (19 September 2008).
	• Large US investment banks Goldman Sachs and Morgan Stanley allowed to convert themselves into bank holding companies following growing market concerns (21 September 2008).
	• Government interventions to support large banks all over the world: UK Bradford & Bingley, European Fortis, German Hypo Real Estate, US Washington Mutual and Wachovia, Irish commercial banks (25–30 September 2008).
	• Various public guarantee and recapitalization schemes are put in place; country sovereign CDS spreads begin to increase, reflecting increasing strains on government finances.
	• UK plan to recapitalize banks (8 October 2008).
	• Sharp devaluation of Iceland's currency following the collapse of major commercial banks; assets of Icelandic Landsbanki bank frozen by UK authorities (8 October 2008).
	• Co-ordinated central bank actions: interest rate cuts, provision of unlimited amounts of US dollars to ease money markets tensions (8–13 October 2008).
	• Hungary receives IMF support programme; US dollar swap lines are extended to key emerging market monetary authorities (28/29 October 2008).

(continued)

Table 4.1 Continued

November 2008–May 2009 Global economic downturn and active policy responses	• G20 countries pledge to reform the financial system (15 November 2008). • US government rescues Citigroup (22 November 2008). • Decisive move by the Federal Reserve to expand unconventional policy measures, in particular with the direct purchases of GSE securities (25 November 2008). • Evidence of a sharp economic downturn; US 10-year government bond yields reach a historical low of 2.05 per cent (30 December 2008). • US government rescues Bank of America (16 January 2009). • UK government rescues Royal Bank of Scotland (19 January 2009). • Expansion of central banks' unconventional actions. • Trough in equity markets: Standard & Poor's (S&P) 500 index back to its October 1996 level, around 50 per cent below the October 2007 highs (9 March 2009). • US Federal Reserve announces purchases of US Treasury Bonds; 10-year yields decline by 47 basis points in one day (18 March 2009). • Renewal of US dollar swap lines (6 April 2009). • Stress tests conducted in the largest US financial institutions support confidence (24 April 2009). • ECB decides to start purchasing covered bonds (7 May 2009).
June–November 2009 Signs of stabilization	• Increasing signs of economic recovery. • End of US recession (June 2009). • Optimism back in financial markets: higher bank earnings; higher risk appetite (for example, rebound in forex carry trades); strong capital flows to emerging markets. • 10 large US financial firms allowed to repay government aid (June 2009).
November 2009–early 2011 onwards Global recovery but financial crisis contagion to sovereigns	• Government-owned Dubai World seeks a moratorium on its debt payments (26 November 2009). • Lowering of Greece's sovereign rating following a major revision of the budget deficit (December 2009). • Rise in volatility and risk aversion in financial markets; spillover of Greek sovereign worries to Ireland, Portugal and Spain as well as to global banks exposed to these countries (mid-January 2010). • US 'Volcker rule' proposal to restrain banks' activities (21 January 2010). • Apart from peripheral Europe, signs that a global recovery is in train. • Start of monetary normalization: discontinuation of US dollar swap lines (1 February 2010); scaling back of US dollar and euro area unconventional measures (first quarter of 2010); policy tightening in emerging market economies. • First EU–IMF support package for Greece (€45 billion, 11 April 2010). • Standard & Poor's downgrades Greece to junk (27 April 2010).

(*continued*)

Table 4.1 Continued

- High volatility in global financial markets: sharp rise in euro area sovereign CDS spreads; renewed widening in Libor/OIS spreads (April 2010).
- Second Greek support package (€110 billion, 2 May 2010) but further contagion to peripheral Europe.
- Flash crash: the US Dow Jones falls by nearly 1,000 points or around 8.5 per cent intra-day before rebounding (6 May 2010).
- EU/IMF €750 billion fiscal stabilization package; the ECB announces direct purchases of securities; reintroduction of US dollar swap lines (10 May 2010).
- Germany restricts naked short selling (18 May 2010).
- US Senate passes the financial reform bill intended to limit large banks' risk-taking (20 May 2010).
- European stress tests publication (23 July 2010).
- Setting up of the European Financial Stability Facility (4 August 2010).
- Basel III framework announced for banks' capital and liquidity standards (July and September 2010).
- Growing concerns of a double dip: renewed fall in major long-term benchmark interest rates and rise in the price of gold (July–September).
- Ireland revises the cost of rescuing its banks to €50 bn, which amounts to almost a third of GDP (30 September 2010), and then to €70 bn (31 March 2011).
- Lingering fiscal concerns in peripheral Europe (October 2010 – April 2011).
- Comprehensive Monetary Easing in Japan (5 October 2010).
- Quantitative Easing Part 2 in the USA (3 November 2010).
- EU/IMF Financial assistance to Ireland (21 November 2010), and portugal request for assistance (7 April 2011).

Note: *10-city composite Case–Shiller Home Price Index (nominal).
Sources: BIS *Annual Reports and Quarterly Reviews.*

Indeed, in June 2007 – only a few weeks before the outbreak of the crisis – the Chairman of the Board of Governors of the US Federal Reserve System noted 'the emergence of some serious stresses in subprime mortgage markets' and that 'the downturn in the housing market has been sharp' but went on to say that 'Thus far, however, we have not seen major spillovers from housing onto other sectors of the economy. On average, over coming quarters, we expect the economy to advance at a moderate pace' (Bernanke, 2007).

Apart from the surprise, a key element of the crisis was its financial stability dimension. Problems in specific financial institutions spread quickly, culminating in September 2008 in the failure of Lehman Brothers, one of the largest US investment banks at that time. Securitization markets dried up, banks stopped lending to each other and forex swap markets were dislocated. This led to huge spreads in these markets. In the event, the 2007 turmoil turned into the most severe financial crisis since the Great Depression in the 1930s.

This crisis has cast doubts on many assumptions and assessments that had previously been taken for granted by the vast majority of economists:

- The crisis was a sign of widespread market failure, particularly in the financial sector. Market discipline, exerted via market prices, failed to prevent excessive risk-taking; markets were not able to self-correct; and large-scale and unprecedented public interventions proved necessary.
- An event in a very specific sector (some types of risky mortgages) in a single country (the USA) quickly contaminated the financial sector worldwide, leading to the bankruptcy of large institutions previously deemed to be 'too big to fail'. In fact, almost all the big names in the financial sector would have become bankrupt had governments not stepped in with large capital injections and guarantees – in addition to the unprecedented actions taken by monetary authorities.
- The crisis was a reminder of the importance of human factors. Cupidity and greed help to explain the massive increase in financial activity in the years before the crisis. Very complex products were developed that only experts understood, and few managers were able to fathom the business their own institutions were involved in. Business managers did not properly manage their teams, boards failed to ask the right questions to management teams, and policy makers were praising the virtues of free market forces and their self-correcting capabilities. And when warnings were expressed by the few who took the risk of looking ridiculous, no one took heed of them.
- The crisis revealed the shortcomings of the statistical techniques used to forecast and manage risks. Many models rest on the assumption that events follow a normal distribution, but in fact extreme events (fat tails) are not that infrequent (Mandelbrot and Hudson, 2004). Events that had been thought of as totally uncorrelated turned out to be highly correlated. Non-linearities appeared to have been understated.

In sum, the crisis brought to the fore complacency, market failure, systemic risk, contingency and fat tails. The overarching lesson is that financial uncertainty tends to be downplayed during boom times. Against this backdrop, financial stability has become a key objective for policy makers, and forecasters will be asked to pay greater attention to financial stability.

What is financial stability?

Financial instability is not that rare

In a sense, it is easier to define financial instability than stability. Financial instability involves severe disruptions in the functioning of financial markets, the failure of large institutions, panic among depositors, investors and other economic agents, and sharp asset price gyrations. Such instability can be triggered by exogenous events, be they non-economic (natural disasters or terrorist attacks, for example) or economic (such as an exchange rate collapse). Alternatively, they can result from the build-up of more endogenous fragilities within the financial system itself (breakdown of a major payment system, or lack of liquidity in a key market, say).

Table 4.2   Selected financial crises in history

1340	King Edward III of England's default on part of external debt
1637	Tulip crisis in the Netherlands
1720	Bursting of the UK South Sea Bubble and John Law's Mississippi Company in France
1813	Denmark-Norway state bankruptcy
1819	Panic and first US financial bust
1825	British bank crisis
1866	Collapse of Overend, Gurney & Company (the last UK bank run before Northern Rock in 2007)
1893	Worst US depression before the 1930s (collapse of banks and rail companies)
1893	Australian banking crisis
1901	Crash of the New York Stock Exchange
1929	Wall Street Crash ('Black Thursday'), followed by the Great Depression
1974	German bank Herstatt bankrupt
1982	Latin-American debt crisis begins in Mexico
1987	'Black Monday' – large falls in US stock markets
1989–91	US Savings & Loan crisis
early 1990s	Scandinavian banking crisis
16 September 1992	Exit of the pound sterling from the European Exchange Rate Mechanism ('Black Wednesday')
1990s–2000s	Lingering financial crisis in Japan
1994–5	Mexican crisis
1997–8	Asian financial crisis
1998–9	Financial crisis in Russia and Brazil
2000–1	Dotcom crash*
2002	Argentina's external debt default and currency peg collapse
2007–	Financial crisis and Great Recession

Note: *While the dotcom crash was not, strictly speaking, a financial crisis, it had significant financial stability implications. One was the sharp decline in stock prices when the IT bubble burst in the early 2000s. A second was the bankruptcy of IT-related companies with system-wide importance (Worldcom, Enron) as well as the weakened financial positions of telecom companies following huge investments made during the bubble.

Indeed, examples of large-scale financial instability have not been that rare historically (see Table 4.2). In the twentieth and twenty-first centuries, global crises have included the Great Depression in the 1930s; the crisis that began in 1997 in South-East Asia and quickly spread to Russia and Latin America; and, of course, the recent global financial crisis that began in summer 2007. More localized crises have included the bankruptcy of the German bank Herstatt in 1974 (which is now widely considered to be the first episode of a systemic risk event in modern history); and the collapse of several domestic banking sectors (Swedish banks in the early 1990s, the lingering Japanese financial crisis in the 1990s and early 2000s, the quasi-failure of the US Long-Term Capital Management hedge fund in 1998 and so on). Therefore, Reinhart and Rogoff (2009) suggest that financial crises should be thought of as being regular rather than extreme events.

Various aspects of financial stability

The concept of financial stability connects at least three distinct dimensions:

- Well-functioning financial intermediation between savers and borrowers. This requires sound financial intermediaries, financial products that can be identified and valued correctly, and adequate market infrastructure, so that financial instruments can be traded and cleared efficiently. A key objective is thus to protect and strengthen the functioning of financial markets to ensure they are resilient when facing 'exogenous' adverse events. Policy efforts since the 1980s had focused on the promotion of sound risk management practices in the industry and of rigorous prudential supervision: both the 1988 Basel I and the Basel II Accords (the latter published in 2004 and still in the process of being implemented across the world) established a framework on minimum capital ratios to preserve the solvency of institutions; the new Basel III framework adopted in 2010 in response to the 2007 financial crisis goes even further to strengthen the resilience of individual financial institutions and of the financial system as a whole. This is in fact an important lesson from the 2007 financial crisis: it is not sufficient merely to take steps based solely on the individual risks of financial institutions, as their impact on the wider financial system also matters.

- Macroeconomic stability. Financial stability also calls for a combination of fairly smooth real output growth (avoidance of large-scale recessions but also of substantial overheating) and low and stable inflation, allowing financial markets to function well almost naturally. Such a focus on stable growth and (consumer price) inflation has been pursued traditionally by modern central banks. Indeed, major departures from macroeconomic stability can lead to financial instability, as with the repercussions on Japanese banks' balance sheets of the bursting of the 1980s bubble and the subsequent deterioration in borrowers' credit quality. But a key lesson of the 2007 crisis is that financial stability may be endangered even in periods of stable growth and inflation, in particular when economic agents are taking on excessive debt while asset prices are booming. Indeed, looking at past episodes of price misalignments, financial distress, volatile exchange rates, property and equity market bubbles and the like, Crockett (2001) argued that financial instability had, if anything, intensified during the past few decades of so-called 'great moderation' (of growth and inflation).

- Economic efficiency and well-being. As with the Great Depression of the 1930s, the 2007 crisis underscored the high costs associated with financial instability, especially in terms of income and unemployment. These costs are not only temporary (large recessions) but also long-lasting as a result of the adverse consequences on potential growth rates and structural unemployment of the bursting of financial bubbles (see Chapter 6). To avoid such high costs, the economy should be protected from financial excesses and excessive risk-taking. In this regard, ensuring financial stability does not rely solely on strengthening the financial system but also on restraining its (negative) externalities. The aim here is to protect not only the banks but also the economy from a 'swollen' financial sector that could grow too big for society. Various measures are currently envisaged throughout the world, such as ensuring a greater loss-absorbing capacity for those institutions that are deemed to be too big to fail, setting up adequate resolution regimes to close failed institutions, taxing financial operations, restricting the scope of banks' activities and so on.

Ways to better understand financial stability issues

To say the least, the 2007 crisis has proved that economists' understanding of financial behaviour remains in its infancy. Indeed, macroeconomic models still do not pay enough attention to financial variables such as debt and asset prices. Sometimes, it is because the interrelations are difficult to assess (for example, the influence of asset prices on demand), while at other times it is because the data do not even exist or are very imperfect. A good example is the information on real estate prices, which cannot be compared readily across or even within countries, a case in point being the conflicting signals delivered in the run-up to the 2007 crisis by various US indicators such as the S&P/Case–Shiller home price indices and the then Office of Federal Housing Enterprise Oversight (OFHEO) national aggregate house price index. Also, there is still insufficient transparent information available on financial valuations, prices, counterparties and concentration of risks. In addition, very rapid market innovation had outstripped statistical systems before the 2007 crisis, implying, for example, that information on banks was not sufficient to reflect the development of the underlying 'shadow banking system'.

The 2007 crisis has already led to numerous calls for more analysis. The aim is to better integrate the financial sector in macroeconomic thinking and modelling (Cecchetti *et al.*, 2009). There is a long list of areas where the modelling of economic activity should be augmented to integrate financial stability aspects, namely:

- The role played by financial intermediaries (Adrian and Shin, 2008): in particular, how is risk assessed at one point in time and projected to evolve over time? What are the linkages both among financial intermediaries and with the real economy (through lenders and borrowers) and policy makers? A key aspect is that the various interconnections among the banking system, capital markets, and payment and settlement systems can lead to unexpected dynamics and amplify shocks (Dudley, 2009). As a result, reinforcing feedback effects between the financial system and the business cycle can lead to procyclicality; that is, the amplification of economic developments in good as well as in bad times. Another important element is the systemic risk represented by financial firms: idiosyncratic difficulties can contaminate the whole system, suggesting that economic models should treat non-financial and financial entities differently. But the difficulty is to define precisely the perimeter of financial institutions: does it include banks, money market funds, insurance companies, financial branches of non-financial firms? For example, the failure of AIG in 2008 was a systemic event resulting mainly from AIG's decision to expand outside its core insurance business and to become a prime actor in credit default swap markets.
- Financial frictions and market imperfections, which can arise from the interrelationship among credit, asset values and financial constraints (the more asset prices rise, everything else being equal, the more debt can be taken on); the departure of asset prices from fundamentals because of the collective aggregation of apparently rational individual decisions (for example, compensation practices that can trigger excessive risk-taking by individuals); the fact that liquidity in financial markets can vary suddenly without being driven by rational forces; and the way that prices of financial products adjust over time to equalize demand and supply at non-market clearing prices (with the possibility of large bid/offer spreads).

- Balance sheet factors: the role of balance sheet variables in affecting economic decisions is still not well understood. Economic models do not pay enough attention to debt and asset prices. Sometimes this is because the interrelations are too difficult to measure – for example, in the case of the influence of financial conditions on consumption and investment, or of the impact of asset prices through so-called 'wealth effects' (see Chapter 3). At other times, it is because the data are very imperfect or do not exist, though significant efforts have been made recently to enhance the provision of financial balance sheet data (OECD, 2011). Finally, microeconomic financial mechanisms are largely ignored, in particular the fact that collateral requirements depend on credit ratings, the occurrence of haircuts and forced sales, the importance of gross versus net amounts of financial assets and liabilities, and counterparty risks.
- The possibility of financial booms/busts: the interrelated dynamics of asset prices, risk premia and leverage suggest that financial stress should be modelled in a dynamic, endogenous way.
- The possibility of irrationality: behavioural economics has argued that individual agents do not always behave rationally, because of excessive self-confidence, the tendency to extrapolate recent trends, and high risk aversion when problems arise. Even rational decisions at the individual level can lead to collective irrationality. Two aspects of financial stability are related to this: herding effects, with the famous example of Chuck Prince, former CEO of Citigroup, who told the *Financial Times* in July 2007 that 'as long as the music is playing, you've got to get up and dance. We're still dancing'; and moral hazard, with large financial firms being encouraged to take excessive, non-rational risks if they are perceived to be benefiting from an implicit government guarantee and thus 'too big to fail' – this is the problem posed by the so-called SIFIs (Systemically Important Financial Institutions).
- The determination of financial prices. The efficient market hypothesis – that the price of a financial asset reflects all available information – has again been questioned by the 2007 crisis: before the crisis, the value of many securitized products was model-based (using flawed models) and did not rightly capture information available on the underlying assets (mortgage delinquencies); during the crisis, prices were largely driven by the degree of liquidity available and by risk aversion.
- The representative agents model. Often it is developments in subsectors or specific institutions that threaten the stability of the entire financial system: looking at representative agents is thus not enough to monitor underlying fragilities. Moreover, the perception of counterparty risk among financial institutions is of key importance in triggering financial stress, and this will not be captured when looking at them collectively. Furthermore, the aggregation of individual decisions can lead to financial instability effects as a result of co-ordination failures; for example, when all individuals are doing what they think is the right thing on the assumption that others are doing something else (Kindleberger and Aliber, 2011).
- Non-linear dynamics, especially when correlations assumed in normal times suddenly change, or when prices overshoot and diverge from fundamentals. This, in particular, requires that analysts find new ways to elaborate extreme scenarios. To date, the practice followed de facto is mainly to derive them by scaling up linearly central, moderate scenarios. The 2007 crisis has shown that this is not enough, and that more 'outside-the-box' thinking is needed.

How will economic forecasting evolve to better deal with financial stability issues?

It is too early to identify the new forecasting techniques and needs that will emerge in response to the 2007 crisis. What is certain is that they will have to address the key objectives identified above, including better integration of the financial sector, better information for policy makers (and the public at large) on financial stability issues, and greater attention to extreme events.

First: more work

Economists' understanding of financial mechanisms needs to improve, addressing the (long list of) shortcomings identified above. An important issue is the trade-off between good fit and good theory. Of course, good fit is needed to ensure that forecasts make sense. But good fit can also be misleading if the underlying theory is based on assumptions that look right in normal times but will prove to be completely wrong in bad times: during the 'calm' years preceding the 2007 financial crisis, mainstream economists developed the concept of the 'great moderation', which turned out to be not as great as imagined. Conversely, the limited number of forecasters who pointed to potential disruptions in the global economy were ridiculed as the economy fared well during the 'good years', though their underlying theory was not so bad. In other words, the fact that one has to be able to deal with two different states of nature (financial stability versus financial instability) greatly complicates forecasters' task and estimation techniques.

Second: monitor fragilities

Forecasters need to pay more attention to the build-up of risk that could materialize and undermine financial stability. This is certainly not a new task: as highlighted in Appendix 4.3, several approaches have been followed to identify economic fragilities and the probability of crises. But this was often a macroeconomic approach, focusing mainly on the analysis of country risk and on variables such as public deficits, inflation or external positions. Moreover, such models have displayed a very limited predictive power in anticipating crises. Furthermore, the 2007 crisis has underscored the importance of the various factors that have a more microeconomic foundation: hidden high leverage in particular sectors, excessive risk-taking by some investors, complexity, and overly rapid financial innovation (imprudent financial alchemy).

Third: devote more attention to tail events

How to balance risks when making forecasts will certainly change. There was a widespread belief before 2007 that financial crises could not be avoided or pre-empted: it was impossible to monitor all the fragilities that develop at a microeconomic level; the rise in asset prices was hard to assess because of the difficulties in evaluating fundamentals; and the liberalization of markets and the conduct of sound macroeconomic policies (characterized by low and stable inflation and healthy public finances) should in itself make markets more efficient and able to self-correct. At the extreme, it was thought to be easier and more efficient to let a crisis occur and clean up the mess afterwards. This changed fundamentally in 2007, when it appeared that the cost of waiting to clean up asset bubbles after they burst can be prohibitive. Indeed, financial sector rescues led to a sharp and durable deterioration in public finances (see Appendix 5.1). Unprecedented monetary policy actions were taken by central banks in uncharted territories (direct interventions in financial markets, provision of financial intermediation services, and sharp expansion of central banks balance sheets), raising widespread concerns about their possible long-term unintended consequences. As a result, policy makers have become more interested in the prevention of low-probability, high-loss scenarios. The notion that one should try to avoid the build-up of fragilities (to 'lean against the wind') rather than clean up after the fact has gained prominence (White, 2009). Forecasters will therefore have to pay more attention to extreme events that are plausible – the tails of the distribution, or 'black swan' events (Taleb, 2007) – through the conduct of stress tests and scenario analyses. They will also have to advise policy makers on how to avoid, or at least limit, these tail events.

Fourth: simplicity

The 2007 crisis has highlighted the risk of using complex techniques that are understood only by specialized experts, so that no one can really see the full picture. It is difficult to envisage a situation where an econometrician would explain to a policy maker that, according to some kind of obscure techniques, s/he sees no threat to financial stability during the projection period. Thus one outcome of the crisis could be a decline in interest in sophisticated techniques understood only by specialists. This might lead to a greater focus on the elaboration of clear and simple economic scenarios, highlighting the associated risks and uncertainties. Forecasters will have to base their work on an encompassing, simple and understandable representation of economic reality.

Fifth: humility

A clear lesson from the crisis is that the economy is too complex to be modelled perfectly, and that forecasts cannot capture all the interactions at play. In retrospect, the 2007 financial crisis could have been identified earlier if sufficient analysis had been made of what was developing in the area of securitization. The economic community has since, and rightly, decided to address this knowledge gap but this not an easy task. Moreover, this may not be helpful in preventing the next financial crisis, which may well arise from some other hidden systemic fragility. Indeed, it might even precipitate the next crisis if it were to foster an unwarranted feeling of security. One reason for this is that financial market structures and practices change over time; and so do the kinds of events that can trigger financial instability as well as their transmission channels to the rest of the economy. In contrast, economic models are backward-looking, because they are based on past experience which has been extrapolated into the future. As a result, forecasters will always have to integrate the possibility that the 'unknown' might happen.

The surprising seizure of the interbank markets in 2007 is a very good reminder of that. The surprise was not the fact that US subprime markets were affected by the decline in house prices but that this distress affected parts of the financial system that were very distant from this specific market. This reflects 'Knightian uncertainty', when the unknowns shift from known to unknown for market participants who suddenly realize that the world is too complex for them to understand. In this view, a crisis is not a bad realization within a known probabilistic environment but rather a change in the environment itself.

Looking forward: the macrofinancial approach

One solution when moving forward is to focus on those indicators that suggest fragilities are developing somewhere in the system, even if it is impossible to know exactly where. For example, a long period of lax financial conditions can give rise to a huge increase in asset prices and credit aggregates, a surge in liabilities in a specific sector (public sector, households, firms) or a disequilibrium at the level of the economy as a whole (balance of payments and net external position). Borio and Drehmann (2009), for example, have argued that banking crises often result from the growing fragility of private-sector balance sheets during booms, sowing the seeds for the subsequent busts, and that these imbalances manifest themselves in the coexistence of rapid credit growth and asset prices. Tracking such indicators could help to inform assessments of the build-up of risks in a pre-emptive way.

A key consideration in this context is that financial conditions are mutually reinforcing on the way up: easy credit boosts output and asset prices, strengthening balance sheets and perceived asset returns, which further reinforces credit extension. And these effects can be compounded by investor optimism and pessimism, which come in waves. At some point, the reversal of such bubbles and the unwinding of excesses and imbalances can only be abrupt and severe, producing financial instability – the so-called 'Minsky moments' (Minsky, 1982). The solution is to be sufficiently alert when booms occur: instead of justifying them – for example, by arguing that there is a 'new economy' – one should be even more cautious when things appear too easy. Here, an analogy can be drawn with speed limits: if cars are allowed to drive at 200 km per hour in cities, nobody can know exactly *ex ante* where an accident will happen, but certainly more accidents will happen; and to prevent them cars should not be allowed to drive so fast. Even if the forecaster has a scenario s/he believes in as the most probable one, s/he should put greater emphasis on downside risks if s/he is observing unusual and rapid developments (for example, a surge in asset prices or in leverage). Attention should thus be focused on mounting fragilities, on the recognition that large uncertainties govern economic developments, and on acknowledging their potential feedback effects with systemic importance.

Appendix 4.2   Technical analysis

Technical analysis – otherwise known as chartism – is widely used by traders in the foreign exchange markets, as documented by Cheung and Chinn (2001). It has also long been popular in other financial markets and in commodity markets. While macroeconomic forecasters focus on the fundamentals driving these markets and on hypothetical equilibrium values, traders try to 'beat the market', or at least try not to be beaten by it, and typically have much shorter horizons. Technical analysis, rather than macroeconomic modelling, often tends to be their favourite tool. Some traders, however, use technical analysis in conjunction with fundamental analysis, doubling their positions when both sets of indicators point in the same direction.

There are several varieties of technical analysis, presented in detail by Edwards and Magee (2001):

- Charting. This involves graphing the history of prices over a period selected by the practitioner, to predict their evolution over some horizon, on the assumption that past patterns are informative. Chartists spot troughs (local minima) and peaks (local maxima), declare them to be support or resistance levels, and identify downtrends and uptrends (stringing together series of troughs or peaks) as well as formations portending market reversals (head-and-shoulders, double tops and bottoms, triple tops and bottoms, V patterns and so on). They also claim that certain round numbers are psychological barriers (say, the 100¥/US$ level), or that markets react to past developments (say, with investors willing to consolidate their positions once their earlier losses are offset by new gains). Furthermore, chartists pay close attention to traded volumes, which reveal the underlying momentum. Chartists argue that, when properly interpreted, this type of evidence helps to predict behaviour. There may be an element of self-fulfilling prophecy here, in so far as a sufficient number of traders see the same patterns at the same time, and react in accordance with chartists' expectations.
- Mechanical rules. A well-known type of rule is the filter rule or trading range break rule, which counsels the buying of an asset when it rises x per cent above its previous local minimum (or conversely for a local maximum), with x typically being chosen somewhere between 0.5 per cent and 3 per cent. Another class of rules rests on moving averages, and will advise buying when a shorter moving average (calculated, say, over five days) crosses a longer moving average (say, 20 days) from below; in other words, when the asset price is rising rapidly (and vice versa). Yet another variety are the rules using so-called Bollinger bands (usually plotted two standard deviations above and below some moving average). While mechanical rules are advertised as a way to avoid the subjectivity inherent in charting, their definition and use are in fact also very subjective.
- Waves. Some chartists proceed on the assumption that prices follow laws and go through certain phases. One such approach rests on Elliott's wave theory, dating back to the 1930s, which states that market prices (and many other phenomena) follow a repetitive rhythm of five-wave advances followed by three-wave declines, with nine

different degrees of trend ranging from a 'grand supercycle' spanning two hundred years to a 'subminuette' degree covering only a few minutes or hours.

Economists have traditionally dismissed the claims of technical analysts on the grounds that they violate the efficient market hypothesis (which in its weak form says that historical data cannot help to forecast future market developments, since this information should be already be embodied in current prices). Indeed, these approaches rely on fairly subjective assumptions and in particular the implicit view that market movements have an inherent logic, whereas they could simply reflect random walk movements.

None the less, there is abundant empirical evidence against the efficient market hypothesis, and the 2007 financial crisis has clearly underscored its shortcomings. Moreover, some technical trading rules have indeed been profitable. Compared with traditional macroeconomic models, some of the chartist approaches have the merit of taking into account real-life factors such as market conditions (the volume of order flows and very short-run volatility), information asymmetries (the whole idea, pioneered over a century by Charles Dow, being that those who know more get in and out before the others), and market psychology (thresholds and herding in particular).

To sum up, the premise of technical analysis is that the inspection of past financial data movements may reveal patterns that allow the prediction of where the financial variable is headed over the coming hours, days, weeks or even months. These methods are embraced by many traders, but economic modellers tend to shy away from or even disparage them. Indeed, the apparent success of some chartists over some past period offers no guarantee that their tools will deliver excess returns when going forward. And, last but not least, these techniques fail to provide forecasters with any economic story.

Appendix 4.3   Country risk analysis

Country risk analysis focused originally on sovereign default risk, but since then its scope has widened. Two approaches can be distinguished. The first is the assessment of a country's fundamentals, which is useful for international investors seeking to diversify their portfolio as well as for forecasters attempting to map out economies' prospects, especially over the medium and long run. The second approach is the *ex ante* evaluation of the likelihood of a structural break, such as a crisis associated with the collapse of the banking system and/or of the exchange rate. Admittedly, neither approach was very successful in predicting the 2007 financial crisis, but even so they can both be informative.

A broadening scope

Macroeconomic models are typically linear: a given exogenous increase in income, say, will boost consumption; and twice as large an increase in income will boost consumption by twice as much. Implicitly, this assumes that agents behave identically irrespective of the circumstances. In contrast, country risk analysis attempts to anticipate changes in economic regime, or at least to quantify their probability. Such breaks are likely to alter behavioural relationships.

The first of the two country risk approaches broadens the analysis of the traditional assessment of sovereign default risk to encompass the overall political, economic and financial situation of a country, including its growth prospects, the sustainability of its public finances and so on. The aim becomes less to quantify sovereign default risk *per se* – which historically has been relatively low – than to get a handle on the factors that will influence the risk/return profile of investments in the country under consideration. The focus is then very much on getting an accurate picture of the fundamentals.

The second perspective on country risk centres on the possible occurrence of crises, which can either be very sudden or drawn-out. It involves the monitoring of indicators that may signal crises ahead of time, with the aim of preventing them or minimizing their costs.

In practice, the two approaches are obviously linked. The first could be described as that followed by international rating agencies, to inform investors. This activity has taken off as countries have opened up and cross-border capital flows have grown. Official international institutions, which are mandated to safeguard global financial stability, combine the first and the second approach in a macro-prudential perspective. The succession of international financial crises (South America in the 1980s, Mexico in 1994–5, East Asia in 1997–8, Russia in 1998, Brazil in 1999, Argentina and Turkey in 2000–1, and the more recent 2007 financial crisis) has stimulated research on the prediction and prevention of crises in the face of the great volatility of capital flows.

Country risk analysis, first and foremost, concerns emerging and developing economies, where evolutions are more hectic and harder to forecast. But country risk is also relevant for advanced economies, since they also experience crises (for example, the European Monetary System shake-up in 1992–3, Japan's prolonged crisis in the 1990s, Iceland's economic meltdown in 2008, or tensions in the euro area in 2010–11).

Rating

Rating agencies (Standard & Poor's, Moody's Investors Service, Fitch Ratings and so on) actively monitor countries issuing securities. The rating takes place at several levels:

- The sovereign dollar rating measures country risk in the narrow sense and focuses on the ability of the government to service its external debt.
- The sovereign local currency rating measures the country's ability to service its local currency-denominated debt. *A priori*, it is easier to reimburse domestic debt, since the question of the availability of foreign exchange reserves does not arise, but at the same time it may be easier for a government to renege on domestic rather than on external debt.
- Rating the country's other issuers takes into account their individual situations. This is connected in some ways to sovereign risk, however, since experience shows that the failure of some large debtors (local governments, firms or banks) can turn into a systemic crisis: a banking sector crisis, for example, will have dire fiscal implications in so far as the government will have to finance the clean-up (or will at the very least see tax receipts decline as activity slumps).
- Rating ranges from the short to the long run; that is, from liquidity to solvency analysis. Indeed, investors have different horizons: for example, in 1998–9, Brazil experienced outflows of short-term capital, because of a heightened perception of exchange rate risk, but at the same time direct investment inflows continued, driven by privatization operations and attractive long-run opportunities.

In practice, and broadly speaking, rating involves analysing a country's fundamentals by looking at different risks and variables (see Table 4.3):

- Political risk: might there be a political upheaval leading to debt repudiation?
- Fiscal risk: are the public finances sound and is there room for manoeuvre if a shock hits?
- Economic risk: is growth broadly based and sustainable?
- Exchange rate risk: is the exchange rate overvalued and are foreign exchange reserves sufficient?
- Financial risk: is the financial system solid and properly supervised?
- External repayment risk: will the country be able to service its external debt?

Each of these risks is rated on the basis of quantitative indicators but also using a fair amount of qualitative judgement. The ratings are then aggregated into an overall rating, which allows the ranking of countries or issuers. While rating is partly subjective, the grades given by different agencies are usually very similar. Table 4.4 displays the scales used by the three leading agencies (taking some liberty with the exact descriptors they use so as to facilitate comparisons).

The higher the rating, the lower the interest rate the issuer can obtain. Ratings are assigned when paper is first issued, and reviewed on a regular basis: if an issuer's creditworthiness is deemed to have improved, its paper may be upgraded. And if the reverse applies, it may be downgraded. Paper that is 'investment grade' is considered to be of good quality and has a rating of Baa or higher from Moody's, a rating of BBB or higher

Table 4.3 Rating criteria

Risk type	Main criteria	Economic indicators
Political	• Conflicts with neighbours or internally • Stability of the regime • Political and social tensions, inequalities	• Demographic data • Literacy rate • Gini income distribution index
Fiscal	• Fiscal balance, taking the economic and debt situation into account • Evolution of public debt, given public sector assets, external and implicit liabilities • Debt service burden • Size and composition of revenue and expenditure • Room for manoeuvre	• Overall, structural and primary balance • Public debt (gross, net, external) • Debt service (fixed rate, variable rate, exchange rate indexed component), in percentage of GDP or of tax receipts • Tax pressure (overall, import duties) • Share of public consumption, and in particular of public sector wage bill • Share of investment spending
Economic	• Overall situation: resources, income level • Position in the cycle • Structural trends • Vulnerability to various types of shocks • Likelihood of catastrophic events (such as earthquakes)	• GDP per capita in current and PPP dollars • GDP growth, inflation, unemployment • Saving and investment rates • Degree of diversification of production and exports
Exchange rate	• Credibility/sustainability of forex policy • Forex reserves given imports and potential capital outflows • Competitiveness (price, quality, investment climate)	• Forex reserves in months of imports and as a share of short-run external liabilities • Effective exchange rate, productivity, surveys of international investors
Financial	• Central bank credibility • Monetary policy stance • Soundness of the financial system • Fragility of domestic borrowers	• Interest rates, monetary aggregates • Credit to government, to private sector • Banks' capital ratios • Share of non-performing loans
Ability to repay external debt	• Liquid forex assets • External financing needs • Prospective evolution • External liabilities: level, composition, likely evolution	• Export and import growth • Terms of trade • Current account balance • Composition of external financing (share of FDI in particular) • Gross external debt, public and private • Net external liabilities • Debt service schedule

Table 4.4   Rating scales

	Moody's	Standard & Poor's	Fitch
Long-term ratings			
Investment grade			
Superior/Highest quality	Aaa	AAA	AAA
Excellent/Very high quality	Aa1, Aa2, Aa3	AA+, AA, AA–	AA+, AA, AA–
Good/High quality	A1, A2, A3	A+, A, A–	A+, A, A–
Adequate/Good quality	Baa1, Baa2, Baa3	BBB+, BBB, BBB–	BBB+, BBB, BBB–
Non-investment grade			
Maybe adequate/ Speculative	Ba1, Ba2, Ba3	BB+, BB, BB–	BB+, BB, BB–
Vulnerable/Highly speculative	B1, B2, B3	B+, B, B–, CCC+, CCC, CCC–	B+, B, B–
Extremely vulnerable/ High default risk	Caa1, Caa2, Caa3	C	CCC, CC, C
Past due payment on interest		CI	
Under regulatory supervision		R	
Has selectively defaulted on some obligations	Ca	SD	
Default	C	D	D
Not publicly rated	D	NR	NR
Short-term ratings			High: F1+, F1
	Superior: P-1	Strong: A-1	Good: F2
	Strong: P-2	Satisfactory: A-2	Fair: F3
	Acceptable: P-3	Adequate: A-3	Speculative: B
	Not prime: NP	Speculative: B	High default: C
		Doubtful: C	Partial default: RD
		Default: D	Default: D

Sources: Moody's, Standard & Poor's, Fitch.

from Standard & Poor's, or both. Paper with lower ratings – or no ratings at all – is termed 'non-investment' or 'speculative' grade (and referred to more colloquially as 'junk'). Many institutional investors have policies that require them to limit their investments to investment-grade issues.

In the wake of the Asian crisis of the late 1990s, rating agencies were denounced for not having predicted the problems they were supposed to warn against, and for amplifying the pain through belated and hasty downgrades. Accusations of myopia and pro-cyclicality resurfaced with a vengeance in the context of the 2007 financial crisis. Rating agencies have been criticized for not foreseeing defaults or for failing to voice more forceful warnings. It has also been argued that they contributed to bringing about the crisis, in so far as their lack of foresight and/or disclosure fuelled unwarranted optimism, and then to worsening the crisis, by lowering their ratings once it had begun. Furthermore, the potential for conflicts of interest that lies at the heart of their business model has been questioned: rating agencies are typically paid by the borrowers for the rating and they often also play an advisory role in which they suggest how to organize securities issues in ways that minimize perceived risk (Brunnermeier, 2009).

Accordingly, a number of reforms have been proposed (Katz *et al.*, 2009). Rating agencies have been called upon to be more transparent about their methodologies and assessments. There has been pressure to regulate and oversee them more strictly, to encourage competition in a sector that is overly dominated by three large firms, and to reduce the reliance of financial regulation on the agencies' ratings so as to encourage investors to perform their own due diligence. The International Organization of Securities Commissions (IOSCO) revised the Code of Conduct for credit rating agencies in 2008, with measures that are meant *inter alia* to strengthen the quality of the rating process, to ensure subsequent monitoring and timeliness of ratings, to prohibit analysts' involvement in the design of structured securities, to differentiate structured finance ratings from others, and to increase public disclosure. Such measures are in the process of being incorporated into US and EU regulations.

Anticipating crises

Though related to traditional country risk analysis, the second approach is less about characterizing the fundamentals than about identifying specific vulnerabilities so as to quantify the probability of a crisis (the likelihood of a favourable regime change tends to get less attention). This is a delicate exercise, as the nature and mechanisms of crises vary greatly across countries and over time, as do the channels of cross-border crisis contagion.

There are at least four different types of crises:

- Traditional sovereign default crises, when a government fails to repay according to schedule. This has been avoided in a number of cases through preventive rescheduling in the Paris Club (for public-sector creditors) or in the London Club (for bank claims).
- Foreign exchange crises, often following the recognition that a country will be unable to service its external debt or to withstand capital outflows. Such crises can break out very suddenly, though they may result from imbalances that have been building up for years.
- Collapses of domestic financial institutions causing systemic, economy-wide crises. Such crises may then last for several years.
- Bond market crises, taking the form of soaring spreads (the latter being defined as the difference in yield compared with US Treasury paper).

The mechanisms producing a crisis are also varied. There are three generations of explanations:

- Balance of payments and thus foreign exchange crises *à la* Krugman (1979): these stem from accumulated imbalances or ill-conceived policies; for example, a fiscal stance that ultimately turns out to be too loose for the exchange rate peg to hold. A number of such crises took place in Latin America in the 1980s.

- Second-generation crises, as described by Obstfeld (1994), can erupt because agents' expectations interact with policy makers' behaviour to become self-fulfilling even when the fundamentals are not intrinsically that weak. Multiple equilibria arise: even in the absence of imbalances *ex ante*, the exchange rate may be attacked if market participants believe that to defend it the authorities will raise interest rates so much that the fundamentals will deteriorate, leading policy makers to abandon the peg; or market participants may simply expect that the authorities will not want to resist attacks in the first place, knowing that ultimately they will be defeated, so the authorities give in immediately. This framework has been used to analyse the speculative attacks on the European Monetary System (EMS) in the early 1990s.
- Third-generation crises, as characterized by Corsetti *et al.* (1999), stem from moral hazard problems: imbalances build up in the form of financial or real estate market bubbles because agents believe, rightly or wrongly, that they will be bailed out by the public sector if things go amiss. The implicit guarantees actually or seemingly offered by national governments or international financial institutions allow for reckless overinvestment and are therefore at the root of the crisis. This model has been used to explain the 1997–8 Asian crises, which were not preceded by large fiscal deficits or poor growth but were related to 'crony capitalism' – namely, the intermingling of interests among financial institutions, political leaders and corporate elites that was seen in the region. This also applies to some extent to the 2007 financial crisis.

As the emerging market upheavals of the late 1990s and the more recent global recession have illustrated, crises can also be triggered by cross-border contagion rather than by the revelation of domestic weaknesses. Innocent, or at least distant, bystanders can thus be hit by what is happening in another part of the world, as was Brazil in 1998 by the Russian crisis, and many countries were by the US financial crisis in 2007. Crisis spillovers occur through a variety of partly interrelated channels:

- Real sector channels: when two countries trade between themselves or compete in the same third markets, an exchange rate crisis-cum-depreciation in one country deteriorates the other's competitiveness, and both may end up with depreciated currencies. Other types of real links, notably foreign direct investment (FDI), may also play a role in contagion.
- Financial market channels: a crisis in one country may heighten risk aversion in financial markets at large and widen bond spreads, hurting all other borrowers and in particular those with large exposures to risk or that were already deemed (rightly or wrongly) to be vulnerable beforehand.
- Psychological channels: a crisis in one country may cause investors to panic and to leave neighbouring countries, in the belief – especially when information on fundamentals is scarce – that they might suffer from an identical problem or because, historically, crises in countries in that region have been correlated.
- Portfolio management channels: open-ended mutual funds foreseeing redemptions after a shock in one country need to raise cash and may sell assets in other countries.

Attempting to foretell crises thus requires to identify potential weaknesses in the fundamentals but also factors that make the economy vulnerable to contagion. A large set of indicators thus needs to be monitored, including most of those listed in Table 4.3. They can serve to underpin a qualitative diagnosis, not unlike the situation in traditional country risk analysis; or a more quantitative approach, by finding coincident or advance crisis indicators or even by constructing a probabilistic crisis signal.

In the latter case, consider a binary set-up: let $Y = 0$ if there is no crisis and $Y = 1$ in the event of a crisis, and suppose that the vulnerability indicators X are distributed normally (probit model) or logistically (logit model). The associated probabilities can be derived based on a panel of countries that have experienced crises. In the logit case:

$$P \equiv P\,(Y = 1) = 1\,/\,[1 + e^{-(\alpha + \beta X)}]$$

This can be estimated in the following form:

$$log\ P/(1 - P) = \alpha + \beta X$$

One challenge here is to define the crisis state empirically. Some studies, for example, consider that an exchange rate movement greater than 25 per cent qualifies. But any such definition is somewhat arbitrary. Moreover, some types of crises, notably banking crises, are difficult to date. In fact, given the relatively limited number of crisis episodes in the historical data, specification searches through the large number of potential right-hand-side variables may well be spuriously effective in predicting past crises (Berg and Patillo, 1999), though even *ex post* it turns out to be more difficult to explain the relative severity of crises than their incidence (Rose and Spiegel, 2009).

The key test, however, is not the ability to fit a set of observations after the fact, but the prediction of future crises. In other words, models need to be judged on their out-of-sample performance. In this regard, while they can help to indicate vulnerability to crisis, the predictive power of even the best models remains limited. In part, this may be a result of endogeneity of policy to the risk of crisis, in so far as country authorities or creditors react to advance crisis signals: an initially successful early warning system might thus cease to work following publication. But, to a large extent, the reason lies in the inherent volatility of capital flows and in the unpredictability of political U-turns.

Chapter 5

Public Finances

Contents

> *A good grasp of the public finance prospects is central to both forecasting and policy advice. Over short- to medium-run horizons, both the influence of the business cycle on public finance outcomes and the effects of fiscal developments on economic activity must be acknowledged, as demonstrated by the 2007 financial crisis and the Great Recession that followed. In the longer run, trend changes, such as the spending pressures from an ageing population, take centre stage. Specific expertise is often required to forecast fiscal developments, including access to fiscal databases, the construction of specialized models, and dedicated human resources. For an overall assessment of fiscal policy, analytical concepts such as structural deficits, tax gaps and others are needed, though they must be used with caution.*

Public finance forecasting is an essential part of government activity. Over time, budgetary institutions have become more complex and fiscal forecasting techniques more sophisticated. These days, public finance projections are made not just by national governments but also by private sector economists, international organizations and central banks.

Fiscal forecasting can be approached from various perspectives. Some take a 'macroeconomic view' (section 5.1): they look at the overall impact of economic conditions on public accounts – and vice versa, the effect of fiscal policy on activity. By contrast, governments need both general and comprehensive information: for practical and policy reasons, they must explore the details of all tax revenues and measures. This is the 'detailed approach' (section 5.2).

All stakeholders may be interested in assessing long-term fiscal trends, which are shaped, among others, by demographic developments (section 5.3).

Deficit and debt forecasts are paid a great deal of attention by policy makers and observers. However, to make sense of these forecasts, it is useful to ask some key questions, such as: What is a result of government decisions (as opposed to exogenous economic shocks)? Are current policies sustainable (or will some policy adjustments be required in the future)? To analyse such questions, economists have developed several concepts and indicators, such as the structural deficit, which are discussed in section 5.4.

Finally, it is worth asking how accurate budget forecasts are, especially in the wake of the Great Recession (section 5.5). While forecasting accuracy as a whole is dealt with in Chapter 7, some specific fiscal aspects are discussed in this chapter.

5.1 The macroeconomic view

The cornerstone of public finance forecasting is its interrelationship with macroeconomic forecasting:

- The economic scenario is a key input in projecting public receipts and outlays.
- In return, the aggregate fiscal stance affects economic activity.

Recent economic history has underscored how crucial both channels are. With the 2008–9 Great Recession, budget deficits ballooned as sagging economies sapped tax revenues and stimulated spending. This illustrates the first channel: economic growth drives budgetary outcomes. But budget deficits in turn helped to mitigate the recession. This happened through both the so-called 'automatic stabilizers' and discretionary fiscal support, reflecting the effects of fiscal developments on economic activity.

Acknowledging both channels is central because of the sheer size of governments in our economies. The general government sector – encompassing central government but also local governments and social security – spends on average more than 40 per cent of GDP in OECD economies.

The 'macroeconomic view' of public finance centres on the aggregate link between the budget and the overall economic forecast. This is not to say that the so-called 'detailed view', taken up in the next section, disregards the connection. But a key characteristic of the macroeconomic view of fiscal forecasting focuses on the interrelationship with the economy and does not go much beyond that: in other words, it does not delve into the fine detail of the budget.

For some purposes, a very streamlined aggregate framework, as described in Box 5.1, may suffice. This may be the case for long-run forecasts (see section 5.3). Such a 'top down' approach may also be the only option when access to the relevant disaggregated budget information is limited.

5.2 The detailed approach

5.2.1 Overview

The detailed approach is followed when one needs to go beyond the bottom line. This is the case for governments. When preparing budget bills, they need to project fiscal developments by subsector and assess any measure under consideration. They are also expected to monitor closely fiscal accounts and adjust both forecasts and possibly policies on an ongoing basis. Other institutions may also thoroughly review fiscal developments, including parliaments, central

---

Box 5.1   The macro-fiscal framework: a starter

For a quick assessment of the budgetary outlook one can start with the following:

$$R_t = R_t(GDP_t, Exo_t, T) \tag{5.1}$$

$$S_t = S_t(Exo_t, T) \tag{5.2}$$

$$GDP_t = GDP_t(GDP_{t-1}, S_t - R_t) \tag{5.3}$$

where R is public revenues, S public spending (hence $S - R$ is the deficit), T a time trend, and Exo budget information, including major new measures.

This is a rather overly simplified framework, yet not that far from what economists use as a quick fix. Of course, it avoids many real-life complications: for example, GDP is a poor proxy of many tax bases; spending as well as revenues may depend on growth and other macroeconomic variables; and the deficit may be a misguided measure of the effect of the budget on growth.

Even so, these three equations capture the core of the macro-fiscal nexus: revenues are highly dependent on growth, public spending is more of an exogenous decision from policy makers, and public deficits may in normal circumstances support growth, at least in the short run. The framework makes it clear that the macroeconomic and fiscal scenarios are interlinked: the consistency of the projections has to be reached by means of an iterative process.

---

banks, international organizations or specialized independent institutions (such as the fiscal councils that have been set up in various OECD countries to monitor the implementation of fiscal policy).

This is a 'bottom-up' approach. Forecasts for each individual revenue and expenditure component are produced and then summed to make aggregate revenue and spending. This requires large resources, good access to information and adequate co-ordination.

The forecasting process is shown in Figure 5.1.

A separate, specialized model is used for each main tax or spending category. In the USA, the Congressional Budget Office (CBO) draws on many such models to produce simulations and forecasts. For example, the projection for personal income tax receipts rests on an analysis of receipts by groups of households (groups are based on criteria such as income bracket, number of children and so on). The idea is to dig as deep as is needed to produce plausible results for each of the specialized models.

Figure 5.1   Forecasting public finances and the macroeconomy

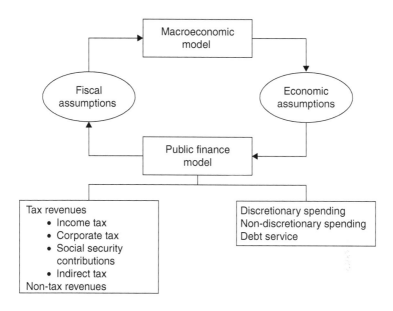

Analysts will typically distinguish between the components of the budget that are directly affected by the economic cycle and others that are not:

- The economic cycle affects most tax revenues and some spending items, such as public debt service (which varies with interest rates) or transfers to the unemployed;
- A sizeable share of spending is not a direct function of the economic cycle but corresponds to nominal appropriations (voted into being by parliament or introduced by decree by the government). Similarly, sales of public assets or transfers from public corporations to the government do not move automatically with the economic cycle. For these discretionary elements, the forecast rests on collecting relevant information, taking into account the lag between the decision and actual outlays or receipts.[1]

The disaggregated results are then assembled to obtain summary fiscal outcomes. Both their consistency and macroeconomic impact can be assessed.

---

[1] This is a standard distinction but it is somewhat simplistic. One could argue that no budget item is completely unrelated to the business cycle: in a cyclical upturn, receipts are abundant and control over spending tends to loosen even as the appetite of spending ministries or agencies sharpens; conversely, lean times lead to tighter spending controls and discretionary tax measures to offset the cyclical tax shortfall. Even within the horizon of the fiscal year, the provisions voted by parliament may be overtaken by supplemental budgets.

This in turn generates new economic assumptions, which can be reinserted into the specialized models to produce a second round of fiscal forecasts. This iterative process continues until some convergence is achieved. In this way, the need to delve into the details of the fiscal outlook can be reconciled, to some extent, with general macroeconomic consistency.[2]

5.2.2 Which approach to follow?

The main advantage of the detailed approach is to provide a full picture of public finance developments. Details are necessary for those involved in the budgetary process: to defend or vote on a budget bill, one should know what the appropriations are for, where the revenues stem from, and the changes that policies entail. But getting into the details also brings some advantages from a forecasting perspective. To name a few:

- Greater precision as to the link between tax receipts and the economic cycle. Rather than relying on aggregate rules of thumb (as suggested in Box 5.1), one will relate each revenue category to its tax base, as detailed in section 5.2.3.
- A better evaluation of the size and impact of new policy measures (or other environmental changes).
- More effective use of the incoming intra-annual data to monitor and update the initial forecasts. Unexpected developments (for example, shifts in interest rates that weigh on debt service) may thus easily be taken on board to adjust forecasts on an ongoing basis.

The detailed approach has limits, however. Two of them stand out. First, it requires good access to reliable information and sizeable resources (exactly how much depends on the degree of detail of the approach). Second, it is of utmost importance to supplement the bottom-up procedure with some kind of top-down assessment.

At the minimum, one should examine the plausibility of summary fiscal indicators. For example, if GDP growth exceeds its potential rate, the fiscal balance, while controlling for any new measures, would be expected to improve. Similarly, a line-by-line calculation adding up to a jump in the forecast ratio of government revenue to GDP might appear rather implausible (if no substantial tax policy changes are envisaged).

In sum, both approaches need to be pursued in parallel, with the aim of ensuring consistency. In the USA, for example, budget forecasting by the Office of Management and Budget (OMB) and the CBO (see Appendix 8.1) involves

---

[2] Practical resource constraints limit the number of feasible iterations, implying that a discrepancy may exist between the aggregation of the specialized models and the global economic scenario.

line-by-line as well as global forecasts, and this process also applies in most
other countries.

5.2.3 Forecasting tax receipts

Forecasters usually proceed tax by tax. More attention is paid to those taxes
that bring in the most revenue: direct taxes (personal and corporate income
taxes), indirect taxes (notably the Value Added Tax (VAT) and import taxes)
and social contributions. In some cases, a more disaggregated approach can be
useful. For example, it may help to forecast profits and tax receipts for specific
enterprises or sectors (say, the oil sector in the UK or in Norway).

Changes in revenues can reflect changes in the tax base or the tax system (see
Figure 5.2).[3] Both economic developments (affecting the tax base) and policy
changes (new measures) are important. Here, starting from Year 0, we first have
growth in the tax base and a tax hike (Year 1), then growth without any new
measures (Year 2), and finally a slowdown in growth combined with a tax cut
(Year 3), causing a fairly dramatic drop in tax revenues.

For each tax, a standard framework is then:

$$\Delta R_t = \beta\, \Delta B_t + NM_t \tag{5.4}$$

where R is revenue, B the base and NM the impact of new revenue measures
(R and B are usually in logs, so the equation is in difference form). The parameter β is the elasticity of revenue R to its base B.

Figure 5.2 Tax receipts: the effects of spontaneous developments and new measures

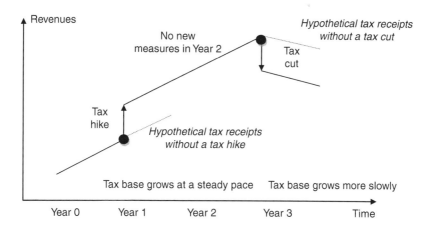

---

[3] Changes in compliance also affect tax receipts. To keep matters simple, we leave this
issue aside in what follows.

The forecasting procedure involves two steps:

- The forecaster starts by predicting receipts on an unchanged legislative basis. This is the first term in the right-hand side of Equation (5.4). It depends on the evolution of the tax base in the absence of any legislative changes (therefore, reflecting mainly the economic environment) and the elasticity.
- Then the forecaster adds his/her best estimate of the impact of any new measures. This is the second term in the right-hand side of the equation. The latter information may or may not be easily available (more below on this).

To forecast receipts using this framework requires an examination of the tax base B, the elasticity β, and the new measures NM.

Tax bases

The legally-defined tax base rarely if ever coincides with a macroeconomic aggregate. A proxy for the tax base therefore has to be used, in the form of an economic base. The latter may depend on activity and its components, inflation (since tax bases are usually nominal), asset prices and the like – both current values and past ones, given taxation lags. For example, household income will be the economic base from which to infer the personal income tax base and receipts, private consumption underlies indirect taxes, and so on.

The approximation of the tax base may not be that good. Tax bases and macroeconomic aggregates may diverge for a variety of reasons: for example, gross private compensation will typically be chosen as the base for social security contributions but that leaves out the self-employed, whose revenues are typically linked less directly to that base. Other issues, such as cross-tax elasticities and lags between macroeconomic developments and actual tax payments also come into play to blur the picture.

The base of the corporate income tax is particularly hard to forecast. Indeed, taxable profits differ from profits as captured in the national accounts, because of tax exemptions, the treatment of provisions and derogatory tax regimes. Moreover, past losses can often be carried forward and deducted from current profits, which can lead to over-projecting tax receipts when activity picks up.

Elasticities

Conceptually, tax elasticities can be obtained in three ways:

- A crude but plausible assumption can be used; for example, it can be decided to set $\beta = 1$. Assuming unitary elasticity means that tax receipts are proportional to the tax base, which may be an acceptable proxy in a number of situations, most obviously for taxes that are proportional by nature, such as social security contributions (at least between lower and upper limits on contributions).
- The detailed legal rules can be examined to try to derive an average elasticity. The OECD follows this route to calculate elasticities of personal income tax

and social security contributions (Girouard and André, 2005): they carry out detailed calculations to take into account marginal tax rates, the distribution of households across income brackets and so on.

- An empirical method can be estimated to calculate β retrospectively using Equation (5.4). This, however, requires a good knowledge of the effects of past measures. In practice, even government experts may find it hard to identify these measures, and estimation of their impacts may be even more challenging. But when it can be used, this method has the added benefit that one can see whether the elasticity was more or less constant in the past, or at least over the most recent subperiod. In that case, analysts may use an average of past elasticities to forecast with some confidence.

Indeed, tax elasticities are likely to be unstable over the cycle. During upturns, unexpected windfall revenues tend to boost receipts beyond what is suggested by standard models, assuming fixed elasticities. Conversely, during downturns, receipts typically plunge even more rapidly than might be assumed based on historical patterns. In other words, elasticities tend to be 'pro-cyclical'. This was apparent in recent years, first in the boom phase (say, in 2004–7), and then in the 2008–9 Great Recession.

Research suggests that these 'missing links' between fiscal receipts and economic growth are partly explained by significant and positive effects of asset prices on revenues (Swiston *et al.*, 2007; Morris and Schuknecht, 2007). Asset prices seem to be most relevant for corporate taxes as well as household income taxes and transaction taxes. Other factors such as a changing composition of aggregate demand or shifts in the distribution of incomes across households may contribute to pro-cyclical elasticities. Also, taking for example personal income tax, which often has a progressive structure, the elasticity is much higher if the base increases because of a rise in income per tax return than if it increases because of a greater number of individual returns. All these features point to the need for a more sophisticated approach encapsulating cyclically-driven changes in elasticities.

New measures

This is a crucial area from a policy perspective. Reliable estimates of the costs and benefits of tax measures are central to the public debate *ex ante* (when proposals are discussed before being adopted) as well as *ex post* (when effects of the measures may be analysed and further changes contemplated). Good estimates of the impact of sizeable tax measures are, of course, also needed by forecasters.

Estimating the costs/savings associated with new measures necessitates large resources, including detailed databases, specific tools and expertise. These resources are typically only found in governmental administrations or highly specialized bodies, such as the Congressional Budget Office (CBO) in the USA, the Institute for Fiscal Studies (IFS) in the UK or the Central Planning Bureau (CPB) in the Netherlands (see Appendix 8.1). Governments and these entities publish information on cost estimates, albeit with more-or-less in-depth explanations. Typically, the outside forecaster has little choice but to rely on these estimates.

When based on adequate data and done properly, costs/savings estimates for new measures may be fairly precise. However, this holds only for their direct impact, barring behavioural responses. Tax changes modify incentives and therefore behaviour so that the direct impact may be quite different from the full-equilibrium effect (Laffer-curve effects are a famous example). Timing considerations may complicate things further as behaviour changes only gradually. Hence, one must distinguish short- and long-run responses. Even *ex post* – say, several years down the road – it often remains difficult to disentangle the contribution of a given policy measure (including the behavioural responses) from other factors.

One particular category of fiscal measures refers to those of a temporary nature. There is no unique definition for these. Loosely defined, they are decisions that change revenues in the short run without creating a permanent basis of higher revenues. Such measures may be widespread, especially when governments pressed to meet budget objectives turn to various 'gimmicks' through one-off factors or creative accounting (Koen and van den Noord, 2005). Box 5.2 provides some examples.

Box 5.2   Temporary fiscal measures

The identification of temporary fiscal measures is a delicate task. This is a grey area with no single operational definition of what can be classified as a 'temporary' or 'one-off' factor. As a rule they are measures that have an effect on the budget balance or debt for a limited period (say, the current year or no more than a few years). Often, they actually do not increase the government's net worth from an intertemporal perspective.

Such measures pertain mainly to public revenues rather than spending. Examples abound: privatization or sales of gold or other assets (such as buildings) lower the level of gross debt with no impact on the deficit (as measured in the national accounts). Other measures may modify the deficit; for example, the acceleration of tax intake, tax amnesties, securitization of tax arrears (or future tax receipts), or sales of mobile phone licences.

Of a somewhat different inspiration were policies in response to the economic and financial crisis in 2008–9. These included two major blocks, both of a temporary nature: first, measures to rescue banks and other financial institutions in distress (see Appendix 5.1); and second, fiscal stimuli to limit the impact of severe financial disruptions on aggregate demand (see Appendix 5.2).

5.2.4 Debt service

Debt service in some cases represents a sizeable share of total public expenditure. Here, a bottom-up approach is typically followed by national governments. This hinges on the intimate knowledge and projection of several components:

- the cost and maturity of the various components of the existing stock of public debt;
- the borrowing schedule for the projected period. This adds the renewal of emissions expiring during that period to additional financing needs for the current year. For the latter, cash-based projections (rather than national accounts on an accrual basis) are relevant, and 'below-the-line' items (such as privatization receipts) that modify the financing requirements need to be taken on board; and
- (government bond) interest rates.

One may then calculate debt service in a detailed manner, bond issue by bond issue. For outside forecasters, less disaggregated approaches based on similar principles may be used (see Box 5.3).

5.2.5 Non-discretionary public spending

Some public spending items, referred to as non-discretionary (or mandatory), are quite sensitive to the cycle. The most prominent examples are unemployment benefits. These items are forecast in relation to the cycle as:

$$S_t = F_t (C_y, Exo, T) \qquad (5.7)$$

where S_t stands for spending on these items, C_y is an indicator of the cycle (say, unemployment), and *Exo* and *T* are as above.

In practice, spending is decomposed by category and the effect of the cycle for each category is estimated separately, looking at their historical elasticity with respect to the cycle and at possible trends. This sort of calculation requires analysts to distinguish clearly what is cyclical (such as unemployment benefits or spending explicitly indexed on inflation) from what is politically decided (say, public works expenditure), what depends on administrative constraints (say, rules forbidding some levels of government from borrowing) and what relates to trends (say, the underlying drift in pensions or health care spending). To enhance the accuracy of the forecast, it will often be useful to take into account more detailed information on demographics (age cohorts and mortality, for example) or social behaviour (divorce rates, say) in the case of social transfer outlays.

As for tax receipts, it is possible first to estimate what the spontaneous change in spending might be, assuming no new measures, and then to add on an estimate for the impact of the latter.

Box 5.3   Projecting debt service

To compute interest payments (IP_t in period t) in a simple formal framework, one may write:

$$IP_t = \Sigma_e \left(\alpha_{e,t} IP_{e,t-1} + r_{e,t} B_{e,t} \right) \tag{5.5}$$

where:

- e is the type of bond: it can be short- or longer-term, at a fixed or at a variable rate, in domestic or in foreign currency (in which case an exchange rate assumption needs to be made) and so on. Depending on the type of bond, the degree of inertia of interest payments, captured by the coefficient $\alpha_{e,t}$, will vary.
- $IP_{e,t}$ stands for the interest payments made on e bonds during period t.
- $r_{e,t}$ is the expected interest rate on e bonds for period t. The assumption used is often a simple one, such as to freeze interest rates at some recent level, though more subtle approaches are possible (see Chapter 4). Future interest rates may, of course, be affected by the evolution of the fiscal position itself.
- $B_{e,t}$ is the borrowing requirement for period t to be covered by issues of e bonds. This borrowing requirement depends on the term structure of the public debt. It is also affected by 'below-the-line' privatization operations, for example, which are not reflected in the national accounts measure of the fiscal balance but which reduce the need for new borrowing.

This approach requires less detailed information on the structure of public debt, especially if some simplifying assumptions are introduced. For example, it may be assumed that $\alpha_{e,t} = \alpha_{e,t-1}$, with $\alpha_{e,t-1}$ computed using Equation (5.5) and actual observations for period $t - 1$. It is also possible to aggregate bonds into a small number of categories – say, short-term fixed-rate bonds; long-term fixed-rate bonds; and variable-rate bonds. Suppose, for example, that public debt D is financed exclusively by fixed-rate 10-year bonds and has a homogeneous age structure (with one tenth arriving at maturity every year), and that the budget is balanced. Then $IP_t = IP_{t-1} + 0.1 \, (r_{t,10} - r_{t-10,10}) D_{t-1}$, where $r_{x,10}$ stands for the interest rate in period x on 10-year fixed-rate bonds issued in that period.

Finally, a fully streamlined approach is simply:

$$IP_t = \alpha_t IP_{t-1} + r_t B_t \tag{5.6}$$

where α_t measures debt service inertia for the whole stock and r_t is the average interest rate on new borrowing.

Over the longer run, the exercise becomes trickier. One might want to extrapolate recent trends, or to assume that the rules or objectives spelt out by governments will be adhered to (for example, that a government will indeed be able to contain spending growth at the announced rate), provided they are sufficiently credible. In the absence of such information, a crude method is to endogenize public spending using some very simple rules of thumb, such as a constant ratio of public expenditure to GDP, or estimating the demand for public goods and services as a function of income levels.

The same holds for the link between unemployment outlays and the cycle, which depends on the share of the unemployment benefit recipients in total unemployment and on the effectiveness of labour market policies: for example, the cyclical component of unemployment spending may be underestimated if costly public employment programmes are put in place to stem the rise in unemployment. This is discussed in more detail by Bouthevillain *et al.* (2001), who also present an even more refined method used by the experts of the Eurosystem to better capture the impact on the budget of changes in the composition of aggregate demand and in the distribution of income.

5.3 Long-run fiscal trends

The above methods are used mainly for short- and medium-run forecasts, although they are sometimes also applied over longer periods; for example by the CBO in the USA. But a different approach is usually followed for long-run projections. Less attention is then paid to the decomposition between various types of taxes. Rather, a broad-brush assumption is imposed, such as a one-to-one relationship between GDP and government revenue, or a trend rate of increase in the ratio of government revenue to GDP is assumed if warranted (in the case of developing countries, for example).

In contrast, more attention is paid to spending trends, and in particular to demographic influences on these. In this context, spending tends to be decomposed into three categories:

- Debt service, which is influenced by the projected evolution of debt and interest rates.
- Spending that is not related directly to demographic determinants. This component is often assumed to be stable in real terms, or to rise at some constant rate, or to remain constant as a share of GDP. Which assumption is most pertinent depends, for example, on what can plausibly be assumed about employment and wages in the public sector.
- Spending that is related directly to demographic developments, such as spending on child benefits, education, pensions and so on. For each of these

categories of spending, calculations are carried out separately, taking into account the number of people concerned (which depends on demographics in the narrow sense, but also on the generosity of benefits and on social trends, such as increasing female participation in the labour force or shifts in the effective retirement age), and spending per head (which changes as entitlements evolve, but is sometimes simply extrapolated from past trends).

The spirit here is not to aim for some illusory projection accuracy, but rather to highlight likely trends that call for immediate preventive action. For example, the CBO regularly publishes 75-year projections of the US Social Security programme's finances (see Table 5.1). While currently the revenues of the programme exceed its outlays, CBO projects a significant increase in expenditure with the retirement of the 'baby boom' generation and rising longevity. The financing gap hovers around 1 per cent of GDP in the long run.

The CBO goes a step further by providing ranges of possible outcomes. This is important, because long-term projections are indeed uncertain and this uncertainty may be a convenient pretext for inaction in public debate. The CBO concludes that a significant long-term financing problem is highly probable in the absence of legislative changes.

Another important example relates to public health expenditure, which absorbs a rising share of national income across OECD countries. In this case, assumptions are made about:

- The elasticity of health spending to GDP, which tends to exceed 1, but with a complicated lag structure because the relation between demand and supply is mediated by the government and insurance providers.
- The price elasticity of demand for health, where it is useful to distinguish between those items that are reimbursed to some extent and those that are paid for in full by patients; again, there are lags.
- The changes in the structure of the market for health care: the evolution of the share of publicly-financed care in total care, the introduction of new management techniques, the substitution between inpatient hospital care and outpatient medical care and so on.

Forecasting health spending over such long periods is, of course, hazardous. One plausibility check is to compare the results derived through this macroeconomic approach with the aggregation of more microeconomic projections of spending on various types of care by sectoral experts. Yet another benchmark might be some normative notion of the evolution of health spending per capita which society is assumed to be ready to pay for.

Table 5.1   The CBO's long-term projections for US Social Security*

Large, albeit uncertain, financing pressures on US Social Security are expected in the long run

	Actual 2008	In 25 years 2033	In 50 years 2058	In 75 years 2083
Revenues	4.8	4.9	4.9	5.0
Outlays	4.4	6.1	5.8	6.2
Surplus or deficit (–)	0.5	1.2	–0.9	–1.3
Surplus or deficit: 80% range of uncertainty**	0.5	–2.0 to –0.6	–2.2 to –0.1	–3.2 to –0.3

*In percent of GDP.
**The actual value will fall within the range with an 80 per cent probability.
Source: CBO (2009a).

5.4   Fiscal policy analysis

To make sense of public finance forecasts requires going one step further and relying more explicitly on an analytical view. After all, fiscal forecasting is useful in so far as it helps to frame budget discussions and policy choices. This means focusing on key questions, including (Blanchard, 1990):

Question 1 (Q1):   To what extent are budget outcomes (present and forecast) affected by macroeconomic developments?

Question 2 (Q2):   What is the discretionary orientation of fiscal policy? Does the government spend money to sustain activity, or does it take steps to improve the fiscal outlook?

Question 3 (Q3):   What is the impact of fiscal policy on the economy? (Through its effect on demand and through relative prices, and hence the allocation of resources.)

Question 4 (Q4):   Are current fiscal arrangements sustainable over the long term? Or will the governments have to increase taxes, cut spending or even monetize or repudiate debt at some point?

These are crucial, interrelated and yet different questions. To address them, economists have developed several concepts and indicators, most of which rely on forecasts (or by-products of forecasts). The focus here is, first, on the structural deficit, then on sustainability analysis. Along the way some light is shed on how (partial) answers can be provided to questions 1 to 4.

5.4.1   The structural balance

In buoyant times, when GDP growth exceeds its potential rate, tax receipts tend to be abundant and some categories of public spending tend to slow, so that the 'headline' fiscal balance improves markedly. The converse holds during downturns, when tax receipts fall short and some spending rises. These changes in budgetary outcomes caused by the business cycle are viewed as being 'automatic fiscal stabilization', which helps to smooth output even in the absence of any discretionary government action.

Hence it is sensible to decompose the fiscal balance into a cyclical and an underlying, or structural, component. The structural deficit gives an answer to Q1: it indicates where the deficit would be if the economy was at mid-cycle (or, in other words, if the economic environment was neutral and the economy operating at 'normal' levels of capacity utilization – with GDP coinciding with potential output). As illustrated in Figure 5.3, headline and structural balances at times send quite different messages.

Structural balances are frequently estimated and published by finance ministries, central banks and international organizations, including the European Commission, the OECD and the IMF. Underscoring the importance of this concept, the interpretation of the European Stability and Growth Pact was amended in 2002–3, to shift the emphasis from the headline balance to the underlying position.

Estimating structural deficits requires the forecaster to remove the cyclical components of revenues and expenditures. In practice, this means using methods that are similar to those used for forecasting fiscal flows and their responses

Figure 5.3   Headline and structural fiscal balance for the OECD region*
Structural and headline balances differ, notably at peaks and troughs of the cycle

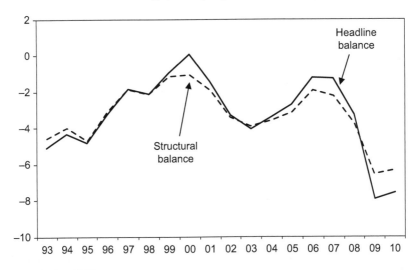

*In percentages of GDP.
Source: OECD Economic Outlook, December 2010.

to economic developments (see section 5.2). The basic technicalities are summarized in Box 5.4.

Using structural deficits: strengths and limitations

As a policy indicator, the structural deficit has two strengths. First, by purging the deficit from business cycle effects, it is indeed better than the headline deficit for assessing the overall stance of fiscal policy. Second, it remains simple enough to be appropriated in policy debates and communicated to policy makers. These two reasons explain both its usefulness and its popularity.

However, a number of caveats ought to be highlighted, related to estimation as well as conceptual issues. Given the wide use of the notion, it is important to keep these limitations in mind:

(i) Estimation problems. Measures of the structural deficit are rather uncertain. One reason is the uncertainty surrounding the output gap itself. Indeed, the observed proclivity of the fiscal authorities to adopt overly optimistic estimates of potential output makes the underlying fiscal situation look stronger than it really is. Another reason is the uncertainty surrounding the elasticities. As was clear from Section 5.2, elasticities are both hard to capture and liable to instability over the cycle.

In practice, this means that several variants may be tried out, based on more-or-less rosy assumptions about potential output and elasticities. Also, measures of the *change* in the structural deficit are usually considered to be more robust, as they rely only on changes in the output gap. Even in that case, however, there remains room for controversy among 'number crunchers'.

(ii) Conceptual issues. The risk here is over-interpretation. As Blanchard (1990) put it, the structural balance tends to be a 'jack-of-all-trades'. In particular, the structural balance often fails as an indicator of the discretionary orientation of fiscal policy (see key question Q2 above). This may be the case for several reasons, including the aforementioned estimation problems but also other factors such as changes in interest rates (which weigh on interest payments), one-off events and so on.

Indeed, it quite frequently happens that governments take active steps to consolidate public finances without any visible improvements in the structural balances (or conversely, that fiscal policy is lax but this is not reflected in a deterioration of the common measures of structural deficits).

Some analysts therefore prefer to use a different approach and to collect and add up all the information on new measures. This is feasible but requires excellent budget information. In practice, it is at best carried out only by finance

Box 5.4   Computing structural deficits

The identification of a cyclical and a structural component requires a consideration of the sensitivity of the fiscal flows to the cycle and the size of the government sector. This allows the budget balance that would be obtained on average over the cycle to be computed.

To this end, the elasticities of receipts and spending *vis-à-vis* GDP are calculated. In the OECD countries, they average 1¼ for corporate income tax, 1 for personal income tax and indirect taxes, ¾ for social contributions and –¼ for public spending: the resulting impact amounts to ½ for the fiscal balance (van den Noord, 2002). In other words, if GDP turns out to be 1 per cent above what was forecast, the fiscal balance will be ½ per cent above the forecast level, and vice versa. However, elasticities vary considerably across countries and even over time: in the USA, for example, the elasticity for the federal fiscal balance to GDP since the mid-1980s is only 0.3, down from 0.4 in the 1960s and 1970s.

Arithmetically, let b denote the budget balance, b^{struc} the structural budget balance, and b^c the cyclical component of the budget balance, all in percentages of GDP. The output gap as a share of potential GDP is $(Y - Y^*)/Y^*$, where Y stands for GDP and the asterisk denotes potential. Let R denote receipts and S spending. With $R^*/R = (Y^*/Y)^\rho$ and $S^*/S = (Y^*/Y)^\eta$, ρ and η are the elasticities of R and S with respect to GDP. Then:

$$b_t^{struc} = b_t - b_t^c \tag{5.8}$$

$$b_t^c = (\rho\, R_t/Y_t - \eta\, S_t/Y_t)\, (Y_t - Y_t^*)/Y_t^* \tag{5.9}$$

R and S can be defined as total receipts and spending, or restricted to the part that is sensitive to the cycle. In the latter case, the excluded components of R and S that are not considered to be cyclically sensitive will be included in the structural balance.

More sophisticated formulations can be used, in particular to take into account the lags associated with tax receipts, which are based partly on income in the previous year.

For example, one might write: $R^*/R = (Y^*/Y)^{(1-h)\,\rho}(Y^*/Y)_{-1}^{h\rho}$, where h reflects the distribution of receipts over the current and previous year. In practice, the Dutch CPB, for example, builds into its estimates a lag of three quarters for both taxes and unemployment benefits (Kranendonk, 2003).

Based on the elasticities prevailing on average in OECD countries, and quoted above, the cyclical component of the budget balance can be estimated roughly as $(R/Y + ¼\, S/Y)$ times the output gap. With an average government size of around 40 per cent of GDP, this implies that, as a rule of thumb, b^c equals about half of the output gap.

ministries or highly specialized institutions.[4] Few such indicators are published and discussed. The US administration has long used a concept of this sort dubbed the 'standardized balance', but publication of this indicator has been suspended in recent years (CBO, 2009b).

Finally, the structural deficit is also of only limited help in answering Q3: what is the impact of fiscal policy on the economy? Indeed, several uncertainties surround the actual impact of any change in the measured fiscal stance itself. This impact depends on a host of factors, including the temporary or permanent nature of the change; the mix between adjustments on both the revenue and the spending side; private agents' confidence in the future, or lack of this; their foresight or myopia concerning future fiscal adjustments and the degree to which they are liquidity-constrained; induced supply-side effects (incentives to work or save more – or less); the uses of public monies (extra spending on the public capital stock may enhance potential output, contrary to some other types of public spending); the economy's openness and so on.

5.4.2 Debt sustainability

The sustainability of public finances (Q4) has become one of the key issues in fiscal policy assessments. Growing concerns over the rising burden imposed by ageing populations had increased public interest in sustainability issues before the 2007 financial crisis. Now that this crisis has propelled public deficits and debts to record levels in many countries, the question of how much fiscal adjustment is needed to repair holes in the budget has gained even more prominence.

The notion of sustainability is intuitive: the idea being whether current policies can be continued indefinitely or whether they will have to be modified because of limits on debt accumulation. Even so, translating this intuition into an operational framework is far from immediate. Headline annual balances and debt figures, or even structural balances, are at best rough indicators of the long-term soundness of public finances. To derive better indicators requires, first, some theoretical considerations to pinpoint the definition of sustainability; and second, an operational specification – the details of which may be the subject of debate.

The first step is to evaluate so-called 'debt-stabilizing deficits'. This is the level of current deficit that keeps the debt-to-GDP ratio unchanged (see Box 5.5 for

---

[4] Moreover, while this approach is straightforward regarding revenues, it raises hard questions when it comes to evaluate spending 'new measures'. What constitutes an unchanged spending policy is, in particular, a matter of debate.

the arithmetic). Higher deficits would lead to increasing debt ratios and vice versa, so it is natural to think of the debt-stabilizing deficit as a benchmark. A common indicator in this context is the primary gap, which is easy to calculate and requires no assumption regarding future developments.

Other approaches try to incorporate more information than primary gaps in sustainability assessments. This is the case with the so-called 'tax gap' methodology, which provides the needed change in taxation to ensure some sustainability condition. This approach analyses future developments in public finances based on a number of economic and demographic assumptions, either over the medium- (say, 5 to 10 years) or long-run (up to 75 years) horizons. In this way one can include views on future growth prospects and possible rising pressures stemming from an ageing population. In addition, one might also test different interpretations of sustainability (for example, should sustainability be viewed as stabilizing the debt-to-GDP ratio, or is a declining debt ratio warranted, and to what extent?).

These tools have the enormous advantage of providing synthetic indicators summarizing a wealth of information. As such, they are better benchmarks of sustainability than headline or even cyclically-adjusted balances. At the same time, it should be stressed that they rest on fragile long-run projections and various conventional assumptions (such as discount factors).

Tax gap indicators have been given greater emphasis in the European context in recent years, with limited actual impact on policies as yet, though this may change in the aftermath of the 2007 financial crisis. The European Commission routinely publishes such indicators for member countries (see Box 5.6) and EU member states are required to outline sustainability strategies in their stability or convergence programmes.

5.4.3 Structural analysis of tax policy

To asses the long-run effects of tax policy, one approach is to turn to the class of computable general equilibrium (CGE) models (see Devarajan and Robinson, 2002). These are general in that they combine an economy-wide framework with strong assumptions about agents' microeconomic behaviour, representing households as utility maximizers and firms as profit maximizers (or cost minimizers), while often also including optimized specifications for governments, trade unions, importers and exporters. They are equilibrium models because they describe how the decisions made by these different economic actors determine the prices of goods and factors, ensuring that in each case demand equals supply. And they are computable models in the sense that they produce numerical results.

The coefficients and parameters in CGE model equations are evaluated with reference to a numerical database, which usually includes a set of input–output

Box 5.5 Debt-stabilizing deficits and primary gaps

Some simple arithmetic can help when thinking about sustainability. A good start is to calculate the debt-stabilizing deficit; that is, the level of the deficit that keeps public debt constant as a share of GDP. Assuming that there are no 'below-the-line' items (such as privatization receipts):

$$D_t = D_{t-1} - b_t Y_t \qquad (5.10)$$

where D is public debt, Y is GDP and b is the budget balance as a share of GDP. A stable debt ratio means $D_{t-1} / Y_{t-1} = D_t / Y_t$. Combining both equations and including the nominal GDP rate of growth θ_t, we get, after a few manipulations (the approximation holds to the extent that θ_t is small):

$$b_t = -\theta_t d_{t-1} / (1+\theta_t) \approx -\theta_t d_{t-1} \qquad (5.11)$$

In other words, the debt-stabilizing deficit is the product of the rate of (nominal) GDP growth and the debt ratio. This is one rationale for the Maastricht Treaty thresholds for euro area countries: a deficit of 3 per cent of GDP is compatible with a stable debt ratio of 60 per cent of GDP multiplied by a trend growth rate for nominal GDP of 5 per cent (assuming 3 per cent for potential growth plus 2 per cent for trend inflation – though these numbers are themselves debatable).

One can infer the associated primary balance consistent with a stable debt ratio. Let bp be the primary balance and i the average interest rate on public debt. We have $bp_t \approx b_t + i_t d_{t-1}$. Dropping the time indices and focusing on the approximate condition, the debt-stabilizing condition becomes:

$$bp \approx d\,(i - \theta) \qquad (5.12)$$

This condition can also be written using the real interest rate r and real GDP growth g, as:

$$bp \approx d\,(r-g) \qquad (5.13)$$

This stability condition is used widely. It simply states that the primary balance should equal the debt ratio multiplied by the spread between the real interest rate and real GDP growth. The primary gap, defined as $bp_t - d_t\,(r-g)$, is a rough but easily computable indicator of fiscal sustainability.

Box 5.6   The European Commission tax gap indicators

The European Commission (EC) regularly publishes two indicators of sustainability that take the form of tax gaps. These indicators rely on long-run projections of the kind discussed in section 5.3.

The first indicator (S1) measures the change in the tax ratio needed to reach a debt ratio of 60 per cent of GDP at the end of the projection period (2060 in the latest set of projections).

The second indicator (S2) measures the adjustment needed to fulfil the intertemporal budget constraint. In practice, this is often a more restrictive condition than S1.

Positive values of S1 and S2 signal the permanent adjustment to fiscal policy that is necessary to ensure sustainability. Overall, the results indicate that large changes are needed, but with considerable variations across countries (see Table 5.2). Of course, only the sign and at best the order of magnitude of the ratios may be taken at face value. The EC's *Sustainability Report* (European Commission, 2009) quantifies the impact of changes to the main assumptions.

Table 5.2   The EC's sustainability indicators S1 and S2*
In the European Union, adjustment amounting to 5.4 per cent of GDP is needed to return to a sustainable path according to the S1 criterion (and 6.5 per cent when based on S2)

	S1	S2
	In per cent of GDP	
European Union (EU27)	5.4	6.5
Euro area	4.8	5.8
Germany	3.1	4.2
France	5.5	5.6
Italy	1.9	1.4
Spain	9.5	11.6
UK	10.8	12.4

*In percentages of GDP.
Source: European Commission (2009).

accounts showing, for a given year, the flows of commodities and factors between agents. They are supplemented by numerical estimates of various elasticity parameters (such as substitution elasticities between inputs in production, price and income elasticities of household demand for different goods, and foreign elasticities of demand for exported products). An alternative name for CGE models is applied general equilibrium (AGE) models: their characteristics are to use data for actual countries or regions, and to produce numerical results relating to specific real-world situations.

This is an ambitious and intellectually appealing approach. It allows fore-casters to estimate the impact of fiscal measures by comparing two equi-libria: one without the measures in place, and the other including them and the endogenous responses of all agents. One example is a US study showing the overwhelmingly favourable effects of unifying corporate and personal income tax and replacing capital taxation with consumption taxation (Jorgenson, 1997). CGE models are also frequently mobilized to examine energy and environmental taxation, which clearly have economy-wide ramifications. Indeed, CGE model results have informed energy policy in many countries – for example, to calculate the level of carbon taxation required to meet the Kyoto protocols. Among the drawbacks of CGE mod-els are their complexity, especially when they are dynamic rather than static, the uncertainty surrounding many of the expert judgements about behaviour and parameter values, and the underlying assumptions about equilibrium.

5.4.4   Analysing spending: project appraisal

One way to assess proposed public spending projects is to carry out a careful *ex ante* cost/benefit analysis, which then feeds into fiscal policy forecasts and decisions. This is often done for large projects, notably by the World Bank (Belli *et al.*, 1997). This methodology compares the costs and benefits of a project with a 'counterfactual'. It is not without some limitations, however.

The starting point is to establish the counterfactual; that is, what would happen in the absence of the project. For example, in the case of transport infrastructure, how will traffic evolve given economic growth, demography and relative prices? Then the net present value (NPV) of the project is derived as the difference between its benefits (planned receipts, welfare gains, posi-tive externalities) and costs (financial outlays, negative externalities). To this end, planned flows of benefits and costs are expressed in present value terms. If F_t is the difference between benefits (B_t) and costs (C_t) in period t, and if d is the discount rate:

$$NPV = \Sigma_t \, F_t \, /(1 + d)^t \qquad (5.14)$$

The project's internal rate of return (IRR) is then the value of d equalizing the projected costs and benefits:

$$\Sigma_t \, (C_t - B_t) \, /(1 + IRR)^t = 0 \qquad (5.15)$$

The project is thus assessed by comparing it to the counterfactual (is NPV positive?) or by checking whether its IRR exceeds the discount rate. In practice, however, numerous difficulties arise:

- Being a partial equilibrium approach, this method ignores sectoral or macroeconomic feedback effects, which can be important.
- The non-monetary elements of the projects are hard to measure;, for example, congestion costs, or the value of human lives saved. Sometimes, competing projects can only be assessed with respect to their effectiveness in reaching non-monetary objectives, and the comparison is then in terms of cost/efficiency rather than cost/benefit.
- *Ex post* results may differ considerably from *ex-ante* plans, because of unexpected events and complications, which add to costs.
- Some of the consequences of the project are difficult to assess, even *ex post*, in particular opportunity costs (for example, when the project displaces other types of public spending) and the impact on agents' behaviour of the tax increase needed to finance the project. The counterfactual itself is often difficult to pin down. One relatively recent approach is to take project irreversibility into account explicitly, through the use of options theory, which emphasizes the value of waiting to go ahead in an environment where some of the costs or benefits of the project are uncertain.
- Most projects begin with negative net benefits that turn positive and remain positive until the end of the project. Then, there is only one IRR, and the IRR and NPV criteria are equivalent. But multiple IRRs arise when net benefits change sign more than once during the life of the project. For example, a project with negative net benefits during the first two years, positive net benefits during the next two, negative net benefits in the fifth (because of new investments, say), and positive net benefits thereafter can have up to three IRRs. More generally, there can be as many IRRs as there are sign changes in the stream of net benefits. For this reason, among others, the NPV criterion (using a predetermined value for the discount rate) is to be preferred.

In addition, there are two important conceptual problems. One relates to the aggregation of preferences. The cost/benefit analysis reflects collective preferences, which may not coincide with microeconomic preferences (since the latter depend on individual circumstances, risk aversion, income and so on). This is all the more troublesome as usually some stand to gain from the project, while others will be affected negatively. Consider a transport infrastructure project that would save human lives by improving safety. From a citizen's point of view, the value of a human life is the same whether that piece of infrastructure is a road, used by private vehicles, or a rail track, for public use. But the government sees things differently: it is fully responsible for train safety (in the case of public ownership), while car drivers can and should insure themselves to some extent (including by driving carefully). The government is thus entitled to put more weight on each human life saved with the rail transport project than with the one related to road transport.

The other conceptual problem concerns the discount rate. First, using discounting mechanically leads to putting less weight on more distant costs and benefits – much less, in fact, when the project has an impact far into the future. This may not be sensible, notably when the project has significant long-run environmental repercussions. Second, there is the issue of the choice of an appropriate discount rate. Opting for a market rate is not a simple solution, given the dispersion of market rates from which to choose. In fact, the discount rate used by private firms is often far above any bond rate, because it reflects high opportunity costs. In the public sector, it is usually lower, albeit still above bond rates, because of budget constraints. That said, the uncertainty about the right discount rate is more of a problem when analysing the intrinsic costs and benefits of a given project than when comparing those of competing projects pursuing the same objective.

5.5   Forecasting performance

How reliable are public finance forecasts? In practice, large fiscal forecast errors do happen. In the USA, the federal fiscal balance has been vastly over- or under-forecast in some years (see Figure 5.4). The mean error for the one-year-ahead forecast over the 1982–2008 period amounted to 0.4 of a percentage point of GDP, and the mean absolute error (which, as discussed in Chapter 7, better measures forecasting accuracy), to 1.3 percentage point of GDP. In the UK, the average absolute forecast error was 0.8 of a percentage point of GDP between 1997 and 2006, bearing in mind that this was a relatively stable period for the UK economy (HM Treasury, 2008a). Not surprisingly, the size of the forecast error increases substantially as the horizon extends further out. Note also that, in general, spending can be forecast better than tax receipts, since it is less dependent on the business cycle.

Care has to be taken with the assessment of forecasting performance, however. Some information that appears to be available when making *ex post* comparisons may not be available *ex ante*, because of lags in the availability of fiscal data, revisions in economic indicators and so on. Most prominently, a large fraction of departures from budget forecasts stem from unannounced policy actions or changes in contemplated measures.

Specifically, three sources of errors are usually distinguished

- policy changes;
- economic assumptions; and
- a residual encompassing various 'technical' factors.

Figure 5.4   Errors in forecasting the US federal budget balance*

The gap between forecast budgets and outcomes can be attributed to a combination of policy measures that were unknown at the time of forecasting, unexpected cyclical developments and more specific technical factors

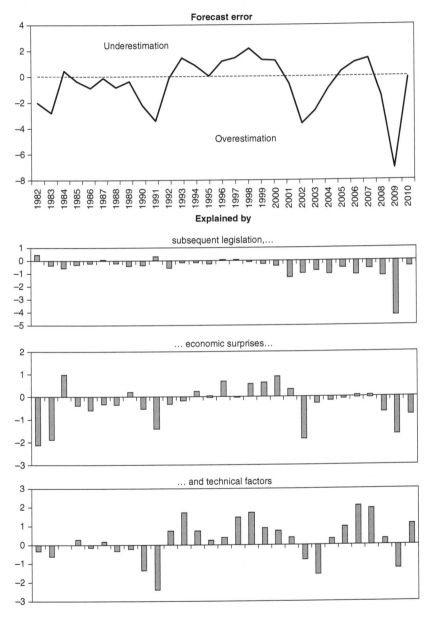

*In percentage of GDP.
Note: The forecast incorporates the expected impact of the budget's policy proposals, thus implicitly assuming that they will be enacted.
Source: OMB (2011); authors' own calculations.

Taking, for example, the fiscal year (FY) 2002, which saw an error amounting to 3.7 percentage points of GDP in the US federal budget balance:

- Economic surprises accounted for half of the forecast error. Nominal GDP, which was expected to grow by 5.3 per cent, instead rose by only 3.5 per cent. This was coupled with a collapse in the stock market, an important factor for several taxes.
- The policy decisions taken in the wake of the 11 September 2001 (9/11) terrorist attacks – which were obviously not envisioned in the president's original budget proposal (tabled in February 2001).

Figure 5.4 illustrates that the largest errors in budget forecasting tend to occur around cyclical turning points. This was particularly noticeable during the recessions of the early 1980s, early 1990s and the 2000s. Errors in the opposite direction can also be considerable, as happened in FY 1998 and FY 2007, reflecting stronger-than-expected economic growth and surges in corporate and personal income tax receipts (including on capital gains), beyond what common tax elasticity estimates would have predicted.

Can forecasting accuracy be improved? Experience suggests a mixed answer. Some estimation 'errors' are unavoidable, since they reflect differences between originally envisaged policies and those actually implemented. The other important factor relates to economic assumptions, and progress there hinges on improving the accuracy of macroeconomic forecasts (see Chapter 7). Even so, some good practices are worth trying, including:

- the use of unbiased economic assumptions;
- close monitoring and regular forecasting updates (especially at turning points); and
- the better capture of elasticities, particularly taking into account their cyclicity and the impact of asset prices on revenues.

However, efforts to improve forecasting accuracy also face a number of obstacles:

- The contours of the general government, often taken as the relevant concept (so that subnational governments and social security administrations are factored in alongside the central government), are less clear in practice than in theory. The accounting rules applying to subnational government, for example, differ from those used elsewhere. Substantial transfers between government levels occur, adding to opacity. Witness the case of Japan, where extra-budgetary funds play a major role.
- Budget and national accounts concepts are not identical. Public enterprises are usually not included in the general government in the national accounts. Privatization receipts (or nationalization outlays) and government loans are treated differently in the two sets of accounts. More generally,

while the national accounts operate on an accruals basis, budget accounts are often established on a cash basis.

- It is hard to capture revenue and expenditure elasticities properly, not least because it is difficult to factor in earlier changes in the tax regime correctly, and to determine whether they were strictly discretionary or not (for example, regarding the indexation of rebates). In addition, assessing the feedback impact of fiscal policy measures on the macroeconomic environment is challenging.
- So-called fiscal forecasts are not always pure forecasting exercises and may incorporate policy factors such as the government's attempt to shape agents' expectations. US legislation, for example, stipulates that official forecasts must be based on assumptions, regarding for example the pace of growth in discretionary spending, which may at times look rather implausible.
- While close monitoring of budget execution during the fiscal year helps, the information available at quarterly or monthly frequencies tends to be incomplete, since it often concerns only the central government (which in Germany, for example, accounts for only a quarter of total public spending), is sometimes heterogeneous, and is frequently expressed in cash rather than in accruals terms. In addition, surprises often spring up in the course of the fiscal year, related to the geopolitical situation or weather conditions, for example.

Against this backdrop, it is useful to be clear at the outset about how uncertain budget forecasts are. One way to do this is to couch the forecast in the form of ranges rather than simple point estimates and/or to present budget outcomes under various economic scenarios (see Chapter 7). In addition, alternative scenarios on policy actions may also be presented. For example, the CBO in its January 2009 *Budget and Economic Outlook* (CBO, 2009f) explored scenarios based on other policy proposals than those in the president's budget, including variants on the funding required for military operations in Iraq and Afghanistan, and policy alternatives on tax code provisions.

Further reading

A recent survey discussing the main issues and challenges in the field of fiscal forecasting is provided by Leal *et al.* (2008). Of interest to practitioners are the publications from the Office of Management and Budget (OMB) and the Congressional Budget Office (CBO) in the USA, from HM Treasury and the Office for Budget Responsibility (OBR) in the UK, and from national treasuries in other countries. The European Commission's annual *Public Finances in EMU* also contains relevant information and research presented from a policy perspective, as do the IMF fiscal monitoring notes. For a more analytical perspective, Blanchard (1990) remains a valuable introduction. The Bank of Italy's annual public finance Perugia workshops are also useful resources.

Appendix 5.1   Fiscal implications of financial sector rescues

As the scale of the 2007 global financial crisis became apparent, governments and central banks across the world, in particular in the advanced economies, stepped in to rescue banks and other financial institutions, with a view to preventing contagion across financial institutions and from the latter to the real economy. In most countries, central banks focused on liquidity support (involving shorter maturities and better collateral), while governments provided solvency support (taking on greater credit risk). The form and magnitude of these interventions, however, varied considerably across countries (see Table 5.3).

Table 5.3   Upfront financial sector support*

	Capital injection	Purchase of assets and lending by treasury	Guarantees	Liquidity provision and other central bank support	Upfront government financing
	(A)	(B)†	(C)$	(D)	(E)$
USA	5.2	1.5	10.6	8.1	6.9
Canada	0.0	10.9	13.5	1.5	10.9
France	1.4	1.3	16.4	...	1.6
Germany	3.8	0.4	18.0	...	3.7
European Central Bank	...	...	...	8.5	...
UK	3.9	13.8	53.2	19.0	20.0
Japan	2.4	11.4	7.3	1.9	0.8
Korea	2.3	5.5	14.5	6.5	0.8
G20 average	2.2	2.7	8.8	9.7	3.7
Advanced economies	3.4	4.1	13.9	7.6	5.7
In US billions	*1160*	*1436*	*4638*	*2804*	*1887*
Emerging economies	0.2	0.3	0.1	13.5	0.4
In US billions	*22*	*38*	*7*	*1581*	*47*

*As of August 2009, in percent of 2008 GDP, averages based on PPP GDP weights. Columns A, B, C, and E indicate announced or pledged amounts, not actual uptake. Column D indicates the actual changes in central bank balance sheets from mid-2007 to mid-2009 (these changes are related mainly to measures aimed at enhancing market liquidity and providing financial sector support, but may occasionally have other causes, and in addition may not capture other types of support).
†Not including treasury funds provided in support of central bank operations. These amount to 0.5 per cent of GDP in the USA, and 12.8 per cent in the United Kingdom.
‡Excluding deposit insurance provided by deposit insurance agencies.
$Includes gross support measures requiring government outlays in advance. Excludes recovery from the sale of acquired assets.
Source: IMF (2009).

While these interventions have helped to contain financial sector disruptions and their knock-on effects on the rest of the economy, they entail some fiscal costs. To assess these costs, it is important to distinguish between the short and the longer run, as well as between gross and net costs, and between the certain and contingent impacts of the different types of intervention. Indeed, some of the interventions were pledges of support that in the event were not used in full, and to a large extent the interventions were to be unwound and repaid later. Moreover, some of the interventions took place against fees, or at a fairly high interest rate, or were conditioned on dividend payments, implying that they also generated significant revenue for the government *ex post*.

Capital injections, which were particularly sizeable in the USA, do not increase the fiscal deficit if they take the form of equity purchases at market prices rather than of outright grants or equity purchases at above-market prices. However, they do raise gross public debt immediately. They do not affect net public debt, since in this case the government's assets increase by the same amount as its liabilities. A similar logic holds for other asset purchases and direct lending by treasuries or central banks, which were carried out on a large scale in the UK and Japan. As these funds were subsequently repaid, which in some countries happened within a few quarters, gross public debt came back down.

Governments also decided to provide or extend the scope of guarantees for bank deposits, interbank loans and, in some cases, bonds. These often represent a large share of annual GDP, but are a contingent liability. Paradoxically, their near-term impact on the government accounts can be favourable, since they involve the payment of fees, thereby improving the fiscal balance without raising gross or net public debt (as long as they are not activated).

The operations carried out by central banks are reflected immediately in their own balance sheet and income statement, but may show up only later in the government accounts, once the associated losses have affected the budget via lower central bank profit transfers to the government or, conversely, recapitalization of the central bank by the government.

Eurostat has quantified the fiscal impact of the various financial sector support measures taken in 2008 and estimated that, for the euro area as a whole and in net terms, they added only 0.04 per cent of GDP to the deficit that year. The estimated impact on gross government debt amounted to 1.9 per cent of GDP, and contingent public liabilities were estimated to have been pushed up by 5.4 per cent of GDP. These impacts were not negligible but were dwarfed by that of the Great Recession on public accounts.

Appendix 5.2 The fiscal response to the 2007 financial crisis

In many economies around the world, fiscal policy was used to limit the extent of the Great Recession, but at the price of a substantial deterioration in the health of public finances.

A large part of the fiscal response has happened without any discretionary intervention, through the automatic decline in tax revenues and increase in public expenditure stemming from the slowdown. At the same time, most governments have also taken new discretionary measures to protect activity and jobs. In mid-2009, the IMF estimated that these amounted on average across the G20 countries to 2 per cent of GDP in 2009, and to 1.6 per cent of GDP in 2010 (see Table 5.4), not counting the cost of the financial sector support initiatives (discussed in Appendix 5.1), nor the cost of tax cuts or spending increases that had been decided before the crisis hit.

Estimating the effectiveness of the fiscal response – often captured by the size of the fiscal multipliers – is difficult and results vary considerably across studies (Spilimbergo *et al.*, 2009). The impact of stimulus packages depends on a number of factors, including their composition. Tax cuts may come into force rapidly but may partly be saved, especially if they are not targeted on low-income and more liquidity-constrained households. However, when saved, tax cuts help in balance sheet repair, which may support consumption later. Discretionary expenditure increases, notably in the form of public investment, may take longer to materialize but may also have more of an impact once they do. Some expenditure rises were pushed through swiftly, however; for example, via the acceleration of extant infrastructure investment programmes.

Some measures may have permanent effects on the level of GDP – for example, tax cuts conducive to higher labour force participation. Others may have only transient effects, notably the 'cash-for-clunkers' schemes adopted in many countries to encourage the scrapping of older cars and the purchase of new ones sooner than would otherwise be the case (though their proponents would argue that, by helping their car industry to survive the downturn, such schemes also support activity over the longer run).

The impact of the fiscal relaxation on activity also hinges on economic agents' perception of the government's room for manoeuvre. If households and firms anticipate future tax increases to pay for today's largesse, they may save part of the income associated with a widening fiscal deficit. If market participants consider that the sustainability of public finances is threatened, they may charge a higher risk premium on government and private borrowing, which will work in the same direction. Increased concerns over the sustainability of public finances in several countries after 2007 have highlighted how painful this impact could be.

Furthermore, fiscal multipliers are larger when expansionary fiscal policy is pursued simultaneously across countries, as leakage via foreign trade is then smaller, and fiscal expansion is accompanied by accommodative monetary policies.

Governments, particularly in the advanced economies, were already facing major long-run fiscal challenges before the crisis, not least in relation to demographic ageing. With debt ratios projected to soar more than at any time since the Second World War, these challenges are now even greater.

Table 5.4 Fiscal expansion in the course of the 2007 financial crisis in the G20 countries*

	2009			2010		
	Stimulus**	Other factors[†]	Total	Stimulus**	Other factors[†]	Total
Argentina	−1.5	−0.3	−1.8	0.0	−0.4	−0.4
Australia	−2.9	−2.9	−5.8	−2.0	−4.8	−6.8
Brazil	−0.6	−0.4	−1.0	−0.6	2.1	1.6
Canada	−1.9	−4.6	−6.5	−1.7	−4.0	−5.7
China	−3.1	−1.7	−4.8	−2.7	−2.1	−4.8
France	−0.7	−5.0	−5.6	−0.8	−5.0	−5.9
Germany	−1.6	−2.1	−3.7	−2.0	−2.2	−4.2
India	−0.6	−5.4	−6.0	−0.6	−5.0	−5.6
Indonesia	−1.4	0.0	−1.4	−0.6	−0.2	−0.9
Italy	−0.2	−3.9	−4.1	−0.1	−4.0	−4.1
Japan	−2.4	−5.0	−7.4	−1.8	−5.7	−7.5
Korea	−3.6	−2.6	−6.2	−4.7	−1.5	−6.2
Mexico	−1.5	−2.0	−3.5	−1.0	−1.3	−2.3
Russia	−4.1	−9.3	−13.4	−1.3	−8.6	−10.0
Saudi Arabia	−3.3	−7.5	−10.8	−3.5	−2.2	−5.7
South Africa	−3.0	−2.6	−5.6	−2.1	−3.8	−5.9
Turkey	−1.2	−3.7	−4.9	−0.5	−2.7	−3.2
UK	−1.6	−7.4	−8.9	0.0	−10.6	−10.6
USA	−2.0	−4.4	−6.4	−1.8	−4.7	−6.5
G20 PPP GDP-weighted average	**−2.0**	**−3.9**	**−5.9**	**−1.6**	**−4.0**	**−5.7**
Including the cost of financial sector support measures:						
USA	−2.0	−7.6	−9.6	−1.8	−5.3	−7.1
Japan	−2.4	−5.5	−7.9	−1.8	−5.9	−7.7
G20 PPP-weighted average	**−2.0**	**−4.9**	**−6.9**	**−1.6**	**−4.2**	**−5.8**

*In percentages of GDP, change in fiscal balance with respect to pre-crisis year 2007.
**Budgetary cost of crisis-related discretionary measures in each year compared to 2007 (baseline). They do not include acquisition of assets (including financial sector support) or measures planned before the crisis.
[†]Estimated impact of automatic stabilizers, plus non-crisis discretionary spending or revenue measures, and non-discretionary effects on revenues beyond the normal cycle (such as the revenue impact of the extraordinary decline in commodity and real estate prices and financial sector profits). A positive amount reflects factors limiting the size of permissible deficits (such as the assumed compliance with fiscal rules).
Source: IMF (2009).

Chapter 6

Medium- and Long-Run Projections

Contents

> *The concept of potential growth (and the associated output gap) is central when making medium-run forecasts – that is, up to five to ten years ahead. There are two main approaches: statistical ones (such as the 'HP filter'); and the ones based on a production function. Longer-run projections usually rely on stylized economic growth models, with a focus on the steady state and on catching-up effects. The resulting scenarios that can be derived for the world economy point to marked changes in the respective ranking of countries in the coming decades.*

Interest in medium- and long-run projections is on the rise, for several reasons. One is related to growing concerns about the economic implications of population ageing in advanced economies but also in some major emerging economies. A second reason is associated with the ongoing rebalancing of global activity towards some large emerging economies with higher potential growth prospects, particularly in Asia. A third reason is that the financial crisis that began in 2007 highlighted that financial disruptions can have lasting effects on long-term economic performance.

Medium- and long-run projections differ from the short-run forecasts discussed in previous chapters. Beyond the next few quarters, it is indeed pointless to try to forecast the entire business cycle. However, it is possible and instructive to look at the underlying trends further out. To differentiate the two types of exercises, the term 'projections' tends to replace that of 'forecasts' for longer-run horizons.

Even so, projections are and should be quantified rather than purely qualitative. In this context, the numbers are not meant to convey what would be an illusory sense of precision. Rather, they serve to illustrate broad trends and to highlight constraints, notably through recourse to alternative scenarios.

Roughly speaking, the medium run can be thought of as extending over the following three, five or even 10 years. The horizon here is the time it usually takes for existing cyclical disequilibria (excess supply, misaligned asset prices and so on) to unwind. Indeed, at the one-to-two-year horizon contemplated in short-run forecasts, these imbalances are typically not expected to be resolved. They often persist at the end of short-run forecasting periods. In contrast, a natural – though not compulsory – assumption over the medium run is that they are worked off.

The long run (10 years or more) can only be thought of in terms of very broad trends. Growth theory is the obvious framework in which to do so, putting emphasis on supply-side factors such as demography and technical progress, and abstracting from cyclical fluctuations.

This chapter first explains how medium-run projections are produced (section 6.1). Macroeconometric models similar to those used for short-run forecasts can be used for this purpose, thereby allowing for fairly detailed depictions.

But it is also common to choose a more streamlined approach, related to growth models, and to focus on concepts such as potential growth and output gaps, which can be seen as summary indicators of, respectively, the trend and the cycle. Potential growth is also at the heart of the longer-run projections (section 6.2).[1]

6.1   The medium run

Usually, the medium-run forecast is added on to a short-run one rather than built from scratch. This is a good way to connect what is projected for the later years with what is known about the recent past. In particular, it is helpful when thinking about the unwinding (or not) of the imbalances that are observed at present or foreseen in the short run. However, the model used for the medium run may contain variables that are not forecast in the short-run model. Hence, there may be a need to start by augmenting the existing short-run forecast so that the path for these variables is mapped out.

Once that is done, the later years can be projected following procedures similar to those described in Annex III for short-run forecasts. Among other things, this involves making assumptions about the exogenous variables (external environment and policies), deciding on how to deal with the residuals, and checking the projection for internal consistency and for plausibility. This exercise, however, does not need be conducted with the same attention to detail as for short-run forecasts. The focus is usually restricted to a few key concepts, notably potential GDP and the output gap.

6.1.1   The concept of potential GDP

Potential GDP is key when looking at long-term economic developments, since it is aimed at measuring the country's productive capacity. When the economy is overheating, actual GDP exceeds potential GDP, and vice versa when there is slack. Productive capacity should not be understood as a technical ceiling but as the maximum sustainable level given the available technology and agents' preferences. Though it cannot be observed directly, economic theory suggests that a gap between actual and potential GDP leads to price movements that may help to restore equilibrium. From this perspective, potential GDP can be defined as the level of GDP consistent with stable inflation; that is, as the level of output at which demand and supply in the economy overall are balanced so that, all else being equal, inflation tends to gravitate to its long-run expected value.

---

[1] This distinction is somewhat arbitrary, since growth models can be viewed as being stripped down and supply-side focused versions of large macroeconomic models. Conversely, the latter can in principle also be used to generate long-run projections, provided they exhibit reasonable long-run properties, namely that they converge on some sustainable growth path.

Potential growth can then be defined as the growth of the level of potential GDP. The output gap is the difference between actual and potential GDP, meaning that this gap is, or becomes, negative during economic downswings. The output gap can thus summarize the position of the economy in the cycle. It is also an indicator of inflationary pressures: a positive output gap denotes tensions in the labour and product markets which may push up inflation; conversely, a negative output gap tends to foreshadow disinflation (see Figure 6.1).[2]

The link between output gaps and the change in inflation is not that precise, however. Other factors influence inflation, such as changes in prices on world markets (associated, for example, with exchange rate movements) as well as expectations. From this perspective, an important factor is the perception of the central bank's reaction function. Many observers have argued that the past few decades of moderate inflation – the 'Great Moderation' – have been the

Figure 6.1 The output gap and inflationary pressures in the USA
There is empirical evidence of a relationship between the output gap and the variation in the rate of inflation

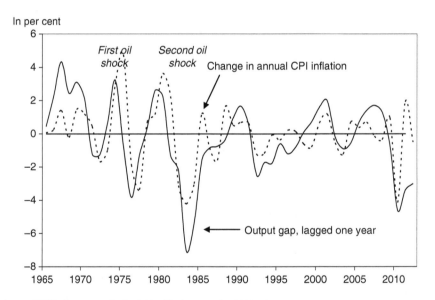

Source: OECD, Economic Outlook No. 88, forecasts for 2011–12.

---

[2] While potential GDP is derived mainly from the supply side, it also reflects demand that can be sustained over the longer run. Hence, the output gap can also be interpreted as an indication of temporary excessive or flagging demand, prompting the use of the expression 'demand-driven inflation/disinflation'.

result of the greater credibility of monetary policy frameworks, contributing to better anchoring inflation expectations at a low level (and possibly reducing the apparent correlation between output gap and inflation).

Moreover, the inflation process evolves over time. The lag between the opening up of a gap and the (demand-driven) reaction of prices varies. There is some price stickiness, and more generally there are various degrees of inertia in the inflation process. There can also be asymmetry effects, with the inflation/output gap relationship depending on the specific position in the business cycle, as well as non-linearities: for example, the impact of a large output gap on inflation could be more than proportionate compared to the impact of a moderate output gap. And there can be so-called 'speed limit' effects, when inflation depends not just on the level but also on the change in the output gap – for example, because of temporary bottlenecks (for a recent review of these various factors, see HM Treasury, 2010).

Furthermore, the output gap/inflation relationship focuses on the impact of domestic slack. But this is becoming less and less relevant with the progressive opening of national economies and the growing importance of emerging countries such as China in international markets. In other words, domestic inflation is influenced increasingly by the world output gap, in particular through its impact on the prices of commodities and manufactured goods that are easily tradable (White, 2008). In addition, inflation may not be where economists traditionally expect it: rather than being in the prices of goods and services, imbalances may be reflected elsewhere, including in asset prices or external positions.

6.1.2 The key role of potential growth beyond the short run

The concept of potential GDP is crucial in both a medium- and a long-run perspective. It provides a baseline for what growth can be expected to be, on average, over such horizons. The assumption is that, in the long run, the paths of potential and actual GDP coincide, on the same trend. Hence, sooner or later, GDP should revert to potential.[3] Figure 6.2 provides a specific illustration of this.

This is, of course, a rather simple scenario, though not necessarily implausible. In reality, complications can arise. One is that the imbalances witnessed prior to T_0 may increase for some time after the start of the projection before they start to unwind, so that the output gap closes later. Another is that it may seem naïve – albeit convenient – to posit that, beyond T_1, the cycle vanishes; indeed, it might be natural to expect that years of negative output gaps will be followed

---

[3] However, it is possible to assume that the output gap does not close over the projection period. Indeed, economies can experience protracted periods of below (or above) potential growth.

Figure 6.2   GDP, potential GDP and the output gap
The output gap can summarize the position of the economy in the cycle

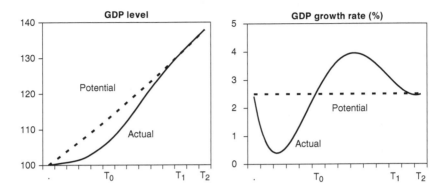

Note: Initially, output and growth are below potential prior to T_0, the start of the projection period, implying a widening negative output gap. The projection then assumes a progressive catch-up; with growth above potential between T_0 and T_1, the output gap gradually closes. Beyond T_1 and until the end of the projection period T_2, it is assumed that growth settles at its potential rate, so the output gap remains nil.

by years of positive output gaps, and vice versa. Indeed, some forecasters prefer to extrapolate past cyclical patterns, on the grounds that this produces a more plausible picture. However, the reason why the back-to-trend scenario is none the less often the best possible assumption is that it is very difficult, if not altogether vain, to try to foresee whether growth will continue above potential or slow beyond T_1. Rather than attempting to fine-tune the projection in this way, it is sensible to opt for a neutral, if artificial, assumption, which gives equal weight to both upside and downside risks.

6.1.3   Estimating potential GDP

Potential GDP is a theoretical construct, not a directly observable variable. Hence it has to be estimated. A variety of methods can be used, which sometimes produce significantly different results.[4] The two main sets of approaches used in economic forecasting are the 'statistical' ones, based on observations of GDP, and the 'economic' ones, relying on a production function.

The first, statistical approach, basically aims at producing a stylized representation of the GDP trend(s), which is/are taken to be potential GDP. A number of different methods are used to that effect (see Box 6.1).[5] Some are based on

---

[4] Output gap estimates are routinely published by national and international institutions (see Further reading). For a comparison of the various methods, see Cotis *et al.* (2004).
[5] There are other ways to separate trend and cycle, as explained in Annex II, but they are used less frequently in a medium-term forecasting context.

Box 6.1   Statistical approaches for estimating potential GDP

Linking 'on-trend' points

One can measure potential GDP by interpolating the rate of actual GDP growth between specific points in the cycle. For example, in the United Kingdom (HM Treasury, 2002, 2008b) average growth is calculated between points where the economy is judged to have been 'on trend'. For these points, GDP is deemed to be at a level close to its average observed for the economic cycle and the factors of production to be employed at 'normal' rates of utilization. To select the 'on-trend' points, economists will draw on wide-ranging evidence, based on business surveys as well as labour market indicators, such as job vacancies, and price and wage inflation.

Potential GDP is then projected forward from 'on-trend' points; for example, by extrapolating into the future the rate of GDP growth observed between the last two 'on-trend' points available. This is certainly not an exact science: the apparent simplicity of the approach should not mask the fact that there is substantial room for informed economic judgement in deciding what constitutes an 'on-trend' point. Nevertheless, it has the merit of considering a comprehensive range of cyclical indicators compared, for example, to the various filtering techniques presented below. In particular, one argument put forward by UK authorities is that the use of a wide range of indicators reduces the influence of data revisions. Moreover, trend output is assumed to follow a deterministic linear trend between 'on-trend' points in the cycle: this limits the volatility of estimated past trend output.

Using Okun's law

Okun's 'law' (Okun, 1962) is based on the observed negative correlation between GDP growth and changes in the unemployment rate. This relationship, however, varies over time and across countries. According to recent estimates by the US Council of Economic Advisors (2010), based on US data for 2000–9:

$$\Delta u = 0.49 \ (2.64 - \Delta y)$$

where:

- Δu is the change in the unemployment rate in percentage points from the fourth quarter of the preceding year to the fourth quarter of the current year;
- Δy is the change in real GDP from the fourth quarter of the preceding year to the fourth quarter of the current year;

- 0.49 indicates the sensitivity of the unemployment rate to growth;
- 2.64 can be seen as the trend growth rate at which unemployment is maintained at its natural level (this is consistent with the US Council of Economic Advisers' own estimation of the US potential GDP growth rate of around 2.5 per cent per year).

Okun's law has the merit of being simple and based on measured economic data. But one drawback is that the relationship it depicts varies over time, not least because of structural breaks in productivity growth. Moreover, the impact of unemployment on GDP growth is blurred by variations in other associated factors, such as labour force participation and working hours. So, in practice, Okun's law is used mainly as rule of thumb to complement or double-check other ways of estimating potential growth.

Trend/cycle decompositions

Another statistical approach relies on quantitative methods to decompose the GDP series into a trend and a cyclical component. As analysed in Annex II, several univariate statistical methods can be utilized for this purpose. In practice, only a few are commonly used in forecasting, with a clear preference for the HP filter (for a comparison of the various filters to determine potential GDP, see, for example, Nilsson and Gyomai, 2007):

(i) The HP filter, proposed by Hodrick and Prescott (1980), is run through the GDP series so as to obtain:

$$\underset{y_t^*}{Min} \;\; \Sigma\left(y_t - y_t^*\right)^2 + \lambda\Sigma\left(\Delta y_t^* - \Delta y_{t-1}^*\right)^2$$

where y is the logarithm of GDP and y^* the logarithm of trend, or potential, GDP. The filter thus takes into account both closeness to actual GDP (the first term of the minimization) and the variability of the trend (second term). The relative weight of these two criteria, and hence the trade-off involved in the smoothing operation, is set by the choice of the parameter λ. In practice, λ is typically set at 1,600 for quarterly data and 100 for annual data. Intuitively, the choice of 1,600 reflects an assumption that the standard deviation of the cycle is 40 times larger than that of the acceleration in the trend for quarterly data: this would be consistent, for example, with an average absolute output gap of 4 per cent and an average absolute change in trend growth of 0.1 per cent.

There are, however, two main caveats. First, the results obtained with the HP filter are quite sensitive to the choice of λ:

- Changing λ alters the amplitude of the cycles: the higher is λ, the smoother the trend and the more pronounced the cycles. However, the

choice of λ generally has little impact on the dates at which actual and trend GDP coincide, so it does not affect the length of the cycles much.
- Empirically, running the HP filter through annual data usually leads to longer cycles (say, 10 to 12 years) than if it is run through quarterly data (which generates cycles of, say, four to six years). Thus the choice of the frequency matters for the length of the cycles.

Most important perhaps, the HP-filter estimated y^* tends to be overly influenced by the latest observations of y. This is the 'end-of-sample bias': because the filter is symmetric, it forces the output gaps to sum to zero over the period being covered, even though the latter corresponds only exceptionally to an exact number of cycles. One way to address this problem is to use an extended HP filter to respect end-point constraints or impose long-term growth rates (for an application to medium-term projections, see Beffy *et al.*, 2006).

(ii) The band-pass filter proposed by Baxter and King (1999) uses centred moving-average techniques to extract from a time series its irregular component (high-frequency noise), the cyclical component (assumed to be within 6 to 32 quarters) and the trend.

(iii) The Christiano–Fitzgerald filter (2003) addresses the main problem posed by band-pass filters, which is that these filters should ideally be applied on a data set of infinite length, by prolonging the observations beyond the end of the series based on a random walk assumption.

the interpolation of the rate of actual GDP growth between selected points in the cycle, or on rules of thumb, such as Okun's law. Others focus instead on extracting the permanent component of GDP – for example, by using Hodrick and Prescott's (1980) filter.

While the statistical methods presented in Box 6.1 are fairly easy to implement or replicate and do not depend on any particular economic theory, they are of limited use when conducting medium-term projections, and even more so for those that are longer-term. One reason is that they rest on somewhat arbitrary assumptions, whether regarding the determination of 'on-trend' points or the separation between transitory and permanent components of a series – for example, the choice of λ for the HP filter is quite arbitrary.

Moreover, these methods do poorly in estimating the current trend, which is a major handicap in a forecasting context. Indeed, for either method to work properly, one needs to be at the end of a cycle rather than somewhere in the middle. The usual remedy involves extrapolating the GDP series forward in some way before extracting the trend. But this introduces a circularity when the aim is indeed to get a handle on potential GDP for forecasting purposes.

Finally, the economic rationale for explaining the projected path of output growth is almost absent and, unlike production-function-based approaches, they do not allow for the decomposition of growth into specific factors. This absence of story-telling properties is a serious drawback when forecasters need to interact with policy makers.

The second type of approach to estimating potential output is based on the use of a production function. The main advantage is to show clearly the contribution of identified factors such as demographics, productivity and so on to trend economic growth. These approaches, presented in Box 6.2, are thus often preferred in forecasting, even if they have their own pitfalls.

Box 6.2   Production-function based approaches for estimating potential GDP

The first choice to be made is that of the production function itself, which should capture the relationship between output and factors of production. Almost always, a constant-returns-to-scale function is used, with two substitutable production factors: capital and labour. A Cobb–Douglas form – which is particularly easy to manipulate* – is usually selected, or speaking more generally, a constant-elasticity-of-substitution (CES) form.

The production function can be written as $Y = F(K, L, A)$, where Y, K, L and A, respectively, stand for output, the capital stock, labour input, and a residual. Y and K are both expressed in real terms. L is usually measured in hours of work rather than as a number of workers, to take into account trend changes in hours worked. A is called total factor productivity (TFP) and captures the contribution of all the factors not incorporated in the measures of capital and labour, such as technical and organizational progress, effort and so on. As Y, K and L are observed, A can be calculated as a residual. Potential output is then $Y^* = F(K^*, L^*, A^*)$, where the asterisks denote trend or potential.

K^* is usually set equal to K, since the capital stock that is in place represents its potential contribution to output. One issue, however, is to assess the level of productive capital correctly, especially when conducting international comparisons. For example, as recalled by Beffy *et al.* (2006), the OECD distinguishes between the gross capital stock (that is, the cumulative flow of investments net of the scrapping rate), the net capital stock (which includes a correction for the declining market value of the assets as their life expectancy grows) and the productive capital stock (an additional correction is provided by an age-efficiency function). The latter measure – capital services – is considered to be better suited to measuring the contribution to the production process of the stock of the various capital assets, which depends on their age and efficiency. A key element is that a greater weight – all else being equal – is placed on those assets that depreciate quickly, since investors want to earn a higher return to compensate for higher depreciation costs. For example, the weight of equipment is greater than for structures, in line with differences in rental values and marginal productivities. Another important feature is the greater weight of rapidly-increasing ICT equipment, implying that capital services tend to grow faster than conventional capital stock measures, and leading to a downward revision in capital productivity gains.

Another challenge is that, via K, potential growth depends on investment so far (assuming no sudden shift in the rate of capital depreciation). So if investment slows down, say, because of rising interest rates, potential growth declines. Since investment is positively correlated with the cycle, estimated potential growth will tend to be pro-cyclical.

A^* is generally derived by smoothing observed TFP. The latter moves with the cycle, because of the lags with which labour and even more so capital adjust to changes in output. However, productivity gains are not, strictly speaking, pro-cyclical since they tend to be the highest during periods when output is accelerating – that is, when the change in the output gap is the largest, not when the economy is peaking. One of two methods is usually employed to smooth TFP:

- Regressing A on a time trend. For example: $logA = a\,T + b + u$, where T is time, a and b are parameters and u is the residual. A^* is then obtained as $logA^* = a^*\,T + b^*$, where a^* and b^* are the estimated parameters. This regression can be improved by adding a variable capturing the cycle on the right-hand side – say, the ratio of capacity utilization in manufacturing (Skoczylas and Tissot, 2005). Note, however, that the period of estimation may affect the results, and that the estimated trend may display some breaks over time.
- Running a smoothing algorithm through A, such as the HP filter. The smoothed series may then retain some pro-cyclicality. This might, however, be justified in so far as technical progress or work effort are pro-cyclical.

Calculating L^* is tricky. Basically, one would write $L^* = POP^*\,PR^*\,(1 - U^*)\,H^*$, where POP^* stands for the trend working-age population, PR^* for the trend participation rate, U^* for structural unemployment and H^* for trend hours worked per job. Estimating each of these requires the analyst to exercise judgement:

- *POP** is usually set equal to *POP* (often the population aged 15 to 65, though different age brackets may be used).
- *PR** is generally obtained through the statistical smoothing of *PR*, to control for the pro-cyclicality of participation rates.
- The same holds for *H**, as *H* is also pro-cyclical (overtime most conspicuously so). When there is a structural shift, this can be problematic, as straight smoothing would not distinguish cyclical effects from other sources of variation – notably in the case of France in the early 2000s, following the introduction of the 35-hour work week.
- *U** is probably the most difficult component, as there are many ways of estimating structural unemployment.

A simple way to define *U** is as the component of *U* that is unrelated to the cycle. Part of *U** corresponds to 'frictional' unemployment, because of the time it takes to find a new job. But *U** may also reflect inadequate skills, minimum wages, the tax wedge, weak job-search incentives, insufficient competition in the goods market, and so on. The impact of these factors is hard to quantify. An apparently easy way around this problem is to derive *U** through the statistical smoothing of *U*. The advantage of a production-function-based approach is then somewhat limited, as compared to directly filtering GDP (to a degree, this caveat extends to the other methods used to estimate *U**). This can be appropriate if the cyclical component of unemployment is not too persistent, which may be the case in flexible labour markets, but has been less so in continental Europe in recent decades. In the USA, the sharp deterioration in the labour market observed after the 2007 financial crisis may also point to a possible structural upward shift in the unemployment rate. In any event, the *U** obtained by statistical smoothing is often fairly close to *U*, so that *Y** does not differ much from *Y*.

One more economic but also complex approach is to compute the NAIRU, understood as the unemployment rate consistent with stable inflation (see Section 3.5, Turner *et al.*, 2001, and Ball and Mankiw, 2002). Several approaches are possible in this respect. The first is to estimate an augmented Phillips curve, allowing forecasters to distinguish a short-run NAIRU, which moves around in response to temporary shocks, and a long-run NAIRU, which is determined by productivity trends. A promising approach is also to estimate the NAIRU using a 'semi-structural' approach (see Appendix 3.3). Yet another way is to use a notion of equilibrium unemployment defined as the rate that stabilizes the share of labour in national income, in the context of a model of wage and price setting *à la* Layard *et al.* (1991). But whatever the method used, the estimates of U^* are fragile, especially in euro area countries, where the cyclical and structural components of unemployment appear to be particularly difficult to disentangle empirically.

---

*A priori, using a production function highlighting the contribution of capital to potential growth makes sense for the medium run but less so for the longer run. Indeed, over the long run, it is often assumed that the evolution of the capital stock is determined by that of labour resources and technology (see below). This would argue for having only labour as an input in a long-run production function. However, it is also possible to keep capital as a factor alongside labour, provided it is projected consistently with the projected labour force and productivity. More fundamentally, perhaps, the capital–output ratio may change over the long run, in response to changes in relative prices (witness the ongoing fall in information technology prices), and taking this into account would require retaining a production function with the two factors.

In addition to the statistical and production function approaches, other methods are used (though less frequently) to estimate potential output. The 'semi-structural' methods focus on the link between the output gap and inflation (see Appendix 3.3 for an example in the case of the estimation of structural unemployment). Alternatively, decompositions based on structural VARs (*à la* Blanchard and Quah, 1989) can be used, as carried out, for example, on US data by Demiroglu and Salomon (2002), who compare the results with traditional CBO estimates of US potential output. Yet another way is to use econometric models, especially dynamic stochastic general equilibrium (DSGE) models, though this avenue is of limited help for forecasting purposes (see Box 6.3).

Box 6.3   Econometric models and potential growth estimates

One can estimate potential GDP by using an econometric model and its simultaneous system of equations that describe the behaviour of certain economic observable variables (such as inflation and unemployment) known to have a link with potential output. The IMF (2008) has, for example, been using its Global Projection Model to develop such model-consistent measures of potential output. To simplify, the model contains two critical equations in which the output gap intervenes (one is the relationship between inflation and the output gap, and the second is a dynamic Okun's law). Since the output gap is an unobservable, 'latent' variable, the procedure followed to estimate it is to select, of all the paths that potential output might take, the one that best predicts the observable variables in the model.

This model-based approach has gained importance with the development of the new class of DSGE models, presented in Annex III. In line with the real business cycle literature, the equilibrium level (the 'natural rate') of output is the result of the maximization of a welfare function. Hence, a wide range of factors can affect potential output, such as technology shocks, propensity to consume, productivity and so on. The new Keynesian variety of DSGE models allows for the existence of rigidities and frictions (resulting, for example, from imperfect competition and adjustment costs) so that, when a shock occurs, variables such as prices adjust only slowly. Edge *et al.* (2007) define potential GDP as the theoretical level of activity if any such frictions were removed, a definition that is widely endorsed in the DSGE literature. In other words, potential output here is the efficient level of output.

DSGE-type output gap estimates may be quite different from simple detrended output, and the two series can even be negatively correlated (Woodford, 2001). This can lead to counterintuitive results. Edge *et al.*, for example, estimate that the US output gap remained negative from the beginning of the 1990s to 2005, a result that is hard to reconcile with the IT-led cycle witnessed during that period.

Furthermore, the major source of economic fluctuations in DSGE representations is associated with productivity shocks, implying that the efficient level of output displays greater volatility than the traditional estimates of potential growth. This, in turn, leads to smaller and less persistent output gaps. Model-based estimates of potential growth at the IMF are also found to display considerably more variation than the more traditional IMF World Economic Outlook (WEO) estimates.

In practice, these two features tend to limit the usefulness of DSGE models for estimating potential growth. More generally, the pitfalls of this class of models do not help. As analysed in Annex III, their estimations are largely model-dependent – they depend on the parameters of the DSGE specification. These models are also quite complex and opaque, and therefore have a poor ability to provide a narrative that can guide economic policy decisions. This is a major drawback compared with the production function approach, which provides, in contrast, a 'story' that is coherent with theory and thereby allows for effective communication between experts and policy makers. Last but not least, the notion that business-cycle fluctuations are efficient limits the scope for active economic stabilization policies, and is therefore unpalatable to policy makers.

One possibility is to use a DSGE model without incorporating the associated estimates of potential GDP that display excessive shocks; this explains why potential GDP is proxied by a moving average of past actual values of GDP in the IMF's Global Integrated Monetary and Fiscal (GIMF) model (Kumhof *et al.*, 2010).

In practice, which concept of potential growth should forecasters use? As a general rule, it is advisable to try out various methods in parallel and see how they compare (keeping in mind that the DSGE approach can lead to quite different estimates). Such cross-checking is particularly welcome given the significant uncertainty surrounding estimates of output gaps. Cerra and Saxena (2000), for example, applied many different methods in the case of Sweden; they found that the Swedish output gap was between –5.5 per cent and 0.2 per cent in 1998, while potential growth ranged from 0.9 per cent to 4.2 per cent. Notwithstanding these wide ranges, they were in a position to conclude that Sweden's large negative output gap – particularly pronounced after the banking crisis of the early 1990s – had closed by 1998 or shortly after. In the United Kingdom, HM Treasury (2008b) also carried out this sort of comparison, concluding that statistical and production function methods deliver broadly similar results. Moreover, different methods can be combined to build forecasts. For example, while UK official output gap estimates rely on trends estimated statistically between 'on–trend' points, future potential output is projected by extrapolating productivity, average hours, employment rate and working-age population (HM Treasury, 2006), which is akin to a production function approach.

6.1.4   Growth accounting and medium-term forecasting

While various methods can be used to estimate potential growth, the production function approach is considered to be the most useful for longer-run forecasting purposes. This is because it requires forecasters to make reasonable assumptions about the evolution of the various drivers of potential growth, and therefore makes for a coherent growth accounting framework. In addition, it is then easier to provide a narrative to policy makers. In contrast, simply extrapolating recent trends determined by statistical methods would add scant value as well as making little sense if important changes regarding the factors driving long-run growth are already foreseeable.[6]

Projecting a consistent growth-accounting framework requires forecasters to make assumptions about a number of key variables:

- TFP trend growth is usually posited to be in line with historical averages.
- Working-age population projections are usually available from demographic studies.
- It is more difficult to foresee the evolution of trend-participation rates, to which the results are quite sensitive, as illustrated by Burniaux *et al.* (2003).

---

[6] This is particularly the case for demographic variables: it would be pointless to prolong a filter-estimated trend of output 10 years ahead if it is known today that the working-age population trend is about to change.

The same holds for working hours. In practice, assessment of structural policies and judgement will be key in determining whether historical trends are
maintained over the projection period, or whether some inflection might
be preferred.

- It may be prudent to keep U^* at its latest estimated level. But, depending on
  the circumstances, it can be useful to explore variants; for example, when it
  is expected that past or ongoing labour market reforms will gradually reduce
  structural unemployment, or that part of a recent increase in unemployment will become structural because of hysteresis effects.
- Capital accumulation cannot be assumed exogenously, as it depends on the
  evolution of output over the projection period. One caveat is that potential
  and actual growth projections are thus interdependent; hence it is frequently
  assumed that the capital–output ratio will remain constant, consistent with
  a long-run approach of economic development (see below).

Such growth accounting has the advantage of highlighting the sources of
growth in a transparent way, as presented in Table 6.1 for the US economy. It
also allows analysts to examine how sensitive the projection of trend output is
to the underlying economic assumptions, including the situation with respect
to productivity (see Box 6.4).

Table 6.1   Components of projected US potential real GDP growth*

Potential real GDP growth is projected at 2.5 per cent per year over 2009–20, driven mainly by labour productivity

Component	Contribution
Civilian non-institutional population aged 16+	1.0
Labour force participation rate**	–0.3
Employment rate[†]	0.0
Ratio of non-farm business employment to household employment	–0.0
Average weekly hours (non-farm business)[‡]	–0.1
Output per hour (productivity, non-farm business)	2.3
Ratio of real GDP to non-farm business output[§]	–0.4
Sum: Real GDP	2.5

* Over 2009–20, percentage points per annum.
** The projected decline stems from the fact that the baby boom generation is entering retirement.
[†] The potential employment rate (= $1 - U^*$) is assumed to remain unchanged.
[‡] The length of the work week has declined by 0.3 per cent per year since the 1950s, but going forward it is assumed to diminish less rapidly as a result of the anticipated decline in labour force participation.
[§] This reflects the empirical regularity that the non-farm business sector tends to grow faster than other sectors.
Source: Council of Economic Advisors (2010).

Box 6.4 Contributions to medium-term growth: the role of productivity

For any production function $Y = F(K, L, A)$, where Y, K, L and A respectively stand for output, the capital stock, labour input, and a residual, one can write:

$$\frac{\dot{Y}}{Y} = \frac{K}{Y}\frac{\partial Y}{\partial K}\frac{\dot{K}}{K} + \frac{L}{Y}\frac{\partial Y}{\partial L}\frac{\dot{L}}{L} + \frac{A}{Y}\frac{\partial Y}{\partial A}\frac{\dot{A}}{A}$$

where dots denote time differentiation. If in addition production factors are remunerated at their marginal productivity:

$$\frac{\dot{Y}}{Y} = \alpha\frac{\dot{K}}{K} + (1-\alpha)\frac{\dot{L}}{L} + \zeta$$

where α is the share of capital in value added, $(1 - \alpha)$ the share of labour and $\zeta = \frac{A}{Y}\frac{\partial Y}{\partial A}\frac{\dot{A}}{A}$ stands for TFP gains (this formula always holds in the simple case of a Cobb–Douglas production function). Thus the contributions to the medium-term evolution of GDP of the stock of capital, the labour force and technical progress can readily be disentangled. Moreover, the likely range of medium-term growth can be identified and communicated, with a clear and transparent explanation of how it depends on a set of alternative economic scenarios.

A key issue of interest is to look at the impact of productivity developments. One common way is to retain a Cobb–Douglas production function:

$$Y = TFP\,K^\alpha\,L^{1-\alpha}$$

The relationship between labour productivity and capital productivity (denoted, respectively, P_l and P_k) and total factor productivity TFP is also straightforward:

$$P_l = Y/L = TFP\,L^{-\alpha}\,K^\alpha = TFP\,(K/L)^\alpha = TFP\,R^\alpha$$

$$P_k = Y/K = TFP\,L^{1-\alpha}\,K^{\alpha-1} = TFP\,(K/L)^{\alpha-1} = TFP\,R^{\alpha-1}$$

where R is the ratio of capital per unit of labour (called capital depth); differentiating these expressions yields directly the relationship between yearly changes in labour and capital productivity (respectively p_l and p_k, using the usual notation in logarithms) and in total factor productivity (*tfp*, in logarithm also):

$$p_l = tfp + \alpha\, r$$

$$p_k = tfp + (\alpha - 1)\, r$$

where $r = \Delta(log\ R)$ is the yearly variation in capital per unit of labour, called capital deepening.

Finally, TFP growth rates can be decomposed into the changes in labour and capital productivity as:

$$tfp = \alpha\, p_k + (1 - \alpha)\, p_l$$

In other words, TFP growth rates are a weighted average of labour and capital productivity growth rates (with the weights equal to the respective shares in the value added of labour and capital).

It should be noted that the factors driving potential growth can be interrelated. Boulhol (2009) finds, for example, that the composition of the working-age population – in particular with regard to educational attainment – does affect variations in both labour utilization (that is, the employment rate) and productivity, thereby accounting for significant differences in GDP per capita across countries. One example is when young, higher-educated cohorts replace lower-educated cohorts: this has a positive impact on productivity but also on labour utilization.

Moreover, projections based on the production-function approach are subject to the statistical uncertainties surrounding both the methods for estimating potential growth and the economic assumptions for projecting its drivers.

Finally, it is important to note that the determination of all the key drivers of potential growth (K^*, L^* and so on) leads to the estimate of medium-term growth from a supply-side perspective. When forecasting or projecting further out, this approach can be complemented by some demand-side adjustments. For example, the OECD medium-term baseline (see Beffy *et al.*, 2006) is updated regularly to extend the short-term forecasts over the following five years (and sometimes over a much longer horizon): this is done based on potential growth estimates resting on a production function; but it also incorporates assumptions regarding the closing of the output gap over the projection period, the return of unemployment to its structural level, and the likely path of exchange rates. This exercise also takes into account a number of behavioural equations, notably for imports and exports.

6.1.5 Dealing with uncertainty

Irrespective of the chosen technique(s), a great deal of uncertainty surrounds any medium-run projections. Indeed, some of the judgement calls needed to anchor these projections are just very difficult, as illustrated in the case of labour productivity in the USA (see Box 6.5). Not only is significant uncertainty attached to the choice of one method versus another, but assessing the current state of the economy correctly is itself crucial: an error of 2 per cent in estimating the present size of the output gap can lead to an error of around half a point in annual GDP growth over several years – if, for example, the output gap is assumed to be closed over the following four to five years.

Box 6.5   What is trend labour productivity in the USA?

One of the most debated issues related to the assessment of recent and future US potential growth has been the evolution of labour productivity, particularly at the time of the two recessions observed in the 2000s. Labour productivity is typically highly pro-cyclical, so that analysts widely expected it to slow down significantly after its sharp expansion in the late 1990s, when the new economy bubble deflated. Instead, the growth in labour productivity measured as output per hour in the non-farm business sector remained strong in the early 2000s, averaging 4.1 per cent over 2002–3 compared to 2.0 per cent in the 1990s and only 1.4 per cent in the 1980s – for a historical average of around 2.3 per cent (see Figure 6.3). Labour productivity surprised again on the upside during the 'Great Recession' caused by the 2007 financial crisis, growing at an annual rate of 2.9 per cent from 2007 to 2009, in the midst of unprecedented financial disruptions. This led to growing concerns regarding a 'jobless recovery' and higher structural unemployment in the USA.

Against this intriguing backdrop, what would be an appropriate medium-run productivity projection? The consensus has tended to move up as productivity outcomes exceeded expectations. The general estimation is that the underlying growth in US productivity is now well above the weak performance of the 1970s and 1980s. One difficult judgement call in this respect relates to the efficiency enhancements associated with information technology. One view is that the massive investments in high-tech equipment made in the recent period are paying off, with some delay, partly because businesses progressively discover unexploited areas of cost reduction. But how large any further gains in the pipeline may be is far from obvious.

It is hard to overstate the importance of these trends. Any variation in US trend productivity growth would have major implications for US potential growth, increases in living standards and fiscal margins in the years to come.

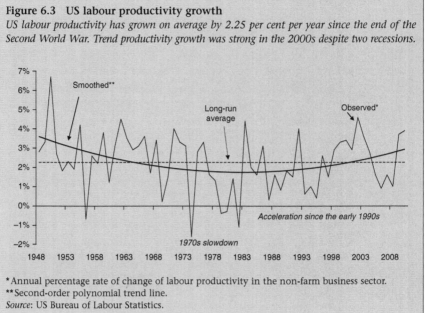

Figure 6.3   US labour productivity growth
US labour productivity has grown on average by 2.25 per cent per year since the end of the Second World War. Trend productivity growth was strong in the 2000s despite two recessions.

*Annual percentage rate of change of labour productivity in the non-farm business sector.
**Second-order polynomial trend line.
Source: US Bureau of Labour Statistics.

Moreover, real world factors can obviously easily throw off any medium-run forecast. This has been the case worldwide, with exogenous shocks such as the oil shocks of the mid- and late 1970s. Another uncertainty pertains to the long-term consequences of the 2007 financial crisis. Past experience with financial crises in various regions, such as Asia in 1997–8, suggests that long-term output growth may be strongly affected (see Box 6.6, and Cerra and Saxena, 2008). It is worth noting, in this respect, that many of the medium-term projections made after the great 2007 financial crisis do not incorporate any sharp downward correction in potential growth prospects. One key example relates to US long-term productivity gains, which are still expected to be close to their historical averages of 2¼ per cent per year by the US administration (see Table 6.1 and Figure 6.3). Finally, policy choices also matter for the evolution of both potential and actual GDP, as they may shape the development of supply-side factors over the medium term; for example, in the case of structural reforms to enhance growth.

Chapter 8 discusses in detail how best to deal with such uncertainties. In a nutshell, it is advisable to use fairly simple and conventional assumptions rather than to try to second-guess future changes in trends. Scenarios can help to illustrate the range of possible outcomes (including the more prudent ones) and should sketch out the likely implications of the alternative policy options that may be under consideration.

Box 6.6 Impact of financial crises on potential growth

The financial crisis that began in 2007 holds two important lessons with respect to long-term economic analysis:

- One is that large financial disruptions can appear relatively frequently, though not as often as the more normal ups and downs of the business cycle (see Appendix 4.1). The IMF (2009b) identifies eight major international financial crises since 1870: the collapse in the German and Austrian stock markets (1873); the end to the lending boom to the Americas (1890); the panic caused by the fall in copper prices (1907); the 1929 Great Depression; the 1981–2 Latin American debt crisis; the bursting of the real estate and equity price bubbles in Japan and Scandinavia in the early 1990s; the 1997–8 Asian and Russian crises; and the recent financial crisis that erupted in 2007.
- A second lesson is that severe financial disruptions can have a long-lasting impact on trend growth. According to calculations by Furceri and Mourougane (2009), a financial crisis (banking or currency) permanently lowers potential output by around 1.5 to 2.4 per cent on average (and even 4 per cent for a 'deep' financial crisis).

In general, it is recognized that financial crises have a direct impact on potential GDP because of lower incentives to invest (thereby limiting capital formation) associated with the combination of lower asset prices, tougher financing conditions and lower growth prospects. A second adverse factor is higher structural unemployment, stemming from the need to restructure the economy in the face of rigidities in the labour market. The effects on TFP and labour force participation are generally negative but can be more ambiguous, depending on how the economy is restructured following the crisis. Regarding productivity, financial disruptions tend to impede the efficient allocation of resources and innovation. However, a crisis can also trigger the end of some inefficient activities ('creative destruction' *à la* Schumpeter). Turning to labour force participation, more workers may be discouraged following the crisis and decide to stay out of the labour force. At the same time, individuals who have seen the value of their assets fall because of the crisis may decide to postpone their retirement.

There are also indirect effects, which mainly depend on the policies taken in response to the crisis. Such effects, for example, could be related to the decision to cut or to expand investment in public infrastructures, the potential change in the size of the government, and the incentives provided by the crisis to implement – or not – structural reforms.

In addition to the usual uncertainties, the impact of a crisis is particularly difficult to assess, for two reasons:

- The absence of a counterfactual: what would have happened if the crisis had not occurred? For example, what policies would have been in place?
- The problem of endogeneity: financial crises are one of the consequences of the pro-cyclicality in the financial system that leads to booms and busts. Hence a crisis can both have an impact on future potential output and be the result of unsustainable activity patterns in the preceding years: merely comparing trend output before and after the crisis will then overstate the change in sustainable output growth.

Nevertheless, historical experience shows that the impact of financial crises on potential GDP has the following main features (IMF, 2009b):

- The level of output is substantially and persistently depressed over the medium term after a banking crisis. On average, the output loss relative to the prevailing pre-crisis trend is close to 10 per cent seven years after the outbreak of the crisis.
- Medium-term growth rates usually tend to return to their pre-crisis rates, except after the major crises associated with very large output losses, which see trend GDP growth fall durably.
- Initial conditions matter: for example, a high pre-crisis investment boom tends to be associated with higher medium-term output losses (possibly because more time is needed to unwind the build-up of excessive capacity observed before the crisis). The pre-existence of macroeconomic imbalances (current account deficits, high inflation and deteriorated fiscal positions) before the crisis can be associated with larger output losses, most probably because there is then less room to engage in expansionary short-term policies limiting the severity of the crisis.
- Losses following currency crises are much smaller, representing about a third of the average loss associated with banking crises. Twin crises (a currency crisis coinciding with a banking crisis) lead to larger output losses.

6.1.6   A case in point: medium-run fiscal programmes in the euro area

Medium-run projections are used, in particular, in the stability or convergence programmes that European countries are required to submit to the European Commission towards the end of each year, in the context of the Stability and Growth Pact. These programmes are focused on budget forecasts but obviously involve a set of underlying macroeconomic projections. Comparing successive vintages of the programmes illustrates how large the uncertainty can be, even when the medium run barely extends beyond the short run.

Figure 6.4   Growth expectations in the euro area: early and late 2000s
It took a significant time to revise euro area GDP growth expectations in both the early and the late 2000s

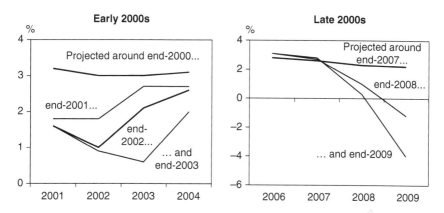

Notes: Real GDP growth in successive versions of stability programmes, as aggregated by the European Commission and published in the annual issue of *Public Finances in EMU* the following year. In late 2000, euro area GDP growth was expected to be around 3 per cent in 2001–4; then projections were cut for 2001–2, but not so much for 2003 and 2004. Despite the start of the financial crisis in 2007, the growth forecast for 2009 was only revised downwards progressively from 2007 to 2009.
Source: European Commission, *Public Finances in EMU*.

As analysed in greater detail in Chapter 7, such projections are subject to significant uncertainty beyond the current year. They nevertheless offer a useful anchor in 'normal' years, providing a scenario for projected output growth compared to the estimated medium-term trend. For example, if a sizeable output gap exists at the beginning of the exercise, reasonable assumptions can be made for closing it, which in turn inform the public finance outlook. However, forecasters often fail to anticipate downturns and to adjust their projections promptly in the face of bad news. The projections associated with European stability programmes over the recent decade are a case in point (see Figure 6.4).

In 2000 (left-hand panel), the programmes initially submitted reflected the euphoria prevailing at a time when aggregate real GDP growth in the euro area exceeded 3½ per cent. GDP growth was estimated to be close to 3 per cent over the following years and this did not seem wildly optimistic. But in the event, the short-run forecasts on which the medium-run ones rested turned out to be well above the mark. Not only were the forecasts for actual growth revised downwards time and again during the next three years, but the projection for GDP growth for the next years was also pulled down by around ½ of a percentage point – in part because of a less optimistic assessment of potential growth. In level terms, these revisions imply that, by end-2003, the level of GDP projected for 2004 was almost 8 percentage points lower than had been expected three years earlier. Based on an elasticity of around ½ for fiscal balances with respect to GDP, this shortfall implies a deterioration of the euro-area-wide fiscal deficit by 4 percentage points of GDP – compared with an actual deficit close to the 3 per cent threshold in 2004.

In the late 2000s (right-hand panel), the programmes submitted were based on a more conservative assessment of medium-term output growth of around 2¼ per cent. But in 2007, it was estimated that euro area GDP growth would remain at this level in 2008–9 despite the start of the financial turmoil. Indeed, it took some time for European policy makers to recognize both the severity of the crisis and the fact that the euro area could not decouple from the global recession. In the event, GDP grew by less than 0.5 per cent in 2008, and shrank by 4.1 per cent in 2009. In terms of levels, GDP in 2009 was 8 percentage points below the level expected at end-2007. The 2009 budget deficit reached 6.2 per cent of GDP; that is, more than 5 percentage points worse than the forecast made in 2008.

What are the lessons to be learnt from the shortcomings of these medium-term projections? It would be naïve to think that in future forecasters will be able to better predict downturns many years in advance. But the sheer size of past forecast errors calls for greater prudence when conducting medium-term fiscal projections. Authorities can become too complacent during 'good times', when the forecasts suggest that they have substantial fiscal room for manoeuvre. They should always keep in mind that, first, the projections might turn out to be completely inaccurate in 'bad times' (when they matter the most) and, second, that downturns tend to be recognized with a considerable lag (implying that they will not have much time to adjust to such bad events).

6.2   The long run

Long-run projections are usually produced using streamlined models: attempting to describe economic developments in any detail a decade or more down the road would be futile, as attested by the considerable uncertainty already hanging over short- and medium-run forecasts.

The purpose of these models is to depict how selected key variables may interact over the long run, keeping in mind that certain regularities can be expected to hold, such as the six 'stylized facts' identified by Kaldor (1961):

1. Output and per capita output grow over time, with no tendency to decline.
2. Capital per worker grows over time.
3. The rate of return to capital is broadly constant, at least in advanced economies.

4. Capital–output ratios are steady over long periods (no rise or fall in the long term).
5. The shares of labour and physical capital in national income are broadly constant in periods when the share of investment in output is constant.
6. The growth rate of output and output per worker differs substantially across countries.

Notwithstanding the considerable margins of error surrounding long-run projections, they can allow forecasters to draw some important qualitative conclusions: for example, they make it clear that, in the absence of major reforms, social security systems in many OECD countries will not be able to cope with the pressure of an ageing population (discussed in more detail later in the chapter).

These long-run projections should not be confused with so-called 'futures research', which attempts to discern the trends and innovations that are likely to reshape the world over the coming decades (see Chapter 8). Long-run projections, in contrast, essentially extrapolate past trends, taking into account only those changes that can be expected with some reasonable confidence.

6.2.1 Solow's model and the golden rule

Growth theory can be a useful theoretical anchor when making long-run economic projections. While it has evolved substantially in recent decades, the starting point remains the model introduced by Solow (1956) and it will be assumed that long-term growth will converge to the steady state of this model (see Box 6.7). This approach has the advantage of being both simple and consistent with the first five of Kaldor's six stylized facts. An additional important feature, moreover, is that in the steady state, the real interest rate equals the economy's real growth rate: this is growth theory's so-called golden rule.

Box 6.7   Steady state in the Solow model

In its basic rendition, the Solow model rests on the following assumptions:

- The production function includes two substitutable inputs, labour and capital, with constant returns to scale. It can be written as $Y = F(K, EL)$, where Y, K and L, respectively, are output, the capital stock and the quantity of labour, while E is labour efficiency, which is assumed to grow at the constant rate μ. E represents the contribution of factors other than capital and labour, and plays the role that *TFP* did in section 6.1. It is necessary to assume that E enters multiplicatively with labour for the model to have a balanced-growth-path solution. Technical progress in this case is said to be labour-augmenting, or 'Harrod-neutral'.

- L expands at a constant, exogenous rate, n, consistent with a long-run perspective where demographic factors dominate.
- The investment rate is also constant and equal to the saving rate (as the economy is assumed to be closed). It is therefore called s. Given that capital depreciates at a rate δ, $dK/dt = s\,Y - \delta K$.

Let $k = K/EL$ and $y = Y/EL$ be the stock of capital and output per unit of 'effective labour', and define $f(k) = F(k,1) = y$ with f satisfying the so-called Inada conditions: it should be strictly increasing ($f' > 0$) and concave ($f'' < 0$), with $f(0) = 0$, $f(\infty) = \infty$, $f'(0) = \infty$ and $f'(\infty) = 0$.

Given that $dK/dt = d(kEL)/dt = k\,d(EL)/dt + EL\,dk/dt$, one has:

$$(s\,Y - \delta K)\,/\,EL = k\,/\,EL\,d(EL)/dt + dk/dt \text{ and } d(EL)/dt = (\mu + n)\,EL$$
$$\text{so that: } dk/dt = s\,f(k) - (n + \mu + \delta)\,k$$

This equation summarizes the model's dynamics. It says that, per unit of effective labour, the increase in the capital stock equals the saving (or investment) minus the investment needed to keep the stock of capital constant given population growth, technical progress and depreciation.

The stock of capital per unit of effective labour converges to k^* (see Figure 6.5), which is such that:

$$s\,f(k^*) = (n + \mu + \delta)\,k^*$$

Figure 6.5   Solow's growth model

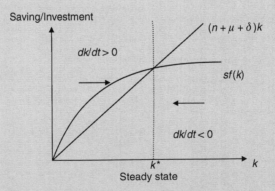

Note: The straight line $y = (n + \mu + \delta)k$ is the investment needed to keep the stock of capital constant and $y = sf(k)$ is the saving curve. For small values of k, $sf(k)$ is above $(n + \mu + \delta)k$ so $dk/dt > 0$: the economy adjusts with an increase in k and thus in investment along the curve $sf(k)$. Conversely, for high values of k, the adjustment proceeds through a reduction in k. The equilibrium is reached when $k = k^*$; at this point $dk/dt = 0$ so k remains constant over time – this is the steady state.

Hence, output per unit of effective labour converges to $y^* = f(k^*)$. Once there, the economy remains on a balanced, or steady state, growth path. Along this long-run path, output per worker and the stock of capital per worker grow at the constant rate μ, while output and the stock of capital grow at the constant rate $(\mu + n)$.

The model thus suggests a simple way to carry out long-term macroeconomic projections; the only variables for which assumptions are indispensable are the growth of the labour force and that of labour efficiency. Assuming the economy is on its steady-state growth path, and assuming that production factors are remunerated at their marginal productivity level (which will be the case under perfect competition), the following holds:

- The profit rate r (equal in this context to the real interest rate) is constant, at $r^* = f'(k^*) - \delta$, which is the constant marginal product of capital per unit of effective labour net of the depreciation rate.
- The share of income going to capital is constant and equals $r^* K/Y$, with the capital–output ratio K/Y constant, since both K and Y grow at the same pace $(\mu + n)$.
- The share of income going to labour is also constant and equals $w L/Y$, where w is the real wage per capita – which rises at the same rate μ as productivity per worker.

In sum, along the steady-state growth path, income shares are constant, the profit rate is constant and wage earners reap all the productivity gains in the form of rising wages. Note, however, that the real interest rate depends on k^*, and hence on the saving rate s (via the above condition $s f(k^*) = (n + \mu + \delta) k^*$). Thus, to project the real interest rate using the result $r^* = f'(k^*) - \delta$, one needs an assumption about s, as well as about the shape of the production function.

One way to go about this is to ask which steady-state path would maximize consumption (production less saving) per capita c. Since $c^* = f(k^*) - s k^* = f(k^*) - (n + \mu + \delta) k^*$, it will be maximized for the value of k^*, for which the first-order condition holds, namely $f'(k^*) = n + \mu + \delta$. This in turn gives the optimal saving rate (plugging the optimal value of k^* into $s f(k^*) = (n + \mu + \delta) k^*$). Using the fact that $r^* = f'(k^*) - \delta$, the real interest rate is:

$$r^* = n + \mu$$

The real interest rate thus equals the economy's real growth rate: this is growth theory's so-called golden rule.

But why would agents spontaneously wish to save at this rate? The golden rule does not allow for any inclination to discount the future, as opposed to the present, and for any risk aversion. One way to bring these elements in is to endogenize saving behaviour in an intertemporal utility maximization model, first proposed by Ramsey (1928). Let θ denote the rate of time preference (or subjective discount rate) and σ risk aversion (which corresponds to the degree of concavity of the utility function). Then it can be shown that the economy will converge on a growth path such that $r^* = f'(k^*) - \delta = n + \mu/\sigma + \theta$. A common simplifying assumption then is that the utility function is logarithmic, so that $\sigma = 1$. Then the relationship reduces to:

$$r^* = n + \mu + \theta$$

This is the 'modified golden rule': the real interest rate is higher than in the golden rule to the extent that agents discount the future.

6.2.2   From the medium-run to the steady state

In practice, few projections are undertaken for horizons spanning several decades. They are often made using simple projections based on the extrapolation of medium-term trends, with the properties embedded in theoretical growth models serving as an anchor for the long-run, steady-state part of the projections (see Box 6.8).

Box 6.8   Extension of medium-term projections to the long run

Building on Box 6.2, the simple Cobb–Douglas production function will be retained:

$$Y = TFP\, K^{\alpha}\, L^{1-\alpha}$$

Differentiating this expression yields a simple relationship between growth rates in GDP, labour, capital and TFP (respectively noted as y, l, k and tfp):

$$y = (1 - \alpha)\, l + \alpha\, k + tfp$$

Let C denote the coefficient of capital (capital per unit of production), so that $C = K/Y$. By differentiation, $c = k - y$. Hence:

$$y = l + (\alpha\, c + tfp) / (1-\alpha)$$

A common simplification, consistent with the steady state in the Solow model presented above, is then to assume that α is constant in the long run (roughly equal to a third for advanced economies); the constant rate of return of capital is compatible with a constant coefficient of capital – that is, capital is growing at the same rate as output in the long run, and $c = 0$. Then:

$$y = l + tfp / (1-\alpha)$$

Another simplification, for advanced economies, is that in the long run they are close to the production frontier, defined as the most efficient use of existing technologies (for developing economies, this cannot be the case, as they are catching up to more advanced economies). Hence one assumes that tfp will be constant for those economies that have already converged to the production frontier (in contrast with catching-up economies, where it makes sense to assume that tfp is higher initially but declining over time).

In the steady-state case, and using the notations from Box 6.4, the relation between TFP and labour productivity can be simplified to:

$$p_l = (y - l) = tfp / (1-\alpha)$$

In sum, along the steady-state growth path, labour productivity growth rates are equal to TFP growth rates divided by the income share of labour. If, for example, $1 - \alpha = \frac{2}{3}$, then a steady-state increase in labour productivity gains of 1 percentage point per year will be matched by an increase in TFP growth rates of $\frac{2}{3}$ percentage point (as noted in Box 6.4, $p_l = tfp + \alpha r$, so the remaining contribution of $\frac{1}{3}$ percentage point reflects the impact of capital deepening).

In the case of France, official estimates (Direction Générale du Trésor et de la Politique Economique, 2006) applying this approach led to a potential growth of a rounded estimate of 1.9 per cent for 2031–50, based on the following assumptions:

- Labour supply growth (estimated at around 0.0 percentage points per year) is equal to the labour force growth based on demographic projections, positing a stability in structural unemployment and in average hours per worker and using some policy assumptions regarding participation rates (a progressive rise in activity rates is assumed as the retirement age is expected to increase over the long run).
- The coefficient of capital is assumed to be constant, leading to a steady contribution of capital to trend growth (0.6 of a percentage point per year).
- The trend in TFP gains is projected in line with developments in the recent past (1.2 percentage points per year).

An important determinant of the projection relates to the demographic scenarios, which are traditionally taken from international organizations (the World Bank provides country projections for a number of demographic variables up to 2050, and the United Nations has estimated demographic trends for major regions up to 2300). The US Census Bureau also produces fairly detailed global population projections and associated analyses (Kinsella and He, 2009). These projections are generally pointing to comparable trends at the global level, though there can be substantial differences across countries.

The approach described in Box 6.8. can be refined, depending on the purpose of the forecasts and the specific issues of interest. For example, in the USA, official long-term forecasts are regularly carried out to assess the budgetary consequences of social security trends. For this purpose, the CBO (2009d, 2009e) has developed an *ad hoc* long-term model called CBOLT, with the following features:

- It relies on extensive demographic inputs (for fertility, mortality, immigration) and on a limited number of key economic assumptions (for total factor productivity, inflation, the difference between GDP and CPI inflation, unemployment, bond rates and the return on equities).
- Total economic output is determined by productivity (TFP is set at its long-term historical average), hours of labour (derived from labour force growth) and the stock of capital, which depends on depreciation rates and, via investment, on private and government saving.
- Instead of simply assuming a constant coefficient of capital, the consistency between assumptions on future savings and the growth in the capital stock compatible with other economic assumptions is examined. In particular, there is an interaction with the fiscal scenario included in the projections, since public dissaving can crowd out private investment and thus weigh on the capital stock and limit output growth.[7]
- There is a distinction between the first 10 years and the outer part of the 75-year projection period.
- There can be a transition between these two subperiods, with phasing-in assumptions over a 5- to 10-year window.
- The impact of policy levers (tax rates, social benefits, retirement ages) can be sizeable.
- Finally, and because the uncertainty surrounding such a long-term horizon is particularly high, the CBO simulates various distributions regarding the model input assumptions around the central projections.

---

[7] For example, calculations by the IMF (2010b) show that a 40 per cent of GDP increase in government debt over five years can lead to a decline in output by around 4½ per cent (assuming a full crowding-out effect, that is a decline in the capital stock by the same amount as the increase in debt).

Yet another approach is to extend medium-run forecasts by making explicit scenarios in the long run. Using this procedure, the OECD (2010) has built a set of alternatives scenarios – depending on fiscal consolidation, exchange rate realignment and structural reform – to project a relatively large number of economic variables 15 years into the future.

6.2.3   More recent approaches in theory...

While simple and operational, the Solow model suffers from two major short-comings. First, it predicts that two economies with identical saving rates and having access to identical technology will ultimately find themselves on identical long-run growth paths. If one starts out with a lower capital stock per head than the other, it will initially grow faster, because the marginal productivity of capital will be higher. But over time it will catch up, and eventually both economies will enjoy the same level and growth rate of GDP per capita. This type of 'absolute convergence' jars with observed cross-country trends. Some countries, notably in East Asia, have indeed caught up to a large extent with the advanced economies, but others, especially in Africa, have clearly failed to do so.[8] In addition, a reasonable calibration of the Solow model implies that convergence to the long-run growth path should be fairly rapid (with half of the gap closed after some 15 years), which is also inconsistent with actual trends.

The second problem is that the most fundamental driver of growth, namely labour efficiency, is treated here as an exogenous variable, rising at a constant rate. The underlying assumption is that technical progress is costless, and that firms and countries can all benefit equally from it, free of charge. The real world is, of course, rather different – not least because of the role played by profit incentives in driving technical progress.

One avenue followed to deal with these problems has been to broaden the concept of capital beyond that of physical capital. Indeed, capital accumulation is correlated with technical progress, since innovations are to a large extent incorporated into new physical assets. At the same time, it is important to focus on the quality of human capital, which depends on education, training and the ability to use new technologies. One solution is to augment the Solow model to incorporate the impact of human capital (see Box 6.9).

Empirically, the augmented Solow model shows convergence towards the steady-state growth path to be twice as slow, which is more realistic. Another

---

[8] While evidence of absolute convergence is weak, there is some indicating conditional convergence – meaning, broadly speaking, that homogeneous groups of countries tend to converge towards a common steady-state level of GDP per capita. For a detailed discussion, see Islam (2003).

Box 6.9 The augmented Solow model

Mankiw *et al.* (1992) have augmented the Solow model to include human capital H alongside physical capital and the sheer volume of labour in the production function. Using a Cobb–Douglas production function, this leads to:

$$Y = K^\alpha H^\beta (EL)^{1-\alpha-\beta}$$

where $(\alpha+\beta) < 1$ (decreasing returns to total capital – physical and human – but constant returns to scale in production).

Assume that a fraction s_k of income is saved to accumulate physical capital and a fraction s_h to accumulate human capital. For simplicity, also assume that both types of capital depreciate at the same rate δ. Keeping the same notations as above and defining $h = H / EL$ and $f(k,h) = Y / EL = F(k,h,1) = k^\alpha h^\beta$, the model's dynamics can be summarized as follows:

$$dk/dt = s_k f(k,h) - (n + \mu + \delta) k$$
$$dh/dt = s_h f(k,h) - (n + \mu + \delta) h$$

As indicated by the arrows in Figure 6.6, the dynamics are stable: the economy converges to a steady-state growth path where both physical and human capital per unit of effective labour are constant, with:

$$k^* = \{s_k^{1-\beta} s_h^{\beta} / (n + \mu + \delta)\}^{1/(1-\alpha-\beta)}$$

and

$$h^* = \{s_h^{1-\alpha} s_k^{\alpha} / (n + \mu + \delta)\}^{1/(1-\alpha-\beta)}$$

Figure 6.6 Convergence to a steady-state growth path with physical and human capital

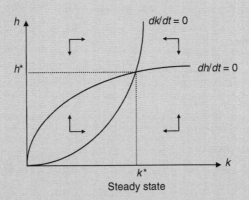

Steady state

Note: For a given value of k, the possible 'equilibrium' values of h are along the curve $(dh/dt = 0)$, since in the steady state h should be constant. Conversely, for a given value of h, a steady-state candidate for k lies along the curve $(dk/dt = 0)$.

The steady-state equilibrium obtains at (k^*, h^*), where the two curves cross. In the bottom-right quadrant, for example, $dk/dt = s_k f(k,h) - (n + \mu + \delta) k < 0$, so k will decrease until it reaches the curve $(dk/dt = 0)$. At the same time, $dh/dt = s_h f(k,h) - (n + \mu + \delta)h > 0$ so h will increase until it reaches the curve $(dh/dt = 0)$.

feature is that the income share of each of the three factors is roughly similar, at around a third, implying that human capital would contribute about as much as physical capital. However, the way the model is tested against the data has its own problems. Human capital is very hard to measure properly, and the enrolment ratios used by Mankiw *et al.* as well as by others may be poor proxies (Wößmann, 2003). Also, the results are highly sensitive to a few outlier observations (Temple, 1998). Moreover, the underlying assumption, shared with the Solow model, that rates of technical progress are identical across countries is rather unrealistic.

The other avenue explored to overcome the Solow model's limitations is to try to describe the forces driving growth in economic terms: this is what endogenous growth theory does (see Romer, 2001). This class of models attempts to reduce the contribution made by the residual in growth accounting – for example by treating research and development (R&D) as a separate factor input. Much of the focus in this context has been on the economics of innovation, highlighting the role played by the trade-off between the cost of R&D and the temporary monopoly rents associated with patents. An important aspect here is that, unlike physical capital, technical knowledge is non-rival in consumption (it can be used in several places at the same time), opening up the possibility of increasing returns to scale.[9]

This approach takes into consideration the factors driving the pace of technical progress – the policies pertaining to R&D, education and training, market regulations, public infrastructures, entrepreneurship, openness and so on. Taking these factors into account is in principle much better than extrapolating past TFP trend in some way. In practice, however, numerous endogenous growth models have been put forward – many of them quite abstract – and it is far from clear which are the most robust to capture actual trends. Hence these elements will at best be used qualitatively, and this approach is of limited direct value for forecasting purposes.

6.2.4 ... and in practice

Nevertheless, with some simplifications one can build long-term projections that partly incorporate the influence of a number of factors on productivity

---

[9] A simple example illustrates this. Consider a firm producing Y in a plant with L workers and a given stock of knowledge. If it opens a second, similar plant, it can produce $2Y$ with $2L$ workers but without needing any additional knowledge, thereby doubling output without having to double all inputs. However, technical knowledge is also partly non-excludable, implying that its owner cannot completely prevent others from using it, especially in the longer run.

(Carone *et al.*, 2006). Catching-up effects in particular can play an essential role. In the case of the IMF long-term growth projections, Batista and Zalduendo (2004) argue that taking into account such determinants as well as cross-country information is important, and they show that convergence is empirically significantly slower than the trend that is usually assumed based on judgement.

Another important element for cross-country comparisons is the projection of exchange rates. A widely held assumption is that in the long run the real exchange rates converge to their PPP rates (see Chapter 4). For emerging economies, the convergence often involves a Balassa–Samuelson type of effect – that is, the real exchange rate appreciation *vis-à-vis* the technological leader is proportionate to productivity growth differentials.

Cross-country analysis is indeed at the core of the approach followed by PricewaterhouseCoopers, one of the prominent private institutions making projections up to 2050 – see Hawksworth and Cookson (2008) for a technical presentation of the long-term forecasting model used for this purpose, updating the initial work conducted on the BRICs (Brazil, Russia, India and China) at Goldman Sachs by Wilson and Purushothaman (2003). This approach rests on Solow-type Cobb–Douglas production functions (with the labour factor adjusted for the quality of education) for all countries. Basic assumptions are used to project the labour force and population, the rate of depreciation and the share of income going to capital. Technical progress is assumed to be more rapid the poorer the country, so the speed of convergence depends on how far behind it lags. TFP is thus determined by the trend of technological progress in the leading country (the USA) and country-specific catch-up factors. Nevertheless, substantial judgement is used to set the various parameters of the model: the depreciation rate of capital, the investment-to-GDP ratio, the employment rate, the trend in education levels, the share of capital and, of course, the catch-up factors.

Others have devoted more attention to the specific modelling of TFP. At Goldman Sachs, O'Neill *et al.* (2005) have augmented Wilson and Purushothaman's methodology by introducing a growth environment score summarizing a set of indicators of structural conditions and policy settings deemed to influence the pace of convergence. Other approaches in the literature rely on variables such as competition, structural reforms and trade openness to explain developments in TFP.

At the OECD, and in the context of work on climate change, Duval and de la Maisonneuve (2009) have set up a conditional growth framework in order to make long-term projections for specific countries and, in aggregate, the global economy. The approach is based on the gradual convergence of each country to its own steady-state level of GDP per capita, determined by a set of variables deemed to drive growth – and, in particular, capital–output ratios, human capital per worker, TFP and employment rates. Specific assumptions allow for the extrapolation of these variables far into the future. Since technology circulates freely across the world, it is assumed that TFP levels in lagging countries could gradually catch up with technological leaders. Hence the global growth scenario is built on the assumption of steady growth in TFP for high-TFP economies and an assumed speed of convergence to the 'frontier' for the lagging countries. This approach leads to a projection of world GDP growth of about 3.75 per cent per year (4 per cent before 2025, and 3.5 per cent between 2025 and 2050). Of course, the results depend greatly on the underlying assumptions, and reasonable alternative scenarios presented by the authors would lead to a world growth rate about 1 percentage point higher or lower compared to the baseline.

One can even formalize this type of approach further, using an integrated economic model to capture the various linkages and feedback effects; for example, higher TFP leads to higher capital accumulation and potential growth. This is done, for example, by Aglietta *et al.* (2007) using the CEPII INGENUE 2 model, a worldwide dynamic computable general equilibrium model that captures demographic trends, geographical differences, saving patterns, technological diffusion and so on.

Yet another approach is to note that an economy's aggregate productivity performance results partly from the reallocation of resources across sectors. In this spirit, Bagnoli *et al.* (1996) use a bottom-up approach based on a general equilibrium model estimated at a sectoral level (the G-Cubed model developed by McKibbin and Wilcoxen, 1998) to project the course of the world economy over the next few decades, allowing for various applications (trade liberalization, climate change and so on).

6.2.5 World growth over the coming decades

Looking far ahead, these long-term projections suggest that major shifts in economic gravity can be expected, partly as a result of demographic differences, but also reflecting catch-up phenomena in productivity and exchange rates. Specifically, some Asian economies, and possibly also Brazil and Russia, could overtake major G7 countries, provided they stick firmly to growth-enhancing policies. A set of projections to 2050, undertaken by Hawksworth and Cookson (2008), can serve to illustrate this prognosis (see Figure 6.7).

With these assumptions, China could overtake the USA as the largest economy by around 2025, and India's catching-up would be almost complete by 2050. The Brazilian economy could be larger than Japan's by 2050. Income per capita levels, however, would remain significantly lower in emerging

Figure 6.7   GDP rankings*

The relative ranking of major economies is expected to change dramatically in the coming decades

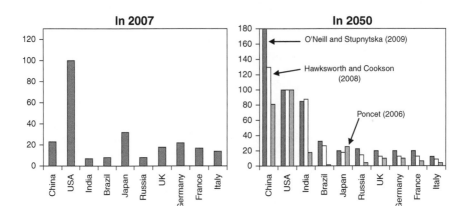

*USA = 100, GDP at market exchange rates in US$ terms.

Note: Hawksworth and Cookson project that China's GDP in US dollars will represent almost 130 per cent of US GDP in 2050 (from around one fifth in 2007). But Poncet foresees less than full convergence at that horizon, while O'Neill and Stupnytska project a much more rapid catching up.

Sources: Hawksworth and Cookson (2008), O'Neill and Stupnytska (2009) and Poncet (2006).

market economies than in the advanced economies, even by 2050. In China – where living standards would be almost twice as high as in India – dollar GDP per capita would still be only 37 per cent of the US level. Hence, compared with the rest of the world, the large OECD economies would remain far ahead in terms of income per capita, but their relative importance would fall dramatically, while some large emerging economies would join the group of dominant players.

Such projections at a very long horizon are, by definition, highly uncertain and very much depend on underlying assumptions. Indeed, Poncet (2006) comes up with a very different scenario. Her projections are built on a more sophisticated modelling of the factors driving long-term growth, with a specific focus on capital accumulation, technology catching-up affects and exchange rates. They show a less rapid development for the emerging economies, because the assumed pace of the TFP catch-up is much slower (implausibly perhaps in some cases, such as Brazil). So is the posited appreciation of their currencies, which would remain far from their PPP levels by 2050. The economic importance of some emerging countries – especially China – would still increase dramatically. But the US economy would keep its top rank (see Figure 6.7, right-hand panel).

Yet the consequences of the 2007 financial crisis may significantly alter these projections. Major emerging market economies weathered this crisis relatively well, while large industrial countries have been sharply and lastingly affected.

As a result, the contribution of the BRIC countries to global growth has increased substantially. Taking these new developments into consideration, and noting in particular that the size of all of the BRIC economies at the end of the 2000s is much larger than originally estimated only five years ago, O'Neill and Stupnytska (2009) updated their long-term projections and estimated that the BRIC as a group could become as big as the G7 countries by 2032, about seven years earlier than they originally believed possible.

6.2.6   The economic consequences of an ageing population

A prominent example of the relevance of long-term projections is the economic consequences of an ageing population, as baby-boom cohorts retire. Many countries, and in particular member countries of the OECD, face massive population ageing during the first half of the twenty-first century. The proportion of the elderly in the total population is set to shoot up, reflecting past fertility declines and continuously increasing life expectancy. As a result, old-age dependency ratios will soar, as illustrated in Figure 6.8 for the USA and in Table 6.2 for the main G20 countries. Indeed, the ratio of those aged 65 and above across the working-age population is projected to

Figure 6.8   US old-age dependency ratio*
The relative importance of the population aged 65 and over is expected to soar and this will strain public finances considerably

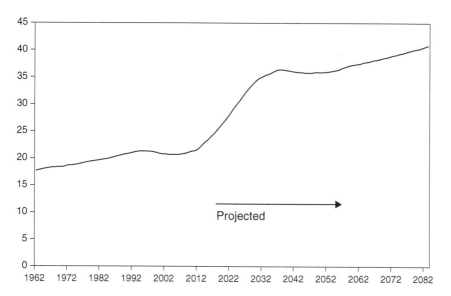

*The US dependency ratio equals the population aged 65 and over divided by the population aged 20–64, in percentages.
Source: Congressional Budget Office (2009b).

Table 6.2 A long-run simulation of ageing-related public spending pressures

By 2050, the old-age dependency ratio is expected to increase substantially in major countries, pushing up pension expenditure and even more so expenditure on public health

	Dependency ratio*		Old-age dependency ratio**		Pension expenditure in % of GDP		Public health expenditure in % of GDP	
	2010	Change to 2050	2010	Change to 2050	2010	Change to 2050	2010	Change to 2050
G20 advanced economies (average)	**51**	**25**	**26**	**24**	**7.1**	**1.2**	**7.0**	**6.9**
of which: France	55	21	26	21	13.5	0.7	8.7	5.9
Germany	51	31	31	28	10.2	2.1	7.9	6.5
Italy	53	35	31	31	14.0	0.7	6.3	4.7
Japan	56	40	35	39	10.3	0.7	6.9	5.9
UK	51	14	25	13	6.7	1.4	8.0	6.2
US	50	13	19	16	4.9	0.8	6.7	8.2
G20 emerging economies (average)	**48**	**10**	**11**	**21**	**3.2**	**2.1**	**2.6**	**2.6**
of which: Brazil	48	11	10	26	8.5	7.3	5.1	5.0
China	39	24	11	27	2.2	0.4	2.2	2.2
India	56	–9	8	12	1.7	–0.8	0.9	0.9
Russia	39	27	18	21	5.1	5.1	3.6	3.1

* Number of persons younger than 15 and older than 64 per 100 persons aged 15 to 64.
** Number of persons older than 64 divided by number of persons aged 15 to 64, in %.
Sources: IMF (2010a); Population Division of the Department of Economic and Social Affairs of the United Nations Secretariat, *World Population Prospects, The 2008 Revision* (medium variant); authors' calculations.

rise from 26 per cent to 44 per cent on average for advanced G20 economies between 2010 and 2050 (and from 11 per cent to 30 per cent for G20 developing economies). This demographic transition has a number of serious macroeconomic implications, notably on real GDP growth, public finances and current accounts. That said, any estimates at that horizon are highly tentative and some of them may not be very plausible, if only because they assume that policies will remain unchanged in the face of dramatic developments.

Past fertility declines translate into slower labour force growth. This will significantly reduce potential growth in typical OECD countries, even if it was mitigated somewhat by higher immigration and fertility rates than are embodied in central projections. In one estimate, the per annum effect may amount to 0.25 per cent in the USA and approach 0.4 per cent in the EU15 and Japan between 2000 and 2050 (Mc Morrow and Röger, 2004). Real GDP and real GDP per capita (and hence overall living standards) would continue to grow, but over time, their level would be affected significantly. By 2050, GDP per capita would be one eighth lower in the USA and around one fifth lower in Europe and Japan than it would have been without the ageing of the population.

Slowing real GDP growth coupled with rising age-related public spending will squeeze budgets (IMF, 2010a). A very large portion of general government spending is indeed sensitive to the population's age structure, most notably health and long-term care, but also publicly-financed old-age pensions and early retirement programmes. The ageing population will drive up pension and public health expenditure significantly in G20 advanced economies between 2010 and 2050, but less so in G20 developing economies. These higher public expenditures will be offset only very partially by a decrease in spending on child benefits and education.

These prospects, combined with the dramatic widening of public debts that has taken place since the 2007 financial crisis, suggest that the fiscal position of almost all advanced countries is not sustainable in the long run and will have to be corrected in coming years. The world fiscal deficit, which widened from 0.3 per cent of GDP in 2007 to 6.7 per cent in 2009 (8.8 per cent for advanced economies), is expected to decline, but would still be around 3 per cent of GDP by 2015 (IMF, 2010b). As a result, the ratio of general government gross debt to GDP is expected to rise to 110 per cent in 2015 for the advanced economies, up from 70 per cent in the early 2000s (in contrast, the public debt ratio is expected to decline slightly, to around 40 per cent of GDP, for the major developing economies). In addition, the simulations suggest that reversing these trends would require substantial fiscal tightening. The average adjustment needed for targeting a debt ratio of, say, 60 per cent for the advanced economies is estimated at almost 9 per cent of GDP between 2010 and 2020. Indeed, a number of countries such as Greece, Portugal and Spain had to take drastic fiscal consolidation measures in 2010 to respond to growing concerns among financial market participants about their long-term fiscal prospects.

To cope with the ageing issue, actions taken in recent years have aimed at increasing retirement ages, reducing average pension benefits, tightening eligibility requirements and so on. Several governments have also encouraged greater private saving, as a complement to existing public schemes. Even so, there is an increasing consensus that much more needs to be done to ensure long-run fiscal sustainability. One difficulty is that growing income redistribution from active to inactive people through public transfers may undermine work incentives and create social tensions. A risk associated with the promotion of private saving schemes is that future pensioners might face an unexpected meltdown in asset prices once they all start consuming their savings at the same time. The demand for and price of these assets (or the exchange rates if past savings had been invested abroad) could fall substantially. A number of studies (such as Takáts, 2010) suggest that global asset prices could therefore face substantial headwinds from the ageing of the population up to around 2050. However, the uncertainty surrounding any such effects at very long horizons is extremely large, in particular with respect to intertemporal consumption/saving decisions (CBO, 2009c). For example, empirical evidence shows that retirees tend to constrain their consumption more than is often thought, because of the uncertainty about their lifespan, and that wealthy old people tend to die leaving sizeable bequests.

Moreover, pension expenditures are only one element in the story. Indeed, public health expenditure is also expected to contribute to the deterioration of fiscal positions in the advanced economies over the next few decades. The key challenge is therefore to increase the pool of resources (that is, national income) from which future social benefits will be drawn so as to limit the tax burden on future generations – assuming that retirees' demands themselves would not grow as much as national income. Boosting productivity gains would help, but might not suffice to offset the demographic drag. Another solution is to boost labour supply and its utilization, not least via higher participation rates for women and older workers. For example, if the female participation rate were to be 5 percentage points higher and if participation rates of older workers were to increase by half as much as they have fallen since 1970, total age-related public spending as a share of GDP might be reduced by as much as 0.75 of a percentage point according to some tentative estimates. Raising the statutory retirement age would help to alleviate future tensions even more, as it would both reduce outlays on pensions and boost GDP and general government revenue. Measures to curtail structural unemployment would also help: in Europe, every percentage point reduction in the unemployment rate boosts potential output and improves the fiscal balance by around a third of a percentage point of GDP (and somewhat more in the longer run) through lower transfer spending and increased tax receipts. Even so, and barring large-scale immigration, all these measures may not be enough to fill the gap, implying hikes in social contributions or tax rates, which in turn are likely to be inimical to potential growth.

As populations do not all grey at the same time or at the same speed across countries, ageing also has international implications. Current account positions within the OECD area and between the latter and the rest of the world may be facing large swings. In theory, developing countries, with their younger populations, could be expected to invest more than they save, and the ensuing current account deficits would be financed by the more rapidly ageing populations of the OECD countries. In practice, however, this is far from certain, witness the large US external deficit since the mid-1990s and the parallel improvement in emerging countries' current account balances, especially in Asia.

Further reading

Regular updates of medium-term projections are provided in the biannual forecasting publications of the IMF (*World Economic Outlook*) and the OECD (*Economic Outlook*). The IMF covers more countries and regions than the OECD, which focuses on industrial countries and the largest emerging market economies but with details for a greater range of variables.

On potential growth estimation, the approaches followed by the CBO in the USA and by the OECD globally are described respectively in CBO (2004), Giorno *et al.* (1995a, 1995b), and Beffy *et al.* (2006). The IMF's production function method is described by De Masi (1997); however, for emerging market economies, IMF estimates often rely on time series techniques, especially the HP filter, and on judgement from country desk economists (IMF, 2008). The IMF also calculates model-based output gap estimates using its Global Projection Model and a DSGE-type approach. The European Commission has switched for most purposes from the 'statistical' (Mc Morrow and Röger, 2001) to the 'economic' approach (Denis *et al.*, 2006).

For longer-run forecasts, the evolution of the labour force is key. In this respect, demographic projections by the United Nations and the World Bank (available on worldbank.org) are a good starting point. Hollmann *et al.* (2000) describe the associated methodological issues, in particular the cohort-component method. Potential productivity trends are also key. They can be extrapolated or derived more formally, as done by Poncet (2006). Theoretical background is provided by Solow (1956) and Romer (2001) as well as Barro (1997) and Weil (2008).

On long-term public finance issues, the IMF's biannual *Fiscal Monitor* provides regular updates. On long-term growth/energy prospects, an authoritative source is the International Energy Agency's annual *World Energy Outlook*.

Chapter 7

Risks and Accuracy

Contents

> *Assessing forecast accuracy is far from straightforward, as it is essentially a relative concept and may be measured in various ways. It is important to look at a variety of indicators and to draw the lessons of past forecast errors. In general, macroeconomic forecasters do a relatively good job but their main shortcoming is their failure to predict turning points. Forecast accuracy can be improved in different ways, including by combining competing forecasts. A good forecast must be accompanied by a thorough and balanced analysis of the associated risks.*

While there is always a demand for economic forecasts, their reliability is frequently questioned and scepticism is widespread among the broader public regarding the accuracy of any forecast. Granted, forecasters often get it wrong, not least when it comes to foreseeing turning points or crises. But uncertainty is part and parcel of the complex economies of the twenty-first century. In addition, the forecasters themselves consider that they tend to be unduly criticized. They argue that their track record is more respectable than is often alleged, noting that professional forecasts have been proved to be more reliant than the so-called 'naïve forecasts' produced using elementary methods. Moreover, accuracy is perhaps not the best criterion against which to judge the value of forecasts. Indeed, their usefulness may have more to do with the associated diagnoses and policy implications.

Yet forecasting accuracy remains a key issue. First, it needs to be properly defined and measured (section 7.1) and forecast errors must be analysed precisely (section 7.2). Looking at forecasters' performance in the past sheds light on what to expect when going forward (section 7.3). It is also worth scrutinizing past forecasting errors to establish what caused them (section 7.4) so that avenues for improvement can be explored (section 7.5), in particular by combining different forecasts.

Nevertheless, the quality of a forecast should not be assessed solely on the basis of the accuracy of its central scenario. What is key is to look at the risks surrounding the projections, in particular by building alternative scenarios (section 7.6).

7.1 Conceptual issues

7.1.1 How to look at forecast accuracy

Many studies try to assess the accuracy of forecasts, taking this concept for granted. Defining accuracy is not straightforward, however. For a start, accuracy should not be confused with certainty. A high degree of accuracy does not mean that the forecast will be 'just right'. Rather, it means that the risks of erring are limited, from a probabilistic perspective. Here lies the first source of misunderstanding between the public and forecasters, since a forecast, by its very nature, cannot offer the kind of certainty for which the broader public may be wishing.

That said, how should one assess whether the risks of error are large or small? Obviously, the size of the 'tolerable' uncertainty depends on the quantitative properties of the variable under consideration. The latter include its intrinsic volatility as well as the precision with which this variable is measured. A 1 per cent forecasting error on a variable that is only measured with a precision of ± 2 per cent is clearly not a big mistake. A relevant measure of accuracy should take such caveats into account: for example, since it is generally considered that uncertainty, as measured by the average revision of output growth in advanced economies, is around 0.5 of a percentage point, one would compare GDP forecasting errors to this kind of benchmark.

Another important point to bear in mind is that the desirable degree of accuracy depends on the purpose of the forecast. In particular, it may hinge on users' room for manoeuvre. For example, in the EU, the Stability and Growth Pact sets a limit of 3 per cent of GDP on fiscal deficits. In that context, if the country is already approaching or has breached the 3 per cent deficit threshold, even a small forecasting error might be seen to be quite significant. A similar example relates to inflation targeting in the United Kingdom: the Governor of the Bank of England is required to write a letter to the Chancellor of the Exchequer every time inflation deviates by more than one percentage point from the targeted 2 per cent. If a forecasting error on the evolution of the degree of slack in the economy causes inflation to overshoot or undershoot by more than one percentage point, it could be deemed to be significant for a Governor wishing to avoid writing the letter.

Yet another complication relates to the frequency of the errors. One might be reassured by a long series of 'accurate' forecasts during a long expansion, only to discover that they subsequently turned out to be completely wrong when a large crisis erupted. For example, the near-term forecasts made during the years preceding the 2007 financial crisis were relatively accurate. But the apparent stability of growth in this period, allowing for greater predictability, was at the cost of the underlying development of large disequilibria – rising real estate prices, low saving rates and widening external imbalances – that contributed to the subsequent turmoil. Hence, should the 'good' forecasts made before the crisis be praised, or instead criticized as they were not pointing to the growing probability of a crisis?

The discussion above has two implications for assessing accuracy. First, users of forecasts need to have a sense of the accuracy of a broad set of forecast variables: for example, governments may want to achieve a range of likely public finance outcomes. Second, the perception of the reliability of a forecast also depends on users' risk aversion, and may not be symmetric. Hence, one may want to put different weights on positive versus negative risks when gauging accuracy. An error leading to an understatement of GDP growth, for example, might be considered benign by governments, in so far as the fiscal position or the labour market will then look better than had been foreseen; but an error of the same size in the opposite direction would create unexpected problems and hence attract more criticism. Similarly, the (rare) cautious growth forecasts made for the period preceding the 2007 financial crisis were, strictly speaking, inaccurate so long as the global economy continued to boom; but they were based on an economic analysis that proved, with the benefit of hindsight, to be relatively prescient.

In sum, the interactions between perceived accuracy and use of the forecast are important: the accuracy of a forecast nobody uses would be irrelevant. Questions about forecast accuracy have therefore gained prominence as governments and central banks, but also private agents, have begun to rely increasingly on economic forecasts.

7.1.2   What should a forecast be compared to?

In principle, the reliability of a forecast is assessed by looking at the size of the errors made. But what is the relevant benchmark? There are at least three main issues to consider.

First, it is not obvious to which strings of data the forecast should ultimately be compared. The data themselves tend to change over time, as statistics are refined and revised. With which vintage should the forecast then be compared? The initial one, some firmer one, or the definitive one, which in principle best describes what actually occurred but may become available only several years down the road? In fact, the revised data often incorporate new information, including changes in methodology, that was not initially available, making the analysis of the forecast error quite difficult. From this perspective, it makes sense to compare the forecast with the first vintage of the data, such as the advance, or 'flash', national account estimates published four to six weeks following the quarter in question – as is indeed the usual practice. Unfortunately, things are usually not quite as clear-cut. A forecast may look mediocre when compared to the initial data, but turn out to do a much better job when set against the final data (Gallo *et al.*, 2002). In such cases, the forecast might in effect have anticipated subsequent statistical revisions. This can happen, for example, with those short-run GDP forecasts that incorporate qualitative survey information: they sometimes approximate the final data better than the flash estimate computed with incomplete hard data.

The second issue is whether one should look at the intrinsic accuracy of a forecast – that is, the size of the forecasting error, duly normalized – or rather, at how it compares with other forecasts. While these two approaches may at first sound similar, the second one is more demanding, since in practice different forecasts cannot readily be compared. They are not carried out at exactly the same time, hence some benefit from having more recent information than others. For example, the *Consensus Forecasts* – a survey of prominent forecasters' predictions published by Consensus Economics Inc. – represents the average of individual forecasts estimated every month; but a number of these individual forecasts are not formally revised with a monthly frequency and thus reflect outdated information at the time of publication (Crowe, 2010). In theory, forecasts that are issued later have a shorter forecast horizon and should therefore be slightly more accurate, all else being equal. Andersson and Aranki (2009) have developed a way to take this into consideration so as to obtain fairer comparisons.

Another caveat in comparing forecasts is that they may pertain to somewhat different time horizons and statistical concepts. For example, when forecasting inflation, a measure based on a CPI index may be forecast in one case, as opposed to the private consumption deflator in another; similarly, GDP growth forecasts may or not incorporate a working-day correction. Furthermore, it is not easy to compare forecasts of different types. A projection based on a macroeconomic model provides a comprehensive and relatively detailed picture, whereas a time-series-based forecast, for example, is restricted to a few aggregates; hence, merely comparing the results of these two exercises would be too simplistic.

Forecasts further differ depending on whether they are published (and therefore possibly normative) or for internal use only. Some are conditioned on specific policy and other assumptions, while others are not: for example, the exchange rate may be frozen or may itself be a forecast. It is therefore difficult in practice to compare institutions' forecasting records in a meaningful way.

A third problem is time consistency. Straight comparisons across forecasts assume that each institution invariably and strictly follows certain well-defined procedures. In practice, this is not the case. For example, in the late 1970s, the US CBO's long-run economic projections were strongly normative, directly reflecting policy goals. Nowadays, however, even if they are not always fully plausible, they are clearly meant to show what will happen if recent historical trends are extrapolated. In Europe, the EC has gradually reduced the normative element of its projections and now bases its 'positive' forecasts on an unchanged policy assumption. Furthermore, forecasting teams, tools and outputs change over time, not least because the forecasts themselves are not generated mechanically but involve considerable discretion. When contrasting institutions' track records, it is thus advisable to focus on only a few key variables, such as growth and inflation, and on a relatively short horizon – say, the current year and the year following.

7.1.3 Measuring accuracy

In practice, four types of method are used to gauge the accuracy of a forecast (see Appendix 7.1). The first is to compute summary statistics describing past errors, in particular the mean error, also called 'bias', and the root mean squared error (RMSE).

The second approach is to compare the forecast of interest to other projections, particularly simple or 'naïve' ones. This benchmarking can be done either by comparing some summary statistics, such as the bias and the RMSE referred to above, or by testing for the respective information content of competing forecasts.

The third way is to test whether the errors in a forecast tend to be one-sided or correlated; if this is the case, the forecast will not be considered to be rational. In particular, analysts will check whether the errors are unbiased (that is, whether they average zero). A further check relates to efficiency, meaning whether all the information available at the time the forecast was produced has been used optimally. In practice, the analyst will focus on testing 'weak efficiency' by checking whether the errors are serially correlated over time or not.

Finally, an important element to gauge the accuracy of a forecast is to conduct directional tests. The aim here is to check whether the forecast is, on average over the period, right in anticipating a decline or a rise in the variable of interest. This approach can be restricted to the periods that see a turning point in the variable, since predicting these episodes correctly is of particular importance.

7.2 Analysing errors

Once forecast errors are measured, how should they be analysed in practice to improve the understanding of economic mechanisms and the quality of future forecasts? Several methods are in common use: post-mortems, analyses of the various factors contributing to the errors, and time series decompositions.

7.2.1 Post-mortem analysis

The first way to learn from past forecasting errors is to undertake periodically a post-mortem analysis. The purpose here is, first and foremost, to examine the errors in order to better understand how the economy has recently been functioning. The focus is on the nature and causes of the unforeseen exogenous shocks that have occurred, and on agents' reactions. This may in turn lead to changes in the behavioural equations of the model, but this is not the primary purpose of the exercise.

The first step is the identification of the shocks that took place unexpectedly after the forecast was made (an oil price shock, a recession in a partner country and so on). Their impact is then quantified through simulation exercises, such as variants around the central forecast. From a formal standpoint, this amounts to ascribing differences between prediction and outcome to two sources: changes in exogenous variables, and deviations of behavioural patterns as reflected in equation residuals.

A key element is the quality of the forecasting tool used, which has to be sufficiently good that misspecification problems can fairly confidently be ruled out. The type of behavioural change can then be of two sorts:

- either the average behavioural patterns, which are the ones embodied in the estimated model equations, are not questioned, but agents are seen as temporarily reacting somewhat differently because of a peculiar context (say, they show more reluctance to spend than normally because of transient geopolitical concerns); or
- the average behavioural patterns are evolving, which is difficult to realize at an early stage because it takes some time for the change to transpire in a statistically significant fashion. In that case, the model's parameters and even its structure will be reconsidered. One example is the influence of interest rates

on private spending in Europe, which changed following financial liberalization in the mid-1980s but became statistically significant only with a lag.

In reality, the distinction between exogenous and endogenous variables is not that clear cut, and sources of errors are not necessarily independent, calling for caution when interpreting individual equation residuals.

In principle, a post-mortem requires a reliable macroeconomic model, and therefore cannot be carried out to analyse forecasts produced with other tools. In practice, however, more 'qualitative' post-mortems are nevertheless undertaken. This is usually done by comparing alternative forecasts to the forecast of the institution. In Sweden, for example, the parliamentary Committee on Finance examines and assesses the monetary policy conducted by the Riksbank every year. It receives specific material for this assessment, especially on the Riksbank's forecasting performance relative to others.

7.2.2   Analysis of the factors contributing to forecasting errors

A second, related approach is to decompose the errors to separate what can be ascribed to the properties of the model used from what is a result of the forecaster's other choices. This is precisely what *ex-ante* versus *ex post* forecast comparisons are aiming at (see Box 7.1). This exercise has some similarities with the post-mortem analysis described above, but the aim is different. It is less to infer a measure of the change in agents' behaviour than to disentangle the sources of errors.

This decomposition is useful because it can help to distinguish between the three main causes of the forecast errors: the model specification, the exogenous assumptions entering the forecasting model, or the degree of judgement employed when using the model. By looking at the contribution of these various factors, the forecaster will be able to focus attention on the main cause of forecasting errors and therefore improve future exercises.

But such a decomposition is also somewhat artificial, in so far as, in practice, the three elements are not independent. For example, the forecaster's choices as regards the residuals of the model's equations may be linked to the treatment of the exogenous variables: if exchange rates are frozen by assumption but the forecaster feels that, say, some depreciation is likely, s/he might adjust the residuals accordingly, at least to some extent. Similarly, the choices on residuals tend to take into account the shortcomings of the model, as a substitute for revamping it fully.

Though the situation differs across forecasts, a general feature is that forecasting ('*ex-ante*') errors are smaller than the ('*ex post*') errors that can be attributed solely to the model used, at least when forecasts are done correctly. This may seem surprising at first, since one might expect the model to perform much

---

Box 7.1 *Ex ante* **versus** *ex post* **errors**

One can define the *ex ante* forecast error Ea_t as the discrepancy between the initial forecast and the outcome; that is:

$$Ea_t = X_t - P(X_t) = X_t - P(X_t(P(EX_t), R_t))$$

where EX_t is the set of exogenous variables and R_t stands for the residuals of the behavioural equations plugged into the forecast. This can be further decomposed as follows:

$$Ea_t \underset{\substack{ex\ ante \\ error}}{} = \underbrace{X_t - P(X_t(EX_t, 0))}_{\substack{ex\ post \\ error}} + \underbrace{P(X_t(EX_t, 0)) - P(X_t(P(EX_t), 0))}_{\substack{error\ on\ the\ exogenous \\ variables}}$$

$$+ \underbrace{P(X_t(P(EX_t), 0)) - P(X_t(P(EX_t), R_t))}_{contribution\ of\ the\ residuals}$$

- The *ex post* forecast error is related to the model: it corresponds to the difference between the outcome and a forecast made by simply plugging the values of the exogenous variables observed *ex post* into the model, without any adjustment.
- The second error is the one made on the values of the exogenous variables (which are themselves either simply assumed or forecast).
- The contribution of the residuals to the forecast error pertains to the forecaster's own decisions – and in particular to his/her judgement calls when deciding to deviate from the 'automatic' forecast produced by the model (with, as input, the assumptions related to the exogenous variables).

If it turns out that the *ex ante* error is mainly a result of the *ex post* error, the model may misspecify some behavioural relationships. If instead, the *ex ante* error principally stems from the exogenous variables, there is a case for trying to build up some more expertise, outside the model, on these exogenous variables. And if the *ex ante* error is principally a result of the residuals, greater attention will need to be paid to how the forecaster uses the model in forecasting.

---

better if the exogenous variables were known with certainty rather than merely assumed or forecast. In fact, the error made on the exogenous variables is often offset by the forecaster through the educated choices made regarding the residuals. In this way, the intervention of the forecaster helps to reduce the errors that would be generated by the mechanical application of the forecasting model.

7.2.3 Using time series methods

As noted in Appendix 7.1, it can be instructive to compare the forecasts with the outcome of time series methods such as the ARIMA and VAR processes. The idea is to assess the value added of the techniques used by the forecaster, compared to a simple statistical extrapolation of the past behaviour of the variables of interest.

The use of time series methods can also be of great help not only to measure but also to analyse forecasting errors, especially in the absence of a fully-fledged model. Forecast errors can be analysed using VARs representing the key endogenous variables that are suspected of having played a role in the errors. For example, the contribution of each of the components of aggregate demand to a revision of the forecast of GDP can be generated. Such an approach is, of course, cruder and less detailed than using a full model, given that it focuses on only a few variables and ignores some of the feedback effects.

Specifically, a VAR representation allows the forecaster to identify the innovations affecting variables compared with their usual dynamics (see Annex II). One can see how these innovations changed between the time of the forecast and the outcome, and quantify their contribution to the forecast error. For example, one will be able to see how the innovation related to investment has changed, and – via the parameters of the VAR representation – have a crude estimate of the impact of the variation of the 'investment shock' on the estimation of GDP in the model, and hence on the error of the GDP forecast.

However, the innovations in a VAR may have a common component, so their 'actual' contributions to the forecast will differ from the crude estimation suggested above. To identify variable-specific innovations, a structural VAR can be run, based on some simple hypotheses. For example, it will be assumed that public consumption, as one element of aggregate demand, is completely exogenous (admittedly a simplification, but not an outrageous one). The other elements will be assumed to be linked through changes in GDP. Then their 'structural' innovations can be obtained as the residuals of the regression of the innovations on the estimated innovation in GDP. They will be considered as specific disturbances to the various components of aggregate demand and their respective contribution to the forecast error of GDP will then be computed.

7.3 Forecasters' track record

Passing an overall judgement on the accuracy of forecasting is difficult. The diagnosis depends on the institution, the country, the period, the variables and the horizon. Generally speaking, however, forecast errors are substantial but forecasting is relatively efficient (in the aforementioned sense). One major problem, however, is that turning points are poorly anticipated.

7.3.1   Errors are substantial but forecasts are generally efficient

The RMSE for short-run GDP forecasts is typically on the order of one to two percentage points. For example, and looking at the European Commission's forecasts for the European Union as a whole, Melander *et al.* (2007) find, for one year-ahead GDP growth forecasts, a ME of 0.3, a MAE of 0.9 and a RMSE of 1.2 (for inflation forecasts: –0.2, 0.8 and 1.3, respectively). Among G7 countries (see Table 7.1) the USA stands out as one of the less difficult to forecast. Moreover, forecast errors are usually larger for smaller countries (Melander *et al.*, 2007). Juhn and Loungani (2002) find that errors for developed economies are smaller than for developing countries, but that taking into account the variability of the underlying data reverses this conclusion. Errors on GDP are often negatively correlated with the cycle, with growth under-predicted when activity accelerates and over-predicted when it slows down. Also, accuracy improves as horizons shorten, since incoming high-frequency data, say quarterly GDP statistics for year *t*, allow analysts to firm up the forecast for year *t* + 1 as time goes by – not too surprisingly, given the important role played by carry-over effects (see Appendix 2.1).

In general terms, forecasts can be described as fairly accurate. Melander *et al.* (2007) confirm this relatively good track record, after looking at the projections

Table 7.1   Accuracy of OECD real GDP growth projections for G7 countries*
The accuracy of one-year-ahead forecasts is significantly lower than for current-year forecasts

	USA	Japan	Germany	France	Italy	UK	G7 average
			Bias**				
Current year	−0.02	0.05	−0.07	0.08	0.19	−0.02	0.07
Year ahead	−0.10	0.84	0.83	0.81	1.11	0.48	0.69
			Over-predictions***				
Current year	44	56	50	63	56	44	54
Year ahead	56	63	75	63	75	63	66
			RMSE				
Current year	0.54	1.17	0.73	0.50	0.61	0.62	0.71
Year ahead	1.55	2.24	1.60	1.42	1.59	1.34	1.64
			R^{2}****				
Current year	0.86	0.56	0.67	0.78	0.61	0.83	0.72
Year ahead	−0.20	−0.63	−0.55	−0.80	−1.57	−0.17	−0.54

*Over the period 1991–2005. Real GDP growth projections published in the *Spring Economic Outlook* editions: current year denotes the projection for year *t* finalized in April of year *t*, and year ahead the projection for year *t* + 1 finalized in April of year *t*; outcomes are the data published one year after the finalization of the projection.
**Average forecast error (in percentage points of GDP).
***Frequency of over-predictions in percentage of the total number of projections.
****See the definition in Appendix 7.1.; R^2 = 1 for a perfect forecast.
Source: Vogel (2007).

of the European Commission, the OECD, the IMF and the *Consensus Forecasts*. In particular, forecasts are not systematically biased one way or the other, even if there are notable exceptions; they are frequently considered to be directionally accurate; and persistence in the forecast errors is relatively modest.

Turning to efficiency, the hypothesis of weak efficiency is normally accepted. However, full informational efficiency is usually rejected: various studies show that forecasters do not use all the information available, and in particular do not exploit other forecasts sufficiently. For example, a country forecast could be enhanced by incorporating information provided by the forecasts made for the larger countries; GDP growth forecasts could be better exploited for forecasting inflation and so on.

Furthermore, 'economic' forecasts tend to outperform naïve projections, as analysed recently by Vogel (2007), who compares OECD forecasts to the naïve extrapolation of trends. In other words, they are better than a coin toss, though this task seems more difficult when forecasting financial variables (see Chapter 4).

Finally, it is also generally recognized that forecast revisions add value: Timmermann (2007) finds that revisions made during the preparation of IMF forecasts typically reduce forecast errors significantly, at least for the same-year forecasts realized for advanced economies.

Even so, there is room to improve the quality of economic forecasts, which in some cases fail to outperform time-series-based forecasts. Specifically, it is generally recognized that forecasts do a relatively good job with regard to projections for the current year but tend to display important shortcomings over a longer term. Indeed, Vogel (2007) finds that OECD one-year-ahead forecasts (as well as the forecasts produced by other institutions) display a positive bias, of as much as 0.7 of a percentage point, for the projections made in the spring of the preceding year. He argues that this mainly reflects a propensity to over-predict during downturns. In addition, he finds that projection revisions do have a significant bias: the revisions analysed show that, on average, GDP projections are being adjusted downwards below the initially established forecast. This pattern could be taken into consideration to enhance the forecasting process, since it will be more efficient for the forecasters to be less optimistic in their initial projections.

Similarly, Timmermann (2007) finds that IMF growth forecasts display a tendency for systematic over-prediction, with the most significant bias being for next-year forecasts, and that forecasts of US GDP are correlated with forecast errors in a substantial number of advanced countries. A key source of error seems to be related to the general assumption in IMF projections that the output gap is eliminated in the medium term (that is, a negative relationship is found between the output gap and the forecast errors for some countries).

Another potential source of bias can be a result of structural changes in the economy that take time to be captured by the forecaster. For example, Batchelor (2007) finds a bias towards optimism in the *Consensus Forecasts* for a number of industrial countries experiencing a decline in their trend growth rates in the 1990s and 2000s, such as Japan and some large euro area economies.

There are also some political economy factors at play. Regarding the IMF's inflation projections in the *World Economic Outlook*, Timmermann (2007) notes a substantial bias towards under-prediction for many emerging countries that have an IMF programme – as can be seen from Table 7.2. One reason is that these projections typically reflect programme targets rather than unconditional forecasts (Musso and Phillips, 2002).

Finally, whether forecasting accuracy has improved over time, as forecasters have learnt from their mistakes and more sophisticated techniques have been developed, is unclear. Prior to the Great Recession, the absolute size of errors for growth and inflation forecasts was declining but this primarily reflected a decline in the volatility of the variables themselves. Vogel (2007) estimates that OECD projection errors have tended to decline in line with the decline of volatility in GDP growth since the 1990s. Melander *et al.* (2007) also find that inflation forecast errors were larger when inflation was higher in the 1970s. Other work, however, has suggested a declining accuracy of US forecasts, derived from the *Survey of Professional Forecasters*, over time (Campbell, 2004). Using the Federal Reserve Greenbook forecasts, Tulip (2005) finds that the reduction in output unpredictability has mainly concerned short horizons, and

Table 7.2 Accuracy of IMF forecasts by regions*

The accuracy of macroeconomic forecasts is much better for advanced economies

Forecasting errors	Real GDP growth**		Inflation**	
	Mean	Standard deviation	Mean	Standard deviation
Advanced economies	−0.5	2.1	−0.1	1.4
Africa	−1.4	4.1	81.7	177.6
Central and Eastern Europe	−1.6	3.9	16.0	34.1
Commonwealth of Independent States	−2.2	8.4	229.7	592.5
Developing Asia	−0.6	2.9	1.4	9.2
Middle East	−1.1	6.6	−0.8	11.3
Western Hemisphere	−1.3	3.1	10.8	62.1

* *World Economic Outlook* next-year forecasts made in April; averages across countries in regions over the period 1990–2003.
** In per cent per year.
Source: Timmermann (2007).

is much less than the reduction in output volatility. Moreover, the post-mortem analyses following the Great Recession are likely to highlight the exceptional mistakes made by many forecasters prior to the 2007 financial crisis.

7.3.2   Forecasts are generally comparable

Different forecasters tend to produce fairly similar predictions. Thus they often err simultaneously. This reflects that they use broadly similar models, fed with the same raw data, and face the same unexpected shocks. In addition, they influence each other, as discussed below. In fact, it is generally acknowledged that no forecasting institution outperforms its counterparts by all measures of accuracy, for all variables and all the time.

One important element is that considering forecasting institutions *per se* is a simplification of reality. Forecasts are, in practice, not generated by a single forecasting model, but involve judgement – and hence personal inputs from the staff involved in the exercises. The forecasts of an institution such as the OECD are not produced by the same individuals for all countries, and, of course, the composition of forecasting teams changes over time. So, over a long period of time, it is not obvious that a given institution should display a specific track record compared to others unless it manages to develop specific internal knowledge that can be shared among its staff members regarding, say, the use of an in-house model or to set up a process to ensure the consistency of the various forecasting inputs.

Certainly, some studies suggest that international institutions such as the OECD perform relatively well (Pons, 2000), a result also found by Vogel (2007) when comparing the OECD to the *Consensus Forecasts*. This might be ascribed to the fact that international institutions take international linkages explicitly into account, so that, for example, imports and exports across countries are consistent with the projections for each of them. In addition, they interact regularly with national authorities, both to exchange data and in the context of multilateral surveillance. But how much of an edge this gives the international institutions remains a moot point, and in practice, the conventional wisdom is that there are no clear major differences in forecast accuracy among public and private institutions. A recent evaluation by Melander *et al.* (2007) finds that the European Commission's track record for GDP forecasts is broadly comparable with the ones of the *Consensus Forecasts*, the IMF and the OECD; the relatively small differences in performance appear to be explained by timing factors. Timmermann (2007) comes to a similar conclusion when comparing IMF forecasts and the *Consensus Forecasts*.

In contrast, forecast accuracy does vary considerably across variables. Relatively less volatile variables, such as GDP or consumption, are easier to pin down than more volatile ones, such as investment – characterized by larger forecast errors, as documented by Melander *et al.* (2007). Uncertainty is also particularly acute in the case of external trade: first, forecast errors for individual countries tend to be correlated; second, international feedback effects stemming from unexpected developments in certain countries are hard to factor in properly; and third, errors made on gross trade flows tend to accumulate, since a significant proportion of exported goods are made up of imported goods that are being re-exported, in the context of growing globalization (a factor particularly relevant for the supply-chain economies located in Asia). Finally, it is also commonly estimated that forecasts of 'balance' variables (that is, the budget and the current account balance) are less accurate.

7.3.3   A typical shortcoming: misgauging turning points

A fundamental and largely shared weakness of forecasting institutions is their poor track record with regard to the anticipation of turning points in activity, be they turnarounds in growth rates or structural breaks. In addition, forecasters have a strong propensity to miss these with disconcerting unanimity – as was cruelly evident in the 2007 financial crisis.

Looking at a sample of 60 past recessions worldwide, Loungani (2001) found that a recession was on average predicted only a third of the time by April of the year in which it occurred (that is, two-thirds of the recessions that took place in a given year had not been recognized by forecasters by April of that year). In other words, recessions tend to arrive before they are forecast![1] This very poor performance in anticipating turning points one year ahead is also confirmed by Vogel (2007) for OECD projections: only 6 per cent of the number of turning points are predicted correctly in the spring of the year before (current year projections, however, manage to get three-quarters of the turning points). Moreover, when recessions are anticipated, their severity is generally under-predicted. In its October 2008 *World Economic Outlook*, the IMF noted that during the period 1991–2007 it had had a tendency to over-predict world growth quite substantially in the years immediately preceding global recessions, confirming the difficulty of predicting tail events. The same holds for the closely monitored US economy, where the recognition lag is also considerable, as noted by Fintzen and Stekler (1999).

Certainly, recessions are relatively rare events. Hence, when judging the quality of a forecaster, one should also recognize his/her ability not to predict recessions that do not happen (recall the long-standing joke that 'economists are so sharp they have predicted eight of the past five recessions'). Recourse to

---

[1] Recessions were defined here as any year in which real GDP declined. Another conventional definition of a recession is that of two consecutive quarters of negative real GDP growth.

directional tests allows this to be taken into account, and thus to soften the critique. Indeed, the directional accuracy of forecasts is generally estimated to be quite high: one-year-ahead OECD forecasts correctly anticipate around 70 per cent of growth pick-ups and slowdowns (Vogel, 2007).

Furthermore, it appears that recoveries are better anticipated than recessions (Loungani, 2002). Since recessions have typically lasted less than a year, forecasting recovery during a recession has been a good bet. In a few cases recessions did drag on, however, and forecasters' ability to predict which ones would do so has been less impressive.

That said, the inability to predict recessions is a major problem. As documented by Stekler (2010), recessions account for a major part of quantitative forecast errors. The apparent accuracy of forecasts during 'normal times' can thus provide a false sense of security, and users of those forecasts will tend to forget that low probability/high loss events can happen at any time – not least because only very small shocks are needed to change the projection in a dramatic, non-linear way. The 2007 financial crisis has been a painful reminder of these limitations and of the fact that economic forecasts are almost always wrong when they matter most (see Appendix 7.2).

7.3.4 The specificities of long-term forecasts

The general features analysed above usually apply to short-term forecasts; that is, for a relatively limited time horizon (one to two years maximum). Studies on the accuracy of medium- to long-term forecasts are much less frequent. One obvious reason is the long lag for such forecasts between the time they are made and the time when the actual numbers are known. As analysed in Chapter 6, none the less, medium- to long-term forecasts are seen as projections. Hence it is generally considered that their degree of accuracy is limited and depends on the specific assumptions retained. This does not mean that there is no interest in reviewing the quality of these projections: as for short-term forecasts, a post-mortem exercise can be particularly useful to enhance the quality of following forecasting exercises. For example, the fact that trend growth in the BRIC countries proved much more rapid in the 2000s than expected at the beginning of that decade has led economists to revise their forecasts up to 2050 significantly upwards (see section 6.2).

One issue that deserves specific attention is the uncertainty surrounding population forecasts, which play a major role in shaping long-term economic projections. As analysed in IMF (2004), the following features characterize long-term demographic projections:

- past projections of world population are generally considered to be relatively accurate, though future world population has tended to be over-estimated.

One benchmark provided by the IMF is that the world population projected in 1957 over-estimated the population in the year 2000 by 3½ percent;

- errors are smaller for industrial than for developing countries;
- the projections become much more uncertain the further into the future one goes: for example, the proportional error of the projection almost doubles when the projection length increases from 15 to 30 years;
- past projections have displayed a tendency to underestimate the proportion of the elderly in the population;
- the main causes of demographic projection errors are the uncertainty surrounding the estimation of the population at the start of the forecasting period; the difficulties in estimating trends in fertility, mortality and migration; and unexpected events (war, disease and so on).

7.4 What causes errors?

Apart from exceptional non-economic events, major sources of errors are the assumptions on which the forecast is based. Other sources include mismeasurement, model misspecification and the forecaster's psychological inclinations.

7.4.1 Changes in forecasts assumptions

A major factor explaining forecasts errors, which is often overlooked, is that the assumptions underpinning the forecast often turn out not to be met. This is why the OECD describes its economic projections as conditional rather than pure forecasts. Indeed, they hinge on specific assumptions regarding exchange rates, commodity prices and macroeconomic policies. Musso and Phillips (2002) find that policy deviations play a dominant role in the forecast errors related to the projections of IMF supported programmes. Turning to the European Commission, Melander *et al.* (2007) recall that problems related to external assumptions (regarding world trade, oil prices and so on) can explain up to 60 per cent of its forecast errors. And, in fact, if a forecast turns out to be wrong because of unexpected shocks, it may still be characterized as optimal in that it reflected the information available at the time of its preparation.

The policy assumptions underlying the forecasts, especially in the fiscal sphere, are particularly important, not least when current policies are unsustainable. In that case, the standard assumption of unchanged policies is very contrived but can serve to point to the development of unsustainable tensions, showing that something will have to give (that is, a policy change, an exchange rate correction and so on). While such forecasts will prove inaccurate *ex post*, they can be useful to provoke desirable policy reactions, as documented by Boughton (2001) in the case of the IMF. A similar issue relates to the IMF forecasts for those countries with an adjustment programme: the forecast assumptions can result from a compromise with the authorities, and experience shows that in practice many programmes are not completed successfully; but if the official IMF forecasts were to deviate greatly from the programmes adopted, they might precipitate a serious crisis and the forecasts could then look even more inaccurate.

7.4.2   'Statistical' hurdles

Economic magnitudes are measured imprecisely and some of them are rather volatile. As discussed in Annex I, there are often significant differences between the first national account estimates published by the statistical office and the final one. In addition, certain aspects of economic activity are poorly captured by the statistical apparatus. Furthermore, forecasters may not have full access to the relevant data: for example, existing information on tax returns may be out of reach. Some forecasters may also fail to fully appreciate how some of the official statistics are put together. And, of course, forecasters may simply overlook less easily available but none the less important information: for example, they may focus too exclusively on the real sector without paying sufficient attention to agents' balance sheets, a weakness highlighted by the 2007 financial crisis.

At the same time, forecasters need to make choices on how to treat the incoming data, knowing that they are at best a lagged image of reality. In particular, after how many unusual observations should they decide that a trend has changed? This question was answered in a variety of ways in the case of the evolution of US productivity since the mid-1990s, for example, with some analysts declaring early on that trend productivity growth had increased, while others long preferred to remain doubtful (see Box 6.5). Another difficulty pertains to the construction of long time series needed for estimation or extrapolation: forecasters have to make some difficult choices – for example, on how to handle breaks, such as the German unification in the early 1990s (which also has implications for long-run euro area series); and the definition of variables can fluctuate over time. Proper treatment requires in-depth knowledge of data construction procedures and peculiarities.

7.4.3   'Economic' sources of errors

More obvious sources of errors involve shocks that forecasters cannot be expected to anticipate. Natural disasters, such as the Great East Japan earthquake in March 2011, belong to this category, as do political and social surprises (such as wars or strikes). Other, more economic, factors are also hard to foresee. In particular, monetary and fiscal policy decisions cannot be predicted with certainty. One recent example from Berger *et al.* (2009) is that forecasters' accuracy in predicting ECB policy rates seems to be partly explained by geographical considerations (notably the country-specific characteristics of the forecaster and his/her closeness to information hubs). In fact, uncertainty regarding these policy decisions is also a problem for official forecasters, since they are not necessarily fully informed about policy makers' intentions, and more fundamentally, the policy makers themselves do not always know the shape or size of future measures. Also complicating the picture is that globalization implies a growing exposure to developments beyond national borders, of which forecasters in any given country know relatively little. In addition, errors may be correlated across countries, because of the existence of common shocks and the systemic importance of the larger economies: if forecasters in Europe align their assumptions for the US economy on the consensus forecast across the Atlantic, and if the latter turns out to be wrong, both sets of forecasts will be off the mark.

Another source of error is related to the nature of economic science. Experimentation is impossible, casting doubts on any theory, and the structure and functioning of economies mutate over time. New production techniques emerge (say, information technologies), aspirations change (say, as regards demand for leisure), institutional arrangements are altered (say, concerning retirement) and regulations evolve (say, deregulation of the network sectors). The 2007 financial crisis also highlighted the difficulty for economists of grasping the interlinkages between the real economy and the financial sphere. In many cases, the forecasting tools need to adapt.

Finally, the central forecast is only an approximation of what might happen, on average, when looking at the whole range of possibilities, based on a linear description of economic relationships. In the real world, non-linear reactions are observed, notably in the case of extreme events, which are rare but can have disproportionate impacts. This also explains why forecast accuracy is higher in normal times, when the relationships among variable are captured correctly by forecasting tools, but not around the time of rare events such as deep recessions.

7.4.4 Forecasters' behaviour

Keynes understood the herd instincts of his fellow economists when writing in the depth of the Great Depression that 'it is better for reputation to fail conventionally than to succeed unconventionally' (Keynes, 1936; see Chapter 4). Forecasters may prefer to cluster around a common prediction rather than issue outlier forecasts, as documented in the case of the USA, Japan and the United Kingdom by Gallo *et al.* (2002), who show that an individual forecaster's predictions are strongly influenced by the consensus forecast of the previous month. This mimetic behaviour sometimes leads the consensus to converge on a forecast that later turns out to be far off the mark. Moreover, the fact that individual forecasts are not independent implies that the standard deviation among the distribution of individual forecasts does not provide an adequate sense of the measure of the uncertainty surrounding the *Consensus Forecasts*.[2]

To some extent, such herd behaviour may reflect the fact that preparing a full-blown forecast is very costly, so that some in the forecast business cut corners and rely on the average view of others. Another explanation is that one forecast, in particular that of the authorities, plays a leading role because it is widely believed that it relies on a superior set of information, including inside knowledge about forthcoming policy decisions. Granger (1996), for example, argues that in the United Kingdom, forecasters tend to cluster around the Treasury's forecast.

Alternatively, some forecasters may crave publicity and try to distinguish themselves from their peers. Individual forecasters may want to build a reputation of relative optimism/pessimism compared to the consensus, and thus tend to produce consistently biased forecasts. Looking at the growth forecasts of the Blue Chip Economic Indicators panel in the USA, Laster *et al.* (1999) found that the forecasters working for banks and industrial corporations (firms that might be expected to make forecast accuracy a priority) tend to stay close to the consensus, whereas independent forecasters, who stand to gain the most from publicity, tend to produce outlier forecasts (see also Ashiya, 2009, who looked at Japanese forecasters), at the cost of forecast accuracy. Yet other forecasters indulge in 'wishful thinking': in a study of foreign exchange forecasts in Japan, Ito (1990) documented that they are biased towards scenarios that would benefit the forecaster's employer, with forecasters working for exporters being more likely to expect yen depreciation, and the reverse for those employed by importers.

Another behavioural reason for forecasting errors is related to the forecaster taking into account users' reactions. A government may be reluctant to predict some developments, even if they are very likely, for fear of political embarrassment or in the belief that such a prediction would become a self-fulfilling prophecy. Dreher *et al.* (2007) argue that IMF forecasts are not based purely on economic considerations, and that forecasts for developing regions can be influenced by 'political' considerations such as the proximity to major countries represented in the IMF Board or the degree of indebtedness to the IMF. Private sector forecasts may also be tainted by market considerations or the intention to influence policies. Furthermore, forecasters try to smooth forecast

---

[2]Nevertheless, Juhn and Loungani (2002) find that greater forecaster discord does provide useful information as it is associated with higher forecast errors.

revisions on the grounds that users would not understand or like a succession of frequent, large up-and-down revisions. Gallo *et al.* (2002) found evidence of the persistence effect of the forecaster's own earlier forecast; this translates into long recognition lags when the economy changes course. Such forecast conservatism can reflect credibility concerns, cost reasons, overconfidence and the learning process, especially in the face of ongoing structural changes (Batchelor, 2007).

Naïve forecasters may also become overly influenced by developments abroad. A well-known example is that of forecasters outside the USA considering that the US cycle must be an advance indicator of their own country's economic situation, without taking into account the possible reasons for divergence.

A further source of error relates to the natural human inclination to put more weight on current or recent developments than on what happened in the more distant past, so that the latest observations often have a disproportionate influence on the forecast. For example, if the oil price suddenly surges, forecasters will either carry the new high price forward or build in a gradual return to a lower price that would be deemed to be consistent with the fundamentals of the oil market. Rarely will they be so bold as to predict a prompt fall.

Yet it might be quite rational for a forecaster to deviate deliberately from optimality. In the past, there was a tendency for authorities to present biased forecasts because of the presumption that they could become self-fulfilling or because of their presumed effect on confidence and behaviour. This attitude has generally disappeared as authorities have realized that it is difficult to lie to everybody all the time. Still, however, policy makers do care about the asymmetric costs of forecast errors (the risk posed to fiscal revenues if growth is lower than expected; and the risk of excessive wage claims if the inflation forecast is too high). If the distribution of the possible outcomes is not symmetric, the (optimal) central forecast may have to differ from the mean and present a bias for rational reasons.

7.5 Can accuracy be improved?

The above diagnosis suggests a number of possible improvements to enhance forecast accuracy. A key caveat is that the dependence on the assumptions incorporated upstream into the forecast may be difficult to change. Generally, forecasters will refrain from second-guessing what lies beyond their field of expertise, such as exceptional natural phenomena, changes in the course of macroeconomic policy compared to what had been promised, and so on. Thus, when terrorists strike, as on 11 September 2001 in the USA, or an earthquake occurs, as on 11 March 2011 in Japan, the forecast is clearly invalidated. But this reflects the limitations of economic science rather than any extraordinary incompetence on the part of forecasters.

Nevertheless, there are a number of ways to attempt to address the other causes of forecast errors, namely statistical hurdles, economic causes and biases related to forecaster behaviour. Combining a variety of forecasts can help, though there are a number of pitfalls. More fundamentally, however, forecasting accuracy is only one of the criteria that should be considered when assessing the quality of a forecast: the forecast should contain a discussion of risks and should not be assessed solely on the accuracy of its central scenario.

7.5.1 Mitigating the causes of forecast errors

One way to improve forecasts is to enhance the quality of the data serving as inputs. In a number of countries, there is considerable scope to do so, witness the overestimation of CPI inflation in the USA, and the efforts made to fix the problems identified in the mid-1990s by the Boskin Commission (Lebow and Rudd, 2003); the endemic problems of Japanese deflators (Ariga and Matsui, 2003); or the deficiencies of euro-area-wide statistics, because of insufficient harmonization across member countries (ECB, 2001a). To date, most attempts have tended to concentrate on 'traditional' economic indicators. But the 2007 financial crisis has highlighted the data shortcomings related to the financial sector, sectoral balance sheets as well as some asset prices (notably housing prices). Significant efforts will be required to address these issues.

More broadly, progress in economic knowledge and in applied economics improves the quality of forecasting. And the more forecasters are involved in the decision-making process, the easier it is for them to serve users' needs, communicate about the limits of their forecasts and thereby avoid misunderstandings. Moreover, putting more effort into estimating the current state of the economy can enhance the accuracy of the forecasts.

7.5.2 Combining forecasts

An alternative and easier approach is to combine all the published forecasts, weighting them according to their track record or simply taking a straight average. The idea is that, since forecasts draw on different information sets but do not systematically outperform each other, taking all of them into account will yield extra information. To the risk averse, an added attraction is that extreme predictions are thereby avoided.

While this may sound appealing, several caveats are in order. As noted, forecasts are often clustered around similar numbers. In practice, there may thus be little diversity from which to profit. Moreover, combining different forecasts amounts to mixing genres, which makes it difficult to interpret the numbers. And if the underlying models and information are relatively similar after all, averaging the forecasts again will not add that much. Ideally, an optimal forecast would use the best information set and the most accomplished model, rather than a mixture of heterogeneous ingredients; from this perspective, pooling information sets is seen as being superior to pooling forecasts (Elliott *et al.*, 2006). For Crowe (2010) this represents the main cause of the consensus forecasts' inefficiency, as even if individual forecasts entering the consensus are rational, they overweight the consensus-shared 'prior' that is based on older information already available.

Against this background, some have tried to find ways to select the most valuable forecasts and eliminate the rest. One criterion for a superior forecast is, of course, that it is unbiased. But the list of forecasts to be retained also depends on the correlation of forecast errors: the forecasts that are combined should display uncorrelated errors. Another issue is to determine the weights that should be assigned to the selected forecasts. This can be very tricky in practice. Taking a straight average for combining forecasts has the advantage of simplicity. Another way is to minimize the RMSE of the combined forecast based on past performance, meaning that forecasts with high variances would count for less, and vice versa. Alternatively, the forecast variable could be regressed on the various forecasts so as to retain those that have the greatest influence. One could also rank the selected forecasts according to some accuracy matrix, and only retain a certain share of the best forecasts (the 'thick modelling' approach of combination). Yet another way to proceed would be to put most weight on those forecasts that performed well recently. A problem with all these methods, however, is that past success is no guarantee for the future.

Empirical work on the subject leads to the following conclusions, not all of them uncontroversial, however:

- *A priori*, accuracy can be improved by combining a model-based forecast with time-series-based forecasts.
- The gains depend on the horizon, and are in principle larger over the longer run, in so far as short-run uncertainty is dominated by unanticipated shocks that neither approach captures.
- While in any one year some forecasters will probably outdo the consensus in terms of accuracy, these top performers vary from year to year and can rarely be identified in advance.
- Conversely, a combination might have outperformed individual forecasts over some past period but could fail to do so in subsequent years.

Theoretical work on the subject is somewhat less conclusive and of limited use for practitioners, not least because it is difficult to know beforehand whether a consensus forecast will be superior. Another debated issue is whether to select first only the forecasts deemed to be encompassing the others before combining them, or not (Kisinbay, 2007). Yet, conducting several theoretical experiments, Clements and Hendry (2004) find that combining forecasts adds value and can even dominate the best individual device. Nevertheless, some theoretical problems are insuperable. In particular, forecasting models are living creatures, and in principle their latest version incorporates the lessons from earlier mistakes, implying that past errors are not bound to recur. And even with a decent consensus forecast, accuracy diminishes as the horizon is extended, some variables remain more difficult to forecast than others, and so on.

None the less, a forecaster can benefit from comparing his/her prediction with that of others. Since the late 1980s, the publication *Consensus Forecasts* (described further in Appendix 8.1) has enabled forecasters to do that in a systematic fashion. The dispersion among individual forecasts is also informative: a high standard deviation of forecasts, as is observed in the case of Japan, signals a more difficult forecasting terrain (Juhn and Loungani, 2002). But, for the reasons spelt out above, forecasters should not rely too much on the consensus.

7.6 Accuracy is not enough – assessing the risks around forecasts

7.6.1 Looking beyond the central scenario

While accuracy is obviously important, it is not a sufficient, nor always an indispensable, condition for a valuable forecast. Other desirable features include the overall coherence of the forecast, but also its timeliness, the relevance of the variants accompanying the central scenario and, more generally the quality of the analysis offered to policy makers. Crucially, a good forecast furthers the understanding of how the economy operates – and using accurate forecasting techniques is a prerequisite – but good 'story-telling' is of uppermost importance as a basis for sound decision-making. So the focus is less on the accuracy of what will happen and more on what might happen, with a clear description of the possible alternative outcomes and the reasons why the forecast may turn out to be wrong. This is particularly important when the forecaster is convinced that his/her forecast is unlikely to be accurate because s/he does not trust the assumptions s/he has to rely on conventionally (see Boughton 2001): the solution in such cases is to emphasize the alternative scenarios.

Moreover, a key element is that, once a forecast is produced, the risks surrounding it also have to be considered – for example, by estimating the consequences of a given shock or even by building complete alternative scenarios. Furthermore, a systematic evaluation of the quality of previous forecasts (both compared to actual outcomes and to other forecasts) should in principle accompany the presentation of any new forecast, to help in understanding the recent past and to give a sense of the inherent degree of uncertainty associated with the forecast. A good example is the regular monetary policy report of the Swedish central bank, which provides systematically statistical tables showing the latest forecasts and the revisions compared to the previous forecast; moreover, an appendix compares the forecasts with outcomes and other forecasts in the context of the annual assessment of monetary policy conducted by the Swedish parliament.

7.6.2 Building variants and alternative scenarios

Each of the numerous assumptions underpinning a forecast is in effect taking a chance on the stability of behavioural relationships, the evolution of exogenous variables, the forthcoming economic policy initiatives and so on. The implied uncertainty and the relevance of the forecast can be better understood by constructing variants or alternative scenarios around the central forecast (also called the reference or baseline scenario). This helps to comprehend the risks of potential shocks and their transmission channels.

A variant can be defined as an alternative scenario resting on a slightly different set of hypotheses, and which is designed to evaluate their impact. For that reason, the results are often presented as deviations from the baseline. Simple variants involve changing only one assumption, regarding, for example, the price of oil, interest rates, the propensity to consume, or investment. Complex variants combine several changes, and tend to become alternative scenarios, telling altogether different stories. This exercise is often conducted by contrasting an optimistic scenario, where several key variables evolve favourably, with a pessimistic one, which causes them all to move in the opposite direction. While a little extreme, this can be a useful pedagogical device.

Macroeconomic models are well suited to this type of analysis. Indeed, many of their exogenous variables – be they command variables (related to monetary and fiscal policy) or variables describing the environment (such as world demand or oil prices) – are precisely those for which forecasters would wish to try out alternative assumptions. Moreover, models highlight the mechanisms through which risks can affect the forecast, which helps analysts to consider the likelihood of alternative scenarios: the first-round effects of changes in assumptions will be quantified, but also their ultimate impact, once all the feedback mechanisms have worked their way through. This is a valuable contribution, which other approaches, such as VARs and indicator-based methods, do not offer. That said, too much should not be expected either: not all of the underlying hypotheses can be tested, nor can all the risks be pinned down *ex ante* (as the unexpectedness of the 11 September, 2001 terrorist attacks illustrated painfully). The best way to proceed, therefore, is to focus on some of the shakiest assumptions that are known to have a strong influence on the shape of the forecast.

For the very long-term forecasts analysed in Chapter 6, these are often presented with a set of variants depending on different assumptions for a limited set of key parameters (such as population or productivity). For example, the demographic projections produced by the United Nations include a central projection but also a low- and a high-variant scenario. Thus, in 2009, the United Nations was projecting world population to grow from 6.9 billion in 2010 to 9.1 billion in 2050 – with a high variant (10.5 billion), a low variant (8.0 billion) and a 'constant fertility variant' (11.0 billion).

7.6.3 Techniques and limitations

A simple variant is typically obtained by altering the level or growth rate of the exogenous variables or the add-on factors. This experimental 'shock' can be confined to the short run or extended indefinitely. Four types of shocks can therefore be envisaged, depending on whether they affect levels or growth rates, and on whether they are temporary or permanent (see Figure 7.1). Suppose, for example, that policy makers decide that an extra €1 billion will be spent as public investment over the forecast period: this would be considered as a permanent level shock. Or suppose that the minimum wage were to be raised: this would be treated as a temporary shock on the growth rate of wages.

This type of analysis may run into a number of difficulties, however:

- It may be hard to calibrate the shock, in particular when the type of shock under consideration cannot be described as a mere shift in the exogenous variables. Consider a tax cut granted to a specific sector that is not treated separately in the model: a proxy then has to be constructed – for example, a change in the economy-wide tax rate scaled down according to the size of the sector in question. It is also possible to draw on other sources of information to establish the first-round effect of the tax cut and then to use the model merely to compute the feedback effects.
- The model may not adequately capture the mechanisms that one would expect to matter most for the shock at hand. For example, in the case of a change in interest rates, it may be that the model does not have a sufficiently rich financial and monetary sector, so that some crucial aspects of the transmission of the shock are missed. It may also be that some behavioural relationships have mutated since the model was last estimated, calling at a minimum for a reconsideration of the obsolete equations.

Figure 7.1   Four types of shocks

Four generic types of shocks can affect the level in output as well as its change over time

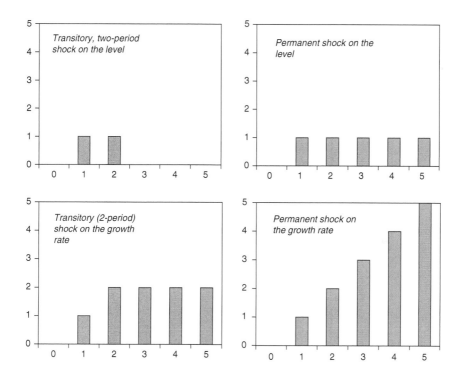

Notes: X-axis: time; Y-axis: change in the level of a fictitious variable in the wake of various shocks.

- Economic policy makers may not react as assumed. Many variants are run on the basis of the conventional hypothesis of unchanged policies, or assuming that policy makers will follow some rule (such as the Taylor rule). This may be unrealistic for some of the less standard shocks. Then, some *ad hoc* policy reaction has to be built in.

While understanding simple variants can be relatively straightforward, more complex combinations do not lend themselves so readily to interpretation. However, if the model is linear, one can treat such combinations as sums of simple variants. This holds more generally, even in models involving a degree of non-linearity, provided the shocks under consideration are small and the forecaster is ready to ignore second-order effects.

Also, in many cases, and in particular for output or prices, deviations from the baseline are presented in level terms. Users have to bear this in mind when comparing growth rates (GDP growth or inflation) across scenarios and over the years.

An important by-product of the presentation of variants and alternative scenarios is to highlight that forecasts are uncertain. Yet another possibility is to complement systematically point forecasts with additional information regarding the underlying probability distribution. This can be done in a rather crude way by providing in a systematic way some of the statistics described in Appendix 7.1 that are calculated on the basis of past forecast errors. Confidence intervals can also be provided, assuming, for example, a normal distribution function. A more complete distribution of the possible value of the variable of interest – a density forecast – can also be provided; for example, by using a fan chart to provide a quantification of the risks to the outlook identified in terms of deviation from the baseline scenario; in other words, the fan chart displays the mean forecast and the associated set of forecast intervals covering 10 per cent, 20 per cent and so on of the estimated probability distribution. This is done in the IMF *World Economic Outlook* projections, with confidence intervals around the projected path of selected economic variables such as growth or inflation. The sources of information to construct these bands incorporate survey-based measures, such as the deviation of individual forecasts provided by the *Consensus Forecasts* or, in the USA, the quarterly *Survey of Professional Forecasters* produced by the Federal Reserve Bank of Philadelphia (which provides mean forecasts as well as the probabilities of different ranges), market-based measures (using financial option prices), the historical track record of the forecasts, judgement[3] and so on. A common assumption when producing these fan charts is that the underlying distribution of the economic variable is skewed. One will, for example, retain a two-piece normal distribution; that is, a combination of two normal distributions with the same mean but different variances (IMF, 2008). There are several sources justifying such potential asymmetry in the balance of risk, such as the zero interest floor or the non-linearity of output–inflation processes. Yet such calculations still rely on *ad hoc* assumptions, and the statistical distribution assumed may still underestimate the probability of extremely adverse events.

7.6.4　A first example: quantifying the impact of the Asian crisis in 1997–8

A telling example is the Asian crisis that began in 1997, causing massive shifts in trade and capital flows and having worldwide repercussions. Looking at its impact on the US and European economies, it can be analysed as four overlapping and interrelated shocks:

- an adverse trade shock stemming from currency depreciation and a decline in demand in the crisis countries;

---

[3] Wallis (2004) emphasizes the role that judgement can play and, comparing inflation outcomes and the fan chart probability distributions, finds that the Bank of England overestimated uncertainty in its inflation forecasts.

- a second and partly related adverse trade shock resulting from yen depreciation and demand contraction in Japan;
- a stimulatory financial shock, with central banks in advanced OECD countries lowering interest rates and the additional downward pressure on bond yields caused by the repatriation of capital from emerging market economies; and
- a commodity price shock, as the price of oil and other raw materials declined.

Using the macroeconomic model software NiGEM, the French Ministry of Finance estimated in its budget documentation around mid-1998 that:

- Together, the two trade shocks would reduce the level of US and EU GDP by some 1.5 per cent by 1999.
- The central banks' policy reaction, coupled with the reflux of capital to US and EU markets and the decline in commodity prices, would partially but significantly offset the impact of the trade shocks on activity.
- The net impact of the Asian crisis on the level of GDP, taking into account short-run feedback effects, would thus be in the order of ½ per cent in 1998 and ¾ per cent in 1999 (implying an impact on annual output growth of, respectively, ½ and ¼ per cent).
- Inflation would be pushed down further, as all four shocks were working in the same direction.

7.6.5 A second example: building a downside scenario for the global economy in 2009–10

Another instructive example regarding the presentation of risks was the downside scenario presented by the IMF in its Spring 2009 *World Economic Outlook* (IMF, 2009b). The aim was to decompose the additional decline in growth (relative to the baseline scenario) between international spillovers and domestic shocks in the various economic regions.

Three types of shocks were considered (financial stress, a housing price correction, and a fall in equity prices), with three intensities (mild, moderate and severe) depending on the region. This was based on substantial judgement, country expertise and the use of NiGEM. This quantified approach allowed forecasters to highlight the regions subject to the greatest risk of additional decline in growth in 2009–10, and to disentangle the respective contribution of domestic factors versus international spillovers.

In this analysis, the risk of an additional decline in growth was deemed to be most severe in emerging Europe, mainly because of domestic factors. Emerging Asia was seen as facing the risk of a moderate decline largely as a result of international spillovers (accounting for the bulk of the estimated decline).

A similar exercise was performed by the OECD. In its Autumn 2009 edition of *Economic Outlook*, the organization selected five possible risks to recovery (fiscal policy tightening; an equity price jump; depreciation of the dollar; an increase in oil prices; and an increase in external demand) and simulated the related shocks using the OECD Global Model to calibrate the possible consequences in terms of growth and inflation for major economic areas.

Because of the increasing interlinkages among economies, there has been a growing policy interest for sharing such exercises at the international level, not just in the context of large international institutions such as the IMF and the OECD, but also among individual countries. In 2009, the G20 leaders launched a 'Framework for Strong, Sustainable and Balanced Growth' in which G20 countries would undertake a mutual assessment of their economic and policy targets. This exercise was built on a base case assessment and on the exploration of alternative scenarios. The intention was to highlight the consequences of individual policy actions and enhance policy collaboration to produce outcomes that could benefit everyone.

7.6.6   A third example: quantifying the economic impact of US policies to alleviate the 2007 financial crisis

A similar approach was used by Blinder and Zandi (2010) to gauge the impact of US policies to deal with the 2007 financial crisis. Using Moody's macroeconomic model, they simulated the counterfactual (that is, a scenario excluding the policy responses) and compared it to the baseline. The effects they found, shown in Table 7.3, are strikingly large.

Indeed, their estimates suggest that, as a result of the policies, real GDP was 15 per cent higher by 2011 compared to what it would otherwise have been; employment was almost 10 million higher, the unemployment rate more than 6 percentage points lower, and the level of the consumer price index

Table 7.3   The 2007 financial crisis: economic impact of policies*
Very expansionary fiscal and monetary policies are estimated to have attenuated significantly the impact of the 2007 financial crisis on the US economy

	2009	2011
Real GDP level (per cent)	+5.8	+15.3
Employment (in millions)	+3.4	+9.8
Unemployment rate (in percentage points)	−2.0	−6.5
Consumer price index level (per cent)	+1.5	+9.0

*Differences between the baseline and the 'no policy response' scenarios for the years 2009 and 2011.
Source: Blinder and Zandi (2010).

9 percentage points higher. The peak-to-trough decline in GDP after the 2007 financial crisis would have been close to 12 per cent with no policy responses, compared to an observed decline of just 4 per cent. In addition, this analysis disentangled the financial policy effects (including monetary policy responses and financial stabilization programmes) and the fiscal policy effects, the former being estimated to be much larger than the latter.

Further reading

For a comprehensive overview of the accuracy of major economic forecasts, especially those of the European Commission, the IMF, the OECD and the *Consensus Forecasts*, see Melander *et al.* (2007). Boughton (2001) provides further insights on the political economy considerations surrounding forecasting habits, evaluation and communication, focusing on the IMF case. In the USA, the CBO publishes an annual assessment of its own forecasting performance in *The CBO's Economic Forecasting Record*. Various aspects of forecasting accuracy are analysed in a dedicated issue of *IMF Staff Papers*, vol. 49, no. 1 (2002). Additional theoretical background can be found in Diebold (2007). The variants for demographic projections are available on the United Nations website (un.org/esa/population/unpop.htm).

Appendix 7.1 Measuring accuracy in practice

In practice, four methods are used to gauge the accuracy of a forecast:

- summary statistics describing past errors;
- benchmarking against other projections, particularly simple or naïve projections;
- testing whether errors tend to be one-sided or correlated; and
- directional tests showing whether turning points in activity are well anticipated.

Summary statistics

An intuitive way to assess accuracy is to characterize the size of past errors. Consider a sequence of T forecasts carried out between time $t = 1$ and $t = T$, with X_t being the forecast variable and $P(X_t)$ the predicted value. Then the errors can be defined as $E_t = P(X_t) - X_t$.

The statistical properties of E_t over the period under consideration can be described using various standard summary statistics, including:

- The mean error (ME), equal to $(\Sigma_1^T E_t) / T$. This is the *bias*. It should be close to zero for a good forecast.
- The mean absolute error (MAE), equal to $(\Sigma_1^T |E_t|) / T$, where $|E_t|$ is the absolute value of E_t.
- The mean squared error (MSE), equal to $(\Sigma_1^T E_t^2) / T$. Its square root is called the RMSE (root mean squared error).

The mean error is a simple and commonly used measure of forecast bias. But as an arithmetical average, it says little about the variance of the errors. A small mean error could indicate that all the errors were small. However, it could also indicate that many of the errors were large but with the over- and under-estimates offsetting each other.

The MAE and the RMSE do not suffer from this ambiguity. They are both measured in the same units as X_t, and should also be small for a good forecast. The RMSE tends to be preferred to the MAE, however, as the RMSE gives more weight to the largest errors, which are the ones forecasters worry the most about. Whether the RMSE or the MAE is 'small' or not should be judged taking into account the following elements:

- The variability of X_t.
- The precision of X_t itself; if X_t is measured imprecisely, the forecast cannot be that precise.
- Whether the errors diminish over time or not. Ideally, the variance of the errors should decrease as the forecast horizon shortens and more information becomes available. Timmermann (2007) finds that this is indeed the case for IMF forecasts, though the positive impact of new incoming information relates mainly to current-year forecasts rather than those for the year ahead.
- The performance of competing forecasts (see below).

If T is relatively small, these summary statistics should be interpreted with extra care, since individual forecast errors can have an unduly large influence in small samples: the mean error, for example, can change sign when a single observation is added.

Generally speaking, a 'decent' forecast of growth or inflation at a one-year horizon would display an RMSE of about 1–2 per cent, which is deemed to be acceptable given the uncertainty surrounding the measurement of such variables.

A drawback of the above summary statistics is that they are expressed in units that depend on the values taken by the variable under consideration. Hence one cannot readily compare them across variables – in order to find out whether it is growth or employment that is forecast most accurately, say, or to compare GDP growth forecasts across those countries that have significantly different trend–growth rates. The use of percentage errors (calculated as $100 \, E_t / X_t$) is scale-independent but is often of little help, since many of the variables of interest, such as inflation or GDP growth, are close to zero. One way to overcome this problem is to 'normalize' the forecasts; that is, to divide them by a statistic describing how large the values of the variable are: for example, by looking at the ratio $RMSE/\sigma$, where σ is the observed standard deviation of the realization X_t, or by dividing the MAE by the mean absolute deviation of X_t.

One useful summary metric for judging the accuracy of a projection in this context is its R-squared, which relates the MSE to the variance of the realization (Campbell, 2004):

$$R^2 = 1 - (\Sigma_1^T E_t^2) \, / \, (\Sigma_1^T (X_t - X)^2)$$

where X is the observed sample mean. R^2 gives an indication of the share of the variance of the realizations correctly accounted for by the projection: it is equal to 1 if there is no error; close to zero if the projection is uninformative; and when it is below zero the projection is considered to be misleading, since the mean of the realizations would be a more accurate predictor (though the sample mean is admittedly not known at the time the projection is made).

Comparison with other projections

Another indicator for judging the relative quality of a forecast that takes into consideration the values of the variable of interest is the following inequality coefficient proposed by Theil (called Theil's U):

$$U = \frac{\sqrt{\sum_1^T (X_t - P(X_t))^2}}{\sqrt{\sum_1^T X_t^2}}$$

where U is the square root of the ratio of the MSE over the average of the squared values of X_t. $U = 0$ indicates that the forecast was perfect.

When X_t is a growth rate, say of the CPI, U can be interpreted in a special way. A naïve projection of the CPI would be that the price level remains unchanged, so that for all periods $P(X_t) = 0$. U would in that case equal 1. So when U is close to 1, the forecast of the growth rate in question does not perform much better than a naïve forecast.

A number of other similar indicators can be set up, depending on the type of simple (naïve) projection used as a benchmark. For example, 'no change in the rate of growth' (as opposed to 'no change in the level') or 'return to the historical mean' can be set as comparator benchmarks. A somewhat more sophisticated approach is to compare the forecast with what purely 'statistical' techniques such as ARIMA and VAR processes would predict, based solely on the past behaviour of the variable.

At the end of the day, the quality of a forecast will be judged compared to what other forecasts (including the naïve ones) can deliver: forecast accuracy is thus a relative concept, which can be measured using the various statistics listed above.

Instead of comparing some summary statistics, yet another approach is to test the respective information content of competing forecasts P and P^*. Two approaches can be followed:

- A test for equal forecast accuracy as proposed by Diebold and Mariano (1995). The following equation will be tested:

$$d_t = \alpha + \varepsilon_t$$

  where $d_t = (E_t)^2 - (E^*_t)^2$ and E_t and E^*_t stand for the errors of, respectively, the forecasts $P(X_t)$ and $P^*(X_t)$ (d can also be estimated differently, depending on the preferred loss function). The test statistic is based on the observed sample mean of d_t corrected with an estimation of the asymptotic variance; if $\alpha = 0$, the two forecasts will be considered as being equally accurate.
- A second option to compare forecasts is to check whether forecast P^* provides valuable information compared to P, or is completely outperformed by it, in which case P would be considered to encompass P^* (the information provided by the second predictor P^* would not enhance the accuracy of P). The equation to test is:

$$X_t = \alpha + \beta\, P^*(X_t) + \gamma\, (P(X_t) - P^*(X_t)) + \varepsilon_t$$

If γ is significantly different from zero, then P^* is said to add useful information compared to P, unless $\beta = \gamma = 1$, in which case P^* is not adding any information and can be disregarded (in other words, P encompasses P^*). Another test here is to use a modified Diebold–Mariano test, with $d_t = (E_t - E^*_t)\, E_t$; if $\alpha = 0$ there is no useful new information provided by P^*, and P is said to encompass P^*.

Bias and efficiency

Forecast errors are said to be rational if they are unbiased (they average zero) and efficient. Efficiency here means that all the information available at the time the forecast was produced has been used optimally. Unbiasedness is in fact a necessary, though not sufficient, condition for efficiency. Another necessary condition in this regard is that the errors are random (white noise) and uncorrelated with past values of X_t or of the errors themselves. Indeed, if such correlations existed, they should have been exploited to reduce the errors and the forecast could have gained in efficiency.

The two types of tests generally carried out are:

- A regression of the forecast errors on lagged values of themselves: $E_t = \alpha + \beta\, E_{t-1} + \varepsilon_t$ (here we consider only one lag for the sake of simplicity, but one could test a higher number of lags). The forecast will be efficient if α and β equal zero. If α differs from zero, the forecast is biased. If β differs from zero, past errors carry over into present ones (serial correlation between the errors; the usual practice when comparing two sets of forecasts is to look at the value of the coefficients of the first-order serial correlation in the forecast errors).

- A regression of the observed values on the predicted values: $X_t = \alpha + \beta \, P(X_t) + \varepsilon_t$. Efficiency requires that the constant α be zero (necessary condition for unbiasedness), that the slope β be equal to 1, and that ε_t be white noise (Mincer and Zarnowitz, 1969). To test unbiasedness on its own, it is sufficient to regress the forecast error on a constant: $E_t = \alpha + \varepsilon_t$. If α is significantly different from zero the forecast is biased.[1]

The concept of efficiency presented above is often characterized as a weak form of informational efficiency, since the information considered relates to the values of the realizations and forecasts of the variable of interest. But a broader concept is that an efficient projection P is optimal if it reflects all the information available at the time of the forecast, including other forecasts. So one can test whether the realization can be explained by different competing forecasts (limited here to two: P and P^*); the equation to test then becomes:

$$X_t = \alpha + \beta \, P(X_t) + \gamma P^*(X_t) + \varepsilon_t$$

Alternatively one can test whether forecast errors can be explained by the deviation from a competing forecast:

$$E_t = \alpha + \beta \, (P(X_t) - P^*(X_t)) + \varepsilon_t$$

Vogel (2007) conducted such tests to for OECD and *Consensus Forecasts*; he found that following the *Consensus Forecasts* more closely would not improve OECD projections systematically.

More generally, testing for efficiency could also check whether additional information – say, past realizations or the concomitant forecasts for a 'large' country – could be used to enhance accuracy. For example, Melander *et al.* (2007) test whether individual country forecasts in Europe fully exploit the information provided by the forecast made for the whole region, or the forecast for Germany.

Another avenue is to test both the rationality of the forecast and its information content (Vuchelen and Gutierrez, 2005), by regressing the actual realization X_t on both its past values and its projections; for example:

$$X_t = \alpha + \beta \, X_{t-1} + \gamma \, (P(X_t) - X_{t-1}) + \varepsilon_t$$

This test allows analysts first to determine the rationality of the forecast: if $\alpha = 0$ and $\beta = \gamma = 1$, one comes back to the equation above for testing weak efficiency. Moreover,

---

[1] This type of test also requires the analyst to check for autocorrelation of the residuals.

if γ is statistically different from zero, the test implies that, even if it is not optimal, the forecast does provide additional useful information, compared to the simple extrapolation of past realizations.

A further element to judge the efficiency of a projection relates to the forecast revision process (since, in general, projections for a given period are made on successive occasions and updated with incoming information). If forecast revisions display a predictable pattern (for example, if they have a positive bias), this should be taken into account in the first stage of the forecasting process to improve the original forecast; for example, if growth forecasts made in the spring are on average revised downwards by 0.5 of a percentage point in the autumn, the first forecasts realized in the spring are not optimal in capturing this pattern. One will thus test whether $\alpha = 0$ in the following equation:

$$\Delta P_t = \alpha + \varepsilon_t$$

The test can also be more sophisticated, as analysts can check whether forecast revisions can be explained systematically by a wide range of indicators (position in the economic cycle and so on). One advantage of such tests is that the optimality of the forecast can be tested without using data on the target variable: this means that the forecast revisions can be tested independently of knowing the value of the realizations.

Finally, it is important to note that the tests described above are carried out on fairly small data samples, limiting the validity of underlying statistical assumptions such as that of a normal distribution. In fact, Musso and Phillips (2002) find statistical evidence that projection errors are not normally distributed, and that accuracy test results are sample-dependent. There are a number of statistical techniques to address the distortions to standard test statistics caused by sample size being limited, in particular to correct for heteroskedasticity and autocorrelation in regression residuals. Melander *et al.* (2007) also use residual bootstrap techniques to construct an empirical distribution function of the forecasts and obtain a large 'bootstrap sample' of forecast errors.

Directional accuracy

Directional tests seek to establish whether the forecast points in the right direction. A simple way to proceed is to group outcomes X_t and predictions $P(X_t)$ in a contingency table, where $N(P_+,O_+)$, for example, stands for the number of cases where both the prediction and the outcome have X_t rising, and $N = T$ is the total number of observations (see Table 7.4):

Table 7.4   Directional tests

		Predictions		
		$\Delta P(X_t) > 0$	$\Delta P(X_t) \leq 0$	Subtotal
Outcomes	$\Delta X_t > 0$	$N(P_+,O_+)$	$N(P_-,O_+)$	$N(O_+)$
	$\Delta X_t \leq 0$	$N(P_+,O_-)$	$N(P_-,O_-)$	$N(O_-)$
	Subtotal	$N(P_+)$	$N(P_-)$	N

A good forecast should have the prediction and the outcome moving in the same direction. In other words, $N(P_+,O_+) + N(P_-,O_-)$ should be large as a share of N (and much larger than $N(P_+,O_-) + N(P_-,O_+))$. A formal statistical test here is the chi-squared independence test. Let

$$\chi^2 = \sum_i \sum_j \frac{(N_{ij} - N_i.N._j/N)^2}{N_i.N._j/N}$$

where i and j take the values + and –, and where, for example, N_{++} is shorthand for $N(P_+,O_+)$ and $N_+.$ for $N(P_+)$.

The null hypothesis is that predictions and outcomes are independent, in which case this statistic follows a chi-squared distribution with one degree of freedom. If the null is rejected, the forecast is deemed to be directionally accurate.

Furthermore, one can build a summary indicator of the right predictions, that is $(N_{++} + N_{--})/N$, to compare how two sets of alternative forecasts compete.

Directional accuracy is particularly important when the concern is to make sure that turning points are not missed too frequently. However, these are two different issues. In general, forecasts are deemed to be directionally accurate because they do a relatively good job at anticipating the direction of macroeconomic variables on average over the cycle; but, sadly, this is far from sufficient to ensure that they predict turning points correctly (Vogel, 2007).

Appendix 7.2   Can forecasters predict severe crises? Recent lessons

As a group, the community of economists did not foresee clearly the financial meltdown that started in 2007 and the economic recession that followed. There is a long history of unexpected downturns, and in particular of financial crises, including the Great Depression of the 1930s. The recurrence of such episodes raises some forecasting questions: can such events be anticipated? If not (or if only partially), what remains as the main role for economic forecasting? What steps may nevertheless be taken to improve forecasters' ability to detect risks of severe crises and thus limit them?

The mainstream view before the crisis: 'Nobody saw it coming'

On a visit to the London School of Economics in November 2008, Queen Elizabeth II asked about the ongoing financial crisis: 'Why did nobody notice it?' Indeed, as the crisis developed and deepened, economic forecasters have been faulted for failing completely to anticipate it. To what extent is this true?

While the idea that 'nobody saw it coming' is an exaggeration (as discussed below), the main message from the forecasting community before the crisis, say in 2005–7, was one of confidence and optimism regarding the continuation of sustained global growth. Moreover, as the crisis began to unfold in financial markets between the summer of 2007 and the summer of 2008, many economists just toned down their assessment of the economic outlook, without predicting a major financial and economic downturn. Only as the crisis deepened in the summer of 2008 did expectations become much gloomier. And then, in the weeks following the collapse of Lehman Brothers in September 2008, forecasters raced to revise their projections downwards, and a number of them actually overshot on the way down, predicting an even more calamitous collapse than the one that eventually occurred.

Not only did economists fail to anticipate the crisis: as a group they nurtured a general climate of confidence and denial of the risk of such a crisis. By the mid-2000s, the notion of the 'Great Moderation' had gained prominence, in reference to a purported decline in the variability of output and inflation, especially in advanced economies, compared to previous decades. The relative mildness of the downturn that followed the bursting of the internet bubble in the late 1990s (in addition to the 11 September 2001 terrorist attacks, which froze global financial markets for a time), the robust world recovery that followed and the rapid integration of emerging countries into global markets underpinned the perception that business cycles had become more benign.

This 'Great Moderation' was interpreted as the result of a combination of structural changes (such as more flexible economies) and improved policies, notably monetary policy. Inflation targeting, whether in a formal or looser framework, was the standard way of thinking. This implied a focus on managing interest rates to ensure low and stable inflation for goods and services, while paying scant attention to financial stability issues (see Chapter 4). True, there were some worries over the sustainability of trade imbalances, rapidly rising asset prices and high leverage in many regions. But the overall mood was one of great confidence.

Willingly or not, Alan Greenspan, who chaired the US Federal Reserve between 1987 and 2006, epitomized such optimism. Before the crisis, he took the view that financial markets work better if left to themselves. He played down the existence of a bubble in the American housing market and minimized the implications of a possible turnaround in this sector. He expressed confidence repeatedly in the 'resilience' of the economy and suggested that it would be easier for policies to clean up the mess after the crisis had occurred rather than to try to lean against the wind beforehand. Only when the crisis unfolded did he modify his views, eventually admitting to being in a state of 'shocked disbelief' when the turmoil reached its height in October 2008.

If exemplary, Greenspan's shifting views are fairly representative of the general mindset as it evolved: optimism and the denial of significant risks before the crisis, underestimation in the early stages of the crisis, and then an abrupt swing to pessimism as the crisis deepened.

Minority views and internal debates

The collective failure of the forecasting community before the 2007 financial crisis should not be exaggerated. The idea that 'no one saw it coming', though popular in the media as well as among many policy makers and executives, is clearly an oversimplification. This may reflect sheer ignorance but may also be self-interested. Indeed, policy makers or financial market participants find it convenient to argue that risks were unanimously overlooked, as this exonerates them from responsibility for not taking action to prevent the crisis (and sometimes for having directly contributed to it).

In fact, prior to the crisis, there were many doubts and debates between economists on the sustainability of the Great Moderation. Bezemer (2009) identifies twelve economists, financial analysts or prominent commentators who warned between 2000 and 2006 of growing financial imbalances and the risks of a housing-led large recession. But such dire scenarios were not part of the main message that the profession as a whole was sending to both policy makers and the general public.

These 'minority views' (at the time) were not merely a reflection of the 'stopped clock syndrome' (a stopped clock is correct twice a day, so the existence of a few bearish forecasters in a flock of bulls may not be evidence of an actual and serious diversity of views). Indeed, these dissenters pointed to some factors that proved central to the dynamics of the crisis. In particular, they voiced concerns regarding debt-driven economies suffering from a growing disconnect between credit and financial assets on the one side, and underlying real-sector fundamentals on the other.

However, the contrast between those who 'were right' and those who 'were wrong' should not be overstated. Reality was more complicated in the sense that many economists (and decision-makers) probably felt uneasy in the face of conflicting signals and theories. For example, central bankers wrestled with a dilemma, as stable and low inflation was accompanied by rocketing asset prices. Even if they worried about the latter, they had neither undeniable measures of bubbles nor necessarily the mandate and tools to prevent them. Or they preferred to take care of the consequences of the crisis rather than trying to pre-empt it.

Global institutions also carried mixed messages: for example, the International Monetary Fund took a sanguine view overall but nevertheless expressed worries on particular issues in its *Global Financial Stability Reports*; for example, on the rapid growth of hedge funds and credit derivatives. The Bank of International Settlements has been credited with recurrently warning on growing financial risks before the crisis. On the other hand, other influential institutions, most prominently the US Federal Reserve and the economic research teams of large financial institutions, tended to discount risks, sticking to a message of confidence.[1] In the financial sphere, risks were largely missed or at least not publicized; for example, rating agencies kept awarding high marks to products that eventually proved to be much riskier than had been thought.

In sum, there were some doubts and uncertainty before the crisis as to the sustainability of growth, but they were largely overlooked. This points to a new question: why does the message from the forecasting community tend to be univocal, even when there is a divergence of views within the community?

Herding of beliefs

In a sense, and while it came as a big surprise, there is nothing really new in the causes and unfolding of the 2007 financial crisis. The typical features of financial boom and bust cycles were present: a housing bubble, a large expansion of credit and debt, financial innovations (in this case, securitization of subprime loans and the creation of new sorts of derivatives) and some structural changes (globalization, greater labour and product market flexibility, inflation targeting) that all supported the belief in a 'new era'. Widespread wishful thinking meant that a very few truly understood the growing complexity of the financial markets, and there was a belief that financial alchemy was able to transform risky financial products into instruments such as AAA-rated CDOs (see Chapter 4), as safe as risk-free assets but with much higher yields. The 2007 episode shares many characteristics with previous ones, the history of which spans many centuries, as noted by Kindleberger and Aliber (2011) and Reinhart and Rogoff (2009). Differences pertain to some of the detailed mechanisms (for example, the subprime market problems that triggered the Great Recession are specific to this crisis, as is the role of poorly supervised securitization) or perhaps to the scale of the crisis, which was magnified by the growing interdependencies within the financial sphere and between financial and real developments. However, other episodes such as the Great Depression of the 1930s or some emerging market crises in past decades would also count as large-scale crises.

With hindsight, what might therefore seem surprising is that so little was heard about the risk of a crisis. Some kind of 'herding in beliefs' in a context of great uncertainty

---

[1] There were some within the Federal Reserve who disagreed with the consensus of not-so-benign neglect, notably the late Governor Gramlich, who voiced serious concerns about the mortgage market in the early 2000s. Other observers pushed for US subprime lenders to adopt a code of best practice and to let outside monitors verify their compliance, but they did so in vain.

seems to have been in operation. Consider the appreciation of US housing prices. It is now acknowledged that a housing bubble had formed, which peaked in 2006 and ended in a sharp turnaround of prices in subsequent years. However, the majority of observers and actors in 2004–7 did not take it for granted that there *was* a bubble, and a fortiori did not anticipate a strong reversal.

These actors or observers had a number of arguments to support their views that the US housing market was not overwhelmingly expensive. One view (admittedly blunt but nevertheless effective) was that (nominal) housing prices had never fallen nationally in any year over the previous 50 years. Another was that there appeared to be a likely long-run upward price trend because of a scarcity of space and tighter land regulations. A third point was market heterogeneity: while there might be a bit of overheating in a few local markets ('froth'), this could not amount to a national bubble. Yet another argument was that, were it to happen, any correction in housing prices would be moderate; and finally, that in any case such a correction would have limited macroeconomic implications, given both the resilience of the economy and the possible reactions of macroeconomic policies. Such arguments and others featured in the speeches of Fed officials, but they were also put forward by many other economists and institutions in both the public and private sectors.

While signs of overheating in the housing market could be detected at the time, notably historically high price-to-rent and price-to-income ratios, very different opinions could be held without the possibility of 'scientifically' proving which one was 'correct'. Before the crisis, it was therefore possible to argue plausibly that housing prices were broadly sustainable or instead that they were strongly overvalued. In fact, even with hindsight, by how much housing prices were unsustainably high remains contentious and cannot be quantified with any precision.

In other words, the situation was both complex and uncertain. In such circumstances, one view tends to become dominant while challenging arguments tend to be played down or even discredited. What emerges from the public debate is not a spectrum of views reflecting the actual uncertainty but rather some form of consensus (embodied in the 'consensus forecast') with only nuances at the margin and not much echo for truly different scenarios.

Which view becomes dominant may be partly the product of chance, but not only this. Complexity makes it possible for factors beyond intellectual analysis to fashion the collective mood. In particular, private interests may come into play, either deliberately or instinctively. For example, many private actors by the mid-2000s had an interest in collectively believing that housing prices would continue to rise. Policy makers are also prone to overconfidence, to the extent it saves them from making hard decisions and makes life easier in the short run, during their mandates.

Because of the inherent uncertainty of the situation, it is difficult to row against the stream. First, it is hard to have clear and unambiguous diagnoses. Second, one analyst cannot really 'prove' that the dominant view is 'wrong', but is able only to express doubts and reservations, which are easily forgotten or simply ignored.

Additionally, common beliefs may have 'self-fulfilling' properties, at least in the short run. As discussed in Chapter 4, beliefs about financial valuations trigger changes in these that seem to validate the initial beliefs. This happened with the US housing market. As time goes by and prices rise, it becomes harder for sceptics to air reservations credibly. Thus the feedback effects of opinions on actual economic developments help to explain the emergence of a dominant opinion.

For macroeconomics at large, something similar seemed to have occurred with the idea of the 'Great Moderation'. As the downturn following the dotcom bubble was mild in the early 2000s (not least as a result of very active policy actions), it was tempting to conclude that indeed economic cycles were smoother and better managed in a 'new era'. In fact, the seeds of the 2007 crisis were sown with the easy credit conditions of the first part of the 2000s. Yet, as long as growth was strong and inflation muted, the notion that economies such as that of the USA were more resilient than before was hard to dismiss.

What cannot be expected from forecasting

One natural question is whether forecasters will be better at anticipating the next crisis. This question is a little paradoxical in the following sense. A crisis by nature comes as a surprise, at least for a critical mass of the populace. Indeed, were a crisis to be foreseen with enough assurance and sufficiently far in advance, then it might not happen, or at least, not have the nature of a 'crisis', in so far as action (painful as this might be) would have been taken to adjust unsustainable behaviour, commitments or policies and make them sustainable.

So, if a crisis is expected, it may simply not happen (because adjustments were made and the forecast was useful, if self-defeating), or it may happen straight away. The latter is likely with financial crises, which are triggered fundamentally by wake-up calls or 'Minsky moments'; that is, the sudden recognition that earlier commitments or promises might not be fulfilled. Investors, fearing that assets are less safe and worth less than previously thought, will try to dispose of them, thus driving down the prices of the assets, or even making them illiquid. Borrowers who are suddenly perceived as being potentially insolvent may not see their credit renewed.

In other words, correctly forecasting a crisis would actually trigger the crisis. If the common perception is that adjustments to financial promises have to be made, then these adjustments are likely to be made quickly. Forecasting in 2005 the vast financial crisis that started in 2007 could not have been 'the consensus forecast'. It had to be a minority and mainly unheard view (as was the case, in fact, leaving aside details on timing and mechanisms); if it had become the dominant view, it would have triggered adjustments that might have either taken the form of an immediate, full-blown crisis (in 2005), or of more gradual changes to avoid the expected crisis. In both cases, the initial forecast would have been invalidated.

As the world goes, crises are not events that occur in a deterministic manner at precise and predictable moments. There is an element of contingency over both timing and mechanisms. This reflects the actions of free individuals, the importance of their changing perceptions, and the complexities of their interrelationships. However, this is certainly not to say that nothing can be done to prevent or minimize the effects of crises. First, it may be preferable to have a crisis sooner rather than later (that is, in 2005 rather than 2007), as built-up imbalances might then be less serious. Second, reactions to 'crisis-prone situations', such as policy changes and mechanisms for orderly resolution, may greatly help to limit the damage, turning severe crises into more acceptable adjustments.

What might be expected from forecasters?

What remains of the role of forecasters if they cannot anticipate large crises with any precision? First, forecasting developments 'in ordinary times' is useful and unavoidable for many purposes. Second, by analysing risks and policies, economic forecasters can contribute significantly to the prevention of large crises, or at least to limiting their consequences.

Ordinary forecasts are typically built on the assumption that no large disruption will occur. This is both normal and without any credible operational alternative since, as already argued, crises and their timing do not occur in a deterministic manner. Meanwhile, routine projections are important as a basic framework for policy decisions, such as preparing budgets or setting interest rates (as discussed in Chapter 8). Indeed, standard forecasting tools do a decent job at detecting short-run ups and downs, predicting ordinary developments and giving an objective basis to macroeconomic assumptions.

At the same time, more prominence could be given to the analysis of medium-run risks and the sustainability of contemporary developments. To do this, economic forecasters must start by drawing on the lessons of the 2007 financial crisis (and of previous similar episodes).

First, the uncertainty of any forecast that goes beyond the near term must be acknowledged, and with it the possibility of a great commotion. What is more, uncertainty often comes 'from within the system', as opposed to 'exogenous shocks'. This is somewhat tautological, if easily forgotten, when one looks at the world economy as a whole, for which exogenous variables are few by nature. The problem is that, while forecasters have found many correlations and partial stories (of which this book gives numerous illustrations, such as, for example, the relationship between the exports of one country and world trade), it is harder to model the workings of the economy as a whole. Hence more efforts could probably be directed at understanding the endogenous mechanisms of economic cycles rather than postulating exogenous shocks.

Second, and related to this, it is by now widely acknowledged that cyclical developments in recent decades have to a large extent been driven by the interactive dynamics of the real and financial sectors. The 1960s and 1970s seemed to be dominated by real sector mechanisms such as the principle of effective demand and inflationary spirals. Since the 1980s, the importance of the interaction between real and financial developments seems to have grown continually, but economists are still struggling to produce a fully convincing representation of this interaction.

This calls for conceptual and modelling work. As reviewed in Annex III, efforts have been made in traditional macroeconomic models to incorporate financial variables in a better way. Dynamic stochastic general equilibrium (DSGE) models are also now being rejuvenated from that perspective. Whether these efforts will prove useful in anticipating future developments remains to be seen, however. Other researchers have argued for a more fundamental rethink of economic models. The so-called 'agent-based models' may be an interesting avenue in this respect. In these models, agents' behaviour is determined partly by direct interactions between them (and not just through prices). As a result of these feedback properties, which *inter alia* lead to herding and non-linear outcomes (small changes occasionally producing large effects), large disruptions such as financial crises may be replicated.

Third, some work on indicators and statistics and the way they are looked at may also be needed. Financial regulators need to scrutinize individual balance sheets more closely. At the macroeconomic level, more emphasis can be put on systemic risk and on some form of macro-prudential regulation. While trying to identify bubbles and taking action to tame them is fraught with danger (as argued by the Federal Reserve before the 2007 crisis), it may eventually be less of an evil than standing still in the face of widening imbalances.

To help in this task, economic forecasters could give more weight to indicators that try to connect the real and financial spheres, such as Tobin's q or the ratio of housing prices to rents. Rules of thumb relating the growth of credit or debt aggregates to the real economy may be useful in helping to identify financial imbalances as they are developing, though such analysis is admittedly rather blunt. In that respect, a more systematic approach could be found in accounting (or flow of fund) models (as advocated by Bezemer, 2009).

More traditionally, the analysis of real sector imbalances can in addition be further developed and given increased prominence in policy discussions, as has been initiated by the G20 countries since September 2009 with the so-called 'Framework for Growth'. In this framework, improved macroeconomic policies and better international policy co-ordination are expected from sharing and discussing national policy plans, building on a forward-looking analysis of the sustainability of global economic developments. Forecasts and risk analysis are thus central to the framework.

To conclude, a final recommendation would be to keep in mind the fundamental uncertainty that was stressed above and, more specifically, to welcome with a good dose of scepticism any future claims that 'this time is different'. Humility and rigour probably remain the best safeguards against the overconfidence that might offer opportunities and profits for some in the short run but bring about hard corrections that are often borne by others in the future.

Chapter 8

Policy Making and Forecasts

Contents

> *Forecasts shape economic policy making and are themselves shaped by it. They also enter other agents' decision-making processes. The government, private sector and social partners all use and produce forecasts, and look at each other's predictions. The role of forecasts in economic policy varies over time and across countries, but on the whole the trend is for more attention being paid to forecasts, especially in the realm of monetary policy. Communicating the forecasts successfully is a challenge, for both technical and political reasons. In that respect, the benefits of transparency are recognized increasingly. Even so, the temptation to produce and use forecasts in an opportunistic fashion endures.*

Forecasts are a key input into policy making but are also a prominent output, in so far as policy makers' choices shape the forecast, and those policy makers need to 'sell' their decisions jointly with a forecast.[1] Official forecasts enter the decision-making processes of other economic agents, notably businesses, social partners and households, some of whom in turn produce their own forecasts.

Demand for forecasts obviously arises from a need to form a view about the future. A government, for example, when preparing the following year's budget, has to rely on a forecast of activity to quantify the foreseeable tax receipts. Firms contemplating investment in new factories try to anticipate demand for the envisaged output. Social partners need to refer to some forecast of inflation when negotiating wage increases. In fact, in virtually all walks of economic life, agents regularly use forecasts as inputs into their decisions. That said, forecast accuracy is far from perfect, as discussed in Chapter 7, and preferences and constraints, along with forecasts, matter when framing decisions.

This chapter therefore begins with a general overview of the virtues and limitations of forecasts (section 8.1). It then turns to the role of forecasts in the

---

[1]In this Chapter and the next, the term 'forecast' will be used throughout even when 'projection' might be more appropriate (on the difference between the two, see Chapter 1).

conduct of economic policy, particularly fiscal and monetary policy (section 8.2) and to the role forecasts play in other forums (section 8.3). The focus then shifts to communication issues. First, some of the technical subtleties are difficult to explain in a simple way, not least with regard to the uncertainties surrounding the forecast (section 8.4). Second, there is the question of how much transparency is desirable: to what extent should governments and central banks publish their forecasts or keep them confidential (section 8.5)? Third, in the case of official forecasts, it is important to acknowledge their ambivalent status: they are both a technical and a political exercise, and this raises tensions that need to be addressed (section 8.6). Complementing the chapter is a world tour of forecasting institutions in Appendix 8.1.

8.1   Economic forecasts' virtues and limitations

8.1.1   The value added by forecasts

The rationale for economic forecasts stems from four basic facts: the existence of lags; the complexity of economic links; the irreversibility of many decisions; and uncertainty.

First, forecasts help to assess the full impact of decisions taken in the present, which materialize with a lag. For example, when a central bank cuts or raises its policy rate, it expects inflation to be affected with a lag, with the bulk of the impact coming one to two years down the road. Even inaction is a decision, and warrants evaluating what the implications are when going forward. And forecasts are a way to reduce, or at least to better circumscribe, the uncertainties surrounding the future.

Second, economies are complex systems, with many interactions. While common sense may grasp economic mechanisms taken individually, it is harder to take a synthetic view of the combined picture that emerges from aggregating numerous interactions. Forecasts make sense of the flow of economic data by integrating these into a consistent view of the economic outlook.

Third, many decisions are largely irreversible. For example, the outlays enshrined in the Budget Law will in principle be disbursed even if growth departs from what was foreseen in the macroeconomic forecast underpinning the budget. Indeed, in practice, governments have only limited means of freezing some spending or adding extra spending in reaction to evolving circumstances during the execution of the budget. Similarly for wages paid by firms, even if the environment has changed since the previous wage negotiation (though part of the compensation may be contingent on firms' fortunes – an example being the bonus system in Japan). In a nutshell, some decisions have very persistent effects as a result of institutional mechanisms such as the automatic renewal of part of public spending commitments, or because bargaining generally takes place over wage increases, as opposed to wage levels.

Finally, interactions and lags are not only complex but also uncertain. The degree of overall economic uncertainty varies over time. It increases considerably following unforeseen shocks, when it is difficult to assess promptly all the reverberations and to anticipate agents' reactions. Moreover, the most important shocks are also the ones for which the consequences are most difficult to quantify (oil shocks, the unification of Germany, the Asian crisis, the 11 September 2001 terrorist attacks, the 2008 Lehman Brothers' bankruptcy and the 11 March 2011 earthquake in Japan are examples of these).

Again, a forecast offers a structured framework with which to address these four basic needs. It does not eliminate risks but provides a way to identify and rank them, to assess the likelihood of alternative scenario, and to quantify the impact of various possible courses of action. A forecast thus helps in the making of 'robust' choices – that is, choices that do not depend on too specific a set of assumptions (see Box 8.1).

8.1.2   How forecasts fit into decision-making processes

Different economic agents obviously have different forecasting needs. A government requires a comprehensive picture, including both the overall trends and a fair amount of detail. In contrast, a portfolio manager, say, is more focused on the variables affecting financial markets. And in manufacturing, business executives are more interested in sector-specific developments (but also in more general variables such as interest rates and the exchange rate).

The type of forecast needed also varies. Some users are only looking for numbers, while others are more interested in explanations. Some agents need only a central scenario – for example, if they are risk-neutral (as opposed to risk-averse) – while others ask for a quantified risk analysis.

Furthermore, some users are seeking an unconditional forecast, notably when they cannot influence events but rather have to adapt to circumstances. Others, notably the authorities, request conditional forecasts, based on assumptions regarding the measures they can take *ex ante* to shape the environment. Moreover, depending on the desired type of forecast, one or other of the forecasting methods is the most suitable.

Not all users are equally reliant on forecasts. In increasing order of importance, forecasts can be:

- treated as one input among many others, provided mainly as background information;
- set apart from the other pieces of information as one important ingredient for decision-making;

Box 8.1   Decision-making under uncertainty

A framework for analysing decisions in an uncertain environment is that of 'decision theory', which stipulates that agents are characterized by a loss function spelling out the loss associated with each decision in each future state of nature. Let $L(d,y)$ denote the loss, where d stands for the decision and y for the state of nature. The latter is random and may in general depend on d. A decision rule then has to be defined. The usual criterion is the minimization of the expected loss: $Min_d \, E_y(L(d,y))$. (Another criterion would be the minimization of the maximum loss, if the agent is particularly risk-averse.)

The decision thus selected generally leads to a relatively favourable, or at least not too unfavourable, result in most of the possible states of nature. Such a decision is called 'robust' because it delivers acceptable results under a variety of circumstances. In contrast, decisions that would only be profitable under a small number of states of nature would be rejected.

By way of illustration, consider an investment project that would be profitable if the average forecast is realized, but not in a fairly large number of less favourable scenarios. If, overall, it appears to be too risky, the project may be abandoned. Alternatively, the project may be shelved until more information becomes available and allows a better assessment of the associated risks.

This illustrates the fact that the forecaster should not confine his or her attention to the central forecast, but should analyse the risks carefully. In practice, however, it may be difficult to explain this to users, as the latter often tend to focus on a scenario in which they believe and/or on the average scenario.

In fact, this attitude may not be irrational. In some cases, knowing the average scenario is sufficient to encourage analysts to make the optimal decision (as defined by the above criterion). This is true in particular when the loss function is quadratic; for example, when $L(d,y) = -A \, y^2 + B(d) \, y$. In this very specific case, the so-called certainty equivalence principle applies: the optimal decision, defined as the one minimizing the average expected losses across all the states of nature, is also the one minimizing the loss for the average state of nature $E(y)$: $Min_d \, L(d,E(y))$.

In practice, however, this condition is rarely met, not least because loss functions are not necessarily quadratic. In fact, loss functions may not even be symmetric, if agents dislike a given loss more than they like a gain of the same amount. Hence, analysing the risks surrounding the central forecast is normally a key part of the forecasting exercise.

- accompanied by more-or-less explicit recommendations, possibly based on alternative scenarios; or
- linked directly to operational decisions through some formalized procedure.

The fourth possibility in the list is sometimes encountered in firms (for example, for inventory management as a function of forecast demand), but rarely if ever in economic policy making. Indeed, policy makers generally do not want to tie their hands in advance by transferring their prerogatives to the technicians who build the forecasts.

More generally, two sets of considerations rule out a direct link between forecast and decision:

- On the one hand, forecasts generally cover only part of the relevant information. For example, a central bank's macroeconomic forecast will help when setting policy interest rates but will be less useful when analysing systemic risk (regarding the stability of the financial system, for example), which a central bank also cares about. Hence policy makers have to take on board information other than that contained in the forecast itself.
- On the other hand, even a forecast that could build in all relevant information would not necessarily dictate what should be decided in a deterministic way, if only because preferences may differ among policy makers. This is noted in the case of monetary policy by Budd (1998), who stresses that agreement among members of the Monetary Policy Committee of the Bank of England on a given collective forecast does not preclude different votes on the interest rate decision.

The role of the forecast is therefore generally to highlight the existing constraints facing policy makers, leaving it to the latter to pursue their objectives (according to the mandates they have). Granted, when forecasts suggest that an objective is unrealistic and thereby embarrass policy makers, they can either be ignored or disparaged in some way. None the less, forecasters for their part are expected to present their results as clearly and informatively as possible, to make sure that users properly grasp all the constraints (see below).

Ultimately, the influence of the forecasts remains difficult to establish, even in specific cases. The policy maker him/herself may not be fully aware of it. The rationale officially provided for decisions may not say much in this respect, since it does not always coincide with the real reasons. In the realm of public policy, where the social or political consequences of decisions are hotly debated, the role of economic forecasts is sometimes overlooked.

8.1.3   Forecasts' alleged shortcomings

Two criticisms are often levelled against forecasts. One is that, given their limited accuracy, they offer at best no more than broad trends, which can be derived at lower cost using simple extrapolations or just common sense. More sophisticated methods only complicate matters, the argument goes, or even serve to divert attention from real problems. The other criticism is that forecasts are instruments for interventionist policies.

Excessive sophistication

Regarding the first criticism, how sensible is it to devote considerable resources to setting up sophisticated forecasts? An alternative approach would rely largely on informal judgements and intuition, drawing on forecasts only if strictly necessary, and would use basic extrapolation algorithms (assuming, for example, that growth will equal the average observed over the last x years), while remaining alert to incoming anecdotal or statistical information.

Such scepticism *vis-à-vis* formalized approaches is not entirely groundless. The cost of certain forecasting tools (such as macroeconomic models) could indeed seem high in view of their limited accuracy. In addition, models are sometimes seen as black boxes, the workings of which are obscure not only for the general public but even at times for the economists who use them. Worse still, economists may be too busy running the models to pay sufficient attention to reality. Refining the forecasting tools may thus come at the expense of observing the facts, leading to a belated recognition of cyclical developments and unrealistic assumptions, in particular those used to assess the impact of economic policy measures. In that case, sophistication would not just be costly, but also plain harmful. These worries highlight the risks stemming from too mechanical a use of quantitative tools. But the latter also have a number of irreplaceable virtues.

Indeed, formalized methods impose a welcome discipline. They make it necessary to think through the underlying assumptions, which can be explained to users and discussed with them; in contrast, mere intuition lends itself less readily to such scrutiny and dialogue. More generally, making explicit assumptions and forecasts helps to structure discussions, and facilitates the convergence of views, or at least clarifies the reasons for divergence. The forecast functions like a common language, enabling the parties involved to better understand each other.

Moreover, the complexity of economic systems is such that the raw information being issued every day often sends mixed and confusing signals. Forecasting tools make it possible to sift through this maze of indicators and to organize that information properly, while keeping track of past mistakes and learning from them.

Finally, the notion that models would distract analysts from the observation of the facts should at the very least be nuanced. Historically, statistical data and tools have been developed jointly with macroeconomic models. One of the main purposes of the models is to help in the interpretation of cyclical developments (see Annex III). And models sometimes help to cast doubts on preliminary data which are indeed subsequently revised.

An excuse for interventionism?

Turning to the second sort of criticism, economic forecasts and the use of alternative scenarios are sometimes viewed as fostering the illusion that the authorities can control economic developments, thereby encouraging interventionist attitudes. In fact, prudence is called for when basing policy recommendations on forecasts. For one thing, forecasts do not eliminate uncertainty, neither with regard to future shocks nor concerning the impact of policy measures, as illustrated in the 1970s with the disappointing results of 'stop and go' policies. There is also a risk that forecasts simply serve to rationalize politically motivated initiatives: governments may use them to engage in unduly expansionary policies, hoping to benefit in the near term in the polls, but at the expense of longer-run stability and growth.

These problems, however, are to be blamed less on the forecasters than on those who misuse their work, even though they should remind forecasters that modesty is called for when they present their results.

Overall, forecasts are useful when they are not used naïvely, when the assumptions are spelt out transparently and rigorously, and when the robustness of the ensuing policy recommendations is adequately tested.

8.2 Forecasts and macroeconomic policy

8.2.1 Macroeconomic stabilization policy

Challenges and constraints

The field of macroeconomics was developed initially based on the notion that policy could steer aggregate demand. In this perspective, forecasting plays a key role in the identification of imbalances and the formulation of remedial measures. Smoothing the cycle at high frequencies ('fine tuning') would, however, be over-ambitious, given the uncertainty regarding where exactly the economy is in the cycle and what the impact of policy measures would be. In addition to recognition and decision lags, the lags with which these measures affect the economy are also uncertain and vary over time: hence, policy initiatives intended to be countercyclical might produce their effects with such a lag that they turn out to be procyclical, thus aggravating rather than reducing macroeconomic volatility.

A further complication is that, in some cases, stabilization might not be desirable. Demand management is an inappropriate tool when permanent supply shocks hit (oil price shocks, say). In that event, the optimal policy response might even be not to try to offset the consequences for growth and inflation.

Countercyclical policies are therefore difficult to get right. Consider, for example, an economy at full employment facing an unanticipated shock that is likely to reduce activity (say, a sudden drop in foreign demand). Before deciding how to react, the authorities should weigh the gains (the reduction in slack) associated with offsetting measures against the costs; such an assessment should take into consideration the uncertainty about the impact of the envisaged measures.

In such a situation, it may well be that the optimal policy reaction is to 'under-react' by taking stimulus measures that can be expected to reduce the slack but not to eliminate it entirely, as famously pointed out by Brainard (1967). Imagine yourself driving a car: sometimes when you turn the steering wheel, it barely responds; but at other times, slightly adjusting the steering wheel produces a sharp change of direction. How should you drive? Very cautiously, according to the Brainard principle. In monetary policy terms, this would translate into the recommendation for a central bank to calculate the optimal interest rate as if it faced no uncertainty, and then to move the policy rate in that direction, but by only part of the way (Blinder, 1998).

However, there may also be a case for 'over-reaction', notably if the authorities' loss function is asymmetric; for example, if they are more eager to avoid under-employment than overheating. To pursue the analogy, suppose you are driving that same unpredictable car along a narrow ridge, buffeted by gusting winds. Should you respond cautiously if a blast suddenly pushes the car towards the edge? The answer is no, since you might be pushed over the edge if the car fails to respond when you turn the wheel slightly. Better to risk over-steering. In the realm of monetary policy, for example, there may be cases where aggressive interest rate movements are called for to avoid a major economic disruption (Giannoni, 2002).

In fact, this rationale was invoked by US Federal Reserve officials during the downturn at the beginning of the 2000s to justify rapid and deep interest rate cuts: deflation was seen as a scenario carrying a low probability but high costs, calling for the Federal Reserve to act more pre-emptively and more aggressively than usual (Bernanke, 2002). More recently, a similar rationale governed the central banks' actions in the face of the 2007 financial crisis. At the US Federal Reserve, for example, it was underscored that, by way of historical comparison, the policy response stood out as being exceptionally rapid and proactive, explaining that 'in taking these actions, we aimed not only to cushion the direct effects of the financial turbulence on the economy, but also to reduce the risk of a so-called adverse feedback loop in which economic weakness exacerbates financial stress, which, in turn, leads to further economic damage' (Bernanke, 2008).

Choosing the right instruments

Against this background, choosing the appropriate policy instrument is not straightforward. Traditional models *à la* Mundell–Fleming suggest that monetary and fiscal policy have similar effects in a closed economy but not in an open one, because of different exchange rate implications. A canonical result is that, when capital mobility is high (as is the case in most advanced economies at the time of writing), fiscal policy is more effective than monetary policy under fixed exchange rates, and vice versa with floating exchange rates. While such models have clear pedagogical merits, they cannot be relied on in practice, as they leave out numerous real-world complications. As one example, the link between monetary policy and exchange rates is far more complex in reality than in those models.

Nevertheless, a long-held view has been that macroeconomic management should rely principally on monetary policy. From this perspective, fiscal policy typically only offers passive support, through the operation of 'automatic stabilizers'.[2] A strong argument supporting this view is that monetary policy is flexible: short-term interest rates can be changed overnight by the central bank. In contrast, fiscal policy decisions go through long gestation periods. Some of them may never even see the light of day, if parliament refuses to endorse the measures proposed by the government. In addition, there is the fear that fiscal policy will be mobilized for countercyclical purposes only during downturns, as fiscal tightening during upturns is much harder to carry out. Furthermore, the room for fiscal manoeuvring may be limited if public debt is already high to start with, or if there are binding rules capping expenditure (such as the US Budget Enforcement Act during the 1990s) or the deficit (such as the Maastricht Treaty during the run-up to the creation of the euro).

These arguments do not close the debate, however. While fiscal policy decisions have longer lead times, their effects can be quicker and more powerful.

---

[2]This term refers to the cushioning role played by public finances over the cycle: during a downturn, for example, tax receipts tend to decline more than does activity, which helps to sustain agents' disposable income and offsets the impact of the slowdown, while some components of public spending, such as unemployment benefit outlays, rise, thus working in the same direction (see Chapter 5). These are 'automatic' stabilizers to the extent that they operate without any need for discretionary government action.

The impact of monetary policy action is usually slower in coming and harder to gauge. In practice, central banks change interest rates more often than governments alter the fiscal stance, but when governments do, the injection or withdrawal of a stimulus often has stronger effects. Furthermore, the scope for monetary policy action may also be limited, in particular when short-term interest rates have essentially reduced to zero, as in Japan in the early 2000s as well as in a number of OECD countries after the 2007 financial crisis. In 2008–9, both monetary and fiscal stimulus were employed, notwithstanding the zero-bound constraint on interest rates and the already challenging fiscal situation prevailing in many countries. Monetary stimulus was engineered via massive injections of liquidity and purchases of various types of securities by central banks (see Box 4.7). Fiscal stimulus took the form of stepping up infrastructure spending and other public outlays, combined with tax cuts of various sorts, with the deficit ceilings embedded in the Stability and Growth Pact or other fiscal rules being effectively suspended (see Appendix 5.1).

Yet the financial crisis also brought to the fore the growing importance of financial regulatory authorities. In particular, it showed that they should not only focus on the microeconomic situation of the institutions they supervise, but also on the system-wide implications of their behaviour. The new Basel III framework will require that these authorities take *ad hoc* measures to limit pro-cyclicality in the financial system (by imposing countercyclical capital charges) and the risks posed by systemically important financial institutions (by ensuring that they have a greater loss-absorption capacity than others). Such measures are likely to have macroeconomic implications that could interfere with the actions of other policy makers. Hence the advent of a macroprudential approach calls for the many public authorities bearing a responsibility for financial stability (central banks, bank regulators and so on) to increase co-operation. In some countries, this has already led to the creation of councils of 'systemic supervisors', sometimes placed under the umbrella of the central banks.

Rule-based approaches

One strand of the economic literature goes further in the criticism of macroeconomic stabilization policies. It claims that almost any discretionary move on the part of the authorities is destabilizing, and suggests the basing of policy decisions on strict compliance with some basic rules. Such rules relate to variables that are deemed to be controlled fairly directly by the authorities. One is that the budget should balance at all times, another that some monetary aggregate should grow at a constant rate, or that the exchange should be fixed. The idea is that, instead of having the authorities assess when to adjust policies, based on forecasts of the evolution of such variables as growth and inflation, their primary goal should be to ensure the stability of some instrument(s) or intermediate objective(s).

The great advantage of rules, the argument goes, is that policy making is then 'depoliticized', which avoids the temptations mentioned above. In addition, the proponents of rules claim that these are required for institutions to function properly, even if politicians are not opportunistic.[3] Indeed, according to this line of thinking, rules foster credibility and thereby stabilize agents' expectations. Uncertainty thus diminishes, increasing the effectiveness of economic agents' decisions. For example, abiding by a fiscal rule helps to anchor long-run expectations as regards public finances, and thereby to contain interest rates (see Chapter 4).

In its most radical rendition, this view implies that forecasts have no practical purpose: policy decisions should be taken in accordance with the rules and without speculating about the business cycle. Monitoring can be restricted to that of the instruments featuring in the rules. For example, a central bank noting that money grows less than the rule prescribes should automatically ease policy. Similarly, the emergence of a fiscal deficit during the execution of the budget should immediately prompt corrective measures.

In practice, however, implementing rules is greatly facilitated by using forecasts (Burns, 1986). The likelihood that the budget will remain balanced at all times will be increased if the authorities do not just look at incoming fiscal data but also try to predict receipts and outlays, taking into account both past experience and the available information on the business cycle: once the deficit has been recorded, it is too late to correct it. The same holds for monetary aggregates, which do not react immediately to interest rate changes and can be predicted to some extent using business cycle information.

More important still, believing that economic policy can be set merely by obeying a few simple rules is naïve. However sound the rule, no rule is fit for all circumstances. But once the door to exceptions is ajar, where do they stop? Strict adherence to the types of rules discussed above is questionable in normal times but becomes particularly undesirable when catastrophes occur (a spectacular example being the 2007 financial crisis). In such cases, discretionary action on the part of the authorities is essential to restore agents' shattered confidence. In fact, rigid rules can themselves cause crises, as illustrated by the collapse of some fixed exchange rate regimes.

---

[3] Seminal references in this vein include Kydland and Prescott (1977) and Barro and Gordon (1983), who assumed that policy makers suffered from an inflation bias. But more recent work points out that, even in the absence of such a bias, rules may help (Clarida *et al.*, 1999).

Finally, the notion that abiding by some rules is a necessary condition for credibility and a good reputation is misguided. These can maintained by following a more flexible strategy which takes into account changes in the economic environment without losing sight of a set of well-defined ultimate objectives.

8.2.2 Fiscal policy

The preparation, discussion and execution of budgets require forecasts for the main public finance aggregates, which generally draw on a broader set of macroeconomic and financial forecasts. The quality of these forecasts is key for the sound management of public finances, since budgetary choices need to be consistent with macroeconomic constraints. The forecasts also provide a basis from which to assess proposed policy options. Hence they help to structure budgets in the public sector, be it at the level of general government, local governments or social security.

The forecasts and the associated macroeconomic framework allow the influence of the business cycle on budget constraints to be factored in.[4] Various channels are important here (these were discussed in more detail in Chapter 5), including:

- Tax receipts are very dependent on the evolution of the corresponding base, which itself depends on developments in activity and its components. For example, the growth (and distribution) of incomes affects direct tax receipts; that of domestic demand matters crucially for indirect tax receipts; and that of the wage bill has a direct bearing on social contributions.
- Some categories of public outlays are quite cyclical; for example, unemployment benefits, which fluctuate with labour market conditions.
- Recorded or forecast inflation affects public sector wages, some tax bases and, more broadly, the size of total budget appropriations.
- Financial conditions – interest rates in particular – affect the cost of public borrowing, whether it is for the roll-over of existing debt or for the funding of the current deficit.

Framing the budget properly bolsters the credibility of fiscal policy. A plausible macroeconomic forecast offers a sound basis for evaluating how much can be spent, given the expected evolution of revenue and the target for the fiscal balance. The forecast thus delineates the contours of what is feasible. In some cases, it will highlight that there is room for manoeuvre, while in others it will nudge policy makers to make choices and prioritize.

---

[4]The budget itself also influences the economic outlook and this has to be taken into account as well. In practice, the forecasts are prepared jointly and iteratively, and ultimately the scenario underpinning the budget is supposed to reflect all the important feedback effects stemming from the budgetary decisions.

The macroeconomic framework is also a co-ordination tool. It is used to help decide on the distribution of total expenditure across sectors, and ensures that various governmental departments or bodies use sensible and consistent assumptions – for example, as regards deflators. Indeed, making good use of the forecasts requires substantial resources and expertise, as well as good co-ordination between the involved parties.

The forecasts needed for fiscal policy purposes are not confined to the next fiscal year, but also encompass the medium or even the long run. In many countries, fiscal policy is embedded in some kind of 'medium-term' framework. Objectives are set for a period of several years, and some of the longer-run implications of today's choices are also considered. One reason to focus more on the medium run is to avoid opportunistic measures that would benefit politicians in the short run but at a cost further out. Another is the disenchantment with fine-tuning. A third reason is that in many OECD countries ageing populations put enormous pressures on pension and health care spending, casting doubts on the sustainability of those policies that are focusing excessively on the short run.

8.2.3   Monetary policy

Economic forecasts are also a key ingredient of monetary policy. Base money or money market interest rates do influence the central banks' final objectives, but with variable lags and potency, meaning that monetary authorities have to anticipate future developments, instead of simply reacting to incoming data. Hence the need for forecasts.

Practitioners generally consider that the bulk of the impact on prices and activity of changes in policy-controlled interest rates occurs one to two years down the road (though they can also have significant effects in the nearer term and continue to work their way through beyond the two-year horizon). Therefore, the forecast should cover at least the current year and the one following, if not slightly more.

Undertaking forecasts enables the central bank to form a view on some key questions, such as: how exchange rate movements will affect import prices and inflation; how the fiscal deficit will affect long-term interest rates; and how growth and unemployment will evolve, since this has indirect implications for inflation and may even be part and parcel of the central bank's direct mandate (witness the US Federal Reserve, which has two legislated goals – price stability and full employment).

In many countries now, central banks enjoy a fair degree of independence from politicians in the conduct of monetary policy, have price stability as their primary goal (though not necessarily as their only objective) and pilot short-term money market rates on a day-to-day basis. In this context, the role of the forecasts depends on their specific operational framework. Put simply, there are three types of regime:

- Monetarist frameworks rest on a target for the growth of a monetary aggregate (typically M2 or M3), and rely relatively less on forecasts. These were in vogue in the 1980s but have since fallen into disrepute, often because of unstable relationships between monetary aggregates and inflation.
- Eclectic frameworks, such as those of the US Federal Reserve of the ECB, rely more heavily on forecasts, but there is no clear and explicit link between forecasts and decisions.
- Inflation-targeting regimes, which had become increasingly popular before the 2007 financial crisis,[5] assign the most prominent role to forecasts. In fact, they are often referred to as 'inflation forecast targeting' regimes, since the central bank takes its interest rate decisions to ensure that forecast inflation coincides with its objective. That said, the 2007 crisis showed that central banks have a larger set of objectives than just aiming at a specific inflation target (see Chapter 4).

As in the case of fiscal policy, effective use of forecasts requires considerable technical and organizational expertise – illustrated *a contrario* by the somewhat hectic beginnings of inflation targeting in some transition countries.

The central bank usually conditions its forecasts on an assumption regarding its own policy actions. A first forecast is often based on the simple and not always realistic assumption of unchanged interest rates, or of the interest rate path expected by financial market participants. An alternative forecast is then included, in which the interest rate is adjusted so that the central bank's inflation objective is met. Forecasts are thus key since they help to calibrate the desirable interest rate moves: even when it seems clear which way they should move, it is important for the central bank to get the size and timing of the interest rate adjustments right. In addition, forecasts also help to factor in the lagged impact of past monetary policy decisions.[6]

Three sets of factors, however, tend to limit the role of forecasts in monetary policy – namely, central banks' imperfect knowledge of transmission mechanisms; their propensity to smooth interest rates; and their systemic responsibilities with respect to the stability of the financial system.

First, the transmission channels of monetary policy are numerous and tend to work differently across countries and over time (Cournède *et al.*, 2008), so that

---

[5] Roger (2010) identifies 29 countries as inflation targeters or, for three of them that joined the euro area, ex-inflation targeters.

[6] For further discussion, see Amato and Laubach (2000).

the impact of monetary policy decisions is difficult to assess, especially *ex ante*. The main channels include the direct impact of changes in the policy rate on household and enterprise spending; their impact on asset prices and thereby on agents' wealth; the rationing of credit by banks; and the effects on the exchange rate, and thereby on imported inflation and the trade balance.

Second, central banks generally try to smooth interest rates over time, implying more gradual policy moves than would be optimal in light of the forecast. This reflects the desire not to surprise market participants with unduly brisk interest rate changes, and in particular to avoid frequent shifts in direction, which could hurt central bank credibility. If forecasts and decisions are well explained, however (see below), there could be less of a need to smooth interest rates.

Finally, central banks also worry about financial system stability. When systemic risks loom large, this objective comes to dominate and the central bank may inject massive amounts of liquidity – for example, to save a large bank or to safeguard the operation of the payment system (as happened following the 11 September 2001 terrorist attacks and after the 2007 global financial crisis). In such circumstances, macroeconomic forecasts may play a more limited role.

8.3   Private sector uses

Businesses and trade unions, as well as households (both as economic agents and as voters) also rely on forecasts for various purposes. To some extent, these agents produce their own forecasts, tailored to their specific concerns. They also rely on published forecasts, including those issued by the government, which may serve as a benchmark.

8.3.1   Firms

Firms tend to use three types of forecasts:

- Operational forecasts, for day-to-day management purposes. In the very short run, the stock of capital is fixed, but the firm needs to plan how much it can sell and at what price, and to optimize its inventory levels. Such forecasts are frequently updated, possibly in *ad hoc* fashion, though more formalized methods can also be used, in particular to plan for seasonal and calendar day fluctuations.
- More elaborate procedures are normally used for annual budget planning purposes. Forecasts for sales, production, prices and costs are put together in a more systematic way. This allows firms to form a broader view and to take decisions, if needed, in response to changes in their environment. This type of exercise is carried out increasingly in the course of the year as well, especially in larger firms, not least to keep shareholders and other stakeholders well informed.

- Economic forecasts are also used for medium-term development plans, in particular when firms are pondering investment decisions. Such forecasts typically have both a macroeconomic and a sectoral dimension. They also include financial components in order to assess investment returns (not unlike the case of the public investment projects discussed in section 5.4.4). In addition, firms usually set medium-term expansion plans and profitability objectives that are contingent on macroeconomic developments.

In all three cases, managers of firms are influenced by the prevailing mood and by the macroeconomic outlook. In good times, managers will be more inclined to take risks, while in more difficult times they will be cautious and may reject or abandon projects that had earlier looked viable.

Macroeconomic forecasts are also particularly useful for firms that operate in a variety of sectors and/or countries. They allow the executives to ensure that the assumptions used are consistent across all the firms' units.

One sector is very sensitive to movements in overall economic activity, and produces vast quantities of forecasts itself: the financial sector. Indeed, lending and portfolio allocation decisions are heavily influenced by forecasts, as are insurance decisions, and their profitability depends directly on the accuracy of these forecasts.

8.3.2 Businesses and trade unions

Businesses and trade unions also rely greatly on forecasts, in particular in the context of wage negotiations, which take into account forecasts of inflation, productivity growth, the evolution of the share of wages and profits in total income, and the labour market. Trend labour productivity is an important indicator when assessing real wages: if both increase at the same rate, the wage share remains constant. The prospective labour market situation is one of the determinants of employers' and employees' bargaining power.

When wage negotiations are decentralized (at the level of the firm or even of the plant), sectoral forecasts matter the most, even if macroeconomic forecasts continue to play a part, notably with respect to inflation. Conversely, in countries where wage negotiations are traditionally centralized, such as in Northern Europe, macroeconomic forecasts take the leading role. Branch-level negotiations lie somewhere in between. In Germany, for example, the wage increases negotiated by the metalworkers' trade union IG Metall have long tended to guide agreements in the other sectors, and analysts are therefore inclined to compare them with macroeconomic rather than sectoral forecasts.

8.3.3 Households

Household decisions also rely on economic forecasts, though more implicitly than explicitly. While relative positions may vary considerably across households at any given point in time, the way each personal situation is perceived is very much coloured by how overall economic conditions appear. For example, households' expectations as regards future income depend heavily on the overall outlook for wages and employment. Changes in household confidence, which are related to their perception of the business cycle but also to non-economic factors, may influence changes in consumption, not least of durables. In the specific and important case of a real estate purchase, the decision is in principle based on a forecast of future income and spending, of the evolution of the housing market, and of nominal as well as real interest rates. Households further rely on financial forecasts when deciding how to invest their savings. And they need to have a sense of the future tax burden and of future social benefits, since these condition how much they should work and save today.

As voters, households need to assess politicians' economic programmes and promises. Forecasts can also play a prominent part in this context. In the Netherlands, for example, the Central Planning Bureau is required to quantify the economic consequences of the proposals set down by each of the main parties during the run-up to general elections. Elsewhere, this role is more typically fulfilled by economic think tanks and the press. The validity of any forecasts in the context of electioneering is, of course, somewhat questionable, but they can none the less contribute to structuring the debate. In so far as they do help to improve households' understanding of the economic issues at stake, they can promote democracy. Cutting through the technicalities and caveats to explain forecasts clearly to the general public is, however, quite a communication challenge.

8.4   Explaining the technicalities

Forecasts are prepared by technicians but destined for an audience that usually lacks familiarity with the underlying methodological issues. Users are mainly interested in some of the salient features of the forecast, and much less in the caveats. Over-simplification or even misunderstandings can thus arise, which is a source of frustration for the technicians.

8.4.1   Numerical ambiguities

Numbers can be misleading if improperly presented or if the recipient does not have the necessary background to interpret them correctly.

At the most basic level, economic statistics are frequently quoted with insufficient context or rigour, notably by the media. For example, a newspaper article might report that 'US GDP increased by 3.5 per cent in the third quarter of 2009'. Precluding any ambiguity would have required the article to specify that this referred to the increase in real GDP from the second to the third quarter, expressed at a seasonally-adjusted and annualized rate, and to the advance – as opposed to the second or third – official estimate. Some European readers might otherwise read the statement in the same way as they read Eurostat press releases, which express growth rates on a non-annualized (albeit seasonally-adjusted) basis.[7] Similarly, a newspaper article saying 'consumer price inflation in September declined and stood at only 0.1 per cent, while analysts expected 0.2 per cent' leaves open the question of which measure of inflation is being described. It could be the month-on-month rate, in which case it is hard to interpret if not deseasonalized, or it could be the 12-month rate (September over September of the previous year).

Such ambiguities may be amplified in the absence of relevant benchmarks. For example, commentators often focus on relatively small differences, of a few decimal points, when comparing official and private sector growth forecasts, overlooking the fact that, in light of the average forecast error and of the degree of precision of national accounts data, these differences are rather insignificant. Such seemingly different forecasts often mask a similar assessment of the cycle, though in some cases they may indeed reflect diverging views. Similarly, when forecasts are updated, sometimes too much attention is paid to minor adjustments which do not alter the overall assessment.

A more delicate issue has to do with carry-over effects (see Appendix 2.1). When news reports focus on average annual growth rates, they may give a seriously distorted picture of the expected growth dynamics. Suppose that, looking ahead at next year from December of the current year, growth is about to pick up strongly following very weak or negative developments in recent quarters. Then annual average growth for the coming year will be very modest, despite the acceleration in activity. A naïve reading of the forecast would ignore the imminent recovery. Presenting quarter-on-quarter forecasts alongside the annual ones can dispel such misunderstandings, though communication can then become somewhat top-heavy.

8.4.2 Keep it simple but not simplistic

Many forecast users are seeking just a few key statistics such as GDP growth and inflation, looking for a simple story that fits with their own view of the economy. In contrast, forecasters normally try to take into account a wide range of variables and possibilities. Hence there is a tension between the need to present a concise and comprehensible story to a broad audience and the need to take on board a wealth of detailed information, some of which is complex and potentially confusing. Simple stories are fine, indeed they are desirable, but only as long as they are not misleading.

---

[7] Other unspecified technical aspects include working-day adjustments or the absence thereof.

The public's perception of the global outlook may differ from that of the fore-caster because it can be shaped by events in some specific sectors or regions. Rural audiences, for example, may tend to look at the overall outlook through the lens of the harvest and put a lot of weight on weather conditions and ani-mal diseases, even when the fortunes of agriculture do not have a significant bearing on nationwide macroeconomic aggregates.

Another complication is related to lags. Employment, for example, is known to react with a lag of several months to slowdowns or accelerations in output. Therefore a recovery may be under way but households may not perceive it until a year later. Conversely, activity may have started to slump without households yet realizing it. This can contribute to a feeling among households that forecasters misconstrue reality.

8.4.3   Misunderstandings

In addition, the meaning of forecasts is often misunderstood. Official forecasts are frequently seen as objectives set by politicians, which they may be in some ways (as discussed below), but not primarily. At the same time, the distinction between conditional and unconditional forecasts is rarely made explicit and is frequently lost on the audience (Don, 2001). Users tend to assume that the forecasts are unconditional, and reflect the assumptions that the forecaster deems to be most plausible.

For example, in the autumn of 1998, the exchange rate assumption used in the draft Budget Law for 1999 in France was criticized harshly by the press. As usual, the assumption was that the exchange rate would remain at the level recorded during the first few months of 1998. But the dollar depreciated sharply in the weeks preceding the presentation of the draft (in connection *inter alia* with the Russian crisis in August), and commentators ridiculed the assumption as being totally obsolete, while forgetting about its status – which was that of a technical hypothesis rather than an attempt to second-guess financial market developments. Ironically, the dollar rebounded in 1999 and *ex post* the assumption turned out to have under- rather than over-estimated the strength of the US currency.

8.4.4   How to describe the uncertainties[8]

Conveying a clear understanding of the uncertainty surrounding a forecast is difficult. The public often underestimates this uncertainty, or, on the contrary, is too sceptical of forecasters' ability to provide any guidance.

---

[8]This subsection analyses the communication challenges associated with forecast uncer-tainty, which Chapter 7 examined from a different angle, discussing how to deal with such uncertainty to enhance forecast accuracy.

Some telling examples drawn from the press illustrate this (Coyle, 2001). The typesetting software used by one newspaper does not enable journalists to write '2½ per cent' with a fraction, to highlight the approximation involved. It has to be a spuriously precise '2.5 per cent', or at best 'around 2.5 per cent'. But 'around' is likely to get subbed out in order to save a line of print. News editors are also allergic to words such as 'probably', 'might' and 'approximately': if it's only worth a 'might', it probably isn't a story, is their line of thinking. Another example is that journalists are encouraged to use superlatives even when none apply – for example, to write about economists 'slashing' their growth forecasts, say, from 1.5 to 1.3 per cent. Obviously, this is not propitious terrain into which to introduce notions of probability distribution, variance and margin of error.

How can the degree of uncertainty be made clear? One traditional approach is to identify the most significant risks (for example, regarding oil prices or exchange rates) and to present alternative scenarios assuming that they materialize, or to present the consequences of different policy options. In a way, this is what has long been done in the Netherlands for budget purposes, with official growth forecasts appearing in pairs, one being a 'favourable' and the other a 'prudent' scenario. This approach is fairly intuitive and can be well understood, provided the number of variants is limited, and that they are sufficiently differentiated without being extreme. One drawback is that users may tend to favour one scenario and avoid the other(s). Another disadvantage is that one cannot infer where the scenarios lie in the complete distribution of possible outcomes: for some users, 'favourable' sounds like 'pie in the sky' and 'prudent' like 'doom and gloom', while for others the terms refer to moderately optimistic and pessimistic variants (Wallis, 2003).

A different approach is to present forecasts in the form of ranges rather than point estimates, as done, for example, by the ECB in its regular forecasts. The ranges usually correspond to statistical confidence intervals: for example, a 95 per cent interval means that the probability that the outcome would fall outside that range is 5 per cent. Such intervals widen as the horizon lengthens, reflecting higher uncertainty as to the more distant future. The intervals need not always be symmetric, as the balance of risks around the central forecast may well be skewed.

In general, such ranges can be generated in two ways:

- Directly from the statistical model used in the forecast. This is only feasible when relatively small systems of linear equations are being used for the forecast, without any *ad hoc* adjustment. In contrast, when large-scale econometric models are used, non-linearities arise and stochastic simulation methods are required to calculate the distribution of estimated outcomes.

- On the basis of past forecast errors. If the sample of past errors is assumed to be normally distributed, its mean and standard error can readily be derived (a non-zero mean denoting a systematic error, or bias). This method requires fewer assumptions and is relatively straightforward to implement.

Showing confidence intervals has tended to become more popular over time (see the survey by Tay and Wallis, 1999). A very complete way to describe uncertainty is the plotting of the density forecast, as done since 1996 by the Bank of England in its quarterly *Inflation Report*, both for inflation (see Figure 8.1) and for growth (not shown). This is called a 'fan chart', because the dispersion of the distribution increases and the intervals 'fan out' as the forecast horizon lengthens. Technically, the fan chart is based on a two-piece normal distribution, with a common mode but different standard errors on the upside and the downside of the forecast. This is a convenient way to represent departures from the symmetry of the normal distribution, while with suitable scaling the

Figure 8.1   Fan chart for inflation forecast*
Uncertainty increases as the forecast horizon lengthens

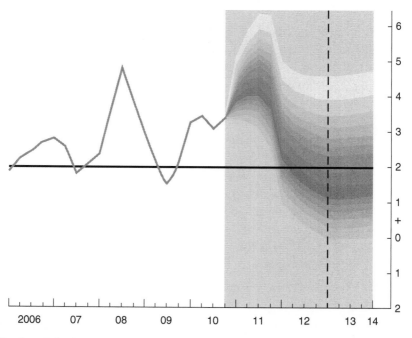

* Based on market interest rate expectations.
** Percentage increase in the consumer price index over a year earlier. The target is 2 per cent. See the Bank of England's February 2011 *Inflation Report* for further details about the underlying assumptions. *Source*: Bank of England.

probability calculations can still be carried out using normal standard tables. The published density forecast pictures the subjective assessment of inflationary pressures by the members of the Bank's Monetary Policy Committee: while the prevailing level of uncertainty is assessed initially based on past forecast errors, the final calibration of the distribution embodies the Committee's collective judgement. Its degree of skewness in particular displays its judgemental view of the balance of risks on the upside and downside of the forecast.

Similar fan charts are published routinely by a number of central banks (from Sweden to Thailand), the IMF (for world output), the European Commission (for euro area GDP) and the United Kingdom's National Institute of Economic and Social Research (NIESR).

An alternative way to describe the uncertainty surrounding the forecast is to use a histogram. The oldest example in macroeconomics is the quarterly *Survey of Professional Forecasters* published by the Federal Reserve Bank of Philadelphia (Diebold *et al.*, 1999). A sample of around 50 forecasters are each asked to provide a stylized distribution of their growth and inflation forecasts for the US economy, based on a given set of intervals. These responses are then averaged (see Table 8.1).

While density forecasts are attractive, they have some limitations. From a practical standpoint, it would be fastidious to produce and present them for all variables. Even when this is done only for a few key indicators, it is not easy to construct intervals that are consistent across variables. More fundamentally, fan charts do not allow a rigorous portrayal of how uncertainty varies as circumstances evolve (for example, if a major shock hits, this will not translate directly into a re-estimation of the size of the risks), even if this can be done *ex post* in an *ad hoc*, heuristic fashion. Histograms based on survey responses may be better instruments from this perspective. However, in neither case is there an explicit link between causes and consequences, in the form of an explanation of how economic events drive the degree of uncertainty attached to the forecasts. Hence, in contrast to the traditional scenario approach, using density forecasts to gauge potential policy decisions is difficult.

8.5   Transparency

8.5.1   A context conducive to transparency

As societies grow richer and more democratic, information demands increase. This trend is particularly conspicuous in financial markets, where participants act instantly on incoming information and penalize opacity (by charging risk premia). But it is linked to a greater need for accountability. Indeed, central

Table 8.1 Density forecast of US growth*

Forecasters' views on the outlook one year ahead vary quite substantially

Growth rate	$x < -2$	$-2 \leq x < -1$	$-1 \leq x < 0$	$0 \leq x < 1$	$1 \leq x < 2$	$2 \leq x < 3$	$3 \leq x < 4$	$4 \leq x < 5$	$5 \leq x < 6$	$x \geq 6$
Probability	0.2	0.1	0.5	2.0	6.0	28.2	45.2	14.4	2.8	0.7

*Mean probability attached to an x per cent increase in real GDP in 2011, on a year-average basis.
Source: Federal Reserve Bank of Philadelphia, *Survey of Professional Forecasters*, First Quarter 2011.

banks have been gaining more autonomy, as politicians disengaged from day-to-day management of monetary policy and set up a framework within which technicians can be in charge. But the granting of greater independence to central banks has gone hand in hand with new obligations to be more transparent and accountable. Few central banks now continue to take decisions based on undisclosed internal forecasts. Similarly, there have been recent tentative suggestions to make producers of fiscal forecasts more independent and, at the same time, more accountable. In 2010, for example, the UK government set up an independent institution (the Office for Budget Responsibility) tasked, *inter alia*, with publishing fiscal projections.

More generally, while government intervention in the economic sphere has been retreating in several ways in recent decades, the authorities' role in providing information and guiding expectations has tended to increase. Undoubtedly, the resources available to government bodies to collect and deal with economic information enable them to play a key role, and indeed private-sector forecasters use government figures as a benchmark.

Last but not least, new means of communication facilitate the dissemination of forecasts. In addition to traditional media such as the economic and financial press, the internet provides rapid and low-cost access to a wide variety of publications, including forecasts and the attendant documentation.

8.5.2   The costs of transparency

Transparency, however, also entails costs. Certainly, preserving some secrecy has in the past been deemed critical to ensure the efficiency of policy decisions. A classic but not such a relevant rationale is that in some circumstances the authorities may want to create and exploit a surprise. But it is difficult to cheat everybody all the time, not least because of the expansion of other sources of forecasts in recent decades. In fact, as the importance of credibility and reputation increases, the authorities prefer to avoid rather than to engineer surprises. From this perspective, the cost of transparency should not be exaggerated.

Two other costs of transparency can, however, be highlighted. The first is that forecast errors hurt the authorities' credibility, even when similar errors are also made by private-sector economists, and can cast doubts on the appropriateness of the policies in place. When this highlights genuine policy deficiencies, it is welcome, but in some cases, sound policies may be abandoned prematurely as a result (Burns, 2001).

The second cost is that, by publishing their forecasts, which can at least reveal policy intentions implicitly, the authorities tie their hands. If an unexpected shock occurs, they face an uncomfortable trade-off: either they implement the policies embedded in their forecasts, which are no longer optimal, or they change course, at the risk of being judged inconsistent with their earlier commitments.

8.5.3   The benefits of transparency

But transparency also offers many benefits. In particular, the regular publication of forecasts including a cogent exposition of the underlying assumptions and of the risks surrounding the central scenario has three virtues.

First, many of the above arguments in favour of confidentiality rest on the hypothesis that the audience does not understand the limitations of a forecast. This is questionable in any event, but especially so in a context where greater dissemination of economic information should improve the public's familiarity with economic issues.

Second, transparency promotes accountability. By making it clear what underpins policy decisions, it facilitates their objective assessment *ex post*, notably after the appearance of surprises. The sources of the forecast errors can be traced and explained more easily. Instead of the somewhat defensive concept of credibility referred to in section 8.5.2 (don't take the risk of error), a more reasonable and sophisticated one is to recognize that some developments are beyond the authorities' control, while others are not. Accountability would only extend to what policy makers actually exert some leverage over.

Finally, transparency facilitates co-ordination and consensus-building. It reduces the uncertainty regarding the authorities' intentions and the reasons to suspect that figures are being massaged. Transparency therefore helps to anchor agents' expectations, not least in the case of monetary policy, where it plays an important part in enabling the central bank to guide financial markets (see Geraats, 2009).

In short, transparency reinforces the credibility of sound policies. And credibility in turn provides policy makers with the flexibility required to react to unexpected events without undermining public trust. Besides, much of the debate on transparency also applies to the private sector, particularly to banks. *A priori*, they might seem to have an interest in keeping their forecasts confidential in order to profit in the financial markets from the associated insights. But, in practice, they have to deal with their clients, who legitimately push for them to disclose their views and forecasts. Hence many of the banks now publish their forecasts and even explain how they are produced.

8.6   Science or politics?

8.6.1   Forecasts rarely appear in isolation

Forecasting is both a technical and a politically charged activity, at least in the case of official forecasts. The attention generated by leaks of government forecasts illustrates how sensitive these can be. Indeed, government forecasts are usually part of political documents such as the budget bill or medium-term fiscal orientations, and serve to justify or support politicians' claims and measures.

Behind a more technical façade, the same holds for central banks, whose decisions also have a political dimension, because of their implications for fiscal policy, but also more generally because of their influence on the outlook and on the relative positions of debtors and creditors. A vivid illustration here is the speculation surrounding the decisions of the Federal Reserve in the USA during the run-up to presidential elections, when commentators fret over whether the central bank will help the incumbent party or be reticent about acting, for fear of appearing partisan.

A key factor is that, within official organizations, forecasting activities cannot be separated completely from policy making advice. In fact, the tools used by the forecasters to project the outlook are also mobilized to simulate and predict the impact of policy measures. In this regard, a telling episode was the fate of a proposal floated in the early 1990s within the British Treasury to outsource forecasting to the private sector: a feasibility study rejected the proposal, noting that, given the intimate relationship between forecasting and advising policy makers, outsourcing was out of the question (Smith, 1998). That said, such a relationship does not necessarily imply a lack of independence – witness the recent growing interest in having independent public bodies carry out fiscal projections.

8.6.2 Prediction or objective?

In these circumstances, official projections inevitably come to resemble policy objectives. This is certainly not fully correct in so far as the published forecasts usually do not depart significantly from what the experts who prepared them really concluded (notwithstanding the dressing-up discussed below).

At the same time, however, these forecasts are also policy objectives, to the extent that they embody the authorities' favourite scenarios. Indeed, the underlying assumptions include the implementation of the announced policies. If the forecast fails to materialize, and in particular if it turns out to have been too optimistic, it may be that the policies were not put in place, or that they were less effective than had been anticipated.

Even when under-performance can be ascribed to exogenous events – say, to a deterioration in the international environment – the responsibility of the public authorities cannot be denied. For example, if forecast errors were mainly a result of unexpected foreign developments, they could also be attributed to a lack of international economic policy co-ordination, or simply to the inability of the public authorities to appreciate the international constraints and risks at the time of the preparation of the forecast.

8.6.3   Dressing up the forecast

The wish to have the forecast reflect policy makers' objectives can lead to dressing up the numbers produced by the technicians, and to the publication of only the adjusted forecast. Some non-public institutions could also be tempted to bias their forecasts in accordance with their political preferences (think tanks) or their strategic plans (private investors). Another, and perhaps more benign, motive may be to smooth revisions – for example, if the new forecast involves a sharp downward revision but it is preferred to recognize this only gradually, for credibility purposes, say.

In most government forecasts, any dressing up will usually translate into a somewhat prettier outlook, where performance is rather better than was actually forecast at the technical level. This may reflect a desire to preserve or boost confidence, in the hope that agents will then be more inclined to spend, which in turn will lead to higher growth – though how much hope policy makers can in practice pin on wished-for self-fulfilling prophecies remains a subject of debate. Or the intention may be to delay the announcement of unpleasant but necessary measures – say, tax increases that could appear necessary if the technical forecasts point to a widening budget shortfall.

In other cases, dressing up the forecast can bias it downwards. Regarding government forecasts, one reason can be prudence, to preserve margins for fiscal policy; or political strategy, in order, say, to be able to show that the situation *ex post* was better than expected as a result of the policies implemented. Turning to central banks, they often prefer to err on the side of caution, by underestimating growth prospects and putting more emphasis on the risks to price stability (be they excessive inflation or deflation). For example, they might be inclined to show a slightly lower growth forecast, to try to influence agents' expectations, with a view to fostering wage moderation.

The extent of such normative adjustments should not be exaggerated, however. Official forecasts do not suffer from major systematic biases, nor do the forecasts of other institutions (Chapter 7). The adjustments are usually far smaller than the uncertainty surrounding the forecast, while any significant modification would be so obvious that it might have a bad effect on decision-makers' future credibility. Dressing up the forecast can thus often be considered to be self-serving 'rounding' of the technicians' numbers rather than blatant manipulation.

8.6.4   Who takes responsibility?

Forecast errors cast doubts on the credibility of the forecaster and of those who have commissioned the forecasts, especially policy makers. They tend to prompt defensive reactions, with sometimes a temptation for the technician to blame the decision-maker and vice versa.

When the international environment deteriorates more than anticipated, the policy maker can justify a change in course fairly easily. At the same time, the forecaster may not be too embarrassed, as s/he typically stakes more credibility on predicting domestic behaviour successfully, based on relatively exogenous assumptions about international developments. An example would be a surge in oil prices: in most cases, the forecaster can argue convincingly that it was not foreseeable.

But often the responsibility for the forecast error is shared, and can be ascribed both to the forecaster, for an inaccurate assessment of the cycle and/or of the effect of policies, and to the decision-maker – for example, for having dressed up the technician's forecast a little too complacently, or for having altered policy unwisely. In the absence of an exogenous scapegoat, the forecaster and the policy maker may then be inclined to engage in denial and to blame each other for the error.

In fact, given that the fragility of any forecast is well known, such reactions may seem a bit futile. Technicians and decision-makers are usually well aware of this, with the former repeatedly highlighting the risks associated with the forecast and the latter trying to avoid staking their reputation on a particular forecast. Some policy makers even try to distance themselves very explicitly from the forecast, presenting it as their staff's work rather than their own. This is the case at the ECB, for example, where the forecast is presented to the Governing Council but not endorsed by them, in contrast to the practice at the Bank of England, where the forecast is prepared by the staff but then amended by the Monetary Policy Committee (MPC), which takes responsibility for the published forecast (Bean, 2001). However, to what extent the broader public perceives such subtle differences, and whether it cares, remains questionable.

8.6.5 Forecasting ethics

In sum, the division of labour should be as follows: the technician presents the central scenario and the relevant variants based on different policy options to the policy maker, and the latter then decides. In practice, however, tensions may arise when the policy maker's objectives are not consistent with what the forecast shows as being feasible, but the policy maker still wants to use the forecast to justify his or her choices. The fact that any projection comes with sizeable margins of uncertainty is in fact an invitation to the policy maker to request that the technician adjusts the original forecast to fit the policy maker's needs.

Hence the forecast (both the central scenario and the variants) is often subject to some negotiation (Mahmoud *et al.*, 1992). The forecaster's bargaining strength depends on his or her status. If the forecaster is seen as a mere number-cruncher, the policy maker may massage the forecast without much restraint. If, instead, the forecaster has more independence, this will be less of a risk. This risk can even be lessened further if the significance of the forecasts is transparent to all.

Further reading

Good discussions of the macroeconomic policy options and actions during the Great Recession include Walsh (2009) for monetary policy, and Auerbach and Gale (2009) for fiscal policy. These questions are also covered at length in the successive issues of the IMF's *World Economic Outlook* and OECD's *Economic Outlook*. Further analysis on how central banks present their projections is provided by Fracasso *et al.* (2003), and technical analysis of the methodology underpinning fan charts by Österholm (2009) and Galbraith and van Norden (2009).

Appendix 8.1 A world tour of the forecasting institutions

Countless public, semi-public and private bodies are engaged in regular or occasional forecasting. Users are also very diverse. On the supply side of the market for forecasts, some producers are driven by profit motives, while others offer a public good. The demand side includes policy makers – in particular finance ministers and central bank governors, but also a broader public – say, the readers of the financial press. The product itself is far from homogeneous: many forecasts cover only the short run, but some extend their predictions over longer horizons, and quality is very uneven. It is also a market with fads, as some forecasters' reputation rides high when they surf on a run of successful predictions, but can suddenly collapse when they fail to foresee a major turning point. Finally, price-setting is rather unclear in this market, since cross-subsidization is rife, including in the private sector. Against this background, this appendix tours some of the main forecasting institutions. First, a general typology is laid out, then the role of forecasting in some of the main public international institutions is described. Finally, a selection of national institutions in some of the largest advanced and emerging countries is presented.

Types of forecasters

There are three main types of forecasters:

- Public international institutions: they produce forecasts that ensure some degree of global consistency, for purposes of multilateral co-operation.
- Public or semi-public national bodies: either they are directly involved in fiscal or monetary policy (economics departments of ministries of finance and central banks) or they have more of a general informational role aimed at a broader public (statistical offices where they are engaged in forecasting, publicly sponsored institutes).
- Private and other entities: economics departments in large financial institutions or enterprises in other sectors, and think tanks attached to business or trade unions, or to political parties.

In practice, the delineation is not that clear-cut. Some think tanks straddle the academic and policy making worlds even as they produce forecasts for clients in the private sector. Moreover, there is the special case of forecasting panels, which pool existing forecasts.

Public international institutions

Public international institutions are themselves of three sorts: some are involved in multilateral surveillance activities; others have less of a macroeconomic focus and are less prominent as forecasters; and some serve economic/monetary unions (see Table 8.2).

The main multilateral surveillance organizations include the Bretton Woods institutions (International Monetary Fund (IMF) and World Bank), the Organisation for Economic Co-operation and Development (OECD), and the Bank for International Settlements (BIS). The first three were created in the wake of the Second World War to promote reconstruction and strengthen economic co-operation, and to avoid a repeat of the debacle of

Table 8.2   International forecasters

Institution	Publication(s)	Website
IMF	*World Economic Outlook*, Article IV consultations	imf.org
OECD	*Economic Outlook*, country surveys	oecd.org
World Bank	*Global Economic Prospects*	worldbank.org/prospects
European Commission	*Economic Forecasts*	ec.europa.eu/economy_finance
ECB	*Monthly Bulletin*	ecb.int
ECRI		businesscycle.com
CEPR	Eurocoin	cepr.org/data/eurocoin
Panels	*Consensus forecasts*	consensuseconomics.com
Global Insight		globalinsight.com
NIESR	*National Institute Economic Review*	niesr.ac.uk
Oxford Economics		oef.com

Note: Some institutions present their most popular forecasts in their flagship publication(s), while others issue them in a variety of formats (not all listed here).

the 1930s. Their global reach and considerable human resources account for their influence and prestige. Their forecasts are milestones in the calendar of the forecasting profession and serve as benchmarks in international forums, but also domestically, especially in the smaller member countries, where national forecasting resources are more limited. They also foster the harmonization of economic statistics across countries. While the IMF, the World Bank and the OECD are inter-governmental bodies, the BIS is a central banking institution, set up in 1930 in the context of the payment of German reparations following the First World War. The BIS brings together the central banks of the advanced economies and of major emerging markets. It monitors global financial developments and hosts several committees in charge of various aspects of financial stability, some of which have regulatory powers. The BIS also monitors economic developments but is not strictly speaking involved in macroeconomic forecasting.

The second group of international organizations is more varied and also less directly involved in the type of forecasting covered in this book. It includes the International Energy Agency (IEA) – a sister organization of the OECD which forecasts energy sector developments – and some United Nations (UN) bodies. The latter include the UN Department of Economic and Social Affairs, its regional economic commissions, the UN Development Programme (UNDP) (which in particular is in charge of elaborating regular Human Development Reports), the UN Conference on Trade and Development (UNCTAD) (which deals with general issues related to trade and development and, more specifically, analyses trends in foreign direct investment), the International Labour Organization (ILO), the World Trade Organization (WTO) and more.

The third group, which serves economic/monetary unions, engages in multilateral surveillance but has a focus on economic policy making in the areas where sovereignty has been pooled. Examples include the European Union (EU) and the European Central Bank (ECB).

Public domestic institutions

At the national level, the most important forecasting bodies are usually those attached directly to policy makers, namely the national government or central bank, who most need forecasts and economic advice, have sufficient resources at their disposal, and are in a position to disseminate forecasts as a public good. They may also be attached to parliament or to subnational governments.

Other public institutions are more independent of the national authorities, even if in some cases they have close links with or are part of the government administration, as is the case with the French statistical office (INSEE) or the Dutch Bureau for Economic Policy Analysis (previously CPB). Their forecasts are typically less normative, in so far as they can depart more easily from official policy assumptions.

There are also a host of publicly sponsored institutions that are further removed from government but play an important role in forecasting, such as the well-known six institutes in Germany, or many of the think tanks in the USA and the UK. Their forecasts are even less normative. A number of them are associated with universities and co-operate in networks, such as the European Forecasting Network (which includes, *inter alia*, Cambridge University's Department of Applied Economics, the French CEPII, the German IWH, the Italian IGIER and the Spanish IFL) or EUROFRAME (which, among others, encompasses the British NIESR, German DIW, Dutch CPB, Irish ESRI, Austrian WIFO and Polish CASE). They often also co-operate with and receive support from international institutions, notably the European Commission.

The private sector

Though it is not their main activity, some of the large private firms engage in economic forecasting, typically of the sector-specific kind (for example, for the oil or automobile market). Private financial institutions – notably banks such as Barclays, Goldman Sachs, HSBC, J.P. Morgan, Morgan Stanley and Nomura – carry out more macroeconomic forecasting activities, both for internal purposes (to inform their traders and fund managers in particular) and for outside clients, not least with a view to enhancing their reputation. Parts of the forecasts are sold (very expensively) to select customers, while other parts are disseminated free of charge. In many cases, the staff in charge of economic forecasts have transferred from central banks, ministries or international institutions. Even in their new capacity, they continue to be in touch with policy makers in various forums where prospects and policies are discussed.

There are also private firms whose main activity is to provide economic forecasts. A number of autonomous businesses, such as Global Insight, sell data, forecasts and analyses to governments or firms. In a similar vein, rating agencies (such as Standard and Poor's, or Moody's) also undertake economic forecasts. Some other firms produce sectoral forecasts or *ad hoc* economic analysis, for example, McKinsey. Finally, political parties or trade unions in some countries have sections engaging in certain forms of forecasting.

Panels

Yet another approach is that of pooling existing forecasts in a panel. This is done by governments (the British Treasury, for example), central banks (often under the 'survey of professional forecasters' label), research institutes (such as the Economic Planning Association in Japan), magazines (*The Economist* in particular), or specialized firms. The most prominent among the latter is Consensus Economics Inc., which follows a rather more systematic and thorough approach than the media in assembling such information in its monthly publication *Consensus Forecasts*. While the average forecast appearing there is influential – to the point that it becomes news itself – it tends to be somewhat behind the curve, particularly around turning points, not least because some of the members of the panel may be slower than others to update their forecast. Finally, the role played by news agencies (such as Reuters) has become increasingly important. They provide the forecasts of key short-term economic indicators on a timely basis – say, monthly US industrial production. These forecasts are usually made by economists working closely with traders, and appear to be highly influential, as financial markets have shown an increased tendency to react to economic 'surprises', understood as the difference between outcomes and consensus expectations.

Futures research

Related to, yet distinct from, forecasting is futures research, which investigates how the world might change over the coming decades. It is produced by institutions such as the Club of Rome (clubofrome.org), the Rand Pardee Center (rand.org), the Hudson Institute (hudson.org), the Institute for the Future (iftf.org), the Institute for Alternative Futures (altfutures.com), SRI International (sri.com) and the World Future Society (wfs.org).

International institutions

The IMF

The IMF, headquartered in Washington, DC, has 187 member countries, each with a voice in decision-making that depends on their economic weight. It is tasked with preventing crises by encouraging countries to adopt sound economic policies, and with lending to members requiring temporary financing to address balance of payments problems. To this end, the IMF monitors economic and financial developments and policies, both in member countries and at the global level, and gives policy advice, including technical assistance to governments and central banks. IMF lending takes place in the context of adjustment programmes negotiated with the country in question and endorsed by the IMF Board.

Since the shift to floating exchange rates in the 1970s, and with the development of international capital markets, IMF lending has been mainly to troubled developing and emerging market countries, though, more recently, the IMF has played a prominent role in rescuing some EU countries. But multilateral surveillance of all member countries' policies has become increasingly important. Alongside the active promotion of statistical harmonization and dissemination, this surveillance takes two forms:

- One is the monitoring and forecasting of national and global economic trends, in the *World Economic Outlook* (WEO), which normally comes out twice a year, in April/May and September/October. The WEO's main forecasts extend two years ahead, but are accompanied by some medium-run projections. The forecasts are more detailed for the advanced economies than for the rest, although not as much as the OECD forecasts. The WEO also contains extensive analysis, including the simulation of variants using the IMF's Global Projection Model. In between WEOs, the IMF also routinely publishes partial, interim updates of its forecasts (for headline variables and for the main countries).

- The second modality of surveillance are the regular country-specific examinations under the heading of the so-called Article IV consultations (in reference to the related Article of Agreement of the Fund). Originally, these reports remained confidential, on the grounds that this allowed them to be more outspoken. But since the late 1990s, many of these reports are published, in response to demands for greater transparency. The reports are usually very thorough and contain useful data (sometimes hard to find in national sources).

Overall, IMF forecasts play an important part. That said, tensions can arise between the IMF's roles as an analyst and as a lender. For example, IMF staff may have concerns with respect to the policies of a country involved in an IMF programme, and may doubt that programme objectives will be met. Yet public criticism on the part of the staff, or the publication of forecasts inconsistent with the programme, might undermine the latter's credibility. The IMF also has to beware of the way it discloses market-sensitive information: drawing attention to or underlining a country's difficulties can send a disquieting signal and prompt capital outflows, while failing to react pre-emptively to worrying developments might mislead economic agents or even give rise to risks of moral hazard.

The OECD

The forerunner of the OECD was the Organisation for European Economic Co-operation (OEEC), formed in 1948 to administer American and Canadian aid under the Marshall Plan for the reconstruction of Europe. Since it took over from the OEEC in 1961, the OECD's mandate has been to help strengthen its member country economies, expand free trade and contribute to development in the wider sense. It includes 34, mainly advanced, economies, but many of the OECD's activities have a more global reach, through its so-called enhanced engagement programme (with Brazil, China, India, Indonesia and South Africa) and through its Development Centre (which focuses on developing economies in Africa, Asia and Latin America). Unlike the Bretton Woods institutions, the OECD does not lend money. It is best known for its publications and data, covering a great variety of fields, including macroeconomics, trade, agriculture, energy, education, the environment, development, and science and innovation; in this context, the OECD actively promotes statistical harmonization and dissemination. Finally, the OECD also produces internationally agreed instruments, decisions and recommendations to promote rules of the game in areas such as taxation and corporate governance. OECD work is conducted in the context of specialized committees.

OECD economic surveillance, as at the IMF, takes place both at a global level and on a country-by-country basis. It involves business cycle monitoring, forecasting and policy analysis to identify and promote best practice, both in the macroeconomic and the structural arenas. The forecasts are published twice a year, in spring and autumn, in the OECD's *Economic Outlook*, accompanied by a global assessment plus country-specific ones. The main projections extend up to two years ahead, with the quarterly detail shown for the key variables. They are complemented by some longer-run projections. Alternative scenarios are often laid out, using the OECD's global economic model. The draft projections are discussed by the Short-Term Economic Prospects working party, where official forecasters from all member countries and some non-member countries meet. The draft projections are then amended and updated, to be presented to the Economic Policy Committee, together with the OECD staff's assessment. Moreover, the OECD regularly updates its quarterly GDP forecasts and every month it publishes leading economic indicators for the main economies.

The OECD also produces detailed country surveys, which are typically published at a one-and-a-half to two-year frequency. They resemble IMF Article IV reports but with a heavier focus on structural problems and in a more integrated and polished format. Unlike the IMF reports, endorsed by the Board but reflecting staff views, the OECD surveys are published under the authority of the Economic and Development Review Committee, which has to reach a consensus on the basis of the draft produced by the staff.

The World Bank and the regional development banks

The World Bank, located across the street from the IMF, now has as its main mission fighting poverty and promoting development. In addition to providing technical assistance in various fields, it finances specific projects or more general sectoral or even economy-wide programmes. The first type of lending involves extensive project analysis, and the second type of activity requires the forecasting of sectoral and macroeconomic developments. The World Bank publishes detailed forecasts and analyses in its annual *Global Economic Prospects*, a key reference on developing countries and international capital flows.

While some of the World Bank's analytical work overlaps with the IMF's, it focuses more than the IMF does on the structural aspects of development, and maintains valuable databases covering these areas.

There are also a number of independent regional development banks which carry out similar functions but in a specific region only, among which the Asian Development Bank (ADB), the Interamerican Development Bank (IADB), the African Development Bank (ADB) and the European Bank for Reconstruction and Development (EBRD).

European institutions

The most prominent institutions engaged in forecasting in a context of pooled sovereignty are the European Commission – which is the executive body of the European Union and one of its five constituting institutions – and the European Central Bank (ECB). Forecasts are needed at the aggregate level, to set common policies – the most important being monetary policy. They are also required on a national basis, since domestic policies have externalities that need to be taken into account. For example, a deterioration in the fiscal position of some euro area countries may lead to higher interest rates for all members, including those who pursue more disciplined fiscal policies.

As well as its important role in statistical harmonization and data dissemination (through Eurostat) the Commission plays a key role in multilateral policy surveillance, along three main dimensions:

- The Commission publishes aggregate and country-specific forecasts twice a year, at about the same time as the OECD, and following a similar format. Variants are presented using the in-house QUEST model. Furthermore, the Commission publishes less detailed interim forecasts between its two main forecasting exercises as well as monthly short-run GDP quarterly forecasts.
- The Commission is also in charge of fiscal policy surveillance in the European Union. Each year, member states have to submit multi-year fiscal 'stability' (for euro area members) or 'convergence' (for other countries) programmes, including a description of the envisaged policy measures and scenario analysis. These plans are scrutinized by the Commission and endorsed or amended by the European Council, which is the EU's main decision-making body and represents the member states – in this case, the Council has its specific configuration devoted to economic and financial affairs (ECOFIN). To a large extent, all this information is published.
- Every year, the Commission also issues *Broad Economic Policy Guidelines*, which are subsequently adopted by the ECOFIN Council. These *Guidelines* pull together business cycle assessments, and analysis and policy recommendations in macroeconomic as well as in structural areas (which are discussed, respectively, in the EU's Economic and Financial Committee and Economic Policy Committee).

When the subject matter concerns only members of the euro area, the ECOFIN and the Economic and Financial Committee gather in the Eurogroup formation, which excludes the United Kingdom, Sweden, Denmark and the newer EU members who are not euro area members.

Monetary policy in the euro area requires euro-area-wide forecasts. These are produced twice a year by the staff of the Eurosystem (the ECB and the national central banks of the euro area member countries), and subsequently published in the June and December issues of the ECB's *Monthly Bulletin*. Between these forecasting rounds, ECB staff alone produce lighter quarterly updates. While the ECB discusses national policies and trends only sparingly in its publications, it monitors country-specific developments closely.

As well as the Commission and ECB, there are also European-wide academic institutions, such as the Centre for Economic Policy Research (CEPR), a network of researchers based in universities, research institutes, central bank research departments and international organizations. It is in many ways the European equivalent of the US NBER (presented below) and indeed has set up its own Euro Area Business Cycle Dating Committee. The CEPR publishes policy-oriented macroeconomic analysis but also EuroCOIN, a coincident indicator of the euro area business cycle.

Forecasting bodies in selected countries

While an exhaustive presentation of the institutions producing forecasts is beyond the scope of this book, a selective tour covering the main ones in the G7 countries (see Table 8.3) and in the large non-OECD economies illustrates the great variety of approaches in this area.

Table 8.3 Forecasting institutions in the G7 economies

Country/institution	Publication(s)	Website
USA		
Federal Reserve Board	*Monetary Policy Report to the Congress*	federalreserve.gov
CEA	*Economic Report of the President*	whitehouse.gov/administration/eop/cea
OMB	Budget and economic outlooks	whitehouse.gov/omb
CBO	Economic and budget projections	cbo.gov
NBER	Business Cycle Dating Committee memos	nber.org
Conference Board	*Business Cycle Indicators*	conference-board.org
Philadelphia Fed	*Survey of Professional Forecasters*	phil.frb.org/econ/spf
Macroeconomic Advisers		macroadvisers.com
Japan		
Cabinet office		cao.go.jp
ESRI		esri.go.jp
Bank of Japan	*Outlook for Economic Activity and Prices*	boj.or.jp
JCER	Short, medium and long-run forecasts	jcer.or.jp
DIR	Research reports	dir.co.jp
United Kingdom		
Bank of England	*Inflation Report*	bankofengland.co.uk
Treasury	*Budget* and *Pre-Budget Report*	hm-treasury.gov.uk
IFS	*Green Budget*	ifs.org.uk
CBI	*Economic Bulletin*	cbi.org.uk
Germany		
Ministry of Economics and Technology	*Jahreswirtschaftsbericht*	bmwi.de
Deutsche Bundesbank	*Monthly Report*	bundesbank.de
Ministry of Finance	Budget documents and forecasts	bundesfinanzministerium.de
Council of Economic Experts	*Annual Report*	sachverstaendigenrat-wirtschaft.de
IFO	*IFO Schnelldienst*	cesifo.de
DIW		diw.de
IfW		ifw-kiel.de
RWI	*Konjonkturbericht*	rwi-essen.de
France		
Ministry of Finance	Budget documents and forecasts	minefe.gouv.fr
INSEE	*Note de conjoncture*	insee.fr
Banque de France	*Monthly Digest*	banque-france.fr
OFCE	*Revue de l'OFCE*	ofce.sciences-po.fr

(continued)

Table 8.3   Continued

Italy		
Treasury	Budget documents and forecasts	dt.tesoro.it
Bank of Italy	Jan. and July issues of *Economic Bulletin*	bancaditalia.it
ISAE		isae.it
Canada		
Department of Finance	Budget documents and forecasts	fin.gc.ca
Bank of Canada	*Monetary Policy Report*	bankofcanada.ca
Conference Board	*Quarterly Canadian Economic Outlook*	conferenceboard.ca

Note: Some institutions present their most popular forecasts in their flagship publication(s), others issue them in a variety of formats (not all listed here).

USA

Like that of statistics, the production of forecasts in the USA is not dominated by a single institution. In addition to government agencies, Congress, the central bank, academia and the private sector all play an important part, reflecting the system of checks and balances characterizing US society.

In the executive branch, forecasting activities are driven mainly by the budgetary process. At the start of each calendar year, the US president tables a budget proposal for the coming fiscal year, which starts in October. The underlying macroeconomic forecast is prepared under the aegis of the Council of Economic Advisers (CEA), a small department attached to the White House, and this appears in the *Economic Report of the President*, published in early February.

Two departments of the administration, endowed with a much larger staff, work at a more disaggregated level: the Treasury, which monitors domestic and international developments, and the Office of Management and Budget (OMB), which twice a year publishes detailed budget forecasts extending over the following five years. In addition, several units in charge of producing statistical information (for example, the Bureau of Economic Analysis, which releases national accounts estimates) also have some forecasting expertise. However, the scope of official forecasts is rather limited compared with other countries: the international context is given short shrift (admittedly in part because the USA is not a small, open economy), and the fiscal projections relate only to the federal government level (including social security), omitting state and local government finances.

The legislative branch of the US government is served in forecasting matters by the Congressional Budget Office (CBO), created in the mid-1970s as an agency independent of the executive branch. The CBO's mission is to provide the objective, timely and non-partisan analyses needed for economic and budget decisions, as well as the information and estimates required for the legislative budget process. The CBO does not make any explicit policy recommendations. It conducts a forecasting exercise similar to the

OMB's, though on a longer (10-year) time frame. The CBO's budget projections and its cost estimates for the bills under consideration enable the House and Senate Budget committees to measure the effects of proposed changes in tax and spending laws – both the president's and their own.

The Federal Reserve monitors economic developments continuously. It is independent of the executive branch and accountable to Congress. The Federal Reserve System, created in 1913, includes 12 regional federal reserve banks plus the Board, located in Washington, DC. The regional banks are to some extent specialized: the one in New York is actively involved in financial market supervision while those in Chicago and Philadelphia have developed widely used tools to follow economic fluctuations closely (such as Philadelphia's *Survey of Professional Forecasters*). The Board staff prepare an official forecast eight times a year but it is available to the public only with a long lag. The policy making Federal Open Market Committee (FOMC) publishes its own GDP, unemployment and inflation forecasts four times a year. Two publications are of special interest: the *Beige Book*, released eight times a year, a fortnight before each FOMC meeting, which synthesizes the anecdotal information on economic conditions collected by the regional banks; and the *Monetary Policy Report to the Congress*, presented in February and July by the chairperson of the Board, in accordance with the 1978 Full Employment and Balanced Growth Act, which contains forecasts in the form of ranges for GDP, unemployment and inflation.

Alongside these official pillars, many other institutions engage in forecasting. Every month, the Conference Board publishes leading, coincident and lagging indicators of the cycle. The Survey Research Center at the University of Michigan issues a well-known monthly index of consumer confidence. Numerous think tanks produce forecasts, be they general or more specialized. So do firms, notably financial institutions, whose economists are located mainly in New York City. The leading private-sector forecaster is Macroeconomic Advisers. The most prominent consensus forecasts are those of the Blue Chip Economic Indicators, based on monthly surveys of leading business economists, for real GDP and 15 other macroeconomic variables.

The Business Cycle Dating Committee of the National Bureau of Economic Research (NBER) closely monitors the US cycle and is the arbiter of recessions, but produces no forecasts.

Japan

In Japan, the government and the central bank play important roles in forecasting. Within the government, economic analysis resources are somewhat dispersed, as is the production of economic statistics. With regard to forecasting in the strict sense, however, responsibilities are more clearly defined. The Cabinet Office of the Prime Minister prepares and publishes the macroeconomic forecasts underpinning the budget as well as longer-run ones. Of particular interest are its comprehensive *Annual Report on the Japanese Economy and Public Finance* and the *Monthly Economic Report*. The Economic and Social Research Institute (ESRI) – attached to the Cabinet Office – carries out surveys, compiles the national accounts, and establishes business cycle peaks and troughs, alongside policy-oriented research work.

The Bank of Japan is the other main pole of economic analysis and forecasting. It produces some of the business cycle indicators, notably in the context of its quarterly Tankan survey, and some statistics, including monetary aggregates, the balance of payments and several producer price indices. It publishes a useful *Monthly Report of Recent Economic and Financial Developments*. The Bank of Japan does not disclose its forecasts, but twice a year the ranges of Policy Board members' forecasts are published in its *Outlook for Economic Activity and Prices*.

Outside government, a number of institutions are playing an increasingly important part in forecasting. One is the Japan Center for Economic Research (JCER), which publishes short-, medium- and long-run forecasts. Financial institutions are also active in this area, both domestic ones such as the Daiwa Institute of Research (DIR) and foreign ones with offices in Tokyo.

United Kingdom

Her Majesty's Treasury and the Bank of England regularly release forecasts. To a large extent, the underlying models are publicly known, and the forecasts themselves quite detailed.

Specifically, HM Treasury traditionally published economic and budget forecasts twice a year, in March/April in the context of the report on the forthcoming Budget, and then mid-way through the fiscal year, in the context of the *Pre-Budget Report*. In 2010, however, an Office for Budget Responsibility (OBR) was created, which has direct control over the forecasts and makes the key judgements underpinning the official projections. To make its independent assessments of public finances and the economy, it has full access to the data and analysis of HM Treasury. The OBR also presents a range of outcomes around its forecasts to illustrate the degree of uncertainty. Furthermore, it is tasked to assess the public sector balance sheet.

On the monetary side, the Bank of England publishes a detailed *Inflation Report* four times a year. The forecasts it contains represent a key pillar of the Bank's inflation-targeting policy, in terms of both credibility and communication. The Bank goes to great lengths to explain the minutiae of the forecast, both in the report itself and during the press conference held when it is released.

Outside the narrowly defined public sector, a number of institutions produce reputable forecasts. Banks in the City play an important role in this respect. Their forecasts are collated every month by the Treasury in *Forecasts for the UK Economy*. The main employers' organization, the Confederation of British Industry (CBI), conducts its own surveys and also publishes forecasts. The National Institute of Economic and Social Research (NIESR) maintains a model of the UK economy as well as a well-known international model, NiGEM. It also publishes a monthly GDP estimate. Similarly, Oxford Economics (OEF) regularly publishes forecasts, using a global macroeconomic model. And the Institute for Fiscal Studies (IFS) is a key actor in public finances forecasts.

Germany

In Germany, the government plays a rather more limited role in economic analysis and forecasting, with the central bank and a series of institutes being more prominent than elsewhere, reflecting a wish to restrain the influence of the central state following the Second World War and maintain the federal structure of the country.

The Federal Ministry of Economics and Technology publishes a *Monthly Report* on the economic situation in Germany and prepares a macroeconomic forecast which is presented in the Federal Government's *Annual Economic Report*, published in January. It also publishes updates in April and November which form the baseline for the estimation of tax receipts as well as for the annual draft budget (*Bundeshaushalt*) and the medium-term fiscal outlook (*Finanzplan des Bundes*). The April vintage comes with medium-term 'trend forecasts'. These forecasts of the German administration, however, do not have a very high profile. One of several reasons is that, within a federal structure, much of the fiscal action takes place at the level of the *Länder* rather than at the national level. In fact, the budget process involves substantial forecasting input from outside the central government: biannually, a working group tasked with estimating the tax receipts for the ongoing and the following year meets, bringing together national and subnational administrations, the central bank and the institutes; and in addition to this, a Financial Planning Council – including representatives of the federal, state and local governments – meets annually to prepare medium-run budget projections.

The Deutsche Bundesbank ('Buba') enjoys a very good reputation, not least because, in the view of the general public, it contributed so importantly to Germany's economic renaissance following the Second World War by safeguarding price stability. The Buba's forecasts are prepared twice yearly in the context of the Eurosystem's forecasting rounds and details are published in its *Monthly Report*.

Economic forecasting and analysis largely takes place in a number of institutes, some of which are publicly subsidized. Most famous, and long-established for some of them, are: the Institut für Wirtschaftsforschung (IFO), in Munich, known for its business climate surveys; the more Keynesian-oriented Deutsche Institut für Wirtschaftsforschung (DIW) in Berlin, which produces its own national accounts data; the more neoclassical-oriented Institut für Weltwirtschaft (IfW) in Kiel; the Hamburgische Welt-Wirtschafts-Institut (HWWI), best known for its monitoring of commodity prices; the Rheinisch-Westfälisches Institut für Wirtschaftsforschung (RIW) in Essen, which focuses mainly on social issues; and the Institut für Wirtschaftsforschung (IWH) in Halle (former East Germany). Most of them publish detailed forecasts at least once a year. Twice a year, four of them jointly publish a common set of forecasts, including some detailed analysis and recommendations. Divergences in views among the institutes can be highlighted in the report, however. There are also many other institutes, especially those working closely with business and trade unions and the academic community. Among them is the Center for European Economic Research (ZEW), which is best known for its monthly indicator of economic sentiment but does not produce its own forecast.

Furthermore, Germany has a Council of Economic Experts which since 1963 has brought together a handful of respected academics. They publish an annual report in November, including forecasts and policy advice, as well as occasional reports on special topics. The tone is often quite critical, reflecting the independence of the members of the Council. Finally, as elsewhere, the private sector and the large German banks (Deutsche Bank, Commerzbank and others) also produce forecasts.

France

In contrast to Germany, forecasting in France is dominated by the central government, even if the landscape has become less polarized over the past few decades. This has reflected the traditional influence of the French administration in economic activity, which was very apparent during the post-Second World War period. Two bodies under the umbrella of the Ministry of Finance take key roles: the Treasury (Direction Générale du Trésor) and the Institut National de la Statistique et des Études Économiques (INSEE), the latter enjoying a fair degree of independence. The Treasury prepares the short-run forecasts underpinning the budget bill as well as the medium-run forecasts appearing in the multi-year stability programmes submitted to the European Commission in the context of EU multilateral surveillance of fiscal policy (see above). The short-run forecasts are updated twice yearly: the spring forecasts are published in *Perspectives Économiques*, and the autumn forecasts in the *Rapport Économique, Social et Financier* (attached to the budget bill). They are discussed in a meeting of the Commission Économique de la Nation, where government officials debate with outside experts. At the same time, the Treasury plays a crucial role in the preparation of economic policy decisions, not least when evaluating the costs and benefits of alternative measures. The INSEE produces almost all economic statistics, including the national accounts, but also analyses and forecasts, unlike its German counterpart. Very short-run forecasts are published quarterly, in the *Notes de Conjoncture*. Though INSEE's forecasts do not commit the government, the INSEE and the Treasury co-operate in many ways, including by sharing information and producing joint work.

Three other public-sector institutions deserve a mention. The Banque de France monitors economic developments, including via its own surveys. It regularly undertakes forecasts, at the national level and in the context of the Eurosystem exercises. The Conseil d'Analyse Économique (CAE) differs from its US homonym, not least in that it has less of an operational function. It brings together some 35 economists, mainly from academia and the private sector, who discuss and publish reports on a great variety of economic topics.

Several independent think tanks also engage in economic forecasting, notably the Observatoire Français des Conjonctures Économiques (OFCE).

Italy

In Italy, the two main official forecasters are the Tesoro, in the context of fiscal policy, and the Bank of Italy, in its January and July *Economic Bulletin*. The Istituto di Studi e Analisi Economica (ISAE) is another prominent forecaster. Confindustria, the main employer organization, also produces macroeconomic forecasts.

Canada

As in most other G7 countries, the Department of Finance and the Bank of Canada are the two leading official institutions publishing regular macroeconomic forecasts. In the private sector, the Conference Board issues quarterly short-term forecasts for the country as a whole and by province, as well as annual long-run forecasts.

BRICS

Economic forecasting has become more important and has also gained international visibility in the so-called BRICS (Brazil, Russia, India, China, South Africa) countries (see Table 8.4).

In Brazil, the Ministry of Finance produces both annual and rolling three-year macroeconomic forecasts for each budget. The central bank (Banco Central do Brasil) publishes inflation and GDP forecasts in its quarterly *Inflation Report*. It also posts a summary of market forecasts for key variables on its website, which is refreshed weekly.

In Russia, the Ministry of Economic Development is in charge of the macroeconomic projections underpinning the budget. The central bank (Bank of Russia) releases projections annually in its *Main Guidelines of State Monetary Policy* but is moving towards the

Table 8.4   Selected forecasters in the BRICS economies

Country/institution	Publication(s)	Website
Brazil		
Ministry of Finance	Budget documents and forecasts	fazenda.gov.br
Banco do Brasil	*Relatório Trimestral de Inflação*	bcb.gov.br
Russia		
Ministry of Economic Development		economy.gov.ru
Bank of Russia		cbr.ru
Economic Expert Group		eeg.ru
Centre for Macroeconomic Analysis and Short-Term Forecasting	forecast.ru	
India		
Ministry of Finance	Budget documents and forecasts	finmin.nic.in
Reserve Bank of India	*Annual Policy Statement*	rbi.org.in
Economic Advisory Council to the Prime Minister	*Economic Outlook, Review of the Economy*	eac.gov.in
Central Statistical Organisation		mospi.nic.in
NCAER	*Quarterly Review of the Economy*	ncaer.org
China		
NDRC		en.ndrc.gov.cn
People's Bank of China		pbc.gov.cn
National Bureau of Statistics		stats.gov.cn
South Africa		
National Treasury	Budget documents and forecasts	finance.gov.za
South African Reserve Bank	*Monetary Policy Review*	reservebank.co.za
Bureau for Economic Research		ber.ac.za

Note: Some institutions present their most popular forecasts in their flagship publication(s), while others issue them in a variety of formats (not all listed here).

publication of inflation and other macroeconomic forecasts in its *Quarterly Inflation Review*. The so-called Economic Expert Group, attached to the Ministry of Finance, produces short-, medium- and long-term projections, which have a semi-official status. The other main forecasting organization is the Centre for Macroeconomic Analysis and Forecasting.

In India, the Ministry of Finance's Department of Economic Affairs prepares a one-year-ahead projection of GDP for budget purposes but it is officially called an assumption rather than a forecast. The Prime Minister's Economic Advisory Council publishes forecasts in its January *Review of the Economy*. The central bank (Reserve Bank of India) publishes its own forecast, but with scant detail. It also conducts and publishes surveys of business confidence and of professional forecasters. All three institutions, as well as the Central Statistical Organisation, publish very short-term forecasts for the ongoing fiscal year before it ends. One of the prominent non-governmental forecasting institutions is the National Council of Applied Economic Research (NCAER).

In China too, official forecasts are still few and far between. The Department of the National Economy of the National Development and Reform Commission (NDRC), which is the former central planning agency and the top economic policy making body, monitors economic developments and produces macroeconomic and other forecasts, mainly in a medium-run (five-year plan) perspective. The central bank (People's Bank of China) produces forecasts, but these are disclosed on a rather *ad hoc* basis. The National Bureau of Statistics occasionally makes public its views about short-term economic prospects. The State Information Centre (an economic analysis unit of the NDRC) makes projections of the economy that are published in the Chinese-language official newspaper *China Securities Journal* from time to time.

In South Africa, the National Treasury produces macroeconomic projections for the annual Budget Statement (February–March) and the Medium-Term Budget Statement (October–November). The central bank (South African Reserve Bank) regularly publishes inflation forecasts in its *Monetary Policy Review*. The main non-official source of economic projections is the Bureau for Economic Research, which also tabulates forecasts from other local sources.

Epilogue

A British Chancellor of the Exchequer who suffered more than others from the major forecasting errors made under his watch decided to take revenge on the technicians and declared in his Budget statement:

> Like long-term weather forecasts, they [economic forecasts] are better than nothing ... but their origin lies in the extrapolation from a partially known past, through an unknown present, to an unknowable future according to theories about the causal relationships between certain economic variables which are hotly disputed by academic economists and may in fact change from country to country or from decade to decade. (Healy, 1990)

Many of the current or recent ministers of finance across the world must have agreed with these sentiments since the 2007 financial crisis.

As mentioned earlier in the book, the Queen of England herself wondered out loud, when meeting representatives of the UK economics profession in late 2008, why no one had seen the financial crisis coming. In response, she received a letter eight months later from the British Academy (2009). It started somewhat defensively:

> Many people did foresee the crisis. However, the exact form that it would take and the timing of its onset and ferocity were foreseen by nobody. What matters in such circumstances is not just to predict the nature of the problem but also its timing. And there is also finding the will to act and being sure that authorities have as part of their powers the right instruments to bring to bear on the problem.

However, the letter continued, sounding more like a confession:

> But against those who warned, most were convinced that banks knew what they were doing. They believed that the financial wizards had found new and clever ways of managing risks. Indeed, some claimed to have so dispersed them through an array of novel financial instruments that they had virtually removed them. It is difficult to recall a greater example of wishful thinking combined with hubris. There was a firm belief, too, that financial markets had changed. And politicians of all types were charmed by the market. These views were abetted by financial and economic models that were good at predicting the short-term and small risks, but few were equipped to say what would happen when things went wrong, as they have ... So in summary, Your Majesty, the failure to foresee the timing, extent and severity of the crisis and to head it off, while it had many causes, was principally a failure of the collective imagination of many bright people, both in this country and internationally, to understand the risks to the system as a whole.

Granted, economic forecasting is almost an art as much as a science, and is eminently fallible. The very etymology of the word 'forecast' combines a reassuring 'fore' – 'in advance' – and a more disquieting 'cast' – as in 'cast the dice'. In fact, even the best forecasters cannot beat what Knight (1921) called uncertainty (as opposed to risk), namely, 'what we don't know we don't know'.[2] Hence, calculated confidence intervals may not properly measure actual forecast uncertainty. Equally disturbing, the best forecasting models may be outperformed by cruder ones, or by merely pooling the forecasts lying around in the marketplace. The reason for this paradox is that any model is at best a simplified representation of reality as observed in the past, and that economies evolve, are hit by unpredictable shocks and undergo sudden shifts.

That said, the past does say a lot about the future and is ignored at one's peril. Models can cope more successfully with measurable uncertainty than can a Chancellor's or anyone else's intuition. While individual future shocks are unpredictable, they can be expected to average out to some extent. If they turn out to be broadly similar, on average, to those witnessed in the past, and if there are no overlooked structural breaks, the model-based projection should be on track.

Moreover, forecasting techniques have seen improvements in recent decades: the statistical infrastructure has become far more elaborate, a wealth of empirical

---

[2] Knight famously contrasted quantifiable risk (randomness with measurable probabilities, which forecasters can cope with), and uncertainty (randomness with unknowable probabilities).

evidence has accumulated, and econometric tools are more sophisticated. Just as important, what forecasting may bring to decision-making (and what it cannot) is clearer than it used to be, at least among practitioners (and policy makers, it is hoped), though it may remain more obscure for outsiders.

Despite their shortcomings, economic forecasts are thus used routinely in the public as well as in the private sector and beyond. Governments, central banks and other official agencies rely heavily on them, as do private firms, citizens and others, both for decisions pertaining to the near term and for ones that have longer-run implications. Like it or not, forecasts are here to stay.

Going forward, the conceptual challenge for forecasters may be to widen their toolbox further in order to better incorporate the evolving cyclical forces of a global economy while streamlining unnecessarily convoluted models. Forecasters also increasingly need to adapt swiftly and learn from events to avoid repeated failure. At the same time, resisting fashions while communicating a rigorous diagnosis to policy makers and wider audiences remains the best contribution they can hope to bring to an uncertain world.

Contents

Measuring and interpreting economic developments requires a set of statistical standards as well as a coherent overall framework. By and large, forecasters around the world use a common language and refer to the same key macroeconomic variables. However, there are differences across time and space regarding the specific empirical content of some of the concepts used. For most practical purposes, at least in forecasting, these differences are relatively minor, but they ought to be borne in mind when comparing national forecasts or performance across countries.

The framework underpinning forecasting is that of the national accounts, which describe the economy at an aggregate level (section AI.1). Economic activity as captured in the national accounts can be seen from three different angles: supply, demand and income. Economic agents are grouped into so-called institutional sectors, whose operations are quantified in a standard set of tables. A key (and tricky) issue is the split of nominal magnitudes between volumes and prices.

The most comprehensive national accounts are constructed with an annual frequency. But forecasters typically reason at higher frequencies, and therefore rely heavily on quarterly national accounts, especially for short-term forecasts (section AI.2). Quarterly accounts are now produced routinely in most countries, albeit with varying degrees of detail and rigour. They are not just a simplified replica of the annual ones, and raise specific technical issues.

While the national accounts provide a coherent analytical ensemble, the quality of the data feeding into this framework is uneven, and methodological problems abound (section AI.3). Statistical observation is an art as much as a science, and some headline variables – say, employment, unemployment or inflation – can be, and are, measured in a variety of ways, with sometimes rather different results. Even when an identical approach is used, there are problems of data heterogeneity. The split between price and volume, which is so central, is not devoid of complications. And last but not least, as better information trickles in and as methods improve, the national accounts data are subject to substantial revisions, which need to be factored in fully.

Stepping back somewhat from run-of-the-mill forecasting, the depiction of economies raises conceptual challenges, some of which are addressed in the course of ongoing revisions to the internationally agreed national accounts framework (section AI.4). Others are more fundamental and are difficult to deal with through mere amendments to the framework; in particular, those concerning the definition and measurement of welfare.

AI.1   The national accounts framework

AI.1.1   Historical background

The origins of today's national accounts framework go back a very long way. For centuries, political authorities have tried to measure the creation of wealth in the territories they controlled. Over 4,000 years ago, in Ancient Egypt, people and property were registered for tax purposes, and a census of raw materials, cattle and produce took place regularly. In the seventeenth century, interest in raising revenue and in assessing England's war potential compared to that of France and the Netherlands led William Petty and later Gregory King to try to estimate national income as the sum of factor incomes or of expenditures. These two were soon followed by Pierre de Boisguillebert and Marshal Vauban, who used similar approaches to estimate France's national income (but Louis XIV disapproved, and their books were suppressed). The eighteenth-century French Physiocrats took a step backwards by restricting the concept of national income to agriculture and the extractive industries, on the grounds that other activities were not productive. But in his *Tableau économique*, François Quesnay, one of the Physiocrats, inaugurated the analysis of intersectoral flows.

It is only with the coming of age of classical economic theory, however, that two key insights came to the fore. First, production became a central concept, understood as a flow of newly created value, as opposed to stocks of wealth; however, the notion that services, and not goods alone, were also part of value-added only emerged in the late nineteenth century. Second, the idea that overall income stemming from production is distributed among the parties involved and then on to other agents gained prominence, subsequently giving rise to the concept of integrated economic accounts and to synoptic representations of the economic dealings between agents.

A number of obstacles stood in the way of the development of national accounts frameworks. Governments and private agents proved reluctant to reveal information about their activities, and there were doubts about the merits of state interventionism, even when the latter was only related to statistical observation. Cyclical crises in the late nineteenth and early twentieth centuries were the focus of much attention, and indicators were designed to assess the positions of economies in the cycle, and to try to anticipate cyclical swings. But the need for an overall framework had not yet become obvious at that time. Budgets were prepared on a purely financial basis, with little, if any, regard for the cycle: outlays and receipts were programmed on the basis of the outcomes of the previous year and of any discretionary changes to spending or taxes, ignoring the impact of the cycle.

The experience of the 1930s, when policies to combat the Great Depression were based on such data as stock price indices, freight car loadings and sketchy indices of industrial production, cruelly underlined the problems of incomplete information and spurred the development of both national accounts and a greater economic role for the government.

In the USA, the Department of Commerce commissioned Simon Kuznets of the NBER to develop a set of national economic accounts, the first version of which was presented in 1937 in a report to Congress. In 1942, annual estimates of gross national product (GNP) were introduced to complement the national income estimates and to facilitate war-time planning. The war also contributed towards stimulating the development of input–output tables, which, following Wassily Leontief's work, became an integral part of the national accounts.

Meanwhile, in the United Kingdom, James Meade and Richard Stone put together a new survey of the country's economic and financial situation, consisting of three tables relating to national income and expenditure, personal income, spending and saving, and the net amount of funds required by, and available from, private sources for government purposes.

This early work led to the development of systems of national accounts (SNAs) in a number of countries after the Second World War. Over time, these SNAs have been improved and harmonized, under the aegis of what is now the Inter-Secretariat Working Group on National Accounts, which brings together experts from the United Nations, the OECD, Eurostat, the IMF, and the World Bank. The first international standard saw the light of day in 1953 and has gone through three major revisions since then – in 1968, 1993 and 2008. The 2008 SNA is to be implemented by countries in the course of the 2010s and is itself intended to evolve over time.[1]

The EU version of the SNA goes by the name of the European System of Accounts (ESA). It imposes stricter harmonization, which is required for policy purposes – for example, for the calculation of budgetary transfers within the European Union or for the assessment of macroeconomic convergence in the context of monetary union. The system in place in Japan is also very close to the SNA framework. The US system, called the National Income and Product Accounts (NIPA), differs somewhat from the international SNA but the basic elements are broadly comparable.

---

[1] Among the changes from SNA 1993 are the extension of the concept of gross fixed capital formation to R&D as well as to large weapons, a new method to calculate insurance sector output, the inclusion of stock options in employee compensation, and a new way of recording import/export processing operations.

In addition to the SNA, there exist several related manuals to promote international consistency, notably those on balance of payments, on government finance statistics, and on monetary and financial statistics.

AI.1.2 Three ways to slice up GDP

National accounting focuses first and foremost on measuring the production of goods and services, which is generally referred to as gross domestic product (GDP). This means delineating the boundaries of GDP and defining which activities fall within its scope and which are excluded. GDP encompasses the production of goods and services that are sold at an 'economically significant' price, but also some other activities which do not lead to a sale on a market at commercial terms, plus an estimate of 'black market' activity (see Box AI.1). GDP excludes some activities, such as domestic services produced and consumed within households (cleaning, preparing meals and child care).

GDP can be compiled from three sides:

* On the production side (resources):

$$GDP = gross\ value\text{-}added\ generated\ in\ the\ economy$$
$$+\ taxes\ net\ of\ subsidies\ on\ products$$

* On the expenditure side (uses):

$$GDP = final\ consumption + gross\ capital\ formation + exports - imports$$

Box AI.1 GDP: a mixed bag

Viewed from the production side, GDP encompasses three types of activity:

* Market output: this is the value added by private entities but also the goods and services provided by the public sector when their price is 'economically significant', a term many national accountants define as a price sufficiently high to cover more than half of their costs. In addition to goods and services, including those rendered by the distribution and transport sectors, market output encompasses the services provided by banks and other financial institutions, measured indirectly by subtracting interest paid to depositors from interest earned on loans and other revenue.
* Non-market output: this includes most of the services (and, less important, goods) provided by the public sector or non-profit institutions

---

(NPIs) free of charge or at an economically non-significant price. They are valued at their cost of production. Non-market output also includes imputed values for the production of some other goods and services by economic agents for their own use, which are not sold in the marketplace but for which the implied notional transaction can be valued. Examples of these are the services provided by owner-occupied dwellings (home owners are assumed to rent their homes, as owners, to themselves, as occupants); the food and other goods produced by households for their own final consumption (farmers who eat some of the food they have grown are assumed to sell it, as producers, to themselves, as consumers); and the services provided by owner-builders in the construction or alteration of dwellings (same type of assumption). The latter two categories are especially significant in developing countries.

- Output produced in the informal, 'shadow', 'hidden', 'underground', or 'non-observed' sector: this relates to economic activities that are not reported to the tax authorities and government statisticians either through ignorance or deliberate intent on the part of producers, or through incompetence or deliberate choice on the part of the authorities. A variety of methods are used to guesstimate the size of this sector (OECD, 2002), including the comparison of tax control files with statistical sources to derive an average rate of fraud (in France, for example) or detailed studies of the labour market (in Italy, for example). Careful estimation is time-consuming and is usually carried out for some base year, with the results being extrapolated for subsequent years.

A separate category of activities are the outright illegal ones. The SNA recommends including productive illegal activities in GDP, for two main reasons. First, the associated incomes tend to be spent mostly on legal goods and services, implying that ignoring illegal activity would entail a mismatch between output and expenditure-based GDP. Second, legislation differs across countries, and the borderlines between legal and illegal activities shift over time, so that abstracting from the latter would be detrimental to the comparability between countries and over time. Not all illegal activities are deemed to be productive, however – only those which involve an exchange of goods and services between willing buyers and sellers. Protection rackets and most kinds of theft or fraud involve forcible transfers but do not add to GDP, hence they are not productive in this sense. Currently, very few countries incorporate explicit estimates of illegal activities in GDP, though most of them have made experimental estimates and European countries are moving towards integrating them into their official accounts.

- On the income side:

GDP = compensation of employees
        + gross operating surplus (including mixed income received by the self-employed)
        + taxes net of subsidies on production and imports

In practice, summing up the components from each side, which use different sources of information, does not lead to exactly the same total. Some countries hide these discrepancies by adjusting one or several components, but others prefer not to. Thus, in the USA, a discrepancy between income- and expenditure-side GDP is shown explicitly (see Table AI.1).

Supply side

In the first approach, also called the supply-side approach, GDP is obtained as the sum of value-added produced by all the economic agents residing in the country during a given period of time, where value-added is total output minus the inputs used in production. Value-added is measured at basic prices; that is, the prices effectively received by producers.[2] When indirect taxes apply, such as value added tax (VAT), or when the product is subsidized so as to lower its price, the basic price differs from the market price, which is the one paid by the purchaser. GDP is computed at market prices, hence the adjustment for taxes and subsidies noted above. The difference between the basic price and the market price also includes trading margins and transport costs, which correspond to the value added by the trading and transport sectors.

The production of goods and services generally requires physical capital (buildings and equipment in particular), which gradually wears out or becomes technologically obsolescent, implying that it needs to be replaced after a number of years. This erosion of the capital stock is called consumption of fixed capital. When subtracting the latter from 'gross' value-added (as calculated above), 'net' value-added is obtained.

Units producing similar goods or services are grouped into the same activity branch (or 'industry'), regardless of ownership. Since, by definition, value-added excludes intermediate consumption, it can be added across units or branches. A branch's value-added is the sum of the value added by each of the units in that branch, and nationwide value-added is the sum of value added across branches of activity. Each unit is classified in one, and only one, branch, in accordance with the International Standard Industrial Classification (ISIC), which provides for several levels of disaggregation. In its most recent version (ISIC Rev. 4), the economy is divided into 21 branches (of which, for example, manufacturing

---

[2] This is the SNA rule. In the USA, however, value-added is compiled at producer prices; that is, basic prices plus indirect taxes less subsidies.

would be one), which are in turn subdivided (there are 24 manufacturing branches at the next level). Each of the subdivisions may be split up itself at the so-called 'four-digit' level into even more specific branches. In the USA and Canada, a slightly different classification is used, the North American Industry Classification System (NAICS). In the European Union, the Classification of Economic Activities in the European Community (NACE) is used.

At any given level of disaggregation in the classification, the relationships between branches can be described in an input–output table. It is a matrix which for each pair of branches (i,j) shows how much branch j uses up of branch i's output as intermediate consumption, which depends on technology and on prices (see Appendix 3.1 for further discussion).

Demand side

Turning to the demand side, GDP equals the sum of final uses of goods and services by residents plus exports less imports. This does not include intermediate consumption, which relates to the goods and services used or consumed in production. It only refers to the purchases by or for the ultimate user, to avoid double counting.

This breaks down into:

- final consumption expenditure C by households, non-profit institutions serving households (NPISH) and government;
- gross capital formation I by enterprises, households (for which investment is mainly residential) and government; it comprises:
  - gross fixed capital formation; that is, capital expenditure on fixed assets and intellectual property products (formerly referred to as intangible fixed assets). It differs from intermediate consumption in that the products involved are not used up within the production process in an accounting period (one can also look at net investment, which corresponds to the increase in the capital stock (excluding revaluations) and is obtained by subtracting the consumption of fixed capital from gross fixed capital formation);
  - changes in inventories. Inventories are what has been produced or imported but not yet consumed, invested or exported. Changes in inventories, or stockbuilding, can be positive or negative. Hence, referring to their rate of growth is unhelpful. When decomposing GDP growth into its components on the expenditure side, it is the change in inventories that comes into play, and the convention is to compute the contribution of stockbuilding to GDP growth, which is the change in stockbuilding as a percentage of the past period's GDP (see Appendix 2.1); and
  - acquisitions less disposals of valuables.

Table AI.1 Main national accounts aggregates in the USA*

	$ billions	% of GDP		$ billions	% of GDP
DOMESTIC INCOME AND PRODUCT ACCOUNT					
Employee compensation	7,819.5	55.4	Personal consumption expenditures	10,001.3	70.8
Wages and salaries	6,286.9	44.5	Durable goods	1,026.5	7.3
Supplements	1,532.6	10.9	Non-durable goods	2,204.2	15.6
+ Taxes on production and imports	1,024.7	7.3	Services	6,770.6	48.0
– Subsidies	60.3	0.4	+ Gross private domestic investment	1,589.3	11.3
+ Net operating surplus of enterprises	3,294.9	23.3	Fixed investment	1,716.5	12.2
Private enterprises	3,308.1	23.4	Nonresidential	1,364.4	9.7
Government enterprises	–13.2	–0.1	Structures	451.6	3.2
+ Consumption of fixed capital	1,861.1	13.2	Equipment and software	912.8	6.5
Private	1,535.8	10.9	Residential	352.1	2.5
Government	325.3	2.3	Change in private inventories	–127.2	–0.9
= Gross domestic income	13,939.9	98.7	+ Net exports of goods and services	–386.3	–2.7
			Exports	1,578.4	11.2
+ Statistical discrepancy	179.1	1.3	Imports	1,964.7	13.9
			+ Government consumption expenditure and gross investment	2,914.9	20.6
			Federal	1,139.6	8.1
			National defence	771.6	5.5
			Non-defence	368.0	2.6
			State and local	1,775.3	12.6
= GDP	14,119.0	100.0	= GDP	14,119.0	100.0
FOREIGN TRANSACTIONS CURRENT ACCOUNT					
Exports of goods and services	1,578.4	11.2	Imports of goods and services	1,964.7	13.9
+ Income receipts from the rest of the world	629.8	4.5	+ Income payments to the rest of the world	483.6	3.4

(continued)

Table A1.1 Continued

	$ billions	% of GDP
Wages and salaries	10.8	0.1
Income payments on assets	472.8	3.3
Interest	344.5	2.4
Dividends	99.5	0.7
Reinvested earnings on FDI in the US	28.8	0.2
+ Net current taxes and transfer payments to the rest of the world	139.5	1.0
+ **Balance on current account**	**−379.7**	**−2.7**
= Current payments to the rest of the world plus balance	2,208.2	15.6
Net saving	−327.4	−2.3
Personal saving	655.3	4.6
Undistributed corporate profits with IVCCA†	284.2	2.0
Nondisbursed accrued wages	5.0	0.0
Net government saving	−1,271.9	−9.0
+ **Consumption of fixed capital**	1,861.1	13.2
= **Gross saving**	1,533.7	10.9
Statistical discrepancy	179.1	1.3
Gross saving and statistical discrepancy	1,712.9	12.1

	$ billions	% of GDP
Wages and salary receipts	2.9	0.0
Income receipts on assets	626.9	4.4
Interest	146.3	1.0
Dividends	206.8	1.5
Reinvested earnings on US direct investment abroad	273.8	1.9
= Current receipts from abroad	2,208.2	15.6
DOMESTIC CAPITAL ACCOUNT		
Gross domestic investment	2,092.7	14.8
Gross private domestic investment	1,589.3	11.3
Gross government investment	503.4	3.6
Net capital account transactions	0.6	0.0
Net lending (+) or net borrowing (−)	−380.3	−2.7
Gross domestic investment, capital account transactions and net lending	1,712.9	12.1
FOREIGN TRANSACTIONS CAPITAL ACCOUNT		
Balance on current account, national income and product accounts	−379.7	−2.7
Net capital account transactions	0.6	0.0
Net lending (+) or net borrowing (−)	−380.3	−2.7

*For year 2009, NIPA presentation.

**Some totals may not exactly match the components due to rounding.

†Inventory valuation and capital consumption adjustments.

Source: US BEA (extracted in August 2010).

- and net exports (that is, exports X minus imports M) or 'trade balance'. For the same reason as in the case for inventories, the focus is on the contribution of net exports to GDP growth and not on their rate of growth. Exports include all sales to non-residents, and are regarded as final spending, since they are final as far as the domestic economy is concerned (though they can be used as intermediate consumption in a foreign economy). Imports are subtracted from demand to obtain GDP, because while they are included directly or indirectly in final expenditure they are not part of domestic production.

Hence the demand-side approach can be summarized as:

$$GDP = C + I + X - M$$

or, equivalently, in supply-equals-demand terms:

$$GDP + M = C + I + X$$

Demand is valued at purchasers' prices, including trade and transport margins, VAT and other taxes on products. Exports are valued 'free on board' (f.o.b.); that is, at the price fetched at the border of the exporting country. In the case of imports, which are part of aggregate supply, flows are valued c.i.f. (that is, including the 'cost of insurance and freight') up to the border of the importing country.

Income side

On the income side, GDP equals the sum of all income earned by resident individuals or corporations in the production of goods and services, plus net taxes on supply. Some types of income are not included – for example, transfer payments such as unemployment benefit, child benefit or state pensions, since they are a redistribution of existing income via taxes and national insurance contributions. To avoid double counting, these payments and other current transfers (for example, taxes on income and wealth) are excluded. GDP on the income side thus breaks down into firms' gross operating surplus, the gross mixed income of the self-employed, compensation of employees (wages plus employee as well as employer social contributions), and taxes on production and imports less subsidies on production. The operating surplus and mixed income are measures of profit excluding any holding gains or losses. Mixed income is the operating surplus of unincorporated enterprises owned by households, which implicitly includes remuneration for work done by the owner or other members of the household. This remuneration cannot be identified separately from the return to the owner as entrepreneur. Some income is not declared to the tax authorities, and to take this into account adjustments are typically made to the GDP income measure.

AI.1.3   Institutional sectors

At an elementary level, economic activity and wealth can be attributed to institutional units, which are the basic transactor units. The SNA groups economic agents with similar economic functions into institutional sectors and subsectors. The economy as a whole consists of the entire set of resident institutional units. The operations carried out by the various institutional sectors are described in a set of integrated economic accounts which includes production accounts, income accounts, capital accounts, financial accounts, balance sheet accounts and external accounts. The following institutional sectors are distinguished: households, non-financial corporations, financial corporations, general government, NPISH and the rest of the world.

The households sector consists of all resident households, defined as small groups of people who share accommodation, pool some or all of their income and wealth, and collectively consume goods and services – mainly housing and food. Households also engage in other forms of economic activity as producers of dwelling rental services (including as owner-occupiers) and through their operation of unincorporated enterprises. The latter are included in the households sector because the owners of ordinary partnerships and sole proprietorships will frequently combine their business and personal transactions, so that complete sets of accounts disentangling these operations will often be unavailable.

Households' gross disposable income principally includes wage earnings, remuneration in kind received from enterprises, mixed income of the self-employed (partly wages, partly profits), property income and social benefits net of taxes and social contributions paid. Gross disposable income minus consumption equals saving. The saving rate is saving divided by gross disposable income. The financial saving rate is the ratio of households' net lending over gross disposable income, where net lending is saving minus households' investment outlays, which mainly consists of residential investment and investment by unincorporated enterprises.

Household consumption is defined in one of two ways:

- Final consumption expenditure, which encompasses all purchases of goods and services by resident households, apart from housing and valuables (defined as expensive durable goods that do not deteriorate over time, are not used up in consumption or production, and are acquired primarily as stores of value) but including imputed expenditure (notably imputed rents in the case of owner-occupied housing) as well as benefits in kind received from employers.
- Actual final consumption of households, which in addition includes social transfers in kind from general government and NPISHs that are part of the output of these institutions or that have been purchased by them from market

producers for onward transmission to households free of charge or at prices that are not economically significant. Spending on health and education falls into this category, but not spending on collective services, such as legislation and regulation, defence, police and environmental protection.

The first of the two concepts of consumption is best suited to study the relationship between household income and consumption, and is often the one referred to in economic forecasting. The second is useful for international comparisons, as the share of social transfers in kind in actual final consumption varies considerably among countries.

The non-financial corporations sector consists of resident corporations engaged mainly in the production of market goods and non-financial services (irrespective of the residence of their shareholders). They are mainly private but can also be government-owned or controlled. Their value-added can be decomposed into wages and gross operating surplus. The margin ratio, defined as gross operating surplus divided by value-added, is a broad measure of profitability.[3] Gross corporate saving is defined as the profit that is left after deducting the remuneration of capital and taxes on corporate income. The extent to which investment can be financed by these retained earnings is measured by the self-financing ratio, which is gross corporate saving divided by gross fixed capital formation.

The financial corporations sector consists of resident corporations engaged mainly in financial intermediation or auxiliary financial activities. Financial corporations principally conduct financial market transactions: borrowing and lending money; providing life, health or other insurance; financial leasing; and investing in financial assets. Financial auxiliaries include stockbrokers, insurance brokers, investment advisers, trustees, custodians, mortgage originators and other entities providing services closely related to financial intermediation even though they do not engage in this themselves.

The general government sector consists of central, state and local government as well as public social security funds. It includes all departments, offices and other bodies engaged mainly in the production of services and sometimes goods outside the normal market mechanism and for consumption by the general public, and in redistributing income. Their costs of production are largely financed from public revenues, enabling them to provide services free of charge or at a nominal price well below production cost. The tax burden (or compulsory levies ratio), defined as the sum of all taxes and social contributions

---

[3] In the USA, profits (defined as the operating surplus minus interest payments and business current transfer payments) rather than the gross operating surplus are usually the focus of attention.

financing general government divided by GDP, is a key measure of fiscal pressure, broadly defined.

The NPISH sector includes non-market entities that are not controlled or financed largely by government, and provide goods or services to their members or other households without charge or at token prices. This sector includes trade unions, professional societies, consumer associations, political parties, churches, sports clubs, charities, and sometimes universities. In some countries, this sector is not recognized separately in the national accounts (for example, in Australia).

In addition to accounts for the resident sectors, the SNA includes external, or rest-of-the-world, accounts, which summarize the transactions of residents with non-residents, businesses and governments. The rest of the world can conveniently be thought of as a separate sector. Its accounts are broadly consistent with the balance of payments (see Table AI.2).[4] In the latter, transactions on goods and services are recorded in the current account, which includes exports and imports, income flows (for example, interest on loans) and current transfers (for example, remittances by migrant workers or intergovernmental grants). The current account balance is the nation's (or region's) net saving; that is, the difference between saving and investment. The capital account encompasses transactions on non-financial assets, such as sales of patents or debt relief operations. The sum of the current plus the capital account is the nation's net lending (or net borrowing). The balance of payments is always 'balanced' in the sense that the aggregate position of the current and capital accounts is always matched, or 'financed', by the financial account (apart from the discrepancy arising from errors and omissions). In the case of a net lending position, for example, the financial account position will be negative: the sum of total net capital outflows plus the change in the central bank's foreign exchange reserves is then positive.[5] In this context, capital flows include foreign direct investment (FDI; the usual definition of FDI is when a significant share – generally over 10 per cent – of a firm's capital is bought by non-residents), portfolio investment, bank lending and the like.

Two additional concepts are often used. First, the balance of 'capital flows' represents the net long-term capital flows into a country, namely the sum of FDI, bonds and equity flows. This aggregate is useful to assess the quality of the financing of a current account deficit, in so far as these flows are perceived to

---

[4] The US balance of payments is presented by the Bureau of Economic Analysis (BEA) in a somewhat different format. For expositional purposes, it is translated in Table AI.2 into the format used in the euro area and Japan.

[5] By convention, albeit somewhat counterintuitively, the sign for these lines of the balance of payments is reversed: for example, accumulation of foreign exchange reserves by the Bank of Japan will be shown as a negative entry.

Table AI.2 Balance of payments*

	USA	Euro area	Japan
Current account	−2.7	−0.6	2.8
Exports of goods	7.6	14.4	10.7
Imports of goods	11.2	13.9	9.9
Balance on goods	−3.6	0.5	0.9
Services (net)	0.9	0.3	−0.4
Income (net)	0.9	−0.4	2.6
Current transfers (net)	−0.9	−1.0	−0.2
Capital account	0.0	0.1	−0.1
Financial account**	1.5	0.5	−3.1
Direct investment (net)	−0.9	−0.9	−1.2
Portfolio investment (net)	−1.3	3.4	−4.4
Financial derivatives (net)	0.4	0.5	0.2
Other investment (net)	3.8	−2.6	2.9
Change in reserve assets (net)	−0.4	0.1	−0.5
Errors and omissions	1.2	0.1	0.4

*For year 2009, in percentages of GDP.
**A negative sign denotes a positive outflow and vice versa.
Sources: US BEA, ECB and Bank of Japan.

be less volatile than other capital flows. Second, the 'basic balance' is defined as the sum of the current account balance and net long-term capital flows.

Gross national income (GNI) – formerly known as gross national product (GNP) – is defined as GDP less primary incomes payable to non-resident units plus primary incomes receivable from non-resident units (primary incomes exclude net insurance claims and other miscellaneous transfers). In other words, GNI equals GDP less net taxes on production and imports, less compensation of employees and property income payable to the rest of the world, plus the corresponding items receivable from the rest of the world. GNI is thus the total income accruing to national residents regardless of the country in which their services were supplied. Net national income is GNI minus fixed capital consumption.

AI.1.4 Key accounts

The national accounts seek to provide a coherent overview of the economic situation, capturing all relevant physical quantities or volumes, incomes and financial positions. A sequence of accounts or tables are used to this effect (see the example of the UK in Table AI.3):

- The goods and services accounts present a comprehensive picture of the supply and use of goods and services (referred to generically as 'products') in the economy and of the income generated from production. They ensure that, in value terms, the flows in each sector and between sectors are consistent.

Table AI.3 Main national accounts aggregates in the UK*

	£ millions	% of GDP
Goods and services account		
GDP (production side)		
Output of goods and services	2,668,184	184.6
– Intermediate consumption	1,372,521	94.9
= Gross value added, at basic prices	1,295,663	89.6
+ VAT and other taxes on products	155,140	10.7
– Subsidies on products	5,223	0.4
= GDP at market prices	**1,445,580**	**100.0**
GDP (expenditure side)		
Household final consumption expenditure	892,194	61.7
+ NPISH final consumption expenditure	35,832	2.5
+ Individual government final consumption expenditure	194,535	13.5
= Total actual individual consumption	1,122,561	77.7
+ Collective government final consumption expenditure	119,509	8.3
= Total final consumption expenditure (1)	1,242,070	85.9
Gross fixed capital formation	240,361	16.6
+ Changes in inventories	295	0.0
+ Acquisition less disposals of valuables	614	0.0
= Total gross capital formation (2)	241,270	16.7
Exports of goods and services	422,905	29.3
– Imports of goods and services	460,665	31.9
= External balance of goods and services (3)	–37,760	–2.6
GDP: (1) + (2) + (3)	**1,445,580**	**100.0**
GDP (income side)		
Gross operating surplus	424,804	29.4
of which : Corporations	349,482	24.2
Households and NPISH	75,322	5.2
+ Mixed income	84,884	5.9
+ Compensation of employees	769,191	53.2
+ Taxes on production and imports	178,312	12.3
– Subsidies	11,611	0.8
= GDP at market prices	**1,445,580**	**100.0**
Current and capital account		
GDP	**1,445,580**	**100.0**
+ Net employee compensation from abroad (receipts minus payments)	–715	0.0
+ Net subsidies from abroad (receipts minus payments)	–1,857	–0.1
+ Property and entrepreneurial income receipts from abroad	260,967	18.1
– Property and entrepreneurial income payments to the rest of the world	232,217	16.1
= Gross national income (GNI)	**1,471,758**	**101.8**
+ Current transfers from abroad (receipts minus payments)	–12,196	–0.8

(continued)

Table AI.3 Continued

= **Gross national disposable income**	1,459,562	101.0
− Total final consumption expenditure	1,242,070	85.9
= **Gross saving**	217,492	15.0
+ Net capital transfers from abroad (receipts minus payments)	3,281	0.2
− Gross capital formation	241,270	16.7
− Acquisition less disposals of non-produced non-financial assets	40	0.0
= **Net lending (+) or net borrowing (−)**	−20,535	−1.4
Financial account		
Net acquisition of financial assets	274,839	19.0
− Net acquisition of financial liabilities	300,650	20.8
− Statistical discrepancy between financial and non-financial accounts	−5,276	−0.4
= **Net lending (+) or net borrowing (−)**	−20,535	−1.4

*For year 2008, in accordance with the 1993 SNA.
Source: Office for National Statistics (2010).

In volume terms, consistency is also ensured but is only approximate when chain-linking is used, as discussed in Box AI.4 below.

- A second set of accounts trace the distribution and use of income. The allocation of the primary income account shows how the income generated in production is distributed. The secondary distribution of the income account shows how primary income is redistributed via taxes, social contributions, benefits and other transfers, and hence the income actually received in the end by each category of agents. The use of a disposable income account shows how disposable income is used in consumption or saved. The capital account then shows what part of saving is mainly invested in non-financial assets, the remainder being net lending or net borrowing.
- The financial and balance sheet accounts record transactions in financial assets and liabilities and show how net worth (total financial and non-financial assets minus total liabilities) increases or decreases. Net worth typically rises when net lending is positive, though its exact variation also depends on fixed capital consumption, on revaluations of assets or liabilities and on other changes (disappearance or emergence of assets or liabilities, say, when oil is discovered after drilling). This third set of accounts is often referred to as the 'flows of funds'.

In principle, the national accounts record transactions on an accrual basis (as opposed to a cash or a payment due basis), reflecting the time when economic value is transferred rather than when cash relating to the transaction is paid or is due for payment. For example, interest flows are recorded as interest accruals, irrespective of payment schedules. The same holds for taxes. In practice, however, some operations may be observable and recorded only on a cash basis, thus calling for statistical corrections.

The above sequence of accounts can be built for each of the institutional sectors, and summarized in a comprehensive table of integrated economic accounts. All these accounts are double-entry, so they balance for each sector and/or between sectors.

At the national level, net worth is the sum of the net worth of all residents, namely their stock of physical assets plus their net financial claims on the rest of the world (since financial assets and liabilities held among residents cancel out).

In practice, the income and financial accounts are often less developed than the goods and services account. Moreover, the producers of the requisite statistical information often differ, with national statistics institutes usually in charge of the 'real sector', while flows of funds are frequently elaborated by central banks. All in all, national balance sheets are difficult to put together, but progress is being made in this regard (see OECD, 2011).

AI.1.5   The split between price and volume

Transactions between economic agents take place and are recorded at current prices. But for analytical purposes, when looking at these transactions over time, it is necessary to distinguish volume and price. In this context, volume refers to all factors other than price that affect valuation at current prices, including sheer quantity but also the quality of the product.

The national accounts provide a description of supply and uses in volume terms. The accounts depicting the distribution of income and the balance sheet accounts are presented only at current prices, even if many of the aggregates involved are then deflated by a relevant price index in order to assess their evolution in real, as opposed to nominal, terms. This is the case, for example, with disposable income and net worth.

Moving from current prices to volumes is not straightforward, as discussed in greater detail below. It is sufficient to stress here that, first, adequate price indices are needed for each component of the account under consideration, which is not always easy. Then the volumes obtained for the components need to be aggregated, which raises a host of problems as soon as relative prices shift over time, as they generally do.

AI.2   Quarterly national accounting

In practice, it would be unthinkable to wait for the release of the previous year's annual accounts before updating economic forecasts. Moreover, exclusive reliance on annual data would make it impossible to capture adequately the dynamic relationships or leads and lags between key economic variables. In addition, there has been an increasing need to have a general framework that allows for the collection and analysis of short-term economic indicators in a coherent way, as in the case of annual data. Therefore, quarterly national accounts have gradually been developed in most OECD countries and in a growing number of emerging market economies. Their coverage and relevance have improved over time. A first estimate of the quarterly accounts is now usually published in the two months following the end of the quarter to which they relate (within one month in the USA and the UK). Partial monthly national accounts are available in a few countries, such as Finland and Canada (Girard, 2009). These can be useful, though there is a trade-off between frequency and quality of the accounts, as there is between timeliness and quality. Constructing quarterly national accounts requires some specific techniques, to control for seasonal variations (as discussed in Chapter 2) and to ensure consistency with the annual accounts, which draw on a richer information set.

For some variables, the quarterly accounts are derived in the same way as the annual accounts. But for many components, there are often no intra-annual source data similar to the annual ones – for example, when dealing with investment or tax data. Econometric techniques can then be used to build 'notional' quarterly accounts. The idea is to exploit the information provided by available higher-frequency series related to the missing national account observations. In effect, the higher-frequency indicators are benchmarked on the actual annual data to construct the quarterly accounts. As an illustration, suppose that household consumption is not observed quarterly but only annually, but that some of its components, such as retail sales and car registrations, *are* observed quarterly. Then a regression of consumption on retail sales and car registrations can be run on annual data and the estimated equation can serve to produce an estimate of quarterly consumption. This can be refined if needed by taking into account explicitly special factors or known trends in some of the components of consumption. In practice, such benchmarking is hard to get right (see Box AI.2), not least because of the appearance of econometric residuals that need to be taken adequately into account.

The challenge is compounded by the fact that, as some key data are missing at the quarterly frequency, notably as regards corporations, some hazardous shortcuts are taken. For example, an estimate of stockbuilding will sometimes be derived as the difference between the sum of estimated value-added across branches and the estimated components of final demand. It will therefore be polluted by the errors made in each estimation (to the extent that they do not offset each other). This is done separately at current prices and in volume terms, and sometimes adjustments for seasonality are not carried out consistently,

Box AI.2   Benchmarking the quarterly national accounts

Benchmarking can serve two purposes. One, dubbed 'quarterization' or interpolation, is to build a quarterly series $X_{t,a}$ (where $t = 1, ...,4$ stands for the quarter and a for the year) when an annual series A_a of better statistical quality exists. The second, extrapolation, is to estimate $X_{t,a}$ when A_a is not yet available. Denote $I_{t,a}$ the quarterly series observed for the indicator used to estimate $X_{t,a}$. In practice, the choice of I depends on its availability and on how closely it mirrors the variations of A_a at the annual frequency.

The simplest way to proceed would be to assume proportionality, namely that:

$X_{t,a} = A_a I_{t,a} / \Sigma_t I_{t,a}$ subject to constraint (1): $\Sigma_t X_{t,a} = A_a$ (interpolation)

or that

$X_{t,a+1} = X_{4,a} I_{t,a+1} / I_{4,a}$ (extrapolation beyond the last known year for A_a)

But if I does not rise as fast as A, there will be a catch-up in the form of a jump in the $X_{t,a}$ series in the first quarter of each year, because of the need to meet constraint (1). This is called the 'step problem'.

For this reason, the *pro rata* distribution technique is generally not advisable. There are several ways to overcome the problem. The best-known is the so-called proportional Denton (1971) method, which is recommended by the IMF. In its basic version, it keeps $X_{t,a}$ as proportional as possible to the indicator by minimizing (in a least squares sense) the difference in relative adjustment to neighbouring quarters subject to the constraint provided by the annual benchmarks. Mathematically, this amounts to minimizing over all quarters the expression:

$$\Sigma_i [(X_i / I_i) - (X_{i-1} / I_{i-1})]^2$$

When the annual data are later released, the whole quarterly series constructed in this way has to be re-estimated, since the adjustment for the errors in the indicator is distributed smoothly over a number of years, not just within a given year.

A number of other benchmarking techniques exist (discussed in greater detail by Bloem *et al.*, 2001). They can be grouped into two categories:

- Numerical methods similar to Denton's, but based on the minimization of somewhat different expressions, with a view to better incorporate information on past systematic movements in the indicator's bias (whose magnitude may, for example, depend on the business cycle).
- Statistical methods, which try to gauge the foreseeable evolution of the indicator's bias; for example, using ARIMA or multivariate models. Such methods are quite heavy to implement and may at times result in over-corrections.

hence the implied quarterly deflators often behave somewhat erratically, in particular the one derived for stockbuilding. In addition, the first quarterly accounts estimates rely on incomplete monthly information. For example, the foreign trade data for the last month of the quarter will often not yet be known. Hence subsequent versions of the quarterly accounts often involve substantial revisions, especially if the initial estimates are published rapidly.

Other problems also arise. In some countries, a price/volume split is not provided for all components of the quarterly accounts, or only with long lags. Moreover, there are usually no accounts for all institutional sectors at the quarterly frequency, so that some key indicators have to be proxied in some way. Another gap is the absence of quarterly financial data, though there are a few exceptions, notably the USA, where the Federal Reserve publishes fairly comprehensive quarterly flow-of-funds statistics.

AI.3   Technical hurdles

Although the national accounts provide a consistent framework, the forecaster faces a number of practical problems related to statistical observation itself, data heterogeneity, the price/volume split and revisions of the source data.

AI.3.1   Statistical observation

Statistical coverage of the economy is very uneven, including in advanced market economies. A key reason is that national accounts have usually been constructed using a pre-existing and heterogeneous set of statistical data, rather than the reverse. Agriculture, which in these countries represents only a tiny share of GDP, is graced with a wealth of data. Conversely, data on the service sector, which is by far the largest one in advanced economies, are typically wanting. Partly, this is historical, but it also stems from the fact that measuring the volume of value-added in services is more difficult than in agriculture or industry. Even in the industrial sector, where data is plentiful, some crucial elements are not captured adequately in the statistics, notably stockbuilding and investment behaviour, or work-in-progress.

These problems are even more acute in the case of higher-frequency data. Industrial production is usually monitored on a monthly basis, but in gross rather than value-added terms. Since the latter is not a constant proportion of the former, this is an extra complication. In addition, relatively few monthly data are available for service sector activities.

Globalization is also producing significant challenges regarding the measurement of trade flows. Customs statistics have to register increasing flows, especially in the closely integrated Asian economies. In general, they also fail to capture illegal/informal exchanges, thus adding further uncertainty. And in the European single market, these problems are compounded because trade flows have proved to be increasingly difficult to measure in the absence of effective borders.

Another difficulty is that economic data are released with a lag, and sometimes with large lags. In the meantime, the forecaster has to make do with other indicators, which are designed for different purposes (for example, administrative uses). It also happens that two series exist for one variable, which send conflicting messages. Controversies surrounding the employment and unemployment data in a number of countries illustrate the confusion that may ensue (see Box AI.3).

In practice, data limitations may mislead analysts. For example, they may put more weight than is warranted by its share of GDP on developments in industry, simply because the data for this sector are much more complete. Consider the Asian crisis in 1997–8: the industrial sector in the USA went through a soft patch, as evidenced by high-frequency indicators such as output and capacity utilization, but the economy at large as measured by GDP continued to expand, benefiting in particular from gains in the terms of trade and the flight of capital away from emerging markets towards safer US shores. The somewhat alarmist high-frequency information probably spurred the Federal Reserve to adopt a more stimulatory monetary stance than would otherwise have been the case. With the benefit of hindsight, the push provided by the Federal Reserve may thus have been pro-cyclical.

While forecasters' conclusions are conditioned by data availability, the reverse also holds, as some data tend to create a diagnosis. For example, data on industrial orders in Germany receive enormous attention. The press and analysts await them eagerly, as if they conveyed precious information about

---

Box AI.3   Capturing labour market trends

In the case of labour markets, the problem is less a lack of data than the contradictory signals sent by alternative employment or unemployment series.

Consider the case of US employment data. The series that the Federal Reserve trusts most – even though it is also subject to sizeable revisions – is the payroll statistic, which is based on a monthly survey of some 400,000 business establishments conducted by the Bureau of Labor Statistics (BLS). This measure showed a decline in US employment by over 0.8 million people in the two years following the November 2001 cyclical trough in real GDP, leading to the description of the recovery as 'jobless', or even 'job-loss'. In contrast, the monthly household survey, conducted by the BLS and the Census Bureau on a sample of about 60,000 households, showed that, over the same period, employment had risen by over 1.5 million. To some extent, this startling dissonance can be explained by differences in coverage between the two surveys: employment in the household survey includes unincorporated self-employed workers, unpaid family workers and farm workers, none of whom are covered in the payroll survey; at the same time, a person holding two jobs counts once in the household survey but twice in the payroll survey. Controlling for these differences, the gap between the two measures narrowed to some extent (partly because of unusually strong growth in the number of self-employed after the 2001 downturn), but it remained huge. Another possible explanation might have been that the payroll survey failed to catch newly-formed businesses, but the BLS adjusts the raw data to take this into account, and subsequent benchmark revisions to the series did not show any systematic bias in this respect. In Canada too, a similar difference was observed in 2002–3, but the most reliable source in that country is the household survey, and little attention is paid to payroll survey data. The choice of the data source matters tremendously over the short run, but it is less important when the focus is on long-run trends, since the two series tend to move much more closely together over longer horizons.

Considerable scope for confusion also exists with regard to unemployment statistics, mainly because the number of people claiming unemployment benefit and the number of those strictly defined as unemployed (who, according to the internationally agreed ILO definition, are people without jobs who are actively looking for work and are immediately available) can differ greatly. For example, a person receiving a benefit may not be looking for a new job and would thus be considered inactive. Conversely, a job-seeker may not receive any benefit at all if his/her rights have expired, but would be considered as unemployed. In addition, the way these populations are measured is often quite different. Information about people receiving unemployment benefits is often produced on an exhaustive basis by public administrations, at a relatively high frequency (usually each month or even each week in the USA). In contrast, determining the total number of people unemployed can be a difficult exercise, requiring surveys to be undertaken and is therefore subject to a certain degree of uncertainty and time lags.

In the United Kingdom, for example, two series compete for attention. One is the Labour Force Survey (LFS) series, conducted using the internationally agreed ILO definition of unemployment. The other is the claimant count series, which measures how many are claiming unemployment-related benefits. In Spring 2009, the LFS measure stood at 7.2 per cent of the labour force, whereas the claimant count was 4.8 per cent. Similarly, in France and Germany, there are also two very different series for unemployment.

the outlook for the German economy. In reality, they are a coincident more than a leading indicator, and often appear less informative than the qualitative opinions expressed by respondents in the smaller sample of industrial firms surveyed by Munich's Ifo Institute. Similarly, the publication of household confidence indicators gives rise to many comments and analyses, despite the fact that they are often of limited value for forecasting purposes.

AI.3.2   Data heterogeneity

The data used in forecasting are very heterogeneous, as they were developed for a variety of reasons and not necessarily to facilitate economic analysis. For example, foreign trade data originally stem from the need to raise taxes at the border, while data on the registered unemployed primarily serve administrative purposes. In addition, data frequency ranges from intra-day or daily (for exchange rates) to annual or multi-annual (some surveys or censuses are conducted only once in so many years).

Another difficulty pertains to data presentation, which differs across countries. For example, in the USA the quarterly national accounts are presented in annualized format, but in contrast in Europe, they are traditionally presented in quarter-on-quarter terms.

Practices regarding deseasonalization also vary. Price data, for example, tend to be presented in seasonally-adjusted form in the USA (with some exceptions, however, notably in the case of foreign trade deflators) but not in Europe. In emerging markets, data are often presented on the basis of the 12-month rate of change, even when seasonally-adjusted series exist. This can be misleading, as 12-month rates are a lagging indicator: thus, in 1999, following the devaluation of Brazil's real, many observers announced a recession, even though the country was already experiencing a recovery. Another example of confusion is the contradictory comments surrounding the release of inflation data, when some analysts describe inflation in terms of the month-on-month increase in the consumer price index, ignoring seasonal factors, while others focus on the 12-month rate of change, which essentially controls for these factors but may not portray the latest price developments adequately. Most national statistical offices have developed measures of core inflation (which exclude certain volatile items) to offer a better gauge of underlying inflation trends. This is useful but compounds data heterogeneity, as the list of excluded items varies.

The diversity of data used has also increased as globalization, financial market development and diversification of public sector activities have prompted forecasters to attempt to factor in information that is not part and parcel of standard national accounts. Examples include capital flows, intra-firm trade across borders, microeconomic balance sheet data and governments' off-balance-sheet operations.

AI.3.3   Measuring inflation

The proper estimation of transaction volumes requires reliable deflators. Depending on the specific purpose, different indices may be used, which are sometimes not adequately kept separate in public commentary. For example, in the case of household consumption, one can use a retail price index (with weights based on retail trade turnover), a consumer price index (CPI) (with weights based on the average basket of a representative household), or a national accounts deflator (which also takes into account items that are not purchased directly by households but none the less are implicitly consumed by them; for instance, owner-occupied imputed rents, which are not included in CPI baskets in all countries). Moreover, in the case of the CPI, countries usually monitor it only for the typical urban household, whose consumption patterns may differ significantly from the nationwide average.

Different measures of inflation at times send conflicting signals. In the UK, for example, no less than three very different indices make headlines on inflation: the old retail price index (RPI), a truncated version thereof (RPIX, which strips out mortgage interest payments) and the European Harmonised Index of Consumer Prices (HICP), which is referred to simply as the CPI. A telling example was in Spring 2009, when CPI inflation was running above 2 per cent (the Bank of England's target), as was RPIX inflation; but, on the RPI measure, deflation had set in, with the index down over 1 per cent over the preceding 12 months.

Finding sound measures of real output or reliable deflators is challenging in large sectors of the economy, especially in most services. Wheat production is easy enough to measure, but the real value of lawyer services is, for example, harder to pin down. Moreover, the share in GDP of 'reasonably measurable' sectors, which include agriculture and manufacturing activities, tends to decline over time as services expand.

Measuring prices in foreign trade is also notoriously complicated. In so far as they record actual quantities (tonnes or number of items, say), the implied unit value indices are useful only if this is done at a very disaggregated level. There is also the aforementioned difference between f.o.b. (for exports) and c.i.f. (for imports) prices, and sometimes much larger differences still between the price of a given good in the importing and in the exporting countries. And while cross-border trade in services is expanding rapidly, their prices are hard to measure. Furthermore, emerging markets and developing countries often monitor foreign trade in US dollar terms only, completely neglecting the price/volume split. This led to some diagnosis errors during the 1997–8 Asian crisis, when the sharp depreciation of a number of currencies translated into steep drops in measured exports, even though actual export volumes were by no means plummeting.

Equally, if not even more, tricky is the pricing of inventories, which, as explained in Chapter 3, matters greatly when attempting to assess cyclical conditions accurately. Firms often value inventories at historical cost; that is, at the price at which they purchased the goods (but using a variety of methods, in particular 'first in, first out' or 'last in, first out'). The standard national accounts convention instead is to value addition to or exit from inventories at the market price prevailing at the exact time of the movement.

Finally, there is also an issue of consistency in valuation. If, for example, imports of computer equipment are valued in a certain way, the same method should be used for the valuation of these items as components of final demand. In practice, however, this is not always the case.

AI.3.4   Dealing with relative price shifts

How aggregation is carried out is important for the estimation of inflation and changes in volume. Consider a national accounts aggregate in periods 0 and 1, with V standing for values at current prices, p^i for the price of elementary item i, and q^i for its quantity. Then:

$$V_1/V_0 = \underset{(1)}{\Sigma\, p^i_1\, q^i_1 /\ \Sigma\, p^i_0\, q^i_0} = \underset{(1)}{(\Sigma\, p^i_0\, q^i_1 /\ \Sigma\, p^i_0\, q^i_0)} \times \underset{(2)}{(\Sigma\, p^i_1\, q^i_1 /\ \Sigma\, p^i_0\, q^i_1)}$$

$$= \underset{(3)}{(\Sigma\, p^i_1\, q^i_1 /\ \Sigma\, p^i_1\, q^i_0)} \times \underset{(4)}{(\Sigma\, p^i_1\, q^i_0 /\ \Sigma\, p^i_0\, q^i_0)}$$

Here, (1) shows the change in volumes holding prices constant at their levels in period 0, which is called a Laspeyres volume index. The weights are the relative values in the base period, which is period 0 in this case.

Symmetrically, (2) shows the change in prices holding quantities constant at their levels in period 1, which is called a Paasche price index.

Alternatively, the change in value can be expressed as the product of a Paasche quantity index (3) by a Laspeyres price index (4). In practice, however, the first decomposition is preferred since it leads to additive volumes.

The following simple numerical example illustrates the importance of the choice of index. Suppose that production of good A has doubled and that its price has increased by 50 per cent, so that the value of the production of A rose threefold, from 1 to 3 (using the price of good A in period 0 as the numeraire). At the same time, suppose that the production and price of good B remained unchanged at 1 in both periods. Now consider a basket including one unit of A and one unit of B. Its value V has doubled since $V_1/V_0 = 4/2 = 2$. The increase in volume is 50 per cent if period 0 prices are used as weights: $[(1\times2) + (1\times1)]/[(1\times1) + (1\times1)] = 1.5$. However, it is 60 per cent if period

1 prices are used: $[(1 \times 3) + (1 \times 1)]/[(0.5 \times 3) + (1 \times 1)] = 1.6$. Correspondingly, inflation is 33 per cent in the first case and 25 per cent in the second.

Hence, changes in the volume of a given national accounts aggregate depend on the weights of its components and on the date used to estimate their relative prices. This can make for large effects when relative prices change substantially. Consider the case of computers, the price of which in the USA dropped by several multiples between the 1990s and the 2000s, resulting in soaring sales: at 1990s prices, the contribution of computer purchases to growth in consumption would be enormous compared with their contribution at 2000s prices. More generally, using a fixed-weight measure of real GDP based on 1990s prices would considerably overstate growth in the 2000s. This substitution bias led to the adoption of chained indices (see Box AI.4).

Box AI.4   Base-year versus chained indices*

Prior to the 1993 SNA, the tradition was to compile volume national account estimates using fixed base-year constant-price estimates, and to shift the base year forward every five or ten years. One major drawback was that the weights used in this approach were the same for the base year, when they reflected actual relative prices and spending patterns, and for periods before or after the base year, when they lost their relevance and biased volume estimates, especially in times of rapid change in the structure of the economy. Moreover, the periodical rebasing often led to uncomfortably large revisions to previously published estimates. Therefore, the 1993 SNA recommended that this approach should be abandoned and chain-linked volume measures, which provide for an annual updating of the weights, be used instead. The growth rates obtained with these chain-linked indices are no longer dependent on the base year. This was implemented in 1996 in the USA by the Bureau of Economic Analysis (BEA) and in 2003 in the UK. Nearly all OECD countries have also adopted chain-linking in recent years.

While chain-linked indices largely overcome the bias problem and mean that in future the revisions associated with rebasing will result mainly from improvements in the quality of source data or methodological changes, they do come with costs. One drawback is greater computational complexity. Fisher indices can be used, which are the geometric average of a Laspeyres and a Paasche index for two adjacent years.** The chain-type quantity index *I* is obtained by multiplying, or 'chaining', together the Fisher indices *F* for each successive pair of periods. If the reference year is 0, the index for year *t* is $I_{t,0} = F_{t,t-1} \times F_{t-1,t-2} \times \dots \times F_{1,0}$. The term 'reference', rather than 'base' year is used, to highlight that the choice of the period 0 does not affect the weights used in the calculation.

Another drawback of chain-linked indices is that, because the weights shift over time, GDP components expressed in volume terms are no longer strictly additive, unlike the constant-price data of the past, and are indeed expressed as indices rather than values computed at base year prices. To assist users in making comparisons across components of GDP for periods at a distance from the reference year, the US BEA publishes so-called chained-dollar indices, which are derived by multiplying the above chain-weighted indices by the current-dollar values of a specific reference year (at the time of writing, the year 2005). None the less, the problem of non-additivity remains and these tables expressed in chained 2005 dollars include a residual line showing the discrepancy between the sum of the components of GDP and total GDP. Furthermore, the growth contributions of the main components of GDP based on chain-type indices cannot easily be calculated. They have therefore to be published by the BEA in specific tables. Statistical offices in other countries proceed in a similar way. For the broad components of GDP, and for periods close to the reference year, this provides a reasonable approximation of their contribution to GDP growth and of their relative importance as a share of GDP. For some subcomponents, however – notably computers and other high-tech equipment with rapid growth in the volume of sales and falling prices – as well as for periods further away from the reference year, chained-dollar levels misrepresent their relative importance.

One further question is how to compute quarterly changes. In the USA, this is done using a Fisher formula incorporating the weights from two adjacent quarters, but before percentage changes are calculated, the quarterlies are adjusted to make them consistent with the annual indices. In general, it is advisable to keep relative prices constant during the course of a year, as quarterly updates would lead to excessive volatility. Table AI.4 provides a numerical illustration in the case of chained Laspeyres indices, and using a one-quarter overlap: estimates for the overlap quarter are compiled at the average prices of the current year as well as at the average prices of the previous year, and the ratio of the former to the latter is the linking factor used to rescale the quarterly data.*** More details and tips on how to use chained indices for analytical and forecasting purposes are provided by Bloem *et al.* (2001) in generic terms, and by Landefeld *et al.* (2003) for the USA.

---

*The exposition in this box relates to volume indices, but applies symmetrically to price indices.
**This is done in the USA and Canada. Other countries use chained annual Laspeyres indices, in particular in the European Union, where this is a Eurostat requirement.
***Alternatively, an annual overlap could be used (see Bloem *et al.*, 2001).

Table AI.4   Annual chain-linking and quarterly data

	q_1	q_2	p_1	p_2	Total at current prices	1997 Level	1997 Index 1997 = 100	At constant prices of 1998 Level	Index 1998Q4 = 100	1999 Level	Index 1999Q4 = 100	Chain-linked index 1997 = 100 Level	q-on-q % rate of change
1997	251.0	236.0	7.0	6.0	3,173.0	3,173.0	100.00					100.00	
1998Q1	67.4	57.6				817.4	103.04					103.04	1.3
1998Q2	69.4	57.1				828.4	104.43					104.43	1.3
1998Q3	71.5	56.5				839.5	105.83					105.83	1.3
1998Q4	73.7	55.8				850.7	107.24	907.55	100.00			107.24	1.3
1998	282.0	227.0	5.5	9.0	3,594.0	3,336.0	105.14	3,594.00				105.14	1.0
1999Q1	76.0	55.4						916.60	101.00			108.31	1.0
1999Q2	78.3	54.8						923.85	101.80			109.17	0.8
1999Q3	80.6	54.2						931.10	102.59			110.03	0.8
1999Q4	83.1	53.6						939.45	103.51	948.80	100.00	111.01	0.9
1999	318.0	218.0	4.0	11.5	3,779.0			3,711.00		3,779.00		109.63	
2000Q1	85.5	53.2								953.80	100.53	111.60	0.5
2000Q2	88.2	52.7								958.85	101.06	112.19	0.5
2000Q3	90.8	52.1								962.35	101.43	112.60	0.4
2000Q4	93.5	52.0								972.00	102.45	113.73	1.0
2000	358.0	210.0	3.0	13.5	3,909.0					3,847.00		112.53	

Steps involved:

1. Compile estimates for each quarter at annual average prices of previous year; annual data obtained as sum of quarters.
2. Compile estimates for the fourth quarter of each year, at annual average price of the same year, for example:
   1998Q4: $5.5 \times 73.7 + 9.0 \times 55.8 = 907.55$
3. Convert constant price estimates for the quarters of the first year following the reference year (here 1997) into a volume index with the average of the reference year set at 100. For example:
   1998Q1: $817.4 / (3173.00 / 4) \times 100 = 103.04$
4. Convert the constant price estimates for each of the other quarters into a volume index with the fourth quarter of last year set at 100. For example: 1999Q1: $916.60 / 907.55 \times 100 = 101.00$
5. Link together the quarterly volume indices with shifting base using the fourth quarter of each year as the link. For example:
   1999Q1: $101.00 \times 107.24 / 100 = 108.31$

Source: Bloem et al. (2001).

AI.3.5   Revisions

Adding to an already lengthy list of technical hurdles are the revisions to earlier estimates carried out either routinely or exceptionally by statistical offices, which in effect alter economic history, in some cases going back several decades (as with the 2009 comprehensive revision of the US NIPA, which affected data all the way back to 1929). Large-scale revisions may be required when better data, based, for example, on more thorough survey evidence, are released, or when methodological changes occur. In practice, comprehensive revisions are only conducted every few years and are often associated with a change in the reference/base year of the national accounts. The aim is to improve the representation of the economy, by refining the definition of some concepts, using more statistical information, and/or updating relative prices.

Though to a much lesser extent, annual national accounts are also routinely revised in order to incorporate the emergence of new information, such as tax rolls, which only become available two or three years after the period to which they relate.

Quarterly national accounts are revised even more frequently. They are affected by the regular revisions of the annual national accounts as well as by the more infrequent revisions. They are also affected, importantly, by the updating of seasonal factors. Furthermore, quarterly national accounts are produced rapidly, sometimes before the release of some of the underlying monthly data themselves, and therefore based on preliminary and often partial statistical information (for example, the first estimate of quarterly GDP will be published when foreign trade flows are only available for the first two months). Given that more information will progressively become available, at least three or four vintages of quarterly national accounts data are produced for any single quarter: 'advance' or 'flash' estimates shortly (one to two months for the major economies) after the end of the quarter, then firmer estimates one month later or so, and then a third set of estimates a number of months later, which themselves may be subject to change when comprehensive historic revisions take place. Even if they complicate forecasters' task, revisions are desirable in so far as they improve data quality significantly, provided, of course, they are well planned, properly documented and not overly frequent.[6]

The size of the revisions depends on the aggregate: revisions to GDP tend to be smaller than revisions to its components. Investment and public sector

---

[6] Against the background of criticism levelled at the UK's statistical office following repeated substantial revisions of the national accounts, its head defended the merits of revisions, underlining in particular the trade-off between timeliness and reliability, and noting that the UK is putting more weight on timeliness than are most continental European countries (Cook, 2004).

accounts in particular are subject to sizeable revisions. Even so, GDP estimates change substantially over time: the average absolute revision to quarterly real GDP growth in the USA over the last three decades of the twentieth century amounted to 1.7 percentage points (at an annualized rate). The magnitude and sign of the revisions also depend on the business cycle: as they are partly based on trends in preceding quarters, early GDP estimates tend to overstate activity when activity is decelerating and to understate it when it is accelerating, as documented for the US case by Dynan and Elmendorf (2001). That said, revisions are hard to predict, though historically they have tended to be more predictable in Italy, Japan and the UK than in the USA (Faust *et al.*, 2005).

The fact that revisions are relatively limited in a specific country does not necessarily imply that the initial estimates are of good quality. It could simply reflect the fact that 'final' national account estimates fail to take sufficient subsequent statistical information into account. That said, a few historical examples can serve to illustrate that some revisions can be quite disconcerting:

- In the case of the US recession of the early 1990s, monetary policy would probably have been different if the final numbers had been known at the time. When the Federal Reserve's Open Market Committee (FOMC) met in November 1990, real GDP was estimated to have risen 1.7, 0.4 and 1.8 per cent, respectively, in the first three quarters of the year (in annualized terms). This suggested that the economy was muddling through a period of slow but positive growth. With the benefit of hindsight, activity was in fact already contracting substantially: after more than half a dozen revisions, the data for this period now show a clear deceleration in economic activity in the course of 1990, from a 4.2 per cent increase in the first quarter to a 1.6 per cent gain in the second, turning into 0.0 per cent in the third and –3.5 per cent in the fourth quarter.
- In early 2004, the Bank of Korea (which in South Korea is responsible for the compilation of the national accounts) adopted most of the provisions of the 1993 SNA, thus extending the coverage of GDP to a wider range of economic activity, and updated the base year. As a result, the estimates for the level of nominal GDP in 2001–3 were raised by more than 10 per cent on average, and the new real GDP series displayed less volatility. The late 2005 upward revision in China's nominal GDP was even larger, at 17 per cent.
- In late 2004, the Japanese statistical authorities released a new set of national accounts, introducing chain linking, with backcasting to 1994. This translated into much lower GDP growth estimates for recent years without altering those for earlier years very much, so that Japan's economic recovery had to be reassessed and no longer appeared that robust compared to previous ones.
- In mid-2009, the comprehensive revisions implemented by the US BEA showed the Great Recession to be more pronounced than had been estimated earlier: the new estimates showed that during the year to the

first quarter of 2009, real GDP decreased by 3.3 per cent, as against 2.5 per cent in the previously so-called 'final' estimates. And by September 2010, the magnitude of the contraction over that year had been revised further downwards, to 3.8 per cent.

AI.4   Open questions and limitations

While the national accounts framework is extremely useful, it does raise a number of questions and has some serious limitations. For example, in an era where quite a few multinational firms operating in dozens of different national economies each generate more value-added than the GDP produced by some of the world's small economies, 'national' accounts may fail to capture fully some of the economic mechanisms at work. Furthermore, the SNA is almost continuously under review as new problems emerge, calling for adjustments to the framework.

AI.4.1   Conundrums

The first limitation is because the focus of the national accounts is more on 'flows' than on 'stocks', even if the latter dwarf quarterly or even annual flows. As agents' behaviour obviously depends heavily on their balance sheets, this is a serious problem, and in recent times more effort has been placed on measuring agents' assets and liabilities. Even so, these are often not well quantified. Some important assets are not always recognized as such, notably vehicles owned by households, which are treated as a consumer good rather than an investment good. Another difficulty is valuation. The valuation of existing fixed assets is uncertain. In principle, it should be carried out at replacement or market prices. In practice, however, businesses record assets at historic acquisition costs in their balance sheet and replacement costs are often derived from bankruptcy procedures and therefore possibly biased downwards. Hence statisticians have to use an indirect method (called the 'perpetual inventory method') to estimate the market value of assets, based on the application of adequate price index numbers to cumulated flows of net fixed capital formation. Turning to financial assets, only some of them are priced in markets on a continuous basis. Even those assets may turn out to be worth very little when they actually are disposed of; for example, if they are sold in a context of generalized financial distress as was the case in 2007–8. Other assets are valued only infrequently; for example, only when they change hands. As a result, price information on the main household asset, houses, is notoriously shaky. Some assets are never explicitly valued at all; for example, in the case of human or ecological capital. The depreciation coefficients are only rough approximations. Furthermore, there is the problem of implicit assets and liabilities, which are not recorded as such but do influence consumption and investment decisions; for example, in the case of the accrual of pension rights in a pay-as-you-go system but also more generally (see Box AI.5).

Box AI.5 Generational accounting

The fiscal deficit and public debt as recorded in the standard government accounts ignore future demographic and other pressures on revenue and spending, even when they are relatively predictable. Hence these measures are not sufficient to fully assess the public finance situation, especially long-term fiscal sustainability and inter-generational equity. One tool used to do so are the so-called generational accounts, inspired by overlapping-generations, general-equilibrium models. Such accounts are now compiled more or less regularly in many countries (see Bonin and Patxot, 2004; and, for country-by-country overviews, Auerbach *et al.*, 1999 and European Commission, 1999). In a nutshell, the idea is to calculate the net tax burden (taxation minus government transfers) that cohorts of individuals will pay over their remaining lifetime, assuming unchanged policy parameters. By comparing the net tax burden faced by the current generation with that of future generations it is possible to examine the extent to which current policy settings imply transfers between generations.

More specifically, generational accounting addresses the following related questions:

- What is the implicit public debt, namely the net government liabilities stemming from current policy?
- How heavy a fiscal burden do current tax and expenditure arrangements imply across generations?
- Is fiscal policy sustainable without increases in taxation on current or future generations or cutbacks in government spending?
- What policy measures would restore generational balance, in the sense that generations face the same fiscal burden – as a share of their lifetime earnings?
- How would such measures affect the remaining lifetime fiscal burdens of those now alive?

Generational accounts compute the present value of net taxes that individuals of different age cohorts are expected, under current policy, to pay over their remaining lifetimes. The sum of the generational accounts of those now alive is their collective contribution toward paying the government's bills, defined as the present value of its current and future purchases of goods and services plus its net debt (financial liabilities minus financial and real assets, including public sector enterprises). The share of the bill left unpaid by current generations must be paid by future generations.

Comparing the generational accounts of current newborns with those of future newborns, adjusting for intervening economic growth, provides a measure of generational imbalance. If future newborns face a higher burden than do current ones, today's policy arrangements are generationally imbalanced; correcting this would call for tax increases or spending cuts today. If, instead, future newborns face a smaller lifetime net tax burden than do current ones, generational balance can be restored by reducing the fiscal burden facing the current generation. A summary measure of the size of the adjustment required to achieve generational balance is the generational balance gap, defined as the ratio to GDP of the difference between the present value of the government's bills and the net taxes it is set to collect under unchanged policies.

In practice, the calculation of generational accounts is far from straightforward. The measurement of the net tax burden of a generation is uneasy, not least because of the difficulty in deciding on who benefits from some of the public transfers (does government spending on education represent a transfer in favour of the young generations or to their parents?). Moreover, it should be borne in mind that generational accounting calculations assume that the fiscal burden of current generations is set by current policies, even when they get older, and that the rest of the burden will be faced by future generations; in reality, this is unlikely to be the case, as illustrated by ongoing reforms of public pensions in OECD economies. Furthermore, as well as a good understanding of the intricacies of the tax and benefits system, generational accounting also necessitates the making of assumptions about future demographic developments, the growth of real GDP and the discount rate; the results are very sensitive to these assumptions, which, as noted in Chapter 7, are quite uncertain. A final limitation is that, in practice, generational accounting often disregards the general equilibrium feedback effects associated with the interaction between tax rates, public spending and growth.

Price measurement is another conundrum. In theory, prices should reflect equilibrium between supply and demand for each good and service, an assumption that is unlikely to be verified in each market at all points in time. In practice, as illustrated above, there are various ways to quantify price developments. One prominent difficulty relates to new goods and services. They are introduced into the price basket only with a lag, meaning that, in the meantime, the price index is incomplete. This was the case of mobile telephone services, which in France, for example, entered the consumer price index eight years after their commercial launch. In addition, some of the new items are very difficult to price. In the case of mobile phone services, there is a great and ever-changing variety of tariff packages. Similarly, for several other products, such as computers and motor vehicles, taking into account the quality of the good is a major challenge. One technique used to do so is hedonic pricing, which involves regressing the price of items, say cars, computers, or even clothing, on a number of technical characteristics (in the case of computers, speed, memory, card type and so on). But hedonic price indices themselves raise a host of new problems, not least because differences in approach across countries hamper international comparability (Triplett, 2001). House prices are also often mis-measured, as many house price indices ignore changes in the physical charac-teristics of housing (partly contributing to a seemingly upward trend in these prices).

A third complication is that a given, apparently well-defined national accounts measure may have a different meaning in two countries depending on institu-tional arrangements. For example, an important institutional factor influencing measured saving rates is differences in pension systems, because transac-tions relating to private pension schemes are treated as financial operations, whereas those related to social security schemes are considered to be current operations.

Finally, one should be wary of spurious precision. Even avoiding the complica-tions listed above, national accounts are no more than estimates, and as such they are subject to a margin of error. The level of GDP in particular is measured with a statistical error reflecting coverage, sampling, processing, non-response and modelling errors. The size of the overall error is hard to establish, given that the notional true value is, by definition, unknown. But the likely error, expressed as a percentage of GDP, is far larger for the level of GDP than for its growth rate, and much larger still when countries are compared, as a result of differences in concepts and techniques. For example, measured GDP growth in Europe would be significantly higher, possibly by as much as half a percent-age point annually in certain years, if statistical methods were more similar to those used in the USA – especially regarding the use of hedonic prices and the measurement of spending on software (Sakellaris and Vijselaar, 2004).

AI.4.2 Measuring welfare

The national accounts focus on the production and exchange of marketed goods and services. As noted in section AI.1, they simply exclude a whole range of activities undertaken at home, which in theory could be included as services pro-vided to other members of the household or to oneself, and would then account for a substantial chunk of GDP. In that sense, the coverage of the national accounts is somewhat incomplete, reflecting statistical hurdles but also underly-ing normative views on the relative value of various human occupations.

There are also other reasons why GDP per capita is a poor measure of welfare. One is that GDP increases when some undesirable events occur: road accidents, for example, add to GDP since they generate business in car manufacturing and repair – and so do traffic jams, which increase spending on transportation. More generally, GDP is recorded without netting out the induced environmental impoverishment in the form of pollution and exhaustion of finite natural resources. That said, attempts have been made to factor in such costs, particularly in the form of satellite systems gravitating around the core SNA such as the integrated environmental and economic accounting system (Box AI.6).

Box AI.6 Greening the national accounts

In recent years, methods have been developed to combine economic and environmental information so as to measure the contribution of the environment to the economy, and the impact of the economy on the environment. The handbook *Integrated Environmental and Economic Accounting 2003*, referred to as SEEA (2003), presents a satellite system of the 1993 SNA allowing the monitoring of these interactions. It comprises:

- Flow accounts for pollution, energy and materials, which provide information at the industry level about the use of energy and materials as inputs to production and the generation of pollutants and solid waste.
- Environmental protection and resource management expenditure accounts, which identify expenditures incurred by industry, government and households to protect the environment or to manage natural resources. They build on the elements of the 1993 SNA that are relevant to the management of the environment to show how environment-related transactions can be made more explicit.
- Non-market valuation techniques, including the calculation of macroeconomic aggregates adjusted for depletion and degradation costs.
- Natural resource asset accounts, which record stocks and changes in stocks of natural resources such as land, fish, forests, water and minerals (see Table AI.5).

Environmentally-modified aggregates can be compiled along the following lines (Bartelmus, 1999):

- Supply-use identity: $GDP + M = EC + C + (I - EC) + X$, where GDP stands for output, and EC for environmental depletion and degradation costs associated with production and consumption.
- Value-added identity for industry i: $EVA_i = O_i - IC_i - CC_i - EC_i = VA_i - EC_i$, where EVA stands for environmentally-adjusted value-added, O for gross output, IC for intermediate consumption, CC for fixed capital consumption, and VA for value-added.

Table AI.5 Illustrative natural resource asset account

Opening stock
+ Increases during the year
  New discoveries of minerals
  Natural growth of plants and animals
  Land reclamation
− Decreases during the year
  Extraction of minerals
  Soil erosion
  Loss of capacity of reservoirs due to silting
  Harvesting of plants and animals
  Natural death of plants and animals
  Loss of animals due to drought
= Closing stock

Source: SEEA (2003).

- Domestic-product identity for the whole economy: $EDP = \Sigma_i\, EVA_i - EC^h = NDP - EC$, where EDP stands for environmentally-adjusted net domestic product and EC^h for the environmental costs generated by households.
- Alternatively: $EDP = C + I - CC - EC + X - M$, where $I - CC - EC$ can be viewed as environmentally-adjusted net capital formation, an indicator that can be used to assess the sustainability of economic performance.

To compute such identities and indicators, a monetary value must be put on natural assets, even if they are not traded in markets. A variety of valuation techniques can be used. In some cases, there are market prices – for example, for traded pollution permits, the price of which represents a market value for environmental waste absorption capacities. Market prices may also allow analysts to estimate pollution costs indirectly – say, in the case of two similar housing units, one of which is in a polluted area and the other not. In other cases, hypothetical maintenance costs can in principle be calculated, defined as what it would have taken to keep the environment unaffected, though in practice, such calculations are very challenging, if not impossible. Yet another approach is contingent valuation, namely estimating what agents would have been ready to pay to avoid environmental costs, which is also difficult to implement.

In addition, this version of 'green GDP' also has conceptual limitations, to the extent that it tries to answer two questions at the same time: one is to measure current well-being, and the other is whether it is sustainable. Netting out environmental costs may answer neither question adequately.

Yet another limitation of GDP as a measure of welfare is that it ignores important dimensions of well-being other than monetary income, such as life expectancy and literacy. The United Nations Development Programme thus monitors a broad set of human development indicators, of which GDP per capita (adjusted for the local cost of living, that is, in PPP terms) is only one component, alongside life expectancy, adult literacy and average years of schooling. Their headline Human Development Index (HDI) is positively correlated with GDP per capita, but not perfectly. In addition, the relationship is by construction non-linear, with income gains at the bottom of the international scale increasing the HDI much more than similar-sized income gains in rich countries. In some cases, the evolution of GDP per capita and the HDI diverge dramatically, for example in those African countries particularly beset by the Aids epidemic, where the narrow economic indicator holds up well or continues to rise even as the HDI collapses.

This strand of analysis further includes work on inequality and poverty indicators: the average welfare level associated with a given level of per capita GDP may not be the same depending on the distribution of income, the presumption being that a very uneven distribution will make for lower welfare.

Jones and Klenow (2010) combine some of these dimensions to construct a synthetic indicator of a nation's flow of welfare, based on average consumption, average leisure, consumption inequality and average life expectancy. This metric is highly correlated with per capita GDP because average consumption differs so much across countries and is strongly correlated with income. On this measure, Western European living standards are much closer to those in the USA: longer lives with more leisure time and more equality largely offset their lower average consumption. In contrast, emerging Asia appears not to have caught up as much, and many African and Latin-American countries are further behind because of lower life expectancy and higher inequality. Another interesting feature is that, in recent decades, rising life expectancy has boosted annual growth in this measure of welfare by more than a full percentage point in much of the world (with the notable exception of Sub-Saharan Africa).

While economists used to pay only limited attention to HDI-type indicators in the past, these concepts have received increased attention in a number of countries, not least in response to the 2007 financial crisis. For example, the French authorities have asked a commission chaired by Professor Joseph Stiglitz to make new proposals to better measure welfare.

Furthermore, increasing attention has been paid to the role of social capital, namely the idea that social relationships play a critical role, alongside individual attributes, in economic activity and human well-being: social networks coupled with shared reciprocity norms, values and understanding favour mutual trust and facilitate co-operation, including in economic pursuits (Healy and Côté, 2001). But, while they would generally have positive spillover effects on the rest of society, some forms of social capital can have a detrimental impact – for example, in the case of mafias. Social capital and its contribution are, in this context, difficult to measure (Durlauf and Fafchamps, 2004).

Finally, a somewhat different approach to welfare has been developed at the World Bank (Dixon and Hamilton, 1996), looking at well-being from the angle of sustainable development. The focus here is on the stocks of assets broadly defined, both natural and man-made, that support well-being: the present value of natural wealth (minerals and fossil fuels, timber, non-timber benefits of forests, cropland, pastureland and protected areas); produced assets (calculated using a perpetual inventory model based on investment data and assumed lifetimes for the different types of assets); and human resources (derived residually, based on GNP minus natural resource rents and the depreciation of produced assets). The estimates carried out in the mid-1990s using this approach showed that the gap between poor and rich countries was several times larger for human than for natural resources.

Further reading

Lequiller and Blades (2006) provide a good cross-country perspective on national accounts. The 2008 SNA and related documentation can be found on unstats.un.org/unsd/nationalaccount. For the NIPA, see Landefeld *et al.* (2008) and go to bea.gov/methodologies. Recent thinking on GDP and well-being can be found on stiglitz-sen-fitoussi.fr.

Annex II

Time series methods

Contents

This Annex discusses how time series methods can be used for forecasting. One can define time series methods broadly as techniques that produce forecasts of specific variables using only their past observations. As mentioned in Chapter 1, the distinguishing feature of these forecasting techniques is that they take a statistical view that, in practice, leaves limited room for economic analysis.

Their appeal stems from the ease with which they allow numerical forecasts to be generated for a host of variables. The drawback is that these forecasts do not lend themselves to much, if any, economic interpretation, which is a major handicap when it comes to disseminating and explaining them. Another limitation that is common to all time series techniques is the so-called 'data snooping' bias. When trying out a large number of estimations on a given data set (also referred to as 'data mining'), a statistical relationship may appear to be significant when in fact it is pure coincidence.[1] This risk is particularly relevant for time series techniques if the statistical relationships deemed to be significant cannot be confirmed by other information (judgement or economic theory, say).

In general, time series methods usually play an ancillary role – as an auxiliary tool or a benchmark. They can be useful for producing necessary forecasts where the available resources are limited, such as *ad hoc* extrapolations in the context of business cycle analysis, or forecasts of exogenous variables in a macroeconomic model. They can also serve as a check on forecasts obtained by other methods. In particular, and as noted in Chapter 7, it is common practice to compare macroeconomic forecasts (which often include judgements) to projections relying purely on time series methods; such comparisons are often carried out in so-called post-mortem exercises, to judge the merits of particular macroeconomic forecasts *vis-à-vis* more 'automatic' tools.

In principle, time series methods can be used for all forecasting horizons. In practice, they assist mainly with short-run forecasting, as an extension of the analysis of the current situation. Indeed, time series methods can capture short-run dynamics quite effectively but lack the economic reasoning needed when thinking about medium- and long-run developments. For example, one application for time series methods is the tracking of releases of economic statistics on a short-term basis – say, weekly statistics on US initial jobless claims. This can be of particular importance given that financial market participants are prone to react abruptly when such economic releases differ too much from the consensus forecast.

---

[1] When conducting a statistical test (for example, testing whether the hypothesis H_0 can be considered as plausible with a probability of 95 per cent), one is subject to errors of type 1 (rejecting the hypothesis H_0 when in fact it is true) or type 2 (accepting the hypothesis H_0 when in fact it is false).

The main objective of time series methods is, generally speaking, to replicate past patterns over the forecast period. In practice, these methods are either univariate (one variable is forecast based on its past realizations) or multivariate (when several variables are). The latter have the advantage of taking into account the observed correlations between variables, albeit at the cost of greater complexity. The methods further differ by the degree of specificity of the model, the attention paid to the statistical validity of the estimations, and the scope to put an economic interpretation on the numbers.

Time series methods are used increasingly for financial forecasting purposes. Many new techniques have been developed, primarily to model the volatility of high-frequency financial markets data, but they don't feature very prominently in the toolkits of macroeconomic forecasters.

This annex is split into two parts. The first is devoted to time series methods that are commonly used for producing macroeconomic forecasts (section AII.1), starting with the univariate methods – including straight extrapolation (AII.1.1), ARIMA models (AII.1.2) and trend-cycle decompositions (AII.1.3) – and then presents VAR analysis as the main multivariate approach (AII.1.4). The second part (section AII.2) focuses more on specific financial forecasting methods, including ARCH/GARCH models (AII.2.1) and multivariate volatility forecasting techniques (AII.2.2). It ends with a presentation of selected applications of volatility forecasts (AII.2.3).

In practice, the two sets of techniques can be used in both areas. For example, a seminal paper on GARCH models was devoted to analysing the variance of inflation in the United Kingdom (Engle, 1982). Conversely, many techniques used for macroeconomic forecasts (VAR, ARIMA) are also applied to the modelling of very short-term financial data.

AII.1   Time series methods used for macroeconomic forecasts

AII.1.1   Empirical extrapolation

Extrapolation is straightforward, and for forecasting purposes it may be sufficient in some cases, even in its simplest form, in particular when resources are scarce. The underlying idea is to extend a range of numbers in a rigorous way, in line with past observations.

Naïve methods

The simplest assumption to forecast a variable X is that it remains unchanged at its latest observed level, so that for τ periods ahead:

$$P(X_{t+\tau}) = X_t$$

where P stands for the forecast function and t is the time of the latest observation (with $\tau > 0$).

This method is in fact optimal when X follows a random walk, with $X_{t+1} = X_t + \varepsilon_t$, where ε_t is a zero mean, white noise process ($E(\varepsilon_t) = 0$, $V(\varepsilon_t) = \sigma^2$ and $\text{Cov}(\varepsilon_t, \varepsilon_{t'}) = 0$ for any $t \neq t'$). The random walk assumption is not necessarily that far-fetched: in a famous article, Meese and Rogoff (1983) show that the best forecast for the exchange rate is precisely its latest observed value.

A variant is to replace the last observation by the historical mean of the data, or an average of recent observations (simple moving average):

$$P(X_{t+\tau}) = 1/k \, \Sigma_{i=0}^{k-1} X_{t-i}$$

For example, for $k = 4$:

$$P(X_{t+\tau}) = (X_t + X_{t-1} + X_{t-2} + X_{t-3})/4$$

One can also use a weighted moving average, which provides the possibility of giving more weight to the latest observations (but the set of weighting factors α_i must ensure that $\Sigma_{i=0}^{k-1} \alpha_i = 1$):

$$P(X_{t+\tau}) = 1/k \, \Sigma_{i=0}^{k-1} \alpha_i X_{t-i}$$

Another elementary method assumes that the latest observed change will persist:

$$P(X_{t+\tau}) = X_t + \tau \, (X_t - X_{t-1})$$

or, in a slightly more sophisticated rendition, that a weighted average of the changes observed over the last three periods can be applied recurrently, as follows:[2]

$$P(X_{t+\tau}) = P(X_{t+\tau-1}) \, \{(X_t/X_{t-1})/2 + (X_{t-1}/X_{t-2})/3 + (X_{t-2}/X_{t-3})/6\}$$

Such methods are said to be naïve because they correspond to what a myopic agent, looking only at very recent information, might forecast, but they fail to predict some very simple dynamic processes, such as geometrical declines. In fact, they serve mainly as a benchmark, to measure what was gained by using more subtle approaches.

---

[2] If one wishes to control for seasonality, with s being the frequency with which seasonal patterns recur, one can use a formula such as $X_{t+\tau} = X_{t+\tau-s} \, \{(X_t/X_{t-s})/2 + (X_{t-1}/X_{t-s-1})/3 + (X_{t-2}/X_{t-s-2})/6\}$.

Exponential smoothing

Exponential smoothing – also referred to as simple exponential smoothing (see below) – derives the forecast as a weighted average of past observations, with the weights declining geometrically:

$$P(X_{t+1}) = \alpha \, (X_t + \beta \, X_{t-1} + \beta^2 \, X_{t-2} + \dots + \beta^j X_{t-j})$$

where $0 < \beta < 1$. It is then necessary to impose a condition so that the declining weights sum to one: $\alpha \, (1 + \beta + \beta^2 + \dots + \beta^j) = 1$. Usually, the number of observations j is sufficiently large to treat the above as an infinite sum:

$$P(X_{t+1}) = \alpha \, (X_t + \beta \, X_{t-1} + \beta^2 \, X_{t-2} + \dots + \beta^j X_{t-j} + \dots)$$

so that the condition boils down to $\alpha = 1 - \beta$; then one can write:

$$P(X_{t+1}) = P(X_t) + \alpha \, (X_t - P(X_t))$$

Turning to the forecast two periods ahead:

$$\begin{aligned}
P(X_{t+2}) &= \alpha \, (P(X_{t+1}) + \beta \, X_t + \beta^2 \, X_{t-1} + \dots + \beta^{j+1} X_{t-j} + \dots) \\
&= \alpha \, P(X_{t+1}) + \beta \, \alpha \, (X_t + \beta \, X_{t-1} + \beta^2 \, X_{t-2} + \dots + \beta^j X_{t-j} + \dots) \\
&= \alpha \, P(X_{t+1}) + \beta \, P(X_{t+1}) \\
&= P(X_{t+1}), \text{ since } \alpha = 1 - \beta
\end{aligned}$$

The forecast made at time t is therefore the same whatever the horizon. But once the realization at $t + 1$ is known, the forecast for X_{t+2} can be updated to become:

$$\begin{aligned}
P_{t+1}(X_{t+2}) &= \alpha \, X_{t+1} + (1-\alpha) \, P_t \, (X_{t+1}) \\
&= \alpha \, X_{t+1} + (1-\alpha) \, P_t \, (X_{t+2})
\end{aligned}$$

where P_{t+1} denotes the forecast made at time $t + 1$ and P_t the forecast made at time t. Updating the forecast then amounts to taking a weighted average of the past forecast (with a weight of $1-\alpha$) and of the realization (with a weight of α).

The simplicity of this approach, developed in the 1950s (Brown, 1963), is one of the main advantages of exponential smoothing. It is a useful method when one has little insight into the factors driving variable X and when the series' trend appears to change rapidly. The weighting scheme puts more emphasis on recent observations, reflecting an intuition that they are the most informative ones.

A drawback, however, is that the choice of the smoothing parameter α (it is often set at 0.2 in the literature) is somewhat arbitrary. To lessen this arbitrariness, one can test various values of α to select the one that seems to be most robust in explaining past observations. In addition, a large range of 'less simple' exponential smoothing methods have been developed in recent years for forecasting purposes, based on the decomposition of time series in various components (see Box AII.1 below).

AII.1.2   ARIMA models

ARIMA (autoregressive integrated moving average) models were popularized by Box and Jenkins (1976),[3] in connection with the rapid development of econometric software. They were designed explicitly to produce forecasts. They offer a more rigorous statistical approach than the extrapolation methods described above (though some judgement still needs to be exercised) and a great flexibility, allowing them to be used in many different contexts. At the same time, they rest on fairly banal functional forms, namely autoregressive and moving average processes.

The standard procedure, described below, involves three steps: identification, estimation and verification.

Definitions

Recall that a stochastic process X_t is said to be autoregressive of order p – AR(p), when it can be written as:

$$X_t = a_1 \, X_{t-1} + a_2 \, X_{t-2} + \ldots + a_p \, X_{t-p} + \varepsilon_t$$

where ε_t is white noise.

A simple AR model is the first-order autoregressive form AR(1):

$$X_t = a_1 \, X_{t-1} + \varepsilon_t$$

A stochastic process is said to be a moving average of order q – MA(q), when:

$$X_t = \varepsilon_t + b_1 \, \varepsilon_{t-1} + b_2 \, \varepsilon_{t-2} + \ldots + b_q \, \varepsilon_{t-q}$$

A simple MA model is the first-order moving average MA(1):

$$X_t = \varepsilon_t + b_1 \, \varepsilon_{t-1}$$

---

[3] The first edition was published in 1970.

X_t is said to follow an ARMA(p, q) process when the two preceding specifications are combined, namely when:

$$X_t - a_1 X_{t-1} - a_2 X_{t-2} - \ldots - a_p X_{t-p} = \varepsilon_t + b_1 \varepsilon_{t-1} + b_2 \varepsilon_{t-2} + \ldots + b_q \varepsilon_{t-q}$$

A simple ARMA model is the ARMA(1,1):

$$X_t - a_1 X_{t-1} = \varepsilon_t + b_1 \varepsilon_{t-1}$$

An ARMA process is stationary (for a definition, see Box 3.1) as its probability distribution is constant over time. In practice, few variables are stationary (for example, they tend to grow over time, or are affected by seasonality) so that ARMA models cannot be used directly. However, they can be used on modified series – namely, series that have been transformed to be stationary. This is at the core of ARIMA(p, d, q) models, which when differenced d times morph into ARMA(p, q) processes. For example, one will use $d = 1$ (respectively, 2 or 3) for a non-stationary process for which one can identify, respectively, a constant trend, a linear trend or a quadratic growth trend.

An ARIMA(p, d, q) process can be written as:

$$(1-L)^d A(L) X_t = B(L) \varepsilon_t$$

where L is the lag operator and $(1 - L)$ the first difference operator (often denoted Δ), while $A(L)$ and $B(L)$ are distributed lag polynomials of order p and q respectively, and ε_t is white noise.

Here p (autoregressive part of the model), d (integrated part) and q (moving average part) are integers. When one of the terms is zero, one usually drops the reference to the AR, I or MA parts in the naming of the ARIMA model. For example:

> ARIMA(1,0,0): AR(1) model;
> ARIMA(0,1,0): I(1) model, which is in fact the random walk
> mentioned above (with $X_{t+1} - X_t = \varepsilon_t$);
> ARIMA(0,0,1): MA(1) model;
> ARIMA(1,0,1): ARMA(1,1) model; and
> ARIMA(0,1,1): IMA(1,1) model.

This last IMA(1,1) specification is indeed the exponential smoothing described in section AII.1.1, since:

$$X_t = \alpha (X_{t-1} + \beta X_{t-2} + \beta^2 X_{t-3} + \ldots + \beta^{j-1} X_{t-j} + \ldots) + \varepsilon_t$$

and

$$X_{t-1} = \alpha (X_{t-2} + \beta X_{t-3} + \beta^2 X_{t-4} + \ldots + \beta^{j-1} X_{t-j-1} + \ldots) + \varepsilon_{t-1}$$

hence

$$X_t = \alpha\,X_{t-1} + \alpha\,\beta\,(X_{t-2} + \beta\,X_{t-3} + \dots + \beta^{\,j-2}\,X_{t-j} + \dots\,) + \varepsilon_t$$
$$X_t = \alpha\,X_{t-1} + \beta\,(X_{t-1} - \varepsilon_{t-1}) + \varepsilon_t$$

so

$$X_t - X_{t-1} = \varepsilon_t - \beta\,\varepsilon_{t-1}$$

which is an ARIMA(0,1,1) process.

Identification

Identification consists of determining the values of p, d and q. First, one has to identify d, the number of times X should be differenced to achieve stationarity (in some cases, d is zero).[4] This is an art as much as a science, as there are many ways to go about it, which do not all deliver the same result. Contemporary methods rest on a variety of stationarity tests, such as the Dickey–Fuller one for testing the presence of a unit root or the Schmidt–Phillips test (for details see, for example, Hamilton, 1994 or Clements and Hendry, 1998).

Note that a non-stationary series is not necessarily integrated. Consider $X_t = 1.5\,X_{t-1}$: no integer number of differencing operations can turn X_t into a stationary series. But taking logarithms can: $Y_t = \log X_t$ is integrated of order 1 (since $Y_t = Y_{t-1} + \log 1.5$). This shows why it can be useful to work with the logarithm of macroeconomic variables that often appear to grow at constant rates in the long run.

Once a stationary series is obtained, one must decide how many autoregressive (p) and moving average (q) parameters are needed to yield an effective but parsimonious model of the process (parsimonious meaning that it has the fewest parameters and greatest number of degrees of freedom among all models that fit the data). To this end, the correlation properties of autoregressive and moving average processes are used (see Table AII.1). Examination of the sample

Table AII.1   Properties of ARMA processes

	Autocorrelations*	Partial autocorrelations**
AR(p)	Exponential decay beyond p	Nil beyond p
MA(q)	Nil beyond q	Decline beyond q
ARMA(p,q)	Exponential decay beyond p	Decline beyond q

*The autocorrelation of order s of series X_t is $\rho_s = Cov(X_t, X_{t-s}) / V(X_t)$.
**The partial autocorrelation of order r is φ_r in the regression: $X_t = \varphi_1 X_{t-1} + \varphi_2 X_{t-2} + \dots + \varphi_r X_{t-r} + \varepsilon_t$.

---

[4] See Chapter 3 for the discussion on stationarity. Recall that if a variable is integrated of order one – noted $I(1)$ – it has a unit root and its first difference is stationary.

correlogram (which plots the autocorrelation coefficient at lag s as a function of lag s) and partial correlogram (similarly for the partial autocorrelation coefficient) helps to decide on p and q, taking into account that:

- If the autocorrelation coefficient converges abruptly towards zero beyond lag q, the presumption is that the process is MA(q).
- If the partial autocorrelation coefficient converges abruptly towards zero beyond lag p, the presumption is that the process is AR(p).
- If neither of these is the case, the presumption is that the process is ARMA(p,q), with $p > 0$ and $q > 0$. In practice, p or q are rarely taken to exceed 2, so that the number of possibilities that need to be tried out is limited. The shape of the two correlograms can help to pin down p and q. Alternatively, various statistical tests can be used for this purpose, especially in order to take the properties of the lags into account (Beveridge and Oickle, 1994). More than one candidate representation may emerge, however, at this stage.

Estimation

The next step is the estimation of the parameters. Different methods are available, which, depending on the process, are more or less convenient, but they all tend to produce similar estimates. Generally, an algorithm is used that maximizes the likelihood (or probability) of the observed series, given the parameter values (by minimizing the implied sum of squared residuals). Standard software packages include such algorithms, which are discussed at greater length by Hamilton (1994), among others.

Verification

The last step prior to using the model in forecasting mode is to check that it is good enough for that purpose. This is also the point at which a choice is made between different possible representations, when more than one is plausible.

Two criteria come into play: the statistical properties of the estimated model on the one hand, and its simplicity and parsimony on the other. The first criterion encompasses the following questions: Are the residuals white noise? Are the parameters statistically significant? How good is the fit on past data? The answer to the last question is *a priori* that the larger are p and q, the better the fit. But this goes against the need for parsimony: while it is easy to enhance the model's fit on past data by adding explanatory variables that happen to be correlated with the explained variable (here, by increasing p and q), this presents a risk of breaking down once the model is used in forecasting mode. In addition, parsimony is key to limiting the risk of data snooping mentioned above. With a more limited number of parameters, the chances are higher that the estimated relationship will be robust going forward. Some formal criteria can be used to decide what is best given this trade-off (for example, the Akaike information criterion, or the Schwarz Bayesian criterion). Another element to consider is how the estimated model performs in out-of-sample forecasting exercises (indeed, since the estimation of an ARMA model is by definition dependent on the sample considered, their out-of-sample fit might be a weakness compared to other forecasting tools).

ARIMA models are relatively easy to implement and therefore widely used, not least in business cycle analysis to extrapolate series over the short run; for example, to add a few points to a series for which one wants to construct a centred moving average.[5] Indeed, just repeating the last observation might introduce bias in that case, and an ARIMA forecast might avoid that problem.

The ARIMA approach, however, shares the usual drawback of statistical models, namely the absence of a straightforward economic interpretation of the model (what is the economic rationale for the chosen *p* and *q*?) and of the forecasts it produces. Their degree of accuracy is also limited when compared to well-designed economic forecasts. For example, Mourougane (2006) showed that for Canadian GDP forecasts on a monthly basis – a frequency for which forecasts are likely to be more volatile and subject to statistical noise – standard autoregressive models do not compare very favourably with indicator-based models. It is also sometimes alleged that the relatively good performance of ARIMA models largely reflects their ability to replicate seasonal movements, in which case it would make more sense to tackle directly the issue of seasonality *per se*. Indeed, software packages can allow for the specification of both the non-seasonal part of the ARIMA model – the three components (*p, d, q*) – and its seasonal part.

AII.1.3 Decomposition into trend and cycle

As noted earlier, one of the key issues in forecasting, when looking at how a variable evolves over time, is to distinguish clearly between what corresponds to a durable trend and what reflects transient movements around that trend. A great variety of alternative techniques have been proposed for this purpose. A selection of statistical approaches is presented here (a more 'economic' approach to the trend–cycle decomposition is laid out in Box 6.1).

In virtually all cases, the decomposition between trend and cycle is either additive or multiplicative:

$$X_t = T_t + C_t + u_t \qquad \text{(additive form)}$$
$$X_t = T_t\, C_t\, u_t \qquad \text{(multiplicative form)}$$

---

[5] The seasonal adjustment techniques discussed in Section 2.4 often rely on ARIMA models to treat the latest points of the time series.

where X_t is the variable under consideration, T_t the trend, C_t the cyclical component and u_t the unpredictable component of the series. A fourth, seasonal component, could be introduced, as discussed in Section 2.4 (see also Makridakis *et al.*, 1998 on time series decompositions with seasonal adjustment). Once these components have been estimated for the past, they can be projected forward to forecast X, generally on the basis of some fairly simple assumptions. The various techniques differ in how T and C (and hence u) are identified. None of them is intrinsically superior to the others, as each hinges on a number of explicit or implicit assumptions, which, depending on the circumstances, are more or less satisfactory. But in practice, the (relatively) simpler approaches – deterministic trends and *ad hoc* smoothing – tend to be used most frequently.

In this context, an important point of controversy is what constitutes a cycle. Broadly speaking, a cycle can be defined as a pattern that repeats itself with some regularity. For one thing, the features of the cycle depend on the chosen horizon, which may be rather short (especially in the financial area) or quite far away (perhaps several decades). In practice, the cycle often referred to in forecasting is the one followed by GDP, which typically spans several years. Also, cycles can be defined in level or first-difference terms. In the first case, peaks and troughs in the level of activity or proxies of these serve to identify the cycle. That is the approach pioneered by Burns and Mitchell (1946) in the USA, at the National Bureau of Economic Research (NBER). The NBER's Business Cycle Dating Committee continues to use this definition, even though it leaves some room for judgement. For example, it defines a recession as 'a significant decline in economic activity spread across the economy, lasting more than a few months, and normally visible in real GDP, real income, employment, industrial production, and wholesale–retail sales'. An alternative approach, used in particular by the OECD when elaborating its leading economic indicators, is to focus on cycles in growth rates rather than in the level of activity. This is particularly relevant for cross-country analyses, since the likelihood of registering negative economic growth in the downturn phase of the cycle is related to the level of the trend growth rate of a country.

When thinking about trend and cycle, forecasters often refer to movements in real GDP, but the same concepts apply to other variables, and notably to the components of GDP: these components contribute more or less to the cyclicity of GDP, depending on their weight in GDP and on their own cyclicity. For example, on the spending side of the national accounts, consumption typically represents about two-thirds of GDP but is not very volatile, as households tend to smooth spending over time, so it may not be the largest contributor to the cyclicity of GDP. Fixed investment is, instead, much more volatile and contributes substantially to fluctuations in GDP, even if its share of GDP is considerably smaller. The same holds for inventory investment. On the output side, manufacturing output contributes more than proportionately to the cyclicity of GDP, though this might in part be because of measurement issues, and in particular to the way that value-added is measured in the non-manufacturing sectors. Finally, it is important to note the role played by international linkages in determining domestic cycles.

Deterministic trends

A simple way to identify an underlying trend in a series is to check whether it follows a deterministic path. The latter can be linear or piecewise linear, when the trend displays one or several kinks because of one or several structural breaks. A typical example of such a break would be the one observed for real GDP in the early 1970s, when in many OECD countries a shift occurred from a relatively high to a lower rate of trend growth. Estimating the trend then respectively involves running the regression:

$$X_t = a + b\,t + \varepsilon_t \qquad \text{(linear trend)} \qquad \text{(AII.1)}$$

$$X_t = a + b\,t + c\,(t - t^*)\,D_t + \varepsilon_t \qquad \text{(piecewise linear trend with one break at time } t^*) \qquad \text{(AII.2)}$$

In the second case, D_t is a dummy variable taking the value 0 for $t \le t^*$ and 1 for $t \ge t^*$. Up to time t^*, equation (AII.2) reduces to equation (AII.1). After t^*, the slope changes from b to $(b + c)$, and the intercept from a to $(a - ct^*)$. This can be generalized to several breaks.

Set against the general framework spelt out above, the residual in these two equations encompasses both the cyclical component C_t and the unexplained u_t. Generally, some *ad hoc* functional form will be assumed for C_t – say, an AR(2) process. One can then characterize the theoretical distribution of ε_t and infer the appropriate estimation method (taking into account in particular any autocorrelation of the error term).

This approach is conveniently simple, but the results are quite sensitive to the selection of the estimation period. It is important to cover an integer number of cycles, lest the estimate suffer from end-of-sample bias. Moreover, identifying changes in regime (that is, points such as t^*) is difficult, even if the choice of t^* can in principle be checked by testing whether coefficient c differs significantly from 0.

Smoothing techniques – exponential smoothing

A different approach rests on *ad hoc* smoothing. The intuition is to try and extract the trend one would see when eyeballing a plot of the series under consideration. One method is to use moving average of various orders, as for deseasonalization purposes or for the calculation of summary indicators of the cycle (see Section 2.4). More complex smoothing techniques can also be applied, such as the Hodrick–Prescott (HP) filter. This filter is presented in detail in Box 6.1, but can be described briefly here as jointly minimizing the distance between the trend and the actual observations, and the variability of the trend – where the weight put on the second criterion depends on a 'smoothing parameter' called λ and often set to a predetermined value in standard econometric packages. A large range of techniques based on exponential smoothing methods have also been developed, in addition to the simple exponential smoothing described above (see Box AII.1).

All these techniques, however, have serious drawbacks. They are subject to end-of-sample biases in so far as they are not run on an integer number of cycles. These techniques also involve some degree of arbitrariness in the selection of the order of the moving average or of the smoothing parameter: depending on these choices, the derived trend may look extremely smooth, or on the contrary rather irregular. Furthermore, the separation between the trend, the cyclical component and the residual is not always clear or based on solid ground.

Spectral analysis

Spectral analysis, in contrast, does allow for the separation of trend, cycle and seasonality (this, in fact, is a generalization of the simple HP filter, which is a specific frequency filter). It draws on the Fourier method of spectral decomposition used in physics (see, for a detailed review of the Fourier analysis of time series, Bloomfield, 2000). The idea is to split up a signal (here, a time series) into different frequency components, based on a search covering the whole range of possible frequencies. Then a subset of the latter is defined as the relevant frequency band and only the components falling within this band are retained. This band may include very low frequencies, extending far beyond the usual business cycle notion, and/or very high ones – for example, when looking at financial market data.

A popular type of spectral analysis is the so-called band-pass filter proposed by Baxter and King (1999). In the empirical application presented by these authors, they define the band based on Burns and Mitchell's definition that business cycles are cyclical components of no fewer than six quarters and their finding that typically they last fewer than 32 quarters in the USA. The filter then passes through components with periodic fluctuations ranging between 6 and 32 quarters, while removing high-frequency ('irregular', or 'noise') and low-frequency ('trend') components. The trend itself may thus fluctuate, but slowly. In theory, the optimal band-pass filter is a moving average of infinite order, so an approximation has to be used in practice. Baxter and King

Box AII.1 Exponential smoothing methods

A significant recent development relates to exponential smoothing methods and the associated state space models (see Hyndman *et al.* (2008) for a detailed introduction). An exponential smoothing method is an algorithm that generates point forecasts only, whereas the underlying 'stochastic state space model' also provides a framework for computing prediction intervals.

There are many methods, depending on how the time series is decomposed in a trend, a cycle, a seasonal component and an error term; how the combination of these components is realized (on an additive or a multiplicative basis, or with some combination of both); and the form of the seasonal component.

For example, assuming that the cyclical component is included in the trend and ignoring the error component, the trend component T can be forecast as T_h over the next h time periods depending on five types of assumptions related to g, the growth term – or 'slope' – of the trend component (estimated at time t as g_t):

- no growth: $T_h = l$ (l being the flat level of the trend, also called the 'smoothed value');
- additive (linear trend): $T_h = l + g\,h$;
- additive damped: $T_h = l + g\,(\phi + \phi^2 + \ldots + \phi^h)$ with $0 < \phi < 1$ (the damping parameter ϕ ensures that the trend of the series dies out over time);
- multiplicative: $T_h = l\,g^h$; and
- multiplicative damped: $T_h = l\,g^{(\phi + \phi^2 + \ldots + \phi^h)}$ with $0 < \phi < 1$;

Given that the seasonal component may be absent, additive or multiplicative, this leads to 15 exponential smoothing methods, some of which are described below.

One is the simple exponential smoothing described in section AII.1.1, with no trend and no seasonal component. We had above:

$$P_t(X_{t+1}) = \alpha\,X_t + (1-\alpha)\,P_{t-1}(X_t)$$

which can be rewritten as

$$P_t(X_{t+1}) = l_t$$
$$l_t = \alpha\,X_t + (1 - \alpha)\,l_{t-1}$$

Another exponential smoothing method is the Holt linear method (Holt, 1957), which is used for forecasting data with linear trends. Since the method relies on an additive trend component and involves no seasonal component, we have:

$$P_t(X_{t+h}) = l_t + g_t\, h \text{ for } h=1, 2, \ldots$$

with

$$l_t = \alpha\, X_t + (1 - \alpha)\, (l_{t-1} + g_{t-1})$$
$$g_t = \alpha\, (l_t - l_{t-1}) + (1 - \beta)\, g_{t-1}$$

Other exponential smoothing methods are the Holt–Winters methods (Winters, 1960) used for seasonal data, relying on an additive trend component with a seasonal component that is modelled either in an additive or a multiplicative way. We have similar equations as for the Holt linear method for both the level and the growth components, plus one equation for the seasonal component.

Hyndman *et al.* (2008) then define 30 'state space models' associated with these 15 methods (depending on whether errors are additive or multiplicative) that provide point forecasts with prediction intervals.

A key point of interest of these models is their variety, allowing for the modelling of a very diverse set of stochastic processes, and the fact that model parameters can be estimated in a quasi-automatic way.

In practice, the specification of these models (notably the determination of the various smoothing parameters such as the above α and β) is obtained by considering the forecast errors generated by the chosen method and minimizing them (using, for example, the likelihood criterion or mean squared errors). In addition, the initial values of the trend components (for $t = t_0$) have to be set up in an *ad hoc* manner, by using the first observation or via some empirical scheme.

recommend a moving average spanning three years on both sides (both for quarterly and for annual data), but band-pass filters can be constructed in many different ways (see, for example, Christiano and Fitzgerald, 2003).

Band-pass filters have some drawbacks, however, quite similar to those of HP filters. When they are symmetric, using them in real time requires prolonging in some way the series of actual observations, in order to compute a moving average centred on the latest one; this can induce a significant end-of-sample bias. In practice, it is advisable to test the sensitivity of the results against alternative choices of the order of the moving average used. Another problem is that the definition of the range of frequencies deemed to encompass the business cycle is rather arbitrary. And, last but not least, it has been argued that, under some circumstances, the band-pass filtered cyclical component can be spurious and may, for example, grossly misrepresent the output gap (Benati, 2001).

Stochastic trends

Another class of models emphasizes the stochastic, as opposed to deterministic, nature of the trend. It posits that random shocks can have effects that are sufficiently persistent to actually have an influence on the long-run trend. In this framework, the trend itself is decomposed into a deterministic component, TD_t, and a stochastic one, TS_t, and the series X_t can be written as:

$$X_t = TD_t + TS_t + C_t + u_t$$

With a deterministic trend, the uncertainty associated with a long-run forecast is limited to the variation in the stationary deviation from that trend, the drift C_t. With a stochastic trend instead, this uncertainty rises as the horizon is extended.

Two methods are commonly used to implement this type of approach. The first, set out by Beveridge and Nelson (1981), applies to series that are integrated of order one. They showed that any ARIMA(p,1,q) process can be decomposed into a random walk stochastic trend (possibly with drift) and a transitory, stationary, zero mean part with a cyclical interpretation.[6] This representation is derived as follows in the simple case of an ARIMA(0,1,1) process. In this case, the first difference of X_t is MA(1): $\Delta X_t = \varepsilon_t + b\,\varepsilon_{t-1}$, where ε_t is independently and identically distributed and b is a constant. Let us normalize the series so that $X_0 = \varepsilon_0 = 0$. Then

$$
\begin{aligned}
X_t &= X_{t-1} + \varepsilon_t + b\,\varepsilon_{t-1} \\
&= X_{t-2} + (\varepsilon_{t-1} + b\,\varepsilon_{t-2}) + (\varepsilon_t + b\,\varepsilon_{t-1}) \\
&= (\varepsilon_1 + \varepsilon_2 + \dots + \varepsilon_t) + b\,(\varepsilon_1 + \varepsilon_2 + \dots + \varepsilon_{t-1}) \\
&= (1 + b)\,(\varepsilon_1 + \varepsilon_2 + \dots + \varepsilon_t) - b\,\varepsilon_t \\
&= T_t + C_t \text{ (defining } T_t \equiv (1 + b)\,(\varepsilon_1 + \varepsilon_2 + \dots + \varepsilon_t) \text{ and } C_t \equiv -\,b\,\varepsilon_t)
\end{aligned}
$$

T_t, the stochastic trend, follows a random walk: $T_t = T_{t-1} + (1 + b)\,\varepsilon_t$. C_t, the cycle, is stationary.

For a more general ARIMA(p,1,q) process, the decomposition becomes:

$$X_t = T_t + C_t, \text{ with } T_t = T_{t-1} + g + \tau\,\varepsilon_t \text{ (random walk with drift } g\text{)}$$
$$C_t = d(L)\,\varepsilon_t$$

---

[6]From a statistical perspective, however, there is no guarantee for uniqueness, and competing decompositions may be unidentifiable (Watson, 1986).

where τ is a constant which is a function of the coefficients in the lag polynomials of order p and q associated with the AR and MA components of the ARIMA process, and $d(L)$ a lag polynomial whose coefficients also depend on these coefficients. Note that, in this decomposition, the trend and the cycle are perfectly correlated, since innovations in the two components are both proportional to ε_t.

In contrast, the second method – proposed by Harvey (1985) and Watson (1986) – assumes that innovations to the trend and to the cycle are orthogonal (perfectly uncorrelated). It is referred to as the unobserved component method and can be formulated as follows:

$$X_t = T_t + C_t, \text{ with } T_t = T_{t-1} + g_t + \eta_t$$
$$g_t = g_{t-1} + \zeta_t$$

where the trend drift itself g_t is allowed to evolve as a random walk and C_t is a cycle with an ARIMA representation, say an AR(2) process of the form $C_t = a\ C_{t-1} + b\ C_{t-2} + \theta_t$. All errors terms ($\eta_t$, ζ_t, θ_t) are white noise. The permanent (η_t) and transitory (θ_t) shocks are independent. Estimation is generally carried out using the Kalman filter procedure. It is often assumed that $\zeta_t = 0$, in which case the third line is dropped (since $g_t = g$) and the second one simplifies to $T_t = T_{t-1} + g + \eta_t$, representing a random walk with drift. If, in addition, $\eta_t = \zeta_t = 0$, the trend is in fact deterministic.

In practice, the two methods yield very different results (Morley *et al.*, 2003). When applied to US real GDP data, the first suggests that much of the variation is that of the trend, and that the cyclical component is small and noisy. In contrast, the second implies a very smooth trend accompanied by an ample and highly persistent cycle. The complexity of these methods makes them difficult to use in everyday business cycle forecasting. However, they can be useful for specific analyses. For example, Sgherri (2005) examines productivity shifts in Italy using unobserved stochastic component techniques, and Vitek (2009) uses them to look at monetary policy forecasting.

Non-linear approaches

All the decompositions described so far implicitly assume that the cycle can be described in linear terms and that it is symmetric. However, it has long been recognized that this is not the case in practice. For example, Keynes (1936) wrote that 'the substitution of a downward for an upward tendency often takes place suddenly and violently, whereas there is, as a rule, no such sharp turning point when an upward is substituted for a downward tendency'. Indeed, the 2007 crisis has highlighted the fundamental asymmetry of financial crises: while vulnerabilities build up slowly, often over years, financial distress emerges quite rapidly, sometimes in a matter of months.

Non-linearity is often associated with asymmetry, which has a number of potentially relevant dimensions, including skewness (do expansions last longer than contractions?), steepness (are contractions steeper than expansions?), depth (are troughs greater than peaks?) and sharpness (are turning points spikier at troughs or at peaks?). Empirical studies have explored some of these dimensions. Using a non-parametric procedure, Neftçi (1984) documents that increases in the US unemployment rate are shorter and sharper than declines. Razzak (2001), based on a different test and focusing on GDP, finds that the degree of symmetry of business cycles varies across countries, with clear evidence of asymmetry for Japan and Australia but much less for the USA, Germany and New Zealand.

A number of non-linear parametric models have been built that capture the stylized feature of steep and short recessions, but with different implications (Figure AII.1). This class of models includes the following univariate ones:

- Hamilton (1989) divides the business cycle into negative and positive trend growth regimes, with the economy switching back and forth between the two according to the transition of a latent state variable that is unobserved – these are the so-called Markov-switching models. During an expansion,

Figure AII.1   Business cycle asymmetry

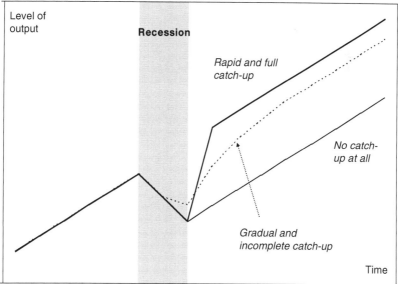

Note: The recession period is shaded.

output does not regain the ground lost in the downturn. Recessions thus permanently lower output, by an estimated 3 per cent in the USA.

- Kim and Nelson (1999) model recessions as regime switches affecting only the cyclical component of output, so that the effect of recessionary shocks is constrained to be completely transitory: following a trough, output first bounces back to catch up with the earlier trend (high growth recovery phase) and then grows again along this trend (normal expansion).

- Another model by Kim *et al.* (2005) augments Hamilton's model with a bounce-back term that generates faster growth in the quarters immediately following the output trough. This yields an effect that lies between the two preceding cases: output does catch up with its pre-recession trend, albeit not completely. The permanent effect of recessions is thus smaller than in Hamilton's model.[7]

In addition, these models can be extended to incorporate multivariate features – for example, to deal with multi-country relationships, as done by Anas *et al.* (2007), who use multivariate Markov-switching models. Other models are threshold auto-regressive (TAR) models (Tong and Lim, 1980) or self-exciting threshold auto-regressive (SETAR) models. These enrich autoregressive models with regime-switching behaviour using a transition variable that is observed (for example, an exogenous threshold variable), or a function of the past values of the series (in the case of SETAR models).

In general, non-linear approaches are interesting in that they suggest that economies respond differently to shocks depending on circumstances. In a linear model, X_t responds in the same way irrespective of the time at which the shock occurs, and the response will be proportional to the shock. In a non-linear setting, in contrast, the response differs according to the economy's position in the cycle and depends in more complex ways on the direction and size of the shock. There has been a growing interest in recent years in these approaches, especially for the purpose of anticipating economic turning points (see section 2.4). More broadly, Markov-switching approaches can be used for analysing/forecasting any behaviour that is deemed to be non-linear and dependent on specific circumstances – see, for example, Kumah (2007) for a recent application to foreign exchange markets in times of monetary contraction and expansion.

---

[7] This holds for US data. Kim *et al.* (2005) also look at Australia, Canada and the United Kingdom, and find that recessions have a greater permanent impact in the latter two countries. Sinclair (2009) focuses on the USA and explores the long-term impact of short-term fluctuations by applying an unobserved components model to real GDP that allows for both asymmetric transitory movements and correlation between the permanent and transitory shocks. She finds that seven out of the past 11 recessions were caused at least partly by temporary asymmetric movements.

In practice, however, such calculations are relatively complex and difficult to communicate to forecast users. Moreover, it is not clear whether allowing for non-linearities improves out-of-sample forecast performance, as documented by Stock and Watson (1999) in the particular case of smooth transition autoregressive (STAR) models – where the economy is switching between two different linear states, depending on specific thresholds. One reason may be that the non-linear features that were prominent in the estimation sample fail to carry over to the forecast period. Another may be that the observed non-linearity is spurious in the sense that it reflects other features of the time series, such as heteroskedasticity or outliers (van Dijk *et al.*, 2002).

AII.1.4   VAR models

Univariate methods provide simple and often fairly robust forecasting tools but they disregard the observed relationships observed empirically across variables, which can be very informative. The most common way to take them into account is to run a vector autoregressive (VAR) model, which is simple to estimate and convenient for forecasting purposes. This approach was pioneered by Sims (1980), as an alternative to structural macroeconomic models (see Annex III). This section provides a brief overview of this class of models (which are presented in more detail in Hamilton, 1994).

Basic principles

Consider, for example, a forecast of the stock of money based on activity, prices and interest rates. One way to proceed would be to estimate the following money demand equation:

$$m_t - p_t = \beta_0 + \beta_1 (m_{t-1} - p_{t-1}) + \beta_2 y_t + \beta_3 i_t + u_t$$

where m_t is the money stock, p_t the general price level, y_t activity (all in logarithms), i_t a representative interest rate and u_t a shock. But p_t, y_t and i_t cannot be considered as exogenous variables, implying a likely simultaneity bias. One could assume that i_t is determined as follows:

$$i_t = \delta_0 + \delta_1 p_t + \delta_2 y_t + \delta_3 m_t + v_t$$

In this case, i_t is correlated with u_t (even if u_t and v_t are uncorrelated) and the estimators of the parameters of the money demand equation would be biased.

The proper way to proceed is to start from the general structural form, which includes all the behavioural equations related to the system under consideration. For example:

$$B_0 Y_t = M + B_1 Y_{t-1} + B_2 Y_{t-2} + \ldots + B_k Y_{t-k} + \omega_t$$

where $Y_t^T = (m_t, i_t, p_t, y_t)$,[8] M is a 4×1 vector of constants (intercepts), the B_i are 4×4 matrices, ω_t is a 4×1 vector of structural disturbances, and the lag structure has been extended to k lags (compared with the above money demand equation), so as not to restrict it unduly *a priori*.

This is a structural form because each equation now lends itself to an economic interpretation (money demand by private agents, interest rate setting by the central bank and so on). However, this system of equations cannot be estimated directly. It has to be transformed into a reduced form for which parameters can be estimated, by multiplying the above equation by B_0^{-1}, which gives:

$$Y_t = A + A_1 Y_{t-1} + A_2 Y_{t-2} + \dots + A_k Y_{t-k} + e_t$$

where $A_i = B_0^{-1} B_i$ and $e_t = B_0^{-1} \omega_t$. This is the general formula for a VAR model, as a simple autoregressive form for a vector of variables.[9] The above derivation of this formula shows that this representation of Y is legitimate, since the VAR is simply a reduced form of the structural representation. The equations defining Y involve reduced-form parameters (the A matrices and the variance–covariance matrix of e_t): these do not themselves have an economic interpretation but are a function of the structural parameters.

The reduced-form parameters can be estimated using straightforward ordinary least squares (OLS) regression, equation by equation, since the OLS estimators are consistent and equal to the maximum likelihood estimators. Forecasting then simply requires Y_t to be computed as a function of its past values, period by period. However, in practice, a number of problems arise.

Choosing the series

Indeed, VARs look deceptively simple. A decisive yet complex and difficult choice is the decision on which of the variables to include in the system. Generally, VAR models are intended to reflect some theoretical model, in line with the sequence presented above. In some cases, the theoretical model is in fact rather loose, and heuristic considerations are brought in to justify the shape of the VAR. In others – see, for example, the 'structural VARs' below which posit the existence of so-called 'structural shocks' – the consideration

---

[8] T is the transpose symbol, indicating that a line vector is turned into a column vector or vice versa.

[9] A further refinement is to posit that A_i are matrices with time-varying coefficients in order to consider potential structural changes over time. This leads to the following time-varying VAR specification: $Y_t = A_{0,t} + A_{1,t} Y_{t-1} + A_{2,t} Y_{t-2} + \dots + A_{k,t} Y_{t-k} + e_t$. For an application to US inflation, unemployment and interest rate, see D'Agostino *et al.* (2009).

of an explicit and fully specified structural model can help to select the variables that should feature in the system. But in all cases, the choice of variables essentially reflects *a priori* ideas and modelling, subject to the practical constraint that the number of variables can only be very limited (usually two to five), to avoid the estimates becoming overly imprecise.

In principle, the variables can be selected on a purely statistical basis, using Granger causality tests:[10] a variable that appears to be exogenous in a Granger sense can be excluded from the vector of endogenous variables of the VAR. However, applying this methodology to a large number of candidate variables, with a sufficient number of lags, requires that a great many observations be available, which is often not the case in macroeconomic analysis.

Thus the VAR approach is not really devoid of theory. On the contrary, the decision to include or omit certain variables usually constitutes a strong *a priori* restriction with important implications as to the underlying model with which the VAR is consistent.

Another delicate issue is whether, and how, to transform the selected time series before running the VAR: can they be kept as they are, or should logs be taken, or first differences? A key question in this respect is how to deal with non-stationarity. Take the above VAR, with Y_t now generalized to a vector of n variables:

$$Y_t = A + A_1 Y_{t-1} + A_2 Y_{t-2} + \ldots + A_k Y_{t-k} + e_t$$

For OLS to be applicable, as indicated above, all the components of Y_t should be stationary. In that case, the estimators are consistent and the usual asymptotic tests of the parameters can be applied. By contrast, if some of the variables are non-stationary (which is likely in the above example for money, prices and activity), they need to be transformed through differencing into stationary variables prior to running the VAR.[11]

---

[10] A variable x is said to 'Granger-cause' variable y if the forecast of the latter is improved by taking into account the information embodied in the former (in fact, this should be described in terms of correlation rather than causation; finding evidence of Granger causality can be an artefact of a spurious correlation, and lack of Granger causality can also be misleading if the true causal link is of a non-linear form). See Berger and Österholm (2008) for a recent analysis of Granger causality links between inflation and money in the USA.
[11] When a variable has to be differenced d times to become stationary, the number d is called the order of integration $I(d)$ of this variable. Output and inflation often appear to be $I(1)$ and prices $I(2)$. See Box 3.1 for more details.

Considering $I(1)$ variables only, two cases can arise. If the variables are not cointegrated,[12] the VAR can be estimated in first differences:

$$\Delta Y_t = A + A_1 \, \Delta Y_{t-1} + A_2 \, \Delta Y_{t-2} + \ldots + A_k \, \Delta Y_{t-k} + e_t$$

Alternatively, if there exist r cointegration relations, an estimation of the VAR in first differences would fail to take into account the information provided by the long-term relationships between the variables. A proper specification of the VAR can then be a vector error correction model (VECM):

$$\Delta Y_t = A + C \, Y_{t-1} + D_1 \, \Delta Y_{t-1} + D_2 \, \Delta Y_{t-2} + \ldots + D_{k-1} \, \Delta Y_{t-k+1} + e_t$$

where the C is called the long-run impact matrix and the D_i are the short-run impact matrices. The transformation used to compute the VECM can be illustrated for the following simple VAR model:

$$Y_t = A + A_1 Y_{t-1} + A_2 Y_{t-2} + e_t$$

Subtracting Y_{t-1} from both sides yields:

$$
\begin{aligned}
\Delta Y_t &= A - Y_{t-1} + A_1 Y_{t-1} + A_2 Y_{t-2} + e_t \\
&= A - Y_{t-1} + A_1 Y_{t-1} + A_2 Y_{t-2} + A_2 Y_{t-1} - A_2 Y_{t-1} + e_t \\
&= A + (A_1 + A_2 - I_n) \, Y_{t-1} - A_2 \, \Delta Y_{t-1} + e_t \text{ (where } I_n \text{ is the } n{\times}n \text{ identity matrix)} \\
&= A + C \, Y_{t-1} + D_1 \, \Delta Y_{t-1} + e_t
\end{aligned}
$$

where

$$C = A_1 + A_2 - I_n \text{ and } D_1 = - A_2$$

Estimation problems

Choosing the right number of lags presents yet another difficulty when estimating a VAR model. In principle, this number can be determined in a fairly objective way. For example, in the case of quarterly series, it would be natural to first try out four and eight lags. Then a Fisher test allows the analyst to check whether lags five to eight can be dropped. If so, one can compare a three- and four-lag specification using the same test, and so on. If not, one might test a six-lag specification, and perhaps a seven-lag one. If eight lags appear to be a minimum, one could even test a 12-lag specification. More generally, statistical software packages provide help with the choice of the lag-selection criteria.

---

[12] A set of non-stationary variables are said to be cointegrated if some linear combination of these variables is stationary. If there exist r independent stationary linear combinations, there are said to be r cointegration relations (see Box 3.1).

In practice, however, the number of lags and variables cannot be that large. The higher they are, the more observations are needed if a reasonable degree of precision is to be preserved. For example, a VAR model with eight lags for three variables requires the estimation of 24 parameters for each of the three equations, and therefore 72 autoregressive parameters, plus the six parameters of the covariance matrix. Given that quarterly time series often do not extend beyond three decades, the number of parameters could easily be of the same order of magnitude as the number of observations. Overparameterization tends to cause multicollinearity and loss of degrees of freedom, leading to large out-of-sample forecasting errors. Hence, VAR estimates obtained on relatively short data sets and/or with a rich structure in terms of variables or lags are not very robust.

Uses of VAR

On the whole, VAR models are a useful tool for business cycle analysis, generating forecasts that can be as good as those obtained through other means (Thomakos and Guerard, 2004). A key additional element is the relatively small size of VAR models, not least when compared to traditional macroeconomic models that are much larger and often difficult to estimate as a whole system (rather than block by block). VAR models also have the advantage of not requiring assumptions to be made about the exogenous variables (though this can be of limited help for out-of-sample exercises).

That said, in addition to their possible lack of robustness, VAR model results are difficult to explain in economic terms. While simulations may work well on historical data, the 'black box' nature of the exercise makes it difficult for VARs to serve as the anchor for the story that is part and parcel of a forecast.

Even so, VAR models contribute to shedding light on the short-run outlook in the following ways:

- They can help to sort survey-based information. Chapter 2 showed that the relations between endogenous, quantitative variables and qualitative balance-of-opinion survey results cannot be viewed as proper behavioural equations. This can make it difficult to choose which information to use. VARs can be of assistance to sort through such survey data (which are often stationary), without needing to worry about causality, simultaneity or links between them.
- They can help to identify some causal relationships. For example, VAR modelling allows analysts to gain a sense of which survey data are ahead of others (this can then be complemented by running *ad hoc* Granger causality tests). The VECM approach, moreover, allows, first, for the impact of these relationships to be characterized over time (by looking at the short- and longer-term dynamics in response to a shock), and second, to consider the various

'cointegrating' relationships between the variables. For example, de Mello and Pisu (2009) used a VECM setting to estimate jointly the determinants of bank loan demand and supply (an appealing approach given that these two variables are affected simultaneously by monetary shocks).

- They can help to interpret ongoing developments. By allowing a comparison of what would have resulted from the VAR with the actual developments, VAR modelling identifies 'innovations'. In turn, one can observe how the model reacts over time (through its 'impulse response' function) to a shock on the exogenous variables. Such analyses help the forecaster to reflect on how 'normal' the current situation is and, if it does not appear to be so, to look for the special factors (say, weather conditions) that might explain deviations from what the VAR predicts.

Structural VARs

As shown above, a VAR can be seen as the reduced form of a structural model. This can be estimated, whereas in general the parameters in a structural model cannot. The latter is said not to be identifiable.

However, when faced with a VAR estimation, it is natural to ask whether one can recover the structural model. This has led to the development of the so-called structural VARs. The idea is to posit that a number of restrictions apply to the parameters of the structural model, so as to be able to identify them based on the reduced-form parameters. Recall that:

$$B_0 Y_t = B_1 Y_{t-1} + B_2 Y_{t-2} + \dots + B_k Y_{t-k} + \omega_t \qquad \text{(structural model)}$$
$$Y_t = A_1 Y_{t-1} + A_2 Y_{t-2} + \dots + A_k Y_{t-k} + e_t \qquad \text{(VAR)}$$

where

$$A_i = B_0^{-1} B_i \text{ and } e_t = B_0^{-1} \omega_t$$

Identification requires the matrix B_0 to be known, as it is needed to compute the structural parameters B_i based on the VAR estimates A_i, and the structural shocks ω_t based on the VAR innovations e_t. Economic considerations can help to pin down B_0. Since B_0 is $n{\times}n$, it initially includes n^2 unknown parameters. The variance–covariance matrix estimated based on the VAR, which is equal to $B_0^{-1} (B_0^{-1})^T$, allows $n (n + 1)/2$ restrictions on these parameters to be identified.[13] Hence, $n (n - 1) / 2$ identifying restrictions remain to be defined in order to arrive at the structural model. The essence of this approach is to identify the structural shocks deemed to be orthogonal according to economic theory.

---

[13] Without loss of generality, it is implicitly assumed here that the structural shocks are orthogonal and that their variance is unity.

A canonical example of this methodology is the bivariate system for unemployment and output growth considered by Blanchard and Quah (1989). They postulate that this system is driven by two orthogonal structural shocks ('supply' and 'demand'). The identifying restriction is that only supply shocks can permanently affect output (just one such restriction is needed here, since for $n = 2$, $n (n - 1) / 2 = 1$). Another classic example of an identifying restriction is that a monetary shock has no long-run impact on real variables.

The structural VAR approach sits halfway between pure VAR analysis and structural macroeconomic models. Once the VAR has been identified, one can study its impulse response functions, which show how variables react over time to structural shocks. This can be useful when thinking about alternative scenarios. One can also retrace the sequence of past structural shocks and decompose the past values of the variables as a function of these shocks. This approach allowed Meurers (2006), for example, to identify the sources of changes in German international price competitiveness over recent decades.

For forecasting purposes, however, structural VARs may not add that much compared to simple VARs, and share the latter's lack of robustness. Also, it may be difficult to properly specify independent structural shocks over the short horizon of near-term analyses. Last but not least, the fact that VARs are run with a small number of variables implies that potentially important information is disregarded, which can lead to puzzling, if not outright misleading, results (Box AII.2).

Bayesian VAR

Another extension of VAR models are Bayesian VARs (BVARs; see Litterman, 1986). The general idea is to estimate a traditional VAR but in addition to impose some restrictions *ex ante* (called 'priors') to shrink the number of parameters instead of allowing unrestricted OLS estimation. The difference with structural VARs is that these priors are not always derived from economic theory or judgement but can be simple assumptions related to the statistical distribution of the coefficients in the equations of the VAR system. More precisely, let δ_{ij}^l be the standard deviation of the prior distribution for the coefficient on lag l of variable j in the equation i of the VAR. Then it can be assumed that this standard deviation declines in harmonic fashion for the dependent variable, and is scaled down closer to zero for the variables other than the dependent variable. In other words:

$$\delta_{ij}^l = \lambda \, / \, l \text{ if } i{=}j$$
$$\delta_{ij}^l = (\theta \, \lambda \, \sigma_i) \, / \, (l \, \sigma_j) \text{ if } i{\neq}j$$

where λ is the 'tightness parameter' set equal to the standard deviation on the first lag of the dependent variable in each equation, θ a scaling factor assumed to be 0.2, and σ_i the coefficients of e, the error vector of the VAR.

Box AII.2   How to use more information in VARs

One of the problems with standard VAR analyses is that to conserve a sufficient number of degrees of freedom, they rarely include more than six to eight variables. In so doing, they discard information that economic agents do take into account when making decisions.

Sims (1992) has illustrated this in the case of a central bank. Suppose that the central bank tightens policy systematically when anticipating rising inflation at a later date. If the signals of future inflationary pressures are not captured adequately by the variables included in the VAR, what is interpreted in VAR analysis as a policy shock may in fact be the central bank's response to new information about inflation. But the policy response to the latter might only partly offset the inflationary pressure, so that the estimated impulse response function will show an interest rate hike, to be followed by a rise in inflation – a counterintuitive finding.

A recent strand of literature has proposed a way to condition VAR analyses on richer information sets without losing the statistical advantages associated with a small number of variables. Bernanke *et al.* (2004), for example, combine standard VAR and factor (principal component) analysis. They build on the finding that, for forecasting purposes, dynamic factor models summarizing the information contained in large data sets outperform univariate autoregressions, small VARs and leading indicator models (Stock and Watson, 2002).

Litterman argues that BVARs compare well with other forecasting techniques and do relatively better at longer horizons, and Adolfson *et al.* (2007) note that BVARs usefully complement more judgement-based forecasts. Such techniques are also used for purposes other than forecasting. For example, Berger and Österholm (2008) use BVARs to study the link between money and inflation in the USA.

AII.2   Volatility modelling

The times series methods described in the first part of this Annex can be used for forecasting many types of data, and in particular financial market data. However, specific additional methods have been developed since the 1980s to deal explicitly with high-frequency data in finance (Engle and Patton, 2001), with a focus on asset prices, the associated returns, moments (volatility) and correlations (see Box AII.3).

Box AII.3   Reminders on autocorrelation

Autocorrelation – also referred to as serial correlation – relates to the correlation between the values of a variable at different points in time. The autocorrelation of order s of a series X_t is:

$$\rho_s = Cov(X_t, X_{t-s}) \,/\, Var(X_t)$$

where Cov stands for covariance and Var for variance.

In practice, for a series X_t observed at $t = 1, 2, ..., T - 1, T$, and denoting the mean as X, ρ_s can be estimated as:

$$\rho_s = \{[\Sigma_{t=1+s}^{T} (X_t - X)(X_{t-s} - X)] \,/\, (T - s)\} \,/\, \{[\Sigma_{t=1}^{T} (X_t - X)^2]\,/\,T\}$$

Then hypothesis tests can be carried out on each of the estimated autocorrelation coefficients ρ_s:

- The Bartlett test on the individual coefficient (assuming a constant variance), to check whether to reject the null hypothesis that the coefficient is equal to zero.
- The White test, to take into consideration that the variance can vary, which leads to 'robust standard errors' that give good estimates of standard errors even in the event of heteroskedasticity.

In practice, the econometric software will display the sample autocorrelation coefficients with confidence intervals calculated using these tests (if the coefficient is outside these intervals, then the hypothesis of non-autocorrelation for a given order will be rejected at the chosen level of confidence).

In addition, when looking at a large number of autocorrelation orders, there is a risk of wrongly rejecting the null hypothesis for a certain order. Hence it is advisable to perform a joint test that all autocorrelation coefficients are equal to 0. One common example is the joint Ljung–Box test ('Q statistic') which serves to establish whether any of a group of autocorrelations of a time series is different from zero. The critical value for rejecting the null follows a χ^2 distribution with the degree of freedom equal to the assumed number of lags (typically, one looks at a maximum of 20 lags, but the choice should depend on the autocorrelation function displayed by the data).

One problem with traditional time series techniques such as ARIMA is the common assumption that the error term ε_t is white noise; that is, with a zero mean (unbiasedness) and a constant variance σ^2 (homoskedasticity). In contrast, ARCH/GARCH models assume heteroskedasticity when forecasting a variable y_t: the variance of the error term (which is in fact the conditional variance of y_t based on the information available at t) can vary over time, even though the unconditional variance of the series is constant. The aim here is thus to model the (conditional) variance. Of course, simpler methods such as those described in section AII.1 can also be applied when forecasting volatility, as for any variables.

Empirically, volatility data tend to display some clustering, especially at high frequencies. In particular, financial data exhibit significant serial correlation, implying that the predictability in the volatility of these data can be used for forecasting purposes. This is of particular interest for asset and risk management tasks.

In terms of macroeconomic forecasts, these methods are rarely used. The seminal paper by Engle (1982) looked at estimates of volatility for UK inflation, and this could be useful for certain forecasting purposes (for example, in countries with inflation targeting). But in general, macroeconomic forecasters are interested in the average volatility of economic indicators, and less in how volatility might evolve over the relatively short horizon of their forecasts. Moreover, the estimation of volatility models usually requires a great number of observations, which typically are available for high-frequency financial market data but less so for macroeconomic indicators. Nevertheless, Barnhill and Souto (2007) have found these techniques useful for analysing monthly macroeconomic time series such as interest rates, exchange rates and commodity prices.

AII.2.1   ARCH/GARCH models

ARCH models

The first ARCH (autoregressive conditional heteroskedasticity) model was presented in Engle (1982)[14] for a random variable y_t assumed to have a zero mean, so that y_t is equal to its error term ε_t:[15]

$$y_t = \eta_t\, h_t^{\frac{1}{2}}\ (= \varepsilon_t)$$
$$h_t = \alpha_0 + \alpha_1\, \varepsilon_{t-1}^2$$

---

[14] In its original specification by Engle ε_t was not the error term but the white noise, called η_t here. The presentation used here follows the more widely used one introduced by Bollerslev for the GARCH models (see below). The same holds for the order q.

[15] Alternatively, $y_t = \varepsilon_t + \mu_t$, to avoid imposing a zero mean.

with η_t a white noise, that is $\eta_t \sim N(0,1)$ and $\varepsilon_t \sim N(0, h_t)$.

In other words, the conditional variance of y_t (also referred to as the variance of the one-period forecast of y_t) is h_t and depends on the information set available at time t – in this case on the constants α_0 and α_1 and on y_{t-1}^2, the square residual observed at the preceding period $t - 1$, which follows an AR(1) process. This is an ARCH(1) model.

More generally an ARCH(q) model with the order q is expressed as:

$$y_t = \eta_t \, h_t^{\frac{1}{2}}$$
$$h_t = \alpha_0 + \Sigma_{i=1}^{i=q} \, \alpha_i \, \varepsilon_{t-i}^2$$

with η_t a white noise and the condition that all α_i should be positive.

The conditional variance h_t of the error term $\eta_t \, h_t^{\frac{1}{2}}$ (= ε_t) is not constant over time and is modelled as a function of the q past errors $\varepsilon_{t-1}, ..., \varepsilon_{t-q}$.

In practice, the estimation of an ARCH(q) model comprises the following steps, using the Lagrange multiplier test procedure proposed originally by Engle:

- Estimation of an AR(q) model for the variable y_t;
- Extraction of the residual ε_t;
- Regression of the square residual on a constant and its q lagged values ($\varepsilon_t^2 = \alpha_0 + \Sigma_{i=1}^{i=q} \, \alpha_i \, \varepsilon_{t-i}^2$); and
- Joint test of whether the coefficients α_i are all equal to 0 for $i = 1$ to q, by testing whether the statistic TR^2 (T being the observations' sample size, multiplied by the R^2 of the regression above) asymptotically follows a $\chi^2(q)$ distribution under the null hypothesis of no ARCH coefficients being different from zero.

GARCH models

The GARCH (generalized ARCH) model was presented by Bollerslev (1986). He described the GARCH(p,q) model as follows (using the same notations as above):

$$y_t = \varepsilon_t$$
$$\varepsilon_t \sim N(0, h_t) \text{ and } \eta_t \sim N(0,1)$$
$$y_t = \varepsilon_t = \eta_t \, h_t^{\frac{1}{2}}$$
$$h_t = \alpha_0 + \Sigma_{i=1}^{i=q} \, \alpha_i \, \varepsilon_{t-i}^2 + \Sigma_{i=1}^{i=p} \, \beta_i \, h_{t-i}$$

with the condition that all α_i and β_i should be positive.

Thus, the GARCH terms h_{t-i} are added to the ARCH terms ε_{t-i}^2 in the variance equation. Bollerslev noted that the extension of the ARCH to a GARCH process bears a resemblance to the extension of an AR time series to the general ARMA process. And indeed an ARCH(q) model is a GARCH(p,q) process with $p = 0$.

In practice, a widely-used specification is the GARCH(1,1) model:

$$y_t = \varepsilon_t \text{ (or } y_t = \mu_t + \varepsilon_t)$$
$$\varepsilon_t \sim N(0, h_t)$$
$$h_t = \alpha_0 + \alpha_1 \varepsilon^2_{t-1} + \beta_1 h_{t-1}$$

Here the variance forecast at t, conditioned on the set of information available at that time, is modelled as a function of the squared residual observed at the preceding period $t - 1$ – as is the case in an ARCH(1) model – plus the lagged variance.

Regarding the estimation of a GARCH(1,1) model, statistical software will typically include the following steps:

- Observation of the series (correlograms) and check that there is strong correlation over a certain number of lags ('volatility clustering');
- Estimation of the equation specifying the GARCH option;
- The output of the software will comprise the coefficient for the squared residual and for the lagged variance (denoted 'GARCH(–1)'); and
- *Ex post* verification of volatility clustering by testing whether the coefficients of the squared residuals regressed on their lagged values are all equal to zero.

Extension of GARCH models

There have been numerous extensions of the family of GARCH models (surveyed in Engel and Patton, 2001). These include:

- TARCH: the 'threshold GARCH' model has a specification similar to a GARCH model but there is an asymmetric effect, since the coefficient for the squared residual depends on the sign of the residual; for example, for a (1,1) process one can estimate the model:

$$h_t = \alpha_0 + \beta_1 h_{t-1} + \alpha_1 \varepsilon^2_{t-1} + 1_{\varepsilon_{t-1} \geq 0} \gamma_1 \varepsilon^2_{t-1}$$

with

$$1_{\varepsilon_{t-1} \geq 0} = 1 \text{ if } \varepsilon_{t-1} \geq 0 \text{ and } 1_{\varepsilon_{t-1} \geq 0} = 0 \text{ if } \varepsilon_{t-1} < 0$$

- EGARCH: the 'exponential GARCH' model is specified in a similar way to a GARCH model but using the logarithms; for example, for an order 1:

$$\ln h_t = \alpha_0 + \beta_1 \ln h_{t-1} + \alpha_1 |\varepsilon_{t-1} / \sigma_{t-1}| + \gamma_1 \varepsilon_{t-1} / \sigma_{t-1}$$

This specification provides for an asymmetric effect, as for the TARCH specification above, and allows for negative coefficients, unlike in a GARCH model (where all coefficients have to be positive).

- ARCH-in-mean models: here the variance equation is the same as in a GARCH specification but the variance is allowed to enter the equation for the variable y_t. For example, $y_t = \mu_t + \varepsilon_t + \delta\, h_t$. Such a specification is useful in the case of financial data for modelling the relation between risk (variance) and return.
- Stochastic volatility models: here an innovation is posited both for the y_t equation (the innovation is ε_t as in a GARCH model) and for the variance equation (the 'new' innovation introduced being η_t). For example:

$$h_t = \alpha_0 + \beta_1\, h_{t-1} + \eta_t$$

- Regime-switching volatility models: depending on a so-called 'state variable' that takes the value 1 or 2, and on the associated probability to switch from one state to the other, the variance could be $h_{1,t}$ or $h_{2,t}$.

Selection of a volatility model

The selection between different volatility models – in particular, the selection of the appropriate orders p and q in a GARCH(p,q) – can be done using some kind of information criteria, as for 'traditional' economic models. In practice, a GARCH(1,1) model often proves to be quite adequate and is not beaten easily by other model specifications. Nevertheless, volatility modelling techniques are still relatively new, and no model is yet widely accepted as the preferred one.

In this context, the specificity of variance forecasting should be underlined. Using all the information available at t, the models provide a forecast denoted h_t of the conditional variance σ_t^2 (which is not observable). In other terms, while one can forecast the conditional variance, one cannot measure *ex post* the error between the forecast and the outcome. So it is different from an (out-of-sample) forecasting exercise where the variable of interest y_t can 'really' be observed at t. But how is it possible to judge the accuracy of the forecast in this context? One possibility is to compute the error of the variance forecast as $(\varepsilon_t^2 - h_t^2)$, in effect using ε_t^2 as an approximation of the unobserved σ_t^2. However, this is only a proxy. Moreover, it has specific implications when judging the fit of a variance forecast. For example, bearing in mind the role played by the R^2 indicator for the y_t equation, one can look at $\sum_{t=1}^{T} (\varepsilon_t^2 - h_t^2)^2$, the sum of the squared proxy errors, when comparing the quality of variance forecasts. One shortcoming, however, is that the squared terms will display much more volatility than the errors themselves. In general, the R^2 of a variance equation will be much lower than the R^2 observed for a 'traditional' equation.

In addition to statistical information criteria, it is also worth focusing on economic goodness-of-fit when judging the quality of a variance model. One example relates to investment decisions. In theory, an investor will decide to invest in different asset classes so as to maximize the return of the aggregate portfolio and minimize the associated risk, depending on his own risk aversion. As a result, the optimal weight of any asset class in the investor's portfolio will depend on the return of the asset (measured by the expected mean of the variable) and its associated risk (measured by its volatility). Hence the modelling of conditional volatility plays an important role for investors who are assessing profit/risk trade-offs.

A second example is option pricing. A widely-used instrument is the Black–Scholes formula for estimating call and put option prices, which depend – among other factors – on the volatility of the underlying variable. This means that the forecast of the variance can be used in a comparison with the implied volatility derived from the observed price of the option on the underlying asset. One important caveat in this case, however, is that the Black–Scholes formula relies on various specific assumptions, including that of a constant variance over time, which is inconsistent with the GARCH approach. Indeed, the implied volatilities derived from the Black–Scholes formula are in general rather different (and often higher) from the GARCH-type estimates.

AII.2.2   Multivariate volatility forecasting

GARCH models have also been extended from one to several variables (Engle, 2002). In general, a multivariate GARCH-type approach is mainly of interest when modelling a portfolio of assets. In most cases, these multivariate models have tended to be quite complex, given the large number of parameters to be estimated. Only a few applications have been able to deal with more than five assets – a very limited number compared with the number of assets typically included in a portfolio.

In the simplest case of two zero-mean variables y_1 and y_2 and with the notations used above (including t as the time subscript), let:

$$y_{1,t} = \varepsilon_{1,t} = \eta_{1,t} h_{1,t}^{\frac{1}{2}} \text{ and } y_{2,t} = \varepsilon_{2,t} = \eta_{2,t} h_{2,t}^{\frac{1}{2}}$$
$$\varepsilon_{1,t} \sim N(0, h_{1,t}) \qquad \text{and } \varepsilon_{2,t} \sim N(0, h_{2,t})$$
$$\eta_{1,t} \sim N(0,1) \qquad \text{and } \eta_{2,t} \sim N(0,1)$$

The conditional correlation between the two variables is

$$\rho_{12,t} = Cov_{t-1}(y_{1,t}, y_{2,t}) / (\sigma_{t-1}(y_{1,t}) \, \sigma_{t-1}(y_{2,t}))$$

or, since the variables have zero mean,

$$\rho_{12,t} = E_{t-1}(y_{1,t} \, y_{2,t}) \, [E_{t-1}(y_{1,t}^2)]^{-1/2} \, [E_{t-1}(y_{2,t}^2)]^{-1/2} \qquad \text{(AII.3)}$$
$$= E_{t-1}(\eta_{1,t} \, \eta_{2,t})$$

Thus the conditional correlation is the conditional covariance between the standardized disturbances.

Empirically, Equation (AII.3) is often estimated in one of two ways:

- the rolling correlation estimator:

$$\rho_{12,t} = [\Sigma_{s=t-n-1}^{t-1} y_{1,s} \, y_{2,s}] \, [\Sigma_{s=t-n-1}^{t-1} y_{1,s}^2]^{-1/2} \, [\Sigma_{s=t-n-1}^{t-1} y_{2,s}^2]^{-1/2}$$

which gives equal weight to all observations less than n periods in the past (and 0 otherwise).

- the exponential smoother developed by RiskMetrics (see the Further Reading section, p. 434):

$$\rho_{12,t} = [\Sigma_{s=1}^{t-1} \lambda^{t-s-1} \, y_{1,s} \, y_{2,s}] \, [\Sigma_{s=1}^{t-1} \lambda^{t-s-1} \, y_{1,s}^2]^{-1/2} \, [\Sigma_{s=1}^{t-1} \lambda^{t-s-1} \, y_{2,s}^2]^{-1/2}$$

where the weights are declining depending on the parameter λ (typically, $\lambda = 0.94$ for daily data).

For multidimensional GARCH models dealing with the returns of k assets, the conditional covariance matrix of returns H is used, which features the k variances $h_{i,t}$ of each asset return $y_{i,t}$ on its diagonal and the $k \, (k-1) \, / \, 2$ covariances between each pair of returns $y_{i,t}$ and $y_{j,t}$. This represents, however, a very large number of parameters to be estimated, limiting the usefulness of these approaches.

However, some models can be estimated by imposing restrictions on the coefficients of H_t. With Y_t denoting the matrix composed of the vectors of the values of the variables over the time sample; that is $(y_{1,t}, y_{2,t}, \ldots y_{k,t})^T$:

- the rolling correlation estimator can be written in matrix notation as:

$$H_t = \Sigma_{j=1}^n (Y_{t-j} \, Y_{t-j}')$$

- the exponential smoother can be written as:

$$H_t = \lambda \, (Y_{t-1} \, Y_{t-1}') + (1 - \lambda) \, H_{t-1}$$

which can be estimated by retaining for H_0 the unconditional covariance matrix; this a very simple method often used for constructing a time-varying conditional covariance matrix.

- the orthogonal GARCH (or principal component) method, resting on uncorrelated linear combinations of the variables derived using principal components techniques to obtain a diagonal matrix H_t.
- the BEKK (after Baba, Engle, Kraft and Kroner) model representation introduced by Engle and Kroner (1995) where:

$$H_t = \Omega + A \ (Y_{t-1} \ Y_{t-1}') \ A' + B \ H_{t-1} \ B'$$

with A and B being matrices for which several assumptions can be made to reduce the number of parameters, and Ω the intercept matrix.
- the CCC (constant conditional correlation) model introduced by Bollerslev, which allows time variation for the variances but not for the correlations:

$$H_t = D_t \ R \ D_t$$

where D_t is a diagonal matrix comprising the $h_{i,t}^{1/2}$ and R is estimated as the unconditional correlation matrix of the standardized residuals ε_t.
- the DCC (dynamic conditional correlation) model, introduced by Engle (2002) which differs from the CCC model in allowing R to be time-varying; in addition, the dynamics of all the correlations over time are the same using simplified parameters:

$$H_t = D_t \ R_t \ D_t$$

- asymmetric multivariate models can also be defined, allowing for different correlations depending on whether the return variables are increasing or decreasing.

AII.2.3   Selected applications of volatility forecasts

Value at risk

A portfolio manager may worry less about the variance of an asset class than about the possible occurrence of excessively large losses, which may matter more to him or her than potential outsize gains. One way to take this into account is to look at the 'value at risk' VaR$_\alpha$ of a variable Y, which can be defined as the threshold such that there is a probability α of observing Y at a given time under this threshold (Jorion, 2006).

Introduced in the 1980s in the US financial markets, the VaR technique has become a popular risk-management tool following its adoption by J.P. Morgan, which decided in the 1990s to release to the public a detailed description of the risk methodologies used by its RiskMetrics service. The concept gained further prominence with the adoption in 2004 of Basel II, the Revised Framework for International Convergence of Capital Measurement and Capital Standards. Financial supervisors were able to allow banks to decide to follow the VaR models' approach (as an alternative to less 'sophisticated' approaches) to calculate the risk weighing on their balance sheets (and thereby the capital that should be kept aside to remain solvent) in case of potential changes in financial market conditions. Such calculations are often based on historically observed volatilities.

A concrete example is that of a US corporation holding a portfolio of US$100 million in euros. The VaR answers the question: what is the maximum that the firm can lose with a probability of x per cent over one day? If one retains a probability of 95 per cent, since the daily standard deviation σ of the €/US$ exchange rate is measured as 0.565 per cent, and under the assumption that the standardized return r/σ is normally distributed (with the mean of the return r equal to zero here), the VaR is calculated as $1.65\sigma = 0.932$ per cent (this is because, for the normal distribution function centred around zero, the probability of having a larger loss and to be on the left side of the –1.65 threshold is 5 per cent; the threshold for a probability of 1 per cent is –2.33). The implication is that 95 per cent of the time the US$100 million portfolio will not lose more than US$932,000 over the following 24 hours.[16]

In practice, there are several ways to compute VaR. It can be done based on the historical observations of returns that can be ordered so as to display their empirical distribution in a histogram (possibly with a greater weight for the most recent observations). Another way – the 'variance–covariance method' – is to assume a normal distribution and to calculate the probability of the variable being below its mean minus a given number of standard deviations. In such cases, modelling the variance with a GARCH-type process can be very useful, since the VaR will vary over time: the potential loss would be much larger in a period of high volatility, implying that the use of a constant variance representation would give risk managers a false sense of security. A third method is to run a Monte Carlo simulation – that is, based on a specific modelling of the variable of interest – to generate a large sample of random outcomes and then to compute their distribution.

Extreme value theory

Extreme value theory (EVT) is somewhat akin to VaR but with a focus on the more extreme tails of the distribution. The distribution assumed here is one with 'fat tails'; that is, excess kurtosis compared to the normal distribution.

---

[16] In practice, a 5 per cent VaR will also be commonly referred to as a 95 per cent VaR. Another idiosyncrasy is that the 5 per cent VaR point is always expressed as a positive number (despite it being a loss).

Consider a series X_t with an unknown distribution and let M_n be the maximum observed for the sample $\{X_1, X_2, ..., X_n\}$. The probability that this maximum will be lower than a certain threshold is $P(M_n \leq x) = F_n(x)$, the distribution function of the sample maxima M_n.

Under certain assumptions, it has been shown that the distribution of F_n, when rescaled, converges to H, the 'extreme value distribution'. There are three main types of such distributions (Fréchet, Weibull and Gumbel, depending on the tail shape; see, for example, Knott and Polenghi (2006) for a recent application) which can be written as the following generalized extreme value distribution:

$$H(x) = exp\{- (1 + \xi\, x)^{-1/\xi}\}$$

where $\xi \neq 0$ is the tail index.

This distribution can be estimated based on observed data for those very rare events. For example, if the focus is on very large losses, a VaR-type forecast will be produced. The observed sequence of extreme events (defined as the observations below the threshold VaR_α) will be used to derive information on the specification to be retained, with the help of the so-called 'Hill estimator' – see Knott and Polenghi (2006) for a presentation.

Density forecasts

Density forecasts go one step further: the purpose here is not to forecast the mean of a variable (as in an ARMA process), nor its variance (as in a GARCH process) nor even a confidence interval (VaR approaches), but the entire distribution of economic variables.

Regarding univariate density functions, the approach followed in practice is to check whether the variable of interest has an (empirical) distribution that is compatible with a specific functional form. A common check is to test whether the distribution observed is compatible with a normal distribution – for example, by using a test for unconditional normality such as the Jarque–Bera test based on the observed skewness and kurtosis of the data; if rejected, the variable cannot be assumed to be normally distributed. A further test using GARCH techniques is to check whether there is conditional normality, assuming that the mean and the variance are time-varying. In general, one will model the mean and the variance of the variable and then check whether the residuals are white noise $(0,1)$. Yet another alternative is to test the compatibility not with a normal distribution but with a distribution with higher kurtosis (say, Student) and fat tails that appear to be more consistent with empirical evidence for financial data.

Turning to multivariate density functions, these have attracted increasing interest in mathematical finance applications in recent years (Cherubini *et al.*,

2004; Patton, 2009). Copulas (or 'dependence functions') allow the estimation of the joint distribution of a number of variables combining the specific distribution of each (as captured by their marginal density functions). The dependence structure is thus modelled as a multivariate distribution of the individual marginal functions; it can the be tested against a known multivariate density function (for example, a multivariate normality distribution function), as in the univariate case. This allows analysts to capture the dependence between variables better than by merely looking at their correlations. For example, copulas can be used to generate asymmetric dependence (say, higher correlations among the variables in good times versus bad times) or tail dependence (say, higher correlations at times of stress). That said, the complexity of these methods and the risks associated with modelling imperfections can be overwhelming. Indeed, copulas had been used across the board for valuing complex derivatives, and these valuations were called into question during the 2007 financial crisis, further contributing to the turmoil (see Appendix 4.1).

Very-high-frequency data

A burgeoning literature is focusing on the forecasting of intra-day, very-high-frequency financial data. In particular, attention is being paid to 'tick data' (the data comprising every price tick observed in the market between a seller and a buyer). These high-frequency, but irregularly spaced, observations can yield useful information regarding the behaviour of financial market participants, and about market characteristics such as liquidity, depth or intra-day patterns. Public interest – including from policy makers – has increased recently regarding the use of these new techniques for high-frequency trading and the potential impact on market functioning (this was particularly the case after the 'Flash Crash' on 6 May 2010, during which the US Dow Jones fell by nearly 1,000 points over a few minutes before rebounding, while some stocks temporarily lost almost all of their value).

The technique for modelling intra-day dynamics or 'diurnality' is inspired by deseasonalization techniques. Basically, a variable will be regressed on diurnal dummy variables spaced at regular intervals. A test will be run to establish whether one of these dummy variables is significant. In essence, diurnal components are thus estimated as if they were seasonal components. Then the standard time series techniques referred to in this Annex are applied to model the mean of the variable, its volatility and to produce estimates of the time of the next trades (duration forecasts). For example, Engle and Patton (2004) have modelled the bid and ask price to analyse the quote price dynamics of US stocks.

Further reading

There is a burgeoning literature on forecasting techniques applying time series methods in economics, as well as in other fields, such as finance, sociology, marketing and so on. Such techniques are useful for some specific business-oriented applications – for example, the modelling of the level of inventories, of monthly sales or of spot prices (Hyndman *et al.*, 2008). RiskMetrics' technical documentation is freely available on riskmetrics.com.

The forecasters.org website of the International Institute of Forecasters (IIF) is a good source of information. So is the forecastingprinciples.com site and Armstrong (2001). The IIF site links to the *International Journal of Forecasting*, which featured a special issue on financial forecasting (April–June 2009). In addition, a good introduction can be found in Poon (2005) and Andersen *et al.* (2009). On volatility modelling more specifically, a brief overview is provided by Engle (2001).

Macroeconomic models

Contents

A macroeconomic (or macroeconometric) model is a quantitative representation of an economy, or of several interdependent countries. It assembles a number of equations and allows analysts to study the behaviour of the economy(ies) when the various relationships between variables are in operation simultaneously. In addition, a model synthesizes data and knowledge with a view to better explaining economic history and forecasting future developments.

Macroeconomic models are created and maintained mainly by governmental agencies, central banks and private forecasting institutions (see Appendix 8.1). They may be used for forecasting purposes, either over the short run (one to two years ahead), or over longer horizons. The central forecast is then called the baseline. The models also serve to experiment with different assumptions regarding the international or domestic environment, as well as regarding policies. These alternative scenarios depart more or less from the baseline.

While macroeconomic models are a precious tool for forecasters, they are sophisticated instruments, to be manipulated with great care. A 'push-button' approach – feed the model with the latest data and let it do the work – would be uninformative at best, and outright misleading at worst. Understanding the model's inner properties and limitations is therefore essential if it is to be used successfully. This annex reviews the general features of macroeconomic models (section AIII.1), their inner logic (section AIII.2) and their simulation properties (section AIII.3). It then turns to the practical uses of models in forecasting (section AIII.4) before assessing the models' merits and limitations (section AIII.5).

AIII.1   General features

From a technical standpoint, a model is a juxtaposition of equations linking economic variables. The latter are of two sorts:

- Endogenous variables, which are explained by the model. They are determined jointly by the system of equations. There are thus as many endogenous variables as there are equations.
- Exogenous variables, which are considered as given, as opposed to being derived by the model. They typically include assumptions about technology, the international environment and economic policy.

The number of equations varies from just a handful to several hundred, or even to thousands for the most disaggregated models, which delve deep into sectoral details, or which include a considerable number of countries (in the case of international models). Generally, these equations fall into one of three categories:

- Behavioural equations: as explained in Chapter 3, they describe how agents behave in relation to consumption, investment, price setting and so on. The specification is normally guided by economic theory, at least to some extent. Most frequently, their parameters are estimated so as to ensure that the equation fits the historical data as closely as possible. But even when they fit well, there always remains some difference between actual observations and the values predicted by the model. This random error term or 'residual' can be added on to the estimated equation so that the historical data can be traced exactly by the model (see below).
- Accounting identities: these stem from the national accounts definitions. For example, a deflator for a given macroeconomic aggregate should equal its nominal value divided by its volume, or the budget balance should be equal to fiscal revenues minus expenditures. Unlike the behavioural equations, the accounting identities are always met exactly. This holds even when there are statistical discrepancies: in this case, they are identified as such and treated like variables.
- Technical relationships: some relations between variables are neither behavioural nor an accounting constraint. Usually, these are equations defining non-observable but important variables, such as production functions, for example, which relate outputs to inputs.

The behavioural equations are at the heart of each macroeconomic model, but the latter's most important value-added lies in its macroeconomic logic: how the equations interact and what this suggests about past and future economic developments.

AIII.2 Macroeconomic logic

Economic reality is always more complex than what may be reflected in a set of equations, even a large one. The 'art of model building' therefore lies in selecting the key relationships that provide a simplified yet relevant view of economic developments for the purpose at hand (Don and Verbruggen, 2006). This 'stylization' process hinges on theory. However, economists would not agree unanimously on theory and what constitutes the essential forces at work in the economy. Moreover, reality at times comes back with a vengeance just when modellers have prided themselves on finding 'the' basic model of the economy. Examples of such reality tests are the stagflation of the 1970s, which discredited simple Keynesian models at the time; and the 2007 financial crisis, which has damaged confidence in some more recent modelling endeavours.

When building or using a model, a natural starting point is therefore to ask what is its underlying framework or 'miniature model' (Fukac and Pagan,

2009). For example, early macroeconomic models of the 1950s or 1960s were associated with the IS/LM framework, the basic demand multiplier and adaptive expectations. Additions and changes were made in the following decades, such as developing supply-side blocks, paying attention to financial channels or building in rational expectations. As a result, the macro-modelling landscape is both diverse at any given time and ever-evolving over time.

At the current juncture one could probably distinguish two strands of macroeconomic models used in forecasting and for economic policy purposes. First are the distant heirs of traditional Keynesian models, though blended with a host of more 'modern' features. The inner logic of such traditional models is perhaps best described as reflecting various versions of a dynamic aggregate supply/aggregate demand (AS/AD) model. Second are dynamic stochastic general equilibrium (DSGE) models, which assume utility-maximizing and forward-looking agents. The following subsections give a brief overview of the 'macroeconomic logic' underlying both approaches.

AIII.2.1   Traditional models

Demand, supply and adjustment

The traditional models are inspired by a blend of Keynesian and neoclassical ideas. The mix varies though. Indeed, this approach is sufficiently flexible to capture adequately many features of observed economic behaviour and to introduce the requisite nuances, where appropriate. Its key elements include the following:

- The starting point is the assumption that, in the short run, output is determined by demand, in a context where prices exhibit some degree of stickiness. Traditional mechanisms such as the investment accelerator and the income multiplier influence the short-run equilibrium significantly. Hence, at a one-to-two-year horizon, effective fiscal and monetary policy action can have a substantial influence on demand.
- The short-run equilibrium often involves over- or under-utilization of labour and capital, but these imbalances are worked off over longer horizons. Trend growth is determined by structural factors such as technical progress, labour market participation and demographics. Typically, Keynesian short-run properties are combined with classical long-run ones.
- A crucial element of medium-run adjustment is the wage–price dynamic centred on some version of the Phillips curve. Tensions or slack on labour or product markets influence wages and prices; in particular, real wages are generally sensitive to unemployment in these models. In this context, if, for example, excess demand pushes up inflation, it will in turn crowd out real spending, via a negative impact on agents' wealth, and affects net exports adversely by reducing price competitiveness: the excess demand pressures are thereby gradually offset. Hence the interaction of real and nominal

variables tends to ensure that, when shocks hit it, the economy will move back, over time, to its long-run growth path.

- Another equilibrating mechanism relates to monetary and financial conditions, notably in so far as they are influenced by monetary policy. If the latter is endogenized into the model in the form of some reaction function – say, a Taylor rule (see Box 4.3) – monetary policy will dampen the cycle. Changes in interest rates will affect real variables directly (for example, consumption and investment) or indirectly (via their impact on exchange rates or asset prices). In this case, it is the interaction between the real and the financial blocks of the model that contributes to macroeconomic stabilization.

Building blocks

As emphasized above, the core of traditional models is the interaction of demand and supply in the goods and services market as well as the labour market, augmented by feedback mechanisms and policy variables. The 'real-side block' describes the Keynesian feedback loop (demand multiplier), household spending, firms' factor demand and foreign trade, while the 'price block' revolves around a couple of equations describing wage formation and price setting.

In this context, the importance of the modelling of supply has been highlighted by past shocks (such as oil shocks or abrupt changes in trend productivity). The demand equations for the production factors, the production function itself (when specified) and the wage–price equations are at the core of what is referred to as supply. Supply-side mechanisms would, for example, include the impact of profitability on investment, or of the cost of labour on labour demand. More fundamentally, modellers pay attention to models' long-run properties. For example, one important question would be whether the model includes an equilibrium unemployment rate, and if so, what are its determinants (see section 3.5).

Models would also typically include a 'financial and monetary block'. This determines the constellation of interest rates, exchange rates and asset prices, which in turn feeds back to real-sector behaviour.

The degree of interdependence between the real and the financial sectors varies across models. Most contemporaneous models feature tangible effects of interest rates on domestic demand, in line with the traditional Keynesian IS curve. But the determination of the interest rates itself differs from one model to the next. It may stem from a money demand equation, a monetary policy rule, or the interest rate may simply be set exogenously. Similarly, the degree of endogeneity of the exchange rate, which influences the speed of adjustment to shocks, is far from uniform across models.

Whether a model incorporates wealth effects or not also makes a big difference. For example, in the case of an inflationary demand shock, its expansionary impact will be mitigated by the erosion of real wealth. However, simulated consumption, when wealth effects are incorporated and asset prices bounce around, may be overly volatile. It should also be borne in mind that, to include wealth effects, the model needs to have a sufficiently fleshed-out financial and monetary block, and that asset prices themselves are hard to predict.

Finally, one could also distinguish an 'income block' linking incomes to the macroeconomic aggregates. This often includes the description of public finances, notably on the revenue side, an important part of models used by some institutions such as national treasuries (see Chapter 5).

Expectations

Agents' expectations are modelled in a variety of ways, with important implications for predicted behaviour. Indeed, this is a major source of simulation differences across models, affecting not only the dynamics of the economic responses to any policy impulse but also their magnitude.

The simplest approach is to assume that agents form expectations by extrapolating from the past and the present: these are the *naïve* and *adaptive expectations* approaches. Alternatively, it can be assumed that agents are more forward-looking, and that they take into account what the model predicts: these are the *rational expectations*, or more precisely 'model-consistent', approaches. The latter, however, involve an element of circularity, since they postulate that agents' decisions hinge on expected variables whose realization depends on these very decisions.

Empirical models sometimes combine adaptive and rational expectations. Some, such as NiGEM, can even be run in either mode. However, rational expectations now tend to be associated with DSGE modelling (see below), while a backward-looking setting remains dominant in more traditional models, especially when it comes to daily forecasting practice. Indeed, for forecasting *per se*, rational expectations are not used that often, in part because of the greater technical difficulties they involve, and because the underlying assumption that economic agents always behave rationally and take into account the future consequences of their current decisions is disputable – not least in the light of the 2007 financial crisis.

AIII.2.2   DSGE models

One of the most significant recent novelties in macroeconomic modelling is the proliferation of dynamic stochastic general equilibrium (DSGE) models. These rest on the paradigm of utility-maximizing and forward-looking agents and push it to the limit. Though initially confined to academia, these tools have become increasingly widespread and influential, especially in central bank circles and in some international institutions (see Box AIII.1). However, these models also raise important problems, and the 2007 financial crisis has exposed some of their shortcomings.

A key characteristic of DSGE models is that they are derived from micro-foundations.[1] For example, households are assumed to maximize a utility function over consumption, saving and labour effort. Firms maximize profits by hiring labour, renting capital and supplying goods. Preferences and techno-logical constraints are specified.

Box AIII.1 From RBC to DSGE models

The DSGE methodology originates from a radical reaction to the failures of traditional macro-modelling in the early 1980s, in the form of the real busi-ness cycle (RBC) literature, initiated by Kydland and Prescott (1982). Like traditional models, RBC (and subsequently DSGE models) seek to explain aggregate growth and fluctuations. Unlike traditional models, however, their specifications rest fully on microeconomic principles.

In the 1980s and early 1990s, the RBC approach was closely connected to a controversial view of the business cycle held by neoclassical economists, namely that macroeconomic fluctuations are merely the product of techno-logical shocks or shifts in preferences. Over time, however, this basic model was extended and modified by the so-called New Keynesians: imperfections and frictions aplenty were added to the Pareto-efficient original structure; and room was made for activist monetary and (less often) fiscal policies (see, for example, Christiano *et al.*, 2005). By the late 1990s, this framework had begun to be widely used, under the DSGE label.

DSGE models are also stochastic: a variety of shocks are posited to affect the economy and to generate fluctuations. Much of modern macroeconom-ics is based on the notion of shocks generating fluctuations, which is not specific to DSGE modelling. But DSGE proponents argue that shocks in DSGE models are truly 'structural' shocks, which are not properly identi-fied in traditional models. A standard list of such shocks would include demand-side shifts (preferences, government spending), supply-side shocks (productivity, labour supply), cost-push shocks and financial (risk premium) and monetary shocks.

---

[1] To what extent DSGE models are truly micro-founded is debated, however (Colander *et al.*, 2008). Similarly, whether microfoundations are the right strategy to investigate macroeconomic phenomena remains disputed.

A number of imperfections and market frictions are then introduced. Mono-polistic competition is typically taken on board, giving agents some price- and wage-setting powers. Nominal rigidities are included in the form of a limited ability to reset prices in each period. Real rigidities are added, especially in the most empirically-oriented models, in the form of habit persistence in consumption, adjustment costs for investment and so on. Finally, some description of the policy environment is incorporated, including, say, some monetary and fiscal rules.

While these ingredients are not original as such, DSGE models differ from standard models (or reduced-form time-series models) in that they encapsulate all specifications in a single, internally-consistent theoretical framework. This contrasts with the traditional approach, in which model equations are inspired by theory but in a fragmented and somewhat eclectic way. Here, a unified view of the economy is formalized explicitly to exert a binding constraint on empirical specifications. Moreover, when taken to the data, system estimation is adopted, again contrasting with the looser equation-by-equation or at best block-by-block estimation of traditional models.

In this sense, DSGE models are of the general equilibrium type, as the name indicates. Furthermore, they are dynamic, showing how the economy evolves over time, and indeed their focus is on explaining short-run fluctuations. Therein lies the difference with the related, earlier computable general equilibrium (CGE) models. These also have microfoundations, but they are static, focusing on the long-run implications of public policies. DSGE models, in contrast, centre on business cycle sources and the dynamic effects of macroeconomic policies.

One feature that deserves emphasis is the treatment of expectations. DSGE models rest on the rational expectations (RE) hypothesis, or at least the assumption that agents' expectations are consistent with the underlying model structure. However, in fact, DSGE models only gained credibility when they found ways to mimic business cycle data, including inertia in prices or spending decisions, despite the prompt adjustments to shocks typically obtained with RE.

The RE assumption remains hotly disputed, and even more so with the 2007 financial crisis. While expectations certainly matter, there are compelling reasons to depart from the RE hypothesis. In the basic DSGE model, changes in expectations of future variables (such as consumption or inflation) translate into one-for-one changes in the current values of these variables. The assumption that agents fully grasp the underlying structure of the economy (as represented in the model) and access information in a costless manner looks rather implausible. Lately, more credible premises have begun to be fed into DSGE models, such as bounded rationality and some form of adaptive learning (see, for example, Milani, 2007 and de Grauwe, 2008).

AIII.3 Estimation and simulation properties

A natural question is whether the behaviour described or predicted by empirical models matches what theory would suggest. As is already clear from the previous discussion, different models emphasize different issues and mechanisms. What is more, even models building on seemingly similar views may display varying properties because of differences in data selection, econometric strategies or mere details in specifications.

AIII.3.1 Theory, empirics and dynamics

In any model, there is a tension between theoretical purity and goodness-of-fit. At a minimum, theory offers some guidance when model builders decide which variables to test in the specification of behavioural equations. The role of theory did not go much further in the first generations of macroeconomic models, which aimed essentially at capturing the mechanisms that were empirically most robust. The bulk of the work then consisted of preparing the data, testing numerous specifications and inspecting model simulations in an iterative process. Good knowledge of the data and their statistical properties were an essential part of the job.

Empirical work still remains central today, but the objective of consistency with theoretical priors has gained ground, especially (though not only) for DSGE models. In more traditional models, theoretical consistency can usually be assessed by checking the implied long-run constraints on the parameters, on the grounds that, if theory is to hold, it is more in the long run rather than at high frequencies. When looking at single equations, an example of such constraints is the unitary elasticity of consumption to revenue (see section 3.2). In the case of a set of equations, it could be the parameters determining factor input demand.

Theory is diverse, however, and choosing between alternative representations reflecting different priors is difficult, because econometric testing on macroeconomic data frequently fails to deliver clear-cut verdicts. Testing for the substitutability of factor inputs, for example, tends to yield mixed results at the aggregate level.

The common modelling strategy is to rely on an econometric estimation of parameters, especially for models used in forecasting, for which a decent match with recent data is an important criterion. Yet it is not uncommon to impose calibrated rather than estimated values of specific parameters. This is done to reflect theoretical priors, but also to fit with broader empirical patterns. More surreptitiously, and perhaps more frequently, 'data mining' comes into play – for example, to pick an estimation period that offers the best arbitrage between conformity of the results with generally held views and empirical robustness.

Moreover, theory generally suggests that, rather than isolated equations, one should test systems of equations, which embody the constraints imposed on parameters that play a role in more than one equation. Progress has been made in estimating equations jointly, though it remains technically heavier and does not always provide informative answers, so that in practice behavioural equations are often estimated individually. Such short cuts, along with the 'data mining' referred to above, imply that model assumptions to some extent have normative features. Faced with a supply shock, for example, models support the reasoning that 'if reality is as assumed in the model, then the impact of the shock will be...', but can offer no certainty as to the shock's actual effects.

The way dynamics is modelled hinges on a similar difficult dilemma. The traditional approach freely uses lagged values of both dependent and explanatory variables. In terms of behaviour, these lags are interpreted as reflecting both adaptive expectations and partial adjustment to a changing environment. Error correction models (see Box 3.1) offer a convenient framework in which to reconcile long-term structural behavioural patterns and the observation of sluggish adjustment in behaviour. However, DSGE models follow another strategy. First, only model-consistent expectations are accepted. Second, dynamics as well as long-run responses are derived from the optimization problem facing firms and households.

Overall, models with few imposed constraints tend to be used for short-run analysis and forecasting, in a spirit akin to that underlying VAR models. Model consistency and stability is more important for medium- or long-run scenario analysis. Hence, the models used for these purposes tend to be more 'structured' and to embody more constraints. But there is always a risk that, by imposing too much structure, one would oversimplify and assess reality incorrectly. Modellers are generally well aware of this risk, but policy makers or the broader public may not be.

AIII.3.2 Actual simulation properties

As noted, models differ in their general approach (see Table AIII.1). Moreover, even when models share important common features, they do not produce identical quantitative or even qualitative results.

Another obvious difference relates to size, which ranges from just a handful of key equations (in small DSGE models) to several thousand (in large international models). Size, however, need not affect the main properties of the model. Rather, models are often expanded to render details more clearly – for example, by disaggregating overall quantity and price variables to show sectoral developments. But a heavier model is not necessarily a more accurate one: adding equations adds information but also extra problems. Indeed, model builders are often reluctant to disaggregate too much, fearing that a very detailed mechanism might become a black box, generating results that are difficult to

Table AIII.1 Selected macroeconomic models

	Institution	Approach	Description
International models			
GEM	IMF	DSGE	Laxton (2008)
Global Projection model (GPM)	IMF	Short-run neo-Keynesian, long-run neoclassical	Carabenciov et al. (2008)
Global model	OECD	Short-run neo-Keynesian, long-run neoclassical	Hervé et al. (2010)
NiGEM	NIESR	Model-consistent expectations, New Keynesian	Barrell and Pomerantz (2004)
World model	OEF	Short-run neo-Keynesian, long-run neoclassical	OEF (2005)
Euro area models			
QUEST III	European Commission	DSGE	Ratto et al. (2009)
New area-wide model	ECB	DSGE	Christoffel et al. (2008)
Country-specific models			
US FRB/US	Central bank	Forward-looking new-Keynesian structural	Reifschneider et al. (1999)
US SIGMA	Central bank	DSGE	Erceg et al. (2005)
Japan CAO model	ESRI	Demand-oriented, Keynesian, with error correction	Hida et al. (2008)
UK BEQM	Central bank	Short-run neo-Keynesian, long-run neoclassical	Harrison et al. (2005)
Germany MEMMOD	Central bank	Neo-Keynesian-neoclassical	Deutsche Bundesbank (2000)
France MÉSANGE	Ministry of Finance	Short-run neo-Keynesian, long-run neoclassical	Klein and Simon (2010)
Canada ToTEM	Central bank	DSGE	Fenton and Murchison (2006)
Australia MM900	KPMG Econtech	CGE	KPMG (2010)
Belgium MODTRIM II	Federal Planning Bureau	Short-run neo-Keynesian, long-run neoclassical	Hertveldt and Lebrun (2003)
Netherlands SAFFIER	CPB	Multipurpose, for short- and medium-term analysis	Kranendonk and Verbruggen (2007)
New Zealand KITT	Central bank	DSGE	Lees (2009)
Norway NEMO	Central bank	DSGE	Brubakk et al. (2006)
Sweden RAMSES	Central bank	DSGE	Adolfson et al. (2007)

comprehend. In practice, there is thus a trade-off between the need to describe the evolution of a large number of variables and the need to have a tractable and transparent tool. The new models that have emerged through the 1990s and 2000s therefore tend to be relatively compact.

More fundamentally, even broadly similar models may differ in some of their main assumptions. Examples include:

- The choice of a production function allowing for substitution between inputs versus one in which factors are complements.
- Endogenization versus an exogenous assumption for the exchange rate.
- Making consumption a function of current income only, or also of expected income and wealth.

Since economic theory leaves room for disagreement on such assumptions, model diversity serves as a reminder that they can and do yield disparate results. This has in fact led some institutions to rely more on what a suite of models suggests than on what any single model predicts.

In other cases, the difference may seem minor at first, but can produce widely divergent outcomes. Seemingly benign differences in numerical values for a key parameter can be responsible for opposite results. For example, the sensitivity of imports to activity has a big influence on the demand multiplier – that is, the additional activity entailed *ex post* by an *ex ante* demand shock (say, an increase in foreign demand or in public spending). The multiplier will be relatively small if imports are very elastic, since in that case the extra demand will be met largely by a rise in imports rather than by domestic producers. Conversely, the multiplier will be large if imports are rather inelastic. Hence the policy implications differ significantly depending on the value of this parameter.[2]

One important way to test differences between models is to impart some basic shocks (such as a change in external demand, a tax cut, an interest rate shift or a wage hike). For the above reasons, the responses differ across models, illustrating that policy prescriptions can be model-dependent. Generally, models deliberately embody some important theoretical properties, therefore one would expect them to deliver results that are in line with the theoretical priors of the models' builders. This is not always self-evident, however, especially with large macroeconomic models combining a great variety of mechanisms, whose interaction may at times lead to surprising results.

Consider, for example, the size of the fiscal multiplier. This is a key simulation in practice as it measures the effect of fiscal policy on economic activity. It is

---

[2] One might object that the value of important parameters is not set arbitrarily, but derived from econometric estimation. Hence, different modellers should work with similar estimates. In practice, however, significant uncertainty attaches to many important parameter estimates.

measured as the final increase in GDP in relation to the *ex ante* size of the fiscal stimulus (see Table AIII.2).

Short-run multipliers from increased government spending tend to be slightly higher than 1 on average, while tax multipliers are smaller, averaging around 0.5. However, estimates vary considerably across models, partly (but not only) because of different underlying assumptions regarding the response of monetary conditions to fiscal loosening. Long-run fiscal multipliers – beyond two years – are generally lower or even occasionally negative when there is large crowding-out.

Table AIII.2   Range of responses to fiscal shocks across models

	All studies	Studies with both 1st and 2nd year multipliers	
	Year 1	Year 1	Year 2
Purchases of goods and services	1.1	1.2	1.3
	0.6–1.9	*0.9–1.9*	*0.5–2.2*
Corporate tax cut	0.3	0.3	0.5
	0.1–0.5	*0.1–0.5*	*0.2–0.8*
Personal income tax cut	0.5	0.5	0.8
	0.1–1.1	*0.1–1.1*	*0.2–1.4*
Indirect tax cut	0.5	0.2	0.4
	0.0–1.4	*0.0–0.6*	*0.0–0.8*
Social security contribution cut	0.4	0.3	0.6
	0.0–1.2	*0.0–0.5*	*0.2–1.0*

Notes: Difference of GDP level between baseline and a scenario with a 1% of GDP *ex ante* fiscal stock. Mean estimate reported on first line; low–high range repeated in *italics* on second line.
Source: OECD (2009), based on various sources.

Table AIII.3   Impact of an oil shock*

Model/Year no.	Impact on real GDP			Impact on CPI inflation		
	USA	Euro area	Japan	USA	Euro area	Japan
MULTIMOD III						
1	−0.3	−0.2	−0.1	0.8	0.7	0.3
2	−0.4	−0.4	−0.2	0.5	0.5	0.2
3	−0.4	−0.4	−0.3	0.3	0.4	0.1
GEM						
1	−0.4	−0.4	−0.2	0.1	0.1	0.1
NiGEM						
1	−0.1	−0.1	n.a.	0.2	0.2	n.a.
2	−0.2	−0.2	n.a.	0.3	0.1	n.a.
3	−0.3	−0.3	n.a.	0.2	0.1	n.a.
Long run	−0.4	−0.5	n.a.	0.1	0.1	n.a.

*Permanent, US$5 a barrel increase; difference between baseline and alternative scenario for GDP level and CPI inflation.
Sources: IMF (2000, 2004); Barrell and Pomerantz (2004).

Similarly, the response to a given oil shock differs across models (see Table AIII.3). Some of the divergences also reflect differences in the precise calibration of the shock and in the ancillary assumptions used in the simulations (notably, again, as regards the central bank's reaction function). In particular, the two IMF models used in this example (MULTIMOD and GEM) generate different results, especially for inflation.

AIII.4 Forecasting with a model

Forecasting with the help of a model is by no means a 'push-button' exercise, which would only require the updating of the series entering the model and then letting the model run freely over the forecast period to collect the results. To begin, assumptions about the evolution of the exogenous variables are needed, since their path is not determined by the model. In addition, the specificities of the ongoing cycle have to be taken into account, both to integrate the conclusions drawn from the short-term diagnosis and to assess the relevance of the relationships embedded in the model. And in the end, it is essential to ensure that the forecast is consistent and convincing.

Far from being a purely mechanical exercise, model-based forecasting is thus a delicate art. This section details the various steps that are involved: reading recent developments through the lens of the model; forecasting the exogenous variables; formulating assumptions about the residuals; and refining the baseline scenario through iteration and amendments. In addition, the forecast should be monitored on an ongoing basis, as new information arrives, which may call for adjustments.

AIII.4.1 Interpreting recent developments

The first step of the forecasting process is to check whether the model accounts fully for recent developments. Indeed, its equations have been estimated over some earlier period, and one should start by examining whether these estimated relationships have continued to hold over the recent past. Most crucial are the most recent observations, since they serve as the jump-off point for the forecast. This work is usually done equation by equation, though model blocks or even the whole model are sometimes simulated to measure their performance over recent periods. For each individual equation, for example, one can evaluate its stability over time by using a Chow test. A more common procedure, however, is to look at the sequence of residuals. Consider the following example:

$$\varphi(L)y_t = \theta(L)x_t + u_t \tag{AIII.1}$$

where y is the explained variable, x the vector of explanatory variables, L the lag operator, $\varphi(L)$ and $\theta(L)$ lag polynomials, and u the residual. This can be rewritten as:

$$u_t = \varphi(L)y_t - \theta(L)x_t \tag{AIII.2}$$

The sequence of u_t can then serve to balance the equation over the period for which observations of x and y are available. For the model as a whole, this operation is generally automatized: the endogenous y are treated as exogenous, the exogenous u as endogenous, and the software 'solves' the model over the stated period.

Examination of the residuals provides a quick diagnosis of how well the equations have performed over the recent past. One usually expects the residuals to have a zero mean and to be uncorrelated over time. If this is not the case, several situations may arise: a positive or negative bias may come to light for the recent observations; the residuals will increase or shrink continuously from a certain date onwards; or there are large changes in the residuals for the latest observation(s). However, before concluding that the equation has broken down, the recent fluctuations in u need to be compared with its behaviour over a longer period, to check whether recent movements are indeed outside the historical range.

If that is the case, four main reasons may explain the deterioration of the model's performance:

- *Measurement problems*. Some of the recent data are provisional and subject to significant subsequent revisions. If the model is right but the data wrong, incorrect measurement of any variable will be reflected in the residual. In fact, one of the often overlooked merits of good models is their ability to highlight potential data problems. This can be very helpful when establishing a proper near-term diagnosis.
- *Incorrect parameter estimation*. Even if the specification is correct, some of the parameter estimates may be inaccurate. Parameters may be unstable or may have moved since the previous estimation period.
- *Erroneous specification*. The specifications used in the model reflect the theoretical knowledge and data available at the time it was constructed and estimated, and are intended to represent the mechanisms that were operating most prominently in the past. When shocks or structural breaks occur, the specification may become obsolete. A frequent problem is the omission of explanatory variables that were unimportant in the past but have recently become influential. For example, the importance of financial developments for real decisions (such as investment or consumption) may have increased over time.
- *Exceptional factors*. A host of special factors may come into play that are difficult to model, including targeted economic policy measures (such as subsidies to the automobile sector or to housing), adverse weather conditions (storms or droughts), political or social events (such as major terrorist attacks or strikes), bunched orders to specific sectors of the economy (say, orders for a batch of aircraft), epidemiological surprises (mad cow disease,

swine flu) and so on. Unforeseen developments abroad may spill over, as was the case with the Asian crisis in 1997–8: capital moved back from the emerging markets to the advanced economies, causing a decline in long-term interest rates that could not otherwise be explained by the evolution of their fundamentals in the advanced economies.

During a forecasting round, one or several of these problems almost invariably arise with some of the equations. It is then important to understand the underlying reasons, and whether the divergence between observed and predicted values is temporary or durable, so that the equation can be used as it should in forecasting. If incorrect parameter estimation and/or erroneous specification are uncovered, one might in principle wish to re-specify and re-estimate these equations. In practice, there is not always the time or resources to do so immediately. In addition, once an equation has been altered, the properties of the model as a whole may change, which calls for further and more ambitious work. Very often, therefore, forecasters prefer to retain the original equations but with some *ad hoc* assumptions with regard to the behaviour of the residuals over the forecast period (see below).

The interpretation of recent developments requires the integration of what the model indicates and what the incoming information suggests. The latter usually encompasses the data released for the variables included in the model, but also other 'hard' or 'soft' indicators, such as survey data, qualitative or sectoral information, and so on. These allow an estimate of the 'present' to be established, for which national accounts data are not yet available (see Chapter 2). Using this type of information can greatly enhance the quality of the model-based forecast by helping to choose the right assumptions for the behaviour of the residuals.

There are several ways to combine the model and other tools for this type of near-term analysis. One is to use all the available information to build a benchmark forecast for the very short run, which is meant to be a stylized version of the more detailed quarterly national accounts data to be published later (see section 2.5 on bridge models). The model-based forecast then starts a couple of quarters later, using this benchmark as a base.

Finally, the model itself can help to refine the diagnosis of the current situation: if the latter is inconsistent with what the relationships in the model imply, and if the model has a good forecasting track record, a reconsideration of the diagnosis may be warranted.

AIII.4.2   Forecasting exogenous variables

For the model to be able to predict the endogenous variables, the exogenous ones need to be forecast. They belong to one of three groups: the international environment (such as growth in partner countries, foreign prices, the price of oil and other raw materials, exchange rates or foreign interest rates); macroeconomic policy (such as taxes, public spending or the monetary stance); and miscellaneous others (such as demography or technical progress).

In the case of an international model, the international environment is, of course, endogenous, even though certain variables such as the oil price or exchange rates may still be treated as exogenous. In the case of a national model, growth in the partner countries enters as an indicator of world demand (see Box 3.3). Similarly, foreign prices enter as a national competitiveness indicator (see Box 3.4). All this assumes that prior forecasts have been produced for the rest of the world, or at least for the country's main trading partners. This may not be feasible in-house. One way to proceed is then to use the forecasts published by international organizations such as the OECD, the IMF or the European Commission, or to use consensus forecasts.

The macroeconomic policy assumptions can be introduced as a conventional set of hypotheses or as the most likely scenario. Alternatively, reaction functions or rules can be used.

In the first approach, announced fiscal policy measures that are deemed to be likely to be implemented are taken into account. For the rest of the time horizon, however, projected budget developments are typically assumed to be in line with past trends, unless there are specific reasons to think otherwise. As regards monetary policy, the convention used in official forecasts is usually to keep policy-controlled interest rates unchanged at their current level. Alternatively, a constant real interest rate assumption is sometimes used, or the interest rate path expected by the market. Similarly, the exchange rate is often assumed to remain frozen at its latest level, which is justified if it follows a random walk (see section 4.7). Such assumptions are not necessarily realistic but they do have the advantage of simplicity. For official forecasts, another advantage is their relative neutrality. For example, central banks may not wish to reveal possible future moves (though they may wish to prepare markets) and governments may not want to be seen to be dictating monetary policy. A forecast based on such assumptions is informative, but only provided its conditional nature is well understood: it shows how things are likely to unfold if, for better or worse, current policies do not change course.

In the second approach, the most plausible – unconditional – economic policy scenario is used, even if it departs from what has been officially announced or if it involves measures that have not yet been unveiled. This approach tends to be favoured by private sector forecasters and clients, who are more interested in what is likely to happen than in what would happen under some more-or-less contrived policy assumptions. It is also pursued alongside the first approach by public sector forecasting teams when they advise policy makers, though the results then often remain confidential.

In fact, this second approach endogenizes economic policy variables, since it usually considers that the latter depend on the near-term outlook. For example, if a slowdown in demand is forecast, the conventional assumption of an unchanged interest rate may be highly implausible and will be replaced by a cut. In a similar vein, one might want to assume some exchange rate appreciation if its current level is widely considered to be significantly undervalued.

Yet another approach is to endogenize the behaviour of policy makers by introducing policy rules. For example, interest rates may be set according to a Taylor-type rule which combines an inflation target, a full-employment objective and some aversion *vis-à-vis* interest rate instability (see Chapter 4). Tax rates can be derived as ensuring the sustainability of public finances (for example, a forecast increase in the deficit or in the public debt ratio would automatically entail an assumed tax rise) or in respect of some rule to which the authorities have committed themselves (see Chapter 5).

None of these approaches is intrinsically superior to the others. Rather, they correspond to different needs.

AIII.4.3   Dealing with residuals: add-on factors

The next challenge is to decide how to deal with the residuals u_t over the forecast period. One might presume *a priori* that u_t should be set at zero over the forecast period, since by construction it should have a zero mean and not display any autocorrelation over time. In practice, however, this may not be appropriate, because of measurement, estimation or specification errors, or special factors causing the residuals not to behave in that fashion. Indeed, in many cases, setting the residuals for all variables to zero throughout the projection period would produce an awkward forecast. Instead, part or even the entirety of the recent residuals will be added on to the result that the equation itself predicts. These additions are sometimes referred to as 'add-on factors' or simply 'add factors'.

Tracing the residuals over the forecast period is done equation by equation, and reflects the views of the forecaster on the magnitude and persistence of factors that are not captured adequately by the model. In particular, future developments in the residuals (the u_t provided by the original estimation of the model) will be extrapolated depending on the interpretation of their past values and on the near-term diagnosis.

To illustrate this procedure, Equation (AIII.1) can be rewritten as follows, after the inversion of φ and differencing:

$$\Delta y_t = \varphi(L)^{-1}\theta(L)\Delta x_t + v_t \qquad\qquad (AIII.3)$$

where $v_t = \varphi(L)^{-1}\Delta u_t$. The right-hand side of Equation (AIII.3) is the sum of two contributions to the growth rate of the endogenous variable: the first term is the contribution from the changes in the explanatory variables, and the second is the contribution of the 'add-on factors' that are not captured by the explanatory variables.

When this equation is used in forecasting, a variety of assumptions can be made regarding the profile of the add-on factor going forward:

- The simplest is to set $u_t = 0$ for the whole forecast period. This is consistent with the model and is indeed warranted if u_t has behaved as white noise over the estimation period and if no disturbances other than those transiting via x_t are foreseen.
- The second option is to freeze u_t at its most recently observed level, or at its average over the recent past, if it is believed that the recent residuals correspond to a permanent shock.
- The third possibility, which is often the preferred one in practice, is to assume that $v_t = 0$ over the forecast period. In a sense, this is a 'neutral' assumption, since it means that only the factors captured explicitly in the model's explanatory variables influence the evolution of y_t.[3]
- Yet another option is to postulate a gradual convergence of u_t or v_t to zero, if it is felt that the factors causing the endogenous variable not to move in line with the model's prediction are likely to wane over time. The speed with which this is posited to happen should in principle be given some justification.

The variables for which this type of exercise is usually conducted are those that are hardest to pin down in a macroeconomic model, because of their great volatility or because they have too many different determinants. Examples include stockbuilding (which is notoriously volatile at quarterly frequencies) and exports of manufactured goods (when irregular orders make for abrupt shifts in the series). Some economic policy measures (one-off investment incentives, for example) are also reflected in the residuals, in so far as they are not integrated in the exogenous variables.

The seemingly *ad hoc* nature of these adjustments is sometimes criticized, but they do have a statistical rationale. In an econometric model, the residual reflects the influence of the factors that the exogenous variables leave out. When relevant information is available that cannot be incorporated adequately into the explanatory variables, it makes sense to adjust the residuals to include

---

[3] Note that the second and third options are clearly different: a constant u_t going forward does not imply that $v_t = 0$, since past values of u also enter v.

it. Ideally, however, such adjustments should be based on some rigorous quantification outside the model.

Furthermore, when a particular econometric equation in the model is open to serious doubts, it may even be preferable to set it aside and use an alternative forecasting method – and in turn to estimate explicitly the future path of the 'add-on factors'. For example, residential investment is often poorly explained econometrically, as it is highly volatile and may react strongly to special fiscal incentives or other temporary elements. Given the considerable gestation lags associated with housing construction, it is frequently preferable to use housing starts as a leading indicator of residential investment in the context of short-term forecasting. But even then, the equation remains of interest: the behaviour of the residual over the forecast period says something about the imbalances that may have built up in the past or about how 'normal' is the forecast path.

In sum, playing around with the residuals gives forecasters some leeway to nuance what the model would mechanically ordain. Therefore, two teams of forecasters using identical models and data may still produce palpably different forecasts.

AIII.4.4 Refining the baseline scenario

Once the exogenous variables and the add-on factors have been set, the model is run to generate the values for the endogenous variables over the forecast period. The fact that, by construction, the model has to be consistent with the national accounts identities imparts some coherence to this initial set of forecasts. But this is not enough, as it does not guarantee that they make economic sense. Indeed, the first run usually has a number of flaws, be it as regards the overall story or some of the components. The next step is thus to identify and correct these shortcomings, in order to re-run the model differently.

Some elements of the forecast may sound implausible to sectoral specialists. There may also be inconsistencies between the different blocks or in relation to the exogenous assumptions. A typical checklist would include such questions as:

- Is the rate of GDP growth consistent with what is assumed for partner countries?
- Are the forecast increases in prices, wages and productivity consistent with the phase of the cycle?
- Is the evolution of the saving rate consistent with household confidence indicators?
- Is the exchange rate assumption sensible given the forecast for activity, interest rates and the external accounts?
- Might the forecast developments prompt an economic policy reaction?

A forecast that fails on some of the above criteria should be reconsidered and the model should be run again – for example, with a different set of assumptions for the exogenous variables or new add-on factors. In principle, this process is iterated until a consistent and plausible forecast emerges.

A common way to help bring out the logic of the forecast is to decompose the latter into different blocks, and to try to tell a credible story for each of the main behavioural aspects, and then a robust overall story that weaves all the elements together. The treatment of the 'add-on factors' will play an important part when communicating these stories.

AIII.4.5   Monitoring the forecast

A forecasting round is thus a heavy undertaking, especially with large models. Very often, it takes place quarterly at best. However, between two forecasting rounds, the world moves on and the forecast needs to be adjusted.

Monitoring first involves checking whether what is observed is in line with the model's forecast. Where the two diverge, the deviation must be analysed, so that the proper adjustments can be effected for the remainder of the forecast period. Broadly speaking, three sorts of discrepancies can arise:

- National accounts data revisions for the recent past, which had previously served as the launchpad for the forecast.
- An inaccurate forecast for an exogenous variable: for example, oil prices may have risen much more than anticipated. In some cases, the implications may be assessed by constructing an alternative scenario, as described below.
- An incorrect choice of add-on factors, which may be redressed by altering their profile for the rest of the forecast period.

AIII.4.6   Forecasting with DSGE models

Policy analysis rather than forecasting *per se* has been the prime motivation for developing DSGE models. The emphasis on theoretical principles and RE has for some time been difficult to reconcile with empirical observations. Data issues (for example, filtering the data before estimating the model, whereas forecasts of actual data are needed to model the RE effects) have also hindered a quick dissemination of academic products to practitioners. Furthermore, the somewhat limited size of DSGE models has acted as an impediment, in so far as forecasters wish to form a view on a wide range of variables rather than just on a few headline ones.

These hurdles are gradually being overcome, however, and a number of DSGE builders now claim that their models have reached sufficient maturity to perform well in forecasting competitions. For example, Smets and Wouters (2007) compare the forecasting performance of their DSGE model of the US economy with that of Bayesian vector autoregressive (BVAR) models: they find similar in-sample fit and comparable or improved forecasting performance out of sample, in particular at medium-term horizons. Encouraging results are also reported, based on real-time data, by Edge *et al.* (2009) for Edo, a detailed DSGE model used at the US Federal Reserve.

One way to improve the forecasting performance of DSGE models is to incorporate available and relevant conditioning information. This may be useful when some variables are observed before the model variables (financial developments or sharp moves in oil prices are cases in point), or else when some other model is believed to be superior to the DSGE model for forecasting the variable used as conditioning information. This approach is now used by several central banks and can significantly improve the usefulness of DSGE models in forecasting (Adolfson *et al.*, 2007; Maih, 2009).

Even so, it is not (yet?) widely accepted that DSGE models should play a decisive part in forecasting. Many policy-oriented economists continue to see these models as being useful for thinking about the workings of the economy, yet potentially highly misleading when taken to actual data (Blanchard, 2008). Good fit may not suffice, as this may be obtained via strong priors that need not hold when forecasting. Not enough is yet known about the forecasting performance of DSGE models to convince daily number crunchers to rely on them.

Hence, in practice, DSGE models are far from having supplanted reduced-form time-series macroeconomic models. Central banks have been the most eager users of DSGE models. Even there, however, they have penetrated the core forecasting process in only a few cases (such as the Bank of Canada and the Swedish Riksbank).

AIII.5   Overall assessment

Models can do a lot. Even so, they have been criticized for lacking theoretical foundations, for using overly restrictive empirical specifications, and for mediocre forecast accuracy. The truth is that the 'art' of model-building consists in striking adequate compromises between conflicting demands. This section discusses these allegations and concludes that, despite their limitations, models are clearly useful.

AIII.5.1   Three criticisms

The first type of critique emphasizes the insufficient theoretical foundations of models. Unsurprisingly, such criticism is often expressed by academics or theory-oriented economists. It stresses, for example, that models often study behaviour in a partial equilibrium framework, ignoring many of the agents' concomitant constraints and decisions (as when analysing household consumption considered apart from residential and financial asset investment choices, or from labour supply decisions). Other examples are when a lack of or poor-quality data entails departures from the theoretical model in the empirical equations, or when the form for dynamic equations is chosen in an *ad hoc* manner rather than based on a theoretical rationale. Some would even question standard simplifying assumptions, such as that of a representative agent.

A well-known theoretical objection to models is the so-called Lucas critique, which states that they are vulnerable to regime shifts (Lucas, 1976): macroeconomic models cannot be used to predict the impact of future shocks or policy initiatives because their estimated parameters reflect average behaviour in the past. If the environment or policies are now different, these parameters might also have changed. The reason is that they are reduced-form parameters reflecting the combination of truly deep structural parameters (such as tastes and technology), which are the only ones that will not change, and regime-dependent characteristics. Hence, the only way out would be to write and estimate an authentically structural model, devoid of any reduced-form parameters.

A second line of criticism stresses empirics. This view was promoted by Sims (1980) in particular, who deplored that empirical model specifications were unduly restrictive, for several reasons. First, the practical distinction between exogenous and endogenous variables is largely arbitrary and is not formally tested. Second, the specifications used in practice are often imposed equation by equation, where economic theory instead implies more complex, cross-equation restrictions. And third, the dynamic structure of the specification is typically *ad hoc* (an objection that overlaps with the first set of criticisms). Sims argued that it was impossible to overcome all these problems in the context of traditional macroeconomic models, and advocated the use of pure time series techniques, such as VARs, which *a priori* seem less restrictive (see Annex II).

Finally, macroeconomic models are frequently criticized for poor forecasting performance. This is the criticism that is heard most often in policy making circles. As discussed at length in Chapter 7, their forecasting accuracy indeed leaves much to be desired. Moreover, the uncertainty relates not only to the baseline scenario, but also to the alternative ones. The assessment of the risks depends on the calibration of the corresponding assumptions, which is difficult not only *ex ante* but even *ex post*. Furthermore, model-based evaluation of economic policy measures is equally delicate. It requires the introduction of assumptions that are not unambiguously supported empirically and for which economic theory does not provide clear-cut answers. For example, will tax cuts stimulate consumption by boosting households' disposable income, or will they encourage precautionary saving because households factor in the tax increases needed in the future to finance today's largesse?

AIII.5.2   A useful toolkit none the less

These are, admittedly, genuine limitations. However, they do not suggest that modellers should stop forecasting but instead that they strike the right balance between conflicting needs and keep improving their instruments. Moreover, though the various criticisms described above are well taken, the profession has tried to address them.

Indeed, the macro-modelling landscape is an ever-changing one, as modellers strive to respond to both criticisms and actual events. For example, the Sims critique has been weakened by later developments in econometric methodology. In particular, the spreading of cointegration techniques and error correction models has allowed the combination of theoretically reasonable long-run properties and data-driven short-term dynamics. In addition, increased use is being made of multivariate systems in which theory sets the identifying constraints, while the technology available to estimate them has improved.

In a similar vein, several leading macroeconomic models have been reconfigured in recent decades to better integrate the different blocks and to strengthen the connection between microeconomic optimization behaviour and the macroeconomic relationships embodied in these models. Much has been done to expand the supply-side of models and to tie in their long-run properties in a theoretically-consistent way. With regard to the Lucas critique, while much ink has been spilt over it, its practical importance is open to doubt. It is dubious that a purely structural, policy-invariant model can ever be constructed (Altissimo *et al.*, 2002).

All things considered, the combined use of techniques such as error correction models and strengthened attention to theoretical priors has to a large extent responded to the early criticisms of theoreticians and econometricians. Moreover, and perhaps more fundamentally, one has to keep in mind the inevitable trade-offs between theoretical views, empirical criteria and the required flexibility to answer policy makers' questions. The latter imperative cannot be underestimated: in a policy context, what matters most are not micro-foundations or test statistics, but looser criteria such as broad conformity with agreed views and suitability for analysing the problem at issue.[4]

---

[4] Don and Verbruggen (2006) list six criteria that a model ought to meet for policy purposes: qualitative plausibility; quantitative plausibility; broad correspondence with the results of empirical studies, including time series analysis; a good match with recent data; good simulation characteristics of the model as a whole; and suitability of the model for the analysis in question.

Other limitations, such as limited actual forecasting power, appear to be more resilient, however. Moreover, new weaknesses have come to the fore with the recent crisis, such as insufficient modelling of real/financial interactions. That said, macroeconomic models do not fare badly in forecasting competitions with other tools (such as purely statistical models), at least at horizons exceeding one year. In addition, while their forecasting performance is especially disappointing around turning points, this weakness is shared by the other forecasting methods. And macroeconomic models provide an explicit economic story when communicating the forecasts, in particular when compared to more 'press button' or 'black box' approaches.

At the same time, models are used more wisely, with more systematic recourse to variants and a more thorough documentation of the underlying assumptions and mechanisms. Notwithstanding their enduring weaknesses, models remain widely used and continue to play a key role in forecasting as well as in policy analysis. On the forecasting side, they allow analysts to put together and to process a wealth of data, in a coherent framework, and provide structure for an internally consistent forecasting narrative. In policy analysis too, models are powerful instruments, allowing analysts to answer 'what if...?' questions. As discussed at greater length in Chapter 8, models can test practitioners' or policy makers' views by working out their implications before any real-life experimentation.

AIII.5.3 Assessing DSGE models

In a sense, DSGE models are the outcome of the rejuvenation of macroeconomic modelling. They are highly sophisticated constructs that constitute a full response to the criticisms of traditional models by theory-oriented economists. They blend forward-looking optimizing behaviour with advanced simulation techniques. To many they have become the incarnation of modern macroeconometrics. Others, however, and in particular practitioners producing daily forecasts, tend to be less convinced.

The major strength of DSGE models is to derive a structural view of the economy that serves as a basis for estimating macroeconomic relationships less arbitrarily than is often done. This is a response to both the Lucas critique and the Sims critique. The former is avoided to the extent that 'deep' parameters describing preferences, technology and 'true' structural shocks are identified. As for the latter, DSGE models are estimated using the equilibrium conditions of the economy, eliminating the requirement to specify exclusionary restrictions, to which Sims objected (Fernandez-Villaverde, 2009). In turn, these features are likely to improve the accuracy of model estimation and make them more robust to regime changes, thereby enhancing forecasting performance. This could pave the way for a new approach to forecasting, possibly with a mix of non-structural methods such as VAR models (see Box AIII.2).

Box AIII.2   Mixing methods: DSGE-VAR

It has long been acknowledged that the advantages of DSGE models in terms of theoretical consistency may come at a cost in terms of model fit. DSGE models remain very simplified representations that impose strong restrictions and therefore may fail to match the data. At the other end of the toolbox, VAR models are prominently data-oriented but maybe overly so, in so far as too few constraints translate into imprecise parameter estimates.

One option is then to get the best of both by feeding a (Bayesian) VAR with a set of DSGE-determined priors. Priors increase the precision of estimates and, if warranted, improve both model fit and forecast accuracy.

Using DSGE models as priors means that restrictions derived from theory will be imposed loosely rather than rigidly (del Negro and Schorfeide, 2007). That is, a restriction will be maintained if it is not clearly rejected by the data, but some flexibility is safeguarded. The 'degree of tightness' in following this approach may vary and indeed be partly data-determined, depending on whether the DSGE appears to fit or to be at odds with the data.

Another interesting by-product of DSGE models is to evaluate the contribution of past shocks to aggregate fluctuations. This may be achieved by exhibiting variance decompositions of, say, GDP or inflation, or historical decompositions of the sources of fluctuations. For example, Smets and Wouters (2003) find that output variations in the euro area are driven primarily by a preference shock and a monetary policy shock at a one-year horizon, with supply-side shocks (labour supply and productivity) growing in importance as the horizon lengthens. Such calculations are highly relevant when attempting to understand the ultimate drivers of business cycles, and are hard to undertake with traditional macroeconomic models containing shocks that do not necessarily have a clear interpretation.

Yet DSGE technology still has a long way to go. One important shortcoming that the 2007 financial crisis has evidenced is the need to take the financial sector better into account (though in fairness, DSGE models were not the only ones that failed in that respect). Finance typically got short shrift in DSGE models before the recent crisis. Financial intermediaries were often ignored completely and financial markets assumed to be efficient, with asset prices reflecting fundamental values. This left little room for instabilities stemming from the financial sector (such as bubbles) or mechanisms that amplify business cycle developments (the so-called pro-cyclicality). Thus, until recently at least, DSGE models have tended to put too much weight on real or monetary disturbances and pay insufficient attention to financial frictions (Tovar, 2009). More fundamentally, perhaps, the 2007 financial crisis was a painful reminder that the hypotheses underpinning these models – notably that markets are efficient and agents behave rationally on the basis of their expectations – are, to say the least, debatable.

Some work has none the less already been done to incorporate financial mechanisms in DSGE models (notably originating in Bernanke *et al.*, 1999). Given the repeated waves of financial disruptions, of which the 2007 episode is a prominent case, modellers face an obvious challenge to go further and enrich their specifications so as to better encompass such phenomena.[5]

Some critics of the DSGE approach go a step further by sketching a more fundamental rethink of the approach. For Blanchard (2008) DSGE models represent an impressive achievement but also have obvious flaws. Bayesian estimation, while being attractive, relies on priors that may be quite arbitrary in practice. There also remains a tension between fully anchoring specifications on first principles and taking the model to the data. This may lead modellers to introduce *ad hoc* micro-foundations, where data determination of short-run dynamics would be more straightforward.

Ultimately, the usefulness of DSGE models has to be assessed by looking at the services they can render. From this standpoint it is not clear that DSGE models are about to supplant more traditional macroeconomic models. One simple reason is that, despite the progress in computing power, DSGE models remain complicated tools that are resource-intensive to build, maintain and use. Size is a related issue, as policy makers need a comprehensive view of the economy involving many variables.

Perhaps more fundamentally, the empirical performance of DSGE models has to be demonstrated further. This means both extending the coverage of current models and finding the right balance between model structure and model fit. For the present it might be best to avoid asking too much from these models. Their greatest contribution is to help frame some policy discussions by developing intuitions about how the economy works. But the more traditional models are likely to remain important in the core forecasting and policy process.

---

[5] There are many other challenges, notably the size and dynamics of fiscal multipliers, a hotly-debated point that is of crucial importance for policy-oriented forecasters.

Further reading

To further understand models, readers would perhaps benefit primarily from actually handling or (co)building one. People outside institutions running models might turn to Fair's books and website (fairmodel.econ.yale.edu), from which Fair's model and a large documentation are available. The papers describing the models in Table AIII.1 are also useful. However, few contributions have taken an across-the-board view of macroeconomic modelling in recent years. Whitley (1994) did so, but more recent developments are not covered in this work.

On the other hand, a burgeoning literature has emerged on DSGE models during the 2000s, as this became the new fashion. Galí (2008) provides an introduction to New Keynesian DSGE models, and Tovar (2009) an overview of DSGE models and their use by central banks. Fernandez-Villaverde (2009) outlines the associated econometric challenges, and Laxton (2008) offers a primer on the IMF's DSGE models. DSGE tools can be found on cepremap.cnrs.fr/dynare.

Bibliography

Adams, B., Bottelier, P., Ozyildirim, A. and Sima-Friedman, J. (2010) On the Selection of Leading Economic Indicators for China, Conference Board Economics Program Working Paper Series, No. 10–02.

Adolfson, M., Laséen, S., Lindé, J. and Villani, M. (2007) RAMSES – a New General Equilibrium Model for Monetary Policy Analysis, *Economic Review*, no. 2.

Adolfson, M., Andersson, M., Lindé, J., Villani, M. and Vredin, A. (2007) Modern Forecasting Models in Action: Improving Macro Economic Analyses at Central Banks, *International Journal of Central Banking*, vol. 3, no. 4.

Adrian, T. and Shin, H. (2008) Financial Intermediaries, Financial Stability and Monetary Policy, Federal Reserve Bank of Kansas City 2008 Jackson Hole Economic Symposium Proceedings.

Aggarwal, R., Lucey, B. and Mohanty, S. (2009) The Forward Exchange Rate Bias Puzzle Is Persistent: Evidence from Stochastic and Nonparametric Cointegration Tests, *Eastern Finance Association Financial Review*, vol. 44, no. 4.

Aglietta, M., Borgy, V., Chateau, J., Juillard, M., le Cacheux, J., Le Garrec, G. and Touzé, V. (2007) Asian Catch Up, World Growth and International Capital Flows in the XXIst Century: A Prospective Analysis with the INGENUE 2 Model, CEPII Working Paper No. 2007-01.

Ahearne, A., Griever, W. and Warnock, F. (2004) Information Costs and Home Bias: An Analysis of US Holdings of Foreign Equities, *Journal of International Economics*, vol. 62, no. 2.

Ahrend, R., Catte, P. and Price, R. (2006) Factors Behind Low Long-Term Interest Rates, OECD Economics Department Working Paper No. 490.

Akritidis, L. (2002) Accuracy Assessment of National Accounts Statistics, *Economic Trends*, no. 589.

Alquist, R., Kilian, L. and Vigfusson, R. (2011) Forcasting the Price of Oil, CEPR Discussion Paper, No. 8388.

Altissimo, F., Siviero, S. and Terlizzese, D. (2002) How Deep are the Deep Parameters?, *Annales d'Économie et de Statistique*, no. 67–8.

Altissimo, F., Cristadoro, R., Forni, M., Lippi, M. and Veronese, G. (2007) New EuroCOIN: Tracking Economic Growth in Real Time, CEPR Discussion Paper No. 5633.

Amato, J. and Laubach, T. (2000) The Role of Forecasts in Monetary Policy, *Federal Reserve Bank of Kansas City Economic Review*, second quarter.

463

Anas, J., Biblio, M., Ferrara, L. and Lo Duca, M. (2007) Business Cycle Analysis with Multivariate Markov Switching Models, in G. Mazzi and G. Savio (eds), *Growth and Cycle in the Euro Zone*, New York: Palgrave Macmillan.

Andersen, T., Davis, R., Mikosch, T. and Kreiss, J.-P. (eds) (2009) *Handbook of Financial Time Series*, New York: Springer-Verlag.

Andersson, E., Bock, D. and Frisén, M. (2004) Detection of Turning Points in Business Cycles, *Journal of Business Cycle Measurement and Analysis*, vol. 1, no. 1.

Andersson, M. and Aranki, T. (2009) A Comparison of Different Forecasters' Ability Given the Publication Date Effect, *Sveriges Riksbank Economic Review*, no. 1.

Ando, A. and Modigliani, F. (1963) The 'Life Cycle' Hypothesis of Saving: Aggregate Implications and Tests, *American Economic Review*, vol. 53, no. 1.

André, C. (2010) A Bird's Eye View of OECD Housing Markets, OECD Economics Department Working Paper No. 746.

Angelini, E., Camba-Méndez, G., Giannone, D., Rünstler, G. and Reichlin, L. (2008) Short-Term Forecasts of Euro Area GDP Growth, ECB Working Paper No. 949.

Ariga, K. and Matsui, K. (2003) Mismeasurement of the CPI, NBER Working Paper No. 9436.

Armstrong, J. (ed.) (2001) *Principles of Forecasting: A Handbook for Researchers and Practitioners*, Norwell, MA: Kluwer.

Artis, M. and Taylor, M. (1995) Misalignment, Debt Accumulation and Fundamental Equilibrium Exchange Rates, *National Institute Economic Review*, no. 153.

Artis, M., Bladen-Hovell, R. and Zhang, W. (1995) Turning Points in the International Business Cycle: An Analysis of the OECD Leading Indicators for the G-7 Countries, *OECD Economic Studies*, no. 24.

Aruoba, S., Diebold, F. and Scotti, C. (2009) Real-Time Measurement of Business Conditions, *Journal of Business and Economic Statistics*, vol. 27, no. 4.

Ashenfelter, O. and Card, D. (eds) (1999) *Handbook of Labor Economics*, Amsterdam: Elsevier.

Ashiya, M. (2009) Strategic Bias and Professional Affiliations of Macroeconomic Forecasters, *Journal of Forecasting*, vol. 28, no. 2.

Ashworth, P. and Davis, P. (2001) Some Evidence on Financial Factors in the Determination of Aggregate Business Investment for the G7 countries, NIESR Discussion Paper No. 187.

Auerbach, A. and Gale, W. (2009) Fiscal Policy to Stabilize Economic Activity, Paper presented at the Jackson Hole Symposium on Financial Stability and Macroeconomic Policy, August.

Auerbach, A., Kotlikoff, L. and Leibfritz, W. (eds) (1999) *Generational Accounting Around the World*, Chicago, IL: University of Chicago Press.

Baffigi, A., Golinelli, R. and Parigi, G. (2004) Bridge Models to Forecast the Euro Area GDP, *International Journal of Forecasting*, vol. 20, no. 3.

Bagnoli, P., McKibbin, W. and Wilcoxen, P. (1996) Global Economic Prospects: Medium-Term Projections and Structural Change, Brookings Discussion Papers in International Economics, no. 121.

Ball, L. and Mankiw, G. (2002) The NAIRU in Theory and Practice, *Journal of Economic Perspectives*, vol. 16, no. 4.

Bandholz, H. and Funke, M. (2003) In Search of Leading Indicators of Economic Activity in Germany, *Journal of Forecasting*, vol. 22, no. 4.

Bank of England (1999) *Economic Models at the Bank of England*, London: Bank of England.

Bank of Japan (2006a) *The Introduction of a New Framework for the Conduct of Monetary Policy*, 9 March.

Bank of Japan (2006b) *The Bank's Thinking on Price Stability*, 10 March.

Barnhill, T. and Souto, M. (2007) Stochastic Volatilities and Correlations, Extreme Values and Modeling the Macroeconomic Environment Under Which Brazilian Banks Operate, IMF Working Paper No. 07/290.

Barrell, R. and Pomerantz, O. (2004) Oil Prices and the World Economy, NIESR Discussion Paper No. 242.

Barro, R. (1997) *Determinants of Economic Growth: A Cross-Country Empirical Study*, Cambridge, MA: MIT Press.

Barro, R. and Gordon, D. (1983) A Positive Theory of Monetary Policy in a Natural Rate Model, *Journal of Political Economy*, vol. 91, no. 4.

Bartelmus, P. (1999) Greening the National Accounts: Approach and Policy Use, United Nations, DESA Discussion Paper No. 3.

Batchelor, R. (2007) Bias in Macroeconomic Forecasts, *International Journal of Forecasting*, vol. 23, no. 2.

Batini, N. and Turnbull, K. (2002) A Dynamic Monetary Conditions Index for the UK, *Journal of Policy Modeling*, vol. 24, no. 3.

Batista, C. and Zalduendo, J. (2004) Can the IMF's Medium-Term Growth Projections be Improved?, IMF Working Paper WP/04/203.

Baxter, M. and King, R. (1999) Measuring Business Cycles: Approximate Band-Pass Filters for Economic Time Series, *Review of Economics and Statistics*, vol. 81, no. 4.

Bean, C. (2001) The Formulation of Monetary Policy at the Bank of England, *Bank of England Quarterly Bulletin*, Winter.

Beffy, P.-O., Ollivaud, P., Richardson, P. and Sédillot, F. (2006) New OECD Methods for Supply-side and Medium-term Assessments: A Capital Services Approach, OECD Economics Department Working Paper No. 482.

Belli, P., Anderson, J., Barnum, H., Dixon, J. and Tan, J. (1997) *Handbook on Economic Analysis of Investment Operations*, Washington, DC: World Bank, Operations Policy Department.

Bénassy-Quéré, A., Béreau, S. and Mignon, V. (2008) Equilibrium Exchange Rates: a Guidebook for the Euro-Dollar Rate, CEPII Working Paper No. 2008-02.

Benati, L. (2001) Band-Pass Filtering, Cointegration and Business Cycle Analysis, Bank of England Working Paper No. 142.

Berg, A. and Patillo, C. (1999) Are Currency Crises Predictable? A Test, *IMF Staff Papers*, vol. 46, no. 2.

Berger, H. and Österholm, P. (2008) Does Money Matter for US Inflation? Evidence from Bayesian VARs, IMF Working Paper No. 08/76.

Berger, H., Ehrmann, M. and Fratzscher, M. (2009) Forecasting ECB Monetary Policy: Accuracy Is a Matter of Geography, *European Economic Review*, vol. 53, no. 8.

Bernanke, B. (2002) Deflation: Making Sure 'It' Doesn't Happen Here, Remarks before the National Economists Club, Washington, DC, 21 November.

Bernanke, B. (2005) The Global Saving Glut and the U.S. Current Account Deficit, Speech at the Homer Jones Lecture, St. Louis, Missouri, 14 April.

Bernanke, B. (2007) The Housing Market and Subprime Lending, Speech at the 2007 International Monetary Conference, Cape Town, South Africa, 5 June.

Bernanke, B. (2008) Federal Reserve Policies in the Financial Crisis, Speech to the Greater Austin Chamber of Commerce, Austin, Texas, 1 December.

Bernanke, B. (2009a) The Crisis and the Policy Response, Speech at the Stamp Lecture, London School of Economics, London, England, 13 January.

Bernanke, B. (2009b) The Federal Reserve's Balance Sheet, Speech at the Federal Reserve Bank of Richmond 2009 Credit Markets Symposium, Charlotte, North Carolina, 3 April.

Bernanke, B. (2010) Monetary Policy and the Housing Bubble, Speech at the Annual Meeting of the American Economic Association, Atlanta, Georgia, 3 January.

Bernanke, B., Boivin, J. and Eliasz, P. (2004) Measuring the Effects of Monetary Policy: A Factor-Augmented Vector Autoregressive (FAVAR) Approach, NBER Working Paper No. 10220.

Bernanke, B., Gertler, M. and Gilchrist, S. (1996) The Financial Accelerator and Flight to Quality, *Review of Economics and Statistics*, vol. 78, no. 1.

Bernanke, B., Gertler, M. and Gilchrist, S. (1999) The Financial Accelerator in a Quantitative Business Cycle Framework, in J. Taylor and M. Woodford (eds), *Handbook of Macroeconomics*, Vol. 1C, North-Holland: Elsevier.

Beveridge, S. and Nelson, C. (1981) A New Approach to Decomposition of Economic Time Series into Permanent and Transitory Components with Particular Attention to Measurement of the 'Business Cycle', *Journal of Monetary Economics*, vol. 7, no. 2.

Beveridge, S. and Oickle, C. (1994) A Comparison of Box–Jenkins and Objective Methods for Determining the Order of a Non-Seasonal ARMA Model, *Journal of Forecasting*, vol. 13, no. 5.

Bezemer, D. (2009) 'No One Saw This Coming': Understanding Financial Crisis through Accounting Models, MPRA Paper No. 15892.

BIS (Bank for International Settlements) (2009a) *MC Compendium, Monetary Policy Frameworks and Central Bank Market Operations*, Markets Committee of Central Banks, May.

BIS (Bank for International Settlements) (2009b) *79th Annual Report*, Basel: BIS.

Blanchard, O. (1990) Suggestions for a New Set of Fiscal Indicators, OECD Economics Department Working Paper No. 79.

Blanchard, O. (2008) The State of Macro, NBER Working Paper No. 14259.

Blanchard, O. and Katz, L. (1999) Wage Dynamics: Reconciling Theory and Evidence, *American Economic Review*, vol. 89, no. 2.

Blanchard, O. and Quah, D. (1989) The Dynamic Effects of Aggregate Demand and Supply Disturbances, *American Economic Review*, vol. 79, no. 4.

Blinder, A. (1990) *Inventory Theory and Consumer Behavior*, Ann Arbor, MI: University of Michigan Press.

Blinder, A. (1998) *Central Banking in Theory and Practice*, Cambridge, MA: MIT Press.

Blinder, A. and Zandi, M. (2010) How the Great Recession Was Brought to an End, Mimeo, July.

Bloem, A., Dippelsman, R. and Mæhle, N. (2001) *Quarterly National Accounts Manual: Concepts, Data Sources, and Compilation*, Washington, DC: IMF.

Bloomfield, P. (2000) *Fourier Analysis of Time Series: An Introduction*, 2nd edn, New York: John Wiley.

Board of Governors of the Federal Reserve System (2010) Credit and Liquidity Programs and the Balance Sheet.

Bollerslev, T. (1986) Generalized Autoregressive Conditional Heteroskedasticity, *Journal of Econometrics*, vol. 31, no. 3.

Bonin, H. and Patxot, C. (2004) Generational Accounting as a Tool to Assess Fiscal Sustainability: An Overview of the Methodology, IZA Discussion Paper No. 990.

Borio, C. and Drehmann, M. (2009) Assessing the Risk of Banking Crises – Revisited, *BIS Quarterly Review*, March.

Borio, C. and Zhu, H. (2008) Capital Regulation, Risk-Taking and Monetary Policy: A Missing Link in the Transmission Mechanism?, BIS Working Paper No. 268.

Boughton, J. (2001) *Silent Revolution, The International Monetary Fund 1979–1989*, Washington, DC: International Monetary Fund.

Boulhol, H. (2009) The Effects of Population Structure on Employment and Productivity, OECD Economics Department Working Paper No. 684.

Bouthevillain, C., Cour-Thimann, P., Hernandez Cos, P., Mohr, M., Tujula, M., Langenus G., Momigliano, S. and Van Den Dool, G. (2001) Cyclically Adjusted Budget Balances: An Alternative Approach, ECB Working Paper No. 77.

Box, G. and Jenkins, A. (1976) *Time Series Analysis: Forecasting and Control*, San Francisco, CA: Holden Day.

Bowman, C. and Husain, A. (2004) Forecasting Commodity Prices: Futures Versus Judgment, IMF Working Paper No. 04/41.

Brainard, W. (1967) Uncertainty and the Effectiveness of Policy, *American Economic Review*, vol. 57, no. 2.

British Academy (2009) The Global Financial Crisis – Why Didn't Anybody Notice?, *British Academy Review*, no. 14.

Brown, R. (1963) *Smoothing, Forecasting and Prediction of Discrete Time Series*, Englewood Cliffs, NJ: Prentice-Hall.

Brubakk, L., Hsebo, T. A., Maih, J., Olsen, K. and Ostnor, M. (2006) Finding NEMO: Documentation of the Norwegian Economy Model, Norges Bank staff memo No. 2006/6.

Brunnermeier, M. (2001) *Asset Pricing under Asymmetric Information: Bubbles, Crashes, Technical Analysis, and Herding*, Oxford, UK: Oxford University Press.

Brunnermeier, M. (2009) Deciphering the Liquidity and Credit Crunch 2007–2008, *Journal of Economic Perspectives*, vol. 23, no. 1.

Budd, A. (1998) Economic Policy, With and Without Forecasts, *Bank of England Quarterly Bulletin*, November.

Burniaux, J.-M., Duval, R. and Jaumotte, F. (2003) Coping with Ageing: A Dynamic Approach to Quantify the Impact of Alternative Policy Options on Future Labour Supply in OECD Countries, OECD Economics Department Working Paper No. 371.

Burns, A. and Mitchell, W. (1946) *Measuring Business Cycles*, New York: NBER.

Burns, T. (1986) The Interpretation and Use of Economic Predictions, *Proceedings of the Royal Society of London, Series A*, vol. 407.

Burns, T. (2001) The Costs of Forecast Errors, in D. Hendry and N. Ericsson (eds), *Understanding Economic Forecasts*, Cambridge, MA: MIT Press.

Camacho, M. and Perez-Quiros, G. (2008) A Model for the Real-Time Forecasting of GDP in the Euro Area (EURO-STING), Banco de España, Monthly Bulletin, April.

Campbell, S. (2004) Macroeconomic Volatility, Predictability and Uncertainty in the Great Moderation: Evidence from the Survey of Professional Forecasters, Board of Governors of the Federal Reserve System, Finance and Economics Discussion Series, 2004-52.

Carabenciov, I., Ermolaev, I., Freedman, C., Juillard, M., Kamenik, O., Korshunov, D., Laxton, D. and Laxton, J. (2008) A Small Quarterly Multi-Country Projection Model with Financial-Real Linkages and Oil Prices, IMF Working Paper No. 08/280.

Carone, G., Denis, C., Mc Morrow, K., Mourre, G. and Röger, W. (2006) Long-Term Labour Productivity and GDP Projections for the EU25 Member States: A Production Function Framework, *European Economy Economic Papers*, no. 253.

Caruana, J. (2010) Systemic Risk: How to Deal With It? *BIS Paper*, 12 February, Bank for International Settlements.

Casey, B., Oxley, H., Whitehouse, E., Antolin, P., Duval, R. and Leibfritz, W. (2003) Policies for an Ageing Society: Recent Measures and Areas for Further Reform, OECD Economics Department Working Paper No. 369.

Cashin, P. and McDermott, J. (2002) The Long-Run Behavior of Commodity Prices: Small Trends and Big Variability, *IMF Staff Papers*, vol. 49, no. 2.

CBO (Congressional Budget Office) (2004) *A Summary of Alternative Methods for Estimating Potential GDP*, Washington, DC: CBO.

CBO (Congressional Budget Office) (2007) *Housing Wealth and Consumer Spending*, Washington, DC: CBO.

CBO (Congressional Budget Office) (2009a) *CBO's Long-Term Projections for Social Security: 2009 Update*, Washington, DC: CBO.

CBO (Congressional Budget Office) (2009b) *Measuring the Effects of the Business Cycle on the Federal Budget*, Washington, DC: CBO.

CBO (Congressional Budget Office) (2009c) *Will the Demand for Assets Fall when the Baby Boomers Retire?*, Background Paper, Washington, DC: CBO.

CBO (Congressional Budget Office) (2009d) *CBO's Long-Term Model: An Overview*, Washington, DC: CBO.

CBO (Congressional Budget Office) (2009e) *The Long-Term Budget Outlook*, Washington, DC: CBO.

CBO (Congressional Budget Office) (2009f) *Budget and Economic Outlook*, Washington, DC: CBO.

CEA (Council of Economic Advisors) (2010) *Economic Report of the President*, Washington DC, February.

Cecchetti, S., Piti D. and Kohler, M. (2009) Integrating Financial Stability: New Models for a New Challenge, Paper prepared for the Joint BIS/ECB Workshop on Monetary Policy and Financial Stability, 10–11 September, Basel, Switzerland.

Cerra, V. and Saxena, S. (2000) Alternative Methods of Estimating Potential Output and the Output Gap – An Application to Sweden, IMF Working Paper No. 00/59.

Cerra, V. and Saxena, S. (2008a) Growth Dynamics: The Myth of Economic Recovery, *American Economic Review*, vol. 98, no. 1.

Cerra, V. and Saxena, S. (2008b) The Monetary Model Strikes Back: Evidence from the World, IMF Working Paper No. 08/73.

CGFS (Committee on the Global Financial System) (2009) *Credit Risk Transfer Statistics*, CGFS Publications No. 35.

CGFS (Committee on the Global Financial System) (2010) *Macroprudential Instruments and Frameworks: A Stocktaking of Issues and Experiences*, CGFS Publications, No. 38.

Chen, Y.-C., Rogoff, K. and Rossi, B. (2008) Can Exchange Rates Forecast Commodity Prices?, NBER Working Paper No. 13901.

Cherubini, U., Luciano, E. and Vecchiato, W. (2004) *Copula Methods in Finance*, New York: John Wiley.

Cheung, Y.-W. and Chinn, M. (2001) Currency Traders and Exchange Rate Dynamics: A Survey of the US Market, *Journal of International Money and Finance*, vol. 20, no. 4.

Cheung, Y., Chinn, M. and Pascual, A. (2005) Empirical Exchange Rate Models of the Nineties: Are Any Fit to Survive?, *Journal of International Money and Finance*, vol. 24, no. 7.

Chirinko, R. (1993) Business Fixed Investment Spending: Modeling Strategies, Empirical Results, and Policy Implications, *Journal of Economic Literature*, vol. 31, no. 4.

Chirinko, R. (2008) The Long and Short of It, CESifo Working Paper No. 2234.

Christensen, I. and Dib, A. (2008) The Financial Accelerator in an Estimated New Keynesian Model, *Review of Economic Dynamics*, vol. 11, no. 1.

Christiano, L. and Fitzgerald, T. (2003) The Band Pass Filter, *International Economic Review*, vol. 44, no. 2.

Christiano, L., Eichenbaum, M. and Evans, C. (2005) Nominal Rigidities and the Dynamic Effects to a Shock of Monetary Policy, *Journal of Political Economy*, vol. 113, no. 1.

Christoffel, K., Coenen, G. and Warne, A. (2008) The New Area-Wide Model of the Euro Area: A Micro-Founded Open-Economy Model for Forecasting and Policy Analysis, ECB Working Paper No. 944.

Clarida, R. and Taylor, M. (1993) The Term Structure of Forward Exchange Premia and the Forecastability of Spot Exchange Rates: Correcting the Errors, Discussion Paper No. 773, Centre for Economic Policy Research.

Clarida, R., Gali, J. and Gertler, M. (1999) The Science of Monetary Policy: A New Keynesian Perspective, *Journal of Economic Literature*, vol. 37, no. 4.

Clarida, R., Sarno, L., Taylor, M. and Valente, G. (2002) The Out-of-Sample Success of Term Structure Models as Exchange Rate Predictors: A Step Beyond, Discussion Paper No. 3281, Centre for Economic Policy Research.

Claus, I. and Li, K. (2003) New Zealand's Production Structure: An International Comparison, New Zealand Treasury Working Paper No. 03/16.

Clements, M. and Hendry, D. (1998) *Forecasting Economic Time Series*, Cambridge, MA: Cambridge University Press.

Clements, M. and Hendry, D. (2004) Pooling of Forecasts, *Econometrics Journal*, vol. 7, no. 1.

Colander, D., Howitt, P., Kirman, A., Leijonhufvud, A. and Mehrling, P. (2008) Beyond DSGE Models: Toward an Empirically Based Macroeconomics, *American Economic Review Papers and Proceedings*, vol. 98, no. 2.

Cook, L. (2004) Revisions to Statistics: Their Role in Measuring Economic Progress, *Economic Trends*, no. 603.

Corsetti, G., Pesenti, P. and Roubini, N. (1999) What Caused the Asian Currency and Financial Crisis?, *Japan and the World Economy*, vol. 11, no. 3.

Cotis, J.-P., Elmeskov, J. and Mourougane, A. (2004) Estimates of Potential Output: Benefits and Pitfalls from a Policy Perspective, in L. Reichlin (ed.), *The Euro Area Business Cycle: Stylized Facts and Measurement Issues*, London: CEPR.

Cotsomitis, J. and Kwan, A. (2006) Can Consumer Confidence Forecast Household Spending? Evidence from the European Commission Business and Consumer Surveys, *Southern Economic Journal*, vol. 72, no. 3.

Cournède, B., Ahrend, R. and Price, R. (2008) Have Long-Term Financial Trends Changed the Transmission of Monetary Policy?, OECD Economics Department Working Paper No. 634.

Coyle, D. (2001) Making Sense of Published Economic Forecasts, in D. Hendry and N. Ericsson (eds), *Understanding Economic Forecasts*, Cambridge, MA: MIT Press.

Crockett, A. (2000) Marrying the Micro- and Macroprudential Dimensions of Financial Stability, *BIS Speeches*, 21 September.

Crockett, A. (2001) Monetary Policy and Financial Stability, Speech at the HKMA Distinguished Lecture, Hong Kong, 13 February.

Croushore, D. (2005) Do Consumer-Confidence Indexes Help Forecast Consumer Spending in Real Time?, *North American Journal of Economics and Finance*, vol. 16, no. 3.

Crowe, C. (2010) Consensus Forecasts and Inefficient Information Aggregation, IMF Working Paper 10/178.

Cummins, J., Hassett K. and Hubbard G. (1996) Tax Reforms and Investment: A Cross-Country Comparison, *Journal of Public Economics*, vol. 62, no. 1–2.

D'Agostino, A., Gambetti, L. and Giannone, D. (2009) Macroeconomic Forecasting and Structural Change, CEPR Discussion Paper No. 7542.

De Grauwe, P. (2008) DSGE Modelling When Agents Are Imperfectly Informed, European Central Bank Working Paper No. 897.

De Masi, P. (1997) IMF Estimates of Potential Output; Theory and Practice, IMF Working Paper No. 97-177.

de Mello, L. and Pisu, M. (2009) The Bank Lending Channel of Monetary Transmission in Brazil: A VECM Approach, OECD Economics Department Working Paper No. 711.

Del Negro, M. and Schorfeide, F. (2007) Monetary Policy Analysis with Potentially Misspecified Models, NBER Working Paper No. 13099.

Demiroglu, U. and Salomon, M. (2002) *Using Time-Series Models to Project Output over the Medium Term*, Technical Paper Series 2002-1, Congressional Budget Office, Washington, DC.

Denis, C., Grenouilleau, D., Mc Morrow K. and Röger W. (2006) Calculating Potential Growth Rates and Output Gaps – A Revised Production Function Approach, *European Economy Economic Papers*, no. 247.

Denton, F. (1971) Adjustment of Monthly or Quarterly Series to Annual Totals: An Approach Based on Quadratic Minimisation, *Journal of the American Statistical Association*, vol. 66, no. 333.

Detken, C., Dieppe, A., Henry, J., Smets, F. and Marin, C. (2002) Determinants of the Effective Real Exchange Rate of the Synthetic Euro: Alternative Methodological Approaches, *Australian Economic Papers*, vol. 41, no. 4.

Deutsche Bundesbank (2000) *Macro-Econometric Multi-Country Model: MEMMOD*, Frankfurt am Main: Deutsche Bundesbank.

Devarajan, S. and Robinson, S. (2002) The Influence of Computable General Equilibrium Models on Policy, International Food Policy Research Institute, TMD Discussion Paper No. 98.

Diebold, F. (2007) *Elements of Forecasting*, 4th edn, Cincinnati, OH: South-Western College Publishing.

Diebold, F. and Mariano, R. (1995) Comparing Predictive Accuracy, *Journal of Business and Economic Statistics*, vol. 13, no. 3.

Diebold, F., Tay, A. and Wallis, K. (1999) Evaluating Density Forecasts of Inflation: The Survey of Professional Forecasters, in R. Engle and H. White. (eds) *Cointegration, Causality, and Forecasting: A Festschrift in Honour of Clive W. J. Granger*, Oxford, UK: Oxford University Press.

Direction de la Prévision (2001) La modélisation macroéconomique des flux de commerce extérieur des principaux pays industriels, *Note de Conjoncture Internationale*, June.

Direction Générale du Trésor et de la Politique Economique (2006) Estimates of French Medium to Long-Term Potential Growth Revisited, *Trésor Economics*, no. 2, November, Ministry of the Economy, Finance and Industry.

Dixit, A. and Stiglitz, J. (1977) Monopolistic Competition and Optimal Product Diversity, *American Economic Review*, vol. 67, no. 3.

Dixon, J. and Hamilton, K. (1996) Expanding the Measure of Wealth, *Finance and Development*, vol. 33, no. 4.

Dixon, R., Freebairn, J. and Lim G. (2004) An Employment Equation for Australia, *Economic Record*, vol. 81, no. 254.

Don, F. (2001) Forecasting in Macroeconomics: A Practitioner's View, *The Economist*, vol. 149, no. 2.

Don, F. and Verbruggen, J. (2006), Models and Methods for Economic Policy: 60 Years of Evolution at CPB, CPB Discussion Paper No. 55.

Dreher, A., Marchesi, S. and Vreeland, J. (2007) The Politics of IMF Forecasts, Working Paper No. 124, University of Milano-Bicocca, Department of Economics.

Dubecq, S., Mojon, N. and Ragot, X. (2009) Fuzzy Capital Requirements, Risk-Shifting and the Risk Taking Channel of Monetary Policy, Working Paper, Banque de France No. 254.

Dudley, W. (2009) Lessons Learned from the Financial Crisis, Speech, Federal Reserve Bank of New York, 26 June.

Durlauf, S. and Fafchamps, M. (2004) Social Capital, NBER Working Paper No. 10485.

Duval, R. and de la Maisonneuve, C. (2009) Long-Run GDP Growth Framework and Scenarios for the World Economy, OECD Economics Department Working Paper No. 663.

Dynan, K. and Elmendorf, D. (2001) Do Provisional Estimates of Output Miss Economic Turning Points? Federal Reserve Board Finance and Economics Discussion Series, No. 2001-52.

ECB (European Central Bank) (2001) Assessment of General Economic Statistics for the Euro Area, *Monthly Bulletin*, April.

ECB (European Central Bank) (2004a) The Impact of the Number of Working Days on Euro Area GDP in 2004, *Monthly Bulletin*, June.

ECB (European Central Bank) (2004b) *The Monetary Policy of the ECB*.

Edge, R., Kiley, M. and Laforte, J.-P. (2007) Natural Rate Measures in an Estimated DSGE Model of the US Economy, Board of Governors of the Federal Reserve System, Finance and Economics Discussion Series 2007-8.

Edge, R., Kiley, M. and Laforte, J.-P. (2009) A Comparison of Forecast Performance between Federal Reserve Staff Forecasts, Simple Reduced-Form Models and a DSGE Model, Federal Reserve Finance and Economics Discussion Series, No. 2009-10.

Edwards, R. and Magee, J. (2001) *Technical Analysis of Stock Trends*, 8th edn, Boca Raton, FL: St Lucie Press.

Elliott, G., Granger, C. and Timmermann, A. (eds) (2006) *Handbook of Economic Forecasting*, North-Holland: Elsevier.

Engen, E. and Hubbard, R. (2004) Federal Government Debt and Interest Rates, NBER Working Paper No. 10681.

Engel, C. and West, K. (2005) Exchange Rates and Fundamentals, *Journal of Political Economy*, vol. 113, no. 3.

Engel, C., Mark, N. and West, K. (2007) Exchange Rate Models Are Not as Bad as You Think, *NBER Macroeconomics Annual*.

Engle, R. (1982) Autoregressive Conditional Heteroskedasticity with Estimates of the Variance of United Kingdom Inflation, *Econometrica*, vol. 50, no. 4.

Engle, R. (2001) GARCH 101: The Use of ARCH/GARCH Models in Applied Econometrics, *Journal of Economic Perspectives*, vol. 15, no. 4.

Engle, R. (2002) Dynamic Conditional Correlation – A Simple Class of Multivariate GARCH Models, *Journal of Business and Economic Statistics*, vol. 20, no. 3.

Engle, R. and Kroner, K. (1995) Multivariate Simultaneous Generalized ARCH, *Econometric Theory*, vol. 11, no. 1.

Engle, R. and Patton, A. (2001) What Good Is a Volatility Model?, *Quantitative Finance*, vol. 1, no. 2.

Engle, R. and Patton, A. (2004) Impacts of Trades in an Error-Correction Model of Quote Prices, *Journal of Financial Markets*, vol. 7, no. 1.

Erceg, C., Guerrieri, L. and Gust, C. (2005) SIGMA: A New Open Economy Model for Policy Analysis, Board of Governors of the Federal Reserve System International Finance Discussion Paper No. 835.

Erkel-Rousse, H. and Minodier, C. (2009) Do Business Tendency Surveys in Industry and Services Help in Forecasting GDP Growth?, INSEE Working Paper No. G2009/03.

Estrella, A. and Trubin, M. (2007) The Yield Curve as a Leading Indicator: Some Practical Issues, *Current Issues in Economics and Finance*, Federal Reserve Bank of New York, vol. 12, no. 5.

European Commission (1999) Generational Accounting in Europe, *European Economy*, no. 6.

European Commission (2007) *The Joint Harmonised EU Programme of Business and Consumer Surveys: User Guide*, Brussels: European Commission.

European Commission (2009) *Sustainability Report 2009, European Economy 9*, Brussels: European Commission.

Fair, R. (2007) Testing Price Equations, Kiel Working Paper No. 1342.

Faust, J., Rogers, J. and Wright, J. (2003) Exchange Rate Forecasting: The Errors We've Really Made, *Journal of International Economics*, vol. 60, no. 1.

Faust, J., Rogers, J. and Wright, J. (2005) News and Noise in G-7 GDP Announcements, *Journal of Money, Credit, and Banking*, vol. 37, no. 3.

Federal Reserve Bank of Philadelphia (2011) *Survey of Professional Forecasters*, First quarter.

Fenton, P. and Murchison, S. (2006) ToTEM: The Bank of Canada's New Projection and Policy Analysis Model, *Bank of Canada Review*, Autumn.

Fernandez-Villaverde, J. (2009) The Econometrics of DSGE Models, NBER Working Paper No. 14677.

Fichtner, F., Rüffer, R. and Schnatz, B. (2009) Leading Indicators in a Globalised World, ECB Working Paper No. 1125.

Filardo, A. (2004) The 2001 US Recession: What Did Recession Prediction Models Tell Us?, BIS Working Paper No. 148.

Financial Stability Forum (2009) *FSF Principles for Sound Compensation Practices*, 2 April.

Fintzen, D. and Stekler, H. (1999) Why Did Forecasters Fail to Predict the 1990 Recession?, *International Journal of Forecasting*, vol. 15, no. 3.

Fracasso, A., Genberg, H. and Wyplosz, C. (2003) *How Do Central Banks Write? An Evaluation of Inflation Reports by Inflation Targeting Central Banks*, Geneva Reports on the World Economy Special Report No. 2, Centre for Economic Policy Research.

Frale, C., Marcellino, M., Mazzi, G. L. and Proietti, T. (2009) Survey Data as Coincident or Leading Indicators, Italian Department of the Treasury Working Paper No. 3.

Freedman, C., Kumhof, M., Laxton, D. and Lee, J. (2009) The Case for Global Fiscal Stimulus, IMF Staff Position Note No. 09/03.

Frenkel, J. (1976) A Monetary Approach to the Exchange Rate: Doctrinal Aspects and Empirical Evidence, *The Scandinavian Journal of Economics*, vol. 78, no. 2.

Friedman, M. (1957) *A Theory of the Consumption Function*, Princeton, NJ: Princeton University Press.

FSA (Financial Services Authority) (2009) *The Turner Review – A Regulatory Response to the Global Banking Crisis*, London: FSA.

Fukac, M. and Pagan, A. (2009), Structural Macro-econometric Modelling in a Policy Environment, Reserve Bank of New Zealand Discussion Paper Series, No. 2009/16.

Furceri, D. and Mourougane, A. (2009) The Effect of Financial Crises on Potential Output: New Empirical Evidence from OECD Countries, OECD Economics Department Working Paper No. 699.

Galbraith, J. and van Norden, S. (2009) *Calibration and Resolution Diagnostics for Bank of England Density Forecasts*, CIRANO Scientific Publications No. 2009s-36.

Galí, J. (2008) *Monetary Policy, Inflation, and the Business Cycle: An Introduction to the New Keynesian Framework*, Princeton, NJ: Princeton University Press.

Gallo, G., Granger, C. and Jeon, Y. (2002) Copycats and Common Swings: The Impact of the Use of Forecasts in Information Sets, *IMF Staff Papers*, vol. 49, no. 1.

Gauthier, C., Graham, C. and Liu, Y. (2004) Financial Condition Indexes in Canada, Bank of Canada Working Paper No. 2004-22.

Gelper, S. and Croux, C. (2010) On the Construction of the European Economic Sentiment Indicator, *Oxford Bulletin of Economics and Statistics*, vol. 72, no. 1.

Geraats, P. (2009) Trends in Monetary Policy Transparency, CESifo Working Paper No. 2584.

Gersbach, H. and Hahn, V. (2009) Banking-on-the-Average Rules, Economics Working Paper No. 09/107, CER-ETH – Centre of Economic Research, ETH Zurich.

Gianella, C., Koske, I., Rusticelli, E. and Chatal, O. (2008) What Drives the Nairu? Evidence from a Panel of OECD Countries, OECD Economics Department Working Paper No. 649.

Giannoni, M. (2002) Does Model Uncertainty Justify Caution? Robust Optimal Monetary Policy in a Forward-Looking Model, *Macroeconomic Dynamics*, vol. 6, no. 1.

Giorno, C., Richarson, P. and Suyker, W. (1995a) Technical Progress, Factor Productivity and Macroeconomic Performance in the Medium Term, OECD Economics Department Working Paper No. 157.

Giorno, C., Richardson, P., Roseveare, D. and van den Noord, P. (1995b) Estimating Potential Output, Output Gaps and Structural Budget Balances, OECD Economics Department Working Paper No. 152.

Girard, M. (2009) Canadian Monthly GDP Estimates, Paper presented at the International Seminar on Timeliness, Methodology and Comparability of Rapid Estimates of Economic Trends, 27–29 May, Ottawa, Canada.

Girouard, N. and André, C. (2005), Measuring Cyclically-Adjusted Budget Balances for OECD Countries, OECD Economics Department Working Paper No. 434.

Girouard, N., Kennedy, M., van den Noord, P. and André, C. (2006) Recent House Price Developments: The Role of Fundamentals, OECD Economics Department Working Paper No. 475.

Granger, C. (1996) Can We Improve the Perceived Quality of Economic Forecasts?, *Journal of Applied Econometrics*, vol. 11, no. 5.

Greenspan, A. (2008) Testimony before the US House of Representatives Committee on Oversight and Government Reform, October 23.

Greer, M. (2003) Directional Accuracy Tests of Long-Term Interest Rate Forecasts, *International Journal of Forecasting*, vol. 19, no. 2.

Gregoir, S. and Lenglart, F. (2000) Measuring the Probability of a Business Cycle Turning Point by Using a Multivariate Qualitative Hidden Markov Model, *Journal of Forecasting*, vol. 19, no. 2.

Guichard, S., Haugh, D. and Turner, D. (2009) Quantifying the Effect of Financial Conditions in the Euro Area, Japan, United Kingdom and United States, OECD Economics Department Working Paper No. 677.

Hahn, E. and Skudelny, F. (2008) Early Estimates of Euro Area Real GDP Growth: A Bottom Up Approach from the Production Side, ECB Working Paper No. 975.

Hamilton, J. (1989) A New Approach to the Economic Analysis of Nonstationary Time Series and the Business Cycle, *Econometrica*, vol. 57, no. 2.

Hamilton, J. (1994) *Time Series Analysis*, Princeton, NJ: Princeton University Press.

Hamilton, J. (2003) What Is an Oil Shock?, *Journal of Econometrics*, vol. 113, no. 2.

Hamilton, J. (2009) Understanding Crude Oil Prices, *Energy Journal*, vol. 30, no. 2.

Hansen, L. and Hodrick, R. (1980) Forward Exchange Rates as Optimal Predictors of Future Spot Rates: An Econometric Analysis, *Journal of Political Economy*, vol. 88, no. 5.

Harding, D. and Pagan, A. (2002) Dissecting the Cycle: A Methodological Investigation, *Journal of Monetary Economics*, vol. 49, no. 2.

Harrison, R., Nikolov, K., Quinn, M., Ramsay, G., Scott, A. and Thomas, R. (2005) *The Bank of England Quarterly Model*, London: Bank of England.

Harvey, A. (1985) Trends and Cycles in Macroeconomic Time Series, *Journal of Business and Economic Statistics*, vol. 3, no. 3.

Harvey, C. (1991) The Term Structure and World Economic Growth, *Journal of Fixed Income*, vol. 1, no. 1.

Hawksworth, J. and Cookson, G. (2008) *The World in 2050 – Beyond the BRICs: A Broader Look at Emerging Market Growth Prospects*, PricewaterhouseCoopers.

Healy, D. (1990) *The Time of My Life*, London: Penguin.

Healy, T. and Côté, S. (2001) *The Well-being of Nations: The Role of Human and Social Capital*, Paris: OECD.

Helbling, T. and Terrones, M. (2003) When Bubbles Burst, *IMF World Economic Outlook*, April.

Hendershott, P. and White, M. (2000) The Rise and Fall of Housing's Favored Investment Status, *Journal of Housing Research*, vol. 11, no. 2.

Heravi, S., Osborn, D. and Birchenhall, C. (2004) Linear Versus Neural Network Forecasts for European Industrial Production Series, *International Journal of Forecasting*, vol. 20, no. 3.

Herring, R. and Wachter, S. (2003) Bubbles in Real Estate Markets, in W. Hunter, G. Kaufman and M. Pomerleano (eds) *Asset Price Bubbles: The Implications for Monetary, Regulatory, and International Policies*, Cambridge, MA: MIT Press.

Hertveldt, B. and Lebrun, I. (2003) MODTRIM II: A Quarterly Model for the Belgian Economy, Federal Planning Bureau Working Paper No. 6-2003.

Hervé, K., Pain, N., Richardson, P., Sédillot, F. and Beffy, P.-O. (2010) The OECD's New Global Model, OECD Economics Department Working Paper No. 768.

Hida, F., Tanaka, K., Umei, H., Iwamoto, K. and Shigihara, H. (2008) The ESRI Short-Run Macroeconometric Model of the Japanese Economy (2008 version): Basic Structure, Multipliers, and Economic Policy Analyses, ESRI Discussion Paper No. 201.

HM Treasury (2002) *Trend Growth: Recent Developments and Prospects*, London, April.

HM Treasury (2006) *Trend Growth: New Evidence and Prospects*, London, December.

HM Treasury (2008a) *End of Year Fiscal Report*, London, November.

HM Treasury (2008b) *Evidence on the Economic Cycle*, London, November.

HM Treasury (2010) Inflation and the Output Gap in the UK, Treasury Economic Working Paper No. 6.

Hodrick, R. and Prescott, E. (1980) Postwar U.S. Business Cycles: An Empirical Investigation, Discussion Paper No. 451, Carnegie Mellon University, reprinted in *Journal of Money, Credit and Banking*, vol. 29, no. 1.

Hollmann, F., Mulder, T. and Kallan, J. (2000) Methodology and Assumptions for the Population Projections of the United States: 1999 to 2100, Population Division Working Paper No. 38, U.S. Census Bureau, Washington, DC.

Holt, C. (1957) Forecasting Seasonals and Trends by Exponentially Weighted Moving Averages, Office of Naval Research, Research Memorandum 52.

Hooper, P., Johnson, K. and Marquez, J. (2000) Trade Elasticities for the G7 Countries, *Princeton Studies in International Economics*, no. 87.

Hördahl, P. and Tristani, O. (2007) Inflation Risk Premia in the Term Structure of Interest Rates, BIS Working Paper No. 228.

Hull, J. (2008) *Options, Futures, and Other Derivatives*, Harlow, UK: Prentice Hall.

Hyndman, R., Koehler, A., Ord, J. and Snyder, R. (2008) *Forecasting with Exponential Smoothing – The State Space Approach*, Berlin: Springer-Verlag.

IEA (International Energy Agency) (2004) *World Energy Outlook*, Paris.

IMF (International Monetary Fund) (2000) The Impact of Higher Oil Prices on the Global Economy, Research Department, December.

IMF (International Monetary Fund) (2004) *World Economic Outlook*, September.

IMF (International Monetary Fund) (2008) Financial Stress, Downturn, and Recoveries, *World Economic Outlook*, October.

IMF (International Monetary Fund) (2009a) *Companion Paper – The State of Public Finances: Outlook and Medium-Term Policies After the 2008 Crisis*, Fiscal Affairs Department, March.

IMF (International Monetary Fund) (2009b) Global Prospects and Policies, *World Economic Outlook*, ch. 1, April.

IMF (International Monetary Fund) (2009c) What's the Damage? Medium-term Output Dynamics After Financial Crises, *World Economic Outlook*, ch. 4, October.

IMF (International Monetary Fund) (2009d) The State of Public Finances, Cross-Country Fiscal Monitor: November 2009, IMF Staff Position Note SPN/09/25.

IMF (International Monetary Fund) (2010a) *From Stimulus to Consolidation: Revenue and Expenditure Policies in Advanced and Emerging Economies*, Washington DC, April.

IMF (International Monetary Fund) (2010b) Navigating the Fiscal Challenges Ahead, *Fiscal Monitor*, May.

IMF (International Monetary Fund) (2011) *Macroprudential Policy: An Organizing Framework*, March.

Isard, P. (2000) The Role of MULTIMOD in the IMF's Policy Analysis, IMF Policy Discussion Paper No. 00/5.

Islam, N. (2003) What Have We Learnt from the Convergence Debate?, *Journal of Economic Surveys*, vol. 17, no. 3.

Ito, T. (1990) Foreign Exchange Rate Expectations: Micro Survey Data, *American Economic Review*, vol. 80, no. 3.

Jones, C. and Klenow P. (2010) Beyond GDP? Welfare Across Countries and Time, NBER Working Paper No. 16352.

Jorgenson, D. (1997) *Tax Policy and the Cost of Capital*, Cambridge, MA: MIT Press.

Jorion, P. (2006) *Value at Risk*, 3rd edn, New York: McGraw-Hill.

Juhn, G. and Loungani, P. (2002) Further Cross-Country Evidence on the Accuracy of the Private Sector's Output Forecasts, *IMF Staff Papers*, vol. 49, no. 1.

Kaashoek, J. and van Dijk, H. (2003) Neural Networks: An Econometric Tool, in D. Giles (ed.), *Computer-Aided Econometrics*, New York/Basel: Marcel Dekker.

Kaldor, N. (1961) Capital Accumulation and Economic Growth, in F. Lutz and D. Hague (eds), *The Theory of Capital*, New York: St Martin's Press.

Kannan, P. (2010) Credit Conditions and Recoveries from Recessions Associated with Financial Crises, IMF Working Paper No. 83.

Katz, J., Salinas, E. and Stephanou C. (2009) *Credit Rating Agencies: No Easy Regulatory Solutions*, World Bank, Crisis Response, no. 8.

Keynes, J. M. (1936) *General Theory of Employment, Interest and Money*, London: Macmillan.

Kilian, L. and Taylor, M. (2003) Why is it So Difficult to Beat the Random Walk Forecast of Exchange Rates?, *Journal of International Economics*, vol. 60, no. 1.

Kim, C.-J. and Nelson, C. (1999) Friedman's Plucking Model of Business Fluctuations: Tests and Estimates of Permanent and Transitory Components, Part 1, *Journal of Money, Credit and Banking*, vol. 31, no. 3.

Kim, D. and Wright, J. (2005) *An Arbitrage-Free Three-Factor Term Structure Model and the Recent Behavior of Long-Term Yields and Distant-Horizon Forward Rates*, Board of Governors of the Federal Reserve System, Finance and Economics Discussion Series, No. 2005-33.

Kim, C.-J., Morley, J. and Piger, J. (2005) Nonlinearity and the Permanent Effects of Recessions, *Journal of Applied Econometrics*, vol. 20, no. 2.

Kindleberger, C. and Aliber, R. (2011) *Manias, Panics and Crashes, A History of Financial Crises*, 6th edn, Basingstoke: Palgrave Macmillan.

Kinsella, K. and He, W. (2009) *An Aging World: 2008*, U.S. Census Bureau, International Population Reports, P95/09-1, Washington, DC.

Kisinbay, T. (2007) The Use of Encompassing Tests for Forecast Combinations, IMF Working Paper 07/264.

Klein, C. and Simon, O. (2010) Le modèle MESANGE nouvelle version réestimée en base 2000, Working Paper DGTPE No. 2010/2.

Klein, L. (1950) *Economic Fluctuations in the United States: 1921–1941*, New York: John Wiley.

Knight, F. (1921) *Risk, Uncertainty and Profit*, Boston, MA: Houghton and Mifflin.

Knott, R. and Polenghi, M. (2006) Assessing Central Counterparty Margin Coverage on Futures Contracts using GARCH Models, Bank of England Working Paper No. 287.

Koen, V. and van den Noord, P. (2005) Fiscal Gimmickry in Europe: One-off Measures and Creative Accounting, OECD Economics Department Working Paper No. 417.

Kohn, D. (2010) Monetary Policy in the Crisis: Past, Present, and Future, Speech at the Brimmer Policy Forum, American Economic Association Annual Meeting, Atlanta, Georgia, 3 January.

Koutsogeorgopoulou, V. (2000) A Post-Mortem on Economic Outlook Projections, OECD Economics Department Working Paper No. 274.

KPMG Econtech (2010) *The MM900 Model*, March.

Kranendonk, H. (2003) *The Cyclically Adjusted Budget Balance: Some Recommendations for Brussels*, CPB Report, No. 2003/3.

Kranendonk, H. and Verbruggen, J. (2007) *SAFFIER: A Multipurpose Model of the Dutch Economy for Short-term and Medium-term Analyses*, CPB Document, No. 144.

Kroszner, R. (2007) Globalization and Capital Markets: Implications for Inflation and the Yield Curve, Speech at the Centre for Financial Stability (CEF), Buenos Aires, Argentina, 16 May.

Krugman, P. (1979) A Model of Balance-of-Payments Crises, *Journal of Money, Credit and Banking*, vol. 11, no. 3.

Kumah, F. (2007) A Markov-Switching Approach to Measuring Exchange Market Pressure, IMF Working Paper No. 07/242.

Kumhof, M., Laxton, D., Muir, D. and Mursula, S. (2010) The Global Integrated Monetary and Fiscal Model (GIMF) – Theoretical Structure, IMF Working Paper No. 10/34.

Kydland, F. and Prescott, E. (1977) Rules Rather than Discretion: the Inconsistency of Optimal Plans, *Journal of Political Economy*, vol. 85, no. 3.

Kydland, F. and Prescott, E. (1982) Time to Build and Aggregate Fluctuations, *Econometrica*, vol. 50, no. 6.

Lafrance, R. and St-Amant, P. (1999) Real Exchange Rate Indexes for the Canadian Dollar, *Bank of Canada Review*, Autumn.

Landefeld, J., Moulton, B. and Vojtech, C. (2003) Chained-Dollar Indexes Issues, Tips on Their Use, and Upcoming Changes, *Survey of Current Business*, vol. 83, no. 11.

Landefeld, J., Seskin, E. and Fraumeni, B. (2008) Taking the Pulse of the Economy: Measuring GDP, *Journal of Economic Perspectives*, vol. 22, no. 2.

Laster, D., Bennett, P. and Geoum, I. (1999) Rational Bias in Macroeconomic Forecasts, *Quarterly Journal of Economics*, vol. 114, no. 1.

Laubach, T. (2003) *New Evidence on the Interest Rate Effects of Budget Deficits and Debt*, Federal Reserve Board Finance and Economics Discussion Series, No. 2003-12.

Laxton, D. (2008) Getting to Know the Global Economy Model and Its Philosophy, *IMF Staff Papers*, vol. 55, no. 2.

Layard, R., Nickell, S. and Jackman, R. (1991) *Unemployment: Macroeconomic Performance and the Labour Market*, Oxford, UK: Oxford University Press.

Leal, T., Pérez, J. J., Tujula, M. and Vidal, J.-P. (2008) Fiscal Forecasting: Lessons from the Literature and Challenges, *Fiscal Studies*, vol. 29, no. 3.

Lebow, D. and Rudd, J. (2003) Measurement Error in the Consumer Price Index: Where Do We Stand?, *Journal of Economic Literature*, vol. XLI, no. 1.

Lees, K. (2009) Introducing KITT: The Reserve Bank of New Zealand New DSGE model for Forecasting and Policy Design, *Reserve Bank of New Zealand Bulletin*, vol. 72, no. 2.

Lequiller, F. (2001) The New Economy and the Measurement of GDP Growth, INSEE Working Paper No. G2001-01.

Lequiller, F. and Blades, D. (2006) *Understanding National Accounts*, Paris: OECD.

L'Horty, Y. and Rault, C. (2003) Why Is French Equilibrium Unemployment So High? An Estimation of the WS-PS Model, *Journal of Applied Economics*, vol. 6, no. 1.

Lin, J.-L. and Liu, T.-S. (2002) Modeling Lunar Calendar Holiday Effects in Taiwan, Mimeo, U.S. Bureau of Census.

Litterman, B. (1986) Forecasting with Bayesian Vector Autoregressions – Five Years of Experience, *Journal of Business and Economic Statistics*, vol. 4, no. 1.

Loungani, P. (2001) How Accurate Are Private Sector Forecasts? Cross-Country Evidence from Consensus Forecasts of Output Growth, *International Journal of Forecasting*, vol. 17, no. 3.

Loungani, P. (2002) 'There Will Be Growth in the Spring': How Credible are Forecasts of Recovery?, *World Economics*, vol. 3, no. 1.

Lucas, R. (1976) Econometric Policy Evaluation: A Critique, *Carnegie-Rochester Conference Series on Public Policy*, vol. 1.

Lucas, R. (2003) Macroeconomic Priorities, *American Economic Review*, vol. 93, no. 1.

Maddison A. (2001) *The World Economy: A Millennium Perspective*, Paris: OECD Development Centre.

Maeso-Fernandez, F., Osbat, C. and Schnatz, B. (2002) Determinants of the Euro Real Effective Exchange Rate: A BEER/PEER Approach, *Australian Economic Papers*, vol. 41, no. 4.

Mahmoud, E., DeRoeck, R., Brown, R. and Rice, G. (1992) Bridging the Gap between Theory and Practice in Forecasting, *International Journal of Forecasting*, vol. 8, no. 2.

Maih, J. (2009) Conditional Forecasts in DSGE Models, Paper presented at the Conference on Forecasting and Monetary Policy, Bundesbank, March.

Makridakis, S., Wheelwright, S. and Hyndman, R. (1998) *Forecasting: Methods and Applications*, 3rd edn, New York: John Wiley.

Malinvaud, E. (1983) *Essais sur la théorie du chômage*, Paris: Calmann-Lévy.

Mandelbrot, B. and Hudson, R. (2004) *The (Mis)behavior of Markets: A Fractal View of Risk, Ruin and Reward*, New York: Basic Books.

Mankiw, N., Romer, D. and Weil, D. (1992) A Contribution to the Empirics of Economic Growth, *Quarterly Journal of Economics*, vol.107, no. 2.

Mark, N. (1995) Exchange Rates and Fundamentals: Evidence on Long-Horizon Predictability, *American Economic Review*, vol. 85, no. 1.

McCauley, R. and McGuire, P. (2009) Dollar Appreciation in 2008: Safe Haven, Carry Trades, Dollar Shortage and Overhedging, *BIS Quarterly Review*, December.

McKibbin, W. and Wilcoxen, P. (1998) The Theoretical and Empirical Structure of the GCubed Model, *Economic Modelling*, vol. 16, no. 1.

Mc Morrow, K. and Röger, W. (2001) Potential Output: Measurement Methods, 'New' Economy Influences and Scenarios for 2001–2010 – A Comparison of the EU15 and the US, *European Commission Economic Paper* No.150.

Mc Morrow, K. and Röger, W. (2004) *The Economic and Financial Market Consequences of Global Ageing*, New York: Springer-Verlag.

Meese, R. and Rogoff, K. (1983) Empirical Exchange Rate Models of the Seventies: Do They Fit out of Sample?, *Journal of International Economics*, vol. 14, no. 1.

Melander, A., Sismanidis, G. and Grenouilleau, D. (2007) The Track Record of the Commission's Forecasts – An Update, *European Economy, Economic Papers*, no. 291.

Meurers, M. (2006) Identifying Determinants of Germany's International Price Competitiveness – A Structural VAR Approach, OECD Economics Department Working Paper No. 523.

Michaud, F.-L., and Upper, C. (2008) What Drives Interbank Rates? Evidence from the Libor Panel, *BIS Quarterly Review*, March.

Milani, F. (2007) Expectations, Learning and Macroeconomic Persistence, *Journal of Monetary Economics*, vol. 54, no. 7.

Mincer, J. and Zarnowitz, V. (1969) *The Evaluation of Economic Forecasts. Economic Forecasts and Expectations*, New York: NBER.

Minegishi, M. and Cournède, B. (2009) The Role of Transparency in the Conduct of Monetary Policy, OECD Economics Department Working Paper No. 724.

Minsky, H. (1982) *Can 'It' Happen Again?, Essays on Instability and Finance*, Armonk, NY: M. E. Sharpe.

Molodtsova, T. and Papell, D. (2009) Out-of-Sample Exchange Rate Predictability with Taylor Rule Fundamentals, *Journal of International Economics*, vol. 77, no. 2.

Morley, J., Nelson, C. and Zivot, E. (2003) Why Are the Beveridge-Nelson and Unobserved-Components Decompositions of GDP So Different?, *Review of Economics and Statistics*, vol. 135, no. 2.

Morris, R. and Schuknecht, L. (2007) Structural Balances and Revenue Windfalls: The Role of Asset Prices Revisited, European Central Bank Working Paper No. 737.

Mourougane, A. (2006) Forecasting Monthly GDP for Canada, OECD Economics Department Working Paper No. 515.

Muellbauer, J. (2008) *Housing, Credit and Consumer Expenditure*, CEPR Discussion Paper No. 6782.

Musso, A. and Phillips S. (2002) Comparing Projections and Outcomes of IMF-Supported Programs, *IMF Staff Papers*, vol. 49, no. 1.

Nardo, M. (2003) The Quantification of Qualitative Survey Data: A Critical Assessment, *Journal of Economic Surveys*, vol. 17, no. 5.

ONS (Office for National Statistics) (2010) *Blue Book*, London: ONS.

Neftçi, S. (1982) Optimal Prediction of Cyclical Downturns, *Journal of Economic Dynamics and Control*, vol. 4, no. 4.

Neftçi, S. (1984) Are Economic Time Series Asymmetric Over the Business Cycle?, *Journal of Political Economy*, vol. 92, no. 2.

Nilsson, R. and Gyomai G. (2007) *OECD System of Leading Indicators, Methodological Changes and Other Improvements*, OECD Statistics Directorate, November.

O'Neill, J. and Stupnytska A. (2009) The Long-Term Outlook for the BRICs and N-11 Post Crisis, *Goldman Sachs Global Economics Papers*, no. 192.

O'Neill, J., Wilson, D., Purushothaman, R. and Stupnytska, A. (2005) How Solid are the BRICs?, *Goldman Sachs Global Economic Papers*, no. 134.

Obstfeld, M. (1994)The Logic of Currency Crises, NBER Working Paper No. 4640.

OECD (Organisation for Economic Co-operation and Development) (2002) *Measuring the Non-Observed Economy: A Handbook*, Paris: OECD.

OECD (Organisation for Economic Co-operation and Development) (2008) *OECD System of Composite Leading Indicators*, Paris: OECD, November.

OECD (Organisation for Economic Co-operation and Development) (2009) The Effectiveness and Scope of Fiscal Stimulus, *OECD Economic Outlook Interim Report*.

OECD (Organisation for Economic Co-operation and Development) (2010) Prospects for Growth and Imbalances Beyond the Short Term, Chapter 4, *Economic Outlook*, no. 87.

OECD (Organisation for Economic Co-operation and Development) (2011) *National Accounts of OECD Countries: Financial Balance Sheets*, Paris: OECD.

OEF (Oxford Economic Forecasting) (2005) The Oxford World Macroeconomic Model: An Overview, Mimeo, Oxford.

Oliveira Martins, J. and Scarpetta, S. (2002) Estimation of the Cyclical Behaviour of Mark-Ups: A Technical Note, *OECD Economic Studies*, no. 34.

OMB (Office of Management and Budget) (2011) *Analytical Perspectives, Budget of the United States Government, Fiscal Year 2012,* Washington, DC.

Okun, A. (1962) Potential GNP: Its Measurement and Significance, *Proceedings of the Business and Economics Section of the American Statistical Association,* pp. 98–104.

Osborn, D., Sensier, M. and van Dijk, D. (2004) Predicting Growth Regimes for European Countries, in L. Reichlin, (ed.), *The Euro Area Business Cycle: Stylized Facts and Measurement Issues,* London: CEPR.

Österholm, P. (2009) Incorporating Judgement in Fan Charts, *Scandinavian Journal of Economics,* vol. 111, no. 2.

Pain, N., Mourougane, A., Sédillot, F. and Le Fouler, L. (2005) The New OECD International Trade Model, OECD Economics Department Working Paper No. 440.

Palumbo, M., Rudd, J. and Whelan, K. (2002) *On the Relationships between Real Consumption, Income, and Wealth,* Federal Reserve Board, Finance and Economics Discussion Series No. 2002-38.

Patton, A. (2009) Copula-Based Models for Financial Time Series, in T. Andersen, R. Davis, J.-P. Kreiss and T. Mikosch (eds), *Handbook of Financial Time Series,* Berlin: Springer-Verlag.

Phillips, A. (1958) The Relationship between Unemployment and the Rate of Change of Money Wage Rates in the United Kingdom, 1861–1957, *Economica,* vol. 25, no.100.

Poncet, S. (2006) The Long Term Growth Prospects of the World Economy: Horizon 2050, CEPII Working Paper No. 2006-16.

Pons, J. (2000) The Accuracy of IMF and OECD Forecasts for G7 countries, *Journal of Forecasting,* vol. 19, no. 1.

Poon, S.-H. (2005) *A Practical Guide to Forecasting Financial Market Volatility,* Chichester, UK: John Wiley.

Poterba, J. (2000) Stock Market Wealth and Consumption, *Journal of Economic Perspectives,* vol. 14, no. 2.

Qi, M. (2001) Predicting US Recessions with Leading Indicators and Neural Network Models, *International Journal of Forecasting,* vol. 17, no. 3.

Ramsey, F. (1928) A Mathematical Theory of Saving, *Economic Journal,* vol. 38, no. 152.

Ratto, M., Roeger W. and in 't Veld J. (2009) QUEST III: An Estimated Open-Economy DSGE Model of the Euro Area with Fiscal and Monetary Policy, *Economic Modelling,* vol. 26, no. 1.

Razzak, W. (2001) Business Cycle Asymmetries: International Evidence, *Review of Economic Dynamics,* vol. 4, no. 1.

Reifschneider, D., Tetlow, R. and Williams, J. (1999) Aggregate Disturbances, Monetary Policy, and the Macroeconomy: The FRB/US Perspective, *Federal Reserve Bulletin,* January.

Reinhart, C. and Rogoff, K. (2009) *This Time Is Different: Eight Centuries of Financial Folly,* Princeton, NJ: Princeton University Press.

Richardson, P., Visco, I. and Giorno, C. (1999) Predicting the Evolution and Effects of the Asia Crisis from the OECD Perspective, *Economic Notes,* vol. 28, no. 3.

Roger, S. (2010) Inflation Targeting Turns 20, *Financial Development,* vol. 47, no. 1.

Romer, D. (2001) *Advanced Macroeconomics,* 2nd edn, New York: McGraw-Hill.

Rose, A. and Spiegel, M. (2009) Cross-Country Causes and Consequences of the 2008 Crisis: Early Warning, FRBSF Working Paper No. 2009-17.

Rossi, B. (2005) Optimal Tests for Nested Model Selection with Underlying Parameter Instability, *Econometric Theory,* vol. 21, no. 5.

Roubini, N. (2006) Summarized talk given at an IMF Seminar, *IMF Survey,* vol. 35, no. 19.

Rudd, J. and Whelan, K. (2007) Modeling Inflation Dynamics: A Critical Review of Recent Research, *Journal of Money Credit and Banking*, vol. 39, no. 2.

Sakellaris, P. and Vijselaar, F. (2004) Capital Quality Improvement and the Sources of Growth in the Euro Area, ECB Working Paper No. 368.

Sarno, L. and Taylor, M. (2002) *The Economics of Exchange Rates*, Cambridge, UK: Cambridge University Press.

Sarno, L. and Valente, G. (2009) Exchange Rates and Fundamentals; Footloose or Evolving Relationship? *Journal of the European Economic Association*, vol. 7, no. 4.

Schnatz, B., Vijselaar, F. and Osbat, C. (2004) Productivity and the Euro–Dollar Exchange Rate, *Weltwirtschaftliches Archiv*, vol. 140, no. 1.

Schumacher, C. and Breitung, J. (2008) Real-Time Forecasting of GDP Based on a Large Factor Model with Monthly and Quarterly Data, *International Journal of Forecasting*, vol. 24, no. 3.

Sédillot, F. and Pain, N. (2005) Indicator Models of Real GDP Growth in the Major OECD Countries, *OECD Economic Studies*, no. 40.

Sensier, M., Artis, M., Osborn, D. and Birchenhall, C. (2004) Domestic and International Influences on Business Cycle Regimes in Europe, *International Journal of Forecasting*, vol. 20, no. 2.

Sgherri, S. (2005) Long-Run Productivity Shifts and Cyclical Fluctuations: Evidence for Italy, IMF Working Paper No. 05/228.

Shiller, R. (2005) *Irrational Exuberance*, 2nd edn, Princeton, NJ: Princeton University Press.

Simpson, P., Osborn, D. and Sensier, M. (2001) Modelling Business Cycle Movements in the UK Economy, *Economica*, vol. 68, no. 270.

Sims, C. (1980) Macroeconomics and Reality, *Econometrica*, vol. 48, no. 1.

Sims, C. (1992) Interpreting the Macroeconomic Time Series Facts: The Effects of Monetary Policy, *European Economic Review*, vol. 36, no. 5.

Sinclair, T. (2009) The Long Term Impacts of Short Term Fluctuations: Evidence from an Asymmetric Model with Correlated Shocks, Paper presented at a Brookings conference, 5–6 November.

Skoczylas, L. and Tissot, B. (2005) Revisiting Recent Productivity Developments Across OECD Countries, BIS Working Paper No. 182.

Skudelny, F. (2009) Euro Area Private Consumption: Is There a Role for Housing Wealth Effects?, European Central Bank Working Paper No. 1057.

Sløk, T. and Kennedy, M. (2004) Factors Driving Risk Premia, OECD Economics Department Working Paper No. 385.

Smets, F. and Wouters, R. (2003) An Estimated Stochastic Dynamic General Model of the Euro Area, *Journal of the European Economic Association*, vol. 1, no. 5.

Smets, F. and Wouters, R. (2007) Shocks and Frictions in the US Business Cycle: A Bayesian DSGE Approach, *American Economic Review*, vol. 97, no. 3.

Smith, J. (2009) World Oil: Market or Mayhem?, *Journal of Economic Perspectives*, vol. 23, no. 3.

Smith, R. (1998) Emergent Policy-Making with Macroeconometric Models, *Economic Modelling*, vol. 15, no. 3.

Solow, R. (1956) A Contribution to the Theory of Economic Growth, *Quarterly Journal of Economics*, vol. 70, no. 1.

Spilimbergo, A., Symansky, S. and Schindler, M. (2009) Fiscal Multipliers, IMF Staff Position Note SPN/09/11.

Stehn, S. (2010) Fiscal Imbalances and Long-Term Interest Rates: How Tight a Link?, Goldman Sachs Global ECS US Research, *US Daily*, 5 May.

Stein, J. (1994) The Natural Exchange Rate of the US Dollar and Determinants of Capital Flows, in J. Williamson (ed.), *Estimating Equilibrium Exchange Rates*, Washington, DC: Institute for International Economics.

Stekler, H. (2010) Perspectives on Evaluating Macroeconomic Forecasts, George Washington University Research Program on Forecasting Working Paper No. 2010-002.

Stock, J. and Watson, M. (1989) New Indexes of Coincident and Leading Economic Indicators, in O. Blanchard and S. Fischer (eds), *NBER Macroeconomics Annual*, Cambridge, MA: MIT Press.

Stock, J. and Watson, M. (1999) A Comparison of Linear and Non-Linear Univariate Models for Forecasting Macroeconomic Time Series, in R. Engle and H. White (eds), *Cointegration, Causality and Forecasting: A Festschrift in Honor of Clive W. J. Granger*, Oxford, UK: Oxford University Press.

Stock, J. and Watson, M. (2002) Macroeconomic Forecasting Using Diffusion Indices, *Journal of Business Economics and Statistics*, vol. 20, no. 2.

Swiston, A., Mühleisen, M. and Mathai, K. (2007) U.S. Revenue Surprises: Are Happy Days Here to Stay?, IMF Working Paper No. 07/143.

Takáts, E. (2010) Ageing and Asset Prices, BIS Working Papers No. 318.

Taleb, N. (2007) *The Black Swan: The Impact of the Highly Improbable*, New York: Random House.

Tay, A. and Wallis, K. (1999) Density Forecasting: A Survey, *Journal of Forecasting*, vol. 19, no. 4.

Taylor, J. (1993) Discretion versus Policy Rules in Practice, *Carnegie-Rochester Conference Series on Public Policy*, vol. 39.

Taylor, J. (2010) The Fed and the Crisis: A Reply to Ben Bernanke, *The Wall Street Journal*, 12 January.

Temple, J. (1998) Robustness Tests of the Augmented Solow Model, *Journal of Applied Econometrics*, vol. 13, no. 4.

Thomakos, D. and Guerard J. (2004) Naïve, ARIMA, Nonparametric, Transfer Function and VAR Models: A Comparison of Forecasting Performance, *International Journal of Forecasting*, vol. 20, no. 1.

Timmermann, A. (2007) An Evaluation of the World Economic Outlook Forecasts, *IMF Staff Papers*, vol. 54, no. 4.

Tinbergen, J. (1939) *Statistical Testing of Business Cycle Theories*, Geneva: League of Nations.

Tong, H. and Lim, K. (1980) Threshold Autoregression, Limit Cycles and Cyclical Data, *Journal of the Royal Statistical Society*, vol. 42, no. 3.

Tovar, C. E. (2009) DSGE Models and Central Banks, *Economics*, vol. 3, 2009-16.

Trichet, J.-C. (2009) The ECB's Enhanced Credit Support, Keynote address at the University of Munich, Germany, 13 July.

Triplett, J. (2001) Hedonic Indexes and Statistical Agencies, Revisited, *Journal of Economic and Social Measurement*, vol. 27, no. 3/4.

Tulip, P. (2005) *Has Output Become More Predictable? Changes in Greenbook Forecast Accuracy*, Board of Governors of the Federal Reserve System, Finance and Economics Discussion Series, 2005-31.

Turner, C., Boone, L., Giorno, C., Meacci, M., Richardson, P. and Rae, D. (2001) Estimating the Structural Rate of Unemployment for the OECD Countries, *OECD Economic Studies*, no. 33.

Vaccara, B. and Zarnowitz, V. (1978) Forecasting with the Index of Leading Indicators, NBER Working Paper No. 244.

van den Noord, P. (2002) The Size and Role of Automatic Stabilisers in the 1990s and Beyond, in M. Buti, J. von Hagen and C. Martinez-Mongay (eds), *The Behaviour of Fiscal Authorities – Stabilisation, Growth and Institutions*, Basingstoke: Palgrave.

van Dijk, D., Teräsvirta, T. and Franses, P. (2002) Smooth Transition Autoregressive Models – A Survey of Recent Developments, *Econometric Review*, vol. 21, no. 1.

Van Horne, J. (2001) *Financial Market Rates and Flows*, 6th edn, Harlow, UK: Prentice Hall.

Vitek, F. (2009) Monetary Policy Analysis and Forecasting in the World Economy: A Panel Unobserved Components Approach, IMF Working Paper No. 09/238.

Vogel, L. (2007) How Do the OECD Growth Projections for the G7 Economies Perform? A Post-Mortem, OECD Economics Department Working Paper No. 573.

Vogel, L., Rusticelli, E., Richardson, P., Guichard, S. and Gianella, C. (2009) Inflation Responses to Recent Shocks: Do G7 Countries Behave Differently?, OECD Economics Department Working Paper No. 689.

Vuchelen, J. and Gutierrez, M.-I. (2005) A Direct Test of the Information Content of the OECD Growth Forecasts, *International Journal of Forecasting*, vol. 21, no. 1.

Wallis, K. (2003) Forecast Uncertainty, Its Representation and Evaluation, *Boletin Inflacion y Analisis Macroeconomico*, no. 100.

Wallis, K. (2004) An Assessment of Bank of England and National Institute Inflation Forecast Uncertainties, *National Institute Economic Review*, no. 189.

Walsh, C. (2009) Monetary Policy to Stabilize Economic Activity, Paper presented at the Jackson Hole Symposium on Financial Stability and Macroeconomic Policy, August.

Wang, J. and Wu, J. (2009) *The Taylor Rule and Interval Forecast for Exchange Rates*, Board of Governors of the Federal Reserve System International Finance Discussion Paper no. 963.

Warnock, F. and Warnock, V. (2005) *International Capital Flows and U.S. Interest Rates*, Board of Governors of the Federal Reserve System International Finance Discussion Paper no. 840.

Watson, M. (1986) Univariate Detrending Methods with Stochastic Trends, *Journal of Monetary Economics*, vol. 18, no. 1.

Weil, D. (2008) *Economic Growth*, 2nd edn, Boston, MA: Addison Wesley.

Wen, Y. (2005) Understanding the Inventory Cycle, *Journal of Monetary Economics*, vol. 52, no. 8.

Wheelock, D. and Wohar, M. (2009) Can the Term Spread Predict Output Growth and Recessions? A Survey of the Literature, *Federal Reserve Bank of St. Louis Review*, September.

White, W. (2008) Globalisation and the Determinants of Domestic Inflation, BIS Working Paper No. 250.

White, W. (2009) Should Monetary Policy 'Lean or Clean'?, Federal Reserve Bank of Dallas Globalization and Monetary Policy Institute Working Paper No. 34.

Whitley, J. (1994) *A Course in Macroeconomic Modelling and Forecasting*, London: Harvester Wheatsheaf.

Wilcox, J. (2007) Forecasting Components of Consumption with Components of Consumer Sentiment, *Business Economics*, vol. 42, no. 4.

Williamson, J. (1983, revised 1985) *The Exchange Rate System*, Washington, DC: Institute of International Economics.

Wilson, D. and Purushothaman, R. (2003) Dreaming with BRICs: The Path to 2050, *Goldman Sachs, Global Economic Papers* no. 99.

Winters, P. (1960) Forecasting Sales by Exponentially Weighted Moving Averages, *Management Science*, vol. 6, no. 3.

Woodford, M. (2001) The Taylor Rule and Optimal Monetary Policy, *American Economic Review*, vol. 91, no. 2.

World Bank (2000) *World Development Report 2000/2001: Attacking Poverty*, Washington, DC: World Bank.

Wren-Lewis, S. (2003) Estimates of Equilibrium Exchange Rates for Sterling Against the Euro, in HM Treasury, *UK Membership of the Single Currency: An Assessment of the Five Economic Tests*, London: HM Treasury.

Wößmann, L. (2003) Specifying Human Capital, *Journal of Economic Surveys*, vol. 17, no. 3.

Wurzel, E., Willard, L. and Ollivaud, P. (2009) Recent Oil Price Movements – Forces and Policy Issues, OECD Economics Department Working Paper No. 737.

Index

Printed and bound by CPI Group (UK) Ltd, Croydon, CR0 4YY